Management for Service Operations

 CPCU

Consisting of Materials from

Management, Third Edition

Kathryn M. Bartol
University of Maryland, College Park

David C. Martin
American University

Service Management: Operations, Strategy, and Information Technology, Second Edition

James A. Fitzsimmons
William H. Seay Centennial Professor of Business
University of Texas at Austin

Mona J. Fitzsimmons

Contemporary Management

Gareth R. Jones
Texas A&M University

Jennifer M. George
Texas A&M University

Charles W.L. Hill
University of Washington

Materials Coordinated by Leonard J. Watson
American Institute for CPCU

The McGraw-Hill Companies, Inc.
Primis Custom Publishing

New York   St. Louis   San Francisco   Auckland   Bogotá
Caracas   Lisbon   London   Madrid   Mexico   Milan   Montreal
New Delhi   Paris   San Juan   Singapore   Sydney   Tokyo   Toronto

McGraw-Hill Higher Education
A Division of The McGraw-Hill Companies

Management for Service Operations
CPCU 7

This book contains select materials from the following sources:
Management, Third Edition, by Kathryn M. Bartol and David C. Martin. Copyright © 1998, 1994, 1991 by The McGraw-Hill Companies, Inc.
Service Management: Operations, Strategy, and Information Technology, Second Edition, by James A. Fitzsimmons and Mona J. Fitzsimmons. Copyright © 1998, 1994 by The McGraw-Hill Companies, Inc.
Contemporary Management by Gareth R. Jones, Jennifer M. George and Charles W.L. Hill. Copyright © 1998 by The McGraw-Hill Companies, Inc.
All are reproduced with permission of the publisher.

2 3 4 5 6 7 8 9 0   CCW CCW   9 0 9

ISBN 0-07-432323-7

Primis Editor: J.D. Ice
Cover Design: Mary P. Clark
Printer/Binder: Courier Corporation, Westford

Contents

CHAPTER 1

The Challenge
of Management

GAINING THE EDGE

QUALITY STANDS OUT AT CORNING

Corning, Inc., has earned a reputation as one of the most quality-oriented companies in the world. The company is probably best known for its popular consumer products, such as its Corning, Corelle, and Pyrex housewares and its fine Steuben crystal. Despite its high-quality products, however, some of the company's competitors, particularly Japanese companies, were catching up with and even surpassing Corning in terms of the overall quality of their products and operations. James R. Houghton, the founder's great-great-grandson, who took over as chairman and chief executive officer of the company in 1983, recognized the threat this situation posed.

After studying quality programs in both Japan and the United States, Houghton found that the very best programs defined "quality" much more broadly than was typically the case. Quality, according to such programs, referred not only to the product itself but also to *every* aspect of the work, such as designing a product, handling a customer, writing a memo, holding a meeting, and making a sales call. By stressing quality in every phase of their operations, companies with these programs were avoiding the rework and waste that undermine profit levels. At the same time, they were pleasing customers.

As a result of these findings, Houghton announced a major commitment to total quality at Corning. He set up the Total Quality Management System in Corning's 49 plants and laboratories in the United States and 6 other countries. Under the system, all 28,000 employees take courses on quality, including an introductory course on quality awareness that emphasizes such factors as understanding the requirements of the customer and meeting those requirements on time, every time. An integral part of the quality thrust is innovation, the development of new ideas to improve processes, services, or product offerings.

Nowhere is the broad quality and innovation effort more evident than at Steuben (pronounced "Stoo-BEN," with the accent on the last syllable), a Corning division that produces fine crystal. Every U.S. president since President Truman has chosen Steuben for gifts of state. Steuben crystal can be found in museum collections all over the world.

Yet even Steuben discovered that it could change for the better. One aspect of the quality efforts at Steuben has involved conducting new research on customer requirements. When results showed that younger customers desire carefully crafted glassware that also has functional value, Steuben changed its product mix from an equal balance to 30 percent ornamental and 70 percent functional (vases, bowls, candlesticks, and the like). Another innovation aimed at quality was the institution of the team approach to making glassware. Now teams of workers follow the whole process of glassmaking from start to finish, a change that has reduced defects by more than 25 percent. There is also a new emphasis at Steuben on the efficient use of resources to make a profit. "We want to do the *right* things right," says Susan B. King, who presided over many of these changes while president of Steuben.

King has recently become senior vice president of corporate affairs at Corning's headquarters. She says that total quality management at Corning continues to be an evolving process and that recently the company has been placing particular emphasis on tools and technology—the mechanisms for producing quality. One example is a new Corning training course on innovation aimed at helping individuals learn an effective process for developing new products and successfully taking them to market.

Such dedication to quality is evident throughout Corning. In addition to its consumer-sector operations, of which Steuben is a part, Corning has businesses in three other global market sectors: specialty glass and ceramics, telecommunications, and laboratory sciences. To help everyone in the company appreciate the importance of the quality effort, "Jamie" (as he likes to be called by everyone at Corning) Houghton annually visits about 50 Corning facilities around the world and stresses the importance of the quality program.[1]

The innovations and quality improvements at Corning are indicative of efforts being made by organizations intent on gaining the competitive edge. This book will examine many such organizations as we consider the management approaches that are critical to organizational success. In the process, we will highlight management techniques that are especially effective at promoting innovation. We will see why even companies like Corning, with an established reputation for quality products and a strong tradition of success, must be receptive to improvements through innovative approaches if they are to continue to compete effectively in today's global marketplace.

We begin this chapter with an overview of the nature of management and the basic processes involved. We then consider what managers actually do by describing the work methods that they use, the different roles that they play, and the work agendas that guide their actions. We also examine the knowledge base and skills that managers need in order to achieve high performance. We explore two major dimensions along which managerial jobs differ, and we consider how the entrepreneurial role at different levels of management can foster innovation. Finally, we investigate what it takes to become an effective manager, taking into account education, experience, and a suitable understanding of future trends and issues.

MANAGEMENT: AN OVERVIEW

Organization Two or more persons engaged in a systematic effort to produce goods or services

For most of us, organizations are an important part of our daily lives. By **organization**, we mean two or more persons engaged in a systematic effort to produce goods or services. We all deal with organizations when we attend classes, deposit money at the bank, buy clothing, and attend a movie. Our lives are indirectly affected by organizations through the products we use. For example, if you have handled a dustpan lately, chances are it was made by Rubbermaid, Inc., the company based in Wooster, Ohio, that makes plastic household and commercial items. The dustpan was a drastic departure from Rubbermaid's original product line of balloons when it was first added to company offerings in 1934. Since then, the lowly dustpan has spawned more than 2000 additional products, giving the company a reputation for innovation and steady growth. What makes Rubbermaid so successful?

Like Corning and Steuben, Rubbermaid began to experience greatly accelerated success after a new chief executive officer (CEO), Stanley C. Gault, took over in 1981. (Gault had previously been a vice-chairman of General Electric, and he is now chairman of Goodyear Tire and Rubber.) By the late 1980s, once-staid Rubbermaid even began appearing among *Fortune* magazine's 10 most admired American companies, and it has continued to do so under Gault's successors. In contrast, over an 11-year period, CEO William H. Bricker transformed Diamond Shamrock from a profitable chemical company with modest oil holdings into a debt-ridden energy company and was forced to resign.[2] To understand how management can make such a difference in an organization, we need to explore the nature of management.

What Is Management?

Management The process of achieving organizational goals by engaging in the four major functions of planning, organizing, leading, and controlling

Management is the process of achieving organizational goals by engaging in the four major functions of planning, organizing, leading, and controlling. This definition recognizes that management is an ongoing activity, entails reaching important goals, and involves knowing how to perform the major functions of management. Since these functions are crucial to effective management, we use them as the basic framework for this book.[3] In this section, we provide a brief overview of the four functions (see Figure 1). Then we consider how they relate to other major aspects of managerial work.

Planning The process of setting goals and deciding how best to achieve them

PLANNING Planning is the management function that involves setting goals and deciding how best to achieve them. This function also includes considering what must be done to encourage necessary levels of change and innovation. For example, Rubbermaid typically sets an annual goal of increasing sales by at least 15 percent. In addition, the company aims to reap 30 percent of those sales from products that are no more than 5 years old—a powerful signal that innovation is important. As a result, the company typically launches at least one new product per *day*. The success rate for the new products is an enviable 90 percent, largely because of the careful planning that goes into new product development and product launches. Rubbermaid's recent successful products include a leakproof, rustproof mailbox that is wide enough for magazines to lie flat and a "litterless lunchbox" that addresses environmental concerns by providing compartments for food.[4]

At Diamond Shamrock, the major goal was to change the chemical company into a major energy company; this was based on Bricker's view in the late 1970s (later proven to be faulty) that energy prices would continue their upward trend. Even so, progress toward the goal was somewhat erratic and reflected poor planning. Diamond Shamrock sold its gas stations to Sigmor Corporation and then bought them back 5 years later. It overpaid by $600 million when purchasing San Francisco–based Natomas, an oil and gas producer, for $1.3 billion. At one point, the company even purchased a stake in a prize bull (partially owned by the CEO).[5]

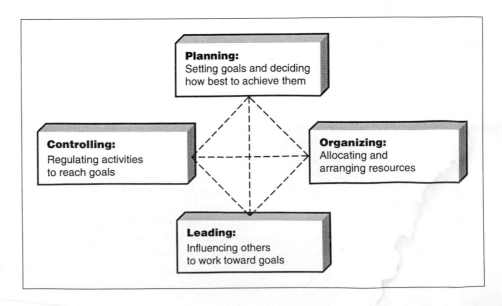

Figure 1 *The functions of management.*

Organizing The process of allocating and arranging human and nonhuman resources so that plans can be carried out successfully

ORGANIZING **Organizing** is the management function that focuses on allocating and arranging human and nonhuman resources so that plans can be carried out successfully. Through the organizing function managers determine which tasks are to be done, how tasks can best be combined into specific jobs, and how jobs can be grouped into various units that make up the structure of the organization. Staffing jobs with individuals who can successfully carry out plans is also part of the organizing function. For example, Rubbermaid recently reorganized to serve customers better by creating five divisions aimed at different customer needs: housewares, office products, commercial products, international operations, and the Little Tikes Company toy subsidiary. In addition, recruiting is done with a careful eye toward bringing in individuals with the potential to take on leadership positions as the company continues to expand. Resources are allocated on the basis of major company goals.[6]

In contrast, at Diamond Shamrock considerable organizing effort was channeled toward developing luxurious facilities for use by top management and the board of directors. Despite the company's difficulties, resources were allocated for such amenities as a 12,000-acre Texas ranch worth $9 million that was used for corporate meetings and entertainment, a $1 million box at the Dallas Cowboys' home stadium, and a fleet of corporate airplanes.[7]

Leading The process of influencing others to engage in the work behaviors necessary to reach organizational goals

LEADING **Leading** is the management function that involves influencing others to engage in the work behaviors necessary to reach organizational goals. Leading includes communicating with others, helping to outline a vision of what can be accomplished, providing direction, and motivating organization members to put forth the substantial effort required. At Rubbermaid the vision is clearly articulated to everyone: Products are to be useful, long-lasting, and inexpensive.[8] To help motivate organization members, Rubbermaid offers an incentive plan that enables eligible managers to receive bonuses based partially on profit levels. In addition, many hourly workers participate in a retirement plan based on profits. One result of these practices is that, in the housewares division alone, employees recently contributed 12,600 suggestions for improvements during a 12-month period, thereby demonstrating their strong commitment to the vision.[9]

At Diamond Shamrock, Bricker had been chosen partially for his support of the company's tradition of participatory management. After becoming CEO, however, he assumed an autocratic style. Many executives concluded that it was useless to fight with Bricker over his high-risk ideas.[10]

Controlling The process of regulating organizational activities so that actual performance conforms to expected organizational standards and goals

CONTROLLING **Controlling** is the management function aimed at regulating organizational activities so that actual performance conforms to expected organizational standards and goals.[11] To do the necessary regulating, managers need to monitor ongoing activities, compare the results with expected standards or progress toward goals, and take corrective action as needed. For example, in order to reach earnings goals, Rubbermaid must keep a careful eye on costs. Recently the costs of certain resins that were a key ingredient in a newly launched plastic desk product suddenly increased 52 percent. Managers quickly took corrective action by changing to a less expensive combination of petrochemicals. Rubbermaid also puts considerable effort into monitoring the quality of its products. This policy has earned the Rubbermaid name such a solid reputation with customers that some stores are allowing the company to set up Rubbermaid boutiques—entire sections stocked exclusively with Rubbermaid products.[12]

On the other hand, as oil prices and earnings began to drop, Diamond Shamrock started to sell assets and cut expenses. Still, the $9 million ranch was retained. Although the original fleet of five company planes was cut back to three, the company leased extra planes for various trips. News of potential conflicts of interest involving company dealings with Bricker's friends began to emerge.[13] As the contrast between Rubbermaid and Diamond Shamrock illustrates, effectively executing the four functions of management can be critical to organizational success.

The Management Process

While the four major functions of management form the basis of the managerial process, there are several additional key elements in the process. These elements were identified by management scholars Steven J. Carroll and Dennis J. Gillen on the basis of their review of major studies on managerial work.[14] As Figure 2 shows, work methods and managerial roles, as well as work agendas, feed into the core management functions. A manager's knowledge base and key management skills are other important factors that contribute to high performance (goal achievement). We consider each of these elements in greater detail in the next two sections of this chapter. Throughout this discussion, keep in mind that the management process applies not only to profit-making organizations, such as Corning and Rubbermaid, but also to not-for-profit organizations.[15] A **not-for-profit organization** (sometimes called a *nonprofit organization*) is an organization whose main purposes center on issues other than making profits. Common examples are government organizations (e.g., the federal government), educational institutions (your college or university), cultural institutions (New York's Carnegie Hall), charitable institutions (United Way), and many health-care facilities (Mayo Clinic).

Not-for-profit organization An organization whose main purposes center on issues other than making profits

WHAT MANAGERS ACTUALLY DO

One of the most famous studies of managers was conducted by management scholar Henry Mintzberg, who followed several top managers around for 1 week each and recorded everything that they did.[16] In documenting their activities, Mintzberg reached some interesting conclusions about the manager's work methods and about several major roles that managers play.

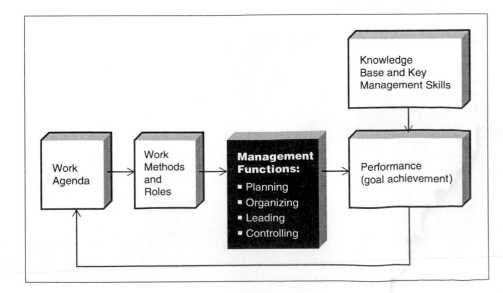

Figure 2 *An extended model of the management process. (Adapted from Stephen J. Carroll and Dennis J. Gillen, "Are the Classical Management Functions Useful in Describing Managerial Work?" Academy of Management Review, vol. 12, 1987, pp. 38–51.)*

Work Methods

Mintzberg found that in their actual work methods, the managers differed drastically from their popular image as reflective, systematic planners who spend considerable quiet time in their offices poring over formal reports. Three of his findings provide particularly intriguing glimpses into the world of high-level managers.

UNRELENTING PACE The managers in Mintzberg's study began working the moment they arrived at the office in the morning and kept working until they left at night. Rather than taking coffee breaks, the managers usually drank their coffee while they attended meetings, which averaged eight each day. Similarly, lunches were almost always eaten in the course of formal or informal meetings. When not in meetings, the managers handled an average of 36 pieces of mail per day, as well as other written and verbal communications. If they happened to have a free minute or two, the time was usually quickly usurped by subordinates anxious to have a word with the boss. Donald Schuenke, head of Northwestern Mutual Life Insurance, estimates that he would have to work no less than 24 hours per day if he were to honor all the requests for just a small amount of his time.[17]

BREVITY, VARIETY, AND FRAGMENTATION Mintzberg found that the managers handled a wide variety of issues throughout the day, ranging from awarding a retirement plaque to discussing the bidding on a multi-million-dollar contract. Many of their activities were surprisingly brief: About half the activities that Mintzberg recorded were completed in less than 9 minutes, and only 10 percent took more than 1 hour. Telephone calls tended to be short, lasting an average of 6 minutes. Work sessions at the manager's desk and informal meetings averaged 15 and 10 minutes, respectively. The managers experienced continual interruptions from telephone calls and subordinates. They often stopped their own desk work to place calls or request that subordinates drop in. Leaving meetings before the end was common. Because of the fragmentation and interruptions, a number of top managers save their major brainwork for times outside the normal workday. For example, Susan King of Corning does much of her important reading, thinking, and planning at the office after 6 p.m., when the workday pace slows. In the process, she puts in about 60 to 70 hours of work per week.

VERBAL CONTACTS AND NETWORKS The managers in Mintzberg's study showed a strong preference for verbal communication, through either phone conversations or meetings, rather than written communication, such as memos and formal reports. For obtaining and transmitting information, they relied heavily on networks. A **network** is a set of cooperative relationships with individuals whose help is needed in order for a manager to function effectively. The network of contacts in Mintzberg's study included superiors, subordinates, peers, and other individuals inside the organization, as well as numerous outside individuals. Some of the contacts were personal, such as friends and peers. Others were professional, such as consultants, lawyers, and insurance underwriters. Still others were trade association contacts, customers, and suppliers.

Network A set of cooperative relationships with individuals whose help is needed in order for a manager to function effectively

IMPLICATIONS OF MINTZBERG'S FINDINGS Although Mintzberg's study focused on top-level managers, his findings apply to a wide variety of managers.[18] For example, one study of factory supervisors found that they engaged in be-

PRACTICALLY SPEAKING

HOW TO BUILD NETWORKS

Experts agree that building networks of influence with others involves the principle of reciprocity. *Reciprocity* means that people generally feel that they should be paid back for the various things they do and that one good (or bad) turn deserves another. For the most part, individuals do not expect to be paid back right away or in specific amounts; approximations will usually do. Because individuals anticipate that their actions will be reimbursed in one way or another, influence and networking are possible.

One way to think about using the reciprocity principle in networking is to view oneself as a "trader" and to use the metaphor of "currencies" as a means of approaching the process of exchange. Just as there are many types of currencies used in the world, there are many different kinds of currencies that are used in organizational life. Too often individuals think only in terms of money, promotions, and status, but there are actually many possibilities.

SOME POSSIBLE CURRENCIES
Some possible currencies that you might be able to trade include:

Resources: giving budget increases, personnel, space, etc.

Assistance: helping with projects or taking on unwanted tasks

Information: furnishing organizational and/or technical knowledge

Recognition: acknowledging effort, accomplishment, or abilities

Visibility: providing the chance to be known by higher-ups

Advancement: giving tasks that can aid in promotion

Personal support: providing personal and emotional backing

Understanding: listening to others' concerns

HOW TO USE CURRENCIES
In using currencies, it helps to consider these four steps:

1 *Think of each individual whom you need to deal with as a potential ally or network member.* If you want to have influence within an organization and get the job done, you will need to create internal network members or allies. Assume that even a difficult person is a potential network member.
2 *Get to know the world of the potential network member, including the pressures that the person is under, as well as the person's needs and goals.* An important factor influencing behavior is how performance is measured and rewarded. If you ask an individual to do things that will be perceived as poor performance within that individual's work unit, you are likely to encounter resistance.
3 *Be aware of your own strengths and potential weaknesses as a networker.* Sometimes networkers underestimate the range of

currencies that they have available to exchange. Make a list of potential currencies and resources that you have to offer. Then think about your own preferred style of interaction with others. Would-be networkers often fail to understand how their preferred style of interaction fits or doesn't fit with the potential ally's preferred style. For instance, does the potential ally like to socialize first and work later? If so, that person may find it difficult to deal with someone who likes to solve the problem first and only then talk about the weather, the family, or office politics. Skilled networkers learn to adapt their own style to that of others in dealing with potential allies.
4 *Gear your exchange transactions so that both parties can come out winners.* For the most part, transactions in organizations are not one-time occurrences. Usually the parties will need to deal with one another again, perhaps frequently. In fact, that is the idea of networks—to have contacts to call on as needed. The implication here is that in most exchange relationships there are two outcomes that ultimately make a difference. One is success in achieving the task goals at hand. The other is maintaining and improving the relationship so that the contact remains a viable one. With networking, it is better to lose the battle than to lose the war.[21]

tween 237 and 1073 activities within a given workday—or more than one activity every 2 minutes.[19] Such research strongly supports the notion that managers need to develop a major network of contacts in order to have influence and to operate effectively.[20] For some ideas on how you might be able to develop such contacts as a manager, see the Practically Speaking discussion, "How to Build Networks."

Managerial Roles

Role An organized set of behaviors associated with a particular office or position

To make sense of the reams of data he collected, Mintzberg attempted to categorize the managers' various activities into roles. A **role** is an organized set of behaviors associated with a particular office or position.[22] Positions usually entail multiple roles. For example, roles for a salesperson position in a retail store might include information giver, stock handler, and cashier.

The three general types of roles that Mintzberg observed were interpersonal, informational, and decisional roles. *Interpersonal* roles grow directly out of the authority of a manager's position and involve developing and maintaining positive relationships with significant others. *Informational* roles pertain to receiving and transmitting information so that managers can serve as the nerve centers of their organizational units. *Decisional* roles involve making significant decisions that affect the organization. Within these role types, Mintzberg outlined 10 more specific roles that managers play. These roles are summarized in Table 1.

Mintzberg's categorization of managerial activities into roles provides some insight into what managers actually do during their workday.[23] The roles also give us clues about the kinds of skills that managers are likely to need to carry out their work effectively.

Mintzberg's role approach provides a somewhat different perspective on management than do the four management functions. At first glance, it might seem that Mintzberg's findings are incompatible with the view that planning, organizing, leading, and controlling are an important part of the management

TABLE 1	Mintzberg's 10 Managerial Roles
Role	Description
INTERPERSONAL	
Figurehead	Performs symbolic duties of a legal or social nature
Leader	Builds relationships with subordinates and communicates with, motivates, and coaches them
Liaison	Maintains networks of contacts outside work unit who provide help and information
INFORMATIONAL	
Monitor	Seeks internal and external information about issues that can affect organization
Disseminator	Transmits information internally that is obtained from either internal or external sources
Spokesperson	Transmits information about the organization to outsiders
DECISIONAL	
Entrepreneur	Acts as initiator, designer, and encourager of change and innovation
Disturbance handler	Takes corrective action when organization faces important, unexpected difficulties
Resource allocator	Distributes resources of all types, including time, funding, equipment, and human resources
Negotiator	Represents the organization in major negotiations affecting the manager's areas of responsibility

Source: Based on Henry Mintzberg, *The Nature of Managerial Work,* Harper & Row, New York, 1980.

process. However, Mintzberg's study did not consider *why* managers were engaging in the different roles that he described. When the *why* is taken into consideration, it becomes clear that the functions of management provide an important blueprint that helps managers channel their role behaviors in ways that will ultimately lead to goal achievement.[24] For example, transmitting information through the disseminator role or representing the organization through the negotiator role has little meaning unless it is linked to a purpose such as a management function. But how do managers tie their various activities and roles into the planning, organizing, leading, and controlling that are necessary to achieve goals? Part of the answer is suggested by another well-known study, conducted by management researcher John Kotter.

Managerial Work Agendas

Kotter's study focused on 15 general managers in 9 different corporations representing a broad range of industries.[25] General managers typically have responsibility for a major business sector of the corporation. On the basis of his findings, Kotter suggested that managers focus their various efforts productively through the use of work agendas.

Work agenda A loosely connected set of tentative goals and tasks that a manager is attempting to accomplish

NATURE OF WORK AGENDAS A **work agenda** is a loosely connected set of tentative goals and tasks that a manager is attempting to accomplish. Managers usually develop work agendas during their first 6 months on a new job, although the agendas are continually subject to reassessment in the face of changing circumstances and emerging opportunities. Typically, such agendas address immediate, as well as more long-run, job responsibilities and are used in addition to more formal organizational plans. Kotter found that to put their work agendas into practice, general managers work hard to establish the extensive networks of relationships identified by Mintzberg.

By making use of work agendas and networking strategies, the managers in Kotter's study were able to engage in short, seemingly disjointed conversations and still accomplish their missions. To illustrate the typical way in which the managers worked, Kotter documented a set of short discussions held by John Thompson, a division manager in a financial services corporation.[26] The conversation began one morning in Thompson's office when two of his subordinates, Anne Dodge and Jud Smith, were present:

Thompson:	"What about Potter?"
Dodge:	"He's OK."
Smith:	"Don't forget about Chicago."
Dodge:	"Oh yeah." *(Makes a note to himself)*
Thompson:	"OK. Then what about next week."
Dodge:	"We're set."
Thompson:	"Good. By the way, how is Ted doing?"
Smith:	"Better. He got back from the hospital on Tuesday. Phyllis says he looks good."
Thompson:	"That's good to hear. I hope he doesn't have a relapse."
Dodge:	"I'll see you this afternoon." *(Leaves the room)*
Thompson:	"OK. *(To Smith)* Are we all set for now?"
Smith:	"Yeah." *(Gets up and starts to leave)*
Lawrence:	*(Steps into the doorway from the hall and speaks to Thompson)* "Have you seen the April numbers yet?"
Thompson:	"No, have you?"

Lawrence:	"Yes, 5 minutes ago. They're good except for CD, which is off by 5 percent."
Thompson:	"That's better than I expected."
Smith:	"I bet George is happy."
Thompson:	*(Laughing)* "If he is, he won't be after I talk to him." *(Turner, Thompson's secretary, sticks her head through the doorway and tells him Bill Larson is on the phone)*
Thompson:	"I'll take it. Will you ask George to stop by later? *(Others leave and Thompson picks up the phone)* Bill, good morning, how are you? . . . Yeah. . . . Is that right? . . . No, don't worry about it. . . . I think about a million and a half. . . . Yeah. . . . OK. . . . Yeah, Sally enjoyed the other night, too. Thanks again. . . . OK. . . . Bye."
Lawrence:	*(Steps back into the office)* "What do you think of the Gerald proposal?"
Thompson:	"I don't like it. It doesn't fit with what we've promised Corporate or Hines."
Lawrence:	"Yeah, that's what I thought, too. What is Jerry going to do about it?"
Thompson:	"I haven't talked to him yet. *(Turns to the phone and dials)* Let's see if he's in."*

Although the dialogue was clear to the participants, it would probably seem somewhat chaotic to outsiders. This is because outsiders lack the specific business and organizational knowledge shared by the managers. For example, an outsider would not be able to readily identify Potter, Ted, Phyllis, Bill Larson, Sally, Hines, or Stacy. Nor would an outside observer understand the full meaning of the references to "Chicago," "April numbers," "CD," or the "Gerald proposal" or, more importantly, know Thompson's agenda and where these various pieces fit in that agenda.

Yet these conversations actually accomplished a great deal. Among other things, Thompson learned the following facts:

■ Mike Potter agreed to help with a problem loan that could otherwise thwart Thompson's business expansion plans in a certain area.
■ Plans for the loan for the following week were moving along as intended.
■ Ted Jenkins, one of Thompson's subordinates and a central figure in his plans for the division over the next 2 years, is feeling better after an operation.
■ Division income for April met budget except for one area, saving Thompson from having to divert attention from other plans to take remedial action.

In addition, Thompson initiated several actions:

■ He set up a meeting with George Masolia about the one off-target area in the April budget report to see what can be done to get things on target again.
■ He passed on some useful information to Bill Larson, a peer who has done him favors in the past and who could help him in the future.
■ He placed a call to Stacy Wilkins, one of his subordinates, to find out her reaction to a proposal that could impact Thompson's division, especially its 5-year revenue goals.

Thompson's discourse shows the fast pace, brevity, variety, and fragmentation that are characteristic of a manager's workday, and it illustrates the use of the verbal contacts and networks that were identified in Mintzberg's study. Many of Thompson's remarks (until he began to speak about the Gerald proposal) reflect mainly the controlling function—checking to be sure that various important activities are moving along as expected. The discussion about the Gerald proposal reflects the planning function. When he talks with George about the budget problem, Thompson will engage in leading and planning.

Without a work agenda (the manager's own working plan), similar discussions could actually be fairly random and far from efficient. Even with an agenda, managers need to make sure that they work within its guidelines. Within a year after he became chief executive officer at First Chicago, a major bank holding company, Barry Sullivan had a solid idea about his priorities. Still, he had a vague sense that in the course of relentless day-to-day activity, he was not spending his time in ways that adequately matched his priorities. With the help of consultants, he learned the cause of his problem: "I was responding to demands on my time in more of an ad hoc manner rather than against some broad idea of how much time I really wanted to allocate to different things." As a result, he now decides how much time he wants to assign to certain activities and tentatively blocks out parts of his calendar up to a year in advance to help him match his time with his priorities.[27]

Work agendas provide rough guidelines within which managers operate in determining how to orient their various activities and roles. But what factors influence the content of work agendas?

FACTORS INFLUENCING WORK AGENDAS According to Rosemary Stewart, a British expert on managerial work, there are three main factors that are likely to have an impact on a manager's work agenda: demands, constraints, and choices.[28]

Job demands are the activities a manager *must* do in a job. For example, managers usually have responsibilities related to the major goals and plans of the organization (such as achieving a 10 percent increase in sales) that are difficult to ignore.

Job constraints are the factors, both inside and outside the organization, that limit what a manager can do. Constraints include such variables as resource limitations, legal restrictions, union contract provisions, technological limitations, and the degree to which the work of a manager's unit is defined.

Job choices are work activities that the manager can do but does not have to do. For example, without a directive to do so, a manager might initiate a proposal to develop a computerized customer service tracking system. Thus work agendas tend to reflect, at least to some extent, the personal preferences and career objectives of individual managers.

MANAGERIAL KNOWLEDGE, SKILLS, AND PERFORMANCE

For managers to develop work agendas, act out roles, and engage in planning, organizing, leading, and controlling, they need a sound knowledge base and key management skills. In this section, we discuss these essential elements in the management process and explain how they relate to the issue of performance.

Knowledge Base

Although managers often switch companies and work in different industries, they are apt to run into difficulties if they don't have a reasonably extensive knowledge base relevant to their particular managerial job. A *knowledge base* can include information about an industry and its technology, company policies and practices, company goals and plans, company culture, the personalities of key organization members, and important suppliers and customers. For example, Kotter found that one reason why the general managers in his study were able to accomplish so much within short periods of time was that they could take action with only small bits of information at their disposal. Their extensive knowledge base enabled them to attach the appropriate meaning to the information fragments they obtained.[29]

Key Management Skills

In addition to having a knowledge base, managers need certain skills to carry out the various functions of management. A *skill* is the ability to engage in a set of behaviors that are functionally related to one another and that lead to a desired performance level in a given area.[30] For managers, three types of skills are necessary: technical, human, and conceptual.

Technical skills Skills that reflect both an understanding of and a proficiency in a specialized field

TECHNICAL SKILLS **Technical skills** are skills that reflect both an understanding of and a proficiency in a specialized field. For example, a manager may have technical skills in accounting, finance, engineering, manufacturing, or computer science.

Human skills Skills associated with a manager's ability to work well with others, both as a member of a group and as a leader who gets things done through others

HUMAN SKILLS **Human skills** are skills associated with a manager's ability to work well with others, both as a member of a group and as a leader who gets things done through others. Managers with effective human skills are typically adept at communicating with others and motivating them to develop themselves and perform well in pursuit of organizational goals.

Conceptual skills Skills related to the ability to visualize the organization as a whole, discern interrelationships among organizational parts, and understand how the organization fits into the wider context of the industry, community, and world

CONCEPTUAL SKILLS **Conceptual skills** are skills related to the ability to visualize the organization as a whole, discern interrelationships among organizational parts, and understand how the organization fits into the wider context of the industry, community, and world. Conceptual skills, coupled with technical skills, human skills, and a knowledge base, are important ingredients in organizational performance, as can be seen in the example of Carnegie Hall, a not-for-profit organization (see the following Case in Point discussion).

CASE IN POINT BEHIND-THE-SCENES SKILLS AT CARNEGIE HALL

As they enjoy performances at New York's Carnegie Hall, few members of the audience probably give any thought to the management knowledge and skills at work behind the scenes of the nation's most celebrated cultural center. Since 1986, Carnegie Hall has been run by Judith Arron, executive and artistic director of the concert landmark. Although she has a university degree in cello and piano, she decided to make concert management her career. Among her previous managerial positions, she served for 10 years as orchestra manager of the Cincinnati Symphony Orchestra before winning the Carnegie Hall position.

She arrived at Carnegie Hall in the midst of a $50 million renovation project, the most extensive in the concert center's history. When concerts resumed in December 1986, Arron's responsibilities included the overseeing of season planning, artist procurement, marketing and promotion, overall supervision of hall operations, and development of community outreach programs. In the latter, Carnegie sponsors musical events in local communities, shelters, and, particularly, elementary schools or brings various special groups to Carnegie Hall for concerts.

Arron's workday typically begins when she leaves home about 7:30 a.m. Usually at her desk by 9, a major part of her day is consumed by meetings with such groups as senior staff members, department heads, the board of directors, orchestra representatives, artists, conductors, and staff members. Although her workday tends to end about 6:30 p.m., she may stay for a weeknight concert, and she frequently comes in for concerts or special events on weekends. "We may have an established superstar or a newcomer I want to hear, or a new orchestra that needs special care." She generally plans to "work 6 days a week and go to two or three concerts."

She is known for being particularly skilled at handling people, including some of the temperamental, but talented, artists who play on Carnegie's stage. Indeed, the cast of artists has been stellar, including such luminaries as Leonard Bernstein, Itzhak Perlman, Mstislav Rostropovich, Alicia de Larrocha, Dame Joan Sutherland, and Benita Valente.[31]   ■ ■ ■

Arron came to her job at Carnegie Hall with an extensive knowledge base about the concert field, gleaned from her years as orchestra manager of the Cincinnati Symphony and several previous jobs. In addition, her strong technical skills in music, human skills in handling people, and conceptual skills in seeing the big picture have been important factors in her high performance and that of Carnegie Hall.

Performance

What constitutes high performance in an organization? Peter Drucker, the noted management writer and consultant, points out that performance achieved through management is actually made up of two important dimensions: effectiveness and efficiency.[32]

Effectiveness The ability to choose appropriate goals and achieve them

EFFECTIVENESS **Effectiveness** is the ability to choose appropriate goals and achieve them. For example, Tokyo-based Honda has become the third-largest automaker in the United States in terms of sales. The company has achieved this admirable position by setting high goals for quality, consistently producing high-quality products, and aggressively promoting these products on value rather than price. In the process, the company has built an exceptionally loyal customer base.[33] Thus Honda illustrates what Drucker means when he points out that effectiveness is essentially doing (accomplishing) *the right things.*

Efficiency The ability to make the best use of available resources in the process of achieving goals

EFFICIENCY **Efficiency** is the ability to make the best use of available resources in the process of achieving goals. In the case of Honda, the company's new Suzuka assembly plant is one of the most efficient in the world. The plant produces Civics using 10.9 hours of direct labor per car. In contrast, at Ford, the most efficient U.S. manufacturer, about 16 direct labor hours go into producing each Escort. At General Motors, it takes an average of 30 direct labor hours to produce a car. Automation helps give Honda an edge, but other factors, such as extensive training of workers and superior working conditions (e.g., clean work areas, quiet enough for conversation), are also important.[34] Through such means, Honda illustrates what Drucker has in mind when he speaks of efficiency as doing *things right.*

In essence, organizations need to exhibit both effectiveness (doing the right things) and efficiency (doing things right) in order to be good performers. Because these dimensions are so closely linked, we will generally use the term ''effectiveness'' in reference to both effectiveness and efficiency. We do this for the sake of simplicity and readability.

MANAGERIAL JOB TYPES

Although we have been discussing the nature of managerial work in general, managerial jobs vary somewhat on the basis of two important dimensions. One is a vertical dimension, focusing on different hierarchical levels in the organization. The other is a horizontal dimension, addressing variations in managers' responsibility areas. We explore these dimensions and their implications in this section. Because of its importance in fostering innovation, we give special attention to the entrepreneurial role at various hierarchical levels.

Vertical Dimension: Hierarchical Levels

Along the vertical dimension, managerial jobs in organizations fall into three categories: first-line, middle, and top management. These categories represent vertical differentiation among managers because they involve three different levels of the organization, as shown in Figure 3.

**First-line managers/
supervisors** Managers at
the lowest level of the
hierarchy who are directly
responsible for the work of
operating (nonmanagerial)
employees

FIRST-LINE MANAGERS   **First-line managers** (or **first-line supervisors**) are managers at the lowest level of the hierarchy who are directly responsible for the work of operating (nonmanagerial) employees. They often have titles that in-

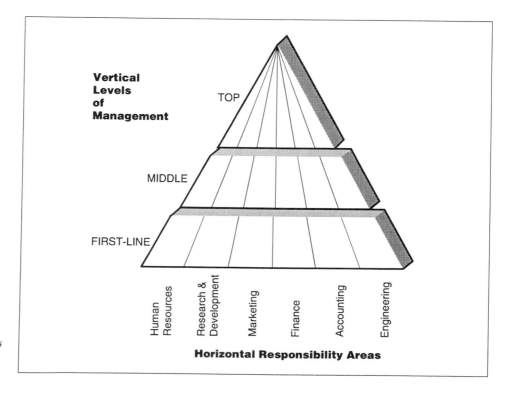

Figure 3 *Types of managers
by hierarchical level and
responsibility area.*

being placed on developing individuals' skills in international management both through classroom training and special job assignments (see Table 3). In essence, effective managers think of management education as a process that continues throughout their careers.

Management Experience

Not surprisingly, experience is also a major factor in learning to be an effective manager. For the CEO respondents in the survey of 800 large U.S. companies, work experience started in high school (79 percent had jobs) and largely continued in college (56 percent had jobs). Another early source of management experience was holding office in college clubs. Approximately 70 percent of the respondent CEOs held at least one office in a club, fraternity, or other campus organization while in college.

A number of the CEOs (38 percent) also participated in intercollegiate sports. Those who did noted that this experience helped them learn teamwork and interpersonal skills that served them well in managerial positions. For example, C. J. Silas, CEO of Phillips Petroleum and winner of a gold medal for basketball at the 1955 Pan American Games, notes that engaging in sports helped him recognize that "you can't do it all yourself."[60]

Although business publications sometimes give the impression that managers, particularly top ones, change jobs frequently, this is not usually the case. Almost 75 percent of the CEOs reported that previous experience with their organization was a major factor in their being selected for the top job. In fact, almost half the CEOs indicated that they had been working for their firm for at

TABLE 3 Learning the Ways of the World	
Company	**Program**
American Express Co.'s Travel-Related Services unit	Gives American business-school students summer jobs in which they work outside the U.S. for up to 10 weeks; also transfers junior managers with at least 2 years' experience to other countries
Colgate-Palmolive Co.	Trains about 15 recent college graduates each year for 15 to 24 months prior to multiple overseas job stints
General Electric Co.'s aircraft-engine unit	Will expose selected midlevel engineers and managers to foreign-language and cross-cultural training even though not all will live abroad
Honda of America Manufacturing Inc.	Has sent about 42 U.S. supervisors and managers to the parent company in Tokyo for up to 3 years, after preparing them with 6 months of Japanese language lessons, cultural training, and lifestyle orientation during work hours
PepsiCo Inc.'s international beverage division	Brings about 25 young foreign managers a year to the U.S. for 1-year assignments in bottling plants
Raychem Corp.	Assigns relatively inexperienced Asian employees (from clerks through middle managers) to the U.S. for 6 months to 2 years

Source: Reprinted from *The Wall Street Journal,* Mar. 31, 1992, p. B1. Reprinted by permission of *The Wall Street Journal,* © 1992 Dow Jones & Company, Inc. All Rights Reserved Worldwide

least 20 years. Furthermore, most of them reported that they had been employed by two or fewer other companies. Still, the situation may be growing more fluid. One study showed that the number of CEOs who had been promoted to the top slot after being with their present company for less than a year grew from 9 to 17 percent in a decade.[61] The researchers speculated that this has been partly brought about by a wave of mergers and takeovers. It may also reflect an increasing willingness of boards of directors to ask for resignations of CEOs when their performance is viewed as inadequate. For example, John Gutfreund was asked to resign as chairman and CEO of Salomon, the brokerage firm, after it was revealed that he knew about a major company violation of Treasury-auction bidding rules but did not report it. In another case, Tom H. Barrett was replaced as chairman and CEO of Goodyear Tire & Rubber Co. when directors concluded that he was not doing enough to rehabilitate the troubled tire maker. In both situations, outsiders were chosen as replacements.[62]

The large number of hours put in by CEOs also tends to accelerate the experience factor. According to a survey by *The Wall Street Journal,* most CEOs work 10 hours or more on weekdays and more than one-third put in 6 hours or more on weekends (see Table 4). For example, Mary Kay Ash, CEO of Mary Kay Cosmetics, rises at 5 a.m. 6 days a week on the premise that the extra work hours provide her with the equivalent of a 9-day week.[63] Most CEOs also travel at least 4 days per month.

The age at which managers tend to be promoted to the CEO position also supports the notion that experience plays an important role. One study showed that 75 percent of CEOs were at least 45 before they were promoted to the position, with more than half being 50 or over at the time of promotion.[64]

Understanding Trends

A solid understanding of business trends is important to those preparing for a career in management. Although it is always difficult to make predictions, four particular trends are likely to impact managerial work in the future:

1 *The growing internationalization of business.* Organizations must increasingly assume an international perspective in conducting their business for two reasons. First, businesses are facing more and more global competition. As Louis Gerstner, CEO of RJR Nabisco, points out, "The world is going to become more competitive in an industrial, commercial sense. More competitive perhaps than we've seen in the history of modern economic society."[65] Second, more and more companies are likely to be doing business in other countries. Corning, Inc., for example, frequently engages in joint ventures with companies in other countries, such as its partnership with the Japan-based Asahi Glass Company to manufacture television-bulb glass.[66] As this trend implies, managers will need to have greater knowledge of international business. We frequently use international companies as examples so that you can learn more about such organizations and the way they do business.

2 *The increasing importance of quality.* Organization managers are becoming more concerned with quality. At Corning, Inc., a quality management program was instituted by Chairman of the Board and CEO Jamie Houghton. Numerous other organizations have also adopted a quality stance, often referred to as *total quality management.* This stance involves a commitment to improve quality in every aspect of the organization's operations.

3 *The expanding public concern with managerial ethics.* Ethical concerns have arisen as a result of recent Wall Street scandals, such as the illegal bidding by the Salomon Brothers investment firm, and the general increase in white-

TABLE 4 CEO Working Hours and Frequency of Travel

WORKING HOURS

Average hours per weekday:

Fewer than 8	1%
8–9	14
10–11	65
12 or more	18

Average hours per weekend:

None	6%
1–5	60
6–10	28
11–15	4
16 or more	1

BUSINESS TRAVEL

Days per month:

Fewer than 4	8%
4–6	35
7–10	43
11 or more	13

Source: Reprinted from *The Wall Street Journal,* Mar. 20, 1987, p. 22D. Reprinted by permission of *The Wall Street Journal,* © 1987 Dow Jones & Company, Inc. All Rights Reserved Worldwide.

collar crimes. Organizations and CEOs are responding by placing greater emphasis on social responsibility.[67] At various points in the text, you will find "Valuing Ethics" boxes that focus on stellar organizational efforts in the areas of social responsibility and managerial ethics.

4 *The growing diversity of the work force.* The impact of demographic diversity on organizations and their managers is enlarging. According to estimates by the U.S. Bureau of Labor Statistics, women will constitute about 47 percent of the work force and minorities and immigrants about 26 percent by the year 2000. Managers themselves will reflect the emerging diversity and, at the same time, will need to be able to effectively utilize an increasingly diverse work force.

Although these four trends are likely to have particularly important future impacts on managerial work, they are not the only emerging developments of consequence. In the chapter on understanding external and internal environments, we consider other issues of future importance to managers and their organizations.

In this chapter, we have provided an overview of the basic challenge of management, including a forward glance at trends that are likely to influence the way managers work in the future.

CHAPTER SUMMARY

Management is the process of achieving organizational goals by engaging in the four major functions of planning, organizing, leading, and controlling. While these functions form the basis of the managerial process, several other elements contribute to an understanding of how managers actually operate. For instance, work methods and managerial roles, as well as work agendas, feed into the management functions aimed at performance. A manager's knowledge base and management skills are also important factors in reaching targeted performance.

Mintzberg's famous study of top managers found that their work methods were characterized by an unrelenting pace, brevity, variety, fragmentation, and heavy use of verbal contacts and networks. In order to make sense of the voluminous data that he collected while observing the managers, Mintzberg isolated three major categories of roles: interpersonal, informational, and decisional. Within these categories, he identified 10 specific roles: figurehead, leader, liaison, monitor, disseminator, spokesperson, entrepreneur, disturbance handler, resource allocator, and negotiator. To a large extent, these work methods and roles are also characteristic of managers at other levels of organizations.

On the basis of his research on general managers, Kotter found that managers channel their various efforts through the use of work agendas, which are loosely connected sets of tentative goals and tasks that a manager is attempting to accomplish. Work agendas usually develop from the demands, constraints, and choices associated with a manager's job. As a result, they tend to reflect, at least to some extent, the personal preferences and career objectives of managers.

For managers to develop work agendas, act out

roles, and engage in planning, organizing, leading, and controlling, they also need a knowledge base and key management skills. The key skills fit into three categories: technical, human, and conceptual. These skills, as well as the other elements in the management process, impact performance. Performance is made up of two important dimensions: effectiveness and efficiency. Effectiveness is the ability to choose appropriate goals and achieve them, while efficiency is the ability to make the best use of available resources in the process of achieving goals.

Managerial jobs differ according to hierarchical level (a vertical dimension) and responsibility areas (a horizontal dimension). They are generally divided into three hierarchical levels: first-line, middle, and top. Managers at these levels vary in the emphasis they place on planning, organizing, leading, and controlling. They also differ in the importance that they place on the key management skills and in the degree to which they use the different types of managerial roles. Although managers at all levels rate the entrepreneurial role as highly important, the way that they use this role to encourage innovation depends on their hierarchical level, as follows: idea champion (first-line), sponsor (middle), and orchestrator (top). In contrast, horizontal managerial job differences focus on responsibility area and involve three major types of managers: functional, general, and project.

The consensus is that it takes a combination of education and experience to be an effective manager. In the educational arena, CEOs for the most part are college graduates, tend to have a graduate degree, and are likely to have participated in formal training and educational programs sponsored or supported by their organization. On the experience side, they usually had some type of job in high school or college, held at least one office in a campus organization, and worked for two or fewer companies prior to joining the one they head. In addition, they tend to put in long hours.

According to several recent informal surveys, managerial work in the future is particularly likely to be affected by the growing internationalization of business, the increasing importance of quality, the expanding public concern with managerial ethics, and the growing diversity of the work force.

QUESTIONS FOR DISCUSSION AND REVIEW

1 Describe each of the major functions of management: planning, organizing, leading, and controlling. For a campus or other organization to which you belong, give an example of a manager engaging in each of these functions. If one or more of the functions are lacking, what are the implications?

2 List three common managerial work methods identified by Mintzberg. How could a manager misuse these work methods, to the extent that they would lead to poor performance?

3 Explain the three general types of roles and the ten specific roles that managers play. Suppose that you opened a ski-and-surf shop near campus that carries clothing, skis, and other accessories for recreation at ski resorts and beaches. Assume that you have six employees. How might you use the ten roles in managing your shop?

4 Outline three major sources of managerial work agendas. How do work agendas help managers channel their efforts toward the appropriate level of performance?

5 Explain why a knowledge base and the key management skills are important to managers. In what ways could managers acquire an appropriate knowledge base and the key skills?

6 Contrast effectiveness and efficiency as they apply to organizational performance. What happens when you have one without the other?

7 Describe how managerial jobs differ according to hierarchical level. What are the implications for managers?

8 Outline how managers at different hierarchical levels use the entrepreneurial role. What do you think is likely to happen if the entrepreneurial role is missing from the middle or top levels of the organization?

9 Indicate how managerial jobs differ according to responsibility area. What are the implications for managers?

10 Summarize what major studies have revealed about the management education and experience of CEOs. How can this information be helpful to beginning managers?

DISCUSSION QUESTIONS FOR CHAPTER OPENING CASE

1 What evidence of planning, organizing, leading, and controlling can you find at Corning, Inc., and its Steuben unit?

2 What entrepreneurial role does Houghton play? What has been the impact?

3 Assess the degree to which technical, human, and conceptual skills are important in King's position. What evidence exists that she uses these skills?

MANAGEMENT EXERCISE: PRODUCING THE NEW BINDING MACHINE

 You are a first-line supervisor in the production department of a local concern that manufactures a variety of office products, such as staplers, binders, and cellophane-tape holders. Recently, the research department developed an innovative small machine that binds reports in one easy operation. According to market research and early sales figures, the demand for the new machine (on which the company holds the patent) is expected to be strong because the machine produces good-looking reports at a very reasonable price. Because sales of the machine are already brisk, the company has decided to add a new production unit. A new first-line supervisor will be hired to head the unit.

You, your boss (who heads the production department), and a few other first-line supervisors who also report to your boss are having a working lunch in a small room off the company cafeteria. The purpose of the meeting is to discuss the basic requirements of the new job and the details that should be explained to job candi-

He became particularly interested in the working and living conditions of his employees while running a cotton mill in New Lanark, Scotland. As was common, the mill employed 400 to 500 young children, who worked 13-hour days that included 1½ hours off for meals. Although his business partners resisted some of his ideas, Owen tried to improve the living conditions of the employees by upgrading streets, houses, sanitation, and the educational system in New Lanark. At the time, Owen was considered to be a radical, but today his views are widely accepted. His ideas laid the groundwork for the human relations movement, which is discussed later in this chapter.[2]

CHARLES BABBAGE   English mathematician Charles Babbage (1792–1871) is widely known as "the father of modern computing." His projects produced the world's first practical mechanical calculator and an "analytical engine" that had the basic elements of a modern-day computer.[3] Difficulties in directing his various projects, however, led him to explore new ways of doing things. In the process, he made direct contributions to management theory.

Babbage was enthralled with the idea of *work specialization,* the degree to which work is divided into various jobs. He recognized that not only physical work but mental work as well could be specialized.[4] In this sense, he foresaw the prospect of specialists, such as accountants who limit their practice to either personal or corporate taxes.

Babbage also devised a profit-sharing plan that had two parts, a bonus that was awarded for useful suggestions and a portion of wages that was dependent on factory profits. His ideas foreshadowed some modern-day group incentive plans, such as the Scanlon Plan, in which workers offer suggestions to improve productivity and then share in the resulting profits.

HENRY R. TOWNE   President of the Yale and Towne Manufacturing Company and a mechanical engineer, Henry R. Towne (1844–1924) articulated the need to consider management as a separate field of *systematic* inquiry on a par with engineering. He outlined his views in a landmark paper titled "The Engineer as an Economist," which was delivered in 1886 to the American Society of Mechanical Engineers in Chicago. He observed that although good engineering skills and good business skills were rarely combined in the same individual, both skills were needed to run an organization effectively. Accordingly, the paper called for the establishment of a science of management and the development of principles that could be applied across management situations. Although the engineering society itself did not become a major force in developing knowledge about management, one of the people who attended Towne's presentation, Frederick Taylor, was subsequently instrumental in building the management field.[5]

ASSESSING THE PRECLASSICAL CONTRIBUTORS   Although the early pioneers explored several different avenues relating to management, their efforts were somewhat fragmentary. They were largely oriented toward developing specific techniques, often to solve visible problems. For example, to overcome chaotic meeting, Henry Robert produced *Robert's Rules of Order,* a publication of the preclassical era that is still used today to run many large, formal meetings (see the following Case in Point discussion).

CASE IN POINT   ROBERT'S RULES BRING ORDER

During the late 1800s, when Henry Martyn Robert, a brigadier general in the U.S. Army, was pursuing his military career as a civil engineer, he frequently attended meetings with people from many backgrounds. Often he had to preside at these meetings.

He quickly learned about the challenge of running meetings when the first meeting over which he presided, involving a group of Baptist ministers, ended in total chaos. Robert was perplexed because nothing was settled or resolved. He had prepared his subject well and had even gathered advice on how to conduct a meeting. He decided that he would never again participate in such a disastrous encounter.

For the next 7 years, he collected information concerning how to conduct a meeting, and he subsequently produced a 176-page book titled *Pocket Manual of Rules of Order for Deliberative Assemblies*. The book provided a set of parliamentary rules for conducting meetings.

He promoted the book, which he had published on his own, by sending 1000 copies to the best parliamentarians in the United States, including governors, legislators, the vice president, and a few attorneys, and he asked the recipients for their comments. After receiving many enthusiastic responses and several very good suggestions, he modified the original text, changing the title to *Robert's Rules of Order*. The book has become a classic source of guidance for running large, formal meetings and is used by many legislative bodies, government councils, associations, and other organizations in which decisions are made by member vote. First published in 1876, the book has not been out of print since. More than 4 million copies have been sold throughout the English-speaking world. It has also been published in Braille.[6] ■ ■ ■

Since they generally came from technical backgrounds, the early pioneers did not tend to think in terms of management as a separate field—that is, until Towne presented his influential paper. Still, they were important innovators who laid the groundwork for other major management thinkers who came after them. Their forward-looking ideas have endured the test of time.

CLASSICAL VIEWPOINT

Classical viewpoint A perspective on management that emphasizes finding ways to manage work and organizations more efficiently

Henry Towne's call for establishing management as a separate field of inquiry helped usher in a major new approach called the classical viewpoint. The **classical viewpoint** is a perspective on management that emphasizes finding ways to manage work and organizations more efficiently. It is made up of three different approaches: scientific management, administrative management, and bureaucratic management. This viewpoint is labeled "classical" because it encompasses early works and related contributions that have formed the main roots of the field of management.[7]

Scientific Management

Scientific management An approach that emphasizes the scientific study of work methods in order to improve worker efficiency

Scientific management is an approach within classical management theory that emphasizes the scientific study of work methods in order to improve worker efficiency. Major representatives of this approach include Frederick Winslow Taylor, Frank and Lillian Gilbreth, and Henry Gantt.

FREDERICK WINSLOW TAYLOR Frederick Winslow Taylor (1856–1915) is known as "the father of scientific management." Born into a relatively wealthy Philadelphia family, Taylor became an apprentice pattern maker and machinist for a local firm before moving on to Midvale Steel. At Midvale, his meteoric rise from laborer to chief engineer in 6 years gave him an opportunity to tackle a

example of a Gantt chart is given in the Supplement to the chapter on Managerial Decision Making.) He also devised a unique pay incentive system that not only paid workers extra for reaching standard in the allotted time but also awarded bonuses to supervisors when workers reached standard. Thus the system encouraged supervisors to coach workers who were having difficulties.

Bureaucratic Management

Bureaucratic management
An approach that emphasizes the need for organizations to operate in a rational manner rather than relying on the arbitrary whims of owners and managers

Another branch of the classical viewpoint is **bureaucratic management,** an approach that emphasizes the need for organizations to operate in a rational manner rather than relying on the arbitrary whims of owners and managers. The bureaucratic management approach is based mainly on the work of prominent German sociologist Max Weber.

Weber (1864–1920) was born into an affluent family with strong political and social connections.[21] He pursued a career as a consultant, professor, and author. Because he was so well read, he was able to make contributions that span a number of academic disciplines, such as management, sociology, economics, and philosophy. Among his most important contributions to the discipline of management are his ideas on the need for organizations to operate on a more rational basis.

In formulating his ideas, Weber was reacting to the prevailing norms of class consciousness and nepotism. For example, it was customary practice to allow only individuals of aristocratic birth to become officers in the Prussian Army or to attain high-level positions in government and industry. Weber felt that the situation not only was unfair but also led to a significant waste of human resources. He also believed that running organizations on the basis of *whom* one knows rather than *what* one knows and engaging in nepotism (the hiring of relatives regardless of their competence) tended to interfere with organizational effectiveness.

In an effort to visualize how the large organizations evolving out of the industrial revolution might ideally operate, Weber formulated characteristics of the "ideal bureaucracy" (see Table 3). He coined the term "bureaucracy" (based on the German *büro*, meaning "office") to identify large organizations that operated on a rational basis. Weber understood clearly that his ideal bureaucracy did not actually exist. In fact, he never intended that his ideas be used as guidelines for managers. Rather, his purpose was to develop ideas that could be used as a starting point in understanding such organizations.[22] However, when his work was translated into English in the late 1940s, many U.S. management scholars used his ideas as a guide to how organizations could be more effectively managed.

Because of the possibility of carrying Weber's ideas to excess, the term "bureaucracy" is sometimes used in a pejorative sense to denote red tape and excessive rules. Yet there clearly are advantages to the bureaucratic characteristics outlined by Weber. For example, recent troubles at family-owned U-Haul can be traced to confusion over roles, secret meetings of the board of directors, hidden rule changes, and advancement determined by family ties—all violations of Weber's ideal. The resulting feuds and court battles among family members are seriously threatening the viability of the national renter of trucks, trailers, and other equipment.[23]

Administrative Management

While the advocates of scientific management concentrated on developing principles that could be used to help organize individual worker tasks more effe

TABLE 3	Major Characteristics of Weber's Ideal Bureaucracy
Characteristic	**Description**
Specialization of labor	Jobs are broken down into routine, well-defined tasks so that members know what is expected of them and can become extremely competent at their particular subset of tasks.
Formal rules and procedures	Written rules and procedures specify the behaviors desired from members facilitate coordination and ensure uniformity.
Impersonality	Rules, procedures, and sanctions are applied uniformly regardless of individual personalities and personal considerations.
Well-defined hierarchy	Multiple levels of positions, with carefully determined reporting relationships among levels, provide supervision of lower offices by higher ones, a means of handling exceptions, and the ability to establish accountability of actions.
Career advancement based on merit	Selection and promotion is based on the qualifications and performance of members.

Administrative management
An approach that focuses on principles that can be used by managers to coordinate the internal activities of organizations

tively and Weber struggled with the concept of bureaucracy, another branch within the classical viewpoint was also developing. The **administrative management** approach focuses on principles that can be used by managers to coordinate the internal activities of organizations. Major contributors include Henri Fayol and Chester Barnard, both of whom were executives of large enterprises.

HENRI FAYOL French industrialist Henri Fayol (1841–1925) was born into a middle-class family near Lyon, France.[24] Trained as a mining engineer, he joined a coal-and-iron combine as an apprentice and rose to the top position of managing director in 1888. He accomplished the difficult task of moving the company out of severe financial difficulties and into a strong position by the time of his retirement at age 77. The company survives today as part of LeCreusot-Loire, a large mining and metallurgical group in central France.

On the basis of his experiences as a top-level manager, Fayol was convinced that it should be possible to develop theories about management that could then be taught to individuals with administrative responsibilities. His efforts toward developing such theories were published in a monograph titled *General and Industrial Management.*

Fayol attempted to isolate the main types of activities involved in industry or business. Within the category of "managerial activities," he delineated five major functions: planning, organizing, commanding, coordinating, and controlling. Thinking of management as encompassing these functions is known as the *functional* approach to management. You have probably noticed the similarity between Fayol's functions and the four functions of management (planning, organizing, leading, and controlling) used as the framework for this book. Many contemporary books on management use a form of the functional approach that has roots in Fayol's work.

Fayol also outlined a number of principles (see Table 4) that he found

---

TABLE 4	**Fayol's General Principles of Management**

1. *Division of work.* Work specialization can result in efficiencies and is applicable to both managerial and technical functions. Yet there are limitations to how much that work should be divided.

2. *Authority.* Authority is the right to give orders and the power to exact obedience. It derives from the formal authority of the office and from personal authority based on factors like intelligence and experience. With authority comes responsibility.

3. *Discipline.* Discipline is absolutely necessary for the smooth running of an organization, but the state of discipline depends essentially on the worthiness of its leaders.

4. *Unity of command.* An employee should receive orders from one superior only.

5. *Unity of direction.* Activities aimed at the same objective should be organized so that there is one plan and one person in charge.

6. *Subordination of individual interest to general interest.* The interests of one employee or group should not prevail over the interests and goals of the organization.

7. *Remuneration.* Compensation should be fair to both the employee and the employer.

8. *Centralization.* The proper amount of centralization or decentralization depends on the situation. The objective is the optimum use of the capabilities of personnel.

9. *Scalar chain.* A scalar (hierarchical) chain of authority extends from the top to the bottom of an organization and defines the communication path. However, horizontal communication is also encouraged as long as the managers in the chain are kept informed.

10. *Order.* Materials should be kept in well-chosen places that facilitate activities. Similarly, due to good organization and selection, the right person should be in the right place.

11. *Equity.* Employees should be treated with kindness and justice.

12. *Stability of personnel tenure.* Because time is required to become effective in new jobs, high turnover should be prevented.

13. *Initiative.* Managers should encourage and develop subordinate initiative to the fullest.

14. *Esprit de corps.* Since union is strength, harmony and teamwork are essential.

Source: Based on data from Henri Fayol, *General and Industrial Management,* Constance Storrs (trans.), Pitman & Sons, Ltd., London, 1949, pp. 19–42.

---

useful in running his large coal-and-iron concern. Although contemporary research has found exceptions to his principles under some conditions, the principles are generally in widespread use today.

CHESTER BARNARD Another major contributor to administrative management was Chester Barnard (1886–1961). Born in Massachusetts, he attended Harvard but did not complete his degree work.[25] After joining AT&T as a statistician, he rose rapidly and was named president of the New Jersey Bell Telephone Company in 1927. Barnard recorded his observations about effective administration in a single classic book, *The Functions of the Executive,* published in 1938.

One of Barnard's best-known contributions is his **acceptance theory of authority.** This theory argues that authority does not depend as much on "persons of authority" who *give* orders as on the willingness to comply of those who *receive*

Acceptance theory of authority A theory that argues that authority does not depend as much on "persons of authority" who *give* orders as on the willingness to comply of those who *receive* the orders

the orders. Thus, in Barnard's view, it is really the employees who decide whether or not to accept orders and directions from above. From a practical point of view, Barnard felt that managers are generally able to exert authority on a day-to-day basis because each individual possesses a "zone of indifference" within which the individual is willing to accept orders and directions without much question.

On the basis of his view that authority flows from the bottom to the top, Barnard argued that employees are more willing to accept directions from a manager if they (1) understand the communication, (2) see the communication as consistent with the purposes of the organization, (3) feel that the actions indicated are in line with their needs and those of other employees, and (4) view themselves as mentally and physically able to comply.

Barnard helped integrate concern with authority, which was growing out of the administrative and bureaucratic approaches, with emphasis on work needs, which was simultaneously developing within the behavioral viewpoint. He also knew of the early behaviorists and the Hawthorne studies, which were a primary force in the development of the behavioral viewpoint, to which we turn next.[26]

BEHAVIORAL VIEWPOINT

Behavioral viewpoint A perspective on management that emphasizes the importance of attempting to understand the various factors that affect human behavior in organizations

The classical theorists generally viewed individuals as mechanisms of production. As a result, they were primarily interested in finding ways for organizations to use these productive mechanisms more efficiently. The idea that an employee's behavior might be influenced by internal reactions to various aspects of the job situation was generally not seen as particularly relevant to the quest for greater efficiency. In contrast, the **behavioral viewpoint** is a perspective that emphasizes the importance of attempting to understand the various factors that affect human behavior in organizations. In exploring this viewpoint, we examine four aspects of its development: the contributions of the early behaviorists, the Hawthorne studies, the human relations movement, and the more contemporary behavioral science approach.

Early Behaviorists

With the growing interest in the subject of management, individuals from other backgrounds began to offer alternatives to the emphasis on engineering that characterized the scientific management approach. Two early behaviorists, psychologist Hugo Münsterberg and political scientist Mary Parker Follett, contributed pioneering ideas that helped make the behavioral perspective a major viewpoint.

HUGO MÜNSTERBERG Born and educated in Germany, Hugo Münsterberg (1863–1916) earned both a Ph.D. in psychology and a medical degree. In 1892, he set up a psychological laboratory at Harvard and began seeking practical applications of psychology. Before long, his attention turned to industrial applications, leading him to publish an important book, *Psychology and Industrial Efficiency,* which appeared in 1913. The book argued that psychologists could help industry in three major ways. The first was closely allied to scientific management: psychologists could study jobs and find ways of identifying the individuals who are best suited to particular jobs. In contrast, the other two ways inherently recognized that factors besides those considered by the classical theorists might influence behavior at work. According to Münsterberg, the second way that psychologists could help industry was by identifying the psychological conditions under which individuals are likely to do their best work. The third was by developing strategies that would influence employees to behave in ways that are compatible with management interests. The ideas and examples he provided ignited the imagination of others and led to the establishment of the field of *industrial psychology*, the study of human behavior in a work setting. Thus, Münsterberg is considered to be "the father of industrial psychology."

MARY PARKER FOLLETT   Another well-known early behaviorist was Mary Parker Follett (1868–1933). Born in Boston and educated in political science at what is now Radcliffe College, Follett was a social worker who became interested in employment and workplace issues.

Follett attributed much greater significance to the functioning of groups in organizations than did proponents of the classical view of management. She argued that members of organizations are continually influenced by the groups within which they operate. In fact, she held that groups have the capacity to exercise control over themselves and their own activities, a concept that is compatible with the recent interest in self-managing teams in American business. For example, at General Motors' new Saturn plant, most of the work is done by teams that have no traditional boss.[27]

Another of Follett's forward-looking ideas was her belief that organizations should operate on the principle of "power with" rather than "power over." Power, to her, was the general ability to influence and bring about change. She argued that power should be a jointly developed, cooperative concept, involving employees and managers working together, rather than a coercive concept based on hierarchical pressure. Although her views probably influenced Barnard's acceptance theory of authority, Follett advocated sharing power whereas Barnard emphasized encouraging the appropriate response from below.[28]

Follett suggested that one way to foster the "power with" concept was by resolving conflict through integration. By *integration* she meant the process of finding a solution that would satisfy both parties. She cited an example involving a dairy cooperative that almost disbanded because of a controversy over the pecking order in unloading milk cans. The creamery was located on the downgrade of a hill, and members who came downhill and those who came uphill both thought they should be given precedence in unloading. The situation was at an impasse until an outsider pointed out that the position of the loading dock could be changed so that both groups could unload their cans at the same time. Follett noted, "Integration involves invention, and the clever thing is to recognize this, and not to let one's thinking stay within the boundaries of two alternatives that are mutually exclusive."[29] Her ideas on integration heralded modern methods of conflict resolution.

Follett placed great importance on achieving what she called *integrative unity*, whereby the organization would operate as a functional whole, with the various interrelated parts working together effectively to achieve organizational goals. Yet she saw the process of working together as a dynamic process because environmental factors would necessitate change. As we will see, her ideas anticipated the systems viewpoint of management.[30] One recent reviewer of her work has argued that its overall significance "rivals the long-standing influence of such giants as Taylor and Fayol."[31]

Hawthorne Studies

Hawthorne studies A group of studies conducted at the Hawthorne plant of the Western Electric Company during the late 1920s and early 1930s whose results ultimately led to the human relations view of management

While Follett was doing her speaking and writing, a number of researchers were involved in the Hawthorne studies. The **Hawthorne studies** are a group of studies conducted at the Hawthorne plant of the Western Electric Company during the late 1920s and early 1930s whose results ultimately led to the human relations view of management, a behavioral approach that emphasized concern for the worker. To understand their significance, we need to trace the studies from their beginning.

When they started, the Hawthorne studies reflected the scientific management tradition of seeking greater efficiency by improving the tools and methods of work—in this case, lighting. The General Electric Company wanted to sell more light bulbs, so, along with other electric companies, it supported studies on the relationship between lighting and productivity that were to be conducted by the National Research Council. The tests were to be held at the Hawthorne Works (Chicago) of the Western Electric Company, an equipment-producing subsidiary of AT&T.[32] Ultimately, three sets of studies were done.

FIRST SET OF STUDIES The first set of studies, called the Illumination Studies, took place between 1924 and 1927 under the direction of several engineers. In one of these studies, light was decreased over successive periods for the experimental group (the group for whom the lighting was altered), while light was held at a constant level for the control group (a comparison group working in a separate area). In both groups, performance rose steadily, even though the lighting for the experimental group became so dim that the workers complained that they could hardly see. At that point, performance in the experimental group finally began to decline (see Figure 2). The researchers concluded that factors other than lighting were at work (since performance rose in both groups), and the project was discontinued.[33] In retrospect, one possibility based on the records of the studies is that the experimental and control groups were in contact and may have begun competing with each other.

SECOND SET OF STUDIES Intrigued with the positive changes in productivity, some of the engineers and company officials decided to attempt to determine the causes through further studies. Accordingly, a second set of experiments took place between 1927 and 1933. The most famous study involved five

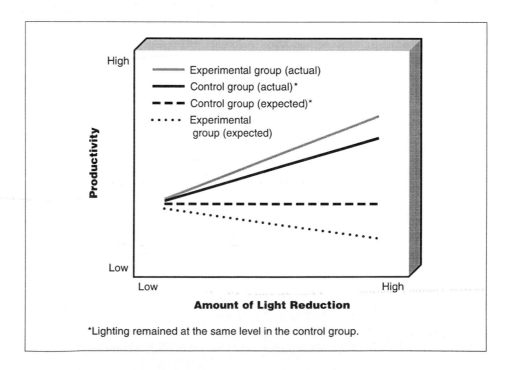

Figure 2 *Actual versus expected results for the experimental and control groups in one of the Hawthorne Illumination Studies.*

women who assembled electrical relays in the Relay Assembly Test Room, where they were away from other workers and the researchers could alter work conditions and evaluate the results. Before the study began, the researchers were apparently concerned about possible negative reactions from the workers who would be included in the experiment. To lessen potential resistance, the researchers changed the usual supervisory arrangement so that there would be no official supervisor. Instead, the workers would operate under the general direction of the experimenters. The workers were also given special privileges, such as being able to leave their workstation without permission, and they received considerable attention from the experimenters and company officials.[34] The study was aimed at exploring the best combination of work and rest periods, but a number of other factors were also varied (sometimes simultaneously), such as pay, length of workday, and provisions for free lunches. Generally, productivity increased over the period of the study, regardless of how the factors under consideration were manipulated.[35]

A Harvard University group (involved in assessing the results) ultimately concluded that the change in the supervisory arrangement was the major reason for the increase in productivity in the Relay Assembly Test Room study and in two related studies involving different work groups. The group felt that the physical changes, such as rest periods, free lunches, and shortened hours, as well as the group incentive pay plans, were factors of lesser importance (largely because adverse changes in some of these factors did not seem to decrease performance).

Since the supervisory arrangement had been set up by the researchers before the study began, this change was not actually part of the study manipulations and was not intended to affect the results. One outcome of the studies was the identification of a famous concept that ultimately came to be known as the Hawthorne effect. The **Hawthorne effect** is the possibility that individuals singled out for a study may improve their performance simply because of the added attention they receive from the researchers, rather than because of any specific factors being tested in the study.[36]

More contemporary investigations now suggest that the Hawthorne-effect concept is too simplistic to explain what happened during the Hawthorne studies and that the concept itself is defective. It now appears likely that the results obtained at the Hawthorne plant stemmed from the fact that the workers interpreted what was going on around them differently than did the researchers (rather than from the idea that the workers reacted positively simply because of attention from the researchers). The workers most likely viewed the altered supervision as an important positive change in their work environment, even though that was not what the researchers intended.[37]

THIRD SET OF STUDIES The third set of Hawthorne studies built on the emerging findings of the second set. It included the famous Bank Wiring Observation Room study (1931–1932), which involved a group of male workers. Studying the group provided knowledge about informal social relations within groups and about the use of group norms to restrict output when doing so seems advantageous to the group. Also included in the third set was a massive interviewing program (1928–1931). Initially aimed at improving supervision, the program evolved and not only enabled researchers to learn what workers had on their minds but also provided workers with a way to let off steam.[38]

IMPACT OF THE HAWTHORNE STUDIES As a result of the Hawthorne studies, the focus of the field of management was drastically altered. In strong contrast to the impersonality that characterized the classical approach, the Haw-

Hawthorne effect The possibility that individuals singled out for a study may improve their performance simply because of the added attention they receive from the researchers, rather than because of any specific factors being tested

thorne studies pointed to the impact that social aspects of the job had on productivity, particularly the effects of personal attention from supervisors and relationships among group members. As one writer has pointed out, "No other theory or set of experiments has stimulated more research and controversy nor contributed more to a change in management thinking than the Hawthorne studies and the human relations movement they spawned."[39]

Human Relations Movement

However flawed the studies, the Hawthorne research set the stage for intense interest in the social dimension of human behavior in organizations. The key to productivity, at that point, appeared to lie in showing greater concern for workers so that they would feel more satisfied with their jobs and be willing to produce more. Emphasis was placed on building more collaborative and cooperative relationships between supervisors and workers. Consequently, managers now needed social skills in addition to technical skills. They also required a better understanding of how to make workers feel more satisfied with their jobs. While the Hawthorne studies provided some clues, managers needed more definitive guidance. Two major theorists, Abraham Maslow and Douglas McGregor, were among those who came forward with ideas that managers found helpful.

ABRAHAM MASLOW Abraham Maslow (1908–1970) received his doctorate in psychology from the University of Wisconsin and eventually became chairman of the psychology department at Brandeis University. He developed a theory of motivation that was based on three assumptions about human nature. First, human beings have needs that are never completely satisfied. Second, human action is aimed at fulfilling the needs that are unsatisfied at a given point in time. Third, needs fit into a somewhat predictable hierarchy, ranging from basic, lower-level needs at the bottom to higher-level needs at the top.[40] The hierarchy outlined by Maslow has five levels of needs: physiological (lowest), safety, belongingness, esteem, and self-actualization (highest). Self-actualization needs refer to the requirement to develop our capabilities and reach our full potential.[41]

Maslow's work dramatized to managers that workers have needs beyond the basic requirement of earning money to put a roof over their heads. This concept conflicted with the views of scientific management, which emphasized the importance of pay. Of all the management-related theories, Maslow's hierarchy of needs theory is probably the best known among managers today.

DOUGLAS MCGREGOR The movement toward having managers think of workers in a new light was also given impetus by the work of Douglas McGregor (1906–1964). McGregor earned a doctorate at Harvard and spent most of his career as a professor of industrial management at the Massachusetts Institute of Technology. A 6-year stint as president of Antioch College led him to realize that the notion of trying to have everyone like the boss (i.e., maintaining good human relations) offered inadequate guidance to managers.

To fill the void, he developed the concept of Theory X versus Theory Y, a dichotomy dealing with the possible assumptions that managers make about workers. McGregor felt that such assumptions exert a heavy influence on how managers operate. Theory X managers (see Table 5) tend to assume that workers are lazy, need to be coerced, have little ambition, and are focused mainly on security needs. In contrast, Theory Y managers (see Table 5) assume that workers do not inherently dislike work, are capable of self-control, have the capacity to be creative and innovative, and generally have higher-level needs that are often unmet on the job.

TABLE 5	Theory X and Theory Y Managerial Assumptions

THEORY X ASSUMPTIONS

1. The average person dislikes work and will try to avoid it.
2. Most people need to be coerced, controlled, directed, and threatened with punishment to get them to work toward organizational goals.
3. The average person wants to be directed, shuns responsibility, has little ambition, and seeks security above all.

THEORY Y ASSUMPTIONS

1. Most people do not inherently dislike work; the physical and mental effort involved is as natural as play or rest.
2. People will exercise self-direction and self-control to reach goals to which they are committed; external control and threat of punishment are not the only means for ensuring effort toward goals.
3. Commitment to goals is a function of the rewards available, particularly rewards that satisfy esteem and self-actualization needs.
4. When conditions are favorable, the average person learns not only to accept but also to seek responsibility.
5. Many people have the capacity to exercise a high degree of creativity and innovation in solving organizational problems.
6. The intellectual potential of most individuals is only partially utilized in most organizations.

McGregor believed that managers who hold Theory X assumptions are likely to treat workers accordingly. Hence, such a manager sets up elaborate controls and attempts to motivate strictly through economic incentives. As a result, workers are likely to respond in a manner that reinforces the manager's original assumptions.

In contrast, managers with Theory Y assumptions have the potential for integrating individual goals with organizational goals. McGregor believed this integration could occur if managers give workers latitude in performing their tasks, encourage creativity and innovation, minimize the use of controls, and attempt to make the work more interesting and satisfying in regard to higher-level needs. Under such conditions, workers are likely to exhibit greater commitment to organizational goals, because the goals coincide more closely with their own. McGregor understood, however, that some relatively immature and dependent workers might require greater controls at first in order to develop the maturity needed for the Theory Y approach.[42]

Like Maslow's hierarchy, McGregor's Theory X and Theory Y approach helped managers develop a broader perspective on the nature of workers and new alternatives for interacting with them. The innovative ideas of both men had an intuitive appeal to managers searching for ways of operating more effectively. Their theories became extremely popular and are still widely applied today.

Behavioral Science Approach

Maslow, McGregor, and others who helped develop the human relations viewpoint tried to show that there was an alternative to the classical school's rational economic perspective of workers. They depicted workers as social creatures, who had a variety of needs to be met on the job. Still, the picture that they drew was fairly general and somewhat simplistic. It often left managers uncertain about the specific actions that they should take and the implications of such actions.

The need for a more complex view of the work situation led to the rise of the behavioral science perspective.

Behavioral science An approach that emphasizes *scientific research* as the basis for developing theories about human behavior in organizations that can be used to establish practical guidelines for managers

The **behavioral science** approach emphasizes *scientific research* as the basis for developing theories about human behavior in organizations that can be used to establish practical guidelines for managers. It draws on findings from a variety of disciplines, including management, psychology, sociology, anthropology, and economics. Concepts are thoroughly tested in business organizations, and sometimes also in laboratory settings, before they are announced as viable approaches for managers. The ultimate aim of the behavioral science approach is to develop theories that managers can use as guides in assessing various situations and deciding on appropriate actions. Since humans themselves are complex and their interactions with others are even more so, the quest for an understanding of organizations and their members is an ongoing activity of considerable challenge.

An example of the useful outcomes of behavioral science research is the idea that individuals perform better with challenging, but attainable, goals than they do without goals. Of course, the goals must be specific and measurable ("I want to get an A in my management course this semester"), rather than vague ("I want to do well in my courses this semester"). The idea that goal setting leads to better performance was the result of extensive research by management researcher Edwin A. Locke and others.[43]

QUANTITATIVE MANAGEMENT VIEWPOINT

The quantitative management viewpoint emerged as a major force during World War II. The sheer magnitude of the war effort caused the British and then the U.S. military services to turn to quantitative methods for help in determining the most effective use of resources. For example, one set of quantitative studies by the U.S. Navy led to eliminating the "catch-as-catch-can" method that airplanes had used in searches for enemy vessels. Instead, quantitative analysis produced a pattern for such airplane searches that not only reduced the number of search planes needed for a given area but also increased the coverage. Aside from conserving scarce resources, the new search pattern in the South Atlantic led to the seizure of enemy ships carrying valuable cargo that significantly aided the Allied effort.[44] This and other important applications of quantitative methods gained the attention of business organizations, particularly as quantitative specialists found jobs in non-military-related organizations after the war.

The quantitative management viewpoint focuses on the use of mathematics, statistics, and information aids to support managerial decision making and organizational effectiveness.[45] Three main branches have evolved: management science, operations management, and management information systems.

Management Science

Management science An approach aimed at increasing decision effectiveness through the use of sophisticated mathematical models and statistical methods

Operations research Another name commonly used for management science

Management science is an approach aimed at increasing decision effectiveness through the use of sophisticated mathematical models and statistical methods. (*Caution:* This term is *not* used synonymously with the term "scientific management," discussed earlier.) Another name commonly used for management science is **operations research**. The increasing power of computers has greatly expanded the possibilities for using the mathematical and statistical tools of management science in organizations. Computers can quickly accomplish the extensive calculations that are often required. Management science was applied, for example, at Avon, the well-known maker of beauty, health-care, and fashion jewelry products. Group Vice President for Planning and Development Robert W. Pratt used statistical methods to analyze the implications of changing the company's common practice of offering heavy product discounts to generate larger orders. His results indicated that the ailing company could improve profits significantly by lowering the discounts, even if doing so meant smaller average orders per salesperson.[46]

Operations Management

Operations management
The function, or field of expertise, that is primarily responsible for managing the production and delivery of an organization's products and services

Operations management is the function, or field of expertise, that is primarily responsible for managing the production and delivery of an organization's products and services.[47] It includes such areas as inventory management, work scheduling, production planning, facilities location and design, and quality assurance. Operations management specialists use quantitatively oriented tools such as forecasting, inventory analysis, materials requirements planning systems, networking models, statistical quality control methods, and project planning and control techniques. Operations management is often applied to manufacturing settings in which various aspects of product production need to be managed, including designing the production process, purchasing raw materials, scheduling employees to work, and storing and shipping the final products. For example, Seeq Technology, a Silicon Valley maker of microchips, relied heavily on operations management when a sudden market glut of its main 128K EPROM chip caused the price to plummet from $15 to $2 in a period of a few months. Since the per-chip costs at that point were $5, the company had to rethink its production process, improve inventory management, and lower machine maintenance costs in order to stay in business while it completed proprietary new technology.[48] Operations management applies to delivering services as well.

Management Information Systems

Management information systems The field of management that focuses on designing and implementing computer-based information systems for use by management

The term **management information systems** refers to the field of management that focuses on designing and implementing computer-based information systems for use by management. Such systems turn raw data into information that is useful to various levels of management. In many industries, computer-based information systems are becoming a powerful competitive weapon because organizations are able to handle large amounts of information in new and better ways. For example, the creation of *USA Today*, the national newspaper, was made feasible by advances in computer-based telecommunication systems.

CONTEMPORARY VIEWPOINTS

While the classical, behavioral, and quantitative approaches continue to make contributions to management, other viewpoints have also emerged. These are contemporary in the sense that they represent major innovations in ways of thinking about management. Two of the most important contemporary viewpoints are the systems and contingency theories. In addition, at any given point in time, there are emerging views that influence the development of the management field even though they have not reached the status of enduring viewpoints.

Systems theory An approach based on the notion that organizations can be visualized as systems

System A set of interrelated parts that operate as a whole in pursuit of common goals

Systems Theory

The **systems theory** approach is based on the notion that organizations can be visualized as systems.[49] A **system** is a set of interrelated parts that operate as a whole in pursuit of common goals. The systems approach as applied to organizations is based largely on work in biology and the physical sciences.[50] In this section, we consider major systems components, open versus closed systems, and the characteristics of open systems.

MAJOR COMPONENTS According to the systems approach, an organizational system has four major components (see Figure 3). **Inputs** are the various human, material, financial, equipment, and informational resources required to produce goods and services. **Transformation processes** are the organization's managerial and technological abilities that are applied to convert inputs into outputs. **Outputs** are the products, services, and other outcomes produced by the organization. **Feedback** is information about results and organizational status relative to the environment.[51]

The systems approach has a number of advantages. First, it can analyze systems at different levels.[52] For example, systems expert J. Miller has outlined a typology of hierarchical levels of living systems, ranging from an individual human cell, including atoms and molecules, up to a supranational system consisting of two or more societies.[53] For the most part, managers consider the organism (individual), group, organization, and society levels, although the growing global emphasis is bringing the supranational level increasingly into play. Second, the systems view provides a framework for assessing how well the various parts of an organization interact to achieve a common purpose. Third, it emphasizes that a change in one part of the system may affect other parts. In thinking about the interrelationships among parts in an organization, you might visualize that the parts are interconnected by rubber bands. A pull on one part may well affect the position of other parts. Fourth, the systems approach considers how an organization interacts with its environment—the factors outside the organization that can affect its operations. In order to consider the environment adequately, an organization needs to operate as an open system.

Inputs The various human, material, financial, equipment, and informational resources required to produce goods and services

Transformation processes The organization's managerial and technological abilities that are applied to convert inputs into outputs

Outputs The products, services, and other outcomes produced by the organization

Feedback Information about results and organizational status relative to the environment

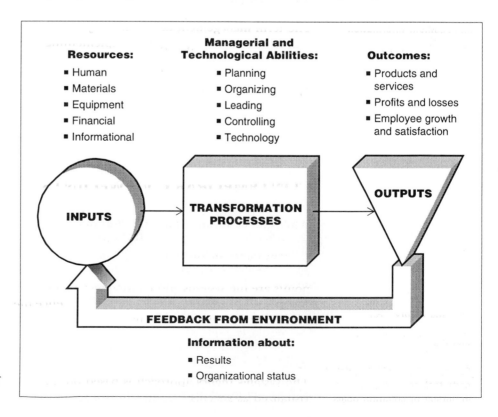

Figure 3 *A systems view of organizations.*

Open system   A system that operates in continual interaction with its environment

Closed system   A system that does little or no interacting with its environment and receives little feedback

OPEN VERSUS CLOSED SYSTEMS   Systems can be open or closed. An **open system** is one that operates in continual interaction with its environment. Through such interaction the system takes in new inputs and learns about how its outputs are received by various important outside elements. In contrast, a **closed system** does little or no interacting with its environment and receives little feedback. From a practical point of view, all organizations are open systems to some extent, since it is virtually impossible for an organization to operate for a significant period of time without some interaction with the environment. Still, organizations can vary tremendously in the degree to which they operate along the open-closed continuum. If an organization operates too closely to the closed end, it might not find out about important environmental factors that can affect it until problems are major.[54] Consider what happened when the Ford Motor Company attempted to launch a new automobile called the Edsel (see the following Case in Point discussion).

CASE IN POINT   FORD'S EDSEL FLOPS

During the late 1940s, managers at Ford realized that they had a problem. According to studies, 1 out of 5 car buyers each year was moving from a low-priced to a medium-priced car. Furthermore, among the owners of General Motors (GM) cars, about 87 percent of those trading up stayed with GM, choosing either a Pontiac, Oldsmobile, or Buick. Almost 47 percent of the Plymouth owners moving to a medium-priced car picked a Dodge or DeSoto—which, like the Plymouth, was within the Chrysler family. Ford, however, had only one medium-priced car, the Mercury, and only 26 percent of the Ford owners trading up selected a Mercury. Accordingly, the company began a decade of elaborate planning and preparation aimed at creating a successful new midpriced car geared to young executives and professionals.

The endeavor proved to be quite a challenge. For one thing, finding the right name turned out to be difficult. After extensive marketing research, 10 names were sent to the executive committee. Even so, the committee chose a name that was not on the list—Edsel, the name of Henry Ford's only son. The name "Edsel" was picked despite the fact that market research had shown that it provoked mixed customer reactions.

Another major issue was styling. The search for a distinctive, yet discreet, design involved 800 stylists, all of whom finally agreed on a vertical front grille shaped like a horse collar. Other features of the car included a body that was 2 inches longer than the largest Oldsmobile, numerous push buttons (e.g., for the transmission), and an extremely powerful engine—all characteristics determined by market research in the early 1950s to appeal to midrange car buyers.

To build and distribute the car, Ford set up a separate division at headquarters and separate Edsel dealers, rather than selling the car through one of its established divisions and chains of experienced dealerships. While it was felt that this would allow the new division and dealers to concentrate totally on the Edsel, the system also added greatly to the overhead associated with the car. To make a profit, Ford would have to sell a large number of Edsels. The executives felt that they were being conservative in estimating that 200,000 cars (or about 650 per day) would be sold the first year.

Although advertising was launched on July 22, 1957, the actual style of the car was kept a closely guarded secret until its introduction day, September 4 (about a month before competitors would be introducing their 1958 models). Sales of the Edsel on the first day were somewhat promising, but they quickly dwindled. In 1958, only about 35,000 Edsels were sold, far short of the conservative target. The 1959 Edsel models were shorter, lighter, less powerful, and less costly, and they were handled through a merged Lincoln-Mercury-Edsel division. Sales that year were about double those of the first year. When the 1960 models failed to generate additional excitement, production of the Edsel was scrapped. Losses reached about $200 million.

What went wrong? First, there was a stock market collapse in August 1957 that had a severe negative impact on purchases of medium-size cars that year. Second, Ford relied heavily on initial marketing data in planning the car. It failed to alter the plans in the face of the growing impact of smaller, more fuel-efficient foreign cars, which were beginning to capture portions of the U.S. market. Third, the first Edsels were prone to oil leaks, mysterious rattles, faulty brakes, and starting difficulties—problems that should have been detected before they reached the newspapers and national visibility. Because of these maladies, the car was quickly labeled a "lemon" and became the source of jokes. Fourth, Ford relied on a network of inexperienced new dealers to woo prospective customers. Fifth, the car was introduced while other carmakers were offering discounts on their previous year's models, making the new Edsel seem expensive. Finally, top management ignored negative marketing information from potential customers when it selected the name "Edsel."

Perhaps the Edsel could have survived one of these difficulties, but in combination, the problems were lethal. The situation illustrates the need to pay close attention to things going on outside that can affect system functioning and success.   ■ ■ ■

CHARACTERISTICS OF OPEN SYSTEMS   Organizations that operate closer to the open end of the continuum share certain characteristics that help them survive and prosper. Three major characteristics of open systems are negative entropy, differentiation, and synergy.[55]

Entropy refers to the tendency of systems to decay over time. In contrast, **negative entropy** is the ability of open systems to bring in new energy, in the form of inputs and feedback from the environment, in order to delay or arrest entropy. One reason the Edsel ran into trouble was that Ford relied on market research conducted in the early 1950s and ignored the newer signs indicating that consumers were turning to more fuel-efficient foreign cars.

Differentiation is the tendency of open systems to become more complex. The increased complexity usually stems from the addition of specialized units to handle particularly troublesome or challenging parts of the environment. Specialized units or positions are also added in response to new organizational tasks or in an attempt to increase controls over existing tasks (e.g., a quality assurance unit may be created). Closed systems are less likely to recognize the need for differentiation or may differentiate in inappropriate ways. For example, Ford engaged in unwarranted differentiation when it ignored the risks inherent in the environment and set up a separate division, along with a network of new dealers, to sell the Edsel. These moves increased the overhead so much that the car had little chance of surviving unless it was a stupendous instant success.

The third major characteristic of open systems is **synergy**, the ability of the whole to equal more than the sum of its parts. This means that an organization ought to be able to achieve its goals more effectively and efficiently than would be possible if the parts operated separately. At Ford, the organization's parts were not operating in synchronization when the top management committee ignored market research and chose the ill-fated "Edsel" tag.

According to the systems viewpoint, managers are likely to be more success-

Negative entropy The ability of open systems to bring in new energy, in the form of inputs and feedback from the environment, in order to delay or arrest entropy

Differentiation The tendency of open systems to become more complex

Synergy The ability of the whole to equal more than the sum of its parts

ful if they attempt to operate their units and organizations as open systems that are carefully attuned to the factors in the environment that could significantly affect them.

Contingency Theory

The classical theorists, such as Taylor and Fayol, were attempting to identify "the one best way" for managers to operate in a variety of situations. If universal principles could be found, then becoming a good manager would essentially involve learning the principles and how to apply them. Unfortunately, things were not to be that simple. Researchers soon found that some classical principles, such as Fayol's unity of command (each person should report to only one boss), could sometimes be violated with positive results. Consequently, contingency theory began to develop. **Contingency theory** is a viewpoint that argues that appropriate managerial action depends on the particular parameters of the situation. Hence, rather than seeking *universal* principles that apply to every situation, contingency theory attempts to identify *contingency* principles that prescribe actions to take depending on the characteristics of the situation (see Figure 4).[56]

Contingency theory A viewpoint that argues that appropriate managerial action depends on the particular parameters of the situation

One of the major pioneering studies that helped establish the contingency viewpoint was conducted in the 1950s by a research team headed by Joan Woodward, an industrial sociologist at the South Essex College of Technology in Great Britain.[57] The study of 100 British firms, which differed in size and product lines, was aimed at determining whether the better-performing companies adhered more closely to classical principles, such as unity of command, than did companies with average and below-average performances. When the comparisons revealed no major differences in the companies' use of classical principles, the researchers began to look elsewhere in their data for an explanation of the performance differences.

They decided to explore the type of technology used by the companies. The researchers divided the companies into three categories: unit or small-batch (products custom-made to customers' specifications), large-batch and mass-production (products produced in large amounts, mainly by assembly lines), and continuous-process (products produced in a noninterrupted flow, as in oil refining or chemical production). When they considered these differences, patterns related to performance began to emerge. The researchers found that suc-

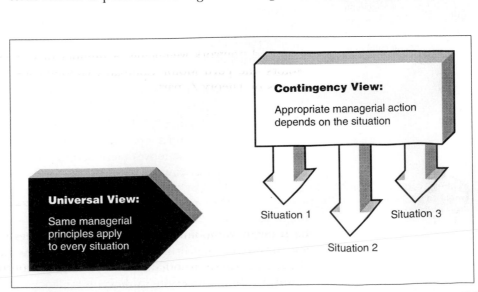

Figure 4 *The contingency managerial viewpoint.*

cessful companies operated somewhat differently depending on their technology category. (For example, small-batch and large-batch companies differed in the number of layers in the hierarchy and the numbers of subordinates reporting to managers at the various levels.) These findings support the contingency viewpoint that appropriate actions by managers often depend on (are contingent on) the situation.

To be fair, Fayol and most of the other classical theorists recognized that some judgment was needed in applying their various principles. Still, they emphasized universal principles and were rather vague about when the principles might *not* apply.[58]

Throughout this book you will encounter theories and concepts related to the contingency viewpoint—that is, areas in which applications of management ideas depend on situational factors. The contingency approach applies particularly well in such areas as environmental factors, strategy, organizational design, technology, and leadership.

Emerging Views

Given that management is a complex endeavor, innovative approaches are constantly needed to help advance the knowledge base. Some new approaches develop into major viewpoints when research and managerial practice show that they are effective. Other new ideas wither after investigations indicate that they are not living up to their promise.

Japanese management An approach that focuses on aspects of management in Japan that may be appropriate for adoption in the United States

One recent perspective that has gained attention can best be termed the **Japanese management** approach, since it focuses on aspects of management in Japan that may be appropriate for adoption in the United States. The interest in Japanese management has arisen because of the recent admirable success of Japanese companies, particularly in manufacturing such items as televisions, videocassette recorders, and computer printers.

Theory Z A concept that combines positive aspects of American and Japanese management into a modified approach aimed at increasing U.S. managerial effectiveness while remaining compatible with the norms and values of American society and culture

On the basis of his research of both American and Japanese management approaches, management expert William Ouchi has outlined Theory Z. **Theory Z** combines positive aspects of American and Japanese management into a modified approach aimed at increasing U.S. managerial effectiveness while remaining compatible with the norms and values of American society and culture (see Figure 5). The Theory Z approach involves giving workers job security; including them in some decision making; emphasizing group responsibility; increasing quality; establishing gradual-advancement policies, more informal controls, and broader career paths; and showing greater concern for employees' work and nonwork well-being. A number of U.S. companies, such as General Motors, the Ford Motor Company, Hewlett-Packard, and Intel, have adopted aspects of Theory Z, particularly the concepts of involving workers in decision making, instituting more informal controls, and encouraging group members to accept responsibility for work in their unit.

PROMOTING INNOVATION: CONTRIBUTIONS OF THE MAJOR VIEWPOINTS

Each major viewpoint has added important ideas to current knowledge about management and, in the process, has changed the way that managers think about and behave in organizations. The main contributions of the major viewpoints are summarized in Table 6.

Figure 5 *Characteristics of Theory Z management. (Adapted from William G. Ouchi and Alfred M. Jaeger, "Theory Z Organizations: Stability in the Midst of Mobility,"* Academy of Management Review, *vol. 3, 1978, pp. 308, 311.)*

TYPE A (American)	TYPE Z (Modified American)	TYPE J (Japanese)
Short-Term Employment	Long-Term Employment	Lifetime Employment
Individual Decision Making	Consensual Decision Making	Consensual Decision Making
Individual Responsibility	Individual Responsibility	Collective Responsibility
Rapid Evaluation and Promotion	Slow Evaluation and Promotion	Slow Evaluation and Promotion
Explicit, Formalized Control	Implicit, Informal Control with Explicit, Formalized Measures	Implicit, Informal Control
Specialized Career Path	Moderately Specialized Career Path	Nonspecialized Career Path
Segmented Concern	Holistic Concern, Including Family	Holistic Concern

TABLE 6	Main Innovative Contributions of Major Viewpoints
Viewpoint	**Innovative Contributions**
Classical	Highlights the need for a scientific approach to management
	Points out that work methods often can be improved through study
	Identifies a number of important principles that are useful in running organizations efficiently
	Emphasizes the potential importance of pay as a motivator
Behavioral	Spotlights the managerial importance of such factors as communication, group dynamics, motivation, and leadership
	Articulates practical applications of behavioral studies
	Draws on the findings of a number of disciplines such as management, psychology, sociology, anthropology, and economics
	Highlights the importance of organization members as active human resources rather than as passive tools
Quantitative	Provides quantitative aids to decision making
	Develops quantitative tools to assist in providing products and services
	Pioneers new computer-based information systems for management
Contemporary (systems and contingency)	Emphasizes that organizations can be visualized as systems of interrelated parts
	Points out the potential importance of the environment and feedback to organizational success
	Argues that there is no one best way to manage and identifies the circumstances or contingencies that influence which particular approach will be effective in a given situation

CHAPTER SUMMARY

Although management practices can be traced back to ancient times, much of the impetus for developing management theories and principles grew out of the industrial revolution and the need for better ways to run the resulting factory systems. Preclassical contributors such as Robert Owen, Charles Babbage, and Henry R. Towne provided some initial ideas that eventually led to the identification of management as an important field of inquiry. From this base, four major viewpoints have developed: classical, behavioral, quantitative, and contemporary.

The classical viewpoint emphasizes finding ways to manage work and organizations more efficiently. It includes three different approaches. The scientific management approach, represented by the work of Frederick Winslow Taylor, Frank and Lillian Gilbreth, and Henry Gantt, emphasizes the scientific study of work methods in order to improve worker efficiency. The bureaucratic approach, pioneered by Max Weber, focuses on the need for organizations to operate in a rational manner rather than relying on the arbitrary whims of owners and managers. The administrative management approach, supported by Henri Fayol and Chester Barnard, explores principles that can be used by managers to coordinate the internal activities of organizations.

The behavioral viewpoint is a perspective that seeks to understand the various factors that affect human behavior in organizations. Hugo Münsterberg and Mary Parker Follett were early behaviorists. It was the Hawthorne studies, though, that dramatically demonstrated that workers were more than mere tools of production. Although flawed, the studies produced insights that led to the establishment of the human relations movement, with its emphasis on concern for the worker. Abraham Maslow's hierarchy of needs theory and Douglas McGregor's Theory X and Theory Y provided some guidance

for managers but were still fairly general. The behavioral science approach, with its emphasis on scientific research, emerged to build more specific theories about behavior in organizations that can be used to provide practical guidelines for managers.

The quantitative viewpoint focuses on the use of mathematics, statistics, and information aids to support managerial decision making and effectiveness. It has three main branches. Operations research is an approach aimed at increasing decision effectiveness through the use of sophisticated mathematical models and statistical methods. Operations management is the field of expertise that is primarily responsible for managing the production and delivery of an organization's products and services. The management information systems field focuses on designing and implementing computer-based information systems for use by management.

The contemporary viewpoints represent recent major innovations in ways of thinking about management. They include the systems and contingency theories, as well as emerging views. The systems theory approach is based on the notion that organizations can be visualized as systems, including inputs, transformation processes, outputs, and feedback. Contingency theory argues that appropriate managerial action depends on the particular parameters of a given situation. Emerging viewpoints include new, promising approaches that may develop into major viewpoints if research supports their relevance. One important emerging view is Japanese management, represented by Theory Z. This theory combines the positive aspects of American and Japanese management into a modified approach appropriate to business in the United States.

All the major viewpoints contribute significantly to innovation in the field of management. Other viewpoints will likely develop as the field progresses.

QUESTIONS FOR DISCUSSION AND REVIEW

1 Explain how the preclassical contributors helped set the stage for the development of management as a science. Identify a situation in which you have used the guidelines in *Robert's Rules of Order* or seen them used. Why have the rules been so popular over a considerable period of time?

2 Contrast the three major approaches within the classical viewpoint: scientific management, bureaucratic management, and administrative management. Give some examples of how these approaches are reflected in an organization with which you are familiar.

3 Review the scientific management principles advocated by Frederick Taylor. How effective do you think these principles would be in eliminating sol-

diering? What might be some disadvantages of his approach? What did Frank and Lillian Gilbreth add to Taylor's approach?

4 Summarize the contributions of Mary Parker Follett. For each contribution, give an example illustrating the relevance of her ideas today.

5 Explain the development of the behavioral viewpoint. How is it possible that a flawed set of studies—the Hawthorne studies—helped bring about the behavioral viewpoint of management?

6 Differentiate among the three major approaches within the quantitative management viewpoint. How have computers aided the development of this viewpoint?

7 Explain the major ideas underlying the systems view-

point. Use this viewpoint to analyze your college or university. To what extent would you consider it to be an open system? Give reasons for your view.

8 Describe the reasoning behind the contingency viewpoint. Why did it emerge? How does Joan Woodward's research on technology illustrate the contingency theory concept?

9 Explain the Theory Z approach to management. Under which system would you prefer to work: American (Type A), Japanese (Type J), or modified American (Type Z)? Why? Which system do you think would work best in the following work environments: research, production, mining, agriculture, service?

10 Show how current management knowledge is the result of innovative processes involving many management pioneers. What can we learn about the process of innovation from studying these people's ideas?

DISCUSSION QUESTIONS FOR CHAPTER OPENING CASE

1 How did scientific management help Henry Ford build the Ford Motor Company?

2 Use the systems view to analyze the reasons for the failure of Ford's first two companies and the success of his third, the Ford Motor Company.

3 If the Hawthorne studies had been conducted in the early 1890s and the human relations movement had been emerging at that time, how might they have influenced Henry Ford's approach?

MANAGEMENT EXERCISE: PROBLEMS AT THE ICE CREAM PLANT

 You are the manager of a plant that produces a special type of extra-creamy ice cream. Sales had been increasing every quarter for the past 4 years, until last quarter. During that quarter sales slipped 17 percent, production was about 15 percent short of projections, absenteeism was about 20 percent higher than it was in the previous quarter, and tardiness increased steadily. You believe that the problems are probably management-related, but you are not sure about their causes or the steps you should take to correct them. You decide to call in a consultant to help you determine what to do next. The consultant tells you that she wholeheartedly supports scientific management and usually looks at problems from that point of view. She mentions that there are other consultants in the area who tend to take other views. In order to get the most complete idea of what should be done at your plant, you call in five other consultants, each of whom supports one of the following approaches: administrative management, bureaucracy, human relations, quantitative management, and systems theory.

Form a group with two of your classmates. Have each member of the group select two of the six management approaches mentioned above. Be sure that all six approaches are included. Each member will play the role of a consultant for one of the approaches that he or she has selected and then repeat the process for his or her second consultant role. The person should analyze the likely problems at the ice cream plant and offer solutions from the point of view of the particular management approach that he or she is representing. The other two group members will critique the explanations presented by the consultant.

REFERENCES

1. Based on Peter F. Drucker, *Management*, Harper & Row, New York, 1973, p. 53; Robert Lacey, *Ford—The Men and the Machine*, Little, Brown, Boston, 1986; and Peter Collier and David Horowitz, *The Fords*, Summit, New York, 1987.

2. Daniel A. Wren, *The Evolution of Management Thought*, 2d ed., Wiley, New York, 1979; W. Jack Duncan, *Great Ideas in Management*, Jossey-Bass, San Francisco, 1989.

3. W. Jack Duncan, *Great Ideas in Management*, Jossey-Bass, San Francisco, 1989; Maurice V. Wilkes, "Charles Babbage—The Great Uncle of Computing?" *Communications of the ACM*, March 1992.

4. Charles Babbage, *On the Economy of Machinery and Manufactures*, Charles Knight, London, 1832, reprinted by Agustus Kelly, New York, 1963.

5. Henry R. Towne, "The Engineer as an Economist," *Transactions of the American Society of Mechanical Engineers*, vol. 7, 1886, pp. 428–432; David F. Noble, *America by Design: Science, Technology and the Rise of Corporate Capitalism*, Knopf, New York, 1977; Daniel A. Wren, "Years of Good Beginnings: 1886 and 1936," in Daniel A. Wren and John A. Pearce II (eds.), *Papers Dedicated to the Development of Modern Management*, Academy of Management, 1986, pp.

1–4; W. Jack Duncan, *Great Ideas in Management,* Jossey-Bass, San Francisco, 1989.

6. Hannah Sampson, "The Army's Clausewitz of the Meeting Room," *Army,* January 1988, pp. 49–50.

7. For a fascinating series of reviews of the works of major contributors to the classical viewpoint, see Allen C. Bluedorn (ed.), "Special Book Review Section on the Classics of Management," *Academy of Management Review,* vol. 11, 1986, pp. 442–464.

8. W. Jack Duncan, *Great Ideas in Management,* Jossey-Bass, San Francisco, 1989.

9. Frederick Winslow Taylor, *The Principles of Scientific Management,* Hive, Easton, Pa., 1985.

10. Edwin A. Locke, "The Ideas of Frederick W. Taylor: An Evaluation," *Academy of Management Review,* vol. 7, 1982, pp. 14–24.

11. Ibid.

12. Daniel A. Wren, *The Evolution of Management Thought,* 2d ed., Wiley, New York, 1979.

13. John Breeze, "Paul Devinat's Scientific Management in Europe— A Historical Perspective," in Daniel A. Wren and John A. Pearce II (eds.), *Papers Dedicated to the Development of Modern Management,* Academy of Management, 1986, pp. 58–63. Critics argue that Taylor failed to acknowledge some previous work by others on the issue of shoveling. On the other hand, supporters state that the issues raised by critics are misguided or involve minor issues. See Charles D. Wrege and Amedeo G. Perroni, "Taylor's Pig Tale: A Historical Analysis of Frederick W. Taylor's Pig Iron Experiment," *Academy of Management Journal,* vol. 17, 1974, pp. 6–27; Charles Wrege and Anne Marie Stotka, "Cooke Creates a Classic: The Story behind F. W. Taylor's Principles of Scientific Management," *Academy of Management Review,* vol. 3, 1978, pp. 736–749; Louis W. Fry, "The Maligned F. W. Taylor: A Reply to Many of His Critics," *Academy of Management Review,* vol. 1, 1976, pp. 124–129; and Edwin A. Locke, "The Ideas of Frederick W. Taylor: An Evaluation," *Academy of Management Review,* vol. 7, 1982, pp. 14–24.

14. Daniel A. Wren, *The Evolution of Management Thought,* 2d ed., Wiley, New York, 1979.

15. Ibid.

16. L. M. Gilbreth, *The Psychology of Management,* Sturgis and Walton, 1914, reissued by Macmillan, New York, 1921.

17. W. Jack Duncan, *Great Ideas in Management,* Jossey-Bass, San Francisco, 1989.

18. Daniel A. Wren, *The Evolution of Management Thought,* 2d ed., Wiley, New York, 1979.

19. Ibid.

20. This section is based on ibid., and W. Jack Duncan, *Great Ideas in Management,* Jossey-Bass, San Francisco, 1989.

21. This section is based mainly on ibid.; see also Arnold Eisen, "The Meanings and Confusions of Weberian 'Rationality,'" *British Journal of Sociology,* March 1978, pp. 57–70.

22. Richard M. Weiss, "Weber on Bureaucracy: Management Consultant or Political Theorist?" *Academy of Management Review,* vol. 8, 1983, pp. 242–248.

23. Jeffrey M. Laderman, "The Family That Hauls Together Brawls Together," *Business Week,* Aug. 29, 1988, pp. 64–68; Robert Tomsho, "U-Haul Patriarch Now Battles Offspring in Bitterest of Feuds," *The Wall Street Journal,* July 16, 1990, pp. A1–A6.

24. This section is based mainly on Daniel A. Wren, *The Evolution of Management Thought,* 2d ed., Wiley, New York, 1979; and W. Jack Duncan, *Great Ideas in Management,* Jossey-Bass, San Francisco, 1989.

25. This section is based mainly on W. Jack Duncan, *Great Ideas in Management,* Jossey-Bass, San Francisco, 1989.

26. Correspondence to Daniel A. Wren from William B. Wolf, cited in Daniel A. Wren, *The Evolution of Management Thought,* 2d ed., Wiley, New York, 1979, p. 250; thirtieth-anniversary edition of Chester I. Barnard, *The Functions of the Executive,* Harvard, Cambridge, Mass., 1968.

27. "How Power Will Be Balanced on Saturn's Shop Floor," *Business Week,* Aug. 4, 1985, pp. 65–66; David

Woodruff, "At Saturn, What Workers Want Is . . . Fewer Defects," *Business Week,* Dec. 2, 1991, pp 117–118.

28. Kenneth R. Andrews, in the introduction to the thirtieth-anniversary edition of Chester I. Barnard, *The Function of the Executive,* Harvard, Cambridge, Mass., 1968; W. Jack Duncan, *Great Ideas in Management,* Jossey-Bass, San Francisco, 1989.

29. Henry C. Metcalf and Lyndall Urwick (eds.), *Dynamic Administration: The Collected Papers of Mary Parker Follett,* Harper & Row, New York, 1940, pp. 32–33.

30. Daniel A. Wren, *The Evolution of Management Thought,* 2d ed., Wiley, New York, 1979; L. D. Parker, "Control in Organizational Life: The Contribution of Mary Parker Follett," *Academy of Management Review,* vol. 9, 1984, pp. 736–745.

31. L. D. Parker, "Control in Organizational Life: The Contribution of Mary Parker Follett," *Academy of Management Review,* vol. 9, 1984, pp. 736–745.

32. Ronald G. Greenwood and Charles D. Wrege, "The Hawthorne Studies," in Daniel A. Wren and John A. Pearce II (eds.), *Papers Dedicated to the Development of Modern Management,* Academy of Management, 1986, pp. 24–35.

33. Ibid.

34. John G. Adair, "The Hawthorne Effect: A Reconsideration of the Methodological Artifact," *Journal of Applied Psychology,* vol. 69, 1984, pp. 334–345.

35. Ronald G. Greenwood and Charles D. Wrege, "The Hawthorne Studies," in Daniel A. Wren and John A. Pearce II (eds.), *Papers Dedicated to the Development of Modern Management,* Academy of Management, 1986, pp. 24–35.

36. Berkeley Rice, "The Hawthorne Defect: Persistence of a Flawed Theory," *Psychology Today,* February 1982, pp. 70–74.

37. John G. Adair, "The Hawthorne Effect: A Reconsideration of the Methodological Artifact," *Journal of Applied Psychology,* vol. 69, 1984, pp. 334–345.

38. Daniel A. Wren, *The Evolution of Management Thought,* 2d ed., Wiley, New York, 1979; Dana Bramel and

Ronald Friend, "Hawthorne, the Myth of the Docile Worker, and Class Bias in Psychology," *American Psychologist*, August 1981, pp. 867–878.

39. John G. Adair, "The Hawthorne Effect: A Reconsideration of the Methodological Artifact," *Journal of Applied Psychology*, vol. 69, 1984, p. 334. The Hawthorne studies have been severely criticized mainly because the studies often had major flaws (such as changing several factors at the same time) and because important data were sometimes ignored in drawing conclusions (especially in discounting the potential importance of pay). In their defense, the studies were conducted at a time when knowledge about how to conduct such studies was fairly embryonic. For criticisms and clarifications, see, for example, Alex Carey, "The Hawthorne Studies: A Radical Criticism," *American Sociological Review*, June 1967, pp. 403–416; John M. Shepard, "On Alex Carey's Radical Criticisms of the Hawthorne Studies," *Academy of Management Journal*, March 1971, pp. 23–32; Dana Bramel and Ronald Friend, "Hawthorne, the Myth of the Docile Worker, and Class Bias in Psychology," *American Psychologist*, August 1981, pp. 867–878; Ronald G. Greenwood, Alfred A. Bolton, and Regina A. Greenwood, "Hawthorne a Half Century Later: Relay Assembly Participants Remember," *Journal of Management*, vol. 9, 1983, pp. 217–231; and Jeffrey A. Sonnenfeld, "Shedding Light on the Hawthorne Studies," *Journal of Occupational Behavior*, vol. 6, 1985, pp. 111–130.

40. W. Jack Duncan, *Great Ideas in Management*, Jossey-Bass, San Francisco, 1989.

41. A. H. Maslow, "A Theory of Human Motivation," *Psychological Review*, vol. 50, 1943, pp. 370–396, and *Motivation and Personality*, Harper & Row, New York, 1954.

42. Douglas McGregor, *The Human Side of Enterprise*, McGraw-Hill, New York, 1960.

43. Edwin A. Locke, Karyll N. Shaw, Lise M. Saari, and Gary P. Latham, "Goal Setting and Task Performance: 1969–1980" *Psychological Bulletin*, vol. 90, 1982, pp. 125–152; Robert D. Pritchard, Steven D. Jones, Philip L. Roth, Karla K. Stuebing, and Steven E. Ekeberg, "Effects of Group Feedback, Goal Setting, and Incentives on Organizational Productivity," *Journal of Applied Psychology*, vol. 73, 1988, pp. 337–358.

44. Norman Gaither, "Historical Development of Operations Research," in Daniel A. Wren and John A. Pearce II (eds.), *Papers Dedicated to the Development of Modern Management*, Academy of Management, 1986, pp. 71–77.

45. James R. Miller and Howard Feldman, "Management Science—Theory, Relevance, and Practice in the 1980s," *Interfaces*, October 1983, pp. 56–60.

46. Hicks Waldon, "Putting a New Face on Avon," *Planning Review*, July 1985, pp. 18–25; John Thackray, "Planning an Avon Turnaround," *Planning Review*, January 1985, pp. 6–11.

47. William J. Sawaya, Jr., and William C. Giauque, *Production and Operations Management*, Harcourt Brace Jovanovich, San Diego, 1986.

48. Edward O. Welles, "The Company Money Almost Killed," *INC.*, November 1988, pp. 46–60.

49. Fremont E. Kast and James E. Rosenzweig, "General Systems Theory: Applications for Organization and Management," *Academy of Management Journal*, vol. 15, pp. 447–465.

50. Ludwig von Bertalanffy, "General Systems Theory: A New Approach to the Unity of Science," *Human Biology*, December 1951, pp. 302–361, and "General Systems Theory—A Critical Review," *General Systems*, vol. 7, 1962, pp. 1–20; Daniel Katz and Robert L. Kahn, *The Social Psychology of Organizations*, Wiley, New York, 1978; see also Kenneth E. Boulding, "General Systems Theory—The Skeleton of Science," *Management Science*, vol. 2, 1956, pp. 197–208.

51. Arkalgud Ramaprasad, "On the Definition of Feedback," *Behavioral Science*, January 1983, pp. 4–13.

52. Donde P. Ashmos and George P. Huber, "The Systems Paradigm in Organization Theory: Correcting the Record and Suggesting the Future," *Academy of Management Review*, vol. 12, 1987, pp. 607–621.

53. J. Miller, *Living Systems*, McGraw-Hill, New York, 1978.

54. Fremont E. Kast and James E. Rosenzweig, *Organization and Management: A Systems Approach*, 2d ed., McGraw-Hill, 1974.

55. Fremont E. Kast and James E. Rosenzweig, "General Systems Theory: Applications for Organization and Management," *Academy of Management Journal*, vol. 15, 1972, pp. 447–465; Daniel Katz and Robert L. Kahn, *The Social Psychology of Organizations*, Wiley, New York, 1978.

56. Fred Luthans, "The Contingency Theory of Management," *Business Horizons*, June 1973, pp. 67–72; Sang M. Lee, Fred Luthans, and David L. Olson, "A Management Science Approach to Contingency Models of Organizational Structure," *Academy of Management Journal*, vol. 25, 1982, pp. 553–566.

57. Joan Woodward, *Industrial Organization: Theory and Practice*, Oxford University, London, 1965.

58. Jay W. Lorsch, "Making Behavioral Science More Useful," *Harvard Business Review*, March–April 1979, pp. 171–180; Henry L. Tosi, Jr., and John W. Slocum, Jr., "Contingency Theory: Some Suggested Directions," *Journal of Management*, vol. 10, 1984, pp. 9–26.

ACKNOWLEDGMENT

Figure

Figure 5: William G. Ouchi and Alfred M. Jaeger, "Theory Z Organizations: Stability in the Midst of Mobility," *Academy of Management Review*, vol. 3, 1978, pp. 308, 311. Adapted by permission of the Academy of Management and the authors.

CONCLUDING CASE

SIEMENS IS GROOMING A NEW GENERATION OF MANAGERS

When German electronics giant Siemens decided to reorganize itself for the 1990s, top management identified a primary need for managers who are oriented to change. Even though the company's sales are in the $50 billion range, Siemens is under intense competitive pressure, particularly from the Japanese. Historically, "European companies take longer to react," says board member Hermann Franz. To stay ahead of competitors in the future, Siemens wants managers who can cut the reaction time and jump ahead of competitors.

To develop and encourage such managers, Siemens is breaking up the massive structure that required talented managers to labor for years at lower levels before attaining promotions. Instead, the company is creating smaller business units and seeking entrepreneurial candidates to head them. In the process, Siemens has identified 500 managers who seem to have the appropriate entrepreneurial bent. Most of them are in their twenties and thirties, although a few are in their forties. These managers are expected to assume senior posts by age 35 to 45, instead of the more usual 50 to 60 range. The 500 have been placed on the fast track and have been given challenging assignments. If they perform at the extraordinary levels expected, they will be moved up quickly. Instead of relying solely on the advanced technology that has been a major strength of Siemens, this group is

also expected to emphasize marketing and sales.

Leading the fast-trackers is the new chief executive officer Heinrich von Pierer. When he was head of Siemens' $3.2 billion energy unit, von Pierer established a solid reputation for recognizing the need for change and taking appropriate action. He foresaw that the nuclear-power-plant business would encounter difficulties in the late 1980s, and he switched emphasis to conventional gas-and-steam turbine production early enough to take full advantage of the market shift. Von Pierer, known as a careful listener and a consensus builder, takes the initiative and breaks through dysfunctional bureaucracies. For example, he typically calls lower-level managers to his office to obtain information firsthand instead of going through a long chain of command.

To become one of the "chosen 500," candidates must be recommended by their immediate superior. They then spend a full week taking a battery of tests, engaging in role playing, and handling case situations at Siemens' management training center, south of Munich. In one exercise, teams of four participants are given a management crisis and limited time to solve it. The team must determine, for example, how to handle the press and demonstrators who are gathering around a factory after a mercury spill. Top managers and a psychologist assess each participant's product knowledge, creativity, and leadership ability. In addition, each participant criticizes his or her colleagues' performance

and rates them on such attributes as risk-taking propensity and information gathering. Candidates who perform exceptionally well are placed in the chosen group.

Selected candidates can expect a fast-paced career, in which they transfer from one challenging job to another, moving across divisions and into foreign countries. The new managers will have a global focus, which will facilitate acquiring and managing companies in faraway lands. Salary is very competitive for excellent performers, starting at about $60,000 and including annual raises that could reach 30 percent of base pay. To remain in the chosen group, however, one's performance must continue to be stellar. Siemens needs exceptional performance from this new cadre of managers because about 50 of its 300 businesses are losing money and another 150 are close to just breaking even. Siemens' long-term strategy is to dominate the global market for electronic systems.*

QUESTIONS FOR CONCLUDING CASE

1 Explain how Siemens is changing to an open system.
2 Explain how Siemens is dealing with entropy through the radical change in its method of selecting managers.
3 How could Siemens effectively use contingency theory to help train its new group of managers?

* Based on Gail E. Schares, "The New Generation at Siemens," *Business Week,* Mar. 9, 1992, pp. 46–48.

FORD MOTOR CHARGES AHEAD AND INTO GLOBALIZATION

Amidst the auto industry downturn of the early 1980s, Henry Ford's motor company was hemorrhaging. Henry Ford II had just retired from his position as chairman of the company that his grandfather had built. Between 1979 and 1982, the company lost $3 billion. It was plagued by a reputation for producing cars designed for yesterday's consumers, and—worse—quality was poor. Wall Street analysts predicted that the company was forever doomed to be an "also-ran" in world car competition.

Cutting costs and raising quality were clear priorities. By the mid-1980s, the company had reduced its hourly work force, cut back on white-collar workers, and shut down eight U.S. plants. The remaining 81 plants were revamped and upgraded technologically to make the work as efficient as possible. Computerized robots and upgraded inventory control were part of the massive changes. At the same time, Ford tied its efficiency and cost-cutting efforts to its quality quest. It adopted the Japanese management view that higher quality ultimately means lower costs. According to one manufacturing manager, "If you don't make bad parts, you won't have bad parts—and if you do, you have to scrap them. This is how cost-conscious plant managers become quality conscious." Such changes reduced costs by $5 billion by the mid-1980s, with another $5 billion in savings by the early 1990s.

The company also redirected the design of its cars. Whereas in the past the tendency had been to follow the competition, top management now told designers to "design the kind of cars you would like to drive." With the new approach, Ford has produced a number of automobiles, including the Taurus, the Sable, and the drastically redesigned Lincoln Continental, that have been big sellers.

Some of the less visible changes at Ford relate to its new approach to internal management. Once considered to have the most autocratic managers in the U.S. auto industry, the company launched a program called Employee Involvement that has pushed decision making to lower levels, including the assembly line. For example, assembly-line workers are now authorized to stop the line if they see a problem. Ford emphasizes teamwork and uses the team concept to involve individuals from various areas, such as design, engineering, and manufacturing, in the development of new models. Ideas come from the bottom of the company as well as from the top.

Ford still has its work cut out for it. The company is considered to be behind in the latest technology to simultaneously improve performance and gasoline mileage. Ford also has to become more competitive in other parts of the world.

Currently, Ford has more than 14 percent of the worldwide automobile market, compared with General Motors' 17 percent share. Ford produces cars, trucks, and accessories in the United States and Canada and in parts of Europe, Asia, Australia, and South America.

Ford also continues to reach toward the Pacific. It owns 25 percent of Mazda, which is developing the next-generation Ford Escort. The Ford Fiesta is made by Kia in Korea, and Ford is in the process of building a new plant in Ohio to produce Nissan-designed minivans that will be sold by both Ford and Nissan. Ford management looks forward to the day when the company can produce an automobile through a joint effort of European, North American, and Japanese designers.*

QUESTIONS FOR CONCLUDING CASE

1 Identify influences from the classical, behavioral, and quantitative viewpoints in the way the Ford Motor Company is managed today.
2 Use systems theory to contrast the way the Ford Motor Company operated at the time the Edsel was introduced with the way the company is currently operating, including its worldwide emphasis.
3 Explain the influence of Japanese management (Theory Z) on current management at the Ford Motor Company.

* Based on Anne B. Fisher, "Ford Is Back on the Track," *Fortune*, Dec. 23, 1985, pp. 18–22; Steve Kichen and Jerry Flint, "Supercharged," *Forbes*, Sept. 5, 1988, pp. 74–78; Paul Ingrassia and Bradley A. Stertz, "Ford's Strong Sales Raise Agonizing Issue of Additional Plants," *The Wall Street Journal*, Oct. 26, 1988, p. 1; Kate Ballen, "The No. 1 Leader Is Petersen of Ford," *Fortune*, Oct. 24, 1988, pp. 69–70; Alex Taylor III, "Why Fords Sell Like Big Macs," *Fortune*, Nov. 21, 1988, pp. 122–125; 1988 Annual Report, Ford Motor Company, Detroit; Joann S. Lublin and Craig Forman, "Ford Snares Jaguar, but $2.5 Billion Is High Price for Prestige," *The Wall Street Journal*, Nov. 3, 1989, p. A1; "How to Go Global—And Why," *Fortune*, Aug. 28, 1989, pp. 73–74; John Marcom, Jr., "Detroit's Euro-Boom," *Forbes*, Mar. 20, 1989, p. 39; Warren Brown, "Ford Chairman Announces He'll Retire 18 Months Early," *The Washington Post*, Nov. 11, 1989, p. D12; Jeff Benkoe, "Ford, Mazda in Talks on New European Car," *The Reuter Business Report*, Apr. 30, 1992; and Neil Winton, "Ford Plans Slow in Eastern Europe," *The Reuter Business Report*, May 5, 1992.

CHAPTER 3

Establishing Organizational Goals and Plans

GAINING THE EDGE

CYPRESS SEMICONDUCTOR THRIVES ON "TURBO MBO"*

When the Cypress Semiconductor Corporation was founded in 1983, the president and CEO, Dr. Thurman John Rodgers (more commonly known as "T. J.") instituted a management by objectives (MBO) program that obtains positive results. Starting from scratch, the organization now has an annual income in excess of $200 million, more than 1500 employees, and 5 subsidiaries.

Cypress's basic mission is to be a profitable $1 billion semiconductor company that ships quickly, operates efficiently, and is a technological leader. The company competes by producing more than 130 complex, state-of-the-art computer chips for specialized markets. For example, Cypress has recently introduced the "hyper-Sparc" microprocessor. Developed for Sun Microsystems, Inc., this chip triples the performance of the fastest earlier microprocessors.

The management by objectives system, which Rodgers likes to call "Turbo MBO," helps the company manage its intricate operations by having employees set goals each week that are then tracked by computer. "Producing a semiconductor is a very unforgiving entity," says Rodgers. "If it takes 1000 tasks to make one and you do 999 right but then you forget one or do one wrong, the semiconductor will not work. The [MBO] system forces management to stick its nose in a big book every single week and find out what is going on. We can't afford surprises."

Under the MBO system, senior management and the board of directors develop broad corporate goals for a 5-year period and engage in strategic planning to determine the best way to reach the goals. In the process, they review the projected sales, marketing, and manufacturing plans and consider other important variables such as the number of employees and the amount of capital involved relative to expected outcomes. The 5-year plan is updated annually. The results are then forwarded to middle managers, who develop goals and related plans (often called tactical goals and plans) at their level that are to be accomplished during the coming year. The tactical goals and plans are given, in turn, to project and program leaders at the next lower level. These leaders develop goals and plans (often called operational goals and plans) that are oriented to the current year and frequently to an even shorter period, such as the immediate quarter. Within the goals and plans developed at the strategic, tactical, and operational levels, the Turbo MBO system operates on a weekly basis.

The weekly goal cycle starts on Monday, when every project leader holds a meeting with the project group to review the status of goals that are due and to map out what each group member will do that week. All the new goals for the week are put into the computer system so that more than 40 managers have access to the data through their personal computers. The system is designed to report goals that are delinquent (past due) and identify individuals who are behind on three or more goals.

On Tuesdays, managers review the goals put into the computer the previous day. They consider such issues as priorities, timeliness, equity of work loads, and appropriate progress on projects. On Wednesday afternoons, Rodgers and his seven vice presidents review the status of goals for significant projects. They also

* Steve Kaufman, "Turbo MBO's Spell Success for Chip Maker," *San Jose Mercury News,* June 1, 1987, p. 2D. Reprinted by permission of *San Jose Mercury News.*

consider critical management ratios, such as revenue per employee, revenue to gross capital, performance to original schedule, sales and administration as a percent of revenue, and other measures for which goals have been set for the company as a whole. By the end of this weekly meeting, goals have been reviewed and revised where appropriate. At this point, a printout of everyone's weekly goals is distributed to each employee. It takes employees about 30 minutes to review and update their goals each week.

A permanent record of each employee's goal accomplishments is made monthly. These records are accumulated and used as input for each employee's annual performance evaluation, which is the basis for annual merit increases.

Employees tend to favor the system because it is "bottom-up." That is, they are able to set their own goals within the overall-goals framework. Managers are enthusiastic because the system provides a high level of communication between themselves and the employees who have goals in their areas. Cypress's financial backers praise it because it keeps the company performing according to plan. Thus using its MBO system for goal setting and planning has generally paid off handsomely for Cypress.[1]

Rodgers learned the value of goals and planning while a project manager at American Microsystems (another high-technology firm). There he filled blackboards with lists of "several hundred things to get done, who would do it, and when." Turbo MBO at Cypress is essentially a computerized refinement of that system, an innovation that has helped Cypress succeed in a very competitive industry. While few organizations set goals as often as weekly, there is strong support in the management literature for the importance of goals and related planning, which jointly form the heart of the planning function. In this chapter, we examine the overall planning process, including the development of the mission of the organization. We also consider the nature of organizational goals and examine a model that helps explain how goals facilitate performance. We next probe the link between goals and plans, considering how plans differ according to level, extent of recurring use, and time horizon and examining the role of goals and plans in promoting innovation. Finally, we explore the steps in the management by objectives process and review the major strengths and weaknesses of MBO.

THE OVERALL PLANNING PROCESS

How was Steve Bostic, head of the American Photo Group, able to increase annual sales from $149,000 to $78 million before selling the high-technology company to Eastman Kodak for a reported $45 million? Bostic attributes his success to having a vision, being able to put specifics down on paper, and having things "well planned and well thought out."[2] As Bostic's experience suggests, having a good idea of the organization's overall mission, as well as more specific, written goals and carefully configured plans, can be important to an organization's success. In this section, we introduce these major components of the planning process.

Major Components of Planning

One could argue that it is virtually impossible for organizations to function without at least some goals and plans. A **goal** is a future target or end result that an organization wishes to achieve. Many managers and researchers use the term "goal" interchangeably with "objective." Others consider "goal" to be a

Goal A future target or end result that an organization wishes to achieve

broader term, encompassing a longer time horizon, and use "objective" to refer to more narrow targets and shorter time frames.[3] We use both terms interchangeably for the sake of simplicity. When distinction between the two is important to the concepts being examined, it will be clear from the context whether a broad or narrow scope or a long or short time frame is involved.

Plan The means devised for attempting to reach a goal

Whereas a goal is a future end result that an organization wants to achieve, a **plan** is the means devised for attempting to reach a goal. *Planning,* then, is the management function that involves setting goals and deciding how best to achieve them. An overall view of the planning process is shown in Figure 1. Hopefully, setting goals and developing plans will lead to goal attainment and, ultimately, to organizational efficiency and effectiveness. As the diagram indicates, the planning process also involves the mission of the organization.

Organizational Mission

Mission The organization's purpose or fundamental reason for existence

Mission statement A broad declaration of the basic, unique purpose and scope of operations that distinguishes the organization from others of its type

Essentially, the planning process builds on the **mission** of the organization, the organization's purpose or fundamental reason for existence. A **mission statement** is a broad declaration of the basic, unique purpose and scope of operations that distinguishes the organization from others of its type.[4] A mission statement serves several purposes. For managers, it can be a benchmark against which to evaluate success. For employees, a mission statement defines a common purpose, nurtures organizational loyalty, and fosters a sense of community among workers. For external parties, such as investors, governmental agencies, and the public at large, the statement helps provide unique insight into the organization's values and future directions.[5] In some organizations, the mission statement is explicitly presented as a formal written document. In others, the statement is implicitly understood. Of course, in the latter case, there is the danger that various organization members may have different perceptions of the organization's mission, perhaps without realizing it.[6]

One study estimates that about 60 percent of the Fortune 500 companies have written mission statements.[7] According to a related study, which examined the statements of 75 firms from the Business Week 1000, mission statements tend to be made up of some or all of the following nine components:[8]

1 *Customers.* Who are the organization's customers?
2 *Products or services.* What are the organization's major products or services?
3 *Location.* Where does the organization compete?
4 *Technology.* What is the firm's basic technology?
5 *Concern for survival.* What is the organization's commitment to economic objectives?
6 *Philosophy.* What are the basic beliefs, values, aspirations, and philosophical priorities of the organization?

Figure 1 *The overall planning process.*

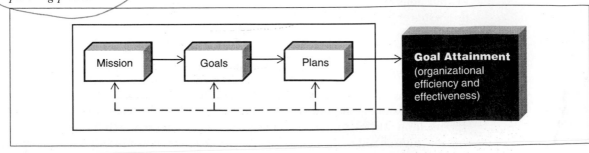

7 *Self-concept.* What are the organization's major strengths and competitive advantages?

8 *Concern for public image.* What are the organization's public responsibilities, and what image is desired?

9 *Concern for employees.* What is the organization's attitude toward employees?

Excerpts from mission statements that match each of these components are shown in Table 1. Laura Nash, a management researcher who has studied mis-

(handwritten note in margin: NOT IN Educational Objectives)

TABLE 1	Major Components of Mission Statements and Sample Excerpts
Major Component	**Sample Excerpt**
Customers	The purpose of Motorola is to honorably serve the needs of the community by providing products and services of superior quality at a fair price to our customers. (Motorola)
Products or services	We provide our customers with retail banking, real estate finance, and corporate banking products which will meet their credit, investment, security, and liquidity needs. (Carteret Savings and Loan Association)
Location	Sara Lee Corporation's mission is to be a leading consumer marketing company in the United States and internationally. (Sara Lee Corporation)
Technology	Du Pont is a diversified chemical, energy, and specialty products company with a strong tradition of discovery. Our global businesses are constantly evolving and continually searching for new and better ways to use our human, technological, and financial resources to improve the quality of life of people around the world. (Du Pont)
Concern for survival	To serve the worldwide need for knowledge at a fair profit by gathering, evaluating, producing, and distributing valuable information in a way that benefits our customers, employees, authors, investors, and our society. (McGraw-Hill)
Philosophy	It's all part of the Mary Kay philosophy—a philosophy based on the golden rule. A spirit of sharing and caring where people give cheerfully of their time, knowledge, and experience. (Mary Kay Cosmetics)
Self-concept	Crown Zellerbach is committed to leapfrogging competition within 1000 days by unleashing the constructive and creative abilities and energies of each of its employees. (Crown Zellerbach)
Concern for public image	The company feels an obligation to be a good corporate citizen wherever it operates. (Eli Lilly and Company)
Concern for employees	To compensate its employees with remuneration and fringe benefits competitive with other employment opportunities in its geographical area and commensurate with their contributions toward efficient corporate operations. (Public Service Electric and Gas Company

Source: Adapted from Fred David, "How Companies Define Their Mission," *Long Range Planning,* February 1989, pp. 92–93.

sion statements, reports that her favorite statement hangs, yellow with age, on the wall of a Boston shoe repair shop. It reads: "We are dedicated to the saving of soles, heeling, and administering to the dyeing."[9]

THE NATURE OF ORGANIZATIONAL GOALS

As we have seen, organizational goals form one of the important elements in the overall planning process.[10] In this section, we assess the major benefits of goals and examine how goals differ according to organizational level.

Benefits of Goals

The use of goals has several major benefits.[11] For one thing, goals can *increase performance*. When challenging goals are set, increases in performance frequently range from 10 to 25 percent, and they are sometimes even higher. Furthermore, such increases have occurred among a variety of employee groups, including clerical personnel, maintenance workers, production workers, salespeople, managers, engineers, and scientists.[12]

Another benefit of goals is that they help *clarify expectations*. With goals, organization members usually have a clear idea of the major outcomes that they are expected to achieve. Without goals, the members lack direction. Thus, even when they are all working very hard, they may collectively accomplish very little—as if they were rowers independently rowing the same boat in different directions and together making little progress.

Goals also *facilitate the controlling function*, because they provide benchmarks against which progress can be assessed so that corrective action can be taken as needed. Thus goals not only help individuals gauge their progress but also assist managers in maintaining control over organizational activities. The situation at W. W. Grainger, Inc., based in Skokie, Illinois, serves as an example. The company sells equipment such as sump pumps, industrial staplers, warehouse fans, and commercial air conditioners to contractors, small manufacturers, and distributors. During the 1970s, Grainger charged premium prices but also provided premium service. Unfortunately, the emphasis on service gradually took a backseat to other priorities, and by the early 1980s, earnings began to slow. The company reacted by placing major displays within reach of its customers in its retail outlets, which now number more than 300, and renewing its emphasis on service. With half its sales stemming from its 24,000-item catalog, Grainger has put considerable effort into training its rows of phone-order clerks. A board at the front of their room keeps a tally on progress. The goal is 0 percent customer waiting. On one day in fall 1989, for example, 1.6 percent of the 367 callers had to wait before placing their orders. Three years earlier, 25 percent had been the norm. The goal of 0 percent customer waiting was reached in 1992.[13]

 Yet another benefit of goals is that they *increase motivation*. Meeting goals, feeling a sense of accomplishment, and receiving recognition and other rewards for reaching targeted outcomes all serve to enhance motivation.

An intriguing study conducted by goal-setting researchers Gary P. Latham and Edwin A. Locke demonstrates the benefits of goal setting. The situation involved truck drivers of a forest-products company in the western United States. The unionized drivers were concerned that if their log-hauling trucks were overloaded, they could be fined by the highway department and subsequently lose their jobs. For this reason, they seldom loaded their trucks to more than 63 percent of capacity. Interestingly, the company had not provided any goals concerning the load level it expected.

In an experiment aimed at improving the situation, the company coordinated a plan with the union that specified the goal of loading to 94 percent of each truck's legal capacity. Under the terms of the agreement, no driver would be reprimanded if the goal was not met. No monetary rewards or fringe benefits were offered as incentives. However, verbal praise was given when drivers loaded their trucks to greater levels than they had previously. During the first month of the experiment, the trucks were hauling 80 percent of their capacity, more than they ever had before. In the second month, however, performance decreased to 70 percent of capacity. Interviews with the drivers revealed that they were testing management to determine whether action would be taken against drivers who did not reach the goal. When the drivers realized that no action was going to be taken, they increased their performance. Loading capacity reached over 90 percent in the third month and remained at that level for more than 7 years. The company saved more than $250,000 in the 9-month period during which the study was conducted.[14] Thus the goal clarified expectations, helped increase motivation, provided a standard against which progress could be gauged, and led to improved performance. This experiment is one of many studies that support the importance of goal setting throughout the organization.[15]

Levels of Goals

Organizations typically have three levels of goals: strategic, tactical, and operational, as shown in Figure 2. (Also shown are three parallel levels of plans, which will be discussed later in this chapter.)

STRATEGIC GOALS **Strategic goals** are broadly defined targets or future end results set by top management. Such goals typically address issues relating to the

Strategic goals Broadly defined targets or future end results set by top management

Figure 2 *Levels of goals and plans.*

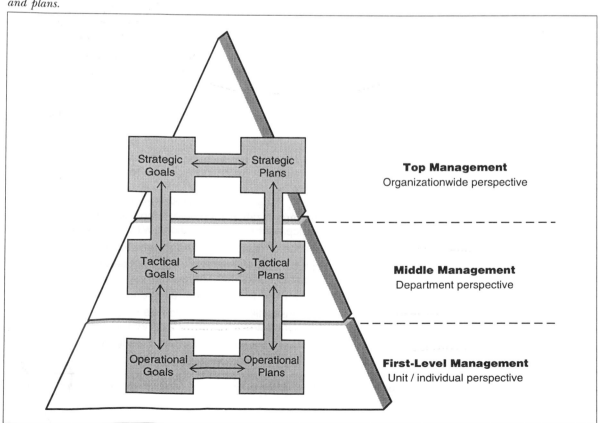

Strategic Goals ⟷ Strategic Plans		**Top Management** Organizationwide perspective
Tactical Goals ⟷ Tactical Plans		**Middle Management** Department perspective
Operational Goals ⟷ Operational Plans		**First-Level Management** Unit / individual perspective

SPECIFIC AND MEASURABLE To be effective, goals need to be specific and measurable so that workers clearly understand what is expected and know when the goal has been achieved. When possible, goals should be stated in quantitative terms. *Quantitative goals* encompass objective numerical standards that are relatively easy to verify. At Rubbermaid, Inc., a company with a reputation for innovative products, a quantitative goal is to derive 30 percent of its sales from products that are less than 5 years old. For some purposes, though, qualitative goals are more appropriate. *Qualitative goals* involve subjective judgment about whether or not a goal is reached. A qualitative goal at Rubbermaid is to develop an idea and prototype for a new plastic desk accessory that is useful, long-lasting, and inexpensive.[24]

TIME-LIMITED Goals also need to be time-limited; that is, there should be a defined period of time within which a goal must be accomplished. Otherwise, goals have little meaning, since individuals can keep putting off achieving them. At Cypress Semiconductor, the weekly goals keep attention focused on meeting goals within the desired time frame. In many organizations, goals are set annually but may be reviewed at various times during the year, such as quarterly.[25]

RELEVANT Goals are more likely to elicit support when they are clearly *relevant* to the major work of the organization and the particular department or work unit. Jack Stack, head of the Springfield Remanufacturing Corporation in Springfield, Missouri, learned an important lesson about goals and relevancy after he took the helm of the ailing equipment manufacturing plant. The company had contracted to ship 800 tractors to Russia, but it lacked some parts needed to complete the machines and the shipping date was less than a month away. In desperation, Stack put up a huge sign that read, "Our Goal: 800 Tractors." The workers responded by coming in at night to figure out what parts were missing from which tractors. They then got the parts through every means they could think of. As a result, the very difficult goal was met.[26]

For guidelines on how to go about actually setting goals, see the Practically Speaking discussion, "How to Set Goals."

Goal Commitment

A critical element in using goals effectively is getting individuals and/or work groups to be committed to the goals they must carry out. **Goal commitment** is one's attachment to, or determination to reach, a goal.[28] Without commitment, setting specific, challenging goals will have little impact on performance. How, then, can managers foster commitment to important organizational goals? They can draw on five major factors that positively influence goal commitment: supervisory authority, peer and group pressure, public display of commitment, expectations of success, and incentives and rewards. A sixth factor, participation, is also sometimes helpful.

Goal commitment One's attachment to, or determination to reach, a goal

SUPERVISORY AUTHORITY Individuals and groups are often willing to commit themselves to a goal when the goal and reasons for it are explained by a person with supervisory authority, usually one's boss. With this approach, goals are essentially assigned by the supervisor, who explains the reason for the goal to his or her employees and provides them with any necessary instructions. The explanation and instructions are likely to be more effective when the supervisor is supportive rather than authoritative. Instead of bluntly telling subordinates to meet the goals, the supervisor should provide encouragement and offer opportunities for individuals to ask questions.

PRACTICALLY SPEAKING

HOW TO SET GOALS

There are six main steps in setting goals to obtain optimal results:

1 *Specify the goal to be reached or tasks to be done.* What do you want to accomplish? Do you want to increase sales? Reduce costs? Improve quality? Boost customer service? Maybe, at the moment, you are thinking that you would like to obtain an A in a particular course this semester (perhaps the one involving this textbook).

2 *Specify how the performance will be measured.* Some outcomes can be measured more easily than others. (e.g., number of units sold and dollar volume of sales). Work outcomes (the results achieved) are typically measured according to one of three parameters:

Physical units: For example, quantity of production, market share, number of errors, number of rejects (quality control)

Time: For example, meeting deadlines, servicing customers, completing a project, coming to work each day, being punctual

Money: For example, profits, sales, costs, budgets, debts, income

Similarly, many course-of-study outcomes can be measured in terms of physical units (such as number of questions answered correctly on examinations and grades received on papers and assignments) and in terms of time (such as meeting deadlines for assignments and attending classes).

Sometimes, outcomes are difficult to measure, perhaps because the measurement process would be too costly or because the outcomes are affected by factors beyond an individual's control. In such cases, it may be necessary to measure behaviors or actions rather than outcomes. For example, if a manager's goal of overcoming worker resistance to certain impending changes is likely to be significantly affected by the actions of others, it may be possible to measure crucial activities instead of outcomes. Such activities might include whether the manager clearly explains why the change is needed, outlines how the change will affect others, and listens to employees' concerns. When possible, though, the goal-setting process should focus on outcomes.

3 *Specify the standard or target to be reached.* This step builds on the type of measure chosen in step 2 by spelling out the *degree* of performance to be included in the goal. For example, the target might be producing 40 units per hour, reducing errors by 2 percent, completing a project by December 15, answering the telephone within three rings, or increasing sales by 10 percent.

In pursuing the objective of attaining an A in a particular course, you might set targets such as correctly answering at least 90 percent of the questions on the midterm and final exams, offering one knowledgeable point during the discussion part of each class, and fulfilling written assignments well enough to earn high grades. Setting subgoals, such as the number of textbook pages to be read and outlined each day, can also help goal achievement.

4 *Specify the time span involved.* To have a positive impact on performance, goals need to have a time span within which they are to be completed. In a production situation, the goal may be stated in terms of production per hour or day. In a service situation, the goal may involve the time it takes to deliver the service. For example, a photocopier repair service may have the goal of responding to customer calls within 2 hours. Other goals, such as major projects, may have time spans involving several months or even years.

For instance, your goals for the semester may involve a few months, while goals associated with obtaining your degree and developing your career may span several years.

5 *Prioritize the goals.* When multiple goals are present, as is likely with most jobs, they need to be prioritized so that effort and action can be directed in proportion to the importance of each goal. Otherwise, individual effort can be focused improperly.

For example, suppose that in the course in which you want to obtain an A, examinations count 70 percent, a paper counts 20 percent, and discussion in class counts 10 percent toward the grade. In this case, a goal related to the examinations should be given first priority, while goals related to the paper and the class discussion should receive second and third priority, respectively.

(*continued on next page*)

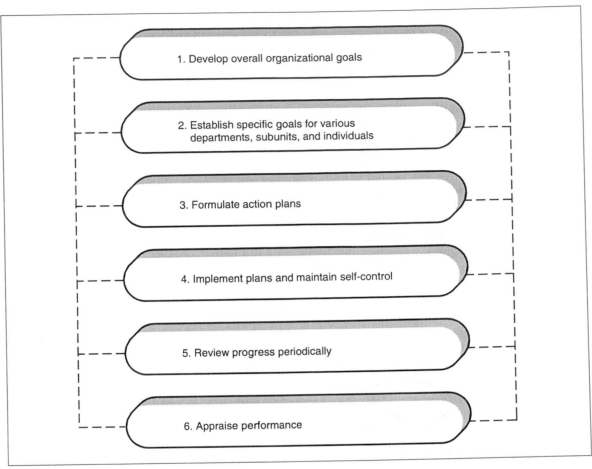

Figure 7   *Steps in the MBO process.*

a whole (e.g., a certain rate of return for a given period or a specific increase in market share). These goals are essentially strategic goals set by top management.

2   *Establish specific goals (or objectives) for various departments, subunits, and individuals.* In this step, coordinating goals are set for various organizational levels so that each goal contributes to reaching the overall goals set in step 1. This stage of the process begins when upper-level managers formulate specific objectives that they plan to accomplish, usually related to their own departments or areas of responsibility (such as marketing or production). These goals are usually developed in collaboration with managers at the next lower level. For example, the head of the marketing department, together with the regional sales managers, may set the goal of increasing a certain product's sales volume to 100,000 during the coming year. Then the regional sales managers confer with their district managers in setting goals at the regional levels. In the eastern region, for instance, the sales manager and district managers may decide on the goal of increasing sales volume to 25,000 for the particular product, thus contributing toward the 100,000 goal at the national level. The process, which is sometimes referred to as the cascading of goals, continues until all units at various levels have specific goals for the coming year. At each level, goals are typically set in key areas, where results are critical to the success of the organization.

Although many organizations follow the top-down process just described, some use a bottom-up approach, in which goal setting begins at the lower levels. These levels propose their goals on the basis of what they believe they can achieve. Goals are then developed at the tactical level that are based on the proposed goals provided by the operational level. The tactical goals are then proposed to the strategic level. Even with a bottom-up approach, however, goal setting usually follows at least some general guidelines developed at the strategic level. In any event, with MBO, there is typically some give-and-take among levels before goals at the various levels are finalized.

3 *Formulate action plans.* Once goals are set, action plans must be developed that focus on the methods or activities necessary to reach particular goals. In essence, an *action plan* is a description of what is to be done, how, when, where, and by whom in order to achieve a goal. Action plans contribute to the feasibility of reaching goals, aid in identifying problem areas, assist in spelling out areas in which resources and assistance will be needed, and facilitate the search for more efficient and effective ways to achieve objectives. Such plans are usually developed by subordinates in conjunction with their supervisors.

4 *Implement and maintain self-control.* A basic notion underlying MBO is that once goals are set and action plans determined, individuals should be given considerable latitude in carrying out their activities. The rationale is that, with MBO, individuals know what they are supposed to achieve, have mapped out plans, and can gauge their progress against set goals. Therefore, it should not be necessary for the supervisor to become as involved in the individual's day-to-day activities as might be the case without goals and action plans. The notion of self-control is particularly true with respect to managerial positions. Of course, supervisors still need to be kept informed about progress and any unanticipated difficulties that arise. They may also need to provide coaching and support if subordinates are having difficulties.

5 *Review progress periodically.* Periodic reviews are important to ensure that plans are being implemented as expected and that goals will ultimately be met. Such reviews provide a good opportunity for checking performance to date, identifying and removing obstacles, solving problems, and altering action plans that are not achieving the expected results. Reviews also make it possible to assess the continuing appropriateness of the goals and to change them or add new ones as necessary. How frequently progress reviews are held will depend on how quickly situations change, but quarterly reviews are common.

6 *Appraise performance.* At the end of the goal-setting cycle, which usually runs for a period of 1 year, managers meet with each of their subordinates to conduct an appraisal of performance over the cycle. The appraisal typically focuses on the extent to which goals were met, as well as on shortfalls, the reasons for them, and actions that can be taken to prevent the same difficulties in the future. The appraisal session includes praise and recognition for areas in which the subordinate has performed effectively, as well as discussion of areas in which he or she could benefit from future development of knowledge and skills. Goals and plans for the next cycle may also be discussed at this point.

As Figure 7 indicates, feedback from each step may lead to the revision of prior goals or the setting of future ones. While constant revision of prior goals tends to defeat the purpose of MBO, some revisions may be necessary to accommodate major changes in circumstances. The purpose of the goal-setting and planning processes is essentially to coordinate efforts toward important organizational goals. If those goals need changing, then efforts probably require redirecting as well; hence corresponding goals at various levels should also be changed.

Strengths and Weaknesses of MBO

As suggested by the successful use of MBO at Cypress Semiconductor, management by objectives has a number of major strengths. On the other hand, MBO also has several weaknesses. The main strengths and weaknesses of MBO are summarized in Table 4.[59]

The possible implications of two of the potential weaknesses—using MBO as a punitive device and overemphasizing quantitative goals—can be seen in the case of MiniScribe, a computer disk-drive company. The Colorado-based firm had been doing poorly before Q. T. Wiles, who had a reputation for resuscitating ill companies, took over the helm. Under Wiles, the value of MiniScribe's stock quintupled within 2 years on the basis of strong financial reports before it was finally revealed that the data were bogus. Interviews with current and former executives, employees, competitors, suppliers, and others familiar with the company revealed major internal difficulties. Wiles had set unrealistic sales goals and used an abusive management style that created intense pressure. In an effort to keep up, managers began to falsify data by booking shipments as sales and simply fabricating figures. MiniScribe ultimately filed for bankruptcy and sold its assets.[60] At Nordstrom's, the Seattle-based retailer, some present and former employees have complained of extreme pressure to meet sales goals. A recent investigation by the Washington State Department of Labor and Industries found that the company systematically violated state law by failing to pay employees for the time spent delivering merchandise to customers or working on inventory.[61]

Assessing MBO

Because of the possible weaknesses, MBO has not always reached its potential. According to one estimate, MBO has been used in almost half the Fortune 500 companies, yet it has been successful only about 20 to 25 percent of the time.[62] Failures of MBO systems seem to stem from a lack of adequate support from top management and poor goal-setting and communication skills among managers who must implement the system. According to a recent study, however, when top management commitment to the MBO program and processes was high, the average gain in productivity was 56 percent.[63] Hence, the way in which managers implement MBO may undermine its effectiveness. While overall organizational or strategic goals are important to the MBO process, they are also a critical element in strategic management.

TABLE 4	Strengths and Weaknesses of MBO	
Strengths		**Weaknesses**
1. Aids coordination of goals and plans		1. Tends to falter without strong, continual commitment from top management
2. Helps clarify priorities and expectations		2. Necessitates considerable training of managers
3. Facilitates vertical and horizontal communication		3. Can be misused as a punitive device
4. Fosters employee motivation		4. May cause overemphasis of quantitative goals

CHAPTER SUMMARY

Major components of the overall planning process are the mission, goals, and plans of the organization. The mission is the organization's purpose or fundamental reason for existence. The mission statement, a broad declaration of the basic, unique purpose and scope of operation that distinguishes the organization from others of its type, has several purposes. The statement can be a benchmark against which to evaluate success; a means of defining a common purpose, nurturing loyalty, and fostering a sense of community among members; and a signal about values and future directions. A goal is a future target or end result that an organization wishes to achieve. A plan is a means devised for attempting to reach the goal.

Goals have several potential benefits. They can increase performance, clarify expectations, facilitate the controlling function, and help increase motivation. Organizations typically have three levels of goals: strategic, tactical, and operational. These levels of goals can be conceptualized as a hierarchy of goals.

A number of key components help explain how goals facilitate performance. Goal content is one component. Goals should be challenging, attainable, specific and measurable, time-limited, and relevant. Goal commitment is another key component. Commitment can usually be positively influenced through supervisory authority, peer and group pressure, public display of commitment, expectations of success, and incentives and rewards. Participation also may engender goal commitment. Work behavior is also a major component. Goal content and goal commitment influence the direction, effort, persistence, and planning aspects of work behavior. Other major components are job knowledge and ability, complexity of task, and situational constraints.

Care must be taken to avoid a number of potential problems with goal setting.

In much the same way that there are levels of goals, plans also differ according to level in the organization. Thus there are strategic, tactical, and operational plans. Plans can also be categorized on the basis of how frequently they will be used. Single-use plans are usually not needed again in the future and include programs and projects. Standing plans are used on a recurring basis and include policies, procedures, and rules. The different levels of goals and plans are related to different time horizons. Strategic goals and plans are usually focused on long-range issues 5 years or more in the future, tactical goals and plans are aimed at intermediate-range issues 1 to 5 years in the future, and operational goals and plans are oriented toward 1 year or less. Research suggests that the planning process can be used to promote innovation in several ways. These include wording the mission statement so that it signals the importance of innovation, setting goals aimed at innovative outcomes, and developing loose plans that allow latitude in the innovation process or focus on innovative means of reaching goals. Managers must take steps to reduce or avoid several potential obstacles to developing plans.

Management by objectives includes the following steps: develop overall organizational goals; establish specific goals for various departments, subunits, and individuals; formulate action plans; implement and maintain self-control; review progress periodically; and appraise performance. MBO has several strengths and weaknesses. Failures of MBO systems seem to step from a lack of adequate support from top management and poor goal-setting and communication skills among managers who must implement the system.

QUESTIONS FOR DISCUSSION AND REVIEW

1 Outline the major components in the overall planning process. Give examples of these components in an organization with which you are familiar.

2 Define the concept of organizational mission, and explain the purposes of a mission statement. Think of an organization that you would like to establish. What type of mission would you develop?

3 Outline the major benefits of goals. Describe a situation in which you have observed these benefits.

4 Explain how goals and plans differ according to organizational level. Describe how goals and plans may be different at the various levels of management at your college or university.

5 Discuss the major components in the diagram indicating how goals facilitate performance. Describe a situation in which you have seen goals work well and one in which goals did not seem to work. Use the diagram to explain the outcome in each situation.

6 Explain how to set goals. List four goals that you might set for yourself during the coming semester.

7 Delineate several potential problems with goal setting. Discuss how two of these problems might apply in an organization with which you are familiar (perhaps an organization on campus). What steps might you take to avoid such problems?

8 Explain the various types of single-use and standing plans. Give an example of each type of plan at your college or university.

9 Assess the role of goals and plans in promoting innovation. Explain how goals and plans helped 3M reduce costs in its manufacturing sector.

10 Explain the steps in the management by objectives process, and assess the strengths and weaknesses of MBO.

Objectives, Scott, Foresman, Glenview, Ill., 1974; Max D. Richards, *Setting Strategic Goals and Objectives,* 2d ed., West, St. Paul, Minn., 1986.

59. Steven J. Carroll and Henry L. Tosi, *Management by Objectives: Applications and Research,* Macmillan, New York, 1973; Anthony P. Raia, *Managing by Objectives,* Scott, Foresman, Glenview, Ill., 1974; Joseph W. Leonard, "Why MBO Fails So Often," *Training and Development Journal,* June 1986, pp. 38–39; Max D. Richards, *Setting Strategic Goals and Objectives,* 2d ed., West, St. Paul, Minn., 1986.

60. Andy Zipser, "How Pressure to Raise Sales Led MiniScribe to Falsify Number," *The Wall Street Journal,* Sept. 11, 1989, pp. A1, A8; Lee Berton, "How MiniScribe Got Its Auditor's Blessing on Questionable Sales," *The Wall Street Journal,* May 14, 1992, pp. A1, A6.

61. Susan C. Faludi, "At Nordstrom Stores, Service Comes First—But at a Big Price," *The Wall Street Journal,* Feb. 20, 1990, pp. A1, A16.

62. Jan P. Muczyk, "Dynamics and Hazards of MBO Application," *Personnel Administrator,* May 1979, pp. 51–61.

63. Robert Rodgers and John E. Hunter, "Impact of Management by Objectives on Organizational Productivity," *Journal of Applied Psychology,* vol. 76, no. 2, 1991, pp. 322–336.

ACKNOWLEDGMENTS

Table

Table 1: Adapted from Fred David, "How Companies Define Their Mission," *Long Range Planning,* February 1989, pp. 92–93. Copyright © 1989, with permission from Pergamon Press Ltd., Headington Hill Hall, Oxford OX3 OBW, UK.

Figures

Figure 3: *Managing in the Tradition of Partnership.* Reprinted by permission of JC Penney.

Figure 4: Gary P. Latham, Thomas W. Lee, and Edwin A. Locke, "Goal Setting Theory and Job Performance," in Lawrence A. Pervin (ed.), *Goal Concepts in Personality and Social Psychology,* Lawrence Erlbaum, 1989. Reprinted by permission of Dr. Lawrence Pervin and Lawrence Erlbaum and Associates.

CONCLUDING CASE

WAL-MART LEAPFROGS THE COMPETITION

Wal-Mart is the world's largest retailing company. Achieving this position was the result of a great deal of hard work by the company's more than 371,000 employees, who are called "associates."

The initial success of the company can be traced directly to founder Samuel Moore Walton. Soon after returning from military duty in World War II, he opened the first Walton's Ben Franklin store (a five-and-dime type of store) in Versailles, Missouri, in the late 1940s. After losing his lease in 1950, Walton moved his business to Bentonville, Arkansas, where he opened a Walton 5 & 10. He also established Ben Franklin franchises and had 15 by 1962, when he opened the first Wal-Mart Discount City. By 1969, when the company became Wal-Mart Stores, Inc., there were 18 Wal-Mart and 15 Ben Franklin stores operating throughout Arkansas, Missouri, Kansas, and Oklahoma. Today there are 1934 stores (including 1720 Wal-Marts, 208 Sam's Wholesale Clubs, and 6 Wal-Mart Supercenters) located in 42 central and southern states, as well as 2 stores owned in a joint venture in Mexico. They have combined revenues of almost $44 billion. The west, northwest, and northeast are considered prime target areas for the future.

Wal-Mart has followed a strategy of building and expanding in areas where the local population is under 50,000. At first, only one or two stores are built. Next, a distribution center is constructed nearby that will support further expansion in the area. Other stores are then built within a day's drive of the distribution center. Wal-Mart currently has 19 distribution centers, which are widely considered to be major factors in the company's spectacular success.

The Wal-Mart organization stresses its relationship with associates, which is based on the premise that they are partners. Associates have access to information about their stores, such as costs, freight charges, and profit margins, that many other organizations show only to general managers. Associates play a major role in achieving overall Wal-Mart and individual store goals.

Goals play an important part in the way that Wal-Mart is managed. They are developed using MBO as part of the planning process. At Wal-Mart, the top level of management provides some guidelines in areas such as profits and growth. These are used as a basis for setting goals at the division and store levels. Most of the more specific tactical goals are developed at the division level. They are then forwarded to the corporate or top level, where they are reviewed and are used to formulate the final goals at the strategic level. Stores also have some input into the goals that are ultimately set, and they have annual operational goals of their own to achieve. Some of the specific goals set at Wal-Mart during a recent annual goal-setting effort included the following:

- Adding 160 new Wal-Mart stores
- Opening 45 new Sam's Wholesale Clubs
- Opening 12 to 15 new Wal-Mart Supercenters
- Increasing sales to more than $54 billion
- Pursuing a "Buy American" plan to give preference to stocking merchandise manufactured in the United States

Individual stores are generally expected to achieve at least a 10 percent increase in sales over the previous year. Stores also have profit goals. Associates receive a share of the profits above the goals set for each store. Once goals are set, the various levels engage in action planning to determine the specific means that will be used to achieve the goals.

Goals are monitored throughout the fiscal year to ensure that they are being achieved as intended. Rarely are they not met, but on a few occasions Wal-Mart has not been pleased with the performance of some stores and has sold them. For example, the Ben Franklin stores were phased out in 1976 to make room for more Wal-Mart stores. A chain of Helen's Arts and Crafts stores and the DOT Discount Drug chain were sold. Wal-Mart also tried a do-it-yourself building concept that failed. Thus not all of Wal-Mart's ventures have been successful from the company's point of view.

On balance, however, Wal-Mart has been extremely successful. A $1000 investment in Wal-Mart's initial stock offering in 1970 would be worth more than half a million dollars today. Wal-Mart is frequently among the leaders in *Fortune*'s survey of the most admired corporations in America. The company is growing at a rate of more than 20 percent a year. Sam Walton died on April 5, 1992. He was succeeded as the chairman of the board by his son S. Robson Walton.*

---

* John Huet, "WAL-MART Will It Take Over the World?" *Fortune,* Jan. 30, 1989, pp. 52–59; "The Five Best," *Business Month,* December 1988, pp. 30–44; "Fact Sheet about Wal-Mart Stores Inc.," Wal-Mart Stores, Inc., Corporate Public Relations Office, Bentonville, Ark., n.d.; Arthur A. Thompson, Jr., and

A. J. Strickland III, *Strategic Management: Concepts and Cases,* 4th ed., Business Publications, Plano, Tex., 1987, pp. 936–954; Steve Weiner, "Gold Balls, Motor Oil and Tomatoes," *Forbes,* Oct. 30, 1989, pp. 130–134; discussion between Brenda Lockhart, corporate coordinator of public relations, and David C. Martin, November 1989; 1992 Annual Report, Wal-Mart Stores, Inc., Bentonville, Ark.; Meg Cox, "Walton's Book Is Big Winner in Advance," *The Wall Street Journal,* Feb. 7, 1992, p. B1; Kevin Helliker, "Sam Walton, the Man Who Made Wal-Mart No. 1 Retailer, Dies," *The Wall Street Journal,* Apr. 6, 1992, p. A1.

QUESTIONS FOR CONCLUDING CASE

1 Trace the overall planning process at Wal-Mart.
2 Use the goal-setting process to explain why the use of goals at Wal-Mart enhances performance.
3 Describe the MBO process at Wal-Mart.

CONCLUDING CASE

PLANNING AT CANON: THE KEY TO SUCCESS

When the Precision Optics Laboratory (the original name for Japan-based Canon) was founded in 1933, there was little advance planning. The company had a single production facility that manufactured cameras for local sale on the basis of rough assessments of likely demand. Today $80 billion Canon produces an array of image, information, and communication products. Production in its numerous worldwide facilities is based on carefully developed plans that include specific goals. Currently, about 75 percent of sales are in business machines, 20 percent in cameras, and 6 percent in optical products.

The Canon planning process began in 1962 with the company's first long-range plan, covering 5 years. At that point, 95 percent of Canon's sales came from cameras, but the company was concerned that market growth for cameras was leveling off. Therefore, its initial plan focused on diversification into other products, mainly business machines. The specific goal was to achieve 20 percent of its sales from products other than cameras in 5 years. The next two 5-year plans included other critical goals, such as furthering diversification, boosting production capacity to meet anticipated demand, establishing a worldwide distribution system for Canon products, and expanding into the image information industry.

In 1975, the company experienced serious difficulties. It had expanded into producing hand-held electronic calculators.

Unfortunately, more than 10 major competitors emerged who aggressively marketed new technologies and/or lowered prices. Moreover, a serious defect in a critical calculator part Canon had purchased from an outside supplier led to massive returns. Overly optimistic estimations of market demand also led to an excessive inventory of products that soon became obsolete. An oil crisis, fluctuations in foreign exchange, and a recession added to the company's woes, causing major losses. Canon was determined never to get in a situation like that again.

From then on, Canon launched a campaign to become a leading global company that would be better able to deal effectively with environmental forces. The company reorganized to provide separate divisions for each major product area, stressed the development of innovative products, and greatly expanded the planning process.

Today the planning system consists of long-range (strategic), medium-range (tactical), and short-range (operational) plans. A central planning staff helps with the planning process.

The long-range (strategic) plan (with a horizon of up to 10 years) outlines broad major directions and goals for the company within the context of the rapidly changing environment. Goals are normally set for the final year of the plan and may include such factors as sales volumes, pretax income, and capital investment. Other parts of the plan are revised annually as necessary. These parts focus mainly on the orientation of the company, changes of structure, and employee motivation and revitalization.

The medium-range (tactical) plans address shorter-term issues that amplify long-range plans and goals. They are normally 3-year plans that are revised annually on the basis of current business considerations. Tactical plans guide the allocation of resources, such as human resources, facilities, equipment, and funding, to achieve tactical goals. They also center on what must be done by the various product divisions to meet overall strategic directives. Contingency plans are also developed to deal with potential serious threats, even when the probabilities of such circumstances are relatively low.

Canon's short-range (operational) goals and plans are oriented to the maximum use of all resources to obtain planned results during the current fiscal year. Operational reports are compared with previously established goals to determine the effectiveness of individual units and the overall company.*

QUESTIONS FOR CONCLUDING CASE

1. Discuss how Canon has used its planning process to position itself as a global business.
2. How would you envision tactical goals and plans flowing from the strategic plans at Canon?
3. Explain how you would implement goal setting and planning in an international organization.

* Toshio Nakahara and Yutaka Isono, "Strategic Planning for Canon; The Crises and the New Vision," *Long Range Planning*, vol. 25, 1992, pp. 63–72.

CHAPTER 4

Managerial Decision Making

COKE GETS BACK ITS KICK

Several times per day, Roberto C. Goizueta (pronounced "Goy-SWET-ah"), the chief executive officer of the Coca-Cola Company, walks from his oak-floored office in Atlanta down the hall to a Quotron machine in order to check Coke's stock price. Since he was awarded the top slot at Coca-Cola in 1981, the news from the Quotron has usually, but not always, been good.

Goizueta, a chemical engineer from Havana, Cuba, who fled the Castro regime, has made major changes in the once-sleepy company and its southern traditions. For one thing, he began emphasizing that management's chief job is maximizing shareholder value so that shareholders receive good returns on their investments in the company's stock. Boosting returns has meant greater risk taking. To encourage such risk taking, Goizueta has worked hard to create an atmosphere in which new ideas can flourish. Yet, to encourage teamwork, he insists that he and his three top officers agree before any major corporate decision is made. Goizueta once vetoed a major acquisition because one member of the team opposed the move.

Perhaps his biggest gamble was putting Coke's name on a diet coke. Although the decision seems simple in retrospect, Goizueta and Donald Keough, Coke's president, say that it was the most difficult one that they have made. They saw horrendous risk in putting the venerable Coke name on a product that could fail. Up until that time, the name "Coca-Cola" was attached to only one product. Nevertheless, they took the gamble in 1982. Within 5 years, Diet Coke became the third-largest-selling soft drink in the United States, and it has accounted for much of Coke's growth in total market share in the country. Since then, the world's most valuable trademark has been attached to several other soft-drink variations.

Then there is the issue of New Coke. Goizueta continues to argue strongly that Coke was correct in offering the new, sweeter-tasting formula in 1985 because of Pepsi's increasing popularity, particularly with children. Looking back, though, he wishes that he had brought old Coke back in 1 month, rather than waiting 3 months before announcing that the old formula would be reintroduced as Coca-Cola Classic. He says he will never forget having to appear on television to tell the American people that he had made a mistake. Coca-Cola Classic continues to be the top-selling cola in the United States. The New Coke situation is particularly famous because, before introducing the new soft drink, the company conducted extensive market tests in over 30 U.S. cities. In obtaining the opinions of more than 40,000 people, Coke sampled eight times the usual number of consumers. Tests, with the brand name hidden, indicated a consumer preference for the new Coke formula when compared with the old formula and with Pepsi. The general consensus is that the company did everything right in terms of following the best market research procedures. Nevertheless, no one predicted the vehemence of customer reactions.

Thus, even though Coke did extensive market research, the efforts did not lead to the best final decision. Still, the managers did follow an appropriate decision-making process, which included generating alternative formulas and evaluating them carefully. Fortunately, in this case, the decision was reversible. Meanwhile, Coke is experiencing some success in reintroducing the new formula in selected markets as Coke II. By following effective decision-making procedures, managers at Coke have increased the likelihood of making good decisions.

For a time, Goizueta led the company toward diversification, but more recently the top managers have decided that Coke will concentrate mainly on being a soft-drink company. A major reason for this shift is that Coke has been able to achieve an exceptionally high return on assets in its soft-drink business and sees considerable room for growth in international markets. Presently, on average, every American annually consumes about 18 gallons of soft-drink products made by Coke. In contrast, consumption is only about 40 percent of that figure in Europe, about 10 percent of that amount in Asia and the Pacific region, and roughly 5 percent of the U.S. figure in Africa. In addition, Coke is generally able to charge relatively high prices in international markets, where competition is usually not as great as it is domestically. Already a leading soft-drink company in 160 countries, the company has between 50 and 60 percent of the market in most of the countries in which it does business. So far, Coke's track record for decision making has been good, and the company's stock has been rising significantly.[1]

Decision making The process through which managers identify organizational problems and attempt to resolve them

As the Coca-Cola situation graphically illustrates, gaining and maintaining a competitive edge requires extensive managerial decision making. **Decision making** is the process through which managers identify organizational problems and attempt to resolve them. In Goizueta's situation, he recognized that Coke was in danger of losing its preeminence in the soft-drink industry. He also saw that the company was not using its tremendous assets to their full capacity. Hence he took steps to solve these problems. Managers may not always make the right decision, but they can use their knowledge of appropriate decision-making processes to increase the odds.

In this chapter we explore the nature of managerial decision making, including the types of problems and decision-making situations that managers are likely to face. We also evaluate managers as decision makers and consider the steps in an effective decision-making process. We examine how major barriers to effective decision making can be overcome, and we weigh the advantages and disadvantages of group decision making. Finally, we show how managers can promote innovation through the use of creativity in the decision-making process.

THE NATURE OF MANAGERIAL DECISION MAKING

Like Goizueta, managers make many different decisions in the course of their work. While managers at lower levels in organizations might not make such monumental decisions as changing the formula for a revered product, many smaller decisions at lower levels have a cumulative effect on organizational effectiveness. For example, Motorola has built its reputation for high quality and innovation (particularly in semiconductors, electronic pagers, and cellular telephones) partially by encouraging individuals from design, manufacturing, and marketing departments to involve themselves early in decision making for new projects.[2] Good decision-making processes are important at all levels.

An effective decision-making process generally includes the four steps shown in Figure 1.[3] Some authors refer to these four steps as "problem solving" and reserve the term "decision making" for the first three steps—the process up to, but not including, implementation and follow-up.[4] Here we use "decision making" and "problem solving" interchangeably to refer to the broad process depicted in Figure 1. We do this because "decision making" is the term more commonly used in business, and we believe that it will be clear when we are using this term in its more narrow sense. We analyze the four steps in the decision-making process in greater detail in a later section of this chapter. First, though, it

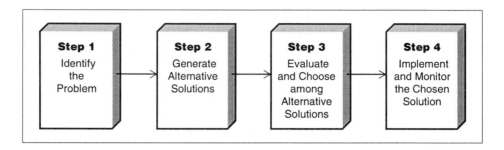

Figure 1 *Steps in the decision-making process. (Adapted from George P. Huber,* Managerial Decision Making, *Scott, Foresman, Glenview, Ill., 1980, p. 8.)*

is useful to examine the major types of problems that managers usually encounter and to consider the important differences in managerial decision-making situations.

Types of Problems Decisions Makers Face

Managerial decision making typically centers on three types of problems: crisis, noncrisis, and opportunity problems.[5]

Crisis problem A serious difficulty requiring immediate action

CRISIS A **crisis problem** is a serious difficulty requiring immediate action. An example of a crisis is the discovery of a severe cash-flow deficiency that has a high potential of quickly evolving into serious losses. Coca-Cola faced a crisis when loyal customers protested the demise of the classic Coke formula.

Noncrisis problem An issue that requires resolution but does not simultaneously have the importance and immediacy characteristics of a crisis

NONCRISIS A **noncrisis problem** is an issue that requires resolution but does not simultaneously have the importance and immediacy characteristics of a crisis. Many of the decisions that managers make center on noncrisis problems. Examples of such problems are a factory that needs to be brought into conformity with new state antipollution standards during the next 3 years and an employee who is frequently late for work. The flat earnings in Coke's troubled food division, which mainly produces Minute Maid orange juice, represented a noncrisis problem. After Goizueta appointed a new president and CEO of the division, the situation began to improve significantly.[6]

Opportunity problem A situation that offers a strong potential for significant organizational gain if appropriate actions are taken

OPPORTUNITY An **opportunity problem** is a situation that offers strong potential for significant organizational gain if appropriate actions are taken. Opportunities typically involve new ideas and novel directions and, therefore, are major vehicles for innovation. Top management at Coca-Cola saw opportunity in the possibility of placing the Coke name on a more extensive line of soft drinks. More recently, the company has been making significant investments in eastern Germany after the breakdown of the old East Germany. So far, Coke has established five bottling plants and about a dozen distribution centers in the region.[7] Opportunities involve ideas that *could* be used, rather than difficulties that *must* be resolved. Noninnovative managers sometimes fall prey to focusing on various crisis and noncrisis problems, and in the process, they may neglect opportunities. In one study of 78 managerial decision-making situations, 13 percent of the situations were crisis problems, 62 percent were noncrisis problems, and 25 percent involved taking advantage of opportunities.[8] In addition to facing three types of decision problems, managers also typically deal with different types of decision-making situations.

Differences in Decision-Making Situations

Managers would be overwhelmed with decision making if they had to handle each and every problem as if it were a completely new situation. Fortunately, that is not the case. Generally, managerial decision situations fall into two categories: programmed and nonprogrammed. Examples of decisions in each category are shown in Table 1.

Programmed decisions
Decisions made in routine, repetitive, well-structured situations through the use of predetermined decision rules

PROGRAMMED DECISIONS **Programmed decisions** are those made in routine, repetitive, well-structured situations through the use of predetermined decision rules. The decision rules may be based on habit, computational techniques, or established policies and procedures. Such rules usually stem from prior experience or technical knowledge about what works in a particular type of situation. For example, most organizations have established policies and procedures for handling basic employee disciplinary problems.

Although programmed decisions are applicable to routine, well-structured situations, they can be quite complex. Computers have enhanced the possibilities for making sophisticated programmed decisions, because they can collect and analyze vast amounts of information that can facilitate programmed managerial decision making. For example, managers at San Diego Gas & Electric switch gas and oil suppliers on the basis of decisions made hourly in the utility's vast computerized "mission control" room.[9] When a person shops with a credit card, a programmed decision is often made by computer regarding the authorization of the purchase. However, if the person wishes to charge an unusually large dollar amount or one that exceeds the ceiling for her or his account, a supervisor may have to engage in further programmed decision making based on policies and procedures governing such situations.

Most of the decisions made by first-line managers and many of those made by middle managers are the programmed type. In contrast, top-level managers make comparatively few programmed decisions (see Figure 2).

Nonprogrammed decisions
Decisions for which predetermined decision rules are impractical because the situations are novel and/or ill-structured

Uncertainty A condition in which the decision maker must choose a course of action without complete knowledge of the consequences that will follow implementation

Risk The possibility that a chosen action could lead to losses rather than the intended results

NONPROGRAMMED DECISIONS **Nonprogrammed decisions** are those for which predetermined decision rules are impractical because the situations are novel and/or ill-structured.[10] Most of the significant decisions that managers make fall into the nonprogrammed category. Because of their nature, nonprogrammed decisions usually involve considerable amounts of **uncertainty,** a condition in which the decision maker must choose a course of action without complete knowledge of the consequences that will follow implementation.

Decisions made under uncertainty involve **risk,** the possibility that a chosen action could lead to losses rather than the intended results. Experts on decision making used to differentiate between uncertainty and risk, but they now view uncertainty as the reason why a situation is risky.[11] Uncertainty can stem from a variety of sources. For example, elements in the environment that are difficult to predict or control can affect the success of a decision. Cost and time constraints can limit the information that can realistically be collected. Social and political factors in the organization, such as poor communication across units, can make relevant information gathering difficult. Finally, situations can change rapidly,

TABLE 1	Examples of Managerial Decision-Making Situations	
Type of Organization	**Programmed Decision**	**Nonprogrammed Decision**
Fast-food restaurant	Determine supplies to be reordered.	Identify location for new franchise.
University	Decide if students meet graduation requirements.	Choose new academic programs.
Automaker	Determine union employee pay rates.	Select new car design.

causing current information to quickly become obsolete.[12] Partially to cope with rapid change and the declining U.S. dollar, Annette Roux, head of France-based Chantiers Bénéteau, decided to open a U.S. manufacturing plant in South Carolina to manufacture the company's line of pleasure craft, including sailboats.[13]

The proportion of nonprogrammed decisions that managers must make increases at each level of the hierarchy (see Figure 2). Because such decisions require effective decision-making skills—and, frequently, creativity—they provide the biggest decision-making challenges to managers. As a result, organizations often expend considerable effort through formal training programs and job experience to develop managers who can effectively handle nonprogrammed decision situations. This chapter focuses mainly on issues related to nonprogrammed decisions.

MANAGERS AS DECISION MAKERS

Because the decisions that managers make have a profound impact on the success of the organization, managerial approaches to decision making have been the subject of considerable curiosity and research. In this section, we describe two major types of models regarding how managers make decisions: rational and nonrational.

The Rational Model

Rational model A model that suggests that managers engage in completely rational decision processes, ultimately make optimal decisions, and possess and understand all information relevant to their decisions at the time they make them

The rational model of managerial decision making, a view that was in vogue during the first half of this century, has roots in the economic theory of the firm. In developing theories about the economic behavior of business firms, economists tended to make the simplifying assumption that managers would always make decisions that were in the best economic interests of their firms. This assumption was accepted by many management theorists. According to the **rational model,** managers engage in completely rational decision processes, ultimately make optimal decisions, and possess and understand all information relevant to their decisions at the time they make them (including all possible alternatives and all potential outcomes and ramifications). If you recently purchased a major competitive item such as a personal computer or an automobile, you most likely experienced the difficulties of obtaining perfect information and

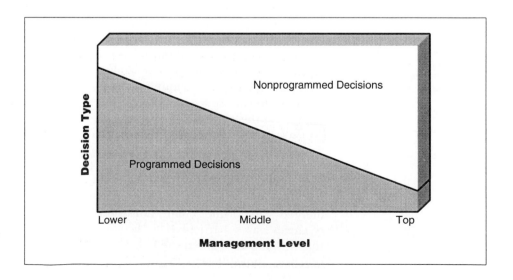

Figure 2 *Relationship of decision-making situation to management level in organizations.*

making "optimal" decisions in complex situations. As a result, you will probably not be surprised to find that there are serious flaws in the rational view of how managers make decisions.[14] Nevertheless, the rational view is useful in providing a benchmark against which to compare actual managerial decision-making patterns.

Nonrational Models

Nonrational models Models that suggest that information-gathering and -processing limitations make it difficult for managers to make optimal decisions

In contrast to the rational view, several **nonrational models** of managerial decision making suggest that information-gathering and -processing limitations make it difficult for managers to make optimal decisions. Within the nonrational framework, researchers have identified three major models of decision making: satisficing, incremental, and garbage can.

SATISFICING MODEL During the 1950s economist Herbert Simon (who later won a Nobel prize for his work in this area) began to study the actual behaviors of managerial decision makers. On the basis of his studies, Simon offered the concept of bounded rationality as a framework through which actual managerial decision making can be better understood.[15] **Bounded rationality** means that the ability of managers to be perfectly rational in making decisions is limited by such factors as cognitive capacity and time constraints. The concept suggests that the following factors commonly limit the degree to which managers are perfectly rational in making decisions:

Bounded rationality A concept that suggests that the ability of managers to be perfectly rational in making decisions is limited by such factors as cognitive capacity and time constraints

- Decision makers may have inadequate information, not only about the nature of the issue to be decided but also about possible alternatives and their strengths and limitations.
- Time and cost factors often constrain the amount of information that can be gathered in regard to a particular decision.
- Decision makers' perceptions about the relative importance of various pieces of data may cause them to overlook or ignore critical information.
- The part of human memory that is used in making decisions can retain only a relatively small amount of information at one time.
- The calculating capacities associated with intelligence limit the degree to which decision makers can determine optimal decisions, even assuming that perfect information has been gathered.[16]

Satisficing model A model stating that managers seek alternatives only until they find one that looks *satisfactory,* rather than seeking the optimal decision

Rather than optimizing their decisions, Simon argued, managers tend to follow the **satisficing model,** which holds that managers seek alternatives only until they find one that looks *satisfactory.* Satisficing can be an appropriate decision-making approach when the cost of delaying a decision or searching for a better alternative outweighs the likely payoff from such a course. For example, if one is driving on an unfamiliar highway with only a little bit of gas left, it might be better to choose a gas station within sight than to hold out for one's favorite brand. On the other hand, managers sometimes make a habit of using the simplistic satisficing approach even in situations in which the cost of searching for further alternatives is justified given the potential gain.[17]

For instance, Sant Singh Chatwal, founder of Bombay Palace Restaurants, Inc., a New York–based chain, wanted to expand in Manhattan but found that leasing property there was extremely expensive. To solve his problem, he quickly merged with another chain, Lifestyle Restaurants, Inc., which owned a number of cheap leases, particularly in very expensive parts of Manhattan. Chatwal says that he had heard about the Lifestyle chairman's "reputation for rough business practices" but still went ahead with the merger. Within 4 months Chatwal was in court attempting to break the contract because of allegedly undisclosed Lifestyle tax liabilities and other problems.[18] Thus Chatwal's haste in selecting what seemed to be a quick solution to his leasing problems illustrates the potential pitfalls of satisficing.

Incremental model A model stating that managers make the smallest response possible that will reduce the problem to at least a tolerable level

INCREMENTAL MODEL Another approach to decision making is the **incremental model,** which holds that managers make the smallest response possible that will reduce the problem to at least a tolerable level.[19] This approach is geared more toward achieving short-run alleviation of a problem than toward making decisions that will facilitate long-term goal attainment. Like the satisficing model, the incremental model does not require that managers process a great deal of information in order to take action. One researcher likened incrementalizing to the actions of a homeowner who deals with the problem of insufficient electric outlets by using various multioutlet adapters, such as extension cords. In the long run, the homeowner's incremental decisions may prove to be unworkable, since additional pieces of electrical equipment (e.g., VCRs and personal computers) may cause fuses to blow.[20]

Garbage-can model A model stating that managers behave in virtually a random pattern in making nonprogrammed decisions

GARBAGE-CAN MODEL The **garbage-can model** of decision making holds that managers behave in virtually a random pattern in making nonprogrammed decisions. In other words, decision outcomes occur by chance, depending on such factors as the participants who happen to be involved, the problems about which they happen to be concerned at the moment, the opportunities that they happen to stumble upon, and the pet solutions that happen to be looking for a problem to solve. The garbage-can strategy is most likely to be used when managers have no goal preferences, the means of achieving goals are unclear, and decision-making participants change rapidly.[21] Desirable outcomes can sometimes be achieved with a garbage-can strategy, but this approach can also lead to serious difficulties. Witness the problems encountered by Gould, Inc., when its former "iron-willed" CEO, William Ylvisaker, decided to remake the company (see the following Case in Point discussion).[22]

CASE IN POINT   GOULD'S ADVENTUROUS SPIRIT RUNS INTO TROUBLE

According to company lore, gambling can be traced far back in the history of Gould, Inc., the Rolling Meadows, Illinois, maker of computers, silicon chips, automation systems, and other electronic gear, whose annual sales once were in the $2 billion range. Founder Lytton J. Shields, company members say, flipped a coin to decide whether to rebuild his battery factory after it was gutted by fire in 1920. More recently, William T. Ylvisaker, former chairman and CEO, earned a reputation for taking excessive amounts of risk based on personal whims.

For example, Gould bought into a Florida real estate development in the late 1970s. The company then invested more than $80 million to improve the properties, including building a polo club (Ylvisaker was a polo buff). Unfortunately, interest rates rose and land values dropped, causing Gould to lose $49.2 million.

Similarly, Gould proceeded to bid on a fixed-price contract to provide a new field radio for the Navy and Marines, despite the fact that designs for the product were still undergoing development. More than 3 years later, the company had not produced any of the radios or even finalized the design.

Most observers agree that during his 18 years as head of the company, Ylvisaker transformed Gould from a small battery maker into a major electronics company. At its peak, Gould was a leader in factory automation, a noted maker of specialty computers for use in such devices as flight simulators, and a well-known defense contractor.

Unfortunately, while Ylvisaker liked to acquire businesses, he had no well-defined plan for Gould. The lack of central focus caused the company to falter from both an organizational and a financial point of view. By the time Ylvisaker was ousted in 1986, the company was in grave difficulty. The new chairman, former IBM executive James F. McDonald, was not able to reverse the situation quickly enough. Finally, the company was taken over by Japan-based Nippon Mining after Nippon made a $1.1 billion offer for what was left of Gould.[23]

■ ■ ■

Thus, while the garbage-can approach can sometimes lead managers to take advantage of unforeseen opportunities, it can also lead to severe problems from which it may be difficult to recover. The garbage-can approach is often used in the absence of solid strategic management.

STEPS IN AN EFFECTIVE DECISION-MAKING PROCESS

Descriptive decision-making models Models of decision making that attempt to document how managers actually *do* make decisions

Normative decision-making models Models of decision making that attempt to prescribe how managers *should* make decisions

The models of managerial decision making just outlined are sometimes referred to as **descriptive decision-making models** because they attempt to document how managers actually *do* make decisions. In contrast, models such as the one outlined in Table 2 are sometimes referred to as **normative decision-making models** because they attempt to prescribe how managers *should* make decisions. According to decision-making experts, managers are more likely to be effective decision makers if they follow the general approach outlined in Table 2. Although following such steps does not guarantee that all decisions will have the desired outcomes, it does increase the likelihood of success.[24] While managers frequently do not have control over many factors affecting the success of their decisions, they do have substantial control over the process that they use to make decisions. In this section, we discuss the four-step decision-making process in greater detail.

TABLE 2	Steps in an Effective Decision-Making Process
Step	**Activities**
Identify the problem.	Scan the environment for changing circumstances. Categorize the situation as a problem (or nonproblem). Diagnose the problem's nature and causes.
Generate alternative solutions.	Restrict criticism of alternatives. Freewheel to stimulate thinking. Offer as many ideas as possible. Combine and improve on ideas.
Evaluate and choose an alternative.	Evaluate feasibility. Evaluate quality. Evaluate acceptability. Evaluate costs. Evaluate reversibility. Evaluate ethics.
Implement and monitor the chosen solution.	Plan the implementation of the solution. Be sensitive to the decision's effects on others. Develop follow-up mechanisms.

Identifying the Problem

Organizational problems
Discrepancies between a
current state or condition and
what is desired

The first step in the decision-making process is identifying the problem. Part of identifying the problem, of course, is recognizing that a problem even exists. **Organizational problems** are discrepancies between a current state or condition and what is desired. This step has three general stages: scanning, categorization, and diagnosis.[25]

SCANNING STAGE The *scanning stage* involves monitoring the work situation for changing circumstances that may signal the emergence of a problem. At this point, a manager may be only vaguely aware that an environmental change could lead to a problem or that an existing situation is constituting a problem. For example, during the 1970s, Swiss watchmakers began to notice the appearance of relatively inexpensive watches being produced in Japan and Hong Kong.[26]

CATEGORIZATION STAGE The *categorization stage* entails attempting to understand and verify signs that there is some type of discrepancy between a current state and what is desired. At this point, the manager attempts to categorize the situation as a problem or a nonproblem, even though it may be difficult to specify the exact nature of the problem, if one exists. For example, sales of the Swiss watches, which were relatively expensive, began to decline rather precipitously.

DIAGNOSIS STAGE The *diagnosis stage* involves gathering additional information and specifying both the nature and the causes of the problem. Without appropriate diagnosis, it is difficult to experience success in the rest of the decision process. At this stage, the problem should be stated in terms of the discrepancy between current conditions and what is desired, and causes of the discrepancy should be specified. At first, the watchmakers thought that the cheaper watches would be a fad that would soon disappear. By 1983, however, the situation had not reversed, and Switzerland's two largest watchmakers, SSIH and Asuag, were deeply in debt. The two firms represented several of the world's best-known watch brands—Omega, Longines, Tissot, and Rado. It was becoming apparent that the new, cheaper watches from Japan and Hong Kong posed a serious long-term threat to the Swiss watchmakers. The banks holding the debt for SSIH and Asuag called in Zurich-based management consultant Nicolas G. Hayek to help generate alternatives.

Generating Alternative Solutions

Brainstorming A technique
that encourages group
members to generate as many
novel ideas as possible on a
given topic without evaluating
them

The second step in the decision-making process is developing alternatives. This practice usually leads to higher-quality solutions,[27] particularly when the situation calls for creative and innovative ones. The development of alternatives can often be facilitated through **brainstorming**, a technique for enhancing creativity that encourages group members to generate as many novel ideas as possible on a given topic without evaluating them. There are four principles involved:

1 *Don't criticize ideas while generating possible solutions.* Criticism during the idea-generation stage inhibits thinking. Also, because discussion tends to get bogged down when early ideas are criticized, only a few ideas are generated.
2 *Freewheel.* Offer even seemingly wild and outrageous ideas. Although they may never be used, they may trigger some usable ideas from others.
3 *Offer as many ideas as possible.* Pushing for a high volume of ideas increases the probability that some of them will be effective solutions.

4   *Combine and improve on ideas that have been offered.* Often the best ideas come from combinations of the ideas of others.[28]

Although brainstorming is typically done in a group, the principles can also be used by individuals. The manager jots down a number of possible solutions, including farfetched ideas, tries to generate a high idea volume, and combines or builds on ideas as he or she proceeds. Brainstorming and other methods of generating ideas will be considered further when we discuss creativity in a later section of this chapter.

At this point, it is important to note that a number of alternatives should be generated during this phase of the decision-making process. For example, Hayek, the bankers, and the heads of the watch companies developed several alternatives, such as liquidating the companies, diversifying into other products, and merging the two companies and mounting an offensive against the overseas threat.

Evaluating and Choosing an Alternative

This step involves carefully considering the advantages and disadvantages of each alternative before choosing one of them. Each alternative should be evaluated systematically according to six general criteria: feasibility, quality, acceptability, costs, reversibility, and ethics.

FEASIBILITY   The feasibility criterion refers to the extent to which an alternative can be accomplished within related organizational constraints, such as time, budgets, technology, and policies. Alternatives that do not meet the criterion of feasibility should be eliminated from further consideration. In the case of the watch companies, at first they did not recognize the feasibility of fighting the overseas threat.

QUALITY   The quality criterion refers to the extent to which an alternative effectively solves the problem under consideration. Alternatives that only partially solve the problem or represent a questionable solution are eliminated at this stage.

ACCEPTABILITY   This criterion refers to the degree to which the decision makers and others who will be affected by the implementation of the alternative are willing to support it. Acceptability has long been recognized as an important criterion against which to judge decisions.[29]

COSTS   The costs criterion refers to both the resource levels required and the extent to which the alternative is likely to have undesirable side effects. Thus the term "costs" is used here in the broad sense to include not only direct monetary expenditures but also more intangible issues such as possible vigorous competitor retaliation.

REVERSIBILITY   This criterion refers to the extent to which the alternative can be reversed, if at all. According to some observers, the importance of a decision is measured not by the amount of money involved but, rather, by how easily the decision can be reversed. For example, when the Coca-Cola Company ran into difficulties in introducing its new formula for Coke in 1985, it was able to reverse the decision by reintroducing its old formula as Coke Classic. Other types of decisions may be much more difficult to reverse.[30] In such cases, the alternative should be reconsidered very carefully before it is selected. For example, liquidating the watchmakers would have been difficult to reverse. Instead, the group decided to merge the two companies, creating the Swiss Corporation for Micro-electronics and Watchmaking (known as SMH), with Hayek as chairman. SMH then launched an inexpensive, technologically innovative plastic Swatch watch, which can be assembled at low cost on a fully automated assembly line. By 1992, the company had sold more than 100 million of the Swatch timepieces and was competing with Hattori Seiko of Japan to be the world's number-one watchmaker. Unlike its Japanese competitors, SMH also continues to produce both medium-priced and luxury watches.

ETHICS   The ethics criterion refers to the extent to which an alternative is compatible with the social responsibilities of the organization and the ethical standards of its managers. For instance, Hayek is considered to be somewhat of a hero in Switzerland for saving the Swiss watchmaking industry and many jobs. Some forward-thinking companies expend considerable effort to ensure that managers consider the ethical implications of their decisions (see, for example, the discussion of Alcoa in the Valuing Ethics box).

Implementing and Monitoring the Chosen Solution

For the decision-making process to be successful, managers must give considerable thought to *implementing* and *monitoring* the chosen solution. It is possible to make a "good" decision in terms of the first three steps and still have the process fail because of difficulties at this final step.

IMPLEMENTING THE SOLUTION   Successful implementation usually depends on two main factors: careful planning and sensitivity to those involved in the implementation and/or affected by it.

VALUING ETHICS

Alcoa's "Core Values"

Shortly after Paul H. O'Neill became chairman of the Aluminum Company of America, he learned that one of the perquisites of his position was a membership in a local, but nationally known, golf resort. When his inquiry determined that women and blacks were not allowed as members, he declined to become a member. He further decreed that no company money should be spent on memberships or activities in such clubs. The action was the first step in what has become a reshaping of the corporate conscience at Alcoa.

At the heart of the reshaping are six "core values" that top management spent 100 hours

hammering out. The values are integrity, safety and health, quality of work, treatment of people, accountability, and profitability. The company has spent millions of dollars and thousands of work hours training Alcoa's more than 60,000 employees to use the values as principles to guide their decision making and actions.

For example, Ken Blevins, president of Alcoa Electronic Packaging, Inc., decided not to release initial shipments of a new Alcoa packaging material for microchips because he was not satisfied with the quality. The new material was ultimately not released for almost 18 months, while company members sought and found solutions to the quality

problems. The delay cost Alcoa "a considerable amount of money" and resulted in negative publicity in which the packaging enterprise was described as "floundering" by a business publication. Blevins says that his decision was aided by the core-values training. The training helped him recognize more clearly that producing a product that measures up to promises made to customers is, in fact, a moral decision. In his view, to do less is a compromise of integrity.

"We are systematically taking our vision and our values and trying to make them a reality in how we run the place," says O'Neill. Company officials willingly acknowledge, though, that living up to the core values is challenging.[31]

In regard to planning, minor changes may require only a small amount of planning, while major changes may call for extensive planning efforts, such as written plans, careful coordination with units inside and outside the organization, and special funding arrangements. In general, the more difficult it is to reverse a solution, the more important it is to plan for effective implementation.

Implementation also tends to occur more smoothly when decision makers show sensitivity in considering the possible reactions of those the decision will affect. For instance, when Pacific Southwest Cable in San Diego, California, decided to place heavy emphasis on service, both to internal (individuals inside the company) and external customers, the company spent considerable time orienting and training workers. Part of the change involved giving employees more latitude in taking service actions, such as allowing service representatives to make billing adjustments without prior management approval. As a result of the careful orientation and training, workers were able to implement the change smoothly. This led, in turn, to considerable increases in market penetration and profits.[32]

MONITORING THE SOLUTION Managers need to monitor decision implementation to be sure that things are progressing as planned and that the problem that triggered the decision-making process has been resolved. The more important the problem, the greater the effort that needs to be expended on appropriate follow-up mechanisms.

OVERCOMING BARRIERS TO EFFECTIVE DECISION MAKING

Unfortunately, as the nonrational models of managerial decision making suggest, managers often do not follow the four-step process just outlined. Despite the fact that this general approach is endorsed by a number of decision experts, managers may not be aware of the experts' recommendations. In addition, managers face several barriers to effective decision making. In this section, we discuss means of overcoming four key decision-making barriers: accepting the problem challenge in the first place, searching for sufficient alternatives, recognizing common decision-making biases, and avoiding the decision escalation phenomenon.

Accepting the Problem Challenge

Decision researchers David Wheeler and Irving Janis have identified four basic reaction patterns that characterize the behavior of individuals when they are faced with a legitimate problem in the form of a difficulty or an opportunity. The first three, complacency, defensive avoidance, and panic, represent barriers to effective decision making. The fourth, deciding to decide, constitutes a more viable approach for decision makers to follow.[33]

Complacency A condition in which individuals either do not see the signs of danger or opportunity or ignore them

COMPLACENCY The **complacency** reaction occurs when individuals either do not see the signs of danger or opportunity or ignore them. With complacency, the failure to detect the signs usually stems from inadequate scanning of the environment. Ignoring the signs altogether is more akin to the "ostrich" effect—putting one's head in the sand and hoping that the danger or opportunity will resolve itself. Complacency can be present even when an individual appears to be responding to the situation. For example, it occurs when an individual immediately accepts a job offer that looks like a good opportunity without devoting any time or effort to assessing the situation thoroughly.

Defensive avoidance A condition in which individuals either deny the importance of a danger or an opportunity or deny any responsibility for taking action

DEFENSIVE AVOIDANCE With **defensive avoidance,** individuals either deny the importance of a danger or an opportunity or deny any responsibility for taking action. Defensive avoidance can take three different forms: rationalization ("It can't happen to me"), procrastination ("It can be taken care of later"), or buck-passing ("It's someone else's problem").

Panic A reaction in which individuals become so upset that they frantically seek a way to solve a problem

PANIC With **panic** or paniclike reactions, individuals become so upset that they frantically seek a way to solve a problem. In their haste, they often seize upon a quickly formulated alternative without noticing its severe disadvantages and without considering other, potentially better, alternatives. Panic is particularly likely to occur with crisis problems.[34]

Deciding to decide A response in which decision makers accept the challenge of deciding what to do about a problem and follow an effective decision-making process

DECIDING TO DECIDE With the **deciding-to-decide** response, decision makers accept the challenge of deciding what to do about a problem and follow an effective decision-making process. Deciding to decide is an important reaction to a legitimate problem situation. Of course, managers cannot attend to every potential problem, no matter how minor and remote, that appears on the horizon. Some guidelines for deciding to decide are presented in Table 3.

Searching for Sufficient Alternatives

For many decision situations, particularly nonprogrammed decisions, it is unrealistic for decision makers to collect enough information to identify *all* potential alternatives and assess *all* possible pluses and minuses. Information acquisition is limited, in large part, because it typically requires time and money. Such costs accrue even when information gathering is confined to checking with knowledgeable organization members or holding a meeting. As a result, decision makers must evaluate how much time, effort, and money should be spent gathering information that will help in making a particular decision.

This information-gathering dilemma is depicted in Figure 3. The horizontal

---

TABLE 3   **Guidelines for Deciding to Decide**

APPRAISE CREDIBILITY OF INFORMATION
Is the source in a position to know the truth?
If so, is the source likely to be honest?
Is there any evidence, and how good is it?

ASCERTAIN IMPORTANCE OF THREAT OR OPPORTUNITY
How likely is a real danger or opportunity?
If a threat, how severe might the losses be?
If an opportunity, how great might the gains be?

DETERMINE THE NEED FOR URGENCY
Is the threat or opportunity likely to occur soon?
Will it develop gradually, or is sudden change likely?
If some action is urgent, can part be done now and the rest later?

Source: Adapted from Daniel D. Wheeler and Irving L. Janis, *A Practical Guide for Making Decisions,* Macmillan, New York, 1980, pp. 34–35.

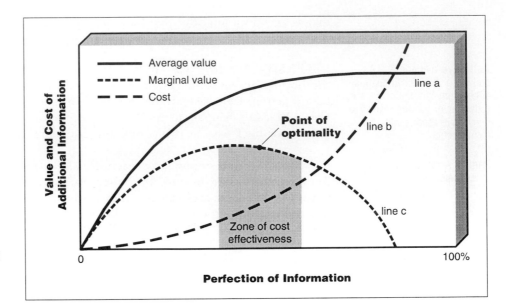

Figure 3 *The cost of additional information. (Adapted from E. Frank Harrison,* The Managerial Decision-Making Process, *3d ed., Houghton Mifflin, Boston, 1987, p. 47.)*

axis indicates potential information about the decision, spanning from 0 to 100 percent. The vertical axis depicts the value and cost of additional information. As indicated by *line a,* as the decision maker collects more and more information, the value of the additional information in many situations begins to level off. At the same time, as shown by *line b,* the cost of additional information during the initial search is usually not very high but tends to get much higher as one moves toward obtaining perfect information. As a result, the marginal, or incremental, value of additional pieces of information *(line c)* rises at first to a point of optimality and then starts to decline as cost begins to exceed the value of additional pieces of information. The area of optimal information gathering is also shown.

Decision makers' efforts tend to fall seriously *below* the zone of cost effectiveness in the process of identifying a sufficient number of potential alternatives. For example, one study of 78 decision-making situations found that in 85 percent of the cases, there was little or no search for viable alternatives. Instead, decision makers tended to quickly copy a solution used by others, accept an off-the-shelf solution offered by a consultant, or seize upon an idea of unknown or debatable value and try to find support for it. Even in the 15 percent of the cases in which a deliberate effort was made to develop viable alternatives, the search process tended to be cut off after only a few possibilities had been identified.[35] Unless countered, the tendency to skip or cut short the search for alternatives is likely to have a stifling effect on innovation. Some approaches that may be helpful in generating decision alternatives will be discussed later in this chapter in the section on creativity. Of course, for rather trivial decisions, managers may correctly feel that the time and effort involved in identifying multiple alternatives are not warranted.

Recognizing Common Decision-Making Biases

Psychologists Daniel Kahneman and Amos Tversky, who for years have been investigating how decision makers operate, have pointed out several biases that tend to characterize the way that decision makers process information.[36] These biases, which are explained below, are framing, representativeness, availability, and anchoring and adjustment. A related issue is decision makers' tendency toward overconfidence under some conditions. These biases are most likely to affect the way that decision makers evaluate alternative solutions, but they may also influence the way that they identify difficulties and opportunities. Consider the following situation:

> Threatened by a superior enemy force, the general faces a dilemma. His intelligence officers say his soldiers will be caught in an ambush in which 600 of them will die unless he leads them to safety by one of two available routes. If he takes the first route, 200 soldiers will be saved. If he takes the second, there's a one-third chance that 600 soldiers will be saved and a two-thirds chance that none will be saved. Which route should he take?

If you are like most people, you chose the first alternative, reasoning that the general should save the 200 rather than risk even higher losses. Suppose, however, that the situation is as follows:

> The general again has to choose between two escape routes. But this time his aides tell him that if he takes the first, 400 soldiers will die. If he takes the second, there's a one-third chance that no soldiers will die and a two-thirds chance that 600 soldiers will die. Which route should he take?

In this situation, most people argue that the general should take the second route. Their rationale is that with the first route 400 will certainly be dead. With the second route there is at least a one-third chance that no one will die, and casualties will only be 50 percent higher if the scheme fails.

Interestingly, most people draw the opposite conclusion from these two problems. In the first problem, people favor the first alternative 3 to 1; in the second problem, they choose the second alternative 4 to 1. Yet a close look will reveal that the problems in both cases are exactly the same—they are just stated differently. The first problem is stated in terms of lives saved, the second in terms of lives lost. The tendency to make different decisions depending on how a problem is presented is called **framing.**

Framing The tendency to make different decisions depending on how a problem is presented

To explain the paradoxical decision pattern exhibited in the general's dilemmas, Kahneman and Tversky have developed the prospect theory. Based on the belief that decision makers tend to be "loss averse," the **prospect theory** posits that they find the prospect of an actual loss more painful than giving up the possibility of a gain.[37] The credit card industry seems to have an intuitive understanding of prospect theory. By a common arrangement, customers receive "discounts for cash" at gas stations rather than being charged "credit surcharges" for using their credit cards. Prospect theory suggests that customers are less willing to pay an *extra* charge for using credit cards (an actual loss) than they are to forgo a discount for paying cash (a potential gain).

Prospect theory A theory positing that decision makers find the prospect of an actual loss more painful than giving up the possibility of a gain

> Linda is 31, single, outspoken, and very bright. She majored in philosophy in college. As a student, she was deeply concerned with discrimination and other social issues and participated in antinuclear demonstrations. Which of the following statements is more likely?
>
> a Linda is a bank teller.
> b Linda is a bank teller and active in the feminist movement.

Most people choose the alternative that says that Linda is both a bank teller and a feminist. Actually, however, the laws of probability suggest that an occurrence (bank teller) is more likely to happen on its own than in conjunction with another occurrence (bank teller *and* feminist). The Linda problem illustrates a common decision shortcut called **representativeness,** the tendency to be overly influenced by stereotypes in making judgments about the likelihood of occurrences. We increase the odds of decision-making difficulties when our judgments run counter to the laws of probability.

Representativeness The tendency to be overly influenced by stereotypes in making judgments about the likelihood of occurrences

> In a typical English text, does the letter "K" appear more often as the first letter in a word or as the third letter?

Availability The tendency to judge the likelihood of an occurrence on the basis of the extent to which other like instances or occurrences can easily be recalled

People generally judge that the letter "K" is more likely to be the first letter in a word even though the letter is almost twice as likely to appear in the third position. We do this because of a bias called **availability,** the tendency to judge the likelihood of an occurrence on the basis of the extent to which other like instances or occurrences can easily be recalled. In this case, it is usually easier to recall words beginning with the letter "K" than words in which "K" is the third letter. Availability also shows up in tendencies to overestimate the likelihood of deaths due to vividly imaginable causes such as airplane accidents, fires, and murder and to underestimate more common, but less spectacular, causes such as emphysema and stroke.[38] Managers may fall victim to the availability bias in a number of ways. For example, they may base annual performance appraisals on the most recent and easily recalled performance of subordinates, judge how well competitors' products are doing by the extent to which the managers have seen them in use, or gauge employee morale by relying on the views of immediate subordinates.

A newly hired engineer for a computer firm in the Boston metropolitan area has 4 years' experience and good all-around qualifications. When asked to estimate the starting salary for this employee, a chemist who had very little knowledge about the profession or industry guessed an annual salary of $17,000. What is your estimate?[39]

Anchoring and adjustment The tendency to be influenced by an initial figure, even when the information is largely irrelevant

Most people do not think that the chemist's guess influenced their own estimate. Yet people tend to give higher salary estimates when the chemist's estimate is stated as $60,000 than when it is $17,000. This tendency to be influenced by an initial figure, even when the information is largely irrelevant, is known as **anchoring and adjustment.** For example, employers often ask a job candidate about her or his current salary and then use the figure as a basis for extending an offer, even though the candidate may currently be underpaid or overpaid.

Overconfidence The tendency to be more certain of judgments regarding the likelihood of a future event than one's actual predictive accuracy warrants

These information-processing biases suggest that decision makers should be cautious about the accuracy of their estimates regarding the likelihood of events. Evidence suggests, however, that decision makers often exhibit **overconfidence,** the tendency to be more certain of judgments regarding the likelihood of a future event than one's actual predictive accuracy warrants.[40] Ironically, overconfidence appears most likely to occur when decision makers are working in unfamiliar areas.[41] The overconfidence stems from a failure to fully understand the potential pitfalls involved. Thus managers may be particularly susceptible to overconfidence when they are planning moves into new, unfamiliar areas of business.

Such a situation produced acute difficulties for the Allied Chemical Corporation. The company and two partners, Gulf Oil and Royal Dutch/Shell, began building a plant to turn years of radioactive waste accumulated from U.S. nuclear power plants into reusable nuclear fuel. Believing it could triumph where others had failed, Allied plunged into the project in the early 1970s without fully considering the multitude of technological questions and the complex political issues involved. In 1971, Allied and its partners began building the Barnwell nuclear fuel plant on a 1587-acre tract next to the federal government's immense Savannah River reserve, a South Carolina nuclear-waste dump. By 1977, the Carter administration had banned plutonium processing, and by 1981, the partners had abandoned the project after spending over $200 million. They conceded that the politics, costs, and technological challenges of the effort were insurmountable—at least for a private enterprise. Nevertheless, Du Pont is now building a nuclear-waste plant in the same area. However, Du Pont is operating as a contractor; the Department of Energy is the owner and financier of the project.[42]

Managers can avoid some of the ill effects of information-processing biases by being aware of how such biases are likely to affect their judgments. Gathering enough information to be fairly well versed about the issues associated with important decisions is also helpful. In addition, decision makers should think about why their judgments might be wrong or far off the target. Such thinking may help reveal contradictions and inaccuracies.[43] Some quantitative methods that can help decision makers make more accurate judgments are covered in the Supplement to this chapter.

Avoiding the Decision Escalation Phenomenon

When a manager makes a decision, it is often only one decision in a series of decisions about a particular issue. Further decisions may be necessary, depending on the results of a previous decision. For example, suppose that you decide to hire a new employee because you expect that the person will be an excellent performer. However, after several months on the job it is apparent that the person is not performing at an acceptable level. Should you take steps to terminate the worker? Of course, at this point you have invested considerable time and money in training the new employee, and it is possible that the individual is still learning the job. So you decide to spend more time helping the worker, and you line up some further training. Even with these additional inputs, 2 months later the worker is still not performing at the necessary level. What do you decide now? Although you have more reason to "cut your losses," you also have even more invested in making the individual productive. When do you discontinue your "investment"?[44]

Decision situations like this one present difficult dilemmas for managers. Substantial costs have already been incurred because of an earlier decision. On the other hand, future actions have the potential of either reversing the situation or compounding the initial losses. Such situations are sometimes referred to as **escalation situations,** because they signal the strong possibility of escalating commitment and accelerating losses.[45]

Research studies indicate that when managers incur costs associated with an initial decision, they often react by allocating more resources to the situation even when the prospects for turning the situation around are dim. Such situations can develop into what decision expert Max H. Bazerman has called nonrational escalation. **Nonrational escalation,** or the escalation phenomenon, is the tendency to increase commitment to a previously selected course of action beyond the level that would be expected if the manager followed an effective decision-making process.[46] As experts in the fields of economics and accounting have pointed out, costs that have already been incurred (e.g., time and money) should be considered **sunk costs.** Such costs, once incurred, are not recoverable and should not enter into considerations of future courses of action. Yet decision makers are often heavily influenced by prior costs when they themselves have made the initial decisions.

Part of the reason for the escalation phenomenon is that decision makers tend to be loss-averse when it comes to writing off prior costs. Thus the tendency may be related to prospect theory, discussed earlier. In addition, the decision maker may be concerned that a change in the course of action may cause others to regard the original decision as a mistake or failure. Methods of avoiding nonrational escalation include setting advance limits on how far to extend the commitment, asking tough questions about why the commitment is being continued, reviewing the costs involved, and watching for escalation situations that may constitute commitment traps.[47] Otherwise, decision makers may find themselves in a situation similar to that which plagued Expo 86 (see the following Case in Point discussion).

Escalation situations Situations that signal the strong possibility of escalating commitment and accelerating losses

Nonrational escalation The tendency to increase commitment to a previously selected course of action beyond the level that would be expected if the manager followed an effective decision-making process; also called *escalation phenomenon*

Sunk costs Costs that, once incurred, are not recoverable and should not enter into considerations of future courses of action

EXPO 86 ESCALATES

Since the late 1970s, British Columbia, Canada, had been planning to host a world's fair, to be held in Vancouver during 1986. The idea for the fair was originally proposed by William Bennett, the provincial premier, and it initially appeared to be something that would bring both visibility and financial benefits to the province. Unfortunately, as the planning progressed, the original estimates of attendance, costs of construction, and projected earnings all proved to be overly optimistic. It became apparent that the city did not have the infrastructure of hotels, parking, and transportation that was needed to host the planned number of visitors. Additionally, the projected cost of the exposition ballooned from $78 million to $1.5 billion, while more realistic revenue projections indicated that the fair would not be a break-even proposition but could be expected to lose over $300 million.

Yet, as this negative news grew in magnitude, the premier of British Columbia became even more committed to the project. Estimates of attendance were raised to justify the project (at one point they were well beyond the city's physical capacity to host the fair's visitors), and the major problems of housing and transportation were minimized. Premier Bennett not only argued strenuously for the fair's continuance but staked his career on the project—withdrawal might cost him his political office.

As the time of the fair approached, the estimated costs of canceling the event were projected to exceed $80 million, making a reversal of the initial decision extremely difficult. Finally, the province instituted a lottery that raised the necessary funds to cover the expected deficit of $300 million, and the fair was held as scheduled.[48]   ■ ■ ■

GROUP DECISION MAKING

Major decisions in organizations are most often made by more than one person. For example, at Coca-Cola, Goizueta and the other three top executives must agree on any major decision. Even at nonsupervisory levels, groups are increasingly involved in making operational decisions. For instance, Gencorp Automotive has geared its new reinforced plastics plant near Indianapolis to run with just three levels: plant manager, team leaders, and 25 teams of 5 to 15 production workers. Each team makes most of the decisions involving its work area.[49] In this section, we consider the advantages and disadvantages of group decision making, as well as means of enhancing group decision-making processes.[50]

Advantages and Disadvantages of Group Decision Making

Group decision making has several advantages over individual decision making. These advantages are summarized in Table 4. According to a study of more than 200 project teams, who were involved in educational courses related to management, the groups outperformed their most proficient group member 97 percent of the time.[51]

Despite its advantages, group decision making also has several potential disadvantages when contrasted with individual decision making. These disadvantages are summarized in Table 4. One of these, the possibility of groupthink, requires further elaboration.

Groupthink is the tendency in cohesive groups to seek agreement about an issue at the expense of realistically appraising the situation.[52] With groupthink,

Groupthink The tendency in cohesive groups to seek agreement about an issue at the expense of realistically appraising the situation

TABLE 4	**Advantages and Disadvantages of Group Decision Making**
Advantages	**Disadvantages**
1. More information and knowledge is focused on the issue. 2. An increased number of alternatives can be developed. 3. Greater understanding and acceptance of the final decision are likely. 4. Members develop knowledge and skills for future use.	1. It is usually more time-consuming. 2. Disagreements may delay decisions and cause hard feelings. 3. The discussion may be dominated by one or a few group members. 4. Groupthink may cause members to overemphasize achieving agreement.

group members are so concerned about preserving the cohesion of the group that they are reluctant to bring up issues that may cause disagreements or to provide information that may prove unsettling to the discussion. Such tendencies can have disastrous consequences when major issues are being considered. For example, the *Challenger* tragedy has been attributed to groupthink. Despite receiving some contrary information, upper-level officials decided to go ahead with the mission. The decision makers included top managers at the National Aeronautics and Space Administration (NASA) and at Morton Thiokol, the company that manufactured the solid rocket boosters. These officials tended to ignore information from engineers at Morton Thiokol and from others about possible malfunctions due to unusually cold weather conditions. Faced with a desire to secure continued funding and with intense public interest in the Teacher in Space program, the decision makers became a cohesive group that was largely unwilling to seriously consider contrary facts. Unfortunately, all seven crew members, including teacher Christa McAuliffe, were killed in the explosion at takeoff.[53] Recent research suggests that groupthink may occur even when groups are not highly cohesive. The problem may stem from a directive leader who states a particular preference early in the discussion. Apparently, when that happens, groups often willingly comply, perhaps partially because their search for alternatives is inhibited by the suggested preference.[54]

Enhancing Group Decision-Making Processes

Managers can take a number of steps that will help them not only avoid the major pitfalls of group decision making but also reap the advantages of the process. One step is involving the group in decisions when the information and knowledge of the group have an important bearing on the decision outcome. That way, the time consumed by group decision making can probably be justified.

Another step is considering carefully the composition of the group. For example, including individuals who are likely to concentrate on major organizational goals helps overcome any tendency toward self-interest. Problems caused by dominating individuals can often be minimized by including someone who is skilled at encouraging the ideas of others.

Yet another step that can be taken to facilitate group decision making is setting up mechanisms that help avoid groupthink. For instance, managers can designate one or more **devil's advocates,** individuals who are assigned the role of making sure that the negative aspects of any attractive decision alternatives are considered.[55] Managers can also encourage the group to engage in **dialectical inquiry,** a procedure in which a decision situation is approached from two opposite points of view.[56]

The group decision-making process can also be improved through the use

Devil's advocates
Individuals who are assigned the role of making sure that the negative aspects of any attractive decision alternatives are considered

Dialectical inquiry A procedure in which a decision situation is approached from two opposite points of view

of techniques that enhance creativity. Creativity is an essential part of the decision-making process because it helps generate novel alternatives that lead to innovation and also fosters the development of unique perspectives on the nature of problems. In the next section, we discuss several approaches for encouraging greater creativity in individuals and groups.

PROMOTING INNOVATION: THE CREATIVITY FACTOR IN DECISION MAKING

Creativity The cognitive process of developing an idea, concept, commodity, or discovery that is viewed as novel by its creator or a target audience

Creativity is the cognitive process of developing an idea, concept, commodity, or discovery that is viewed as novel by its creator or a target audience.[57] Hence creativity is usually identified by assessing outcomes.[58] In fact, creativity researcher Teresa M. Amabile argues, "Creativity is not a quality of a person; it is a quality of ideas, of behaviors, or products."[59] Creativity is crucial to solving problems in ways that result in important organizational innovations. As worldwide competition heats up, greater emphasis is being placed on creativity. Japan, in particular, is trying to overcome its reputation as a copycat of the technology of other countries through increased efforts at creativity. For example, at the Matsushita Electronics Corporation, semiconductor executives wear badges stating "Create." At the Nippon Electric Company (NEC), posters and placards encourage workers to "invent the new VCR" and offer $100 awards for creative ideas.[60]

Try your hand at the classic creativity problem shown in Figure 4. Then look at Figure 5, which presents some possible solutions to the problem. Many individuals are unable to solve the nine-dot problem because they make the assumption that the lines cannot go outside the nine dots. As this problem illustrates, creativity requires both convergent and divergent thinking. **Convergent thinking** is the effort to solve problems by beginning with a problem and attempting to move logically to a solution. One might liken convergent thinking to searching for oil by digging an ever bigger and deeper hole.[61] **Divergent thinking,** on the other hand, is the effort to solve problems by generating new ways of viewing a problem and seeking novel alternatives. Rather than digging in the same hole, a divergent thinker digs in many different places to generate new perspectives. In the creative process, convergent thinking helps define a problem and evaluate

Convergent thinking The effort to solve problems by beginning with a problem and attempting to move logically to a solution

Divergent thinking The effort to solve problems by generating new ways of viewing a problem and seeking novel alternatives

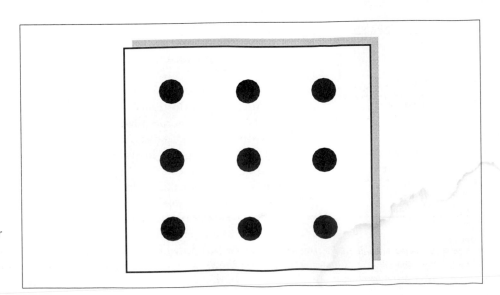

Figure 4 *The nine-dot problem. Without lifting your pencil from the paper, draw no more than four straight lines that will cross through all nine dots.*

This puzzle is difficult to solve if the imaginary boundary (limit) enclosing the nine dots is not exceeded. A surprising number of people will not exceed the imaginary boundary, for often this constraint is unconsciously in the mind of the problem-solver, even though it is not in the definition of the problem at all. The overly strict limits are a block in the mind of the solver. The widepread nature of this block is what makes this puzzle classic. (Adams, 1980, p. 24)

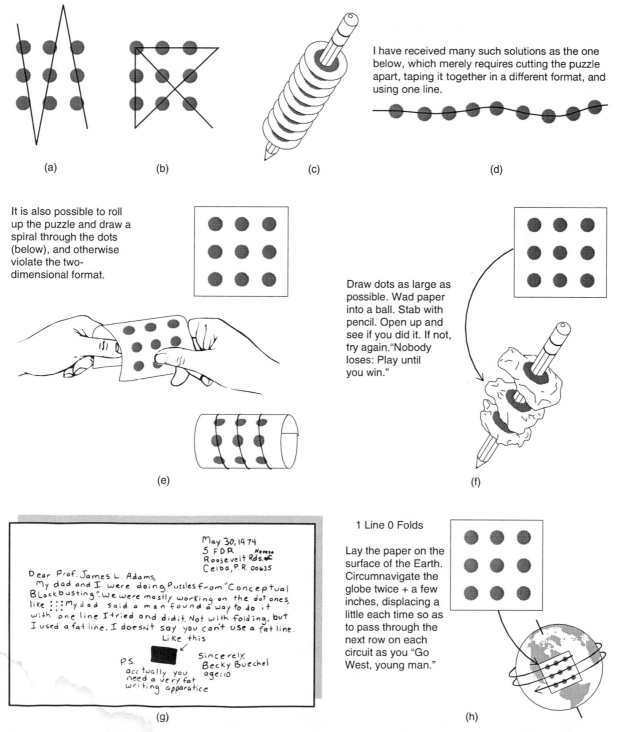

I have received many such solutions as the one below, which merely requires cutting the puzzle apart, taping it together in a different format, and using one line.

(a)　　　　(b)　　　　(c)　　　　(d)

It is also possible to roll up the puzzle and draw a spiral through the dots (below), and otherwise violate the two-dimensional format.

Draw dots as large as possible. Wad paper into a ball. Stab with pencil. Open up and see if you did it. If not, try again."Nobody loses: Play until you win."

(e)　　　　(f)

May 30, 1974
5 FDR　Nowsa
Roosevelt Rds. ℄
Ceiba, P. R. 00635

Dear Prof. James L. Adams,
　My dad and I were doing Puzzles from "Conceptual Blockbusting". We were mostly working on the dot ones, like ::: my dad said a man found a way to do it with one line. I tried and did it. Not with folding, but I used a fat line. I doesn't say you can't use a fat line. Like this

P.S.
acctually you need a very fat writing apparatice

Sincerely,
Becky Buechel
age:10

1 Line 0 Folds

Lay the paper on the surface of the Earth. Circumnavigate the globe twice + a few inches, displacing a little each time so as to pass through the next row on each circuit as you "Go West, young man."

(g)　　　　(h)

Figure 5 *Some possible solutions to the nine-dot problem. (Based on J. L. Adams,* Conceptual Blockbusting: A Guide to Better Ideas, *2d ed., Norton, New York, pp. 25–30; reprinted from Diane E. Papalia and Sally Wendkos Olds,* Psychology, *McGraw-Hill, New York, 1985, p. 297.)*

proposed solutions. Divergent thinking helps develop alternative views of problems, as well as seek novel ways of dealing with them. In this section, we examine the basic ingredients of creativity, describe the stages of the creative process, and offer some major techniques for enhancing group creativity that can be used by managers.

Basic Ingredients

According to creativity expert Amabile, the following three basic ingredients are necessary for creativity.

DOMAIN-RELEVANT SKILLS These skills are associated with expertise in the relevant field. They include related technical skills or artistic ability, talent in the area, and factual knowledge.

CREATIVITY-RELEVANT SKILLS These skills include a cognitive style, or method, of thinking that is oriented to exploring new directions, knowledge of approaches that can be used for generating novel ideas, and a work style that is conducive to developing creative ideas. A creative work style is characterized by the ability to concentrate effort and attention for long periods of time, the ability to abandon unproductive avenues, persistence, and a high energy level.

TASK MOTIVATION The individual must be genuinely interested in the task for its own sake, rather than because of some external reward possibility, such as money. Recent evidence suggests that primary concern with external rewards tends to inhibit the creative process. For example, a scientist attempting to develop a new drug in order to obtain a bonus or prize is not likely to be as creative as a scientist whose primary interest is learning more about a promising new direction.[62] For some ideas on how to boost your creativity, see the Practically Speaking discussion, "How to Be More Creative."

Stages of Creativity

The creativity process involves several stages. One commonly used model of creativity has four stages,[64] which are shown in Figure 6 and described below.

PREPARATION This stage involves gathering initial information, defining the problem or task requiring creativity, generating alternatives, and seeking and carefully analyzing further data relating to the problem. At this stage, the individual becomes thoroughly immersed in every relevant aspect of the problem. For complex technical problems, this stage may take months or even years.

INCUBATION This stage of the creativity process involves mainly subconscious mental activity and divergent thinking to explore unusual alternatives. During this stage, the individual generally does not consciously focus on the problem; this allows the subconscious to work on a solution.

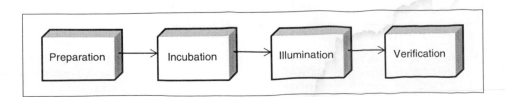

Figure 6 *Stages of creativity.*

PRACTICALLY SPEAKING

HOW TO BE MORE CREATIVE

Some of the following suggestions, which are based on research and thinking on creativity, may help you be more creative in your work and your daily life.

What Do You Want to Do?

- Take time to understand a problem before you begin trying to solve it.
- Get all the facts clearly in mind.
- Identify the facts that seem to be the most important before you try to work out a detailed solution.

How Can You Do It?

- Set aside a sizable block of time to focus on a particular problem, rather than attending to it in scattered sessions.
- Work out a plan for attacking the problem.
- Establish subgoals. Solve part of the problem and go on from there. You don't have to do everything at once. Write out your thoughts. This allows you to capture important points and to come back to them later. It also allows you to look for patterns.
- Imagine yourself acting out the problem. *Actually* act out the problem.
- Think of a similar problem you've solved in the past and build on the strategy you used then.
- Use analogies whenever possible. See whether you can generalize from a similar situation to your current problem.
- Use several different problem-solving strategies—verbal, visual, mathematical, acting. Draw a diagram to help you visualize the problem, or talk to yourself out loud, or "walk through" a situation.
- Look for relationships among various facts.
- Trust your intuition. Take a guess and see whether you can back it up.
- Play with ideas and possible approaches. Try looking at the same situation in a number of different ways.

How Can You Do It Better?

- Try consciously to be original, to come up with new ideas.
- Don't worry about looking foolish if you say or suggest something unusual or if you come up with the wrong answer.
- Eliminate cultural taboos in your thinking (such as gender stereotyping) that might interfere with your ability to come up with a novel solution.
- Try to be right the first time, but if you're not, explore as many alternatives as you need to.
- Keep an open mind. If your initial approach doesn't work, ask whether you made assumptions that might not be true.
- If you get stuck on one approach, try to get to the solution by another route.
- Be alert to odd or puzzling facts. If you can explain them, your solution may be at hand.
- Think of unconventional ways to use objects and the environment. Look at familiar things as if you've never seen them before.
- Consider taking a detour that delays your goal but eventually leads to it.
- Discard habitual ways of doing things, and force yourself to figure out new ways.
- Do some brainstorming with one or more other people. This involves trying to produce as many new and original ideas as possible, without evaluating any of them until the end of the session.
- Strive for objectivity. Evaluate your own ideas as you would those of a stranger.[63]

ILLUMINATION   At this stage, a new level of insight is achieved, often through a sudden breakthrough in "eureka" fashion.

VERIFICATION   This stage involves testing the ideas to determine the validity of the insight. At this point, convergent, logical thinking is needed to evaluate the solution. If the solution does not prove feasible, it may be necessary to cycle back through all or some of the previous stages.

The invention of the computerized axial tomography scanner (often referred to as the CAT scanner) illustrates the creativity process. This revolutionary device allows radiologists to take three-dimensional pictures of the inside of the body with much greater clarity than conventional X rays. Inventor Godfrey Hounsfield received a Nobel prize for his work (see the following Case in Point discussion).

CASE IN POINT

THE CAT SCANNER GREETS AN ASTONISHED WORLD

CAT scanner inventor Godfrey Hounsfield worked as an electrical engineer for EMI, Ltd., a British pioneer in entertainment and electronic technologies, which is located in Hayes, England. Although Hounsfield made some major breakthroughs in computer memory storage in the 1960s, EMI elected not to pursue the technology because the company did not want to take on IBM. So Hounsfield's boss told him to find another idea to work on. Armed with computer knowledge from his previous work, Hounsfield was comparing notes with a colleague when they made an interesting observation. If one were able to take readings that could detect the presence of materials from all angles through a box, in three dimensions, it would be possible to determine what was in the box without opening it. The notion was related to pattern recognition, a highly theoretical field that was gaining attention from scientists in engineering and mathematics. Scientists were trying to find ways by which computers could recognize images as swiftly as the eye and brain and take appropriate action.

For some reason, Hounsfield's mind leaped to a different vision—a mathematical puzzle so vast that solving it by conventional means would be impossible. He also kept thinking about the box. He speculated that if the object was reduced to "picture points," like the tiny dots that make the picture on a TV screen, then all the picture points could be assigned a mathematical value. The picture points could be recorded through the use of X rays, and each point could be viewed as the result of a mathematical equation. Then, if one assembled all the relevant mathematical equations outside the box and had a computer reassemble them, one could show the object inside the box on a computer screen.

Hounsfield mulled over his notion for some time. Then, suddenly, his thoughts joined two unrelated planes, linking his knowledge of computerized pattern recognition with that of medical radiology. What if one could make pictures of what is inside the human body? As he thought about it, he realized that the pictures could be three-dimensional, giving the medical profession vastly improved information about a patient's condition. Formidable obstacles still lay ahead in developing a practical means of implementing his ideas. Hounsfield worked with an enormous dedication, often until midnight each night, to develop a practical prototype. Finally, in 1972, a demonstration of the first head scanner was made in Chicago to an enraptured audience at a meeting of the Radiological Society of North America. Since then, the device has eliminated much exploratory surgery and greatly enhanced effective treatment prospects for many patients throughout the world.[65] ■ ■ ■

Techniques for Enhancing Group Creativity

Whereas the preceding discussion focused on an individual's creative efforts, this section examines techniques for enhancing creativity in group settings. Two major techniques are brainstorming and the nominal group technique. (We discuss another method that can be used to enhance group creativity, the Delphi method, in the Supplement to this chapter, "Planning and Decision Aids.")

BRAINSTORMING The brainstorming technique is a means of enhancing creativity that encourages group members to generate as many novel ideas as possible on a given topic without evaluating them. The four basic rules—do not criticize during idea generation, freewheel, offer many ideas, and improve on already offered ideas—were discussed earlier in the chapter.

Brainstorming is often coupled with other approaches, such as choosing a word in the dictionary and brainstorming associations between the word and aspects of the problem. This approach worked for Current, Inc., a Colorado Springs greeting-card company. Focusing on the word "shrink" led artists and writers to develop Wee Greetings, a line of business-size cards that fit well in lunch boxes and shirt pockets. Using the word "enlarge," they envisioned Greeting Gifts, cards that come with balloons or confetti.[66]

Nominal group technique (NGT) A technique that integrates both individual work and group interaction within certain ground rules

NOMINAL GROUP TECHNIQUE The **nominal group technique (NGT)** is a means of enhancing creativity and decision making that integrates both individual work and group interaction within certain ground rules. The technique was developed to foster individual, as well as group, creativity and to overcome the tendency of group members to criticize ideas when they are offered. The ground rules, or steps, involved in NGT are as follows:

1 The individual members independently prepare lists of their ideas on a problem.
2 Each group member presents his or her ideas in a round-robin session (one idea at a time from each group member in turn) without discussion. The ideas are recorded on a blackboard or flip chart so that everyone can see them. If a presented idea triggers a new idea for someone else, that member adds the new idea to her or his list for presentation on a future round-robin turn.
3 When all the individual ideas are recorded on the group list, the members discuss the ideas for clarification and evaluation purposes.
4 The members silently and independently vote on the ideas, using a rank-ordering or rating procedure. The final outcome is determined by pooling the individual votes.[67]

Evidence generally supports the effectiveness of NGT in developing large numbers of creative alternatives while maintaining group satisfaction. In fact, a growing number of studies support the notion that nominal groups are more effective than brainstorming groups at generating ideas. In brainstorming groups, the problem seems to be that individuals must typically wait until someone stops talking before they can offer an idea. While waiting, they may either forget their ideas or keep rehearsing what they are going to say so that they do not forget (thereby using up time that could otherwise be spent on thinking of more ideas).[68]

Thus there are a number of means that managers can use to encourage creativity and innovation in work settings. While this chapter has focused on understanding various aspects of decision processes in organizations, the Supplement to this chapter highlights a variety of specific tools that can assist organization members in both planning and decision making.

CHAPTER SUMMARY

Decision making is the process through which managers identify organizational problems and attempt to resolve them. Managers deal with three types of problems: crisis, noncrisis, and opportunity. Opportunity problems are major vehicles for organizational innovation. Because opportunities involve ideas that could be used, rather than difficulties that must be resolved, they sometimes receive insufficient attention.

Generally, managerial decision situations fall into two categories: programmed and nonprogrammed. Because of their nature, nonprogrammed decisions usually involve significant amounts of uncertainty and risk.

man, *Judgment in Managerial Decision Making*, Wiley, New York, 1986.

12. Ronald N. Taylor, *Behavioral Decision Making*, Scott, Foresman, Glenview, Ill., 1984, pp. 121–122.

13. Katherine Weisman, "Safe Harbor," *Forbes*, Sept. 4, 1989, pp. 58–62.

14. Bernard M. Bass, *Organizational Decision Making*, Irwin, Homewood, Ill., 1983, pp. 27–28.

15. See, for example, Herbert A. Simon, "A Behavioral Model of Rational Choice," *Quarterly Journal of Economics*, vol. 69, 1955, pp. 99–118, and "Rational Choice and the Structure of the Environment," *Psychological Review*, vol. 63, 1956, pp. 129–138.

16. Max H. Bazerman, *Judgment in Managerial Decision Making*, Wiley, New York, 1986, p. 5.

17. George P. Huber, *Managerial Decision Making*, Scott, Foresman, Glenview, Ill., 1980.

18. Pranay Gupte, "Merge in Haste, Repent in Leisure," *Forbes*, Aug. 22, 1988, p. 85.

19. Charles E. Lindblom, *The Intelligence of Democracy*, Free Press, New York, 1965; Bernard M. Bass, *Organizational Decision Making*, Irwin, Homewood, Ill., 1983, pp. 34–35.

20. George P. Huber, *Managerial Decision Making*, Scott, Foresman, Glenview, Ill., 1980, p. 27.

21. Michael D. Cohen, James G. March, and Johan P. Olsen, "A Garbage Can Model of Organizational Choice," *Administrative Science Quarterly*, vol. 17, 1972, pp. 1–25; Anna Grandori, "A Prescriptive Contingency View of Organizational Decision Making," *Administrative Science Quarterly*, vol. 29, 1984, pp. 192–209.

22. Myron Magnet, "How Top Managers Make a Company's Toughest Decisions," *Fortune*, Mar. 18, 1985, pp. 52–57.

23. Steve Weiner, "Taking the Pledge," *Forbes*, June 29, 1987, pp. 41–42; Stephen Kindel, "The 10 Worst Managed Companies in America," *Financial World*, July 26, 1988, pp. 28–39; Michael Oneal, "Gould Is So Thin You Can Hardly See It," *Business Week*, Aug. 29, 1988, p. 74; "Japan Makes a Bid for the Merger Business," *The Economist*, Sept. 17, 1988, pp. 85–86.

24. Daniel D. Wheeler and Irving L. Janis, *A Practical Guide for Making Decisions*, Free Press, New York, 1980.

25. This section is based on David A. Cowan, "Developing a Process Model of Problem Recognition," *Academy of Management Review*, vol. 11, 1986, pp. 763–776.

26. The Swiss watchmaker example is based mainly on Margaret Studer, "SMH Leads a Revival of Swiss Watchmaker Industry," *The Wall Street Journal*, Jan. 20, 1992, p. B4; and Peter Fuhrman, "Jewelry for the Wrist," *Forbes*, Nov. 23, 1992, pp. 173–178.

27. Ronald N. Taylor, *Behavioral Decision Making*, Scott, Foresman, Glenview, Ill., 1984, pp. 36–59.

28. A. F. Osborn, *Applied Imagination*, Scribner, New York, 1963.

29. Norman R. F. Maier, *Problem-Solving Discussions and Conferences: Leadership Methods and Skills*, McGraw-Hill, New York, 1963.

30. Harvey Gittler, "Decisions Are Only as Good as Those Who Can Change Them," *The Wall Street Journal*, Oct. 7, 1985, p. 22.

31. Laura Sessions Stepp, "In Search of Ethics: Alcoa Pursues a Corporate Conscience through Emphasis on 'Core Values,'" *The Washington Post*, Mar. 31, 1991, pp. H1, H4, and "New Test of Values," *The Washington Post*, Aug. 4, 1991, pp. H1, H4.

32. Robert L. Desatnick, "Service: A CEO's Perspective," *Management Review*, October 1987, pp. 41–45.

33. Daniel D. Wheeler and Irving L. Janis, *A Practical Guide for Making Decisions*, Free Press, New York, 1980, pp. 17–36.

34. Giora Keinan, "Decision Making under Stress: Scanning of Alternatives under Controllable and Uncontrollable Threats," *Journal of Personality and Social Psychology*, vol. 52, 1987, pp. 639–644.

35. Paul C. Nutt, "Types of Organizational Decision Processes," *Administrative Science Quarterly*, vol. 29, 1984, pp. 414–450.

36. This section, including the problems, is based on Kevin McKean, "Decisions," *Discover*, June 1985, pp. 22–31.

37. For recent research on prospect theory and the framing effect, see David V. Budescu and Wendy Weiss, "Reflection of Transitive and Intransitive Preferences: A Test of Prospect Theory," *Organizational Behavior and Human Decision Processes*, vol. 39, 1987, pp. 184–202; N. S. Fagley and Paul M. Miller, "The Effects of Decision Framing on Choice of Risky vs. Certain Options," *Organizational Behavior and Human Decision Processes*, vol. 39, 1987, pp. 264–277; Margaret A. Neale, Vandra L. Huber, and Gregory B. Northcraft, "The Framing of Negotiations: Contextual versus Task Frames," *Organizational Behavior and Human Decision Processes*, vol. 39, 1987, pp. 228–241; Howard Rachlin, *Judgment, Decisions, and Choice*, Freeman, New York, 1989; and Marc Jegers, "Prospect Theory and the Risk-Return Relation: Some Belgian Evidence," *Academy of Management Journal*, vol. 34, 1991, pp. 215–225.

38. S. Lichtenstein, P. Slovic, B. Fischhoff, M. Layman, and B. Combs, "Judged Frequency of Lethal Events," *Journal of Experimental Psychology: Human Learning and Memory*, vol. 4, 1978, pp. 551–578.

39. Adapted from Max H. Bazerman, *Judgment in Managerial Decision Making*, Wiley, New York, 1986, p. 28.

40. Ronald N. Taylor, *Behavioral Decision Making*, Scott, Foresman, Glenview, Ill., 1984, p. 141.

41. Max H. Bazerman, *Judgment in Managerial Decision Making*, Wiley, New York, 1986, p. 36.

42. John Merwin, "A Billion in Blunders," *Forbes*, Dec. 1, 1986, p. 111.

43. A. Koriat, S. Lichtenstein, and B. Fischoff, "Reasons for Confidence," *Journal of Experimental Psychology: Human Learning and Memory*, vol. 6, 1980, pp. 107–118.

44. This example and section rely heavily on work by Max H. Bazerman, *Judgment in Managerial Decision Making*, Wiley, New York, 1986, pp. 67–69.

45. Barry M. Staw and Jerry Ross, "Behavior in Escalation Situations: Antecedents, Prototypes, and Solutions," in L. L. Cummings and Barry M. Staw (eds.), *Research in Organizational Behavior*, vol. 9, JAI, Greenwich, Conn., 1987, pp. 39–78.

46. Max H. Bazerman, *Judgment in Managerial Decision Making*, Wiley, New York, 1986, p. 69.

47. J. Z. Rubin, "Experimental Research on Third Party Intervention in Conflict: Toward Some Generalizations," *Psychological Bulletin*, vol. 87, 1980, pp. 379–391; Joel Brockner, "The Escalation of Commitment to a Failing Course of Action: Toward Theoretical Progress," *Academy of Management Review*, vol. 17, 1992, pp. 39–61.

48. Adapted from Barry M. Staw and Jerry Ross, "Behavior in Escalation Situations: Antecedents, Prototypes, and Solutions," in L. L. Cummings and Barry M. Staw (eds.), *Research in Organizational Behavior*, vol. 9, JAI, Greenwich, Conn., 1987, pp. 67–68; see also Barry M. Staw and Jerry Ross, "Good Money after Bad," *Psychology Today*, February 1988, pp. 30–33. For an extended treatment, see Jerry Ross and Barry M. Staw, "Expo 86: An Escalation Prototype," *Administrative Science Quarterly*, vol. 31, 1986, pp. 274–297.

49. Elizabeth M. Fowler, "Management Participation by Workers," *The New York Times*, Dec. 27, 1988, p. D6.

50. This section is based largely on George P. Huber, *Managerial Decision Making*, Scott, Foresman, Glenview, Ill., 1980; and Norman R. F. Maier, "Assets and Liabilities in Group Problem Solving: The Need for an Integrative Function," in Michael T. Matteson and John M. Ivancevich (eds.), *Management and Organizational Behavior Classics*, 4th ed., BPI/Irwin, Homewood, Ill., 1989.

51. Larry K. Michaelsen, Warren E. Watson, and Robert H. Black, "A Realistic Test of Individual versus Group Consensus Decision Making," *Journal of Applied Psychology*, vol. 74, 1989, pp. 834–839.

52. Irving L. Janis, *Groupthink*, 2d ed., Houghton Mifflin, Boston, 1982.

53. Arie W. Kruglanski, "Freezethink and the Challenger," *Psychology Today*, August 1986, pp. 48–49.

54. Carrie R. Leana, "A Partial Test of Janis' Groupthink Model: Effects of Group Cohesiveness and Leader Behavior on Defective Decision Making," *Journal of Management*, vol. 11, 1985, pp. 5–17. For alternative explanations of groupthink, see Glen Whyte, "Groupthink Reconsidered," *Academy of Management Review*, vol. 14, 1989, pp. 40–56.

55. Daniel D. Wheeler and Irving L. Janis, *A Practical Guide for Making Decisions*, Free Press, New York, 1980.

56. Charles R. Schwenk and Richard A. Cosier, "Effect of the Expert, Devil's Advocate, and Dialectic Inquiry Methods on Prediction Performance," *Organizational Behavior and Human Performance*, vol. 26, 1980, pp. 409–424; David M. Schweiger and Phyllis A. Finger, "The Comparative Effectiveness of Dialectical Inquiry and Devil's Advocate: The Impact of Task Biases on Previous Research Findings," *Strategic Management Journal*, vol. 5, 1984, pp. 335–350; David M. Schweiger, William R. Sandberg, and Paul L. Rechner, "Experiential Effects of Dialectic Inquiry, Devil's Advocacy, and Consensus Approaches to Strategic Decision Making," *Academy of Management Journal*, vol. 32, 1989, pp. 745–772.

57. Max H. Bazerman, *Judgment in Managerial Decision Making*, Wiley, New York, 1986, p. 81.

58. Teresa M. Amabile, *The Social Psychology of Creativity*, Springer-Verlag, New York, 1983, p. 31.

59. Quoted in Alfie Kohn, "Art for Art's Sake," *Psychology Today*, September 1987, p. 54.

60. Gene Bylinsky, "Trying to Transcend Copycat Science," *Fortune*, Mar. 30, 1987, pp. 42–46.

61. This analogy is based on Edward de Bono, *New Think*, Basic Books, New York, 1968; see also Edward de Bono, *Lateral Thinking for Management*, American Management Association, New York, 1971.

62. Teresa M. Amabile, *The Social Psychology of Creativity*, Springer-Verlag, New York, 1983, pp. 67–77.

63. Reprinted from Diane E. Papalia and Sally Wendkos Olds, *Psychology*, 2d ed., McGraw-Hill, New York, 1988, p. 293.

64. J. W. Haefele, *Creativity and Innovation*, Reinhold, New York, 1962; Max H. Bazerman, *Judgment in Managerial Decision Making*, Wiley, New York, 1986, pp. 89–91.

65. Based on "Problems! We've Got to Have Problems!" in P. Ranganath Nayak and John M. Ketteringham, *Breakthroughs*, Rawson Associates, New York, 1986, pp. 151–178.

66. Emily T. Smith, "Are You Creative?" *Business Week*, Sept. 30, 1985, pp. 80–84.

67. Andre L. Delbecq, Andrew H. Van de Ven, and D. H. Gustafson, *Group Techniques for Program Planning*, Scott, Foresman, Glenview, Ill., 1975, pp. 66–69; see also George P. Huber, *Managerial Decision Making*, Scott, Foresman, Glenview, Ill., 1980, pp. 200–205.

68. See W. R. Street, "Brainstorming by Individuals, Coacting and Interacting Groups," *Journal of Applied Psychology*, vol. 59, 1974, pp. 433–436; A. H. Van de Ven and A. L. Delbecq, "The Effectiveness of Nominal, Delphi, and Interacting Group Processes," *Academy of Management Journal*, vol. 17, 1974, pp. 605–621; T. B. Green, "An Empirical Analysis of Nominal and Interacting Groups," *Academy of Management Journal*, vol. 18, 1975, pp. 63–73; and Michael Diehl and Wolfgang Stroebe, "Productivity Loss in Idea-Generating Groups: Tracking Down the Blocking Effect," *Journal of Personality and Social Psychology*, vol. 61, 1991, pp. 392–403.

69. Adapted from Laurie Hays, "Book Maps *USA Today*'s Costly Road," *The Wall Street Journal*, July 14, 1987, p. 6.

ACKNOWLEDGMENTS

Table

Table 3: Reprinted with the permission of The Free Press, a division of Macmillan, Inc., from *A Practical Guide for Making Decisions* by Daniel D. Wheeler and Irving L. Janis. Copyright © 1980 by The Free Press.

Figures

Figure 1: George P. Huber, *Managerial Decision Making*, Scott, Foresman, 1980, p. 8. Reprinted by permission of George Huber.

Figure 3: E. Frank Harrison, *The Managerial Decision-Making Process*, 3d ed. Copyright © 1987 by Houghton Mifflin Company. Used with permission.

Figure 5: *Conceptual Blockbusting*, figures pp. 25–30. Copyright © 1990 by James L. Adams. Reprinted by permission of Addison-Wesley Publishing Company, Inc.

CONCLUDING CASE

PROFITS FINALLY COME TO *USA TODAY**

Allen H. Neuharth, Gannett Company's chairman, threw a little champagne party in June 1987 at company headquarters in Arlington, Virginia, to celebrate the first profitable month for Gannett's national newspaper, *USA Today*. Buoyed by advertising and circulation gains, Neuharth savored the triumph. He told his staff to expect a long and successful future for the venture they had launched in the fall of 1982.

But as glasses clicked and trays of oysters and pâté made the rounds, many people in the room knew that *USA Today*'s success had come at a high price. The project, which had become Neuharth's obsession, had made and broken careers at Gannett. Meanwhile, 5 years of heavy operating losses had severely pinched the media chain's 90 other newspapers and disheartened their staffs.

The publication of *The Making of McPaper* stirred up fresh discord. A Neuharth-authorized book, it described the obstacles and sacrifices involved in creating and expanding *USA Today*. Reactions within the Gannett organization were strong, renewing the clash between Neuharth's backers and the financial and production executives who had early doubts.

The book airs plenty of dirty linen. It describes the bitter infighting at Gannett and reveals tales of those who suffered breakdowns in the anxious, early

* Laurie Hays, "Book Maps *USA Today's* Costly Road," *The Wall Street Journal*, July 14, 1987, p. 6. Copyright © 1987 Dow Jones & Company, Inc. Reprinted by permission of *The Wall Street Journal*. All rights reserved worldwide.

days of *USA Today*'s publication. Even the book's title causes resentment among staffers, dredging up the derogatory nickname assigned to the paper by critics who viewed it as "fast-food" journalism.

Some Gannett executives believe that the book unfairly casts as villains people who Neuharth apparently felt had plotted to thwart his project. Douglas H. McCorkindale, the company's chief financial officer, for instance, is described by Neuharth as one of the "enemies within" who "planned for failure" instead of success. According to Peter Prichard, the book's author, questions McCorkindale raised about the project cost him the chief executive's job, now held by John J. Curley.

Though a supporter now, McCorkindale says he did oppose the way the *USA Today* project was carried out. Neuharth and Curley abandoned Gannett's usually careful procedures for planning major capital expenditures, such as new printing plants, McCorkindale says. In addition, the management and staff of *USA Today* in Arlington were allowed to spend large sums of money, while Gannett's other daily newspapers were forced to pinch pennies.

"There's a lackadaisical attitude toward a lot of things now because of what many in the company saw as the inordinate waste involved in the project," states McCorkindale in the book. "They say, 'Why should we kill ourselves in Gitchagumee, Idaho (to make money), when they'll just waste it over there (at *USA Today*) anyway.'"

"*USA Today* should have been playing by the same rules" as Gannett's other papers,

McCorkindale says. "The planning wasn't complete. It was full of holes. They didn't want questions raised because it would raise more questions, and people don't like that."

Indeed, *USA Today*'s financial cost to Gannett exceeded even McCorkindale's forecasts. Excluding capital expenditures and the costs of employees that *USA Today* borrowed from other newspapers, the publication amassed operating losses of more than $230 million in the 5 years after its launch.

The *USA Today* staff has itself experienced heavy turnover. Both those who left and those who are still with Gannett cite the organization's disarray, the new rules that were made up daily, and the intense pressure that resulted from Neuharth's direct involvement in the project. Neuharth made it clear that the venture would be a test of everyone's character and that everyone's future with Gannett was on the line, according to Prichard, who has become editor of the newspaper.[69]

Since becoming marginally profitable, the paper has slipped back into the red ink, amassing losses by 1992 estimated to be about $800 million. Even though circulation continues to grow and is now in the 1.8 million range, *USA Today* has continued to experience serious difficulties in attracting enough advertising to make consistent profits.[†]

† Paul Farhi, "*USA Today:* Looking Ahead to Tomorrow," *The Washington Post,* Aug. 29, 1988, Washington Business section, pp. 1, 22; Joshua Hammer, "The McPaper Route," *Newsweek*, Apr. 27, 1992, p. 58.

QUESTIONS FOR
CONCLUDING CASE

1 Which model of decision
   making best matches the
   situation involving the birth of
   USA Today?

2 Evaluate the extent to which
   Gannett top executives used an
   effective decision-making
   approach in deciding to launch
   USA Today and in dealing with
   subsequent problems. What was
   the impact?

3 Evaluate the extent to which
   the *USA Today* situation
   represented an escalation
   situation (between the time the
   paper was launched and the
   time it began to make money).

CONCLUDING CASE

ROYAL DUTCH/SHELL VIGOROUSLY PURSUES OPPORTUNITIES

Risks are enormous in the petroleum business. The price of raw materials can swing from $4 to $40 per unit, dictators can affect the business climate at will, and human error resulting in an oil spill can cost $3 billion or more. Royal Dutch/Shell, an Anglo-Dutch multinational corporation, has earned an admirable reputation for handling the risks. Despite soft prices in the oil industry, mounting costs for development of new oil fields, and greater environmental requirements, Royal Dutch/Shell has adopted a growth strategy.

In contrast, at troubled British Petroleum a former chief executive, believing that energy prices would rise, invested heavily in the development of new sources. When prices remained low, the company ran into financial trouble. Given the uncertainties, competitor Exxon has cut back on spending and is using its extra cash to buy back stock rather than seek growth.

At Royal Dutch/Shell, pursuing growth amid uncertainty has led to significant rewards. In 1990, the company passed Exxon to become the world's largest oil company. The company has annual revenues exceeding $100 billion and is able to handle most of its capital spending through cash flow.

Royal Dutch/Shell has developed several approaches to help handle the uncertainties of the industry. Within a culture that encourages individual initiative, the approximately 260 operating units generally make their own decisions, with the help of service units that offer research and technical support. The relative autonomy allows managers of operating units, such as Shell Oil Company, a U.S. subsidiary, to consider local conditions, monitor regulatory requirements, and shift quickly to handle customer needs or crises.

The strategic directions for Royal Dutch/Shell are determined by the committee of managing directors. The six members are chosen from the top ranks of Royal Dutch Petroleum and Shell Transport & Trading, the Dutch and British holding companies that own Royal Dutch/Shell.

The committee operates on the basis of consensus; key strategic and personnel decisions must be unanimous; and the focus is long-term. Shell uses three major mechanisms to deal with uncertainty: geographic diversification, concentric product diversification, and speedy adaptation to change. For example, Shell explores for oil and gas in about 50 countries, has refineries in 34, and sells its products in 100. As a result, political or economic upheaval in a particular country cannot severely damage the company. Shell expects particularly high returns in high-risk countries; otherwise, it does not do business there. In the area of product diversification, Shell stays close to the energy and chemical businesses that it knows best. It balances emphasis on upstream processes, such as exploration and production, with that on downstream processes, such as refining and marketing.

Speed is also a key factor. When Spain discontinued the state monopoly over service stations, Shell quickly began developing a network of stations there. Similarly, with the opening of eastern Europe, Shell invested in Interag, the state-owned company that had been distributing its products in Hungary.

Shell's managing directors try to identify changes in the industry by studying and debating scenarios prepared by their planning department. The scenarios attempt to depict reasonable, but alternative, pictures of conditions

in the world 10 years in the future. Each of the geographic regions and operating companies then uses the scenarios to formulate its own strategies within the overall strategic plan.

The two current scenarios are labeled "Sustainable World" and "Global Mercantilism." The first assumes that major international economic disputes are resolved: the United States and Japan avoid a trade war, Europe's economic unity is successful, free trade expands, and so on. In this scenario, Shell expects that more attention will be given to environmental issues and that greater emphasis will be placed on restricting emissions and developing energy alternatives to oil and natural gas. The second scenario sketches a world of trade wars, recessions, and destabilization: efforts to create trade blocs are not successful, and there is little consensus on environmental issues. With this scenario, regulations will be fewer and more varied, and oil consumption will increase. While the reality will likely fall somewhere in between, Shell is attempting to position itself to handle a variety of circumstances. The emphasis is on stretching conventional thinking and considering a wide variety of possibilities.

Supplementing the scenario process, war gaming helps Shell handle the unexpected. For example, local operating companies are expected to simulate supply disruptions and prepare alternatives. As a result, when the Gulf war disrupted supplies from the Middle East, Shell was able to quickly redirect alternative supplies.*

* Based mainly on Christopher Knowlton, "Shell Gets Rich by Beating Risk," *Fortune,* Aug. 26, 1991, pp. 79–82; also on James R. Norman, "The Opportunities Are Enormous," *Forbes,* Nov. 9, 1992, pp. 92–94.

QUESTIONS FOR
CONCLUDING CASE

1 To what extent does Shell
appear to emphasize the
handling of crisis, noncrisis,
and opportunity problems?

2 What evidence exists that Shell
uses an effective decision-
making process in making
various decisions?

3 How do Shell's managing
directors try to avoid group
think? What role does divergent
thinking play in the process?

SUPPLEMENT

PLANNING AND DECISION AIDS

During the early 1980s, United Airlines embarked on a significant expansion of flight schedules. The expansion was part of its response to increased rivalry among major competitors, including American, Delta, and Northwest. During a single month, for example, United added 67 departures to its operations at Chicago's O'Hare Airport. It soon became the first airline with service to cities in all 50 states. While the expansion brought the desired increase in passenger volume, it also began to strain the work-force scheduling and planning systems. Because of airline-ticket price pressures and heavy discounting by competitors, it was imperative that United control its labor costs and, at the same time, maintain desired customer service levels. As a result, the schedules and plans that the managers prepared by hand were no longer adequate.

To meet the challenge of providing good reservation and airport service while controlling costs, the airline turned to management science. *Management science* (also often called *operations research*) is a management perspective aimed at increasing decision effectiveness through the use of sophisticated mathematical models and statistical methods. Management science offers a variety of quantitative techniques that can greatly help managers in planning for and making decisions about complex situations such as those facing United. By combining management science techniques and computers, United was able to develop a very successful scheduling and work planning system called the Station Manpower Planning System (SMPS). The SMPS, which continues to be changed to meet expanding needs, has helped United realize significant labor cost savings, improve customer service, and increase employee satisfaction.

The success of the SMPS at United is the result of a growing number of aids available to help managers gain the competitive edge through innovations in the areas of planning and decision making. Many, but not all, of these aids rely heavily on quantitative techniques associated with the field of management science.

Generally, managers do not require in-depth knowledge of mathematics and computers to utilize management science tools. Rather, they need to have a basic knowledge of the major tools available so that they can visualize possible applications of such tools. Under some circumstances, managers will need to obtain advice and help from management science experts. However, with the growing availability of packaged software that can be adapted to a variety of work settings, several of the techniques in this supplement are more accessible and much less costly than they were in the past. As a result, the importance of these planning and decision-making aids is likely to increase in the future.

In this supplement, we describe a number of the major aids to planning and decision making. In so doing, we consider several forecasting methods, including one that is useful for promoting innovation. We also examine tools that are widely used for planning and controlling projects and explore a variety of useful quantitative planning techniques. Finally, we investigate several quantitative aids for decision making.

FORECASTING

Forecasting The process of making predictions about changing conditions and future events that may significantly affect the business of an organization

Forecasting is the process of making predictions about changing conditions and future events that may significantly affect the business of an organization.[1] The forecasting process is important to both planning and decision making because each depends heavily on assessments of future conditions. Forecasting is used in a variety of areas, such as production planning, budgeting, strategic planning, sales analysis, inventory control, marketing planning, logistics planning, purchasing, material requirements planning, and product planning.[2] Forecasting methods fall into three major categories: quantitative; technological, or qualitative; and judgmental.[3]

Quantitative Forecasting

Quantitative forecasting A type of forecasting that relies on numerical data and mathematical models to predict future conditions

Quantitative forecasting relies on numerical data and mathematical models to predict future conditions. The two main types of quantitative forecasting methods are time-series and explanatory methods.

Time-series methods Methods that use historical data to develop forecasts of the future

TIME-SERIES METHODS Time-series methods use historical data to develop forecasts of the future. The assumption underlying time-series models is that there are patterns or combinations of patterns that repeat over time. Time-series models use extensive amounts of historical data, such as weekly sales figures, to identify such patterns, and then they base future projections on those patterns.

Examples of the types of patterns that may be identified by time-series methods are shown in Figure S-1. A *trend* reflects a long-range general movement in either an upward or a downward direction. For example, after identifying a general decline in coffee consumption, Hillside Coffee, Inc., of Carmel, California, began to try out coffees with chocolate and nut flavorings. The experiments with the new, flavored coffees began after the company learned that many of its restaurant customers were adding sweet liquors to coffee to make appealing hot

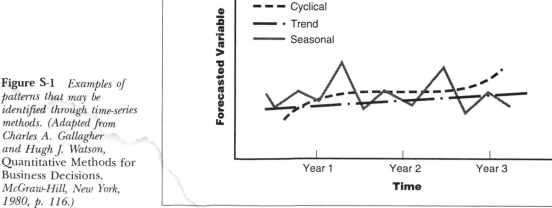

Figure S-1 *Examples of patterns that may be identified through time-series methods. (Adapted from Charles A. Gallagher and Hugh J. Watson,* Quantitative Methods for Business Decisions, *McGraw-Hill, New York, 1980, p. 116.)*

drinks. The company wanted to create similar types of flavors without alcohol for use in the home. Free samples and recommendations from customers have helped the company gain a strong group of consumers, particularly teenagers and individuals in their early twenties. A *seasonal* pattern indicates upward or downward changes that coincide with particular points in a given year, such as particular seasons of the year. The Toro Company sells both lawn mowers and snow throwers as a means of handling seasonal differences in customer demand patterns (see Figure S-2). A *cyclical* pattern involves changes at particular points in time that span longer than a year. For example, sunspot intensity varies over an 11-year cycle and has an effect on the agriculture industry.[4]

Because time-series methods rely strictly on historical data, they are not very useful in predicting the impact of present or future actions that managers might take to bring about change. Instead, they are more suited to predicting broad environmental factors, such as general economic prospects, employment levels, general sales levels, or cost trends, that may be heavily influenced by past events. There are a variety of methods for analyzing time series, many of them quite sophisticated and requiring the use of computers. Although time-series methods attempt to predict the future by identifying patterns, they do not concern themselves with the causes of such patterns.

While time-series approaches can be useful, there are dangers in relying too heavily on past trends. Miller Brewing learned about such dangers the hard way. On the basis of a decade in which the company grew at a hefty 640 percent, while the beer industry as a whole grew at only about 40 percent, Miller decided to build a huge new brewery in Trenton, Ohio. In 1982, just as the brewery was completed, American sales of beer leveled off for the first time in 25 years. At the same time, Miller's archrival, Anheuser-Busch, began an expensive, but highly successful, expansion and marketing campaign. Within 5 years, sales of Miller High Life, once the number-two beer in America, declined by 50 percent. The new Trenton brewery, which never opened, led to a $280 million write-off for Miller.[5]

Figure S-2 *Toro consumer division's retail sales percentages for two major product lines. (Courtesy of The Toro Company.)*

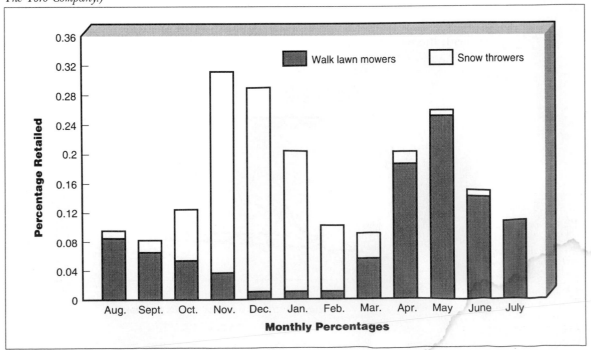

Explanatory, or causal, models Models that attempt to identify the major variables that are related to or have caused particular past conditions and then use current measures of those variables (predictors) to predict future conditions

Regression models
Equations that express the fluctuations in the variable being forecasted in terms of fluctuations in one or more other variables (predictors)

EXPLANATORY, OR CAUSAL, MODELS **Explanatory**, or **causal**, **models** attempt to identify the major variables that are related to or have caused particular past conditions and then use current measures of those variables (predictors) to predict future conditions. Developing such models often leads to a better understanding of the situations being forecasted than time-series models offer. Explanatory models also allow managers to assess the probable impact of changes in the predictors. For example, a manager may be able to estimate how future sales will be affected by changes such as adding more sales personnel or expanding shelf space. Thus explanatory models are generally more amenable than time-series models to assessing the probable impact of managerial actions relative to the variables.

Three major categories of explanatory models are regression models, econometric models, and leading indicators. **Regression models** are equations that express the fluctuations in the variable being forecasted in terms of fluctuations in one or more other variables. An example of simple regression, in which one variable (a predictor) is used to predict the future level of another (forecasted) variable, is shown in Figure S-3.[6] Here, a company that sells burglar alarm systems for homes is attempting to predict the demand for alarm systems (forecasted variable) on the basis of the number of information leaflets (predictor variable) requested by the public. The leaflets are offered in an advertisement run in newspapers in a major metropolitan area. The various data points plotted in Figure S-3 represent leaflets requested and sales within 1 month of the leaflet request. In a simple regression, the relationship between the predictor and the forecasted variables is stated in mathematical form. The form is $y = a + bx$, where y is the forecasted variable, x is the predictor variable, a is a constant representing the point where the regression line crosses the vertical axis, and b indicates how much the value of y changes when the value of x changes 1 unit. A statistical technique is used to develop the straight line that best fits the data points and to provide the values for a and b. Then future projections can be made by substituting different values for x in the equation and determining the impact on y. For example, if our equation came out to be $y = 1.5 + .085x$, then substituting 350 leaflets for x would predict sales of 27 alarm systems.

More complex multiple regression models incorporating multiple predictor variables are also used for forecasting. Relying on such a model, Elaine Garzarelli, executive vice president for research at Shearson Lehman Brothers, was

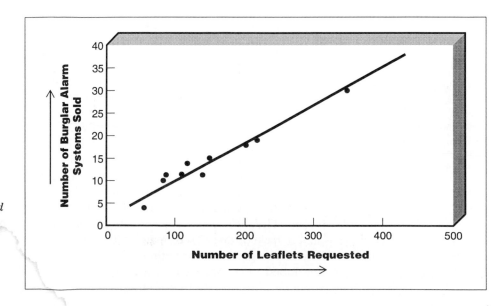

Figure S-3 *Data points and regression line for number of leaflets requested and number of burglar alarm systems sold. (Adapted from Charles A. Gallagher and Hugh J. Watson,* Quantitative Methods for Business Decisions, *McGraw-Hill, New York, 1980, p. 134.)*

one of the rare Wall Street figures who predicted "black Monday." In forecasting the market crash that occurred on October 19, 1987, she used quantitative analysis of thirteen pieces of data, three relating to economic cycles, several pertaining to monetary issues, and three concerning market valuation. Garzarelli continues to use the thirteen indicators in her efforts to build a successful forecasting track record on Wall Street.[7]

Econometric models
Systems of simultaneous multiple regression equations involving several predictor variables that are used to identify and measure relationships or interrelationships that exist in the economy

The second major category of explanatory models is **econometric models.** The term "econometric model" most often refers to systems of simultaneous multiple regression equations involving several predictor variables that are used to identify and measure relationships or interrelationships that exist in the economy. Such models attempt to predict the likely future directions of the economy and, often, the impact of changes such as proposed tax legislation on various segments of the economy. The development of econometric models is complex and expensive. As a result, these models are beyond the scope of most managerial jobs and all but very large organizations. However, companies can subscribe to a number of econometric forecasting services, such as the Wharton School, Chase Econometric Associates, and Mapcast (GE). By doing so, a company obtains many of the benefits of econometric forecasting at a cost that is substantially less than the cost of developing its own econometric model.

Leading indicators
Variables that tend to be correlated with the phenomenon of major interest but also tend to occur in advance of that phenomenon

The third major category of explanatory models is **leading indicators,** variables that tend to be correlated with the phenomenon of major interest but also tend to occur in advance of that phenomenon. In general, the use of leading indicators is a fairly simple method of forecasting, although the methods of analysis involved can be quite sophisticated. For example, the growth of the gross national product (GNP) works very well as a leading indicator for Pitney Bowes's Data Documents, Inc., division. For a number of years, sales of the division's business forms have generally trailed changes in GNP growth by about 6 months. However, locating appropriate leading indicators is not always a simple task. To predict outboard-motor sales, the Brunswick Corporation's Mercury Marine division uses the monthly consumer confidence index published by the Conference Board, a research group. Unfortunately, so far Brunswick has not been able to find a good leading indicator for sales of the inboard-outboard units that are typically found in middle-of-the-market boats.[8] Thus it can be difficult to identify a useful leading indicator that provides reasonably accurate predictions.

Technological, or qualitative, forecasting A type of forecasting aimed primarily at predicting long-term trends in technology and other important aspects of the environment

Promoting Innovation: Technological, or Qualitative, Forecasting

Technological, or **qualitative, forecasting** is aimed primarily at predicting long-term trends in technology and other important aspects of the environment. Particular emphasis is placed on technology, since the ability of organizations to innovate and remain competitive is often related to being able to take advantage of opportunities evolving from technological change. Technological, or qualitative, forecasting differs from quantitative approaches in that it focuses more heavily on longer-term issues that are less amenable to numerical analysis. Therefore, rather than relying on quantitative methods, technological forecasting depends on such qualitative factors as expert knowledge, creativity, and judgment. This type of forecasting provides an excellent opportunity to generate innovative thinking among participants because the emphasis is on future possibilities. The difficulties of accurately predicting the future are obvious, and predictors have often missed major shifts, such as the magnitude and speed of the increase in global competition. Although a number of approaches have been developed to facilitate technological, or qualitative, forecasting, two of the most prominent are the Delphi method and the La Prospective approach.

Delphi method A structured approach to gaining the judgments of a number of experts on a specific issue relating to the future

THE DELPHI METHOD The **Delphi method** is a structured approach to gaining the judgments of a number of experts on a specific issue relating to the future. One unique aspect of the Delphi method is that the experts are not brought together to discuss their views. On the contrary, they are intentionally kept apart so that each one's initial judgments will not be influenced by those of other participants in the process.[9] The Delphi method has been used in a variety of organizations, including TRW, IBM, AT&T, Corning Glass Works, Goodyear, and ICL in Britain. Although experts participating in the Delphi method can come from inside or outside the organization, many organizations prefer to use internal experts in order to retain better control over the results.[10] The Delphi method can be used to seek creative solutions to problems; however, its most frequent function is forecasting, particularly predicting technological change.

There are three basic steps in the Delphi method:

1 A panel of experts is asked to anonymously identify likely scientific breakthroughs in a given area within a specific long-term period (e.g., over the next 50 years). The experts are also asked to estimate when, within the specified period, they expect the breakthroughs to occur. On the basis of the information received, a list of potential breakthroughs is compiled, including information regarding the estimated time frame within which each is likely to occur.

2 The list is sent back to the experts, who are asked to estimate (often on the basis of a 50-50 probability) whether each breakthrough is likely to occur earlier or later than the average estimated time frame. They may also be permitted to specify that they do not believe the breakthrough will occur during the time period (e.g., the 50 years) under consideration.

3 The experts are provided with a new list that represents the information gathered in step 2. If there is consensus, those who disagree with the majority are asked to explain why they do. If there are major differences among the experts, the participants may be asked to furnish reasons for their views. Experts can, and often do, alter their estimates at this point. If there continues to be a wide divergence of opinion, step 3 may be repeated and may include a reassessment of the explanations previously given.

Although these steps outline the basic approach used in the Delphi method, organizations frequently make minor alterations to suit their particular needs. The Delphi method was used by the Alaska Department of Commerce and Economic Development to assess Alaska's energy, economy, and resource development future.[11] It was also used in technological forecasting for power generation by Bharat Heavy Electricals, Ltd. (BHEL), a billion-dollar company in India (see the following Case in Point discussion).[12]

CASE IN POINT   THE DELPHI METHOD AT BHEL

Bharat Heavy Electricals, Ltd., the largest heavy-electrical-equipment company in India, has used the Delphi process to explore the future direction of power development, especially in the areas of electric energy and electric transportation. The company's products form systems for the generation of electric power through thermal, nuclear, and hydro sources, as well as for the transmission of power to the industrial and transportation sectors. The Delphi process involved 286 company members from a variety of engineering disciplines.

In the first step, or round, an open-ended questionnaire was sent to prospective respondents. The purpose of this round was to gather as many ideas as possible regarding major technological breakthroughs that could conceivably be developed within the next 30 to 40 years. Participants also estimated when they expected the technological breakthroughs to occur.

In the second round, the list of technological breakthroughs and the estimated timings of the breakthroughs were fed back to the participants. The participants were then asked to reconsider their earlier timing estimates and give fresh ones, provide reasons if their estimates were outside the general range of timings projected in the first round, and supply a priority ranking for each technological development in terms of the urgency of each requirement. The replies from the second round led to an emerging trend toward consensus on most issues.

In the third round, participants were given the collated comments and the new information about estimated timings that had been collected in round 2. In this round, participants were asked for their final estimates as well as their rationale for their forecasts.

Not only did the process identify the likely development of 19 different forms of energy sources, but it also provided "refined guesstimates" regarding when such new energy sources would appear. Bharat felt that these and other estimates would be useful in corporate planning. In addition, the results were extremely useful in formulating R&D projects related to corporate plans.[13]

■ ■ ■

LA PROSPECTIVE Developed in France and used widely in Europe, the La Prospective view (sometimes also called the *futuristics* or *futuribles* view) argues that there are many different possible futures depending on such factors as confrontations among actors, the continuation of current trends, regulatory and other constraints, and the relative power of the actors involved. As a result, organizations need to consider a number of futures and attempt to make decisions and take actions that do not greatly inhibit further freedom of choice. Otherwise, taking inflexible and irreversible actions may lead to severe difficulties if forecasts turn out to be grossly off the mark. The **La Prospective** approach addresses a variety of possible futures by evaluating major environmental variables, assessing the likely strategies of other significant actors (e.g., other organizations), devising possible counterstrategies, developing ranked hypotheses about the variables, and formulating alternative scenarios. Scenarios are outlines of possible future conditions, including paths the organization could take that would likely lead to these conditions.[14]

Judgmental Forecasting

Judgmental forecasting relies mainly on individual judgments or committee agreements regarding future conditions. Although judgmental forecasting is the most widely used forecasting method in industry, this approach typically relies on informal opinion gathering and is the least systematic of the forecasting methods. As a result, judgmental forecasting methods are highly susceptible to common decision-making biases.[15] Two major means of judgmental forecasting are the jury of executive opinion and sales-force composites.

THE JURY OF EXECUTIVE OPINION The **jury of executive opinion** is a means of forecasting in which organization executives hold a meeting and estimate, as a group, a forecast for a particular item. However, since the estimators are in direct contact with one another, the outcome may be heavily weighted by

---

La Prospective An approach that addresses a variety of possible futures by evaluating major environmental variables, assessing the likely strategies of other significant actors, devising possible counterstrategies, developing ranked hypotheses about the variables, and formulating alternative scenarios that do not greatly inhibit freedom of choice

Judgmental forecasting A type of forecasting that relies mainly on individual judgments or committee agreements regarding future conditions

Jury of executive opinion A means of forecasting in which organization executives hold a meeting and estimate, as a group, a forecast for a particular item

if preparing the site was shortened by 3 weeks. Then the path 10-20-40-50-70-80 would become the critical path (46.83 weeks). On the noncritical paths, there is some latitude about when various activities can be started without endangering the completion date of the entire project. This latitude is commonly referred to as **slack**.

Once the critical path is developed, it is important to periodically record the actual time it takes to complete the various activities and then to review the implications. For example, when activities on the critical path take longer than estimated, action must be taken to rectify the situation. Otherwise, the entire project will be delayed. Similarly, if an activity on a noncritical path takes substantially longer than expected, the critical path could change. Thus PERT helps managers not only plan but also control projects. The ability of individual managers to use PERT to plan and control both small and large projects has vastly increased with the widespread availability of software packages that are relatively easy to use.[20]

Slack Latitude about when various activities on the noncritical paths can be started without endangering the completion date of the entire project

OTHER PLANNING TECHNIQUES

A number of other quantitatively oriented planning techniques exist that can greatly assist managers. Some of the most prominent include the use of linear programming; queuing, or waiting-line, models; routing, or distribution, models; and simulation models. We discuss each of these techniques very briefly. Typically, the development of effective applications of these techniques requires the help of a management science expert.

Linear Programming

Linear programming (LP) A quantitative tool for planning how to allocate limited or scarce resources so that a single criterion or goal (often profits) is optimized

Linear programming (LP) is a quantitative tool for planning how to allocate limited or scarce resources so that a single criterion or goal (often profits) is optimized. It is the most widely used quantitative planning tool in business. Linear programming is most likely to be applicable when a single objective (such as maximizing profits) must be achieved, constraints exist that must be satisfied, and variables are linearly related to the objective.[21] A variable is linearly related to an objective when an increase (or decrease) in the variable leads to a proportional increase (or decrease) in the objective. For example, a linear relationship would apply if one chair (variable) produced can be sold for $30 profit (objective), four chairs for $120 profit, and six chairs for $180 profit. The technique has been applied to a variety of situations, including minimizing the cost of "hen scratch" (a combination of cereal grains) while maintaining a proper nutritional balance, finding the most profitable product mix in a manufacturing operation, and maximizing capacity usage at modern oil refineries.[22]

Queuing, or Waiting-Line, Models

Queuing, or waiting-line, models Mathematical models that describe the operating characteristics of queuing situations, in which service is provided to persons or units waiting in line

Managers are frequently responsible for providing services under conditions that may require the persons or units needing service to wait in lines, or queues. **Queuing, or waiting-line, models** are mathematical models that describe the operating characteristics of queuing situations. Many different queuing models exist because of the need to describe a variety of different queuing situations (such as a single service window at a small post office versus multiple service points that one must pass through in getting a driver's license). Unlike linear programming, queuing, or waiting-line, models do not provide an optimal solution. Rather, the models allow managers to vary the parameters of the situation and determine the probable effects. Queuing models were an important part of the Station Manpower Planning System developed by United. The airline needed models of situations in which customers would be waiting in lines so that it could determine how to schedule its staff effectively.

Routing, or Distribution, Models

Routing, or distribution, models Quantitative methods that can assist managers in planning the most effective and economical approaches to distribution problems

Many organizations distribute a product or service to multiple customers. **Routing, or distribution, models** are quantitative tools designed to assist managers in planning the most effective and economical approaches to distribution problems.[23] The development and use of these models is sometimes referred to as *network optimization analysis*. Among the companies that use routing models is Joyce Beverages, a bottler that delivers a variety of soft-drink products to approximately 5000 customers in Maryland, Virginia, and Washington, D.C. Delivery personnel visit between 500 and 600 customers daily; about 65 percent of them need the deliveries within a specified time frame; and vehicle routes must be changed dramatically from day to day. Adopting a computerized vehicle-routing model helped the company both improve customer service and save money.[24]

Simulation Models

Simulation A mathematical imitation of reality

Simulation is a mathematical imitation of reality. The technique is used when the situation of interest is too complex for more narrow techniques such as linear programming or queuing theory. Rather than constituting a standardized set of formulas that can be applied to a broad set of problems, simulations are usually custom-made to fit a situation.[25] As a result, they can be very expensive to develop. Simulations allow managers to change parameters so that different assumptions and/or approaches can be evaluated. Canadian National Railway (CN) developed a simulation model to help managers determine the most advantageous areas for laying more than $1 billion of double track that would handle expanding rail traffic through rugged mountain terrain.[26] Simulation has been utilized in production, inventory control, transportation systems, market strategy analysis, industrial and urban growth patterns, environmental control, and a variety of other areas.[27]

QUANTITATIVE AIDS FOR DECISION MAKING

Although the aids that we have discussed so far are mainly considered planning tools, they often also assist managers in making the decisions that are part of the planning process. In addition, there are a number of aids that are aimed specifically at helping managers make certain types of decisions. Two particularly well known quantitative aids for decision making are payoff tables and decision trees.

Payoff Tables

Payoff table or **decision matrix** A two-dimensional matrix that allows a decision maker to compare how different future conditions are likely to affect the respective outcomes of two or more decision alternatives

Payoff The amount of decision-maker value associated with a particular decision alternative and future condition

One helpful method of framing managerial decision situations is the use of the payoff table. A **payoff table** is a two-dimensional matrix that allows a decision maker to compare how different future conditions are likely to affect the respective outcomes of two or more decision alternatives. The payoff table is often referred to as a **decision matrix**.[28] Typically, in a payoff table, the decision alternatives are shown as row headings in the matrix, and the possible future conditions are shown as column headings. The number at the intersection of a row and a column represents the **payoff**, the amount of decision-maker value associated with a particular decision alternative and future condition. An example will be helpful in clarifying these concepts.[29]

Put yourself in the place of a decision maker at a college where there is a good possibility that enrollments may increase but existing classroom space is being used to capacity. Investigation of the situation reveals that there are three viable alternatives for increasing space: Construct a new building, expand an old building, or rent or lease another building. These alternatives are shown as row headings in Table S-3. There are also three possible future conditions. Student enrollments may go up, go down, or remain unchanged. These conditions are shown as column headings in the table. The potential payoff for each combination of alternative and possible future condition is listed at the appropriate intersection in the table. If it were clear which future condition would occur, then it would be a simple matter to select the alternative that has the highest payoff for that condition. Unfortunately, it is not possible to know exactly which condition will occur. However, on the basis of past experience, current enrollment trends, and personal judgment, the decision maker is able to assign probabilities to the possible future conditions. A *probability* is a decision maker's best estimate regarding the likelihood that a future condition will occur.[30] Such estimates are usually made in the form of a percentage ranging from 0 to 100. For example, as shown in the table, the decision maker estimates that there is a 50 percent probability that student enrollments will go up, while probabilities that enrollments will go down or remain unchanged are each estimated at 25 percent. Which alternative should the decision maker choose?

Expected value The sum of the payoffs times the respective probabilities for a given alternative

Decision-making experts recommend choosing the alternative with the highest expected value. The **expected value** for a given alternative is the sum of the payoffs times the respective probabilities for that alternative. For example, the expected value (EV) for expanding an old building is determined as follows:

$$EV = .50(400,000) + .25(100,000) + .25(100,000) = \$250,000$$

Likewise, the expected value for constructing a new building is

$$EV = .50(500,000) - .25(200,000) - .25(100,000) = \$175,000$$

Similar computations show an expected value of $225,000 for renting or leasing another building. Therefore, the alternative with the highest expected value in this case is expand an old building.

TABLE S-3	**Payoff Table for Classroom Space Problem**			
	Possible Future Conditions			
Alternatives	**Student Enrollments Up [.50]***	**Student Enrollments Down [.25]**	**Student Enrollments Unchanged [.25]**	**Expected Value**
Construct new building	$500,000	($200,000)†	($100,000)	$175,000
Expand old building	$400,000	$100,000	$100,000	$250,000
Rent or lease another building	$400,000	($100,000)	$200,000	$225,000

*Numbers in brackets are probability estimates for possible future conditions.
†Numbers in parentheses represent losses.
Source: Adapted from E. Frank Harrison, *The Managerial Decision-Making Process,* Houghton Mifflin, Boston, 1987, p. 375.

The value of payoff tables is that they help decision makers evaluate situations in which the outcomes of various alternatives depend on the likelihood of future conditions. As such, payoff tables are most useful when the decision maker is able to determine the major relevant alternatives, the payoffs can be quantified, and reasonably accurate judgments can be made regarding future probabilities.[31] For example, payoff tables have been used to decide which new products to introduce, real estate investments to select, crops to plant, and restaurant staffing levels to implement.[32] Managers at Hallmark, the greeting-card company, use payoff matrixes to help determine the production quantities of unique products, such as a special Muppet promotion that includes albums, plaques, gift wrap, stickers, party patterns, and other items.[33]

Decision tree A graphic model that displays the structure of a sequence of alternative courses of action and usually shows the payoffs associated with various paths and the probabilities associated with potential future conditions

Decision Trees

A **decision tree** (shown in Figure S-6) is a graphic model that displays the structure of a sequence of alternative courses of action. It usually also shows the payoffs associated with various paths and the probabilities associated with potential future conditions.

Figure S-6 *Decision tree and expected values for building a large or a small manufacturing plant.*

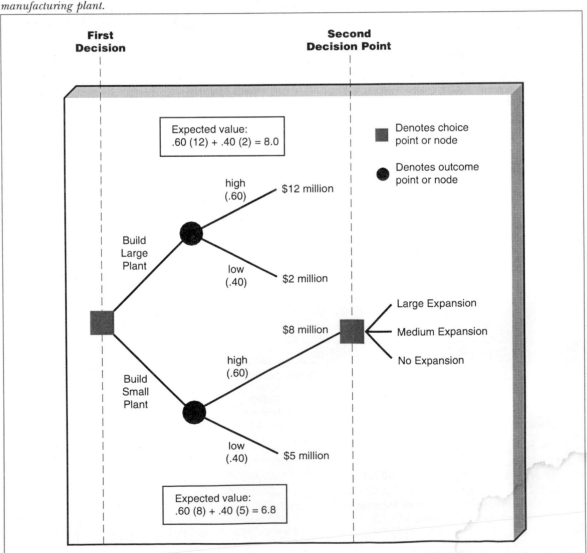

In the simple decision tree shown in Figure S-6, the manager is faced with an initial decision about whether to build a large or a small manufacturing plant, given some uncertainty regarding future demand for the product. If a large plant is built and demand is high, the company will make a $12 million profit. However, if demand is low, it will make only a $2 million profit (the profit is low because of the overhead on the large plant). The latter amount is less than the profit that will be made with a small plant under conditions of either high or low demand ($8 million and $5 million, respectively). To help make the decision, we compute the expected value for each alternative. The expected value for the large-plant alternative is $8 million [(.60 × $12 million) + (.40 × $2 million)]. The expected value for the small-plant alternative is $6.8 million [(.60 × $8 million) + (.40 × $5 million)]. This analysis suggests that the manager should seriously consider building the large plant.

So far, the decision tree operates as a graphic alternative to the payoff table. However, a major advantage of a decision tree is that it allows decision makers to consider more complex alternatives. For example, a manager may want to consider the implications of initially building a small plant and then possibly expanding it when the nature of the demand becomes more obvious. In our example in Figure S-6, building a small plant and then facing high demand for the product would raise the possibility of a second, later decision point, at which time a manager could take further action ranging from a large plant expansion to no expansion. These later decision possibilities can be considered and their expected values computed by using complex decision trees involving multiple decision points. A decision tree can help managers identify different options, as well as consider the potential impact of various alternative branches of the tree. The device was used to assist the U.S. Postal Service in its decision to continue the nine-digit zip code (zip + 4) for first-class business mailers and to purchase additional capital equipment in conjunction with its postal automation efforts.[34]

Break-Even Analysis

Break-even analysis A graphic model that helps decision makers understand the relationships among sales volume, costs, and revenues in an organization

Break-even analysis is a technique that helps decision makers understand the relationships among sales volume, costs, and revenues in an organization.[35] Although break-even analysis is often conducted graphically, as shown in Figure S-7, it also can be done mathematically.[36] The technique allows managers to determine the break-even point, which is the level of sales volume at which total revenues equal total costs. At the break-even point the organization neither loses nor makes money—that is, it just breaks even. The break-even point is important because only with a sales volume beyond that point does the organization begin to make a profit.

Several major elements are included in the break-even analysis shown in Figure S-7. *Fixed costs* are costs that remain the same regardless of volume of output (e.g., the costs of heating, lighting, administration, mortgage on building, and insurance). Fixed costs in Figure S-7 are illustrated by the horizontal line at $600,000. *Variable costs* are costs that vary depending on the level of output (e.g., the costs of raw materials, labor, packaging, and freight). In this particular situation, variable costs are $40 per unit for a unit that sells for $60. These data can be used to draw the lines on the graph for total costs (fixed costs plus variable costs) and total revenues, respectively. The break-even point, shown graphically, is at 30,000 units. At this point, fixed costs of $600,000 plus variable costs of $1,200,000 [30,000 × $40 (variable costs per unit)] equal $1,800,000. Revenues also equal $1,800,000 [30,000 × $60 (sale price per unit)] at this point. Hence the organization would break even at 30,000 units.

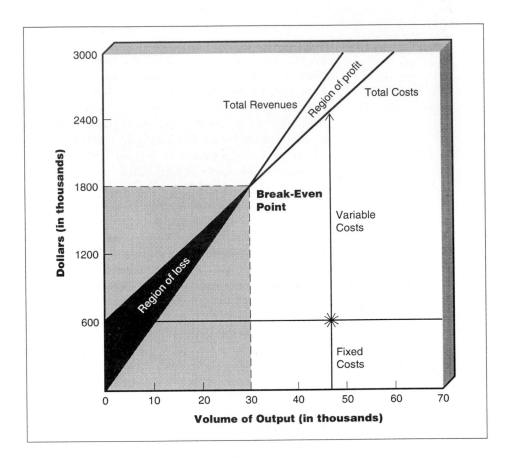

Figure S-7 *Break-even analysis.*

Break-even analysis is useful because it is a rough means of determining how many units of a product or service the organization must sell before it begins to make a profit. The analysis also provides a means of assessing the impact of cutting costs when profits begin. For example, if the organization lowered its fixed and/or variable costs, the total cost line in Figure S-7 would drop, lowering the break-even point.

This type of analysis has been conducted by John Sculley, head of Apple Computer. At one point, concluding that Apple's operations had become too large and expensive, he initiated a cost-cutting program that ultimately reduced Apple's break-even point from $400 million to $325 million per quarter. As a result, profits climbed 23 percent, despite a 23 percent drop in revenues, and cash on hand rose to an unprecedented $441 million at Apple.[37] Break-even analysis is also used to assess the impact of raising prices (and, thereby, total revenues), causing the total revenues line to rise more steeply and the break-even point to be lower.

Break-even analysis makes some simplifying assumptions. For instance, it assumes that a given price will be charged for all units (yet, some customers may get discounts) and that the fixed costs will remain the same across a wide range of outputs. Such assumptions suggest that the technique is valuable for doing rough analyses, rather than for precisely fine-tuning volumes, costs, and revenues. More complex types of break-even analyses, particularly those involving computers, are available for more precise needs.[38]

REFERENCES

1. Hans Levenbach and James P. Cleary, *The Modern Forecaster: The Forecasting Process through Data Analysis,* Lifetime Learning, Belmont, Calif., 1984, p. 3.

2. J. T. Mentzer and J. E. Cox, "Familiarity, Application and Performance of Sales Forecasting Techniques," *Journal of Forecasting,* vol. 3, 1984, pp. 27–36.

3. This section relies heavily on Steven C. Wheelwright and Spyros Makridakis, *Forecasting Methods for Management,* Wiley, New York, 1985.

4. Charles A. Gallagher and Hugh J. Watson, *Quantitative Methods for Business Decisions,* McGraw-Hill, New York, 1980, p. 116.

5. John Merwin, "A Billion in Blunders," *Forbes,* Dec. 1, 1986, p. 104.

6. This example is based on Charles A. Gallagher and Hugh J. Watson, *Quantitative Methods for Business Decisions,* McGraw-Hill, New York, 1980, pp. 131–135.

7. Peter Finch and Marc Frons, "Gurus Who Called the Crash—Or Fell on Their Faces," *Business Week,* Nov. 30, 1985, pp. 124–125; Susan Antilla, "The Hottest Woman on Wall Street," *Working Woman,* August 1991, pp. 49–51.

8. Dexter Hutchins, "And Now, the Home-Brewed Forecast," *Fortune,* Jan. 20, 1986, pp. 53–54.

9. George P. Huger, *Managerial Decision Making,* Scott, Foresman, Glenview, Ill., 1980, p. 206.

10. John F. Preble, "The Selection of Delphi Panels for Strategic Planning Purposes," *Strategic Management Journal,* vol. 5, 1984, pp. 157–170.

11. Ted G. Eschenbach and George A. Geistauts, "A Delphi Forecast for Alaska," *Interfaces,* November–December 1985, pp. 100–109.

12. Other examples can be found in George P. Huber, *Managerial Decision Making,* Scott, Foresman, Glenview, Ill., 1980, pp. 206–209; and Steven C. Wheelwright and Spyros Makridakis, *Forecasting Methods for Management,* Wiley, New York, 1985, pp. 289–290.

13. V. D. Garde and R. R. Patel, "Technological Forecasting for Power Generation—A Study Using the Delphi Technique," *Long Range Planning,* August 1985, pp. 73–79.

14. M. Godet, "From Forecasting to 'La Prospective': A New Way of Looking at Futures," *Journal of Forecasting,* vol. 1, 1982, pp. 293–301.

15. Steven C. Wheelwright and Spyros Makridakis, *Forecasting Methods for Management,* Wiley, New York, 1985, pp. 311–366.

16. For a recent review of forecasting literature, as well as commentary by several forecasting experts, see J. Scott Armstrong, "The Ombudsman: Research on Forecasting: A Quarter-Century Review, 1960–1984," *Interfaces,* January–February 1986, pp. 89–109.

17. See, for example, Mike Hack, "Harvard Project Manager Serves Pros, Casual Users," *InfoWorld,* Jan. 30, 1989, pp. 54–55.

18. John O. McClain and L. Joseph Thomas, *Operations Management: Production of Goods and Services,* Prentice-Hall, Englewood Cliffs, N.J., 1985, pp. 50–51.

19. These steps and the following material on PERT are based heavily on Everett E. Adam, Jr., and Ronald J. Ebert, *Production and Operations Management,* 3d ed., Prentice-Hall, Englewood Cliffs, N.J., 1986, pp. 533–538.

20. For a recent review of software packages that include Gantt charts and PERT, see Edward A. Wasil and Arjang A. Assad, "Project Management on the PC: Software, Applications, and Trends," *Interfaces,* March–April 1988, pp. 75–84.

21. K. Roscoe Davis and Patrick G. McKeown, *Quantitative Models for Management,* 2d ed., Kent, Boston, 1984, pp. 24–25.

22. William E. Pinney and Donald B. McWilliams, *Management Science: An Introduction to Quantitative Analysis for Management,* Harper & Row, New York, 1982, p. 95.

23. For recent advances in this area, see Bruce L. Golden and Arjang Assad (eds.), *Vehicle Routing: Methods and Studies,* North-Holland, Amsterdam, 1988.

24. Bruce L. Golden and Edward A. Wasil, "Computerized Vehicle Routing in the Soft Drink Industry," *Operations Research,* vol. 35, 1987, pp. 6–17.

25. William E. Pinney and Donald B. McWilliams, *Management Science: An Introduction to Quantitative Analysis for Management,* Harper & Row, New York, 1982, pp. 460–461.

26. Adapted from Norma Welch and James Gussow, "Expansion of Canadian National Railway's Line Capacity," *Interfaces,* January–February 1986, pp. 51–64; see also John F. Burns, "Trains to Be Cut in Canada," *The New York Times,* Oct. 5, 1989, pp. D1, D2.

27. K. Roscoe Davis and Patrick G. McKeown, *Quantitative Models for Management,* 2d ed., Kent, Boston, 1984, p. 625.

28. George P. Huber, *Managerial Decision Making,* Scott, Foresman, Glenview, Ill., 1980, p. 91.

29. The example is based on E. Frank Harrison, *The Managerial Decision-Making Process,* 2d ed., Houghton Mifflin, Boston, 1981, p. 279.

30. For several different definitions of probability, see William E. Pinney and Donald B. McWilliams, *Management Science: An Introduction to Quantitative Analysis for Management,* Harper & Row, New York, 1982, pp. 48–49.

31. E. Frank Harrison, *The Managerial Decision-Making Process,* 2d ed., Houghton Mifflin, Boston, 1981, p. 280.

32. George P. Huber, *Managerial Decision Making,* Scott, Foresman, Glenview, Ill., 1980, p. 90; Dennis H. Ferguson and Thomas I. Selling, "Probability Analysis: A System for Making Better Decisions," *The Cornell H.R.A. Quarterly,* August 1985, pp. 35–42.

33. F. Hutton Barron, "Payoff Matrices Pay Off at Hallmark," *Interfaces,* July–August 1985, pp. 20–25.

34. Jacob W. Ulvila, "Postal Automation (ZIP + 4) Technology: A Decision Analysis," *Interfaces,* March–April 1987, pp. 1–12.

35. Everett E. Adam, Jr., and Ronald J. Ebert, *Production and Operations Management,* 3d ed., Prentice-Hall, Englewood Cliffs, N.J., 1986.

36. See Jerry A.Viscione and Gordon S. Roberts, *Contemporary Financial Management,* Merrill, Columbus, Ohio, 1987, for a mathematical treatment of break-even analysis.

37. Deborah C. Wise and Geoff Lewis, "Apple, Part 2: The No-Nonsense Era of John Sculley," *Business Week,* Jan. 27, 1986, pp. 96–98.

38. See, for example, Thomas L. Powers, "Breakeven Analysis with Semifixed Costs," *Industrial Marketing Management,* vol. 16, 1987, pp. 35–41.

ACKNOWLEDGMENTS

Tables

Table S-1: Adapted from Spyrous Makridakis and Steven C. Wheelwright, "Forecasting an Organization's Futures," in Paul C. Nystrom and William H. Starbuck (eds.), *Handbook of Organizational Design,* 1981, p. 132. Copyright © Oxford University Press 1981. Reprinted by permission of Oxford University Press.

Table S-2: Adapted from Joseph G. Monks, *Operations Management,* 3rd ed., McGraw-Hill, New York, 1978, p. 561.

Table S-3: E. Frank Harrison, *The Managerial Decision-Making Process,* 3d ed., p. 375. Copyright © 1987 by Houghton Mifflin Company. Used with permission.

Figures

Figure S-1: Charles A. Gallagher and Hugh J. Watson, *Quantitative Methods for Business Decisions,* McGraw-Hill, 1980, p. 116. Reproduced by permission of McGraw-Hill, Inc.

Figure S-3: Charles A. Gallagher and Hugh J. Watson, *Quantitative Methods for Business Decisions,* McGraw-Hill, 1980, p. 134. Reproduced by permission of McGraw-Hill, Inc.

Figure S-5: Adapted from Joseph G. Monks, *Operations Management,* 3rd ed., McGraw-Hill, New York, 1987, p. 560.

CHAPTER 5

Strategic Management

THE MAGIC RETURNS TO DISNEY

By the early 1980s, the magical kingdom of Walt Disney Productions had lost its sparkle. It seemed that the creative juices in the company had slowly ebbed after the death in 1966 of Walt Disney, creator of such well-known characters as Mickey Mouse, Minnie Mouse, and Donald Duck. Walt Disney's immediate successors were wary of tampering with what had been a successful formula and, thus, made changes only slowly. As a result, attendance at the Disney theme parks in California and Florida began to level off, Tomorrowland began to lose its forward look, and, for the first time in almost three decades, no Disney-produced show was on network television. With few exceptions, Disney movies were dismal failures at the box office.

The dire situation reversed dramatically after the board brought in Michael D. Eisner as chairman and chief executive officer and Frank G. Wells as president and chief operating officer. Eisner, who has a creative bent, had been an extremely successful president of Paramount Pictures. Frank Wells, a lawyer with a strong financial background, had been a noteworthy vice-chairman of Warner Brothers. When the two took charge at Disney in September 1984, they quickly began to infuse the company with a renewed entrepreneurial spirit. Eisner and Wells concluded that the company's major assets were the Disney name, the Disney culture, its movies, and its library. Therefore, they planned to revitalize these assets and, at the same time, to embellish them with new assets. In doing so, they introduced new movies, new ideas, new theme parks, and new executives.

The company, now called the Walt Disney Company, has three main operating divisions: filmed entertainment, consumer products, and theme parks and resorts. In the filmed entertainment division, the new management team has converted Walt Disney Studios from a lackluster performer to a leader of the pack with such hits as *Aladdin, The Little Mermaid, Beauty and the Beast,* and *Dick Tracy* and the re-release of earlier successes such as *Fantasia.* Many of its films are adult fare, released under Touchstone and Hollywood Pictures. In addition, Disney has introduced the *Mickey and Donald* cartoon series on China Central Television, where it is the most popular children's program.

The consumer-products division ensures that Disney products, such as Mickey Mouse watches, sweatshirts, stuffed animals, and crib linen, are available throughout the world. The items are all manufactured under license. Notable recent agreements include a joint venture to manufacture Disney products in Guangzhou, China, and a 10-year contract with Mattel, Inc., which will make a wide range of toys to be distributed through Disney facilities. Disney retail stores, introduced by the Eisner and Wells regime, have performed well beyond expectations. Currently, there are 180 Disney stores in the United States, 13 in Europe, and 2 in Japan. By the end of 1995, the company expects to have 300 Mic-Kids outlets in China, which are part of the joint venture to make Disney products there.

The theme parks and resorts division, which accounts for 60 to 65 percent of Disney revenues, is moving forward at a rapid pace. Under Eisner and Wells, the company has revamped Walt Disney World and Disneyland to such an extent that the number of visitors to the parks has increased dramatically. A "WESTCOT Center" theme park near Disneyland is expected to be completed by 1999. Disney also opened Euro Disneyland near Paris in 1992.

Many of the ideas for films, consumer products, and park attractions originate with Eisner himself, who counts on Wells to squelch his more impractical suggestions, such as his vision of a 43-story hotel in the shape of Mickey Mouse. Other ideas begin with the famous Disney Imagineering division, an innovative group that is mainly responsible for dreaming up new ideas and figuring out how they can become realities. One of its concepts, for example, is now the "Body Wars" attraction at Walt Disney World, which simulates zipping along the path of the human bloodstream, as well as visiting the heart and brain.

After Imagineering develops design and engineering requirements for a project, it submits them to a six-person strategic planning group, which reviews the project's compatibility with strategic directions and checks to make sure that the financial aspects make sense. Then, together, the two groups outline a budget and a schedule before the package goes to Wells and Eisner, who quickly make the final decision about whether or not to proceed.

In providing strategic directions, Eisner and Wells encourage synergy among various divisions, so the efforts of one division often help those of others. For example, if the animation studio creates a cartoon character like Roger Rabbit to appear in films, the consumer-products division often licenses the character to merchandisers. These manufacturers produce stuffed animals, T-shirts, and other products based on the character, and the items are sold in Disney retail stores and theme parks. The character may also become the basis for a costumed figure in the parks and possibly the subject of new rides or attractions.

In Eisner's view, his chief duty at Disney is leading creatively and being an orchestrator, thinker, inventor, and cheerleader for new ideas. Wells keeps close tabs on financial aspects. So far, their efforts have returned the magic to Disney and pleased investors as well. Eisner's goal is to produce 20 percent earnings growth and return on equity compounded annually. He is doing well at meeting this goal.[1]

How were Eisner and Wells able to take a languishing company and make it so visibly prosperous again? Their success stems in part from their strong commitment to Disney's growth and their ability to map out important strategic directions for the company. Strategic goals and plans are a particularly important part of the managerial planning function because they ultimately determine the overall direction of the organization. Accordingly, in this chapter, we take a more thorough look at strategic-level planning issues, exploring how companies like Disney are managed strategically. We begin by examining the concept of strategic management. We then consider how competitive analysis can form the basis for developing effective strategies aimed at gaining an edge over competitors. We next analyze policy formulation at the corporate, business, and functional levels. Finally, we probe the process of strategy implementation.

THE CONCEPT OF STRATEGIC MANAGEMENT

Strategies Large-scale action plans for interacting with the environment in order to achieve long-term goals

Strategic management A process through which managers formulate and implement strategies geared toward optimizing strategic goal achievement, given available environmental and internal conditions

Most well-run organizations attempt to develop and follow **strategies**, large-scale action plans for interacting with the environment in order to achieve long-term goals.[2] A comprehensive statement of an organization's strategies, along with its mission and goals, constitutes an organization's strategic plan.[3] To learn where such strategies originate and how they are put into action, we need to examine carefully an aspect of the planning function called strategic management. **Strategic management** is a process through which managers formulate and implement strategies geared toward optimizing strategic goal achievement, given available environmental and internal conditions.[4] This definition recognizes that strategic management is oriented toward reaching long-term goals, weighs important environmental elements, considers major internal characteristics of the organization, and involves developing specific strategies.

The Strategic Management Process

The strategic management process is made up of several major components, as shown in Figure 1. The process begins with identifying the organization's mission and strategic goals. Next, it involves analyzing the competitive situation, taking into consideration both the external environment and relevant organizational factors. After such an analysis, managers can begin to develop, or formulate, various strategies that can be used to reach strategic goals. The part of the strategic management process that includes identifying the mission and strategic goals, conducting competitive analysis, and developing specific strategies is often referred to as **strategy formulation.** In contrast, the part of the process that focuses on carrying out strategic plans and maintaining control over how those plans are carried out is known as **strategy implementation.**[5] Strategy implementation is increasingly highlighted as a distinct part of the strategic management process because even the most brilliantly formulated strategies will achieve nothing if they are not implemented effectively.

Importance of Strategic Management

Strategic management is important for several reasons.[6] For one thing, the process helps organizations identify and develop a **competitive advantage,** which is a

Strategy formulation The process of identifying the mission and strategic goals, conducting competitive analysis, and developing specific strategies

Strategy implementation The process of carrying out strategic plans and maintaining control over how those plans are carried out

Competitive advantage A significant edge over the competition in dealing with competitive forces

Figure 1 *The strategic management process.*

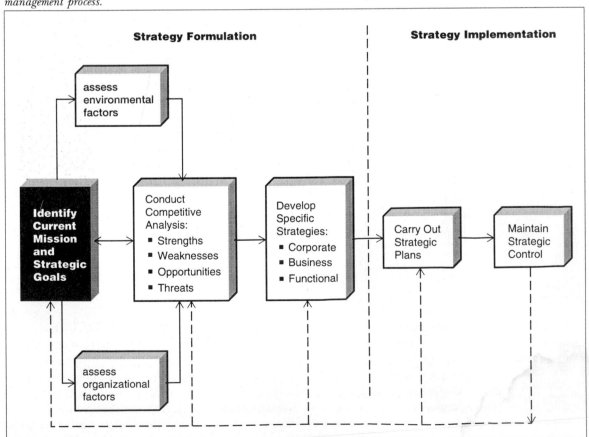

significant edge over the competition in dealing with competitive forces.[7] For example, Disney has been able to gain a competitive advantage in the family entertainment industry by creating amusement parks, movies, and products based on the renowned Disney characters.

Strategic management is also important because it provides a sense of direction so that organization members know where to expend their efforts. Without a strategic plan, managers may concentrate on day-to-day activities only to find that a competitor has maneuvered itself into a favorable position by taking a more comprehensive, long-term view of strategic directions. This was the case at the Rayovac Corporation, a battery and flashlight maker based in Madison, Wisconsin. Rayovac had fallen behind competitors in the early 1980s because of its aging product line, outdated packaging, and slowness in entering the market for alkaline batteries (which became the industry standard). Since that time, a new chairman and vice-chairman, the husband-and-wife team of Thomas and Judith Pyle, have rejuvenated the company, partially through a variety of innovative products. For instance, the Luma 2 is a sleek flashlight with an extremely bright krypton light and a lithium-powered, long-lasting backup bulb. Rayovac says that with the backup system, the flashlight should work for about 10 years.[8]

Strategic management can also help highlight the need for innovation and provide an organized approach for encouraging new ideas related to strategies.[9] In addition, the process can be used to involve managers at various levels in planning, thus making it more likely that they will understand the resulting plans and be committed to their implementation.[10]

Levels of Strategy

Many organizations develop strategies at three different levels: corporate, business, and functional. The three levels are shown in Figure 2.[11]

CORPORATE-LEVEL STRATEGY **Corporate-level strategy** addresses what businesses the organization will operate, how the strategies of those businesses will be coordinated to strengthen the organization's competitive position, and how resources will be allocated among the businesses. Strategy at this level is

Corporate-level strategy
A type of strategy that addresses what businesses the organization will operate, how the strategies of those businesses will be coordinated to strengthen the organization's competitive position, and how resources will be allocated among the businesses

Figure 2 *Levels of strategy.* *(Adapted from John A. Pearce II and Richard B. Robinson, Jr.,* Management, *McGraw-Hill, 1989, p. 206.)*

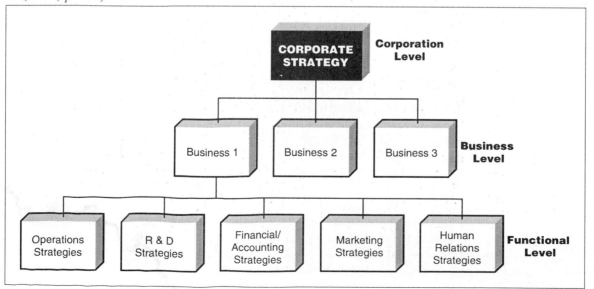

typically developed by top management, often with the assistance of strategic planning personnel, at least in large organizations.[12]

The board of directors is also involved in developing corporate-level strategy, although the degree of board participation varies. Within the strategic management process, a board of directors can typically be most helpful by advising on new directions for growth, suggesting when major changes in strategy are needed, and providing input on the timing of major investments.[13]

Strategic business unit (SBU)
A distinct business, with its own set of competitors, that can be managed relatively independently of other businesses within the organization

Business-level strategy
A type of strategy that concentrates on the best means of competing within a particular business while also supporting the corporate-level strategy

BUSINESS-LEVEL STRATEGY   Many organizations include a number of strategic business units. A **strategic business unit (SBU)** is a distinct business, with its own set of competitors, that can be managed relatively independently of other businesses within the organization.[14] **Business-level strategy** concentrates on the best means of competing within a particular business while also supporting the corporate-level strategy. Strategies at this level are aimed at deciding the type of competitive advantage to build, determining responses to changing environmental and competitive conditions, allocating resources within the business unit, and coordinating functional-level strategies. Most often, the heads of the respective business units develop business strategies, although such strategies are typically subject to the approval of top management. When an organization comprises only a single business, corporate-level and business-level strategies are essentially the same. Thus the corporate-level and business-level distinction applies only to organizations with separate divisions that compete in different industries.[15]

Functional-level strategy
A type of strategy that focuses on action plans for managing a particular functional area within a business in a way that supports the business-level strategy

FUNCTIONAL-LEVEL STRATEGY   **Functional-level strategy** focuses on action plans for managing a particular functional area within a business in a way that supports the business-level strategy. Strategies at this level address main directions for each of the major functional areas within a business, such as manufacturing or operations, marketing, finance, human resource management, accounting, research and development, and engineering. Functional-level strategies are important because they often reflect strong functional competencies that can be used to competitive advantage.

COORDINATING LEVELS OF STRATEGY   Coordinating strategies across the three levels is critical in maximizing strategic impact. The business-level strategy is enhanced when functional-level strategies support its basic thrust. Similarly, the corporate-level strategy is likely to have greater impact when it is bolstered by business-level strategies that complement one another.[16] Thus the three levels must be closely coordinated as part of the strategic management process.

THE ROLE OF COMPETITIVE ANALYSIS IN STRATEGY FORMULATION

SWOT analysis   A method of analyzing an organization's competitive situation that involves assessing organizational strengths (S) and weaknesses (W), as well as environmental opportunities (O) and threats (T)

Before managers can devise an effective strategy for gaining a competitive edge, they need to carefully analyze the organization's competitive situation. This involves assessing both the environmental and the organizational factors that influence an organization's ability to compete effectively. Such an assessment can be made with SWOT analysis.[17] **SWOT analysis** is a method of analyzing an organization's competitive situation that involves assessing organizational strengths (S) and weaknesses (W), as well as environmental opportunities (O) and threats (T). Identifying strengths and weaknesses requires assessing internal characteristics, while detecting opportunities and threats involves evaluating relevant environmental factors.

For SWOT analysis purposes, a *strength* is an internal characteristic that has the potential of improving the organization's competitive situation. In contrast, a *weakness* is an internal characteristic that leaves the organization potentially vulnerable to strategic moves by competitors. An *opportunity* is an environmental condition that offers significant prospects for improving an organization's situation relative to competitors. Conversely, a *threat* is an environmental condition that offers significant prospects for undermining an organization's competitive situation. Some issues that might be considered in SWOT analysis are shown in Table 1.

Environmental Assessment

In analyzing opportunities and threats, managers need to consider elements in the general environment, or mega-environment, that can positively or adversely influence an organization's ability to reach its strategic goals. Such elements are broad factors, including technological, economic, legal-political, sociocultural, and international influences. Managers also need to assess major elements in the organization's task environment, which includes the more specific outside elements with which the organization interfaces in conducting its business. Such elements include customers, competitors, and suppliers.

TABLE 1   **SWOT Analysis: An Illustrative Framework**

Strengths	Weaknesses	Opportunities	Threats
Effective material and inventory control systems	Outdated equipment compared to that of key competitors	Diversification into related product-market areas	Market penetration by foreign competitors
Innovative sales promotion and advertising	Inadequate market research to identify customer segments and needs	Forward or backward integration to enhance competitive position	Intensifying domestic competition
Promptness of attention to customer complaints	Delays in providing replacement parts and repair services	Increase in the height of entry barriers	Decreasing entry barriers
Timely and accurate information to management on general and competitive environments	Inadequate information support in making strategic and routine decisions	Decreasing labor costs	Better and cheaper substitute products
Effective procedures for recruiting, training, and promoting employees	Unfavorable relations with trade unions	Appeal to additional customer segments	Increasing material costs
Success of research and development activities (in leading to product and process innovations)	Ineffective working relationships between R&D personnel and other departments	Demographic changes leading to increased market demand	Increasing concentration among buyer groups
Good, long-term relationships with reliable suppliers	Excessive dependence on a single supplier	Unfavorable sociocultural changes	Adverse demographic changes
Favorable relationships with the public	Inadequate strategic planning systems	Deregulation providing new market opportunities	Sociocultural changes that depress demand
Liquidity, leverage, activity, and profitability ratios superior to industry norms and key competitors	Inability to raise additional funds	Technological developments that help extend the growth plan of the product life cycle	Increased environmental legislation
Capacity to adapt and evolve, consistent with demands of changes in environment and strategy	Inability of the culture to foster innovation, creativity, and openness to new ideas	Decreasing cost of funds	Potential product obsolescence because of technological developments
Good relationships with policy makers and government officials	Poor relationships with the media	Declining trade barriers in foreign countries	Rising interest rates
Thorough understanding of overall strategy by functional-area managers	A lack of effective integration of activities across functional areas		Political instability in countries where foreign operations are located

Source: G. G. Dess and A. Miller, *Strategic Management,* McGraw-Hill, 1993, p. 364.

Five competitive forces model Porter's approach to analyzing the nature and intensity of competition in a given industry in terms of five major forces

PORTER'S FIVE COMPETITIVE FORCES MODEL Strategy expert Michael E. Porter developed the **five competitive forces model** to analyze the nature and intensity of competition in a given industry in terms of five major forces. The forces are rivalry, bargaining power of customers, bargaining power of suppliers, threat of new entrants, and threat of substitute products or services. The collective strength of these forces directly affects the profit potential, or long-term return on investment, available to businesses operating in the particular industry. The major reasons for lower profit potential are summarized in Table 2.

Rivalry is the extent to which competitors continually jockey for position by using such tactics as price competition, advertising battles, product introductions, and increased customer service or warranties. All these tactics have the ability to lower profits for the various competitors in the industry either by lowering the prices that can be charged or by raising the costs of doing business. For example, the magazine industry has become so competitive that a number of magazines are being forced out of business. Several publishers have been reporting lower profit margins because they are selling subscriptions at a discount, offering bargain cover prices at newsstands, and accommodating advertiser pressures for special rates (rather than running the risk of losing advertisers to rival publications.)[18] Thus the magazine industry illustrates Porter's premise that the greater the rivalry, the lower the profit potential for businesses operating in the industry.

The *bargaining power of customers* is the extent to which customers are able to force prices down, bargain for higher quality or more service at the same price, and play competitors against each other. Customers tend to be powerful when the quantities they purchase are large in proportion to a seller's total sales, when the products or services represent a significant portion of a customer's costs, or when the items needed are standard in the supplier industry. For instance, U.S. suppliers in the auto-parts industry have found that they must offer better quality at lower prices than they did in the past to gain orders from Japanese automakers operating plants in the United States. Such measures are necessary particularly because many Japan-based auto-parts suppliers have built U.S. plants, providing alternative sources of supplies.[19] The greater the bargaining power of customers, the lower the profit potential in the industry.

TABLE 2	**Porter's Five Competitive Forces Model**
Competitive Forces	**Reasons for Lower Profit Potential**
Rivalry	Various competitive tactics among rivals lower prices that can be charged or raise costs of doing business.
Bargaining power of customers	Customers force price reductions or negotiate increases in product quality and service at the same price.
Bargaining power of suppliers	Suppliers threaten price increases and/or reductions in the quality of goods or services.
Threat of new entrants	New entrants bid prices down or cause incumbents to increase costs in order to maintain market position.
Threat of substitute products or services	Availability of substitutes limits the prices that can be charged.

Source: Based on Michael E. Porter, *Competitive Strategy,* Free Press, New York, 1980, pp. 3–28.

The *bargaining power of suppliers* is the extent to which suppliers can exert power over businesses in an industry by threatening to raise their prices or reduce the quality of their goods and services. Suppliers tend to be powerful when there are only a few of them selling to many businesses in an industry, when there are no substitutes for their products or services, or when their products or services are critical to the buyer's business. The greater the bargaining power of suppliers, the lower the profit potential for businesses operating in the industry.

For example, French makers of champagne are running into difficulties because of a shortage of grape-growing land in the Champagne region of France. The region is famous for producing ideal grapes that have made the sparkling wine increasingly popular throughout the world. Thus suppliers of grapes in that area can command premium prices. To remedy the supply shortage, Moët and other French champagne makers, such as Pommery et Greno and Laurent-Perrier, are purchasing wineries and land suitable for growing grapes in the United States (mainly in California and Oregon), as well as in Australia, Spain, Latin America, and elsewhere. Still, a debate rages over the comparative virtues of grapes grown in France versus those grown in other locations. Some champagne producers argue that top-quality champagne requires grapes from France's Champagne region, affording area growers considerable power as suppliers.[20]

The *threat of new entrants* is the extent to which new competitors can enter the same product or service markets. New entrants bring added capacity and possibly substantial resources. The results are price wars and/or increases in costs for existing businesses, which frequently must increase expenditures (for additional advertising, a larger sales force, better service, etc.) in order to just maintain market position. The threat of entry depends on how hard it is to break into the market. High barriers to entry exist when large capital investments are required to start a business (as is the case in the steel industry) or when economies of scale make it difficult for a new entrant to start small and gradually build up volume (as with television manufacturing). High barriers also exist when established competitors have products or services that are perceived as unique by loyal customers (e.g., a brand-name perfume).

When barriers to entry are high and new entrants can expect vigorous reaction from existing competitors, the threat of new entrants is low. For example, Anheuser-Busch, the nation's largest brewer, at one point announced that it would start matching the steep discounts that smaller competitors were offering in their attempt to invade some of the brewer's markets. Because of economies of scale, Anheuser-Busch's costs per barrel of beer are substantially lower than those of competitors, giving it heavy ammunition in a price war. With the handwriting on the wall, the smaller brewers quickly discontinued much of their heavy price-cutting.[21] In contrast, when barriers are low and new entrants can expect mild reactions from incumbent competitors, the threat of new entrants is high and, consequently, the profit potential in the industry is low.

The *threat of substitute products or services* is the extent to which businesses in other industries offer substitute products for an established product line. For example, artificial sweeteners can be substituted for sugar, electricity can often be substituted for gas in producing energy, and paint can be substituted for wallpaper. The Coca-Cola Company has been attempting to get workers in small offices to switch from coffee to Coke by providing a compact new machine called the BreakMate. This machine chills water, carbonates it, and mixes it with Coca-Cola syrup before dispensing the soft drink into 6½-ounce cups.[22] The availability of substitutes constrains the prices that firms in an industry (such as the coffee industry) can charge, since price increases might encourage customers to switch to a substitute (such as Coca-Cola). As a result, the availability of substitute products or services reduces the profit potential in the industry.

Organizational Assessment

In conducting a competitive analysis, managers need to give considerable attention to how factors within the organization affect the competitive situation. More specifically, they need to assess major internal strengths and weaknesses that influence the organization's ability to compete.

Distinctive competence A strength that is unique and that competitors cannot easily match or imitate

Strengths are potential sources of competitive advantage. A strength that is unique and that competitors cannot easily match or imitate is known as a **distinctive competence**. Distinctive competences can be exploited in gaining a competitive advantage precisely because competitors will have difficulty following suit.[23] For example, by taking advantage of its distinctive competence in research and development, 3M has produced a broad range of useful product innovations over a sustained period of time.[24]

On the other hand, organizational weaknesses can leave the organization vulnerable to competitors' actions. For instance, the Kerr-McGee Corporation, an Oklahoma City–based energy company, ran into trouble when its salary levels failed to keep up with those offered by competitors. Lured by higher salaries, most of its exploration and production talent defected to other firms. The compensation system was later streamlined, and since then the company has been rebuilding its work force. As a result, the exploration staff made two significant oil-reserve finds in the North Sea.[25]

Functional audit An exhaustive appraisal of the important positive and negative attributes of each major functional area

One common aid in assessing internal organizational strengths and weaknesses is a functional audit. A **functional audit** is an exhaustive appraisal of the important positive and negative attributes of each major functional area.[26] For instance, a functional audit might assess the appropriate segmentation and targeting of markets by the marketing department, the currency of equipment in the operations department, and the availability of working capital from the finance department. Of course, a functional audit would cover many more aspects of each department and consider other departments as well.[27]

In determining which aspects to include in a functional audit, managers might find it useful to compile a list of the internal characteristics that appear to be the *key success factors* in the industry.[28] (In compiling the list, managers will need to have information about competitors. Some ideas about obtaining such data are given in the chapter, "Understanding External and Internal Environments," in the Practically Speaking discussion, "Keeping Tabs on Competitors.") Analysis of environmental opportunities and threats, as well as organizational strengths and weaknesses, sets the stage for developing corporate-level strategies.

FORMULATING CORPORATE-LEVEL STRATEGY

Corporate-level strategy comprises the overall strategy that an organization will follow. Its development generally involves selecting a grand strategy and using portfolio strategy approaches to determine the various businesses that will make up the organization.

Grand strategy A master strategy that provides the basic strategic direction at the corporate level

Grand Strategies

A **grand strategy** (sometimes called a *master strategy*) provides the basic strategic direction at the corporate level.[29] There are several generic types, which can be grouped into three basic categories: growth, stability, and defensive grand strategies.[30] These strategies and their major subcategories are shown in Figure 3.

Growth strategies Grand strategies that involve organizational expansion along some major dimension

Concentration An approach that focuses on effecting the growth of a single product or service or a small number of closely related products or services

GROWTH **Growth strategies** are grand strategies that involve organizational expansion along some major dimension. In business organizations, growth typically means increasing sales and earnings, although other criteria (such as number of geographic locations) are possible. Similarly, not-for-profit organizations can grow in terms of revenue, clients served, or other criteria. Three major growth strategies are concentration, vertical integration, and diversification.

Concentration focuses on effecting the growth of a single product or service or a small number of closely related products or services. Concentration usually takes place through *market development* (gaining a larger share of a current market or expanding into new ones), *product development* (improving a basic product

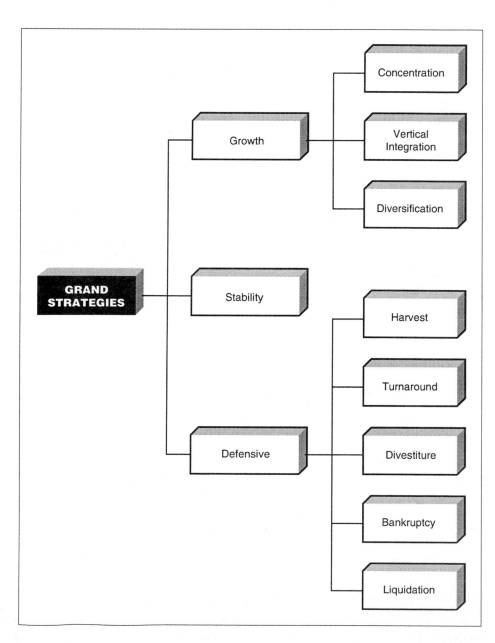

Figure 3 *Types of grand strategies.*

or service or expanding into closely related products or services), or *horizontal integration* (adding one or more businesses that are similar, usually by purchasing such businesses). For example, France-based Groupe Michelin engaged in horizontal integration when it took over the Uniroyal Goodrich Tire Company, making Michelin the world's largest tire manufacturer. Indicative of its strategy of high concentration, more than 90 percent of Michelin's annual sales are based on tires.[31]

Vertical integration An approach that involves effecting growth through the production of inputs previously provided by suppliers or through the replacement of a customer role by disposing of one's own outputs

Vertical integration involves effecting growth through the production of inputs previously provided by suppliers or through the replacement of a customer role (such as that of a distributor) by disposing of one's own outputs. When a business grows by becoming its own supplier, the process is known as *backward integration*.[32] One interesting organization that is prospering partially through backward integration is PGA Tour, Inc., the professional golf association headed by Commissioner Deane Beaman. When Beaman took over the organization in 1973, its annual revenues from professional golfing events were $3.1 million. Today, annual revenues top $100 million. This is partly because Tour now owns, operates, or licenses more than 13 courses and clubs used each year for Tour events. The remainder of the time, the courses and clubs are available to members, who pay dues. Thus Tour not only has become its own supplier of sites for tournaments but also receives revenues. In addition, it often gets close to 20 percent of the gains from residential development on certain properties next to courses. In another move toward vertical integration, Tour has been working on producing its own telecasts of tournaments for national television, rather than having relatively high-cost network personnel supply the production services. Contracts have been signed with the major television networks through the 1996 tour season.[33]

When organizational growth encompasses a role previously fulfilled by a customer, the process is known as *forward integration*. Liz Claiborne, Inc., has recently engaged in forward integration by opening Liz Claiborne and First Issue retail stores. This move has enabled the company to sell directly to consumers, rather than selling exclusively through department stores and outlets owned by others. According to one study, organizations are more likely to use a vertical integration strategy when product or service demand is reasonably certain, rather than highly uncertain.[34]

Diversification An approach that entails effecting growth through the development of new areas that are clearly distinct from current businesses

Diversification entails effecting growth through the development of new areas that are clearly distinct from current businesses. In addition to diversifying for growth reasons, organizations often diversify to reduce the risk that can be associated with single-product or -industry operations.[35] There are two types of diversification: conglomerate and concentric. *Conglomerate diversification* takes place when an organization diversifies into areas that are unrelated to its current business. Organizations that adopt a conglomerate diversification strategy are often referred to as *conglomerates*. For example, Textron, Inc., a conglomerate, has an aerospace business that is being adversely affected by the current downturn in defense spending. However, its two other major businesses, commercial products (auto parts, lawn mowers, fasteners, etc.) and financial services (Paul Revere Insurance and other financial and leasing services) have helped cushion the effects.[36] Because of the variety of businesses involved, conglomerates can be difficult for top management to administrate effectively. *Concentric diversification* occurs when an organization diversifies into a related, but distinct, business. With concentric diversification, businesses can be related through products, markets, or technology. In the case of The Limited, Inc., the concentric diversification involved related products, mainly women's clothing (see the following Case in Point discussion).

CASE IN POINT   THE UNLIMITED LIMITED

When Leslie Wexner opened his first women's clothing store in Columbus, Ohio, in 1963 with a $5000 stake, few would have predicted that the shop was the beginning of a major women's clothing empire. Wexner called his first shop "The Limited" because it offered only women's sportswear. He got the idea of specializing after working in his parents' clothing store and noticing that office garments and fancy dresses did not sell nearly as fast as sportswear. When he attempted to persuade his parents to concentrate on sportswear and eliminate the other merchandise, they insisted that the shop needed a wide variety of clothing to attract customers. In fact, his father told him: "You'll never be a merchant." Within a year, the son's new shop proved to be so successful that the parents closed up their store and joined forces with their "merchant" son. By 1969, when The Limited, Inc., made a public stock offering, Wexner had opened six stores. Seven years later, there were 100 The Limited stores; the number increased to more than 700 by the end of the 1980s.

Along with the growth of The Limited stores, there have been shifts in emphasis. Since The Limited originally targeted women between 15 and 25, Wexner found that he was losing his customers as they grew older. Accordingly, he repositioned The Limited to appeal to women in the 20-to-35 age bracket, and he started a new chain, the Limited Express, to appeal to teenagers and women in their early twenties. This highly successful chain, now called simply Express, has more than 600 stores and is growing at more than 18 percent annually, three times the industry average.

In order to keep the company growing at a fast pace, Wexner has expanded into other areas related to women's clothing. For example, in 1981, he bought a small chain of lingerie stores, called Victoria's Secret, and has expanded it to more than 600 outlets. This chain has also been eminently successful. He also purchased the Lane Bryant stores in 1982 and eliminated the tall and largest sizes because of the relatively small market. Instead, he expanded offerings in sizes 14 through 20, noting that 40 percent of women are size 14 or larger.

Next, Wexner bought the huge Lerner chain. It was close to bankruptcy, owing largely to poor management, including abysmal inventory control. Lerner now carries the same type of merchandise found in The Limited Stores, but the items are geared to a lower-priced market.

In 1988 Wexner bought Abercrombie & Fitch, a 27-store chain that sells men's and women's sportswear and gift items. Today it has more than 40 stores and is thriving. In 1990 the Structure, a men's apparel chain, was opened as part of The Limited's strategy of having several stores colocated in shopping centers. Currently, there are more than 200 of these stores located adjacent to Express stores. Wexner recently opened two more new chains, Cacique, a more conservative women's lingerie chain than Victoria's Secret, and Bath & Body, a women's cosmetics chain.

Wexner has also developed a larger version of The Limited stores. The new International Fashion stores, with about 12,500 square feet of floor space (compared with 3700 at regular The Limited stores), can accommodate The Limited's usual fare along with career clothing, lingerie, and children's apparel. The Limited's flagship store, Henri Bendel, located in Manhattan, New York, continues to perform admirably. Thus The Limited and its various related chains, now numbering more than 4000 outlets, continue to experiment with creative ways to keep the company growing, mainly in women's clothing or closely related areas, such as men's and children's clothing. Wexner's goal is to have revenues of more than $10 billion by the mid 1990s.[37]   ■ ■ ■

All three growth strategies, including the diversification approach used by The Limited, can be implemented through internal growth or through acquisition, merger, or joint venture. With internal growth the organization expands by building on its own internal resources. The organization's core characteristics can be coupled with changes in technology and marketing, resulting in increased profit and growth.[38] An **acquisition** is the purchase of all or part of one organization by another, while a **merger** is the combining of two or more companies into one organization. Finally, a joint venture occurs when two or more organizations provide resources to support a given project or product offering. Thus there are several alternative routes to implementing particular growth strategies.

Acquisition The purchase of all or part of one organization by another

Merger The combining of two or more companies into one organization

STABILITY A **stability strategy** involves maintaining the status quo or growing in a methodical, but slow, manner. Organizations might choose a stability strategy for a number of reasons. For instance, if a company is doing reasonably well, managers may not want the risks or hassles associated with more aggressive growth. This is often the case in small, privately owned businesses, which constitute the largest group likely to adopt a strategy of stability. For example, Bob Sidell started California Cosmetics after formulating special cosmetics to cope with the skin problems of teenage actors appearing in the TV show *The Waltons.* Within 3 years, Sidell and his partner, Paula Levey, had developed their mail-order operation into a company with annual sales of $10 million. Such fast growth, though, brought botched orders, rising complaints, and returns and nondeliveries in the 17 percent range. After some initial cutbacks to gain stability, the company plans to grow much more slowly. "We'll probably never be the richest folks on the block," says Levey. "But we're going to be around years from now."[39] Another reason for choosing stability is that it provides a chance to recover. An organization that stretched its resources during a period of accelerated growth may need to attain stability before it attempts further accelerated growth. On the other hand, if managers believe that growth prospects are low, they may choose a stability strategy in an attempt to hold on to current market share. (Worsening situations, however, may call for defensive strategies.) Finally, a stability strategy may even occur through default if managers are unconcerned with their strategic direction.

Stability strategy A strategy that involves maintaining the status quo or growing in a methodical, but slow, manner

DEFENSIVE **Defensive strategies** (sometimes called *retrenchment strategies*) focus on the desire or need to reduce organizational operations, usually through cost reductions (such as cutting back on nonessential expenditures and instituting hiring freezes) and/or asset reductions (such as selling land, equipment, and businesses).[40] Defensive strategies include harvest, turnaround, divestiture, bankruptcy, and liquidation.

Harvest entails minimizing investments while attempting to maximize short-run profits and cash flow, with the long-run intention of exiting the market.[41] A harvest strategy is often used when future growth in the market is doubtful or will require investments that do not appear to be cost-effective. For example, the vacuum-tube market collapsed because of the late 1940s' invention of the transistor and subsequent advanced solid-state circuitry. Consequently, many large producers of vacuum tubes (e.g., Western Electric, General Electric, and Westinghouse) gradually phased out their production.[42] With a harvest strategy, the resulting short-run profits are often used to build other businesses with better future prospects.

A **turnaround** is designed to reverse a negative trend and restore the organization to appropriate levels of profitability. Such efforts often require at least temporary reductions in order to conserve funds. (The term "turnaround" is

Defensive strategies Strategies that focus on the desire or need to reduce organizational operations, usually through cost and/or asset reductions

Harvest A strategy that entails minimizing investments while attempting to maximize short-run profits and cash flow, with the long-run intention of exiting the market

Turnaround A strategy designed to reverse a negative trend and restore the organization to appropriate levels of profitability

Divestiture A strategy that involves an organization's selling or divesting of a business or part of a business

Bankruptcy A strategy in which an organization that is unable to pay its debts can seek court protection from creditors and from certain contract obligations while it attempts to regain financial stability

Liquidation A strategy that entails selling or dissolving an entire organization

Portfolio strategy approach A method of analyzing an organization's mix of businesses in terms of both individual and collective contributions to strategic goals

BCG growth-share matrix A four-cell matrix (developed by the Boston Consulting Group) that compares various businesses in an organization's portfolio on the basis of relative market share and market growth rate

sometimes used more loosely to denote a major shift from a negative direction to a positive one.) A **divestiture** involves an organization's selling or divesting of a business or part of a business. According to one study, when divestitures are congruent with the corporate or business strategies outlined in company publications, they have a positive effect on the price of the firm's stock. Conversely, when divestitures are conducted in the absence of clear strategic goals, they generally have a negative market effect.[43]

Under Chapter 11 of the Federal Bankruptcy Act, **bankruptcy** is a means whereby an organization that is unable to pay its debts can seek court protection from creditors and from certain contract obligations while it attempts to regain financial stability. For example, two U.S. subsidiaries of the Canada-based Campeau Corporation, the Allied Stores Corporation and Federated Department Stores, Inc., filed for bankruptcy in January 1990. Constituting the largest retailing bankruptcy in U.S. history, the chains include such well-known stores as Bloomingdale's, Abraham & Straus in New York, Rich's in Atlanta, and Burdines in Florida. The Campeau empire ran into a cash-flow problem when sales were slower than expected, and the company experienced difficulty in paying debts associated with its recent acquisitions.[44] **Liquidation** entails selling or dissolving an entire organization. Liquidation usually occurs when serious difficulties, such as bankruptcy, cannot be resolved.

Portfolio Strategy Approaches

While grand strategies address an organization's overall direction, portfolio strategy approaches help managers determine the types of businesses in which the organization should be engaged. More specifically, a **portfolio strategy approach** is a method of analyzing an organization's mix of businesses in terms of both individual and collective contributions to strategic goals. The concept is similar to the approach an individual takes when attempting to assemble a group, or portfolio, of stocks that will provide balance in terms of risk, long-term growth, and other important factors. Three of the most frequently used portfolio approaches are the BCG growth-share matrix, the GE business screen, and the product/market evolution matrix. Each uses a two-dimensional matrix, which measures one variable along one dimension and another along a second dimension to form four or more cells. Portfolio approaches apply to analyzing existing or potential strategic business units.

BCG GROWTH-SHARE MATRIX One of the earliest portfolio approaches to gain extensive use is the four-cell matrix developed by the Boston Consulting Group (BCG), a prominent management consulting firm. The **BCG growth-share matrix,** shown in Figure 4, compares various businesses in an organization's portfolio on the basis of relative market share and market growth rate. Relative market share is the ratio of a business's market share (in terms of unit volume) compared with the market share of its largest rival. Market growth rate is the growth in the market during the previous year relative to growth in the economy as a whole.[45] In the BCG matrix shown in Figure 4, each business, represented by a circle, is plotted on the matrix according to its position along both dimensions. The size of the circle indicates the business's percent revenue relative to the revenues generated by other businesses in the portfolio. The resulting matrix divides the businesses into four categories.

The *star* has a high market share in a rapidly growing market. Because of their high growth potential, stars often initially require substantial investment capital beyond what they are able to earn themselves. For example, General Electric recently spent $2.3 billion to acquire a chemical business that was part of

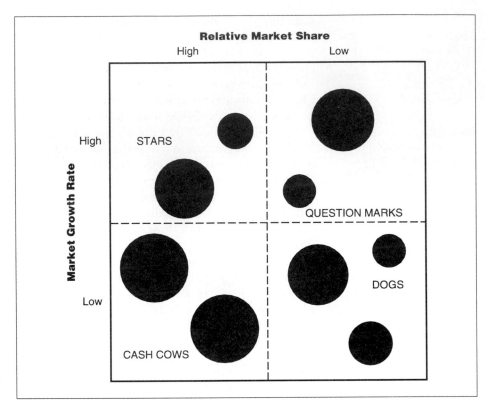

Relative Market Share

Figure 4 *BCG growth-share matrix.*

the Borg-Warner Corporation. Combined with GE's other chemical operations, this acquisition gives GE a larger presence and a star in the fast-growing plastics business.[46]

A *question mark* (often also called a *problem child*) has a low market share in a rapidly growing market. Question marks present somewhat of a dilemma for their organizations. Like stars, they require substantial investment to take advantage of the rapidly growing market, yet their low market share usually means that they have limited ability to generate large amounts of cash themselves. Thus, they are "cash hogs." For example, Cincinnati-headquartered Roto-Rooter, Inc., is best known as a service that uses a motor-driven auger to unclog drains and sewer lines. Since acquiring Roto-Rooter in the early 1980s, the Chemed Corporation has attempted to expand the company into residential plumbing repair work and industrial pipe cleaning. So far, Roto-Rooter has about 1 percent of the plumbing market, but it will take considerable further funding to build up what might be the first large national plumbing company.[47] With question marks, managers must usually either provide substantial cash to fuel growth or divest the business.

The *cash cow* has a high market share in a slowly growing market. As a result, it tends to generate more cash than is necessary to maintain its market position. Cash cows, often former stars, can be valuable in a portfolio because they can be "milked" to provide cash for stars and question marks. For instance, the drain-cleaning business of Roto-Rooter provides excess cash that has been used to open new company outlets and buy back old franchises to facilitate the buildup of the plumbing business.[48]

A *dog* has a low market share in an area of low growth. Thus it typically generates only a modest cash flow or may even have a small negative cash flow. Usually, dogs are harvested, divested, or liquidated. For example, General Electric sold a consumer electronics division that was only marginally profitable to the French electronics giant Thomson S.A. in 1988. Thomson was interested in the acquisition as a means of acquiring operations in the United States.[49]

Overall, the BCG matrix suggests using revenues from cash cows to fund the growth of stars, as well as to build the market share of the question marks with the best prospects. Dogs and the remaining question marks are usually divested unless they provide sufficient positive cash flow to justify retaining them, at least in the short run. One recent study suggests that dogs may generate more cash than they are generally given credit for and that managers, therefore, should evaluate them carefully before taking the divestiture step.[50]

The BCG matrix is useful in providing a means of viewing a set of businesses as a portfolio with differing cash flows and cash requirements.[51] The matrix also helps develop a rationale for prioritizing resource allocations across businesses, thereby assisting managers in formulating strategies for building some businesses and divesting others.

Still, the BCG matrix does have a number of shortcomings.[52] Among the most important is that it does not directly pertain to the majority of businesses that have average market shares in markets of average growth (note that the matrix has only two categories, high and low, for each dimension). In addition, generalizations based on the matrix may be misleading, since organizations with low market shares are not necessarily question marks. For example, at Germany-based Daimler-Benz, managers raise car production only after careful debate, lest the Mercedes lose its exclusive image.[53] Similarly, businesses with large market shares in slow growth markets are not necessarily cash cows. Some may actually need substantial investments to retain their market position. For example, Nabisco Brands (a division of RJR Nabisco) has about 30 percent of the cookie market (e.g., Oreos) and about half the cracker market (e.g., Ritz), with both markets growing relatively slowly. Still, RJR Nabisco had planned to spend $4 billion in capital investments to retain the division's position as a low-cost producer. The expenditures were placed on hold in 1989 because Nabisco had to pay off massive debts associated with its takeover by the investment firm of Kohlberg, Kravis, Roberts & Company.[54] Another shortcoming of the matrix is that it provides little guidance regarding which question marks to support and which dogs to salvage. Finally, one survey suggests that executives dislike the BCG terminology. According to one executive, "We try to avoid the use of words such as 'cash cow' or 'dog' like the plague. If you call a business a dog, it'll respond like one. It's one thing to know that you are an ugly duckling; much worse to be told explicitly that you are."[55] Despite these shortcomings, the BCG matrix does have research support in regard to its ability to differentiate among businesses for purposes of thinking about strategy.[56]

GE business screen A nine-cell matrix (developed by General Electric with McKinsey & Company) that is based on long-term industry attractiveness and on business strength

GE BUSINESS SCREEN Another popular portfolio matrix is the GE business screen, developed by General Electric with the help of McKinsey & Company.[57] The **GE business screen** (also often called the *GE planning grid*) is a nine-cell matrix that is based on long-term industry attractiveness and on business strength (see Figure 5). The major factors to consider in assessing these two dimensions are summarized in Figure 5. On the screen, or grid, each business is represented by a circle, with the size of the circle proportional to the size of the industry (measured by total industry sales) in which the business competes. (Note that the meaning of the circle differs from that in the BCG matrix, in which the circle represents the business's percent revenue relative to the revenues generated by other portfolio businesses.) The pie slice within the circle shows the business's market share within the industry.

In the GE screen, the three cells at the upper left corner of the matrix represent situations of long-term industry attractiveness and business strength.

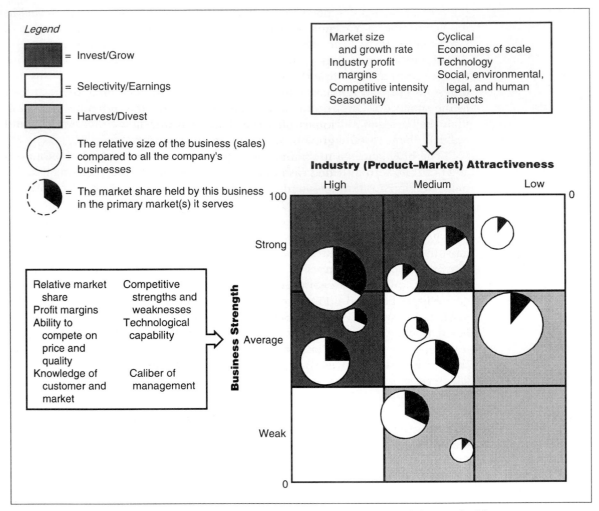

Legend

■ = Invest/Grow

□ = Selectivity/Earnings

▨ = Harvest/Divest

○ = The relative size of the business (sales) compared to all the company's businesses

◔ = The market share held by this business in the primary market(s) it serves

Relative market share
Profit margins
Ability to compete on price and quality
Knowledge of customer and market

Competitive strengths and weaknesses
Technological capability
Caliber of management

Market size and growth rate
Industry profit margins
Competitive intensity
Seasonality

Cyclical
Economies of scale
Technology
Social, environmental, legal, and human impacts

Industry (Product–Market) Attractiveness

High   Medium   Low

Business Strength

Strong
Average
Weak

Figure 5 *GE business screen. (Adapted from John A. Pearce II and Richard B. Robinson, Jr.,* Management, *McGraw-Hill, 1989, p. 209.)*

The strategic prescription for businesses in these cells is *grow and build*. The three cells at the opposite corner of the matrix (lower right) represent situations of relatively low industry attractiveness and weak business strength. The strategy here should generally be *harvest and/or divest*. The remaining cells depict mixed situations, in which the strategy is usually *hold and maintain*.

The GE business screen has three main advantages over the BCG matrix.[58] For one thing, the terminology is more palatable to managers, particularly in the harvest and/or divest section of the grid. In addition, multiple factors are considered in determining where a business fits on the two dimensions. Thus the GE screen includes more information about businesses. Finally, the three categories for industry attractiveness and business strength result in finer distinctions among businesses, particularly those that are average. Still, the screen does not specify the strategies that should be followed by various businesses, nor does it provide a means for identifying businesses that are just about to move into a period of high growth.[59]

Product/market evolution matrix A 15-cell matrix (developed by Hofer) in which businesses are plotted according to the business unit's business strength, or competitive position, and the industry's stage in the evolutionary product/market life cycle

PRODUCT/MARKET EVOLUTION MATRIX To help resolve the issue of identifying companies, particularly new businesses, that are about to accelerate their growth, strategy researcher Charles W. Hofer has suggested a further refinement.[60] The **product/market evolution matrix** (sometimes called the *life-cycle* *portfolio matrix*) is a 15-cell matrix in which businesses are plotted according to the business unit's strength, or competitive position, and the industry's stage in the evolutionary product/market life cycle (see Figure 6). The first dimension, the business unit's competitive position, is similar to the business strength, or competitive position, dimension in the GE screen. On the second dimension, however, the two approaches differ. Whereas the GE screen measures long-term industry attractiveness, the product/market evolution matrix shows the industry's stage in the evolutionary life cycle. This starts with initial development and proceeds through the growth, shakeout, maturity and saturation, and decline stages. The maturity and saturation stage is particularly important because it often lasts for an extended period of time. An industry is said to have reached *maturity* when growth slows and the market moves toward the saturation point, where demand is limited to replacement of the product or service.[61] The challenge in the maturity and saturation stage is preserving or slowly expanding market share while avoiding the decline stage.[62] As in the GE screen, the size of the circle representing each business is proportional to the size of the industry in which the business competes, while the pie slice within the circle shows the business's market share within the industry.

The data shown in Figure 6 suggest that business A has good prospects for growth and should be developed. Business B is in a rather weak competitive position and likely would be considered a dog in BCG matrix terminology. Business E is well established and would be considered a star, although it is moving toward maturity. Business F is gradually losing its competitive position but is a

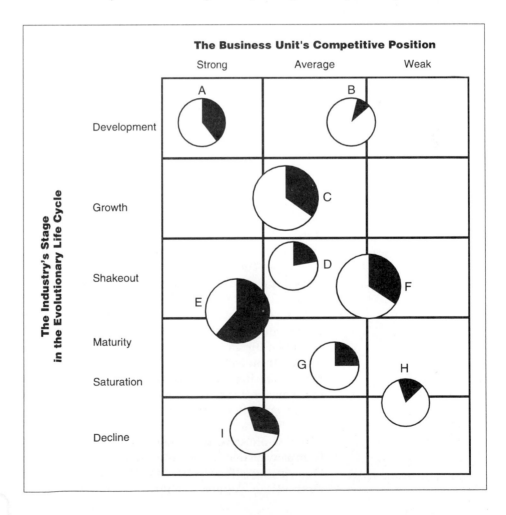

Figure 6 *Product/market evolution matrix.*

probable cash cow. Business H is most likely a candidate for divesting or liquidating and would be considered a dog.

ASSESSING THE PORTFOLIO MATRIXES   Each portfolio matrix offers a somewhat different perspective that is likely to be useful in the strategy formulation process. Therefore, it is possible to use one or more. Regardless of the number of matrixes used, each one enhances thinking about the mix of businesses in an organization's portfolio. For example, the Westinghouse Electric Corporation has recently been using a portfolio approach to divest many of its traditional businesses (e.g., light bulbs, electric motors, and transformers) in favor of more than 70 small new businesses, mainly in high-growth service sectors (such as broadcasting, financial services, truck refrigeration, and waste disposal). The new configuration of businesses, which makes the company less vulnerable to an economic downturn, has led to a significant boost in profits for Westinghouse.[63] Portfolio matrixes, however, do not provide advice about specific strategies for businesses. Such specifics are covered by strategies at the business level.

FORMULATING BUSINESS-LEVEL STRATEGY

Business-level strategy is concerned with how a particular business competes. The best-known approach for developing strategy at the SBU level is based on the research of strategy expert Michael E. Porter.

Porter's Competitive Strategies

Porter has outlined three generic business-level strategies that can be used to gain competitive advantage over other firms operating in the same industry.[64] The strategies are termed "generic" because they are applicable to a variety of situations. Still, they are more specific than the generic corporate-level strategies discussed in the previous section. Porter's competitive strategies are cost leadership, differentiation, and focus. Common requirements for successfully pursuing these strategies are summarized in Table 3.

Cost leadership strategy
A strategy outlined by Porter that involves emphasizing organizational efficiency so that the overall costs of providing products and services are lower than those of competitors

COST LEADERSHIP   A **cost leadership strategy** involves emphasizing organizational efficiency so that the overall costs of providing products and services are lower than those of competitors. With this low-cost approach, careful attention must be paid to minimizing necessary costs in every aspect of the business. This entails developing efficient production methods, keeping tight controls on overhead and administrative costs, seeking savings by procuring supplies at low prices, and monitoring costs in other areas (such as promotion, distribution, and service). Lower costs enable an organization to offer lower prices and thus gain an edge over competitors. They can also lead to above-average profits because of higher profit margins or large sales volumes. For instance, Louisville-based Humana, Inc., a publicly owned health-care company, has recently been achieving a significantly higher return on equity than others in the industry and has been realizing pretax profit margins of around 10 percent. According to Humana, this success stems from the fact that the company is the lowest-cost producer of health care in the United States.[65]

Of course, for a cost leadership strategy to be effective, lower costs cannot come at the expense of necessary quality. This was shown at the H. J. Heinz Company when its low-cost strategy led to difficulties at its Ore-Ida division. Cost-cutting efforts related to the strategy caused changes in manufacturing methods for popular Tater Tots frozen spuds. As a result, the Tater Tot insides

TABLE 3	Common Requirements for Successfully Pursuing Porter's Competitive Strategies	
Generic Strategy	**Commonly Required Skills and Resources**	**Common Organizational Requirements**
Overall cost leadership	Sustained capital investment and access to capital Process engineering skills Intense supervision of labor Products designed for ease in manufacture Low-cost distribution system	Tight cost control Frequent, detailed control reports Structured organization and responsibilities Incentives based on meeting strict quantitative targets
Differentiation	Strong marketing abilities Product engineering Creative flair Strong capability in basic research Corporate reputation for quality or technological leadership Long tradition in the industry or unique combination of skills drawn from other businesses Strong cooperation from channels	Strong coordination among functions in R&D, product development, and marketing Subjective measurement and incentives instead of quantitative measures Amenities to attract highly skilled labor, scientists, or creative people
Focus	Combination of the above policies directed at the particular strategic target	Combination of the above policies directed at the particular strategic target

Source: Reprinted from Michael E. Porter, *Competitive Strategy,* Free Press, New York, 1980, pp. 40–41.

were mushy and the outsides had lost their light and crispy coating. Ultimately, sales began to decline. With the changes reversed, Tater Tots now have more than 55 percent of the market for frozen fried potatoes.[66]

A low-cost strategy is not without risks. To be effective, the strategy usually requires that a business be *the* cost leader, not just one of several. Two or more businesses vying for cost leadership can engage in a rivalry that drives profits down to extremely low levels. Therefore, the business must have a cost advantage that is not easily or inexpensively imitated, and it must stay abreast of new technologies that can alter the cost curve. In addition, managers must still consider making some product or service innovations, at least the ones that are very important to customers. Otherwise, competitors using a differentiation strategy may lure customers away with significant product or service improvements.

Differentiation strategy A strategy outlined by Porter that involves attempting to develop products and services that are viewed as unique in the industry

DIFFERENTIATION A **differentiation strategy** involves attempting to develop products and services that are viewed as unique in the industry. Successful differentiation allows the business to charge premium prices, leading to above-average profits. Differentiation can take many forms; for example, design or brand image (Coach in handbags, Ralph Lauren in menswear), technology (Hewlett-Packard in laser printers, Coleman in camping equipment), customer service (IBM in computers, Nordstrom's in apparel retailing), features (Jenn-Air in electric ranges), quality (Xerox in copiers, Swarovski in rhinestones), and selection (Echlin in auto parts). Kimberly-Clark adopted this strategy with the introduction of its Huggies Pull-Ups, disposable training pants that are a cross between absorbable diapers and underwear. This unique product brought sales of more than $500 million in its first year on the market, and it is expected to be the industry leader for some time, as no other manufacturer has a similar offering.[67] With differentiation, perceptions of product or service uniqueness are more important than costs. However, a company still cannot afford to ignore costs.

There are a few vulnerabilities associated with a differentiation strategy. If prices are too high, customers may choose less costly alternatives, even though they forego some desirable features. Also, customer tastes and needs can change, so businesses following a differentiation strategy must carefully assess customers' shifting requirements. Differentiation, of course, works best when the differentiating factor is both important to customers and difficult for competitors to imitate. While differentiation is usually aimed at a fairly broad market, a focus strategy concentrates on a narrow niche.

Focus strategy A strategy outlined by Porter that entails specializing by establishing a position of overall cost leadership, differentiation, or both, but only within a particular portion, or segment, of an entire market

FOCUS A **focus strategy** entails specializing by establishing a position of overall cost leadership, differentiation, or both, but only within a particular portion, or segment, of an entire market. The segment may be a group of customers, a geographic area, or a part of the product or service line. The rationale is that a market segment can be served more effectively by an organization that specializes than by competitors that attempt to cover the entire market. The focus strategy still relies on a low-cost or a differentiation approach, or perhaps both, to establish a strong position within the particular market segment, or niche. Differentiation within a focus strategy can occur by tailoring products to the specialized needs of the market segment. This may simultaneously produce a cost advantage, since a firm that specializes may be able to offer better prices on custom orders than a firm that has the cost of leadership in serving the larger-volume needs of the broader market. A company that has successfully used a focus strategy is Baxters of Speyside (see the following Case in Point discussion).

CASE IN POINT

BAXTERS OF SPEYSIDE FOCUSES ON SPECIALTY FOODS

"We take the produce of the hills and glens of Bonnie Scotland and make beautiful things," says Gordon Baxter, chairman, summing up the basic approach that has made Scotland's specialty food producer, Baxters of Speyside, a major success. Baxters of Speyside has become a popular brand name in Britain and is increasingly well known elsewhere for its premium soups, jams, and other specialties. For example, the company offers soups with such intriguing names as Cream of Pheasant, Cream of Scampi, Cock-a-Leekie, and Royal Game. These innovative products have helped establish the company's reputation in Britain's premium-food market, where overseas customers are willing to pay as much as twice the price of competing brands for Baxters specialties. Baxter's wife, Ena, developed most of the exotic recipes. Now, a team of chefs and food technologists help her.

The family-run company, with annual sales topping $40 million, has evolved from a grocery store founded in 1868 by Baxter's grandfather. Baxter's father added a jam factory and began selling items to two of Britain's best-known department stores, Harrods and Fortnum & Mason, during the 1920s and 1930s. After the company nearly went out of business during World War II, Baxter and his brother rebuilt and expanded it. Since then, several of Baxter's children have joined the company, adding a fourth generation of involvement.

Capitalizing on its unusual products and location, Baxter and his entourage often wear kilts and even bring along bagpipes on sales trips to the United States.

''Scotland is very projectable,'' he says. According to one salesperson at Harrods in London, Baxters of Speyside products sell partly because customers visualize the product being carefully stirred by hand in a pot, even though the foods are made in a modern factory.

Sales began to grow significantly when Baxter was able to persuade some of Britain's chain retailers to carry the premium brand. As a result, the company has about 77 percent of Britain's premium soup market.

With only about 4 percent of its total sales in the United States, the potential for growth is great. Not surprisingly, Baxter's files contain letters from many U.S. companies, such as General Foods, General Mills, Campbell, and Heinz, expressing interest in purchasing Baxters of Speyside. Baxters operates within its cash flow; the company has no debt. The Baxter family owns 96.5 percent of the shares. Profit margins are above the industry average.[68] ■ ■ ■

Despite the success of Baxters of Speyside, adopting a focus strategy involves several risks that a business needs to guard against. For one thing, costs for the focused firm may become too great relative to those of less focused competitors. As time goes on, differentiation can become less of an advantage, since competitors serving broader markets may embellish their products. In addition, competitors may begin focusing on a group *within* the customer population being served by the focused firm. For example, Roadway Package Systems (RPS) is attempting to invade the market for door-to-door ground delivery of packages, currently dominated by United Parcel Service (UPS). RPS has contracts with 2500 individuals, who lease or buy distinctive white RPS delivery trucks. Each individual picks up and delivers packages in a particular territory for RPS. These independents are paid only for work performed, whereas UPS employees typically receive higher, unionized wages and generous benefits. While UPS limits packages to 70 pounds and delivers to residents as well as businesses, RPS has set a 100-pound limit and restricts delivery to businesses. With about 150 terminals so far, RPS can deliver to approximately 75 percent of the United States, and another 80 terminals are planned by the late 1990s.[69]

Regardless of which generic strategy is used, the ability to carry it out successfully depends on distinctive competencies. Such competencies typically develop at the functional level.

FORMULATING FUNCTIONAL-LEVEL STRATEGY

Functional-level strategies spell out the specific ways that functional areas can be used to bolster the business-level strategy. For example, under a product differentiation strategy, the R&D department might be called upon to accelerate the innovation process in order to provide new products in advance of the competition. Similarly, to support the new product lines, marketing might develop a plan that calls for premium prices, distribution through prestigious locations, and a special promotion scheme aimed at targeted market segments. Operations, the function that is responsible for actually producing the product, might devise a functional strategy based on using excellent raw materials, incorporating the latest technology, and subcontracting some components in order to produce a premium product.

In essence, strategies at the functional level can be extremely important in supporting a business-level strategy. Typically, the functional areas develop the distinctive competencies that lead to potential competitive advantages. Such competencies do not usually occur by chance. Instead, they need to be carefully conceived and may take several years to develop. For example, the talent that Disney has accumulated in its Imagineering group provides a distinctive competence that helps the company continually innovate.

STRATEGY IMPLEMENTATION

While strategy formulation is an important part of the strategic management process, strategies are unlikely to have the intended impact unless they are implemented effectively. Strategy implementation involves any management activities that are needed to put the strategy in motion, institute strategic controls for monitoring progress, and ultimately achieve organizational goals (see Figure 7).

Carrying Out Strategic Plans

Strategy implementation experts Jay R. Galbraith and Robert K. Kazanjian suggest that several major internal aspects of the organization may need to be synchronized in order to put a chosen strategy into action. Principal factors (shown in Figure 7) are technology, human resources, reward systems, decision processes, and structure.[70] The factors tend to be interconnected, so a change in one may necessitate changes in one or more others.

TECHNOLOGY Technology comprises the knowledge, tools, equipment, and work techniques used by an organization in delivering its product or service. Technology is often an important factor in strategy implementation because the technological emphasis must fit the strategic thrust. Organizational strategy, at all levels, must consider the technical functions of the business.[71] For example, if an organization pursues a low-cost strategy, changes in technology may be necessary to reduce costs. Following a differentiation strategy may also entail technological change in order to develop and/or produce the enhanced products or services.

HUMAN RESOURCES Human resources are the individuals who are members of the organization. Having the individuals with the necessary skills in the appropriate positions is a prerequisite for effective strategy implementation.[72] This is accomplished by conducting strategic human resource planning, which links the human resource needs with the strategies to be pursued. Furthermore, the skills and experience of an organization's human resources are often a source of competitive advantage. A skilled work force usually has a greater ability to find

Figure 7 *The strategy implementation phase of the strategic management process.*

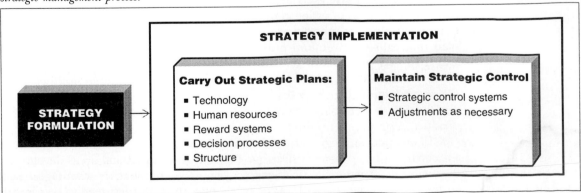

ways to reduce costs or produce new products or services than does a less experienced staff.

REWARD SYSTEMS Reward systems include bonuses, awards, or promotions provided by others, as well as intangible rewards such as personal feelings of achievement and challenge. Carefully considered reward systems are likely to constitute an important source of motivation to support a given strategy. For example, at Albertson's, Inc., a major food and drug retail chain with stores in 17 Sunbelt and western states, employee bonuses are based on profits in order to encourage productivity and better service.[73] Specific rewards may be matched to the type of strategy being pursued. Thus a manager in an organization following a stability strategy might receive a bonus for a job well done, whereas a manager following a growth strategy may be given stock in the expanded venture as a reward for meeting organizational goals.[74]

DECISION PROCESSES Decision processes include the means of resolving questions and problems that occur in organizations. Issues of resource allocation are particularly important to strategy implementation because strategic plans are more likely to be successful when the resources they call for are readily available. Decision-making processes can also help resolve specific problems and issues that arise during the course of implementing the plan.

STRUCTURE Organization structure is the formal pattern of interactions and coordination designed by management to link the tasks of individuals and groups in achieving organizational goals. Such patterns help various parts of the organization coordinate their efforts. The broad outline of an organization's structure is often depicted in an organization chart. Current research suggests that strategies may be more successful when the structure supports the strategic direction.

Maintaining Strategic Control

While a variety of factors must be considered in carrying out strategic plans, managers also need to be able to monitor progress. They do so through strategic control. This involves monitoring critical environmental factors that could affect the viability of strategic plans, assessing the effects of organizational strategic actions, and ensuring that strategic plans are implemented as intended. Instituting strategic control includes designing information systems that provide feedback on the way strategic plans are being carried out, as well as on their apparent effects. Such systems enable managers to make adjustments in the implementation of strategic plans, as necessary.

CHAPTER SUMMARY

Strategic management is a process through which managers formulate and implement strategies geared toward optimizing strategic goal achievement. The part of the strategic management process that includes identifying the mission and strategic goals, conducting competitive analysis, and developing specific strategies is often referred to as strategy formulation. The part of the process that focuses on carrying out strategic plans and maintaining control over how those plans are carried out is known

as strategy implementation. The overall process helps organizations identify and develop a competitive advantage, a significant edge over the competition in dealing with competitive forces.

Many organizations develop strategies at three different levels: corporate, business, and functional. Corporate-level strategy addresses what businesses the organization will operate, how the strategies of those businesses will be coordinated to strengthen the organization's competitive position, and how resources will be allocated among the businesses. Business-level strategy concentrates on the best means of competing within a particular business while also supporting the corporate-level strategy. Functional-level strategy focuses on action plans for managing a particular functional area within a business in a way that supports the business-level strategy.

Before attempting to devise an effective strategy, managers need to assess both the environmental and the organizational factors that influence an organization's ability to compete effectively. One general method is SWOT analysis, which involves assessing organizational strengths (S) and weaknesses (W), as well as environmental opportunities (O) and threats (T). Porter's five competitive forces model helps analyze the nature and intensity of competition in a given industry in terms of five major forces: rivalry, bargaining power of customers, bargaining power of suppliers, threat of new entrants, and threat of substitute products or services. A common aid in assessing internal organizational strengths and weaknesses is the functional audit.

Corporate strategy development generally involves selecting a grand strategy and using portfolio strategy approaches to determine the various businesses that will make up the organization. The three basic types of grand strategies are growth (including concentration, vertical integration, and diversification), stability, and defensive (including harvest, turnaround, divestiture, bankruptcy, and liquidation). Three of the most frequently used portfolio approaches are the BCG growth-share matrix, the GE business screen, and the product/market evolution matrix.

At the business level, use of Porter's competitive strategies, which include cost leadership, differentiation, and focus strategies, constitutes the best-known approach. Functional-level strategies specify major ways that functional areas can be used to bolster the business-level strategy.

In carrying out strategic plans, managers need to consider major internal aspects of the organization that may need to be synchronized. Such aspects include technology, human resources, reward systems, decision processes, and structure. Strategy implementation also includes maintaining strategic control. This involves monitoring critical environmental factors that could affect the viability of strategic plans, assessing the effects of organizational strategic actions, and ensuring that strategic plans are implemented as intended.

QUESTIONS FOR DISCUSSION AND REVIEW

1 Explain the concept of strategic management and the notion of competitive advantage. Identify an organization that you think has a competitive advantage in its industry, and describe the nature of its advantage.

2 Outline the major components of the strategic management process. Explain why engaging in strategic management is likely to be beneficial for an organization.

3 Distinguish among the three levels of strategy. Explain the role of each in an organization that has separate divisions that compete in different industries.

4 Explain SWOT analysis. Conduct a brief SWOT analysis of your college or university by developing two items for each of the four SWOT categories.

5 Outline Porter's five competitive forces model. Use the model to assess the nature and intensity of competition in an industry with which you are familiar.

6 Describe the three major generic strategies available at the corporate level, and explain the subcategories within each. For each generic strategy, identify an organization that appears to be pursuing that particular strategy.

7 Contrast the three major approaches to portfolio strategy at the corporate level. If you were on the strategic planning staff of a major company with 35 different businesses, which approach would you recommend and why?

8 Describe Porter's competitive strategies for the business level. Assess the competitive strategy of an organization with which you are familiar, and explain its usefulness in dealing with Porter's five competitive forces.

9 Explain the role of strategies at the functional level. Describe the connection between functional strategies and distinctive competence. What distinctive competencies exist at Baxters of Speyside?

10 Outline the process of strategy implementation. Which corporate-level generic strategy do you believe is being pursued by your college or university? Evaluate the effectiveness of strategy implementation at your college or university.

DISCUSSION QUESTIONS FOR CHAPTER OPENING CASE

1 What type of grand strategy does the Walt Disney Company appear to be pursuing? Cite evidence to support your conclusion.

2 Use Porter's five competitive forces model to analyze the competitive situation facing the Walt Disney Company.

3 Which of Porter's competitive strategies best characterizes the strategy being used by the various Disney businesses, such as the theme parks and resorts, consumer-products, and filmed entertainment divisions?

Assess the appropriateness of the strategy. To what extent would each of Porter's competitive strategies be appropriate for each of the divisions?

MANAGEMENT EXERCISE: DEVELOPING A STRATEGY FOR PMB

 You have been an extremely successful entrepreneur. Your Pedal More Bicycle (PMB) Company has more than doubled its sales each year for the past 10 years. PMB manufactures various types of bicycles, including racing and mountain bikes. PMB also makes accessories, such as seat covers, travel packs, and reflectors, and does a brisk business in bicycle parts. Your company has been successful by offering better quality and more innovative designs and features than can be obtained from competitors. Last year, your firm went public and was an instant hit on the market, making the controlling interest that you retained worth a great deal of money. PMB still has considerable growth potential. Nevertheless, you are now ready to take on new challenges. PMB has a sound reputation, which will be an asset if you want to borrow money to expand your business. You are aware of several current business opportunities:

1 The Winston Roller Bearing Company, a manufacturer of fabricated steel products and roller bearings, can be purchased for a fair price. The company is currently family-owned.

2 The Roxborough Leather Company, which produces leather goods for automobiles and shoes, can be acquired or leased on a long-term basis.

3 A Harley-Davidson motorcycle sales franchise is available in your area.

4 A very good location for an auto-parts outlet is going to be available within the next year. The information you have at this time indicates that such an outlet would be received very well in the area.

5 A small chain of three retail bicycle outlets will soon be offered for sale because the owners want to move back to their hometown, about 800 miles away. The outlets have done reasonably well, but improvements could be made that would probably increase sales dramatically.

6 The XYZ computer outlet, a retailer of home computers and software, is looking for a buyer. The current owners, who have been very successful, want to retire and move to the family farm in southern California.

You believe that sufficient funds could be raised to acquire two of these businesses. However, there are probably other considerations. Assume that PMB has strong manufacturing and marketing capabilities and no glaring internal weaknesses relative to competitors in the bicycle business. Develop a grand strategy for PMB, and use a portfolio strategy approach to analyze the various business alternatives. Choose one of Porter's generic strategies for each business that you select. Be prepared to explain the reasoning behind your choices.

REFERENCES

1. Based on Stephen J. Sansweet, "Disney's "Imagineers' Build Space Attraction Using High-Tech Gear," *The Wall Street Journal*, Jan. 6, 1987, pp. 1, 24; Ronald Grover, "Disney's Magic," *Business Week*, Mar. 9, 1987, pp. 62–69; Walter Roessing, "Michael D. Eisner, Frank G. Wells, the Walt Disney Company," *Sky*, September 1987, pp. 50–56; Stephen Koepp, "Do You Believe in Magic?" *Time*, Apr. 25, 1988, pp. 66–73; Howard Rudnitsky, "Mickey Is Eating My Lunch!" *Forbes*, Sept. 18, 1989, pp. 86–92; Christopher Knowlton, "How Disney Keeps the Magic Going," *Fortune*, Dec. 4, 1989, pp. 111–132;

Richard Turner, "Disney's Ship May Come in at Long Beach," *The Wall Street Journal*, Feb. 6, 1990, p. B1; "Disney Plans Massive Mall, Residential Project in Florida," *The Washington Post*, Mar. 13, 1990, p. C4; Pauline Yoshihashi, "Disney, Mattel to Strengthen Ties in Toyland," *The Wall Street Journal*, Nov. 12, 1991, p. B1; Thomas R. King, "Disney Plans Resort in Home Sweet Anaheim," *The Wall Street Journal*, Dec. 13, 1991, p. B1; Michael Duckworth, "Disney Plans to Re-enter China Market as Beijing Promises Copyright Reforms," *The Wall Street Journal*, Mar. 23, 1992, p. A7B; "Walt Disney to

Close Disney Kitchens at Its Retail Stores," *The Wall Street Journal*, Mar. 30, 1992, p. B15; and Richard Turner and Peter Gumbel, "As Euro Disney Braces for Its Grand Opening, the French Go Goofy," *The Wall Street Journal*, Apr. 10, 1992, p. A1.

2. Lawrence R. Jauch and William F. Glueck, *Business Policy and Strategic Management*, 5th ed., McGraw-Hill, New York, 1988; John A. Pearce II and Richard B. Robinson, Jr., *Strategic Management: Strategy Formulation and Implementation*, 3d ed., Irwin, Homewood, Ill., 1988.

3. Arthur A. Thompson, Jr., and A. J. Strickland III, *Strategic Management:*

Concepts and Cases, 6th ed., BPI/Irwin, Homewood, Ill., 1992.

4. Ibid., and Leslie W. Rue and Phyllis G. Holland, *Strategic Management: Concepts and Experiences,* 2d ed., McGraw-Hill, New York, 1989.

5. Arthur A. Thompson, Jr., and A. J. Strickland III, *Strategic Management: Concepts and Cases,* 6th ed., BPI/Irwin, Homewood, Ill., 1992.

6. Ibid.

7. Michael E. Porter, *Competitive Advantage: Creating and Sustaining Superior Performance,* Free Press, New York, 1985.

8. Steve Weiner, "Electrifying," *Forbes,* Nov. 30, 1987, pp. 196–198.

9. Warren Keith Schilit, "An Examination of the Influence of Middle-Level Managers in Formulating and Implementing Strategic Decisions," *Journal of Management Studies,* May 1987, pp. 271–293.

10. Ibid.

11. Arthur A. Thompson, Jr., and A. J. Strickland III, *Strategic Management: Concepts and Cases,* 6th ed., BPI/Irwin, Homewood, Ill., 1992. Thompson and Strickland also include an operating strategy level that addresses strategy for managers within functional areas.

12. Ibid.

13. Robert Mueller, "Criteria for the Appraisal of Directors," *Harvard Business Review,* vol. 57, 1979, pp. 48–56.

14. Leslie W. Rue and Phyllis G. Holland, *Strategic Management: Concepts and Experiences,* 2d ed., McGraw-Hill, New York, 1989.

15. John A. Pearce II and Richard B. Robinson, Jr., *Strategic Management: Strategy Formulation and Implementation,* 3d ed., Irwin, Homewood, Ill., 1988.

16. Arthur A. Thompson, Jr., and A. J. Strickland III, *Strategic Management: Concepts and Cases,* 6th ed., BPI/Irwin, Homewood, Ill., 1992.

17. Ibid.

18. Patrick M. Reilly, "As Magazine Industry Faces a Shakeout, Some Publishers Start to Close the Books," *The Wall Street Journal,* Jan. 31, 1990, pp. B1, B4.

19. Norm Alster, "Unlevel Playing Field," *Forbes,* June 26, 1989, pp. 53–57.

20. Stewart Toy, "Waiter, a Magnum of Your Best Portland Champagne," *Business Week,* Dec. 11, 1989, pp. 92–94.

21. Julia Flynn Siler, "A Warning Shot from the King of Beers," *Business Week,* Dec. 18, 1989, p. 124.

22. Betsy Morris, "Coke Unveils Compact Dispenser, Hoping to Sell More Soft Drinks in Small Offices," *The Wall Street Journal,* Nov. 17, 1988, p. B1.

23. Charles W. L. Hill and Gareth R. Jones, *Strategic Management: An Integrated Approach,* Houghton Mifflin, Boston, 1989.

24. Ibid.

25. Toni Mack, "Playing with the Majors," *Forbes,* Nov. 13, 1989, pp. 92–94.

26. Leslie W. Rue and Phyllis G. Holland, *Strategic Management: Concepts and Experiences,* 2d ed., McGraw-Hill, New York, 1989.

27. Ibid.

28. Arthur A. Thompson, Jr., and A. J. Strickland III, *Strategic Management: Concepts and Cases,* 6th ed., BPI/Irwin, Homewood, Ill., 1992.

29. John A. Pearce II and Richard B. Robinson, Jr., *Strategic Management: Strategy Formulation and Implementation,* 3d ed., Irwin, Homewood, Ill., 1988.

30. This section relies heavily on Leslie W. Rue and Phyllis G. Holland, *Strategic Management: Concepts and Experiences,* 2d ed., McGraw-Hill, New York, 1989.

31. E. S. Browning, "Long-Term Thinking and Paternalistic Ways Carry Michelin to Top," *The Wall Street Journal,* Jan. 5, 1990, pp. A1, A8.

32. Ted Kumpecb and Piet T. Bolwijn, "Manufacturing: The New Case for Vertical Integration," *Harvard Business Review,* March–April 1988, pp. 75–81.

33. Richard Behar, "Spreading the Wealth," *Forbes,* Aug. 10, 1987, pp. 74–81; Leonard Shapiro, "To Beaman, It's a Flat-Out Tour de Force," *The Washington Post,* Jan. 9, 1992, p. B3.

34. Kathryn Rudie Harrigan, "Vertical Integration and Corporate Strategy," *Academy of Management Journal,* vol. 28, 1985, pp. 397–425.

35. Raphael Amit and Joshua Livnat,

"A Concept of Conglomerate Diversification," *Journal of Management,* vol. 14, 1988, pp. 593–604.

36. Howard Banks, "Being a Conglomerate Is Not All Bad," *Forbes,* Dec. 11, 1989, pp. 40–41.

37. Based on Brian O'Reilly, "Leslie Wexner Knows What Women Want," *Fortune,* Aug. 19, 1985, pp. 154–160; Steven B. Weiner, "The Unlimited?" *Forbes,* Apr. 6, 1987, pp. 76–80; Carol Hymowitz, "Limited Inc. Struggles to Lure Back Customers," *The Wall Street Journal,* Oct. 13, 1988, p. B6; "The Limited's Approach," *Chain Store Age Executive,* December 1988, pp. 28–36; Carol Hymowitz, "Upscale Look for Limited Puts Retailer Back on Track," *The Wall Street Journal,* Feb. 24, 1989, pp. B1, B5; Laura Zinn, "Maybe the Limited Has Limits after All," *Business Week,* Mar. 18, 1991; "Michael Jeffries Named Head of Abercrombie & Fitch," *Women's Wear Daily,* Feb. 18, 1992, p. 27; "Urban Warfare; The Gap and The Limited in Manhattan," *Women's Wear Daily,* Apr. 21, 1992, p. 10; and Stephanie Strom, "Chain Takes Fashion Tongue—in Chic," *The New York Times,* Apr. 21, 1992, p. D1.

38. John A. Pearce and James W. Harvey, "Concentrated Growth Strategies," *Academy of Management Executive,* vol. 4, no. 1, 1990, pp. 61–68.

39. David J. Jefferson, "Dream to Nightmare: When Growth Gets Out of Hand," *The Wall Street Journal,* Jan. 23, 1990, p. B2.

40. John A. Pearce II and Richard B. Robinson, Jr., *Strategic Management: Strategy Formulation and Implementation,* 3d ed., Irwin, Homewood, Ill., 1988.

41. Arthur A. Thompson, Jr., and A. J. Strickland III, *Strategic Management: Concepts and Cases,* 6th ed., BPI/Irwin, Homewood, Ill., 1992.

42. Jack Willoughby, "The Last Iceman," *Forbes,* July 13, 1987, pp. 183–204.

43. Cynthia A. Montgomery, Ann R. Thomas, and Rajan Kamath, "Divestiture, Market Valuation, and Strategy," *Academy of Management Journal,* vol. 27, 1984, pp. 830–840.

44. "Bankruptcy Petition Brings Fresh Risks for Allied, Federated,"

The Wall Street Journal, Jan. 16, 1990, pp. A1, A10; Todd Mason, "It'll Be a Hard Sell," *Business Week,* Jan. 29, 1990, pp. 30–31.

45. Sometimes other criteria, such as a 10 percent growth rate, are used to gauge high and low market growth; see Leslie W. Rue and Phyllis G. Holland, *Strategic Management: Concepts and Experiences,* 2d ed., McGraw-Hill, New York, 1989.

46. Janet Guyon, "GE to Acquire Borg-Warner's Chemical Lines," *The Wall Street Journal,* June 17, 1988, p. 3.

47. Richard Phalon, "Roto-Rooter's New Drill," *Forbes,* Dec. 11, 1989, pp. 176–178.

48. Ibid.

49. Laura Landro and Douglas R. Sease, "General Electric to Sell Consumer Electronics Lines to Thomson SA for Its Medical Gear Business, Cash," *The Wall Street Journal,* July 23, 1987, p. 3; Janet Guyon, "GE Chairman Welch, Though Much Praised, Starts to Draw Critics," *The Wall Street Journal,* Aug. 4, 1988, pp. 1, 8.

50. Donald C. Hambrick, Ian C. MacMillan, and Diana L. Day, "Strategic Attributes and Performance in the BCG Matrix: A PIMS-Based Analysis of Industrial Product Businesses," *Academy of Management Journal,* vol. 25, 1982, pp. 510–531.

51. Arthur A. Thompson, Jr., and A. J. Strickland III, *Strategic Management: Concepts and Cases,* 6th ed., BPI/Irwin, Homewood, Ill., 1992.

52. Ibid.

53. Graham Turner, "Inside Europe's Giant Companies: Daimler-Benz Goes Top of the League," *Long Range Planning,* vol. 19, 1986, pp. 12–17.

54. Bill Saporito, "The Tough Cookie at RJR Nabisco," *Fortune,* July 18, 1988, pp. 32–46; Peter Waldman, "New RJR Chief Faces a Daunting Challenge at Debt-Heavy Firm," *The Wall Street Journal,* Mar. 14, 1989, pp. A1, A19.

55. Anil K. Gupta and V. Govindarajan, "Build, Hold, Harvest: Converting Strategic Intentions into Reality," *Journal of Business Strategy,* March 1984, pp. 34–47.

56. Donald C. Hambrick, Ian C. Macmillan, and Diana L. Day, "Strategic Attributes and Performance in the BCG Matrix: A PIMS-Based Analysis of Industrial Product Businesses," *Academy of Management Journal,* vol. 25, 1982, pp. 510–531.

57. This section is based mainly on Charles W. L. Hill and Gareth R. Jones, *Strategic Management: An Integrated Approach,* Houghton Mifflin, Boston, 1989; and Arthur A. Thompson, Jr., and A. J. Strickland III, *Strategic Management: Concepts and Cases,* 6th ed., BPI/Irwin, Homewood, Ill., 1992.

58. John A. Pearce II and Richard B. Robinson, Jr., *Strategic Management: Strategy Formulation and Implementation,* 3d ed., Irwin, Homewood, Ill., 1988.

59. Charles W. Hofer and Dan Schendel, *Strategy Formulation: Analytical Concepts,* West, St. Paul, Minn., 1978.

60. Arthur A. Thompson, Jr., and A. J. Strickland III, *Strategic Management: Concepts and Cases,* 6th ed., BPI/Irwin, Homewood, Ill., 1992.

61. Charles W. L. Hill and Gareth R. Jones, *Strategic Management: An Integrated Approach,* Houghton Mifflin, Boston, 1989.

62. Malcolm Schofield and David Arnold, "Strategies for Mature Businesses," *Long Range Planning,* vol. 21, 1988, pp. 69–76.

63. Gregory Stricharchuk, "Westinghouse Relies on Ruthless Pruning," *The Wall Street Journal,* Jan. 24, 1990, p. A4.

64. This section is based mainly on Michael E. Porter, *Competitive Strategy: Techniques for Analyzing Industries and Competitors,* Free Press, New York, 1980.

65. James Cook, "We're the Low-Cost Producer," *Forbes,* Dec. 25, 1989, pp. 65–66.

66. Gregory L. Miles, "Heinz Ain't Broke, but It's Doing a Lot of Fixing," *Business Week,* Dec. 11, 1989, pp. 84–88.

67. Alecia Swasy, "Kimberly-Clark Bets, Wins on Innovation," *The Wall Street Journal,* Nov. 22, 1991, p. A5.

68. Based on Richard C. Morais, "Cock-a-Leekie," *Forbes,* Sept. 7, 1987, pp. 68–69.

69. Kerry Hannon, "Shifting Gears," *Forbes,* Dec. 11, 1989, pp. 124–130.

70. Jay R. Galbraith and Robert K. Kazanjian, *Strategy Implementation: Structure, Systems and Process,* 2d ed., West, St. Paul, Minn., 1986.

71. Paul S. Adler, D. William McDonald, and Fred MacDonald, "Strategic Management of Technical Functions," *Sloan Management Review,* Winter 1992, pp. 19–26.

72. Charles W. L. Hill and Gareth R. Jones, *Strategic Management: An Integrated Approach,* Houghton Mifflin, Boston, 1989.

73. Marc Beauchamp, "Food for Thought," *Forbes,* Apr. 17, 1989, p. 73.

74. Helen Deresky and Theodore Herbert, "Senior Management Implications of Strategic Human Resource Management Programs," in *Proceedings, Human Resources Management Organizational Behavior Conference,* Association of Management, November 1986.

ACKNOWLEDGMENTS

Tables

Table 1: G. G. Dess and A. Miller, *Strategic Management,* McGraw-Hill, 1993, p. 364.

Tables 2, 3: Reprinted with the permission of The Free Press, a division of Macmillan, Inc. from *Competitive Strategy: Techniques for Analyzing Industries and Competitors* by Michael E. Porter. Copyright © 1980 by The Free Press.

Figures

Figure 2: Adapted from John A. Pearce II and Richard B. Robinson, Jr., "Levels of Strategy," *Management:* p. 206, 1989. Copyright © McGraw-Hill, 1989.

Figure 5: Adapted from John A. Pearce II and Richard B. Robinson, Jr., *Management,* McGraw-Hill, 1989, p. 209.

CONCLUDING CASE

CRAY RESEARCH, INC., FACES STIFF COMPETITION

In the field of supercomputers, one name stands out: Cray. Cray Research, Inc., was founded in Minneapolis, Minnesota, by Seymour Cray in 1972, with the goal of building the world's fastest computers.

Originally, the Cray staff estimated that there was a world market for about 80 to 100 of the ultraspeed computers, which currently can cost more than $30 million each. The market, made up primarily of government agencies and very large firms, has grown to well over $1 billion in sales and leases. Supercomputers are used for such business applications as analyzing billions of pieces of data to determine which stocks to buy and sell, assessing how new car designs will fare on the road without building expensive prototypes, and testing supersonic aircraft designs to determine how aircraft will perform at speeds that are difficult to simulate.

Cray's strategy is based on two broad thrusts: build supercomputers that dominate the high end, middle range, and low end of the supercomputer market, and develop and provide the software to be used with Cray machines. Cray pursues this strategy in several ways.

At the high end of the market, Cray Research is continuing to make and improve the Y-MP series introduced in 1988. The latest version, which costs $30.5 million, has a central processing unit that can perform 1 billion mathematical operations a second, or one gigaflop. The system has a peak capacity of 16 gigaflops. Cray is currently working on a project with Sun Microsystems that will link 1000 or more microprocessors,

producing computer speeds of up to 1 trillion calculations a second.

Separately, the Cray Computer Corporation, a company owned by Cray Research, Inc., and headed by Cray Research founder Seymour Cray, has been struggling with the development of the Cray 3. This midrange supercomputer is based on new technology involving semiconductors that are significantly faster at handling data than are the silicon chips used by other supercomputers. This is to be followed by the even more sophisticated Cray 4 in the mid-1990s. Cray Computer Corporation is currently reviewing a joint marketing arrangement with rival supercomputer makers for producing and distributing massively parallel supercomputer systems in which several microprocessors are linked.

At the low end of the market, Cray Research has introduced a computer that sells for about $300,000. Through a cooperative arrangement, the machine is being sold by the Digital Equipment Corporation's sales staff. This computer is very popular, and annual sales of more than 350 units are being projected for the future.

At Cray, software is designed while the supercomputers are being developed. This arrangement gives Cray a competitive edge because Cray is currently the only company that both builds supercomputers and develops its own custom-prepared software for the machines.

However, the competition is close on the heels of Cray. HSNX, a U.S. subsidiary of NEC, recently bested Cray when it secured a contract to build a supercomputer for the Canadian Meteorological Center. Both NEC and Fujitsu are bidding against Cray for the sale of several supercomputers to U.S.

government agencies. Convex Computer, based in Richardson, Texas, recently sold a mini-supercomputer to Northwest Airlines, which needed the computing power for crew and maintenance scheduling. Elroy Olson, Northwest's director of crew utilization, explained that "the Cray was faster than the Convex, but the cost was prohibitive."

The success of the Y-MP 90 computers and the anticipated completion of the Cray 3 give Cray Research, Inc., a great deal of confidence. Yet the market demands dictate that Cray develop further advanced supercomputers as soon as possible to retain the coveted position of being the best in the world.[*]

QUESTIONS FOR CONCLUDING CASE

1 Using SWOT analysis, how would you characterize the competitive situation facing Cray Research?
2 Which of Porter's competitive strategies best matches the strategy being used by Cray Research?
3 What major alterations in distinctive competence have occurred at Cray? How might these changes affect the firm's competitive advantage?

* Based on Tom Alexander, "Cray's Way of Staying Super-Duper," *Fortune*, Mar. 18, 1985, pp. 56–76; John W. Verity, "Street Smarts: The Supercomputer Becomes a Stock Strategist," *Business Week*, June 1, 1987, pp. 84–85; Richard Gibson, "Cray Research Cancels a Supercomputer Plan and Loses a Superstar," *The Wall Street Journal*, Sept. 3, 1987, pp. 1, 10; George Melloan, "Staying Ahead of the Pack at Cray Research," *The Wall Street Journal*, Feb. 23, 1988, p. 31; John Burgess and Evelyn Richards, "Can U.S. Protect Lead in Supercomputers?" *The Washington Post*,

May 7, 1989, pp. H1, H7; Richard Gibson, "Cray Plans to Spin Off Founder's Efforts on New Computer; Cites Research Costs," *The Wall Street Journal,* May 16, 1989, p. A3; William M. Bulkeley, "Long a U.S. Province, Supercomputer Market Feels a Japanese Threat," *The Wall Street Journal,* May 24, 1989, pp. A1, A9; Russell Mitchell, "Now Cray Faces Life without Cray," *Business Week,* May 29, 1989, p. 31; Carla Lazzareschi, "Cray Left His Company to Prevent Internal Conflict," *Los Angeles Times,* June 4, 1989, part IV, p. 4; Willy Schatz,

"Cray to Offer New Low-End Supercomputer," *The Washington Post,* Nov. 15, 1989, p. F3; Jim Bartimo, "Can Convex Throw the Big Boys a Curve?" *Business Week,* Dec. 18, 1989, p. 104D; Bryan Borys and David B. Jemison, "Hybrid Arrangements as Strategic Alliances: Theoretical Issues in Organizational Combinations," *Academy of Management Review,* vol. 14, no. 2, 1989, pp. 234–249; Russell Mitchell, "The Genius," *Business Week,* Apr. 30, 1990, pp. 81–88; "NEC Steals Cray Thunder at Weather Center," *The Wall Street Journal,* July 2,

1991, p. B1; Hal Lancaster, "Cray Will Offer New Computer at $30.5 Million," *The Wall Street Journal,* Nov. 19, 1991, p. A8; Stephen Kreider Yoder, "Cray Research, Sun to Launch 'Parallel Project,'" *The Wall Street Journal,* Jan. 22, 1992, p. B1; "For the High-Tech Duffer, a Cray-Designed Club," *Business Week,* Feb. 24, 1992, p. 34; Russell Mitchell, "The Problem a Cray Couldn't Solve," *Business Week,* May 4, 1992, p. 72; and Russell Mitchell, "The Numbers Aren't Crunching Cray Research," *Business Week,* June 1, 1992, p. 35.

CONCLUDING CASE

STAR TV: THE FIRST PAN-ASIAN TV NETWORK

Most of the 2.7 billion people living in the 38 countries extending from Egypt through India to Japan and from the Russian Far East to Indonesia do not have television sets and satellite dishes. Yet, in 1991, STAR TV debuted a 24-hour all-sports television program, beaming the U.S. Open tennis tournament via satellite to this vast potential audience in Asia.

STAR TV, which is an acronym for Satellite Television Asian Region, is owned by the Hong Kong based HutchVision Group and was launched at an initial cost of $300 million. Originally offering only one channel, STAR TV has since added four more to its menu. Its second channel, MTV Asia, ties into Viacom International's MTV networks. The third, which broadcasts in Mandarin Chinese, is aimed at the many Chinese people spread throughout Asia. It offers dramas, comedies, movies, and financial news. The fourth channel provides 24-hour English-language news programs through a joint venture with BBC World Service Television. The fifth channel is oriented to family entertainment and broadcasts movies, soap operas, comedies, and sitcoms.

STAR TV has initially targeted a select 5 percent of the population in major markets in Hong Kong, Taiwan, South Korea, Indonesia, and India. This segment of the potential audience is made up of English-speaking, well-educated, well-traveled, wealthy Asians. Japan is not a major target for STAR TV because that country already has a well-developed satellite TV network of its own.

Currently, STAR TV is making its money solely from advertising. However, there are plans to introduce pay channels in the near future. Although it offers the only TV available in some areas, there are regions where competitive networks exist. For example, an Indonesian-run satellite TV system, Palapa B2P, is capable of broadcasting into parts of the area covered by STAR TV. However, to receive the signals from both the STAR TV and the Palapa satellites, a subscriber needs a large (8 feet in diameter), expensive ($2500) antenna dish. As an alternative, the companies could beam broadcasts to a few big dishes for metropolitan areas. The signals could then be redistributed to single households via coaxial or fiber-optic cable. Such a plan is being developed for Hong Kong.

The central-dish concept is likely to be implemented in a number of countries where governments are anxious to retain their historic control over the broadcast media. Otherwise, individuals with their own antenna dishes could receive broadcasts direct via satellite, making government regulation difficult. In Singapore and Malaysia, for example, selling satellite dishes to households is illegal. Such regulations will become harder to enforce as satellites with more powerful signals are launched, since the receiving dishes will then be smaller and less expensive.

Some observers have predicted that STAR TV will lose massive amounts of money attempting to build an audience. However, the availability of the network appears to have inspired a number of entrepreneurs to become aggressive in offering cable and

master-antenna systems. When the STAR TV sports channel offered the World Cup cricket championships in 1992, sales of satellite dishes skyrocketed, particularly in areas that had once been British colonies. A recent survey commissioned by the network shows that STAR TV had reached 3.75 million households in eight countries, an increase of 66 percent within a 6-month period. These figures do not include unaudited markets, such as China, where an estimated 3 million households have the technical capability to receive broadcasts. One surprise has been the rapid penetration in India, where 1.2 million households can receive broadcasts. Taiwan is the second-largest market, with about 1.2 million households, and Israel is third, with 272,000. More than 200 advertisers now appear on the network, including Coca-Cola, Johnson & Johnson, and Procter & Gamble.

A number of additional competitors are arising. For example, ESPN and Turner Broadcasting's CNN are already transmitting in part of the market. Singapore has licensed three new pay-TV channels, one of which has an agreement with STAR TV to carry its MTV programming. The Malaysia state government is establishing its own pay-TV network. As one observer pointed out, whether STAR TV succeeds or fails, it has drastically altered the nature of the broadcast media in Asia.*

* Andrew Tanzer, "The Asian Village," *Forbes*, Nov. 11, 1991, pp. 58–60; Laurence Zuckerman, "Satellite TV Makes Broadcasting Waves," *International Herald Tribune*, Dec. 10, 1992, p. 1.

QUESTIONS FOR
CONCLUDING CASE

1   What factors should the senior
    management of STAR TV
    consider in making an
    environmental assessment at
    this point?

2   Which generic grand strategy
    and which of its subcategories
    best describe the strategy STAR
    TV is pursuing? Which of
    Porter's competitive strategies
    does the network appear to be
    following?

3   What types of strategies should
    the senior management at
    STAR TV be reviewing for the
    future (for the years 1997 to
    2003)?

CHAPTER 6

Basic Elements of Organization Structure

GAINING THE EDGE

STRUCTURAL CHANGES HELP HEWLETT-PACKARD EXCEL

Although Hewlett-Packard (H-P) had a solid reputation for innovation, by 1990 the electronics firm was trailing several major competitors in important areas like personal computers and workstations. So when John A. Young, H-P's chief executive, learned that an important workstation project was falling seriously behind schedule, he began to contemplate making major structural changes.

For one thing, Young found that H-P's elaborate network of committees was slowing the company's ability to introduce new products. The committees had been introduced several years earlier to help H-P coordinate its growing array of computer-related products. Now, however, they were obstacles to market responsiveness because they seriously delayed important decisions.

To correct the situation, Young wanted the company to follow the lead of its printer group, based in Boise, Idaho. The printer group has operated largely independently of the committee structure because its printers are used with various brands of IBM PC clones, not just those made by H-P.

With its considerable latitude, the group developed a popular line of laser printers that quickly captured about 60 percent of the U.S. laser printer market despite formidable competition from Apple, IBM, and many Japanese companies. Part of the printer group's success was its ability to translate economies of scale into lower prices, which made it more difficult for competitors to mount serious challenges. The group also introduced a well-timed series of technological advances calculated to stay ahead of the competition. A particular coup was the introduction of the Deskjet line, a series of relatively low-priced printers based on ink-jet technology which quickly became best-sellers.

In addition to dismantling the committee network, as part of its reorganization H-P cut a layer of management from the hierarchy and decentralized decision making to a greater degree. The company also divided its computer business into two primary groups. One group was made responsible for personal computers, printers, and other products sold through dealers; the other, for workstations and minicomputers sold to big customers. To further facilitate making quick changes in response to market needs, each group was given its own sales and marketing team.

The changes have helped Hewlett-Packard be more nimble in pursuing its businesses. As a result, the company has gained market share in workstations and increased sales of minicomputers. Its printers continue to constitute formidable competition. While acknowledging that their changes to date have produced positive results, Young's successor, Lewis E. Platt, and other H-P executives recognize that future structural changes may well be necessary to keep the company competitive.[1]

Put yourself in the shoes of Hewlett-Packard's top management. If you were managing an internationally known, highly successful company that was starting to fall behind competitors in meeting customer needs, you might do what John Young did. Young engaged in the managerial function of *organizing*, the process of allocating and arranging human and nonhuman resources so that planned goals can be achieved. Organizing is important to managers because it is the means they use to align work with resources so that organizational plans and decisions can be made and carried out effectively.

As the Hewlett-Packard situation illustrates, even the best intentions and plans can go awry when the way in which the organization is structured and resources are used encourages counterproductive actions. Often, means of organizing that work under one set of circumstances become inappropriate as the situation changes. As a result, organizing is an ongoing management function. Managers need to give frequent consideration to organizing issues in order to keep the company moving on target. As we begin this chapter, we initially probe the nature of organization structure. We also explore major considerations in dividing work in ways that are meaningful to individuals and that are likely to energize their efforts to put forth their best performance. We then review major ways of grouping jobs and units in developing an overall organization structure. We next investigate several important methods of coordinating efforts up and down the hierarchy. Finally, we examine methods of horizontal coordination that not only help various departments and units synchronize their efforts but also encourage innovation.

THE NATURE OF ORGANIZATION STRUCTURE

If you are like most people, you have probably had the experience of running into a problem that made you want to speak to the supervisor or next in command in an organization. Under such conditions, you would probably respond with disbelief if you were told that no one knew who the supervisor was or whose job it was to handle a complaint like yours. We expect such matters to be worked out—at least by organizations that have some hope of long-run survival. In essence, we expect organizations to have developed reasonably effective organization structures.

Organization Structure Defined

Organization structure The formal pattern of interactions and coordination designed by management to link the tasks of individuals and groups in achieving organizational goals

Organization structure is the formal pattern of interactions and coordination designed by management to link the tasks of individuals and groups in achieving organizational goals. The word "formal" in this context refers to the fact that organization structures are typically created by management for specific purposes and, hence, are official, or formal, outcomes of the organizing function. Organizations also have informal structures, or patterns of interaction, which are not designed by management but which usually emerge because of common interests or friendship.

Organization structure consists mainly of four elements:[2]

1 The assignment of tasks and responsibilities that define the jobs of individuals and units
2 The clustering of individual positions into units and of units into departments and larger units to form an organization's hierarchy
3 The various mechanisms required to facilitate vertical (top-to-bottom) coordination, such as the number of individuals reporting to any given managerial position and the degree of delegation of authority
4 The various mechanisms needed to foster horizontal (across departments) coordination, such as task forces and interdepartmental teams

Organization design The process of developing an organization structure

The process of developing an organization structure is sometimes referred to as **organization design.** One aid to visualizing structure is the organization chart. Therefore, we briefly discuss this chart before analyzing the four main elements of organization structure in greater detail.

The Organization Chart

Organization chart A line diagram that depicts the broad outlines of an organization's structure

Chain of command The unbroken line of authority that ultimately links each individual with the top organizational position through a managerial position at each successive layer in between

Figure 1 *Organization chart for the Acacia Mutual Life Insurance Company.*

The **organization chart** is a line diagram that depicts the broad outlines of an organization's structure. Organization charts vary in detail, but they typically show the major positions or departments in the organization. They also indicate the way the positions are grouped into specific units, the reporting relationships from lower to higher levels, and the official channels for communicating information.[3] Some charts show titles associated with the positions, as well as the current position holders. An overall organization chart indicating the major managerial positions and departments in the Acacia Mutual Life Insurance Company, based in Washington, D.C., is shown in Figure 1.

Such charts are particularly helpful in providing a visual map of the chain of command. The **chain of command** is the unbroken line of authority that ultimately links each individual with the top organizational position through a managerial position at each successive layer in between.[4] The basic idea is that each

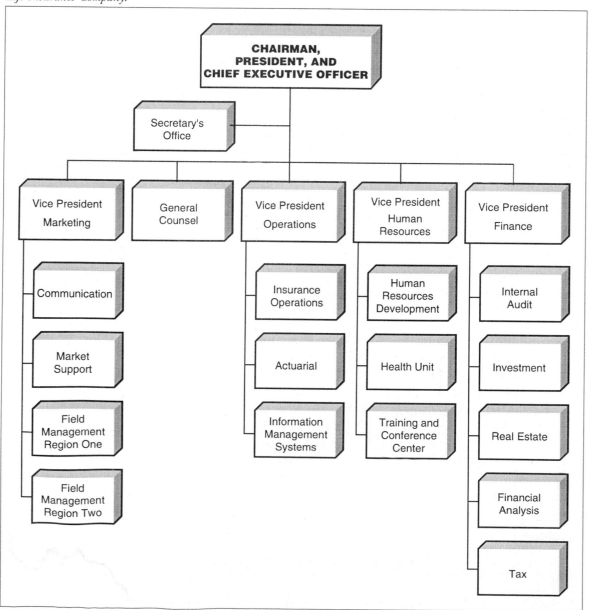

individual in an organization should be able to identify his or her boss and trace the line of authority through the organization all the way to the top position.

Today, most organizations that include more than a few individuals are likely to have organization charts showing the chain of command and the basic structure of the organization. Although such charts provide a broad view, they do not include all aspects of the structure picture. For example, organization charts do not normally include detailed information about how work is divided into specific jobs. Yet, as noted earlier in the definition of organization structure, the design of jobs is an important aspect of structure. Therefore, it is the subject to which we now turn.

JOB DESIGN

Work specialization The degree to which the work necessary to achieve organizational goals is broken down into various jobs

Different types of jobs can involve very different activities. A job as a buyer for Macy's, the New York–based department store chain, may involve keeping in contact with various suppliers in a certain specialty area (such as shoes), previewing new offerings, developing sources for in-house brands, and studying trends in consumer tastes. In contrast, the job of a salesperson may include learning about new items in certain departments, keeping merchandise neatly arranged, helping customers, and ringing up sales at the register. The differing activities of the buyer and the salesperson reflect **work specialization,** the degree to which the work necessary to achieve organizational goals is broken down into various jobs. Without some specialization, it would be difficult for most organizations to function. This is because it is usually impossible for every organization member to have the entire range of skills necessary to run an effective organization.

Job design The specification of task activities associated with a particular job

On the other hand, even jobs with similar titles can differ substantially in the activities performed. For example, a job as an administrative assistant may include typing, filing, and photocopying, or it could involve such activities as coordinating meetings and travel, investigating trouble spots, and making decisions about a certain range of issues. What is included in a given job depends on **job design,** the specification of task activities associated with a particular job.

Job design is important to the organizing function for two major reasons. For one thing, task activities need to be grouped in reasonably logical ways. Otherwise, it may be very difficult for organization members to function efficiently. For another, the way that jobs are configured, or designed, has an important influence on employee motivation to perform well. Thus managers need to consider both efficiency and motivational issues in designing jobs that will facilitate effective performance.

Approaches to Job Design

There are four major approaches to job design: job simplification, job rotation, job enlargement, and job enrichment.[5]

Job simplification The process of configuring jobs so that jobholders have only a small number of narrow activities to perform

JOB SIMPLIFICATION **Job simplification** is the process of designing jobs so that jobholders have only a small number of narrow activities to perform (see Figure 2a). Economist Adam Smith was one of the first to highlight the advantages of work specialization and simplification. Using his now-famous example involving pins, Smith pointed out that an individual working alone could make 20 pins per day, while 10 people working on specialized tasks could make 48,000 pins per day.[6] The simplification idea was further popularized by Frederick Taylor through his scientific management viewpoint, which emphasizes reducing jobs to narrow tasks and training workers in the best way to do them.

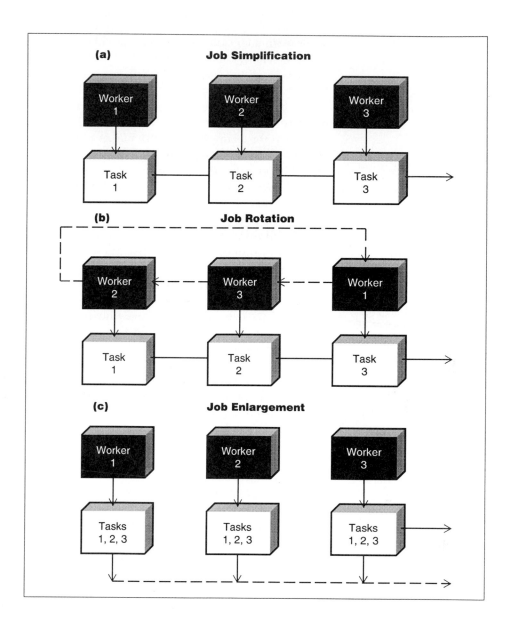

Figure 2 *Major approaches to job design.*

Because the jobs involved in job simplification are simple and repetitive, workers are almost interchangeable, making training new workers relatively easy. Perhaps the most obvious example of job simplification is the assembly-line approach commonly used to make automobiles. Unfortunately, job simplification can be carried too far, creating narrow, repetitive jobs that are not conducive to motivating employees. Instead, such jobs often result in negative side effects, such as worker boredom, low job satisfaction, absenteeism, turnover, and sabotage.[7]

Job rotation The practice of periodically shifting workers through a set of jobs in a planned sequence

JOB ROTATION Job rotation is the practice of periodically shifting workers through a set of jobs in a planned sequence (see Figure 2*b*). The approach is often aimed at reducing the boredom associated with job simplification by providing some task variety. Job rotation also has the advantage of *cross-training* workers (training them to do the tasks involved in several jobs) so that there is maximum flexibility in job assignments. Although job rotation can be useful in alleviating monotony and boredom, its advantage with simple jobs may be short-lived. With such jobs, employees are likely to learn the new jobs quickly and become relatively bored again.

Job rotation is generally more successful as an employee development tool. In this approach, employees are rotated through a series of more challenging jobs in order to increase their capabilities, expand job assignment flexibility, and increase their understanding of various aspects of the organization. At Morgan Guaranty, for example, the bank makes a regular practice of rotating managers through various departments. As a result, the managers tend to be more cooperative with one another because they either have been or will be in the other person's job at some point.[8] Job rotation across different units or geographic locations may also help stimulate innovation, since it promotes the exchange of ideas.[9] Potential problems with job rotation are that departments may view the rotating individuals as temporary help (and give them only trivial things to do) and may also question their departmental loyalty.

JOB ENLARGEMENT   **Job enlargement** is the allocation of a wider variety of similar tasks to a job in order to make it more challenging (see Figure 2c). For example, Maytag changed the assembly process for washing-machine pumps so that each worker could assemble a complete pump rather than apply only one part on an assembly line.[10] Job enlargement broadens **job scope,** the number of different tasks an employee performs in a particular job. Although it is an improvement over narrow job specialization, job enlargement has generally had somewhat limited success in motivating employees. This is primarily because a few more similar tasks often do not provide sufficient challenge and stimulation.

JOB ENRICHMENT   **Job enrichment** is the process of upgrading the job-task mix in order to increase significantly the potential for growth, achievement, responsibility, and recognition. The concept of job enrichment was pioneered by Frederick Herzberg, whose work during the late 1960s highlighted the importance of job content as a significant force in motivation.[11] Job enrichment increases **job depth,** the degree to which individuals can plan and control the work involved in their jobs.

To guide job enrichment efforts, job design researchers Richard Hackman and Greg Oldham developed the **job characteristics model.**[12] The model, shown in Figure 3, involves three main elements: core job characteristics, critical psychological states, and outcomes. There are five *core job characteristics:*

1   **Skill variety** is the extent to which the job entails a number of activities that require different skills.
2   **Task identity** is the degree to which the job allows the completion of a major identifiable piece of work, rather than just a fragment.
3   **Task significance** is the extent to which the worker sees the job output as having an important impact on others.
4   **Autonomy** is the amount of discretion allowed in determining schedules and work methods for achieving the required output.
5   **Feedback** is the degree to which the job provides for clear, timely information about performance results.

The more that these core characteristics are reflected in jobs, the more motivating the jobs are likely to be.

The motivational value of these characteristics stems from workers' experiencing three *critical psychological states:* feeling the work is meaningful, knowing that they are responsible for the outcomes, and actually finding out about results. According to the model, these critical states then lead to the major out-

---

Job enlargement   The allocation of a wider variety of similar tasks to a job in order to make it more challenging

Job scope   The number of different tasks an employee performs in a particular job

Job enrichment   The process of upgrading the job-task mix in order to increase significantly the potential for growth, achievement, responsibility, and recognition

Job depth   The degree to which individuals can plan and control the work involved in their jobs

Job characteristics model   A model developed to guide job enrichment efforts that include consideration of core job characteristics, critical psychological states, and outcomes

Skill variety   The extent to which the job entails a number of activities that require different skills

Task identity   The degree to which the job allows the completion of a major identifiable piece of work, rather than just a fragment

Task significance   The extent to which the worker sees the job output as having an important impact on others

Autonomy   The amount of discretion allowed in determining schedules and work methods for achieving the required output

Feedback   The degree to which the job provides for clear, timely information about performance results

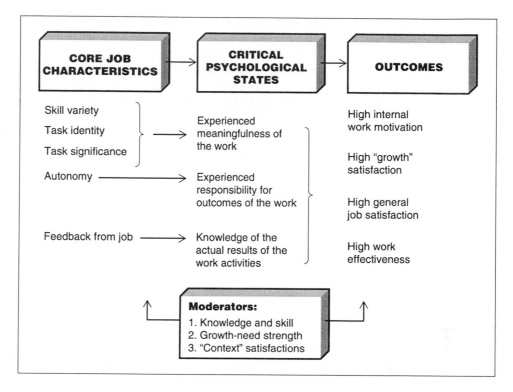

Figure 3 *Job characteristics model. (Adapted from J. Richard Hackman and Greg R. Oldham,* Work Redesign, *Addison-Wesley, Reading, Mass., 1980, p. 90. Used by permission of J. Richard Hackman.)*

comes (listed in Figure 3), including higher internal work motivation, greater satisfaction of growth needs, higher general job satisfaction, and increased work effectiveness. The increased work effectiveness usually stems from higher work quality, although greater quantity may sometimes result, depending largely on the improvements made in the flow of work.

Research indicates that workers may differ in their reactions to increases in the core job characteristics (see the moderators listed in Figure 3). Not surprisingly, individuals are more likely to feel motivated by job changes if they have the knowledge and skills necessary to perform well in the redesigned job, if they have high **growth-need strength** (the degree to which an individual needs personal growth and development on the job), and if they feel satisfied with other aspects of the job context (such as supervision, pay, coworkers, and job security).[13] One organization that has successfully used the job characteristics model to implement job enrichment is First National Bank of Chicago (see the following Case in Point discussion).

Growth-need strength The degree to which an individual needs personal growth and development on the job

---

CASE IN POINT   JOB ENRICHMENT AT FIRST NATIONAL BANK OF CHICAGO

First National Bank of Chicago has used the job characteristics model to redesign jobs in its unit that prepares letters of credit for businesses. Before the redesign, preparation of the letters, which let businesses know how much credit the bank is willing to extend, was fragmented into a "paperwork assembly." The jobs involved narrow skills, little sense of the overall product and its impact on client businesses, limited autonomy, and virtually no feedback from clients. For example, one person's whole job was feeding tape into a Telex machine.

Although the unit was notorious for poor service, managers had little success in their attempts to improve the quality and speed of the process. One survey of employees in the line-of-credit department showed that 80 percent of the staff members were dissatisfied with their jobs. The 20 percent who were satisfied were managers and technical professionals. Even the managerial jobs were limited. There was one manager for about every five workers. On the basis of the survey, a group of workers were asked to help with the redesign of their jobs. The aim was to involve the entire staff in bringing about change.

The redesign ultimately eliminated a layer of management and changed the nature of the jobs. Each employee now performs customer contact work (resulting in higher task identity, task significance, and feedback) as well as research, writing, costing, and other letter-preparation tasks (resulting in increased skill variety, autonomy, and task identity) associated with a specific client group. The changes also led to staff reductions (mainly through attrition and transfers) of about 40 percent, extensive staff training, and pay increases of $7000 to $8000 per year for the individuals remaining (because they now had higher-skilled jobs). Within a year, profits related to the department rose by $2 million, employee morale rose dramatically, and customer satisfaction increased significantly.[14]   ■ ■ ■

Considering the job content is one method of organizing work to meet organizational and worker needs; another is devising alternative work schedules.

Alternative Work Schedules

Alternative work schedules
Schedules based on adjustments in the normal work schedule rather than in the job content or activities

A related aspect of designing jobs is creating **alternative work schedules,** schedules based on adjustments in the normal work schedule rather than in the job content or activities. The basic objective of this approach is to increase workers' job satisfaction and motivation by arranging work schedules that allow individuals to meet the needs associated with both personal life and work life. Three major types of alternative work schedules are flextime, the compressed workweek, and job sharing.

Flextime A work schedule that specifies certain core hours when individuals are expected to be on the job and then allows flexibility in starting and quitting times as long as individuals work the total number of required hours per day

FLEXTIME **Flextime** is a work schedule that specifies certain core hours when individuals are expected to be on the job and then allows flexibility in starting and quitting times as long as individuals work the total number of required hours per day. For example, a company may have core hours between 10 a.m. and 3 p.m. (with an hour for lunch). Workers may then choose various schedules, such as 7 a.m. to 4 p.m. or 10 a.m. to 7 p.m., that comprise 8 hours of work per day and include the core hours. One recent study showed that the most popular core period is 9 a.m. to 3 p.m.

Major advantages of flextime are improvements in employee morale, accommodation of the needs of working parents, decreased tardiness, and reductions in traffic problems because workers can avoid the peak congestion times. Flextime often also results in lower absenteeism and lower turnover. Major disadvantages include lack of supervision during some hours of work, unavailability of key people during certain periods, understaffing during some periods, and coordination difficulties if the outputs of some employees are inputs for other employees. Also, keeping track of the various schedules may increase administrative work. Overall, however, flextime has been a successful innovation, and its use appears to be growing.[15]

Compressed workweek
A work schedule whereby employees work four 10-hour days or some similar combination, rather than the usual five 8-hour days

COMPRESSED WORKWEEK The **compressed workweek** is a work schedule whereby employees work four 10-hour days or some similar combination, rather than the usual five 8-hour days. Some companies close for 3 days each week. This often provides operating economies, such as reductions in energy use that result from cutting down on heating and cooling for the 3 days off. For example, at the

Alabama-based Birmingham Steel Corporation, workers put in 12-hour days, working 3 days one week and 4 days the following week. The schedule has had a major positive effect on productivity by cutting the number of shifts and time-consuming changeovers from three to two.[16]

Other organizations coordinate employee schedules to remain open for 5 days each week. The basic idea behind the compressed workweek, sometimes called the 4/40 workweek, is to make the job attractive to employees by providing 3 (usually consecutive) days off per week. Potential disadvantages include possible fatigue, loss of productivity, and accidents, as well as difficulties interfacing with other organizations that operate on traditional workweek schedules. More research is needed on the effects of the compressed workweek. According to one study, the compressed schedule initially led to greater job satisfaction and higher performance, but the positive effects disappeared within 2 years.[17]

Job sharing A work practice in which two or more people share a single full-time job

JOB SHARING **Job sharing** is a work practice in which two or more people share a single full-time job. With job sharing, one person can work in the morning and the other in the afternoon, or they can alternate days or develop some other sharing schedule. Individuals who share jobs may be parents who are sharing work and family responsibilities or mothers attempting to juggle both home and work activities. One survey of 348 U.S. and Canadian firms found that 11 percent had job sharing.[18]

TYPES OF DEPARTMENTALIZATION

Departmentalization The clustering of individuals into units and of units into departments and larger units in order to facilitate achieving organizational goals.

While the way in which individual jobs are arranged is one important dimension of organization structure, another important aspect is departmentalization. **Departmentalization** is the clustering of individuals into units and of units into departments and larger units to facilitate achieving organizational goals.[19] Differing overall patterns of departmentalization are often referred to as *organization designs*.

Four of the most commonly used patterns of departmentalization are functional, divisional, hybrid, and matrix.[20] Briefly, the *functional structure* groups positions into units on the basis of similarity of expertise, skills, and work activities (e.g., marketing, accounting, production or operations, and human resources). In contrast, the *divisional structure* groups positions into units according to the similarity of products or markets (e.g., a separate division for each of several products). The *hybrid structure* combines aspects of both the functional and divisional forms, with some jobs grouped into departments by function and others grouped by products or markets. Finally, the *matrix structure* superimposes, or overlays, a horizontal set of divisional reporting relationships onto a hierarchical functional structure.

Regardless of the organization design, however, managers typically need to take further steps to achieve the vertical and horizontal coordination that makes a structure effective. In the next section, we discuss methods of vertical coordination.

METHODS OF VERTICAL COORDINATION

Vertical coordination The linking of activities at the top of the organization with those at the middle and lower levels in order to achieve organizational goals

Although the various types of departmentalization provide basic structures within which individuals carry out organizational work activities, a number of additional mechanisms are important to effective vertical coordination. **Vertical coordination** is the linking of activities at the top of the organization with those at the middle and lower levels in order to achieve organizational goals. Without such coordination, the various parts of the organization have difficulty working effectively together. Five particularly important means of achieving effective vertical coordination are formalization, span of management, centralization versus decentralization, delegation, and line and staff positions.[21]

The Role of Formalization

Formalization The degree to which written policies, rules, procedures, job descriptions, and other documents specify what actions are (or are not) to be taken under a given set of circumstances

One common method of achieving vertical coordination is formalization. **Formalization** is the degree to which written policies, rules, procedures, job descriptions, and other documents specify what actions are (or are not) to be taken under a given set of circumstances.[22] Formalization helps bring about vertical coordination by specifying expected behaviors in advance.[23] For example, policies provide general guidelines within which organization members are expected to operate; procedures spell out actions to be taken under certain recurring circumstances; and rules specify what should or should not be done in a given situation. Job descriptions detail the tasks and activities associated with particular jobs.

Most organizations rely on at least some means of formalization. For example, major student organizations are likely to have written policies about basic qualifications for office, as well as procedures governing how elections should be conducted. Without such means of formalization, it would be necessary to decide these issues every year, a situation that could be time-consuming and might lead to significant inequities. On the other hand, extensive rules and procedures can be stifling and discourage necessary amounts of change and innovation.[24]

This occurred at J. Bildner & Sons, Inc., a Boston-based upscale grocery store. When it began an ill-fated expansion attempt, the company developed formal policies and rules that unwittingly sometimes thwarted its intended emphasis on service. In one instance, a customer at a recently opened New York store inquired about the cost of buying a roasted turkey for Christmas. Rather than quoting a price based on the cost of the turkey and a reasonable markup for profit, the manager followed the rules and multiplied the price per slice by the number of slices in a turkey. Naturally, the price was absurd and the customer walked out.[25]

When organizations are small, they can usually run very informally, with few written documents specifying policies and procedures. As they grow, however, organizations tend to require additional degrees of formalization to coordinate the efforts of increasing numbers of individuals. The challenge is to avoid becoming overly formalized. Consider the experience of Celestial Seasonings as it grew larger, became part of a giant company, and then became an independent company again (see the following Case in Point discussion).

CASE IN POINT   CELESTIAL SEASONINGS RETAINS ITS INNOVATIVE FLAIR

The origins of Celestial Seasonings, makers of herbal tea, are legendary. In 1970, Mo Siegel and his friend Wyck Hay gathered herbs in the mountains of Colorado, mixed their first blend of herb tea, loaded the mixture in muslin bags sewn by their wives, and began selling the tea to local health food stores.

The company took the name "Celestial Seasonings," which was the nickname of an early investor's girlfriend. Tea names, chosen by Mo's friends and company members, were equally whimsical, beginning with Mo's 24 Herb Tea, Red Zinger Herb Tea, and Morning Thunder Tea. The tea was packaged in colorful recyclable boxes that featured such idyllic scenes as roaming buffalo and picnicking couples. Up to that time, herb teas had largely been somewhat bitter-tasting brews used for medicinal purposes. The fledgling company changed all that with its flavorful new creations, which soon found themselves on supermarket shelves, and virtually created the herb tea industry.

From the start, the company operated relatively informally, encouraged employee participation in decision making, and was dedicated to all-natural ingredients. In the early days, major decisions were made in all-company meetings lasting as long as 8 hours, volleyball games were played every lunch hour, and toddling children could be found playing in Mo's office. As Celestial grew, the company brought in managers from such major corporations as Pepsi, Coca-Cola, Smuckers, and Lipton to help. Automation became a necessity as the amount of tea blended per day approached 8 tons. Still, the company managed to retain its informality, avoiding such symbols of hierarchical status as time clocks and reserved parking places. Employees were asked to contribute ideas in such areas as new ways to automate, possible new teas, and names for new flavors (often chosen through employee contests).

The success of the innovative company attracted the attention of Kraft, Inc., which bought Celestial from Mo Siegel in 1984 for approximately $40 million, with assurances that the company would be left alone to continue its solid growth. By 1989, Kraft had decided to leave the beverage business, and it attempted to sell Celestial to the tea company's archrival, Thomas J. Lipton, Inc. However, an antitrust suit filed by R. C. Bigelow, Inc., a small competitor in the herb tea market, blocked the sale. Kraft then agreed to sell Celestial Seasonings to its management and a venture capital firm.

"Although Kraft let us operate as an independent business," says Barnet Feinblum, who was promoted to president when Siegel left, "little by little we were having to comply with Kraft's policies, whether it was employee benefit plans or decisions on purchasing equipment. If we had continued that way, Celestial Seasonings would have gradually and inexorably become just like Kraft." For example, Feinblum remembers missing one opportunity because of Kraft's lengthy lead time in purchasing Italian tea-bagging machines. Still, Kraft did double Celestial Seasonings' advertising budget, and sales were approaching $50 million in 1989 when Celestial became independent again.

Unfortunately, sales began to level off. The company then offered founder Mo Siegel an opportunity to acquire 25 percent equity if he would return as chairman and CEO. By this time, Mo, who had been working with a variety of nonprofit organizations, missed the corporate environment and agreed to return. Mo has brought a renewed sense of excitement to Celestial. He combines a flair for selecting winning tea flavors with strong philosophical views about such things as health, the environment, and recycling.[26] Optimism once again pervades Celestial. ■ ■ ■

As the Celestial Seasonings situation illustrates, too much formalization can begin to stifle an organization, particularly when it is relatively small. On the other hand, even Celestial Seasonings has had to develop policies, such as using only natural ingredients, and rules, such as procedures for cleaning various spice ingredients imported from all over the world. In addition to formalization, span of management is an important means of vertical coordination.

Span of management, or **span of control** The number of subordinates who report directly to a specific manager

Span of Management

Span of management, or **span of control,** is the number of subordinates who report directly to a specific manager. Span of management is important to vertical coordination because it has a direct bearing on the degree to which managers can interact with and supervise subordinates. With too many subordinates, managers can become overloaded, experience difficulty coordinating activities, and lose control of what is occurring in their work units. On the other hand, with too few subordinates, managers are underutilized and tend to engage in excessive supervision, leaving subordinates little discretion in doing their work.[27]

FACTORS INFLUENCING SPAN OF MANAGEMENT In general, spans of management can be wider under the following conditions:[28]

- *Low interaction requirements.* When the work is such that subordinates are able to operate without frequent interaction with each other and/or with their superiors, managers can supervise more individuals.
- *High competence levels.* High job-related skills and abilities of managers and/or subordinates make it possible for managers to handle more subordinates.
- *Work similarity.* When employees in a given unit do similar work, it is easier for a manager to maintain adequate supervision than when tasks vary widely.
- *Low problem frequency and seriousness.* When problems, particularly serious ones, are infrequent, there is less need for managerial attention.
- *Physical proximity.* When subordinates are located within close physical proximity of one another, managers can coordinate activities more easily.
- *Few nonsupervisory duties of manager.* Managers can handle more subordinates when they have few nonsupervisory duties to perform, such as doing part of the subordinates' work themselves.
- *Considerable available assistance.* Managers can supervise more subordinates when they have considerable additional help, such as assistant and secretarial support.
- *High motivational possibilities of work.* When the work itself offers a high challenge, subordinates are more likely to increase their performance levels because of opportunities to exercise discretion, making it less necessary for continual managerial involvement.

Tall structure A structure that has many hierarchical levels and narrow spans of control

Flat structure A structure that has few hierarchical levels and wide spans of control

LEVELS IN THE HIERARCHY Although it is not always obvious to the casual observer, spans of management for various managerial positions directly influence the number of hierarchical levels in an organization. A **tall structure** is one that has many hierarchical levels and narrow spans of control. In contrast, a **flat structure** is one that has few hierarchical levels and wide spans of control.

To understand how span of control is related to the number of levels, it is helpful to contrast the two hypothetical organizations depicted in Figure 4. Organization A, the taller structure on the left, has seven levels; while organization B, the flatter organization on the right, has five levels. If we assume a span of control of 4 in organization A, then the number of managers (beginning with the top level) would be 1, 4, 16, 64, 256, and 1,024, respectively, for a total of 1,396 managers (levels 1 through 6). At the seventh (bottom) level, there would be 4,096 nonmanagerial employees. In contrast, if we assume that organization B has a span of control of 8, then the number of managers (beginning with the top level) would be 1, 8, 64, and 512, respectively, for a total of 585 managers (levels 1 through 4). Organization B also has 4,096 nonmanagerial employees in its bottom level, which is level five. Hence organization A requires 811 *more* managers than does organization B.[29]

If one wanted to reduce the number of hierarchical levels in organization A, the only way to do so without reducing the number of employees at the bottom would be to increase spans of control. Of course, in a real organization, spans of control are not the same throughout the whole organization. Still, the principle

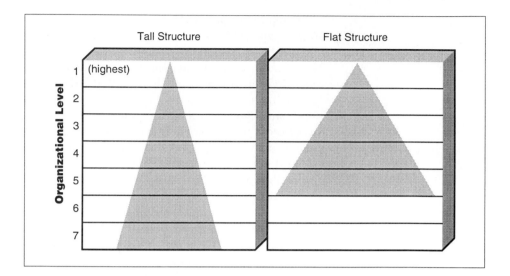

Figure 4 *Tall versus flat structure.*

is the same. When average spans of control in an organization are narrow, the organization most likely has a tall structure. Very tall organizations raise administrative overhead (because there are more managers to be paid, given office space, etc.), slow communication and decision making (because of the many levels), make it more difficult to pinpoint responsibility for various tasks, and encourage the formation of dull, routine jobs.[30]

Because of such problems with tall structures, many companies have recently been downsizing. **Downsizing** is the process of significantly reducing the layers of middle management, increasing the spans of control, and shrinking the size of the work force.[31] Its purpose is to improve organizational efficiency and effectiveness. A closely related term that is often used synonymously with "downsizing" is "restructuring." **Restructuring** is the process of making a major change in organization structure that often involves reducing management levels and possibly changing some major components of the organization through divestiture and/or acquisition.[32] Again, the purpose is to boost efficiency and effectiveness. Restructuring frequently, but not always, involves reducing the size of an organization's work force.

In one example of downsizing, the Ford Motor Company reduced its number of management levels after finding that it was laboring under 12 layers of management, compared with 7 layers at Toyota.[33] The additional levels at Ford represented expensive overhead not borne by a significant competitor, causing a competitive disadvantage for Ford. In addition, having many levels made it more difficult for the company to move quickly in its increasingly competitive situation. Soon after Ford made its reductions, Toyota was back cutting management levels of its own (see the following Case in Point discussion).

Downsizing The process of significantly reducing the layers of middle management, increasing the spans of control, and shrinking the size of the work force

Restructuring The process of making a major change in organization structure that often involves reducing management levels and possibly changing components of the organization through divestiture and/or acquisition, as well as shrinking the size of the work force

---

CASE IN POINT

TOYOTA SHEDS MANAGEMENT LEVELS

Faced with increasing global competition, management at the Toyota Motor Corporation recently undertook a restructuring aimed at eliminating two management levels. In keeping with the Japanese tradition of attempting to avoid layoffs, the company shifted a number of middle managers to "hands-on work," rather than cutting their jobs.

Toyota's primary aim in restructuring was to streamline decision making by

reducing the number of layers through which decisions must travel. The changes affected about 25,000 of the approximately 65,000 Toyota employees, including about 1000 managers. Cost cutting did not seem to be a major factor for the Toyota move because the company has been making admirable profits in recent years. In fact, it has so much cash that it is often referred to as "the Bank of Toyota."

Instead, the restructuring appeared to stem from the fact that the company was often slower to take competitive action than were its smaller Japanese rivals. For instance, Toyota opened its own U.S. assembly plant only after Honda, Nissan, and Mazda were already manufacturing in the United States. The company also trailed behind Honda in making its entry in the luxury-car market.

At Toyota, there were "so many, many steps to reach top management that it [took] time to make a decision," noted a Toyota spokesperson. Furthermore, there were significant numbers of middle managers whose main activities could be summarized as "sit quietly without doing anything," the spokesperson added. Now the displaced managers will need to "become involved in the process of creating and doing hands-on work."[34]   ■ ■ ■

Still, downsizing must be planned and implemented carefully. Done well, it can significantly reduce costs, speed up decision making, energize employees through more challenging jobs, reduce redundancies, and increase innovation. Done poorly, it can cause the loss of valuable employees (either because they are laid off or because they decide to leave), demoralize survivors, and result in short-run productivity declines as employees attempt to pick up additional responsibilities.[35] This was the situation at Waterford Glass Group PLC, Ireland's venerable maker of lead crystal goblets and related items. The company ran into difficulty in the mid-1980s when it attempted to downsize in part by reducing the size of its highly paid labor force through an early retirement offer. A related step was the purchase of new glass furnaces and diamond-cutting wheels that could speed production. Unfortunately, too many of the most experienced glass-blowers chose early retirement. It took several years for the remaining, less experienced work force to achieve the firm's previous productivity levels, even with the new equipment.[36] While the downsizing trend may reduce the overall number of managerial positions in organizations, it is also likely to provide more challenging and interesting jobs at various levels. Many organizations are placing less emphasis on hierarchical level, stressing instead horizontal influence, teamwork, increased access to information, and greater decision-making latitude at lower levels.

Centralization versus Decentralization

Centralization The extent to which power and authority are retained at the top organizational levels

Decentralization The extent to which power and authority are delegated to lower levels

To foster vertical coordination, managers also need to consider the appropriate level of **centralization,** the extent to which power and authority are retained at the top organizational levels. The opposite of centralization is **decentralization,** the extent to which power and authority are delegated to lower levels. Centralization and decentralization form a continuum, with many possible degrees of delegation of power and authority in between. The extent of centralization affects vertical coordination by influencing the amount of decision making at the upper and lower levels.

Centralization has several positive aspects.[37] If all major decisions are made at the top levels, it can be easier to coordinate the activities of various units and individuals. Coordination from the top can help reduce duplication of effort and resources by ensuring that similar activities are not carried on by different organizational units. In addition, top managers usually have the most experience and may make better decisions than individuals at lower levels. Similarly, top-level managers usually have a broader perspective and can better balance the needs of various parts of the organization. Finally, centralization promotes strong leadership in an organization because much of the power remains at the top.

Decentralization also has a number of major advantages.[38] Encouraging decision making at lower levels tends to ease the heavy work loads of executives, leaving them more time to focus on major issues. Decentralization also enriches the jobs of lower-level employees by offering workers the challenge associated with making significant decisions that affect their work. In addition, it leads to faster decision making at the lower levels, because most decisions do not have to be referred up the hierarchy. Individuals at lower levels may be closer to the problem and, therefore, in a better position to make good decisions. Finally, decentralization often leads to the establishment of relatively independent units, such as divisions, whose output is easier to measure than that of units in a functional design. It is worth noting, though that a divisional structure is not synonymous with decentralization. In some divisional structures, much of the power and authority is still held at the top, and most decisions of significance must be referred to the executive levels.

Given that both approaches have advantages, how does top management decide on the degree of centralization versus decentralization? There are four main factors that begin to tilt the scale away from the centralization side of the continuum and toward the decentralization side:[39]

Large size: It is more difficult for top-level managers in large organizations to have either the time or the knowledge to make all the major decisions.

Geographic dispersion: Top executives frequently find it impossible to keep abreast of the details of operations at various locations.

Technological complexity: It is typically difficult for upper management to keep up technologically.

Environmental uncertainty: The fast pace of change interferes with top management's ability to assess situations with the speed required for timely decisions.

In one recent move toward decentralization, Paul H. O'Neill, chairman of the Aluminum Company of America (Alcoa), stunned a meeting of worldwide Alcoa executives by announcing that he planned to eliminate 2 layers of upper management and give Alcoa's 25 business-unit managers much greater latitude in managing their businesses. "We felt liberated," said Australian business-unit manager Robert F. Slagle.[40]

Delegation

Responsibility The obligation to carry out duties and achieve goals related to a position

Authority The right to make decisions, carry out actions, and direct others in matters related to the duties and goals of a position

Another means of vertical coordination that is closely related to the centralization-decentralization issue is delegation. Suppose that you have just become the manager of a restaurant that is part of a chain. Let's assume that you are one of ten restaurant managers who report to a district manager. When you take over as restaurant manager, you probably expect to be assigned **responsibility,** the obligation to carry out duties and achieve goals related to a position. For example, you might have the responsibility of keeping the restaurant open during certain hours, seeing that food is served, making sure the customers are satisfied, and achieving a certain profit margin. You probably also expect to be given **authority,** the right to make decisions, carry out actions, and direct others in matters related to the duties and goals of a position. For example, as the restaurant manager, you might expect to have the authority to hire employees, assign work, and order the food and supplies necessary to keep things running smoothly. You would also expect the position to involve **accountability,** the requirement to provide satisfactory reasons for significant deviations from duties or expected results.

Accountability The requirement to provide satisfactory reasons for significant deviations from duties or expected results

Carrying our story a step further, suppose you soon found that when you attempted to make decisions, such as hiring a new worker, the district manager tended to interfere and even frequently reversed your decisions. Yet, when the end of the month came and you had not achieved your expected profit margin (largely because of interference from the district manager), the district manager still held you accountable for the shortfall in results. Under this set of circumstances, you might correctly conclude that you had been given the responsibility but not the authority needed to do your job.

Delegation The assignment of part of a manager's work to others, along with both the responsibility and the authority necessary to achieve expected results

In this situation, the district manager failed to engage in adequate **delegation,** the assignment of part of a manager's work to others, along with both the responsibility and the authority necessary to achieve expected results. Delegation involves moving decision-making authority and responsibility from one level of the organization to the next lower level. The delegating managers, though, are still ultimately responsible for achieving the results and will be held accountable by their own bosses. Delegation is important to vertical coordination because it allows the hierarchy to be both more efficient and more effective by enabling work to be done at the lowest level possible.[41] In addition, delegation facilitates developing subordinates to fill future managerial positions, thus strengthening prospects for adequate vertical coordination in the future. Generally, more delegating is done with a decentralized structure than with a centralized one. Even within a centralized structure, though, top managers must do some delegating. They cannot do everything themselves.

Although even classical theorists placed considerable emphasis on the need to delegate, many managers still find delegation difficult. Some managers are reluctant to delegate because they fear blame if subordinates fail, believe they lack the time to train subordinates, or wish to hold onto their authority and power. Others avoid delegating because they enjoy doing tasks that subordinates could perform, feel threatened that competent subordinates may perform too well and possibly make the manager look poor by comparison, or simply feel that they do not know how to delegate effectively.[42]

The failure to delegate can hurt managerial careers. A study by the Center for Creative Leadership showed that overmanaging, or the inability to delegate and build a team, was one of the "fatal flaws" that caused executives on the fast track to become derailed.[43] For some guidelines on how to delegate, see the Practically Speaking discussion, "Guidelines for Effective Delegating."

Line and Staff Positions

Line position A position that has authority and responsibility for achieving the major goals of the organization

Staff position A position whose primary purpose is providing specialized expertise and assistance to line positions

Another issue related to vertical coordination is the configuration of line and staff positions. A **line position** is a position that has authority and responsibility for achieving the major goals of the organization. A **staff position** is a position whose primary purpose is providing specialized expertise and assistance to line positions. Sometimes the term "staff" is also used to refer to personal staff, individuals who provide assistance to a particular position as required (e.g., an administrative assistant to a division head).

The positions and related departments that are considered either line or staff vary with the type of organization. For example, in a grocery chain, line

PRACTICALLY SPEAKING

GUIDELINES FOR EFFECTIVE DELEGATING

These guidelines will help you be an effective delegator:

- The secret of delegating is determining what each member of a work unit can do. Carefully choose the subordinate who should take on the project. Usually it is someone immediately below you in the corporate hierarchy. If you want to skip down two ranks, work through that person's supervisor.
- Next, decide whether you want the subordinate to pinpoint the problem or propose a solution. If the latter, should he or she take action or just present you with alternatives? And do you choose the solution jointly or by yourself?
- Once you define your goals, consider whether the person you have chosen can handle the responsibility. Will the task be a

challenge, but not so difficult that the subordinate gets frustrated? "The art of managing is to figure out what each person is capable of, and create assignments that are within their reach, or slightly above, so they can learn," according to one expert.

- Do not make the mistake of spelling out in detail how the subordinate should approach the task. Be clear in your objectives, though, because some people fear that they will appear ignorant if they ask questions. Encourage questions. To give a sense of purpose, explain why the task is important. If it is something that seems menial or insignificant, note that it is a prelude to more meaningful assignments later on.
- Make sure that the subordinate has the time, budget, and data or equipment needed to get the job done—on a deadline. If someone needs training to accomplish the task, be

prepared to make the investment. Yes, you could do the job yourself in the time it takes to train someone else, but the hours spent training the individual will be recouped many times over in the future.

- Unless the project is relatively simple, set up specific checkpoints to review progress so that both you and your subordinate can be sure that work is progressing as planned. That way you can provide additional help, if needed, before the project is in serious trouble. If things are going well, you can let the subordinate know that you appreciate good work.
- Be prepared, too, to live with a less than perfect result. Let subordinates know you will support the outcome of their efforts, good or bad. Take responsibility for an occasional blooper, says an expert, and you will have loyal followers for life.[44]

departments might be store operations, pharmacy operations, and food operations (directly related to major organizational goals), while staff departments might be human resources and consumer affairs (more indirectly related to major goals). In a manufacturing organization, production and sales are typically considered line departments, while purchasing and accounting are normally staff departments. Among the departments that are considered staff in many organizations are human resources, legal, research and development, and purchasing. However, each organization must be evaluated in terms of its own major goals in designating line and staff.[45] For instance, in a major law firm, the legal function would be a line department, despite the fact that it often is a staff department in other types of organizations.

The usefulness of the distinction between line and staff departments becomes more clear when one considers the differences between line authority and staff authority. Line departments have **line authority,** which is authority that follows the chain of command established by the formal hierarchy. On the other hand, staff departments have **functional authority,** which is authority over others in the organization in matters related directly to their respective functions. For example, in the structure for a bank, shown in Figure 5, the line departments receive their authority through the chain of command connected to the president. The bank's staff departments have functional authority in relation to other departments, that is, authority only in their area of staff expertise. Staff depart-

Line authority The authority that follows the chain of command established by the formal hierarchy

Functional authority The authority of staff departments over others in the organization in matters related directly to their respective functions

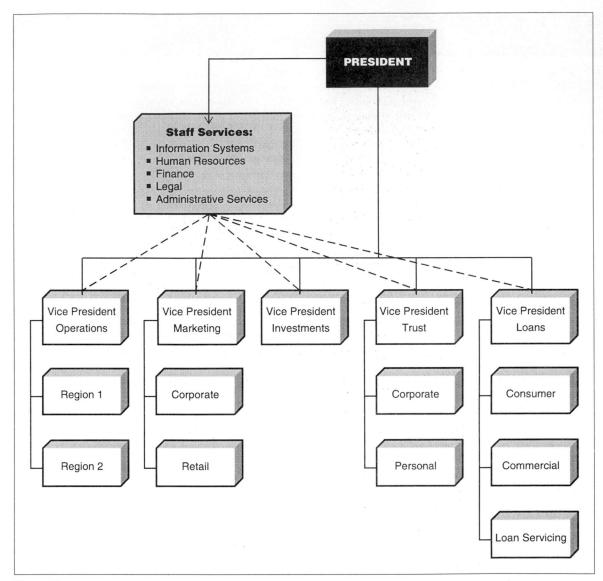

Figure 5 *Line and staff departments of a bank.*

ments facilitate vertical coordination by making their considerable expertise available where it is needed, rather than following the strict chain of command.

Still, conflicts frequently arise. For example, staff departments sometimes grow very large and begin to oversee the departments that they are supposed to assist. Before they were cut back, burgeoning staffs at Xerox second-guessed managers to such a point that they were counterproductive. The ability to adapt existing products to local markets or develop technological breakthroughs was seriously impaired. One former manager explained that moving from the conceptual to the detailed engineering phase of a product, a step that should have taken 2 to 4 weeks, took 2 years because of continual reviews by staff units.[46] Nevertheless, such conflicts are not inevitable, particularly if areas of responsibility are clarified and line and staff personnel are encouraged to operate as a team with joint accountability for final results.[47]

Recently, there has been a trend toward reducing the number of corporate-level staff personnel, as companies attempt to cut costs and speed up decision making. This can be seen, for example, at Nucor, a South Carolina–based company that runs steel minimills. Although it has annual revenues that exceed $800 million, Nucor operates with a corporate staff of less than 20. The small central office mainly monitors budgets, cash flow, and overall operations.[48] Enhancing vertical coordination is one structural issue in organizations; promoting horizontal coordination is another.

PROMOTING INNOVATION: METHODS OF HORIZONTAL COORDINATION

Suppose that you purchased a television set at a large local department store with the understanding that the TV would be delivered within 3 days but the set failed to arrive on time. Imagine that when you called to inquire about the delay, your call was passed up the hierarchy until you were talking with a vice president of the department store. You would probably begin to wonder about an organization in which a vice president is drawn into what should have been a routine transaction between sales and shipping. If all such problems had to be handled vertically, organizations would quickly become paralyzed.

Horizontal coordination The linking of activities across departments at similar levels

Instead, most organizations take steps to facilitate **horizontal coordination**, the linking of activities across departments at similar levels. Horizontal coordination provides an additional means of processing information in organizations. Organization structure specialist Jay R. Galbraith argues that the more organizations need to process information in the course of producing their products or services, the more methods of horizontal coordination they will need to use.[49] Organizations typically need to process more information when they face complex and/or changing technology, environmental uncertainty, and growing size. For example, when William H. Wilson founded the Pioneer/Eclipse Corporation, a small company that specializes in a floor-cleaning system, he was able to provide most of the necessary coordination himself within a traditional functional structure. As the company grew larger and more complex, it began to lose money because of insufficient horizontal coordination. In one situation, the sales department launched a promotion only to find that manufacturing and purchasing knew nothing about it and had insufficient materials and stock on hand to fill orders. In another instance, the credit department denied credit to a major account before the sales department could resolve the conflict more amicably. "The left hand," says one observer, "did not know what the right hand was doing."[50]

Because horizontal coordination facilitates processing information across the organization, it also helps promote innovation.[51] There are three reasons for this: First, new ideas are more likely to emerge when a diversity of views are shared. Second, awareness of problems and opportunities across areas can spark creative ideas. Third, involving others in the development of ideas often positively influences their willingness to help implement new ideas.

By facilitating the exchange of information across units at similar levels, horizontal coordination mechanisms, in essence, supplement the basic hierarchy and related methods of vertical coordination. Three major means that are particularly useful in promoting horizontal coordination are slack resources, information systems, and lateral relations (see Figure 6).[52]

Slack Resources

Slack resources A cushion of resources that facilitates adaptation to internal and external pressures, as well as initiation of changes

One interesting means of supporting horizontal coordination is the use of **slack resources,** a cushion of resources that facilitates adaptation to internal and external pressures, as well as initiation of changes.[53] You have probably benefited from the availability of slack resources in your personal life. For example, in your

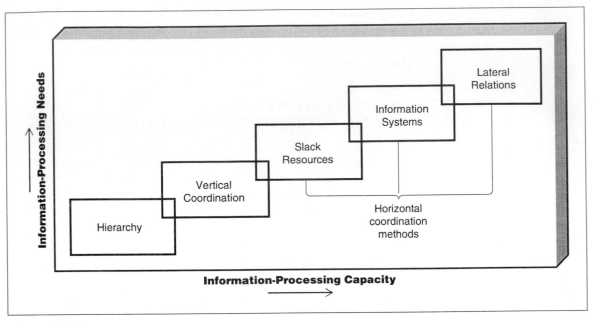

Figure 6 *Horizontal coordination methods for increasing information-processing capacity as needed.*

family, a slack resource might be an extra car, an extra television set, or your own telephone line. Through coordination and tighter programming of mutual schedules, your family might be able to get by with less, but doing so would take more effort and might hinder quick changes in plans. Because organizations face similar choices, they, too, often use slack resources, such as extra people, time, equipment, and inventory, to reduce the need for constant coordination among units and to provide some latitude in how resources are used.

Slack resources can also can help foster creativity and innovation.[54] For example, 3M encourages researchers to spend 15 percent of their time on projects of their own choice that have potential for long-term payoff (a practice the company calls "bootlegging"). In essence, this practice promotes the use of slack resources (time, equipment, and materials) to enhance the prospects for innovation.[55]

Information Systems

Another important and growing means of horizontal coordination is the use of information systems, particularly computerized ones, to coordinate various parts of organizations. For example, because of its far-flung international operations and its use of divisional structures, Citicorp experienced horizontal coordination difficulties. The company was frequently embarrassed when a client of one Citicorp unit would use the services of other units, perhaps even in other parts of the world, and receive conflicting advice. Even when the advice did not actually conflict, the fragmented guidance offered to clients did not maximize Citicorp's capacity to provide good service. The solution? Citicorp greatly enhanced the ability of various departments to exchange information by instituting a new computerized conferencing system. Called PARTICIPATE, the system allows offices around the world to communicate and coordinate their efforts quickly.[56]

Lateral Relations

Lateral relations The coordination of efforts through communicating and problem solving with peers in other departments or units, rather than referring most issues up the hierarchy for resolution

Another approach to horizontal coordination that is increasingly being used is lateral relations. **Lateral relations** is the coordination of efforts through communicating and problem solving with peers in other departments or units, rather than referring most issues up the hierarchy for consideration. Such collaboration promotes innovative solutions to difficulties and fosters creative responses to opportunities. Major means of lateral relations are direct contact, liaison roles, task forces, teams, and managerial integrators.[57]

Direct contact
Communication between two or more persons at similar levels in different work units for purposes of coordinating work and solving problems

DIRECT CONTACT   One means of lateral relations is **direct contact,** communication between two or more persons at similar levels in different work units for purposes of coordinating work and solving problems. Direct contact allows many managers at middle and lower levels to resolve issues without having to involve upper-level managers. In fact, problems can frequently be handled better by lower-level managers because they may be more familiar with the issues involved.

Liaison role   A role to which a specific individual is appointed to facilitate communication and resolution of issues between two or more departments

LIAISON ROLES   A **liaison role,** another means of lateral relations, is a role to which a specific individual is appointed to facilitate communication and resolution of issues between two or more departments. Liaison roles are typically reserved for situations in which there is a need for almost continuous coordination between the departments in order to function effectively. For example, an engineer may be appointed to maintain contact between the engineering and manufacturing departments.[58]

Liaison roles are becoming more common between private businesses and major customers. In this type of situation, the liaison person enhances horizontal coordination by working with various internal departments, as well as with the customer. The advantage of liaison roles in dealing with customers is illustrated by the comments of a steel company executive (who wished to remain anonymous). The executive maintains a full-time liaison person on site at Honda's plant in Marysville, Ohio. He explained that if there is a problem with stamping steel to make fenders and other car-body parts and if there were no liaison person, the scenario would go like this: The Honda people affected by the problem would go to their purchasing department. The purchasing department would contact the steel company salesperson. The salesperson would complain to the steel company product office. The product office would pass the issue on to the steel company department that made the steel for Honda. At that point, said the executive, the offending department is likely to deny responsibility for the problem and argue that ''it's a Honda stamping problem'' (i.e., the problem is not caused by the way in which the steel is made but, rather, by the way in which the steel is being stamped at the Honda plant).[59,*] A liaison person helps cut through such red tape by dealing directly with the departments closely associated with the problem.

TASK FORCES AND TEAMS   A *task force* is a temporary interdepartmental group usually formed to make recommendations on a specific issue. Task-force recommendations typically constitute advice. The person or group that appointed the task force can then decide whether or not to implement the recommendations. Task forces promote horizontal coordination by providing a vehicle through which individuals from different organizational units can share their ideas on specific issues and plan viable courses of action.

Teams, on the other hand, are either temporary or ongoing groups that are

---

* Jerry Flint and William Heuslein, ''An Urge to Service,'' *Forbes,* Sept. 18, 1989, pp. 172–176. Reprinted by permission of *Forbes* magazine.

expected to solve problems and implement solutions related to a particular issue or area. Teams are often composed of individuals from different departments, but they may also be made up of members from the same organizational unit. At its nylon fiber plant in Pensacola, Florida, Monsanto uses an interesting combination of liaison roles and teams in its new Adopt A Customer program, aimed at offering outstanding customer service. Under the program, Monsanto matches top customers with key employees who act as liaison persons. When problems arise, the liaison employees become "resource team leaders" who help bring about quick resolution of problems. For example, if a customer notifies the liaison employee that yarn is breaking during processing, the liaison person then becomes an internal resource team leader. He or she notifies the technical salespeople and quickly puts together a team with the necessary expertise and resources to resolve the difficulty promptly and offer innovative solutions if necessary. "The whole idea of Adopt A Customer is to give top priority to that problem not in three days, but on day one, with the first phone call from our customer," says Monsanto's manager of technical sales for carpet fibers.[60,*]

Managerial integrator
A separate manager who is given the task of coordinating related work that involves several functional departments

MANAGERIAL INTEGRATORS   A **managerial integrator,** another means of lateral relations, is a separate manager who is given the task of coordinating related work that involves several functional departments. Such managers typically have titles such as "project manager," "product manager," or "brand manager" and are not members of any of the departments whose activities they help coordinate. *Project managers* are usually responsible for coordinating the work associated with a particular project until its completion. They are used extensively in the aerospace, defense, and construction industries, in which large, technically complex projects must be completed within specified time limits and at contracted costs. *Product managers* orchestrate the launching of new products and services and may then continue coordinating interdepartmental work related to those products and services. For example, until recently, the Buick-Oldsmobile-Cadillac group of General Motors had a functional structure but used product managers to facilitate horizontal coordination across functional lines.[61] *Brand managers* coordinate organizational efforts involving particular name-brand products, most often within the soap, food, and toiletries industries. Brand managers help devise and implement brand strategies and plans, monitor results, and correct problems as they occur. In essence, managerial integrators act as horizontal coordinating agents. The use of managerial integrators allows fast reaction to environmental change and efficient use of resources because functional resources can be switched among various projects relatively easily. In addition, managerial integrators are in a good position to act as sponsors of innovative ideas.

They typically do not have line authority over the individuals and functional departments that they are attempting to coordinate. Rather, they must obtain the cooperation of the functional managers who control the major resources. In doing so, they must compete with others (e.g., managerial integrators for other projects) who also want the help of various functional departments in making their projects, products, or brands a success. As a result, managerial integrators must use their knowledge, competence, personality, group management skills, and persuasion abilities in working with functional managers and individuals who work within the functional departments and are assigned to their project.[62]

* Jerry Flint and William Heuslein, "An Urge to Service," *Forbes,* Sept. 18, 1989, pp. 172–176. Reprinted by permission of *Forbes* magazine.

CHAPTER SUMMARY

Organizing is the process of arranging work and resources so that planned goals can be achieved. One important part of the organizing function is determining organization structure. Organization structure consists of four main elements: job design, departmentalization of positions and units, methods of vertical coordination, and methods of horizontal coordination. Organization charts provide a graphic depiction of the broad outlines of an organization's structure and help employees trace the chain of command.

There are four main approaches to job design: job simplification, job rotation, job enlargement, and job enrichment. The job characteristics model helps guide job enrichment efforts by explaining the importance of core job characteristics, critical psychological states, and high growth-need strength to job outcomes. A related aspect of designing jobs is providing alternative work schedules. Major types of alternative work schedules include flextime, the compressed workweek, and job sharing.

Among the most commonly used forms of departmentalization are functional, divisional, hybrid, and matrix. There are five major means of achieving vertical coordination, which is the linking of activities at the top of the organization with those at the middle and lower levels: formalization, span of management, centralization versus decentralization, delegation, and line and staff positions.

Three major means that are particularly useful in facilitating horizontal coordination are slack resources, information systems, and lateral relations. Slack resources provide a cushion of resources that allows adaptation to change, while information systems enhance information exchange. Lateral relations, which involves coordinating efforts with peers in other departments and units, has several main forms: direct contact, liaison roles, task forces, teams, and managerial integrators. Methods of horizontal coordination are particularly useful in promoting innovation because they facilitate the exchange of ideas across organizational units.

QUESTIONS FOR DISCUSSION AND REVIEW

1 Explain the four elements that make up organization structure. What evidence can you see of these elements at your college or university?

2 Describe the relationship between an organization chart and an organization's chain of command. If you were new to an organization, how could an organization chart help you become oriented?

3 Contrast the various major approaches to job design. Use the job characteristics model to explain how you might go about enriching a particular job.

4 Distinguish among the three main types of alternative work schedules. What adjustments might be required to accommodate nontraditional work schedules?

5 Explain the role that formalization plays in vertical coordination. Give an example of a policy or rule that is likely to have a dysfunctional impact on organizational effectiveness. In what way should the policy or rule be changed to have a positive influence?

6 Explain the relationship between span of management and the extent to which an organization is flat or tall. Why are a number of major organizations attempting to make their structures more flat? What are some potential pitfalls associated with the process of making an organization structure flatter?

7 Contrast the advantages of centralization and those of decentralization, and explain when each approach is likely to be most appropriate. Why is delegation important to both?

8 Explain the differences between a line position and a staff position. Which type of position would you prefer to hold? Why?

9 Explain the concepts of slack resources and computer-based information systems as they apply to horizontal coordination. Cite examples showing how each one has been used to facilitate horizontal coordination in organizations?

10 Distinguish among the various types of lateral relations. How could they be used effectively in your college or university?

DISCUSSION QUESTIONS FOR CHAPTER OPENING CASE

1 What changes in vertical coordination were made at Hewlett-Packard? What other vertical coordination changes might you suggest?

2 What methods of horizontal coordination are apparent at Hewlett-Packard? What changes might be necessary?

3 What type of departmentalization is in use at Hewlett-Packard? What alternatives might be available?

MANAGEMENT EXERCISE: DESIGNING AN INNOVATING ORGANIZATION

 You have just landed a job as the administrative assistant to the CEO of Chameleon Technology, a fast-growing high-technology firm. You took the job because you want to learn more about how to manage high-technology firms. Also, you figure that because the company is growing rapidly, some very good career opportunities will open up quickly.

Chameleon has had tremendous success with its initial product, a small hard-disk drive for personal computers that holds considerably more data and costs less than offerings from competitors. Recently, the company introduced a new high-resolution video screen for use with personal computers that is also selling better than anticipated. Because the company is growing so quickly, the CEO is experiencing acute difficulties trying to handle long-range planning as well as the day-to-day developments in a rapidly changing competitive environment. For example, in a number of recent instances, sales were made but products were not shipped in a timely manner. In another case, although production was expanded to meet the rising demand, the human resource area was not notified of the need for additional workers. In both situations, the bottleneck occurred because the CEO's office did not coordinate these activities as well as it had in the past.

In addition, the CEO is concerned with fostering the kind of innovative thinking that will lead not only to improvements in existing products but also to new offerings. The CEO feels that Chameleon is too dependent on its two products and that the company is not moving fast enough in improving the disk drive and developing new products.

Because of your recent management studies, the CEO asks you to develop some ideas about how to achieve better coordination of the company's activities and also foster innovation. Chameleon is currently organized in a functional structure, with major departments in the following areas: manufacturing, sales, human resources, finance and accounting, and engineering. The company currently has about 600 employees.

Prepare a proposal to present to the CEO outlining the steps that could be taken to achieve better vertical and horizontal coordination, as well as to encourage more innovation.

REFERENCES

1. Based on Barbara Buell and Robert D. Hof, "Hewlett-Packard Rethinks Itself," *Business Week*, Apr. 1, 1991, pp. 76–79; Robert D. Hof, "Suddenly, Hewlett-Packard Is Doing Everything Right," *Business Week*, Mar. 23, 1992, pp. 88–89; Stephen Kreider Yoder, "Hewlett-Packard Is Too Busy to Notice Industry Slump," *The Wall Street Journal*, May 11, 1992, p. B4; and Ken Yamada, "Hewlett-Packard Names Lewis E. Platt President and Chief, Succeeding Young," *The Wall Street Journal*, July 7, 1992, p. B2.

2. John Child, *Organization: A Guide to Problems and Practice*, Harper & Row, New York, 1977, p. 10.

3. Alfred D. Chandler, Jr., "Origins of the Organization Chart," *Harvard Business Review*, March–April 1988, pp. 156–157.

4. W. Jack Duncan, *Great Ideas in Management*, Jossey-Bass, San Francisco, 1989.

5. George T. Milkovich and William F. Glueck, *Personnel/Human Resource Management: A Diagnostic Approach*, 4th ed., Business Publications, Plano, Tex., 1985.

6. Adam Smith, *The Wealth of Nations*, Dent, London, 1910.

7. J. Richard Hackman and Greg R. Oldham, *Work Redesign*, Addison-Wesley, Reading, Mass., 1980.

8. Robert H. Waterman, Jr., "The Power of Teamwork," *Best of Business Quarterly*, Spring 1988, pp. 17–25.

9. Beverly L. Kaye, *Up Is Not the Only Way: A Guide for Career Development Practitioners*, Prentice Hall, Englewood Cliffs, N.J., 1982; Joan E. Rigdon, "Using Lateral Moves to Spur Employees," *The Wall Street Journal*, May 26, 1992, p. B1.

10. M. D. Kilbridge, "Reduced Costs through Job Enrichment: A Case," *Journal of Business*, vol. 33, 1960, pp. 357–362.

11. Frederick Herzberg, *Work and the Nature of Man*, World Publishing, Cleveland, Ohio, 1966, and "One More Time: How Do You Motivate Employees?" *Harvard Business Review*, January–February 1968, pp. 53–62.

12. J. Richard Hackman and Greg R. Oldham, *Work Redesign*, Addison-Wesley, Reading, Mass., 1980.

13. Considerable research support exists for the importance of the job characteristics model, particularly as it relates to the job satisfaction of workers. See, for example, Brian T. Lohner, Raymond A. Noe, Nancy L. Moeller, and Michael P. Fitzgerald, "A Meta-Analysis of the Relation of Job Characteristics to Job Satisfaction," *Journal of Applied Psychology*, vol. 70, 1985, pp. 280–289; Ricky W. Griffin, "Effects of Work Redesign on Employee Perceptions, Attitudes, and Behaviors: A Long-Term Investigation," *Academy of Management Journal*, vol. 34, 1991, pp. 425–435; and Michael A. Campion and Carol L. McClelland, "Interdisciplinary Examination of the Costs and Benefits

of Enlarged Jobs: A Job Design Quasi-Experiment," *Journal of Applied Psychology,* vol. 76, 1991, pp. 186–198.

14. F. K. Plous, Jr., "Focus on Innovation: Chicago Bank Eliminates Paperwork Assembly Line," *World of Work Report,* November 1986, pp. 1–2.

15. R. T. Golembiewski and C. W. Proehl, "A Survey of the Empirical Literature on Flexible Workhours: Character and Consequences of a Major Innovation," *Academy of Management Review,* vol. 3, 1978, pp. 837–853; Simcha Ronen and Sophia B. Primps, "The Compressed Work Week as Organizational Change: Behavioral and Attitudinal Outcomes," *Academy of Management Review,* vol. 6, 1981, pp. 61–74; Dan R. Dalton and Debra J. Mesch, "The Impact of Flexible Scheduling on Employee Attendance and Turnover," *Administrative Science Quarterly,* vol. 35, 1990, pp. 370–387; Cathy Trost, "To Cut Costs and Keep the Best People, More Concerns Offer Flexible Work Plans," *The Wall Street Journal,* Feb. 2, 1992, p. B1.

16. "Why a Big Steelmaker Is Mimicking the Minimills," *Business Week,* Mar. 27, 1989, p. 92.

17. J. M. Ivancevich and H. L. Lyon, "The Shortened Workweek: A Field Experiment," *Journal of Applied Psychology,* vol. 62, 1977, pp. 34–37.

18. Edward G. Thomas, "Flextime Doubles in a Decade," *Management World,* April–May 1987, pp. 18–19.

19. John Child, *Organization: A Guide to Problems and Practice,* Harper & Row, London, 1984.

20. This section is based largely on Robert Duncan, "What Is the Right Organization Structure? Decision Tree Analysis Provides the Answer," *Organizational Dynamics,* Winter, 1979, pp. 59–80; and Daniel Robey, *Designing Organizations,* Irwin, Homewood, Ill., 1986, pp. 210–213.

21. Richard L. Daft, *Organization Theory and Design,* 3d ed., West, St. Paul, Minn., 1989; John Child, *Organization: A Guide to Problems and Practice,* Harper & Row, London, 1984.

22. Richard H. Hall, *Structures, Processes, and Outcomes,* Prentice-Hall, Englewood Cliffs, N.J., 1987; John

Child, *Organization: A Guide to Problems and Practice,* Harper & Row, London, 1984.

23. Jay Galbraith, *Organization Design,* Addison-Wesley, Reading, Mass., 1977, p. 43.

24. James W. Frederickson, "The Strategic Decision Process and Organizational Structure," *Academy of Management Review,* vol. 11, 1986, pp. 280–297; Alfred A. Marcus, "Responses to Externally Induced Innovation: Their Effects on Organizational Performance," *Strategic Management Journal,* vol. 9, 1988, pp. 387–402.

25. Buck Brown, "James Bildner's Spectacular Rise and Fall," *The Wall Street Journal,* Oct. 24, 1988, p. B1.

26. Eric Morgenthaler, "Herb Tea's Pioneer: From Hippie Origins to $16 Million a Year," *The Wall Street Journal,* May 6, 1981, p. 1; Nora Gallagher, "We're More Aggressive Than Our Tea," *Across the Board,* July–August 1983, pp. 45–50; Sandra D. Atchinson, "An Herbal Tea Party Gets a Bitter Response," *Business Week,* June 20, 1988, p. 52, "Kraft Is Celestial Seasonings' Cut of Tea," *Business Week,* July 28, 1986, p. 73; John Birmingham, "Strange Brew," *Adweeks' Marketing Week,* Nov. 21, 1988, pp. 18–22; Robert Ebisch, "Celestial after the LBO," *Business Plus/Daily Camera* (Denver, Colo.), July 4, 1989, pp. 1, 8–9; Susan D. Atchison, "Putting the Red Zinger Bank into Celestial," *Business Week,* Nov. 4, 1991, pp. 74–78.

27. John Child, *Organization: A Guide to Problems and Practice,* Harper & Row, London, 1984.

28. Dan R. Dalton, William D. Todor, Michael J. Spendolini, Gordon J. Fielding, and Lyman W. Porter, "Organization Structure and Performance: A Critical Review," *Academy of Management Review,* vol. 5, 1980, pp. 49–64; Robert D. Dewar and Donald P. Simet, "A Level Specific Prediction of Spans of Control Examining the Effects of Size, Technology, and Specialization," *Academy of Management Journal,* vol. 24, 1981, pp. 5–24; David D. Van Fleet, "Span of Management Research and Issues," *Academy of Management Journal,* vol. 26, 1983, pp. 546–552; C. W.

Barkdull, "Span of Control: A Method of Evaluation," *Michigan Business Review,* vol. 15, 1963, pp. 25–32; John Child, *Organization: A Guide to Problems and Practice,* Harper & Row, London, 1984, pp. 58–59.

29. This example is based on Stephen P. Robbins, *Organization Theory: Structure, Design, and Applications,* 3d ed., Prentice-Hall, Englewood Cliffs, N.J., 1990.

30. John Child, *Organization: A Guide to Problems and Practice,* Harper & Row, London, 1984, p. 53.

31. W. Norman Smallwood and Eliot Jacobsen, "Is There Life after Downsizing?" *Personnel,* December 1987, pp. 42–46; George Bailey and Julia Szerdy, "Is There Life after Downsizing?" *The Journal of Business Strategy,* January–February 1988, pp. 8–11.

32. Norman R. Horton, "Restructurings and Dismemberments," *Management Review,* March 1988, pp. 5–6; George Bailey and David Sherman, "Downsizing: The Alternatives May Be Cheaper," *Management Review,* April 1988, pp. 54–55.

33. Phil Nienstedt and Richard Wintermantel, "Motorola Restructures to Improve Productivity," *Management Review,* January 1987, p. 47 (reprinted from *Personnel,* August 1985).

34. Joseph B. White, "Toyota Wants More Managers Out on the Line," *The Wall Street Journal,* Aug. 2, 1989, p. A10; Yumiko Ono and Marcus W. Brauchli, "Japan Cuts the Middle-Management Fat," *The Wall Street Journal,* Aug. 8, 1989, p. B1.

35. Robert M. Tomasko, "Planned Downsizing: A Sustainable Alternative," *Management Review,* April 1988, pp. 55–58; Philip R. Nienstedt, "Effectively Downsizing Management Structures," *Human Resource Planning,* vol 12, 1989, pp. 155–156; Amanda Bennett, "Downsizing Doesn't Necessarily Bring an Upswing in Corporate Profitability," *The Wall Street Journal,* June 6, 1991, p. B1; Andrea Knox, "The Downside and Dangers of Downsizing," *The Washington Post,* Mar. 15, 1992, p. H2.

36. Mark Maremont, "Waterford Is Showing a Few Cracks," *Business Week,* Feb. 20, 1989, pp. 60–61; Cotton Timberlake, "Waterford Crystal

Appears on the Way to Recovery after Major Cost-Cutting," *The Wall Street Journal*, Jan. 24, 1992, p. A7A.

37. Howard M. Carlisle, "A Contingency Approach to Decentralization," *Advanced Management Journal*, July 1974, pp. 9–18.

38. Ibid.

39. John Child, *Organization: A Guide to Problems and Practice*, Harper & Row, London, 1984.

40. Michael Schroeder, "The Recasting of Alcoa," *Business Week*, Sept. 9, 1991, pp. 62–64; Dana Milbank, "Changes at Alcoa Point Up Challenges and Benefits of Decentralized Authority," *The Wall Street Journal*, Nov. 7, 1991, pp. B1–B2.

41. W. Jack Duncan, *Great Ideas in Management*, Jossey-Bass, San Francisco, 1989.

42. Carrie R. Leana, "Predictors and Consequences of Delegation," *Academy of Management Journal*, vol. 29, 1986, pp. 754–774. For an interesting treatment of lessons to be learned about delegation from U.S. presidents, see Edward J. Mayo and Lance P. Jarvis, "Delegation 101: Lessons from the White House," *Business Horizons*, September–October 1988, pp. 2–12.

43. Morgan W. McCall, Jr., and Michael M. Lombardo, "What Makes a Top Executive?" *Psychology Today*, February 1983, pp. 26–31.

44. Adapted from Laurie Baum, "Delegating Your Way to Job Survival," *Business Week*, Nov. 2, 1987, p. 206.

45. Vivian Nossiter, "A New Approach toward Resolving the Line and Staff Dilemma," *Academy of Management Review*, vol. 4, 1979, pp. 103–106.

46. "The Shrinking of Middle Management," *Business Week*, Apr. 25, 1983, pp. 53–54.

47. Edward C. Schleh, "Using Central Staff to Boost Line Initiative," *Management Review*, May 1976, pp. 17–23.

48. Thomas Moore, "Goodbye, Corporate Staff," *Fortune*, Dec. 21, 1987, pp. 65–76.

49. Jay R. Galbraith, *Organization Design*, Addison-Wesley, Reading, Mass., 1977.

50. Lucien Rodes, "At the Crossroads," *INC.*, February 1988, pp. 66–76.

51. Michael Tushman and David Nadler, "Organizing for Innovation," *California Management Review*, vol. 28, 1986, pp. 74–92; Andrew H. Van de Ven, "Central Problems in the Management of Innovation," *Management Science*, vol. 32, 1966, pp. 590–607; Rosabeth Moss Kanter, "When a Thousand Flowers Bloom: Structural, Collective, and Social Conditions for Innovation in Organizations," *Research in Organizational Behavior*, vol. 10, 1988, pp. 169–211.

52. This section relies heavily on Jay R. Galbraith, *Organization Design*, Addison-Wesley, Reading, Mass., 1977.

53. L. J. Bourgeois, "On the Measurement of Organizational Slack," *Academy of Management Review*, vol. 6, 1981, pp. 29–39.

54. Ibid.

55. Thomas J. Peters and Robert H. Waterman, Jr., *In Search of Excellence: Lessons from America's Best-Run Companies*, Harper & Row, New York, 1982.

56. Henry C. Mishkoff, "The Network Nation Emerges," *Management Review*, August 1986, pp. 29–31.

57. The material in this section is based largely on Jay R. Galbraith, *Organization Design*, Addison-Wesley, Reading, Mass., 1977.

58. Elizabeth V. Reynolds and J. David Johnson, "Liaison Emergence: Relating Theoretical Perspectives," *Academy of Management Review*, vol. 7, 1982, pp. 551–559.

59. Jerry Flint with William Heuslein, "An Urge to Service," *Forbes*, Sept. 18, 1989, pp. 172–176.

60. Ibid.

61. David E. Whiteside, "Roger Smith's Campaign to Change the GM Culture," *Business Week*, Apr. 7, 1986, pp. 84–85.

62. John R. Adams and Nicki S. Kirchof, "The Practice of Matrix Management," in David I. Cleland (ed.), *Matrix Management Systems Handbook*, Van Nostrand Reinhold, New York, 1984, p. 21; Ralph Katz and Thomas J. Allen, "Project Performance and the Locus of Influence in the R&D Matrix," *Academy of Management Journal*, vol. 28, 1985, pp. 67–87.

ACKNOWLEDGMENT

Figure

Figure 3: J. R. Hackman and G. R. Oldham, *Work Redesign*. Copyright © 1980 by Addison-Wesley Publishing Company, Inc. Reprinted with permission of the publisher.

CONCLUDING CASE

TEACHING AN ELEPHANT TO DANCE— GM REORGANIZES

When Roger B. Smith became chairman of General Motors in 1981, the automobile giant's share of the U.S. car market was crumbling and the company had just reported its first loss since 1921. Smith quickly appointed a task force of 10 select executives to consider a massive reorganization of a structure that had been in existence for decades. At that point, the major skeleton of the company consisted of two huge fiefdoms, Fisher Body and the General Motors Assembly Division (GMAD), as well as the five famous car divisions: Chevrolet, Pontiac, Oldsmobile, Buick, and Cadillac. With centralized design, engineering, and manufacturing, all GM's cars had begun to look remarkably similar, regardless of the nameplate and price tag. The situation had become so bad that Ford's Lincoln-Mercury division scored big with ads that poked fun at owners of GM luxury cars who were trying to pick their cars out from a sea of moderately priced, moderately altered clones.

At the same time, GM was criticized because it responded to the popular smaller cars of its Japanese competitors merely by making shrunken versions of its larger cars, a strategy that was essentially a failure. In addition, the company's structure made responsibility difficult to pinpoint, even though multiple organizational units had to sign their agreement for most decisions. Smith wanted a structure that would enable GM to respond more quickly to the market and to measure more easily the performance of its major organizational units.

After 15 months of planning, the world's largest corporation (the first to top $100 billion in sales) began a major structural overhaul in 1984 that was destined to take several years because of GM's monstrous size. The main reorganization created two new car groups: Buick, Oldsmobile, Cadillac (BOC) and Chevrolet, Pontiac, GM of Canada (CPC). The BOC group concentrated on large cars, while CPC was in charge of smaller cars. Each group had its own design, engineering, and manufacturing resources, while Fisher Body and GMAD were dissolved.

Smith's bold moves were aimed at giving GM "the key to the twenty-first century." Unfortunately, the reorganization took longer than planned, and critics argue that Smith did not move quickly enough to cut costs. GM's share of the U.S. auto market, which was about 45 percent when Smith took over, dropped to around 35 percent by the time he retired in 1990. His successor, Robert C. Stempel, faced a formidable competitive situation.

After GM posted a record loss of $4.45 billion in 1991, Stempel announced that the company would cut 74,000 employees and 21 production facilities by the mid-1990s. Because losses in GM's core North American automobile operations had been as much as $7 billion, GM's board of directors became impatient with the pace of change and, in an unusual move, forced a reshuffling of the company's top management. Among the major changes, Lloyd E. Reuss, GM's president and the individual who had been in charge of the hemorrhaging North American automobile operations, was demoted. John F. Smith, formerly head of GM's highly profitable European operations, was made president and chief operating officer of the company. Stempel remained CEO, but he lost his position as chairman of the executive committee of the board.

Under pressure from the board, Stempel and John Smith soon announced a management reorganization. The car design and manufacturing activities of the two major car groups, BOC and CPC, were merged into one group, North American Passenger Car Platforms. In addition, all vehicle sales and marketing operations were combined into one group, North American Vehicles Sales and Marketing. The heads of these two groups reported directly to Smith, eliminating a layer of management and enabling the company to more readily make fundamental changes and cut costs. Within a few months, GM announced plans to cut 74 percent of its corporate headquarters, which would reduce the size of the corporate staff from 13,500 to 3500. Still, impatient with the pace of change, the board named John Smith as CEO and ousted Stempel.*

---

* Tom Nicholson, James C. Jones, and Erik Ipsen, "GM Plans a Great Divide," *Newsweek,* Jan. 9, 1984, pp. 68–69; Urban C. Lehner and Robert L. Simpson, "GM Unveils Plan for Realigning Auto Making," *The Wall Street Journal,* Jan. 11, 1984, p. 3; Michael Brody, "Can GM Manage It All?" *Fortune,* July 8, 1985, pp. 22–28; David E. Whiteside, "Roger Smith's Campaign to Change the GM Culture," *Business Week,* Apr. 7, 1986, pp. 84–85; Paul Ingrassia and Jacob M. Schlesinger, "GM's Market Share Declined Last Year Even as Net Set a Mark," *The Wall Street Journal,* Feb. 15, 1989, pp. A1, A7; Warren Brown, "If You Were at the Helm of GM," *The Washington Post,* Jan. 14, 1990, pp. H1, H4; Paul Ingrassia, "GM Is to Name Stempel Today Chairman, Chief," *The Wall Street Journal,* Apr. 3, 1990, p. A3; Paul Ingrassia, "GM Posts Record '91 Loss of $4.45 Billion and Identified a Dozen Plants for Closing," *The Wall Street Journal,* Feb. 25, 1992, pp. A3, A8; Warren Brown and Frank Swoboda,

"GM Moves to Consolidate, Trip Top Management," *The Washington Post,* Apr. 25, 1992, pp. A1, A16; Alex Taylor III, "The Road Ahead at General Motors," *Fortune,* May 4, 1992, pp. 94–95; Frank Swoboda and Warren Brown, "GM Cutting Headquarters Staff by 74%," *The Washington Post,* July 15, 1992, pp. D1, D4; Jerry Flint, "Darkness before Dawn," *Forbes,* Nov. 23, 1992, pp. 42–43.

QUESTIONS FOR CONCLUDING CASE

1 How would you characterize the new changes in organization structure at GM? What difficulties might they create?

2 What can John Smith do to enhance vertical coordination?

3 What can John Smith do to boost horizontal coordination?

CONCLUDING CASE

VOLKSWAGEN GEARS UP FOR GLOBAL COMPETITION

During most of the 1980s and into the 1990s, Volkswagen AG has pursued a daring expansion strategy. The company acquired two major carmakers, Seat in Spain and Skoda in Czechoslovakia. According to Carl Hahn, head of Volkswagen during the period, the strategy was aimed at creating a "federated" European company: a true multinational emerging from the European theater, gaining the capacities to compete across the board worldwide." As part of the federated notion, there are separate divisions for each of the company's two existing *marques,* or brands, Volkswagen and Audi, and separate divisions for both Seat and Skoda. Each division was given a great deal of operating autonomy.

The rationale behind the structure is to allow the different brands to customize their products to meet the requirements of their particular groups of customers. Volkswagen believes that profits in the automobile industry of the future will be earned mainly from meeting the needs of increasingly narrow groups of customers. Having separate divisions provides flexibility. For example, if young drivers in Europe develop an appreciation for Mediterranean styling, then Seat can take the lead in appealing to this group.

At the same time, each division is to emphasize Volkswagen's traditional strength—namely, solid engineering and drivability. For this reason, a major research and development center is maintained in Germany for the use of all the divisions. Even with their autonomy, the divisions are still expected to cooperate and share when it is in the best interest of the company.

To facilitate cooperation, the chief executive of each division participates in the board of management of Volkswagen AG. In Germany, the principle of "codetermination" applies, whereby publicly traded companies have both a board of management and a supervisory board. The board of management usually has about 10 members, who are top executives in the company. This board is responsible for the day-to-day management and operation of the company. In contrast, the supervisory board exercises oversight. Half of its 12 to 20 members are employee representatives, and half represent owners and are elected in a manner similar to the election of board directors in the United States. The supervisory board has the exclusive power to appoint members of the management board, and it awards each executive a contract for from 1 to 5 years (renewable if the executive is performing satisfactorily). The supervisory board also participates in matters that can significantly affect employment. Hence its approval is necessary for foreign acquisitions (such as those of Seat and Skoda) and plans to establish factories abroad.

Indeed, Volkswagen has been building or retooling plants in various parts of the world, such as former East Germany, China, and Mexico. This expansion has enabled the company to serve national markets more effectively, as well as to reduce labor costs. The town of Wolfsburg, Germany, which is the site of Volkswagen headquarters, also contains the world's largest automotive plant under one roof. Partially because labor costs are exceptionally high, Volkswagen has expended considerable effort to automate the plant. Workers have been freed to concentrate on less routine aspects, such as customization, that are difficult for robots to do. In 1990, about 60 percent of Volkswagen's automobiles were made in the company's nine German plants. Less automation is used in other parts of the world, where labor costs are lower.

Although the expansion has led to greater market share, it has been expensive. The company is spending $50 billion over a 5-year period to expand across Europe from Czechoslovakia to Spain, including a $3 billion production line being established in Swickau in eastern Germany. Unfortunately, profits have been modest. The challenge facing the current Volkswagen chief executive, Ferdinand Piëch, is to cut costs and make Volkswagen's various expansion projects pay off. The company faces increased competition from Japanese cars that are made at less cost and from U.S. car manufacturers with operations in Europe.*

QUESTIONS FOR CONCLUDING CASE

1 Identify the type of departmentalization used by Volkswagen. What methods of vertical coordination are apparent at the company?
2 What mechanisms for promoting horizontal coordination and innovation can be identified? What could Volkswagen do to increase them?
3 Assess the impact of automation on job design at Volkswagen. Suggest some future possibilities for using job enrichment to enhance results at Volkswagen.

* Based on Bernard Avishai, "A European Platform for Global Competition: An Interview with VW's Carl Hahn," *Harvard Business Review,* July–August 1991, pp. 104–113; and John Templeman, "VW's New Boss Has the Beetle in His Blood," *Business Week,* Apr. 13, 1992, p. 56.

CHAPTER 7

Human Resource Management

GAINING THE EDGE

CHANGES IN HUMAN RESOURCE MANAGEMENT BOOST CARE

CARE, a not-for-profit organization based in New York City, was founded after World War II to provide a means by which Americans could send packages of food and clothing to European victims of the war. Gradually CARE, which stands for Cooperative for American Relief Everywhere, shifted its emphasis to sponsoring school-lunch, maternal-health, disaster relief, forestation, agribusiness development, and job training programs in Europe, Asia, Latin America, and Africa.

By 1980, CARE itself was experiencing serious difficulties, and its human resource management problems were particularly acute. Little human resource planning was being done. Job descriptions, when they existed at all, were poorly written. Many employees did not have appropriate skills for performing their jobs effectively. Yet few formalized training programs were available to help them improve their job-related skills. There were virtually no standards for performance, and performance appraisals were rarely conducted. The compensation system dispensed inconsistent and inequitable rewards.

As a result, a new team was brought in to revamp human resource management at CARE. In a dramatic change, human resources became an integral part of the management process. Today, the president for human resources reports directly to the chief operating officer and is included in all parts of the strategic management process. One of the organization's six major strategic areas is devoted to human resource management.

Current job descriptions now exist for every job. A human resource information system allows ready access to various types of information about employees, including an inventory of their skills. A formal orientation program introduces new employees to the organization, and training programs help them develop technical and other skills that they need to operate effectively. The company's new compensation system allocates pay on a more equitable basis, and a streamlined salary structure has helped recruit excellent professional and managerial talent. For example, CARE increased management salaries by 35 to 75 percent in order to attract more experienced people. The salaries are still not generous, but they are more competitive with small companies and other not-for-profit organizations. Performance standards are now a part of the company's new performance evaluation system, which is based on management by objectives. As a result, annual pay raises are awarded on the basis of merit. The standards have also induced a portion of the management staff to resign over a period of time rather than meet the new expectations for performance.

Although numerous changes have been made in various areas at CARE, many of the positive results are attributable to the improved management of human resources. CARE was singled out by *Fortune* magazine in 1987 as one of America's best-run charities—very different, indeed, from the manner in which the organization operated earlier. Human resource management improvement continues to be the order of the day at CARE.[1]

While there were multiple causes for the problems that beset CARE by 1980, many of the difficulties can be traced to shortcomings in acquiring, developing, and utilizing human resources. In this chapter, we discuss the organizing function by examining how organizations, like CARE, can acquire and develop the human resources needed to activate structural elements. Without employees who can perform the necessary tasks, organizations have little hope of achieving their goals.

Human resource management (HRM) is the management of various activities designed to enhance the effectiveness of an organization's work force in achieving organizational goals.[2] In exploring this topic, we look first at the human resource management process and consider its strategic importance. We next investigate human resource planning and various aspects of staffing the organization. We also examine methods of developing organization members and evaluating their performance. Finally, we consider important issues in the areas of compensating organization members and maintaining effective work-force relationships.

Human resource management (HRM) The management of various activities designed to enhance the effectiveness of an organization's work force in achieving organizational goals

STRATEGIC HUMAN RESOURCE MANAGEMENT

In a growing number of organizations, such as CARE and 3M, high-level managers within the human resource management function participate directly in strategy formulation and implementation.[3] These organizations are at the forefront of a trend toward recognizing human resources as a crucial element in the strategic success of organizations.[4] In this section, we introduce the major aspects of the human resource management process before exploring in greater depth the main reasons for its increasingly important strategic role.

The HRM Process: An Overview

As indicated in Figure 1, human resource management encompasses a number of important activities. One critical aspect of the process is human resource planning. This involves assessing the human resource needs associated with an organization's strategic plan and developing plans to meet those needs. The staffing component includes attracting and selecting individuals for appropriate positions. Once individuals become part of the organization, their ability to contribute effectively is usually enhanced by various development and evaluation efforts, such as training and periodic performance evaluations. Compensating employees is another important factor in the HRM process, because adequate rewards are critical not only to attracting but also to motivating and retaining valuable employees. Finally, managers must respond to various issues that influence work-force perceptions of the organization and its treatment of employees.

In order to explore human resource management in an orderly fashion, the activities that make up the HRM process are discussed sequentially in this chapter. The components, though, are actually highly interrelated. A situation at F. W. Woolworth highlights the importance of this relationship. When a group of British financiers took over the British arm of Woolworth from its American parent, the chain of 1000 stores had a tarnished image and 30,000 employees with a reputation for poor service. Investigation revealed many interrelated problems, such as poor employment interviewing practices (interviews typically

Figure 1 *The human resource management process.*

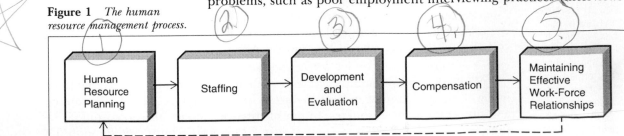

| Human Resource Planning | Staffing | Development and Evaluation | Compensation | Maintaining Effective Work-Force Relationships |

lasted only 10 minutes), little training for either sales staff or managers, and a compensation system that failed to reward good performance. Thus various components of the HRM process collectively reinforced the service problems.[5]

Human resource professionals operating within human resource departments typically play a major role in designing the elements in the HRM process and in supporting their use by line managers. Nevertheless, line managers are ultimately responsible for the effective utilization of human resources within their units. Thus they carry out many aspects of the HRM process, particularly in relation to implementing strategic plans.

The Strategic Importance of HRM

Understanding the strategic potential of human resource management in organizations is a relatively recent phenomenon, one that has evolved through three main stages.[6] From early in this century until the mid-1960s, HRM activities were in the *file maintenance* stage. During this period, much of the emphasis was on screening applicants, orienting new employees, recording employee-related data for personnel purposes, and planning company social functions (such as the company picnic).

The second stage, *government accountability*, began with the passage of the Civil Rights Act of 1964. (Title VII of the act forbids employment discrimination based on race, color, religion, sex, or national origin.) It continued as additional laws, court rulings, and federal regulatory guidelines increasingly influenced various aspects of employment, such as hiring and promotion decisions, pension plans, and health and safety issues. (We discuss several of these laws in this chapter.) Of course, some laws, particularly those governing relations with unions, existed before 1964. But the mid-1960s ushered in an era of accelerated governmental regulation of employment issues, which continues to a large degree today.

The third stage, which began in the late 1970s and early 1980s, is the *competitive advantage* stage. In this stage, human resource management is increasingly viewed as important for both the formulation and the implementation of strategy. Thus, under some circumstances, human resources can be a source of distinct competence that forms a basis for strategy formulation. For example, 3M's noted scientists enable the company to pursue a differentiation strategy based on innovative products. Under other circumstances, HRM activities may be used to support strategy implementation.[7] At the competitive advantage stage, then, human resources are considered explicitly in conjunction with strategic management, particularly through the mechanism of human resource planning.[8]

HUMAN RESOURCE PLANNING

Human resource planning
The process of determining future human resource needs relative to an organization's strategic plan and devising the steps necessary to meet those needs

Job analysis The systematic collection and recording of information concerning the purpose of a job, its major duties, the conditions under which it is performed, the contacts with others that job performance requires, and the knowledge, skills, and abilities needed to perform the job effectively

Human resource planning is the process of determining future human resource needs relative to an organization's strategic plan and devising the steps necessary to meet those needs.[9] Human resource professionals and line managers consider both demand and supply issues, as well as potential steps for addressing any imbalances. Such planning often relies on job analysis as a means of understanding the nature of jobs under consideration.

Job Analysis

Job analysis is the systematic collection and recording of information concerning the purpose of a job, its major duties, the conditions under which it is performed, the contacts with others that job performance requires, and the knowledge, skills, and abilities needed to perform the job effectively. Job analysis information can be collected in a variety of ways. These include observing individuals as they do their jobs, conducting interviews with individuals and their superiors, having individuals keep diaries of job-related activities, and distributing questionnaires to be completed by job incumbents and their supervisors.[10]

The results of job analysis are often used to develop job descriptions. A **job description** is a statement of the duties, working conditions, and other significant requirements associated with a particular job. Job descriptions are frequently combined with job specifications (see Table 1). A **job specification** is a statement of the skills, abilities, education, and previous work experience that are required to perform a particular job. Formats for job descriptions and job specifications tend to vary among organizations, but the information is typically used for activities that require a solid understanding of the job and the qualifications necessary for performing it. Such activities include human resource planning, recruitment, selection, and performance appraisal.[11]

Job description A statement of the duties, working conditions, and other significant requirements associated with a particular job

Job specification A statement of the skills, abilities, education, and previous work experience that are required to perform a particular job

Demand for Human Resources

A significant aspect of human resource planning is assessing the demand for human resources. Such an assessment involves considering the major forces that affect the demand and using basic forecasting aids to predict it.

TABLE 1	Sample Job Description and Job Specification

THE PORT AUTHORITY OF NEW YORK AND NEW JERSEY

Data Control Clerk (1127)

Under immediate supervision receives and reviews input and output data for recurring computer reports and records. Receives detailed instructions on assignments which are not routine. Work is checked through standard controls.

DUTIES
Job Description

Operates data-processing equipment such as Sorters (IBM 083), Bursters (Std Register and Moore), decollators (Std Register), Communications Terminal (IBM 3775), and interactive operation of IBM 327X family of terminals to process accounting, personnel, and other statistical reports.

Feeds and tends machine according to standard instructions.

Makes minor operating adjustments to equipment.

Submits data with necessary documentation for computer processing.

Reviews output data and corrects problems causing incorrect output.

Revises and maintains lists, control records, and source data necessary to produce reports.

Distributes output reports by predetermined instructions.

Operates magnetic-tape cleaning and testing equipment.

Corrects and/or adjusts files via use of time-sharing terminals.

QUALIFICATIONS
Job Specification

Six months' experience in operating data-processing equipment.

Ability to reconcile differences and errors in computer data.

Source: Reprinted from David J. Rachman, Michael H. Mescon, Courtland L. Bovée, and John V. Thill, *Business Today,* 6th ed., McGraw-Hill, New York, 1990, p. 244.

MAJOR FORCES   Human resource demand is affected by an organization's *environment,* including factors in both the general environment, or mega-environment, and the task environment. For example, an aspect of the general environment, such as the economy, can alter demand for a product or service and, thus, affect the need for certain types of employees.

In addition to environmental factors, *changing organizational requirements,* such as alterations in the strategic plan, can also influence the demand for human resources. Similarly, internal *work-force changes,* such as retirements, resignations, terminations, deaths, and leaves of absence, frequently cause major shifts in the need for human resources.

FORECASTING AIDS   Several basic techniques are used to forecast human resource demand in organizations.[12] Judgmental forecasting is based mainly on the views of knowledgeable individuals, particularly line managers, who are often in a good position to make estimates about future needs for various types of workers. Quantitative forecasting, which relies on numerical data and mathematical models, is another frequently used approach. Finally, technological, or qualitative, forecasting, which is aimed mainly at predicting long-term trends in technology and other important aspects of the environment, can also help predict future demand.

Supply of Human Resources

Demand is only one side of the equation governing whether an organization will have sufficient human resources to operate effectively. In assessing the other side, supply, human resource professionals and managers consider both internal and external labor supplies.

INTERNAL LABOR SUPPLY   One prime supply source is the pool of current employees who can be transferred or promoted to help meet demands for human resources. Major means of assessing the internal labor supply include skills inventories, replacement planning, and succession planning.[13]

A **skills inventory** is a data bank (usually computerized) containing basic information about each employee that can be used to assess the likely availability of individuals for meeting current and future human resource needs. A skills inventory typically contains information regarding each employee's performance, knowledge, skills, experience, interests, and relevant personal characteristics.

Replacement planning is a means of identifying potential candidates to fill specific managerial positions. This is done through the use of replacement charts. A **replacement chart** is a partial organization chart showing major managerial positions, current incumbents, potential replacements for each position (usually including, for each individual, a current performance rating and an assessment of preparedness to assume the position), and the age of each person on the chart (see Figure 2). With replacement charts, age is used to track possible retirements, but it is not considered in determining promotions. On the contrary, managers must be careful not to discriminate against older workers in making such choices. The Age Discrimination in Employment Act of 1967, as amended in 1978 and 1986, prohibits discrimination against employees and job applicants who are more than 40 years old. The law covers promotion, as well as hiring and termination decisions. Under one of its provisions, organizations cannot force employees to retire because of age (with a few exceptions, including law enforcement officers and fire fighters).[14]

Replacement planning focuses on specific candidates who could fill desig-

Skills inventory   A data bank (usually computerized) containing basic information about each employee that can be used to assess the likely availability of individuals for meeting current and future human resource needs

Replacement chart   A partial organization chart showing the major managerial positions in an organization, current incumbents, potential replacements for each position, and the age of each person on the chart

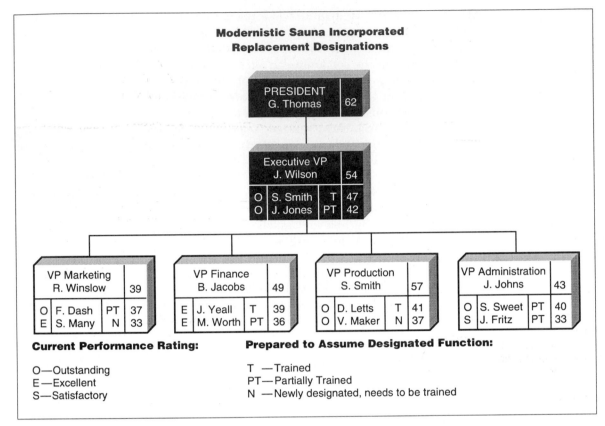

Figure 2 *Replacement chart for Modernistic Sauna, Inc.*

nated managerial positions. In contrast, *succession planning* is a means of identifying individuals with high potential and ensuring that they receive appropriate training and job assignments aimed at their long-run growth and development. Thus succession planning provides the organization with a well-qualified pool of individuals from which middle and top managers can be drawn in the future.

EXTERNAL LABOR SUPPLY Some reliance on the external labor supply is usually necessary because of organizational expansion and/or employee attrition. Periodic estimates of labor supplies in a variety of categories are made by government agencies, including the Bureau of Labor Statistics of the U.S. Department of Labor, and by industry and human resource associations. In addition, human resource professionals, particularly those heavily engaged in recruitment and selection, are often knowledgeable about supply trends in given areas and can supplement the knowledge of line managers.[15]

Reconciling Demand and Supply

After estimating the demand and supply of human resources, managers must often take steps to balance the two.[16] If estimates show that the internal supply of labor is too large, then managers need to make plans to reduce the number of employees through such measures as resignations and retirements, early retirement programs, or, possibly, layoffs. On the other hand, if additional employees are necessary, then plans must be made for promoting and transferring current organization members, if desirable, as well as for hiring new workers.

AFFIRMATIVE ACTION ISSUES One important aspect of reconciling supply and demand is considering the affirmative action implications. **Affirmative ac-**

Affirmative action Any special activity undertaken by employers to increase equal employment opportunities for groups protected by federal equal employment opportunity laws and related regulations

tion is any special activity undertaken by employers to increase equal employment opportunities for groups protected by federal equal employment opportunity laws and related regulations. As mentioned earlier, Title VII of the Civil Rights Act of 1964 (as amended by the Equal Employment Opportunity Act of 1972) forbids employment discrimination on the basis of race, color, religion, sex, or national origin.[17] Groups covered by Title VII and related laws and regulations are often referred to as "protected groups."

More recently, the Americans with Disabilities Act (ADA) of 1990, which was implemented in mid-1992, prohibits private employers, state and local governments, employment agencies, and labor unions from engaging in employment discrimination against qualified individuals with disabilities. The law covers recruitment, firing, promotions, compensation, job training, and other terms, conditions, and privileges of employment. Furthermore, the law requires that employers make reasonable accommodations so that a qualified disabled individual can perform a job, unless the adjustments would impose an undue hardship on the employer.

Affirmative action plan A written, systematic plan that specifies goals and timetables for hiring, training, promoting, and retaining groups protected by federal equal employment laws and related regulations

Organizations often have patterns of employment in which protected groups are underrepresented in certain areas, such as management, relative to the number of group members who have appropriate credentials in the marketplace. To remedy this, an organization may adopt an **affirmative action plan**, a written, systematic plan that specifies goals and timetables for hiring, training, promoting, and retaining groups protected by federal equal employment laws and related regulations.[18] Such plans are required, by federal regulations, in organizations with federal contracts greater than $50,000 and with 50 or more employees. The plans, which must be filed with the Department of Labor, have to include provisions for hiring the disabled (as stipulated by the Rehabilitation Act of 1973). Courts sometimes require that organizations formulate affirmative action plans because of evidence of past discriminatory practices. Many organizations, though, establish affirmative action programs on a voluntary basis.[19]

Such programs must balance efforts to assist women and minorities against the rights of others who may be competing for the same jobs. For example, courts have generally been unwilling to approve plans that cause individuals to lose their jobs in order to make room for members of protected groups, but they have allowed more limited burdens, such as postponements of promotions.[20] Affirmative action programs continue to be challenged in the courts by individuals and groups who do not fit into the protected category and, therefore, charge reverse discrimination.

POPULATION TRENDS Demographic shifts are also causing organizations to place emphasis on hiring women and minorities. Bureau of Labor Statistics' projections indicate that annual work-force growth has slowed since 1988 and will not increase until at least the year 2000. This is partly because most of the baby-boomers wishing to work have already been absorbed into the work force and there is no similar bulge of workers behind them. It is estimated that, out of necessity, women will constitute about 47 percent of the work force and minorities and immigrants about 26 percent by the year 2000. As a result, organizations are taking steps to more effectively manage the increasing diversity. One such company is the Digital Equipment Corporation. At its factory in Boston, which makes computer keyboards, the 350 employees represent 44 countries. Because of the 19 different languages spoken, written plant announcements are printed in English, Chinese, French, Spanish, Portuguese, Vietnamese, and Haitian Creole.[21] Some organizations are filling vacancies with part-time workers, many of whom are senior citizens who have retired from full-time jobs. For instance, the Travelers Corporation, an insurance company based in Hartford, Connecticut, runs a job bank for area retirees in order to have workers available for part-time and temporary clerical and administrative jobs.[22] Diversity issues and other considerations that grow out of human resource planning then become the basis for staffing efforts.

STAFFING

Staffing The set of activities aimed at attracting and selecting individuals for positions in a way that will facilitate the achievement of organizational goals

Staffing is the set of activities aimed at attracting and selecting individuals for positions in a way that will facilitate the achievement of organizational goals. Given the slower growth of the work force, such activities are taking on new meaning as organizations begin to experience greater difficulty in attracting and retaining needed employees. With fewer workers entering the labor force, recruitment can be more challenging, particularly in regard to entry-level workers.

Recruitment

Recruitment The process of finding and attempting to attract job candidates who are capable of effectively filling job vacancies

Recruitment is the process of finding and attempting to attract job candidates who are capable of effectively filling job vacancies.[23] Job descriptions and job specifications, both mentioned earlier, are important in the recruiting process because they specify the nature of the job and the qualifications required of job candidates. Recruiting can be conducted both internally and externally.

INTERNAL RECRUITMENT Most vacant positions in organizations are filled through internal recruitment, the process of finding potential *internal* candidates and encouraging them to apply for and/or be willing to accept organizational jobs that are open.[24] CARE, for example, has a policy of filling job vacancies from within and conducts recruiting through external sources only when a job cannot be filled internally. The advantages and disadvantages of internal recruitment are summarized in Table 2.[25]

TABLE 2	Advantages and Disadvantages of Internal and External Recruitment
Advantages	**Disadvantages**
INTERNAL RECRUITMENT	
1. Candidates are already oriented to the organization.	1. There may be fewer new ideas.
2. Reliable information is available about candidates.	2. Unsuccessful contenders may become upset.
3. Recruitment costs are lower.	3. Selection is more susceptible to office politics.
4. Internal morale is increased due to upward-mobility opportunities.	4. Expensive training may be necessary.
5. Good performance is rewarded.	5. Candidates' current work may be disrupted.
EXTERNAL RECRUITMENT	
1. Candidates are a potential source of new ideas.	1. The probability of mistake is higher because of less reliable information.
2. Candidates may have broader experience.	2. Potential internal candidates may be resentful.
3. Candidates may be familiar with competitors.	3. The new employee may have a slower start because of the need for orientation to the organization.
4. Candidates may have new specialties.	4. The recruitment process may be expensive.

Job posting A practice whereby information about job vacancies is placed in conspicuous places in an organization, such as on bulletin boards or in organizational newsletters

One major method of recruiting internally is **job posting,** a practice whereby information about job vacancies is placed in conspicuous places in an organization, such as on bulletin boards or in organizational newsletters. At CARE, for instance, all nonunion jobs are posted for at least 15 working days, while union jobs are posted for at least 3 working days, in conformance with union contracts. Skills inventories and replacement charts, mentioned earlier, are also used to locate potential candidates for internal recruiting.

EXTERNAL RECRUITMENT External recruitment is the process of finding potential *external* candidates and encouraging them to apply for and/or be willing to accept organizational jobs that are open. The advantages and disadvantages of external recruitment are listed in Table 2.

A variety of sources exist for obtaining external job candidates. Advertising is generally the most heavily used recruiting source. Other sources include college recruiting programs, employment agencies, and referrals by employees. Rather than focusing on a particular recruitment source per se, recruiters should usually concentrate first on the types of qualifications that are required and then think of the best way to locate individuals who have those qualifications.[26]

One major issue related to external recruiting is the tendency of recruiters and managers to provide candidates with an overly positive view of the organization in order to attract new employees. Unfortunately, this strategy can backfire: an individual who accepts a position on such terms may become dissatisfied and leave when the position fails to meet his or her inflated expectations. An alternative approach is the **realistic job preview,** a technique used during the recruiting process in which the job candidate is presented with a balanced view of both the positive and the negative aspects of the job and the organization.[27] Even though realistic job previews may reduce the number of candidates interested in a position, such previews are likely to have a positive effect on job satisfaction, performance, and the length of employment of those ultimately hired.[28] Recruiting, though, is only one part of the staffing process. Decisions must also be made about the candidates to whom job offers will be extended.

Realistic job preview A technique used during the recruiting process in which the job candidate is presented with a balanced view of both the positive and the negative aspects of the job and the organization

Selection

Selection The process of determining which job candidates best suit organizational needs

Selection is the process of determining which job candidates best suit organizational needs.[29] During this process, managers must determine the extent to which job candidates have the skills, abilities, and knowledge required to perform effectively in the positions for which they are being considered. Before discussing more specifically the most commonly used selection methods, we examine an important concept underlying their use, validity.

Validity The degree to which a measure actually assesses the attribute that it is designed to measure

VALIDITY In order to make adequate assessments of candidates, selection methods must have validity. **Validity** is the degree to which a measure actually assesses the attribute that it is designed to measure. As applied to selection, validity addresses how well a selection device (such as a test) actually predicts a candidate's future job performance.[30]

Organizations often conduct studies to determine the validity of selection methods, particularly if the methods have an adverse impact on groups protected by equal employment opportunity laws and regulations. A selection method is generally considered to have an **adverse impact** when the job selection rate for a protected group is less than 80 percent of the rate for the majority group. For example, requiring a high school diploma for entry-level positions might have an adverse impact because the percentage of minority-group mem-

Adverse impact The effect produced when a job selection rate for a protected group is less than 80 percent of the rate for the majority group

bers with high school diplomas tends to be smaller than that of majority-group members. Under such conditions, an organization can continue to use the selection method only if it can demonstrate that the method is a valid predictor of job performance and that there is no other approach that would have similar validity without the adverse impact.

Organizations are permitted to discriminate against certain groups in employment when a **bona fide occupational qualification (BFOQ)** exists. A BFOQ is a legitimate job qualification that necessitates an employer's selecting an individual in a certain sex, religion, national-origin, or age group.[31] For example, in hiring models to display men's clothing, a mail-order firm can limit the job to males. Generally, there are few circumstances under which employers can use a BFOQ as a justification for employment discrimination.

MAJOR SELECTION METHODS More than one selection method is typically used in assessing job candidates. The most prevalent methods include the use of application blanks, selection interviews, tests, assessment centers, and reference checks.[32]

An **application blank** is a form containing a series of inquiries about an applicant's educational background, previous job experience, physical health, and other information that may be useful in assessing an individual's ability to perform a job. It serves as a prescreening device to help determine whether an applicant meets the minimum requirements of a position, and it allows preliminary comparisons with the credentials of other candidates.[33] Résumés furnished by job applicants often also provide useful background information.

Another selection method, the **selection interview,** is a relatively formal, in-depth conversation conducted for the purpose of assessing a candidate's knowledge, skills, and abilities, as well as providing information to the candidate about the organization and potential jobs.[34] A survey of national firms found that most outside job candidates who are considered seriously enough to warrant an interview are interviewed at least twice. Typically, one interview is conducted by a professional recruiter from the human resource department and the other by the supervisor of the unit with the open position.[35]

As an indication of the perceived importance of the interview, 90 percent of the responding companies in one large survey reported that they placed more confidence in the selection interview than in any other selection method.[36] Ironically, despite their popularity, interviews, as they are widely conducted, have relatively low validity as a selection device. A major reason for this is that many interviewers follow a format that constitutes an *unstructured interview*. With this type of interview, little planning is done regarding the information to be collected, and the interviewer asks whatever questions happen to come to mind.[37] Because of the lack of structure, data about candidates are collected in a nonsystematic way that yields insufficient information for evaluating or comparing candidates adequately.

One potential remedy is the *structured interview,* in which the interviewer has a predetermined set of questions that are asked in sequence, with virtually no deviations. This type of interview is sometimes used to advantage if a large number of candidates are to be prescreened or if interviewers are relatively untrained. While a structured interview yields more valid data than an unstructured one, a structured interview is almost mechanical and may convey disinterest to the candidate. It also does not allow the interviewer to probe interesting or unusual issues that may arise.

To overcome these disadvantages and still acquire reasonably valid data for making a selection decision, interviewers can use a *semistructured interview.* With this format, the interviewer relies on a number of predetermined questions but

---

Bona fide occupational qualification (BFOQ) A legitimate job qualification that necessitates an employer's selecting an individual in a certain sex, religion, national-origin, or age group

Application blank A form containing a series of inquiries about such issues as an applicant's educational background, previous job experience, physical health, and other information that may be useful in assessing an individual's ability to perform a job

Selection interview A relatively formal, in-depth conversation conducted for the purpose of assessing a candidate's knowledge, skills, and abilities, as well as providing information to the candidate about the organization and potential jobs

also asks spontaneous questions to explore any unique issues that arise in regard to a particular candidate (such as an unexplained break in work history, unusual work experience, or the individual's particular strengths and weaknesses). A semistructured approach can make the interview process more comfortable for the candidate and can create a better impression of the organization because the interview is more conversational. For some hints on conducting a semistructured interview, see the Practically Speaking discussion, "How to Conduct an Effective Interview."

Employment test A means of assessing a job applicant's characteristics through paper-and-pencil responses or simulated exercises

Another selection device is an **employment test,** a means of assessing a job applicant's characteristics through paper-and-pencil responses or simulated exercises. Three major types of tests used in the selection process are ability, personality, and performance tests.[39]

Ability tests measure mainly mental (such as intelligence), mechanical, and clerical abilities or sensory capacities (such as vision and hearing). Except for measures of sensory capacities, the tests are usually the paper-and-pencil type.

Personality tests are means of measuring characteristics, such as patterns of thoughts, feelings, and behaviors, that are distinctly combined in a particular individual and influence that individual's interactions in various situations. Paper-and-pencil personality tests measure such characteristics as sociability, independence, and need for achievement. The use of personality tests for selection purposes is subject to considerable debate because of both the difficulty of accurately measuring personality characteristics and the problems associated with matching them appropriately to job requirements. They should be used with caution in selection processes.[40]

Performance, or *work sample, tests* are means of measuring practical ability on a specific job. In this type of test, the applicant completes some job activity under structured conditions. For example, a word-processing applicant might be asked to prepare materials on equipment that would be used on the job, while a service representative may be asked to handle a simulated situation involving a complaining customer. Although they can be costly if special facilities and equipment are needed, performance tests, when devised to closely reflect important aspects of the job, tend to be valid predictors of future performance. They also tend to be less susceptible to the adverse-impact problems that plague many paper-and-pencil tests.

Assessment center A controlled environment used to predict the probable managerial success of individuals mainly on the basis of evaluations of their behaviors in a variety of simulated situations

An **assessment center** is a controlled environment used to predict the probable managerial success of individuals mainly on the basis of evaluations of their behaviors in a variety of simulated situations. The situations (or exercises) are essentially performance tests that reflect the type of work done in managerial positions. According to one estimate, assessment center programs are in operation in more than 2000 organizations, including AT&T, where the technique was originally pioneered.[41]

Reference checks Attempts to obtain job-related information about job applicants from individuals who are knowledgeable about the applicants' qualifications

Reference checks are attempts to obtain job-related information about job applicants from individuals who are knowledgeable about the applicants' qualifications. Reference checks can be obtained by mail, by telephone, and in person. Such checks are conducted to verify information on application blanks and résumés and, sometimes, to collect additional data that will facilitate the selection decision. One reason for the widespread use of reference checks is that, according to one estimate, between 20 and 25 percent of all candidate application blanks and résumés contain at least one major fabrication.[42]

DEVELOPMENT AND EVALUATION

After individuals are hired, both they and their employing organizations will ultimately gain from efforts aimed at enhancing their knowledge, skills, and

PRACTICALLY SPEAKING

HOW TO CONDUCT AN EFFECTIVE INTERVIEW

You have a job vacancy in your unit and need to interview several job candidates. What should you do? There are a number of steps you can take before, during, and after the interview to increase the likelihood of obtaining information that will be useful in making your selection decision.

BEFORE THE INTERVIEW

Much of the secret of conducting an effective interview is in the preparation. The following guidelines will enhance your preparatory skills:

Determine the job requirements. Using the job description and job specification, prepare a list of characteristics that the person will need to possess in order to perform the job. For example, suppose that you are a bank manager and have a job opening for a teller. Important characteristics would include oral communication skills, a willingness to check for errors, the ability to get along with others, and a service orientation in handling customers. Once the major characteristics are identified, you can develop an interview guide.

Prepare a written interview guide. A written guide of what you wish to cover during the interview will ensure that major points are addressed with each interviewee. You need to plan questions that assess the degree to which job candidates possess the characteristics necessary for the job.

Past performance is often a good predictor of future performance. Therefore, it is useful to ask questions about what a person has actually done, rather than focusing on generalities or speculations about what the person will do in the future. For example, in assessing how well the individual interacts with customers, a relatively *poor* question would be: "How well do you handle problem customers?" For the most part, a candidate is unlikely to answer that he or she has difficulty handling problem customers, even if that is the case.

A *good* question would be framed in terms of how the individual has dealt with customers in the past. For example, you might say, "Please describe a time when a customer paid you an especially nice compliment because of something you did. What were the circumstances?" You might follow up by asking, "Tell me about a time when you had to deal with a particularly irritating customer. How did you handle the situation?" Answers to these types of specific questions can provide insight into how an individual is likely to treat customers and handle trying situations in the future. (If the individual has no job experience, questions can be adjusted accordingly—for example, " . . . a time when you had to deal with a particularly irritating *person.*")

Next, prepare a step-by-step plan outlining how you will present the position to the job candidate. Develop a similar plan for the points you wish to make about the work unit and the organization. Such plans will help you present the information in an organized fashion and will ensure that you cover all the important points you wish to make.

Review the candidate's application and/or résumé. By reviewing the candidate's background materials, you will be familiar with the particular experiences and accomplishments that are most relevant to the requirements of the job. Read the application and/or résumé before the interview; otherwise, you may appear (correctly so) unprepared. In addition, it is easy to miss gaps, discrepancies, and relevant experience when the materials are reviewed quickly in front of the candidate.

DURING THE INTERVIEW

Your carefully prepared questions will help you maintain control of the dialogue during the interview. Here are some additional guidelines for actually conducting the interview:

Establish rapport. Small talk at the beginning of the interview will often help put the candidate at ease. You may be able to comment about some item on the résumé, such as a hobby that you and the candidate have in common or a place where you both have lived. Be careful, though, not to let the interview get too far off track with an extended discussion of, say, your respective golf games.

Avoid conveying the response you seek. Suppose that you are attempting to determine the candidate's ability to work with other tellers, all of whom must work within a relatively small area. You ask, "Do you think that you will be able to work well with the other tellers, especially given our space constraints?" The candidate easily replies, "Of course, no problem." A bright

(continued on next page)

interviewee can quickly realize, from your question, the answer that you are seeking. A better approach would be to say something like this: "We all sometimes have unpleasant experiences with coworkers. Tell me about the most difficult time that you have ever had working with a coworker."

Listen and take notes. Be sure to do a great deal of listening. Some experts recommend that the interviewer should talk 20 to 30 percent of the time and allow the interviewee to talk (the interviewer listens) 70 to 80

percent of the time. You want to learn as much as possible about the job candidate in the relatively limited time that you have available. Take a few notes to help you remember important points.

Ask only job-relevant questions. Interviewers sometimes stray into asking questions that are discriminatory. One example is asking a female applicant what kind of work her spouse does. Such a question is discriminatory since it is seldom directed at a male candidate and is irrelevant to job requirements or the

person's qualifications. The best policy is to ask only questions that are clearly and directly related to job requirements.

AFTER THE INTERVIEW
Write a short report right after the interview, scoring the candidate on the characteristics required for functioning effectively in the job. Briefly indicate your rationale, perhaps using examples or summaries of responses. By documenting your ratings immediately after the interview, you will have good data to help you with your selection decision.[38]

---

abilities. Major approaches to increasing the effectiveness of organization members include training and development, as well as performance appraisal.

Training and Development

Training and development
A planned effort to facilitate employee learning of job-related behaviors in order to improve employee performance

Training and development is a planned effort to facilitate employee learning of job-related behaviors in order to improve employee performance.[43] Experts sometimes distinguish between the terms "training" and "development": "training" denotes efforts to increase employee skills on present jobs, while "development" refers to efforts oriented toward improvements relevant to future jobs.[44] In practice, though, the distinction is often blurred (mainly because upgrading skills in present jobs usually improves performance in future jobs). We adopt the increasingly common practice of using both terms interchangeably.[45] According to one estimate, U.S. businesses spend close to $60 billion annually on internally run training and education programs.[46]

PHASES OF THE TRAINING PROCESS Training efforts generally encompass three main phases.[47] All three typically involve human resource professionals and managers. In addition, outside consultants are sometimes brought in to help with various aspects of the process.

The training process begins with the *assessment phase.* This phase involves identifying training needs, setting training objectives, and developing criteria against which to evaluate the results of the training program. In the assessment phase, training requirements are determined by conducting a needs analysis. A **needs analysis** is an assessment of an organization's training needs that is developed by considering overall organizational requirements, tasks (identified through job analysis) associated with jobs for which training is needed, and the degree to which individuals are able to perform those tasks effectively.[48]

Needs analysis An assessment of an organization's training needs that is developed by considering overall organizational requirements, tasks associated with jobs for which training is needed, and the degree to which individuals are able to perform those tasks effectively

The next part of the process is the *training design and implementation phase.* This involves determining training methods, developing training materials, and actually conducting the training. During this phase, a number of training methods can be used, which fall into three main categories.[49] With *information presentation methods,* trainees are taught facts, skills, attitudes, or concepts but are not expected to put what they are learning into practice during the training. Examples are lectures, reading lists, videotapes, and most computerized instruction. In *simulation training methods,* artificial situations offer trainees a means of practicing what they learn during the training. Examples include case analysis, role plays (in which trainees act out the roles of individuals in a described situation), and in-basket exercises (in which a trainee must decide how to handle a number of items, such as memos, letters, and telephone messages, while under time pressure). With *on-the-job training (OJT) methods,* the trainee learns while actually performing a job, usually with the help of a knowledgeable trainer.

The final part of the training process is the *evaluation phase.* This entails evaluating the results of the training in terms of the criteria developed during the assessment phase. Major ways to evaluate training include measuring participants' reactions to the training to determine how useful they thought it was, assessing actual learning (perhaps through tests before and after training), determining the extent of behavioral change (possibly by having the supervisor or subordinates of a trainee assess changes in the individual's behavior), and measuring actual results on the job (such as increased output).[50]

TYPES OF TRAINING PROGRAMS   The most common types of training programs are orientation training, technical skill training, and management development training.[51] *Orientation training* is usually a formal program designed to provide new employees with information about the company and their jobs. *Technical skill training* is oriented toward providing specialized knowledge and developing facility in the use of methods, processes, and techniques associated with a particular discipline or trade. Training that helps individuals learn various aspects of their jobs falls into the category of technical skill training. *Management development programs* focus on developing managerial skills for use at the supervisory, managerial, and executive levels. Training can have a positive impact on both productivity and employee morale (see the following Case in Point discussion).

CASE IN POINT   TRAINING MAKES A DIFFERENCE AT FIRST SERVICE BANK

Service is an important factor in the success of First Service Bank, a small thrift institution headquartered in Leominster, Massachusetts. Yet the bank found its competitive position threatened by high turnover of competent bank tellers. In assessing the situation, bank managers and human resource professionals decided that raising pay was not the only answer, although the pay scale was adjusted upward somewhat. They believed that growth opportunities were also likely to be important to the type of employee that the bank hoped to attract and retain. Thus an extensive training program was devised.

Job analysis revealed that the teller position involved a broader range of skills and abilities than it had in the past. The employees' duties now included such tasks as entering information into the data base and retrieving it when necessary for customers, explaining numerous products and services to customers, recognizing opportunities to sell additional products and services, and handling diverse transactions such as commercial checking accounts and credit card payments. To reflect the expanded scope of the position, the bank changed the title of the teller job to "bank service representative" (BSR).

On the basis of needs analysis, a trilevel training and certification program—

BSR I, BSR II, and BSR III—was developed. Training methods include the use of workbooks, videotapes, and participatory exercises, such as role playing. Seminars average 2 to 4 hours per week and extend over a 3- to 6-month period.

For new hires, the BSR I course begins with a 7-day orientation that includes an overview of various bank policies, as well as training in specific procedures. After subsequent on-the-job training, individuals are encouraged to sign up for other sessions that cover a variety of topics, including government regulations, insurance issues, and effective presentation skills. A series of comprehensive proficiency skills tests must be passed before certification at the BSR I level.

The BSR II course includes skill-building sessions related to product knowledge, sales referral, security, and telephone etiquette, as well as a stress reduction session led by a licensed psychologist. Individuals who pass the various proficiency exams and become certified at the BSR II level can then move to BSR III. The third-level course covers more advanced topics and includes train-the-trainer seminars in which BSRs learn to train new hires.

As part of the program, raises are tied to BSR certifications, as well as to on-the-job standards for quality (such as degree of overages and shortages), absenteeism, and punctuality. Through a sales commission and bonus system, the BSRs receive cash, trips, and tickets to cultural events for meeting certain sales goals. Individuals who aspire to be managers can enroll in additional courses aimed at management development. Within 1 year of the training program's institution, productivity rose by more than 25 percent, turnover declined by 50 percent, and the bank's assets increased by more than 70 percent.[52]

■ ■ ■

At First Service Bank, the BSR training system, with its built-in potential career progression, was also tied to the performance appraisal system.

Performance Appraisal

Performance appraisal The process of defining expectations for employee performance; measuring, evaluating, and recording employee performance relative to those expectations; and providing feedback to the employee

Performance appraisal is the process of defining expectations for employee performance; measuring, evaluating, and recording employee performance relative to those expectations; and providing feedback to the employee.[53] A major purpose of performance appraisal is to influence, in a positive way, employee performance and development. In addition, the process is used for a variety of other organizational purposes, such as determining merit pay increases, planning future performance goals, determining training and development needs, and assessing the promotional potential of employees.[54]

MAJOR METHODS FOR RATING PERFORMANCE   Because performance is multidimensional, performance appraisal methods must consider various aspects of a job. The most widely used approaches focus on employee behavior (behavior-oriented) or performance results (results-oriented).[55]

Graphic rating scales
Scales that list a number of factors, including general behaviors and characteristics, on which an employee is rated by the supervisor

Within the behavior-oriented category, two important assessment means are graphic rating scales and behaviorally anchored rating scales. **Graphic rating scales** list a number of factors, including general behaviors and characteristics (such as attendance, appearance, dependability, quality of work, quantity of work, and relationships with people) on which an employee is rated by the supervisor. (See Figure 3 for an example of a graphic rating scale.) Supervisors rate individuals on each factor, using a scale that typically has about five gradations (e.g., unsatisfactory, conditional, satisfactory, above satisfactory, and outstanding). Because the rating factors tend to be fairly general, they are relatively flexible and can be used to evaluate individuals in a number of different jobs.

Rating Factors	LEVEL OF PERFORMANCE				
	Unsatisfactory	Conditional	Satisfactory	Above Satisfactory	Outstanding
ATTENDANCE					
APPEARANCE					
DEPENDABILITY					
QUALITY OF WORK					
QUANTITY OF WORK					
RELATIONSHIP WITH PEOPLE					
JOB KNOWLEDGE					

Figure 3 *A portion of a graphic rating scale. (Reprinted from Wayne F. Cascio,* Managing Human Resources, *2d ed., McGraw-Hill, New York, 1989, p. 326.)*

Behaviorally anchored rating scales (BARS) Scales that contain sets of specific behaviors that represent gradations of performance used as common reference points (or anchors) for rating employees on various job dimensions

However, the general nature of graphic rating scales makes them somewhat susceptible to inconsistent and inaccurate ratings of employees. This is mainly because considerable interpretation is needed to apply the factors to specific jobs (e.g., what does "quality" mean in different jobs?).[56]

In an effort to reduce the subjective interpretation inherent in graphic rating scales, performance appraisal experts have developed **behaviorally anchored rating scales (BARS)**. BARS contain sets of specific behaviors that represent gradations of performance used as common reference points (or anchors) for rating employees on various job dimensions. Figure 4 shows one scale, or set of specific behaviors, from a BARS series developed to assess various aspects of police patrol officer performance. An officer being rated on this scale can be allocated points ranging from 1 through 9 for job knowledge, depending upon where the supervisor places the individual relative to the anchors. Of course, the officer would be rated on other BARS dimensions as well, such as judgment, use of equipment, relations with the public, oral and written communication, and dependability.[57] Developing a BARS series involves extensive job analysis and the collection of critical incidents (examples of very good and very bad performance). Therefore, creating the scales for a particular job is expensive and time-consuming. As a result, BARS tend to be used mainly in situations in which relatively large numbers of individuals perform similar jobs. For example, a BARS approach was used successfully to develop a performance appraisal system for reporters, copy editors, and supervising editors at the *Times-Union* and the *Democrat and Chronicle*, two metropolitan newspapers in Rochester, New York, that are owned by the Gannett Company, Inc.[58]

An alternative and widely used results-oriented rating method is *management by objectives* (MBO), a process through which specific goals are set collaboratively for the organization as a whole, various subunits, and each individual member. With MBO, individuals are evaluated, usually annually (although more frequent discussions of progress are often held), on the basis of how well they have achieved the results specified by the goals. MBO, or goal setting, is particularly applicable to nonroutine jobs, such as those of managers. For example, the various projects undertaken by CARE lend themselves to the MBO approach, which is used extensively by the agency.

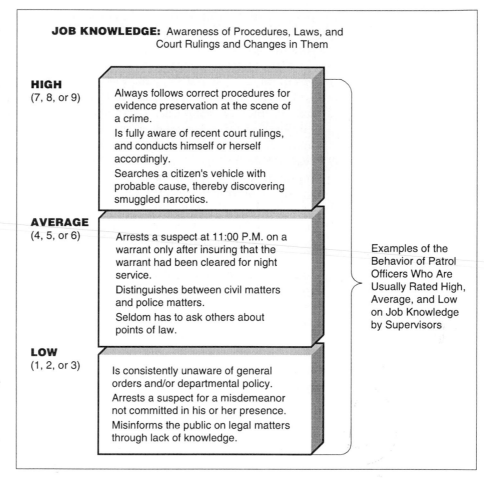

JOB KNOWLEDGE: Awareness of Procedures, Laws, and Court Rulings and Changes in Them

HIGH
(7, 8, or 9)

Always follows correct procedures for evidence preservation at the scene of a crime.

Is fully aware of recent court rulings, and conducts himself or herself accordingly.

Searches a citizen's vehicle with probable cause, thereby discovering smuggled narcotics.

AVERAGE
(4, 5, or 6)

Arrests a suspect at 11:00 P.M. on a warrant only after insuring that the warrant had been cleared for night service.

Distinguishes between civil matters and police matters.

Seldom has to ask others about points of law.

LOW
(1, 2, or 3)

Is consistently unaware of general orders and/or departmental policy.

Arrests a suspect for a misdemeanor not committed in his or her presence.

Misinforms the public on legal matters through lack of knowledge.

Examples of the Behavior of Patrol Officers Who Are Usually Rated High, Average, and Low on Job Knowledge by Supervisors

Figure 4 *A behaviorally anchored rating scale for assessing the job knowledge of police patrol officers. (Reprinted from Wayne F. Cascio,* Managing Human Resources, *2d ed., McGraw-Hill, New York, 1989, p. 327.)*

COMMON RATING ERRORS The performance appraisal process is complicated by the fact that raters' memories are somewhat fallible and raters are susceptible to biases that produce rating errors.[59] One such bias is the *halo effect,* the tendency to use a general impression based on one or a few characteristics of an individual in order to judge other characteristics of that individual. Another bias is the *contrast error,* the tendency to compare subordinates with one another rather than against a performance standard. Thus, when compared with two unsatisfactory workers, an average worker may end up being rated "outstanding." In the *recency error,* supervisors assign ratings on the basis of the employee's more recent performance. In the *leniency error,* raters tend to be unjustifiably easy in evaluating employee performance, while in the *severity error,* they tend to be unjustifiably harsh. Finally, the *self-serving bias* is the tendency to perceive oneself as responsible for successes and to see others as responsible for failures. Efforts to use rater training as a means of overcoming these biases have met with mixed success. One review of a number of studies involving rater training suggested that results may be better with simulation training methods that actively involve participants in the training process.[60]

THE PERFORMANCE APPRAISAL INTERVIEW In a performance appraisal interview, the self-serving bias is not limited to raters only. According to numerous studies, about 80 percent of the interviewees in performance appraisal interviews initially believe that they have been performing at an above-average level.[61] The statistical reality, however, at least in large organizations, is that no more than 50 percent of a company's employees can be above-average performers. Hence the performance appraisal interview is a challenging situation for supervisors to handle.

To perform effectively as raters, supervisors must essentially play three different, and somewhat incompatible, roles during the interview: leader, coach, and judge.[62] As leader, the rater must assign work duties; work with the subordinate to establish standards, or expectations, about the level of performance required; and furnish resources, such as additional personnel, equipment, time, materials, and space, that are required to do the job. As coach, the rater is responsible for ensuring that the individual is trained adequately to reach the required level of performance and must provide support and encouragement for the subordinate's efforts. Yet, as judge, the rater must evaluate the accomplishments of the employee as objectively as possible. The rater's judge role makes it somewhat difficult to simultaneously build the trust and openness that are necessary, in particular, for the coaching role.

Given this context, it is not surprising that interviews with 60 managers indicate that they are generally more concerned with using the appraisal process to motivate and retain subordinates than with using it to assess performance accurately.[63] Yet the general tendency to inflate ratings gives subordinates false feedback. It can also lead to serious lawsuits should the managers subsequently need to terminate employees who have received positive performance appraisals.[64] In addition to being used for motivation and assessment, performance appraisals often influence pay raises allocated through the organization's compensation system.

COMPENSATION

Compensation Wages paid directly for time worked, as well as more indirect benefits that employees receive as part of their employment relationship with an organization

Benefits Forms of compensation beyond wages for time worked, including various protection plans, services, pay for time not worked, and income supplements

Compensation consists of wages paid directly for time worked, as well as more indirect benefits that employees receive as part of their employment relationship with an organization.[65] Wages paid for time worked are typically payments made in cashable form that reflect direct work-related remuneration such as base pay, merit increases, or bonuses. **Benefits,** on the other hand, are forms of compensation beyond wages for time worked, including various protection plans (such as health insurance or life insurance), services (such as an organizational cafeteria or drug counseling), pay for time not worked (such as vacations or sick leave), and income supplements (such as stock ownership plans). Benefits are considered a more indirect form of compensation because they are generally not as closely tied to job and performance issues as are other forms of remuneration.

Types of Equity

Most organizations attempt to develop compensation systems that carefully consider issues of equity, or fairness. Equity issues are important because, as equity theory points out, individuals tend to compare their own relative inputs and outcomes with those of others in assessing the degree of equitable treatment that they receive. In practice, though, developing fair compensation systems is quite challenging, primarily because three major types of equity are involved.[66] *External equity* is the extent to which the organization's pay rates for particular jobs correspond to rates paid for similar jobs in the external job market. *Internal equity* is the degree to which pay rates for various jobs inside the organization reflect the relative worth of those jobs. *Individual equity* is the extent to which pay rates allocated to specific individuals within the organization reflect variations in individual merit. How, then, are these three types of equity incorporated into compensation systems?

Designing the Pay Structure

Job evaluation A systematic process of establishing the relative worth of jobs within a single organization in order to determine equitable pay differentials among jobs

Because of the complexity involved, many organizations, particularly large ones, have compensation specialists in the human resource department who oversee the compensation system development process. At the foundation of most major compensation systems is evaluation. **Job evaluation** is a systematic process of establishing the relative worth of jobs within a single organization in order to determine equitable pay differentials among jobs. Such evaluations typically rely on job analysis and resulting job descriptions for the specific information used to compare jobs.

Although there are a number of different approaches to job evaluation, the most popular approach is the point factor method, which was used by CARE in designing its new compensation system. The **point factor method** is a job evaluation approach in which points are assigned to jobs on the basis of the degree to which the jobs contain selected compensable factors. *Compensable factors* are any characteristics that jobs have in common that can be used for comparing job content.

Point factor method A job evaluation approach in which points are assigned to jobs on the basis of the degree to which the jobs contain selected compensable factors

The first step of job evaluation with the point factor method is selecting the compensable factors that will be used to rate each job. The most commonly used factors are responsibility, skill required, effort required, and working conditions, although others, such as education required and experience required, are also frequently used.

The second step is developing a set of levels, or scale, for each compensable factor and assigning weighted points to each level. The total points allocated to each factor differ, depending on how much weight top management (advised by a compensation specialist) wants to give a specific factor in evaluating all jobs. For example, Table 3 shows a point factor scale for assessing the contribution of education to the relative worth of jobs in an organization. Note that education is divided into five different levels, ranging from eighth-grade education to graduate degree. Each level has been assigned points that constitute the level's weighting within the total of 300 points allocated to the education factor. Of course, the job would be rated on other compensable factors as well. Other scales being

---

TABLE 3   Point Factor Scale for Education

Education—300 Points

This factor measures the amount of formal education required to satisfactorily perform the job. Experience or knowledge received through experience is not to be considered in evaluating jobs on this scale.

POINTS		
20	Level 1	Eighth-grade education
90	Level 2	High school diploma or eighth-grade education and four years of formal apprenticeship
160	Level 3	Two-year college degree or high school diploma and three years of formal apprenticeship
230	Level 4	Four-year college degree
300	Level 5	Graduate degree

Source: Reprinted from Marc J. Wallace, Jr., and Charles H. Fay, *Compensation Theory and Practice,* 2d ed., PWS-Kent, Boston, 1988, p. 214.

used in this situation might be experience, worth a maximum of 300 points; responsibility, worth up to 200 points; and physical demands and working conditions, each worth a possible 100 points.

The third step in the point factor method is measuring each job on each compensable factor and adding the points to obtain a total score reflecting the worth of each job. Thus, in the above situation, a job could receive a maximum of 1000 points if it rated the highest number of points on each compensable factor. The total scores are used to establish a wage rate for each job. As is probably obvious from the description so far, job evaluation helps establish internal equity by grading the worth of each job relative to that of others in the organization. How, then, does external equity figure into the pay scheme?

In order to address the external-equity issue, most organizations utilize information from pay surveys. A **pay survey** (often called a *wage-and-salary survey*) is a survey of the labor market to determine the current rates of pay for benchmark, or key, jobs. *Benchmark,* or *key, jobs* represent a cross section of the jobs in an organization, usually reflecting a mix of scores on the compensable factors, various levels in the organization, and a sizable proportion of the organization's work force. At least 25 to 30 percent of an organization's jobs are typically designated as benchmark jobs.

Most pay surveys are conducted by mailing questionnaires or using the telephone (for relatively short surveys). Organizations may conduct their own surveys and/or use surveys from other sources, such as other organizations (which often share their surveys with companies that participate in them), the Bureau of Labor Statistics and other government agencies, professional groups (such as industry associations), and private companies that specialize in compensation issues (such as Sibson and Company). One of the key considerations in evaluating survey data is which organizations should be used for comparisons. After carefully considering the organizations with which it competes for talent, CARE has developed comparative indicators that are based on a weighted survey of nonprofit organizations, midsize private-sector companies, and public organizations.

Pay-survey information for benchmark jobs is matched to job evaluation points in order to develop a pay policy line (see Figure 5). The pay policy line is the basis for developing the pay grades and the associated minimum and maximum pay rates for each grade that make up the organization's pay structure.

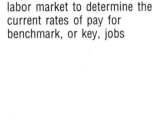

Pay survey   A survey of the labor market to determine the current rates of pay for benchmark, or key, jobs

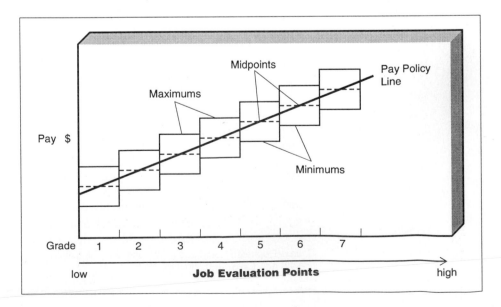

Figure 5   *Pay structure.*

Other jobs are then allocated to the pay grades on the basis of their job evaluation points. Thus organizations do not typically have a wage rate for each job. Instead, jobs are usually grouped into grades, or classifications, within some type of pay structure.

Individual equity becomes an issue when specific pay raises are allocated to individuals. The main determinants of pay increases within the specified pay range for a given grade are typically seniority and/or performance. Many organizations have recently placed renewed emphasis on the notion of pay for performance by awarding pay on the basis of merit and/or offering various incentive pay programs tied to performance.

Skill-based pay A compensation system in which employees' rates of pay are based on the number of predetermined skills the employees have mastered

Efforts are also being made in a number of organizations to foster innovation through nontraditional forms of compensation. One idea that is growing in popularity is **skill-based pay,** a compensation system in which employees' rates of pay are based on the number of predetermined skills the employees have mastered.[67] For example, at the Santa Clara, California, plant of Northern Telecom, a leading supplier of digital-communication switching systems, workers receive a pay increase for each new skill that they master. Workers who once performed narrow tasks now move freely among several different tasks, allowing the company to cut the number of job grades from 25 to 5 and to capitalize on the innovative ideas that result.[68] Another approach that is attracting increased attention is **gainsharing**, in which employees throughout an organization are encouraged to become involved in solving problems and are then given bonuses tied to organizationwide performance improvements.[69]

Gainsharing A compensation system in which employees throughout an organization are encouraged to become involved in solving problems and are then given bonuses tied to organizationwide performance improvements

Employee Benefits

Benefits account for a growing portion of total compensation. According to the U.S. Chamber of Commerce, which annually surveys a national cross section of private-sector firms, benefits rose, on average, from 18.7 percent of direct payroll costs in 1951 to 38.4 percent by 1990.[70] Thus an employee who earns an annual salary of $20,000 is likely to receive another $7680 in benefits. The rise in benefits is attributable to several factors.[71] Among the most important are the rise in employer costs for social security, federal tax policies that provide tax advantages to employers and allow employees to receive the benefits on a tax-free or tax-deferred basis, pressure from labor unions for generous benefit packages, employer concern for employee needs, and attempts to encourage productivity improvements through rewards provided by benefits.

Employers are legally required to make payments so that employees are covered by social security, unemployment compensation, and workers' compensation (in case of injury on the job). However, most benefits provided by employers are not required by law (even though some may be governed by law if they are offered). One organization that has a reputation for being particularly generous with benefits is privately owned Hallmark Cards, Inc. Employee benefits at Hallmark include low-interest, $2500-per-year college loans for employees' children, interest-free loans of up to $1000 for emergencies, adoption assistance of up to $3000, paternity or maternity leave of up to 6 months for the parent of a newborn or newly adopted baby, and a physical fitness facility combined with an extensive wellness program.[72]

5 MAINTAINING EFFECTIVE WORK-FORCE RELATIONSHIPS

Maintaining positive relations between an organization and its employees is an important aspect of human resource management. Two areas of particular relevance are labor-management relations and employee rights.

Labor-Management Relations

Labor-management relations
The process through which
employers and unions
negotiate pay, hours of work,
and other conditions of
employment; sign a contract
governing such conditions for
a specific period of time; and
share responsibilities for
administering the resulting
contract

Unions Employee groups
formed for the purpose of
negotiating with management
about conditions relating to
their work

Labor-management relations is the process through which employers and unions negotiate pay, hours of work, and other conditions of employment; sign a contract governing such conditions for a specific period of time; and share responsibilities for administering the resulting contract.[73] **Unions** are employee groups formed for the purpose of negotiating with management about conditions relating to their work. Some employee groups call themselves associations rather than unions (e.g., the American Nurses Association). When recognized by the National Labor Relations Board (NLRB), unions have the legal right to negotiate with employers and help administer the resulting contract.

A number of studies have addressed why employees join unions. A main factor is dissatisfaction with various working conditions, such as wages, job security, benefits, treatment by supervisors, and prospects for promotion. Still, even dissatisfied workers will typically not join a union unless they believe that it will be effective in remedying the situation.[74]

The number of employees who are dues-paying union members has been declining, from a peak of 22,618,000 in 1979 to 16,568,000 in 1991.[75] Although the causes of the decline are not completely clear, some reasons given are more effective human resource management in organizations, a decrease in union organizing attempts, a decline in the economic well-being of companies (making it more difficult for unions to pressure for better wages and benefits), and increasingly effective management opposition to unions.[76]

CERTIFICATION PROCESS Unions are normally established in organizations through an *organizing drive*.[77] The drive begins when employees sign authorization cards designating the union as their exclusive bargaining representative. At least 30 percent of employees within the group to be represented must sign cards before the union can petition the National Labor Relations Board to conduct an election. Once the NLRB verifies that the required percentage of employees seek union representation, the board notifies management of that fact. At this point, management and the union can attempt to agree on union representation and the group of employees that will be considered the bargaining unit. Usually, though, the two parties do not agree, and the NLRB must determine the unit. Next, an election is held. The union must receive a majority of the votes cast in order to be certified as the exclusive representative for the bargaining unit. Regardless of the outcome, no further union elections associated with the bargaining unit can take place for 1 year. Recent trends indicate that although unions are experiencing considerable success in obtaining authorization cards from the necessary 30 percent of affected workers, they are subsequently winning certification elections less than half the time (see the following Case in Point discussion).

CASE IN POINT

THE UAW VERSUS NISSAN

The United Auto Workers (UAW) represents production workers at the ''Big Three'' automakers (General Motors, Ford, and Chrysler). For almost 6 years, it had been working to unionize a plant owned by the Japan-based Nissan Motor Manufacturing Corporation in Smyrna, Tennessee. The task facing the UAW was formidable.

When the Smyrna plant opened in 1983, it was welcomed by a community that was experiencing double-digit unemployment. More than 120,000 local residents applied for the initial 3200 hourly and salaried jobs at the plant. Those who were hired were reportedly told that they were the "cream of the crop" and that they had become part of a "family" work group. Considering workers as part of an organizational family, attempting to ensure lifetime employment, and involving employees in decisions affecting their work are some of the common characteristics of Japanese management.

Six years later, the $14.80 hourly wage paid to the average worker with 3 years' seniority was slightly lower than wages paid at Ford Motor but 37 percent higher than the average manufacturing wage in the nearby Nashville area. In benefits, UAW workers were slightly better off.

Nissan had built considerable loyalty through its community activities. For instance, the company sponsored an international folk festival, donated funds for civic causes such as the Murfreesboro Symphony, and provided robotics and electronics equipment for high school classes. Its annual tax payments of $2 million allowed local property taxes to be reduced by 25 percent. The company also established a fitness center and offered workers attractive discounts on leasing new Nissans each year.

For its part, the UAW was able to get the required 30 percent of employees to sign union authorization cards to force an election. Nevertheless, union officials recognized that many workers did not view paying $30 each month in union dues as a good investment, largely because they doubted that the union could improve things appreciably. One important issue emphasized by the UAW was health and safety. At the Nissan plant, workers received paid breaks totaling 23 minutes per day, compared with the 48 minutes allocated to Ford workers. The UAW charged that the pace at the Smyrna plant resulted in higher injury rates of workers. In its campaign, the UAW brought in 30 professional organizers, distributed leaflets to workers as they entered and left the plant, and had representatives visit more than two-thirds of the employees at their homes.

Company officials used the plant's closed-circuit television system to deliver carefully developed messages, such as one blaming the union for layoffs at GM and pointing out Nissan's no-layoff policy. The company also highlighted the possibility of strikes with the UAW as the bargaining agent. Prounion workers began to wear shirts that said, "Vote Yes for a Safer Workplace," while antiunion workers wore shirts stating, "I Can Speak for Myself."

Finally, the big day of the election arrived—July 27, 1989. The results were lopsided, with 1622 workers voting against the union and 711 voting in favor.[78]

■ ■ ■

In some instances unions and management have produced partnerships, such as the one created at Corning's Big Flats, New York, plant. Over a 2-year period, teams of management and union workers redesigned jobs, modified work hours, eliminated unnecessary tasks, and cut costs. The result is a plant where "partnership" is a way of life. Quality, productivity, morale, and profits have increased since the program began.[79]

UNION DECERTIFICATION If a union does win an election, it can be decertified in the future, but not earlier than 1 year after the certification election. If there is evidence that at least 30 percent of the employees want to decertify the union, the NLRB can be asked to hold a decertification election. Recent trends indicate that unions have been losing such elections about three-fourths of the time, although about six times more certification than decertification elections are held each year (e.g., 3623 versus 587 in 1990).[80]

Current Employee Issues

Maintaining effective work-force relationships requires that both human resource professionals and line managers stay abreast of and make appropriate responses to issues affecting employees. Several areas of current concern are protection from arbitrary dismissal, sexual harassment, drug and alcohol abuse, privacy rights, and family issues.[81]

PROTECTION FROM ARBITRARY DISMISSAL Issues of job security and protection from arbitrary dismissal are the subject of a growing number of laws and lawsuits.[82] In the United States, the legal principle that has mainly been followed during the past century is **employment at will**, which holds that either employee or employer can terminate employment at any time for any reason. Recently, the notion of employment at will has been increasingly challenged because of various federal and state laws (such as those forbidding the termination of employees for whistle-blowing or for complaining about safety hazards in the workplace) and certain court rulings (such as one holding that some employment arrangements constitute implied contracts). Adopting a policy of discharging employees only for good cause, following a progressive disciplinary process (e.g., giving oral and written warnings and suspensions before attempting to terminate an individual), and carefully documenting the reasons for dismissal will aid in protecting the rights of both employees and employers.

Employment at will The legal principle that holds that either employee or employer can terminate employment at any time for any reason

SEXUAL HARASSMENT Sexual harassment is an issue of growing concern in organizations. According to the Equal Employment Opportunity Commission, sexual harassment involves "unwelcome sexual advances" and "requests for sexual favors." It also includes "other verbal or physical conduct of a sexual nature" when submission to such conduct is explicitly or implicitly a condition of employment; when submission to or rejection of such conduct affects employment decisions, such as promotions; or when such conduct unreasonably interferes with work performance or creates a hostile or offensive working environment. To a large extent, employers are legally responsible for sexual harassment, particularly by managers and others with authority to make employment-related decisions. To discourage sexual harassment, employers should widely disseminate written policies against such behavior, have written complaint procedures, guarantee safety against retaliation for sexual harassment complaints, and take prompt action to redress claims that are found to be justified.[83]

DRUG AND ALCOHOL ABUSE Another important issue affecting employees and their employers is drug and alcohol abuse. Such abuse typically leads to increases in absenteeism, workplace accidents, and use of medical benefits and causes declines in productivity. A recent report indicates that productivity losses related to alcohol problems amount to about $86 billion per year and drug-related losses cost more than $54 billion.[84]

In a constructive response to substance abuse problems, more than 10,000 employers have established employee assistance programs.[85] An **employee assistance program (EAP)** is a program through which employers help employees overcome personal problems that are adversely affecting their job performance. Under such programs, supervisors may refer workers to EAP counselors or outside counselors who help identify problems and arrange for appropriate assistance. Workers can usually also contact EAP counselors themselves. Although drug and alcohol abuse are the major problems covered, such programs increasingly provide assistance for a broader range of issues, including stress, smoking cessation, weight control, financial matters, legal difficulties, and other personal issues that cause difficulties for employees.

Employee assistance program (EAP) A program through which employers help employees overcome personal problems that are adversely affecting their job performance

PRIVACY RIGHTS The employee's right to privacy is another human resource issue of current importance. One privacy concern related to the drug abuse problem just discussed is *drug testing*, the attempt to detect drug usage through analysis of blood, urine, or other body substances. According to one estimate, at least 30 percent of the employers of recent college graduates engage in drug testing of new employees, and the number is growing.[86] Although the legal issues are far from resolved, courts have generally been willing to allow employers to test job applicants, on the premise that applicants choose to submit to the tests in order to obtain a job. On the other hand, courts are generally much less tolerant of mandatory drug and alcohol testing of employees. This type of testing is more likely to survive legal challenge under the following conditions: The employees have jobs that involve public safety (e.g., airline pilots) or that are dangerous (e.g., electricians); testing is limited to situations in which there is reasonable suspicion of on-the-job impairment; there is a written and publicized substance abuse policy; there are procedural protections (such as careful labeling and secondary tests to confirm positive results); and employers offer voluntary rehabilitation programs rather than firing employees for first offenses.

A related privacy issue is *genetic screening*, the attempt to detect, through tests, genetic factors that may contribute to certain occupational diseases. So far, only a few companies, mainly in the chemical industry, are using genetic screening as a means of identifying those workers who are more likely to contract diseases after exposure to certain chemicals or toxins. While the screening has the potential of protecting workers from hazardous working conditions, it could also possibly be used to deny employment to individuals on the basis of their genetic makeup.[87] As a result, genetic screening appears likely to generate considerable controversy in the future.

Another current privacy-rights issue is the use of *polygraphs* and other mechanical lie detectors by employers. The practice has been severely limited by the Employee Polygraph Protection Act of 1988. The law was passed because of concerns about the accuracy and validity of polygraphs, particularly in routine use. It largely forbids the use of polygraph tests by private employers for screening job applicants, except in the pharmaceutical industry (because the work involves the handling of controlled substances) and in the security industry.

FAMILY ISSUES Given the rising proportion of women in the workplace, the growing number of dual-career couples, and the frequency of single parenting, family issues as they affect workers are increasing in importance. To help employees more effectively handle the often conflicting responsibilities of work and family, several major companies, such as Du Pont, now have family issues specialists on their human resource staffs. The specialists help develop policies and also assist employees in regard to such issues as leaves from work, child care, and elder care.[88] This type of approach is likely to promote positive working relationships with employees and facilitate the management function of leading.

CHAPTER SUMMARY

Human resource management is the management of various activities designed to enhance the effectiveness of an organization's work force. Major activities include human resource planning, staffing, development and evaluation, compensation, and maintenance of effective work-force relationships. The strategic importance of HRM has been increasing, particularly since the late 1970s and early 1980s.

Human resource planning considers both demand for and supply of human resources relative to an organization's strategic plan. Such planning relies on job analysis and resulting job descriptions and job specifications.

Assessing demand involves considering the major forces that can influence demand and using basic forecasting techniques to predict future demand. Assessing supply entails determining internal and external labor supplies. In reconciling demand and supply, organizations need to consider affirmative action implications.

Staffing is the set of activities aimed at attracting and selecting individuals for positions in a way that will facilitate the achievement of organizational goals. The attraction aspect of staffing involves recruitment. Most organizations engage in extensive internal recruitment in order to offer job opportunities to current employees. For the most part, organizations engage in external recruiting only when there are no suitable internal candidates for particular positions. The selection aspect of staffing focuses on determining which job candidates best suit organizational needs. An important issue in selection is validity, which addresses how well a selection device or method actually predicts a candidate's future job performance. The most prevalent selection methods include the use of application blanks, selection interviews, tests, assessment centers, and reference checks.

Training and development is a planned effort to facilitate employee learning of job-related behaviors in order to improve employee performance. Training typically includes three main phases: assessment, training design and implementation, and evaluation. The major types of training programs are orientation training, technical skill training, and management development programs.

Performance appraisal is the process of defining expectations for employee performance; measuring, evaluating, and recording employee performance relative to those expectations; and providing feedback to the employee. Major methods of performance appraisal include behavior-oriented approaches, such as the use of graphic rating scales and behaviorally anchored rating scales, and results-oriented approaches, such as management by objectives. Because performance raters tend to be susceptible to biases that produce rating errors, they must engage in three somewhat incompatible roles (leader, coach, and judge) in carrying out an effective performance appraisal interview.

Compensation systems need to consider internal, external, and individual equity in developing pay structures and allocating individual pay. The most common approach to devising pay structures is the point factor method of job evaluation. Organizations are attempting to reward intrapreneurs through specialized pay approaches, such as bonus programs, and are encouraging work-force flexibility and innovation through such means as skill-based pay and gainsharing.

Maintaining positive work-force relationships involves engaging in effective labor-management relations and making appropriate responses to current employee issues. Organizations become unionized through a certification process regulated by the National Labor Relations Board. Unions can become decertified through a similar process. Among the employee issues of current concern are protection from arbitrary dismissal, sexual harassment, drug and alcohol abuse, privacy rights, and family matters as they affect workers.

QUESTIONS FOR DISCUSSION AND REVIEW

1 Briefly describe the major elements in the human resource management process, and explain why HRM has gradually increased in strategic importance in organizations. To what extent do you believe that effective human resource management is strategically important for your college or university? Explain your reasoning.

2 Discuss the role of job analysis in human resource planning. Why would job descriptions (and job specifications) based on job analysis be useful in a variety of human resource activities, such as recruitment, selection, and performance appraisal?

3 Identify the major factors that managers need to consider in attempting to predict future demand for human resources. How can forecasting methods help? What factors do managers need to examine in assessing the future supply of human resources? What options do managers have in reconciling demand and supply imbalances?

4 Distinguish between internal and external recruiting. What are the major advantages and disadvantages of each?

5 Explain the role of validity in selection. Identify the most widely used selection methods, and assess their usefulness as valid means of making selection decisions. Evaluate the validity of a selection device used in an organization with which you are familiar.

6 Identify the main phases of training, the major categories of training methods, and the most common types of training programs. Give an example of each type of training method from your own experience either as an individual being trained or as a trainer.

7 Explain the major methods for rating employee performance, the common biases that affect ratings, and the roles that supervisors must play during the performance appraisal interview. Think of a time when your performance was appraised by someone. How well did the individual balance the roles of leader, coach, and judge? Explain your view.

8 Describe how pay structures are developed using the point factor method. Why might nontraditional compensation systems, such as the ones described in the chapter, be better at encouraging innovation than more traditional approaches?

9 Explain the nature of benefits. Why are they growing as a portion of total compensation? List several benefits that either you or someone in your family receives as part of job compensation.

10 Describe the processes through which unions are certified and decertified. What role might employee-rights issues potentially play in unionization efforts?

DISCUSSION QUESTIONS FOR CHAPTER OPENING CASE

1 Explain the strategic importance of human resource management at CARE.
2 Present evidence of various elements of the HRM process at CARE.

3 Identify and evaluate the organization's recent changes in HRM.

MANAGEMENT EXERCISE: MANAGING HUMAN RESOURCES IN RETAIL HARDWARE

 You have just accepted a position as a department head in a large hardware store. The owner, who is the store manager, likes to involve others in decisions. During your interviews for the job, the store manager mentioned that if you became department head, he would ask for your views on ways to improve human resource management in the store. He is particularly interested in your input because he is thinking about opening up several other stores in the region. (In fact, you are taking the job partially because you believe that such expansion can only help your career.)

The manager said that he, the assistant manager, and all ten department heads will soon be holding some strategic planning meetings at which they will consider the impact of human resources in regard to the expansion plans. Also, he anticipates holding subsequent meetings that focus on various aspects of human resource management. He further stated that he wants to maintain a working environment that is stimulating, challenging, and exciting. At the same time, he would prefer to avoid having the store become unionized, since he feels that opening up new stores in the area would be more complicated if a union was involved.

From what you have been able to learn, the 18 percent annual growth of the store and the 15 percent return on investment could definitely be improved. In addition, human resource management seems to be almost nonexistent at this point.

To prepare for the upcoming meeting, outline the suggestions you will offer on the following topics:

1 What issues should be considered as part of human resource planning?
2 What approaches can be taken in regard to recruiting and selecting human resources?
3 What are the store's options for training, performance appraisal, and compensation?

REFERENCES

1. Amanda Bennett, "CARE Makes a Comeback after Drive to Revamp Its Management Practices," *The Wall Street Journal*, Feb. 9, 1987, p. B1; Gwen Kinhead, "America's Best-Run Charities," *Fortune*, Nov. 9, 1987, pp. 145–150; additional information obtained from telephone interviews with Jack McBride and Al Warner of CARE, Inc., on Apr. 15 and Apr. 20, 1987, as well as written materials furnished by Mr. McBride, July 8, 1992.
2. Herbert G. Heneman III, Donald P. Schwab, John A. Fossum, and Lee D. Dyer, *Personnel/Human Resource Management*, 4th ed., Irwin,
Homewood, Ill., 1989; William B. Werther, Jr., and Keith Davis, *Personnel Management and Human Resources*, 2d ed., McGraw-Hill, New York, 1985.
3. Randall S. Schuler and Susan E. Jackson, "Linking Competitive Strategies with Human Resource Management Practices," *Academy of Management Executive*, vol. 1, 1987, pp. 207–219; Stella M. Nkomo, "Strategic Planning for Human Resources—Let's Get Started," *Long Range Planning*, vol. 21, 1988, pp. 66–72; Cynthia A. Lengnick-Hall and Mark L. Lengnick-Hall, "Strategic Human
Resources Management: A Review of the Literature and a Proposed Typology," *Academy of Management Review*, vol. 13, 1988, pp. 454–470; Lloyd Baird and Ilan Meshoulam, "Managing Two Fits of Strategic Human Resource Management," *Academy of Management Review*, vol. 13, 1988, pp. 116–128.
4. Harold L. Angle, Charles C. Manz, and Andrew H. Van de Ven, "Integrating Human Resource Management and Corporate Strategy: A Preview of the 3M Story," *Human Resource Management*, Spring 1985, pp. 51–68.

5. Don Rose, "Woolworth's Drive for Excellence," *Long Range Planning,* vol. 22, 1989, pp. 28–31.

6. Wayne F. Cascio, *Managing Human Resources,* 2d ed., McGraw-Hill, New York, 1989.

7. Cynthia A. Lengnick-Hall and Mark L. Lengnick-Hall, "Strategic Human Resources Management: A Review of the Literature and a Proposed Typology," *Academy of Management Review,* vol. 13, 1988, pp. 454–470; Randall Schuler and Susan E. Jackson, "Linking Competitive Strategies with Human Resource Management Practices," *Academy of Management Executive,* vol. 1, 1987, pp. 207–219.

8. Thomas A. Mahoney and John R. Deckop, "Evolution of Concept and Practice in Personnel Administration/Human Resource Management (PA/HRM)," *Journal of Management,* vol. 12, 1986, pp. 223–241.

9. James W. Walker, *Human Resource Planning,* McGraw-Hill, New York, 1980; Cynthia A. Lengnick-Hall and Mark L. Lengnick-Hall, "Strategic Human Resources Management: A Review of the Literature and a Proposed Typology," *Academy of Management Review,* vol. 13, 1988, pp. 454–470.

10. Edward L. Levine, "Everything You Always Wanted to Know about Job Analysis," Mariner, Tampa, Fla., 1983; George T. Milkovich and John W. Boudreau, *Personnel/Human Resource Management,* 5th ed., Business Publications, Plano, Tex., 1988.

11. Patrick M. Wright and Kenneth N. Wexley, "How to Choose the Kind of Job Analysis You Really Need," *Personnel,* May 1985, pp. 51–55.

12. James W. Walker, *Human Resource Planning,* McGraw-Hill, New York, 1980; William B. Werther, Jr., and Keith Davis, *Personnel Management and Human Resources,* 3d ed., McGraw-Hill, New York, 1989.

13. This section is based on Douglas T. Hall and James G. Goodale, *Human Resource Management: Strategy, Design, and Implementation,* Scott, Foresman, Glenview, Ill., 1986; and Randall S. Schuler and Vandra L. Huber, *Personnel and Human Resource Management,* 4th ed., West, St. Paul, Minn., 1990.

14. Bartley A. Brennan and Nancy Kubasek, *The Legal Environment of Business,* Macmillan, New York, 1988; Randall S. Schuler and Vandra L. Huber, *Personnel and Human Resource Management,* 4th ed., West, St. Paul, Minn., 1990.

15. Wayne F. Cascio, *Managing Human Resources,* 2d ed., McGraw-Hill, New York, 1989.

16. Douglas T. Hall and James G. Goodale, *Human Resource Management: Strategy, Design, and Implementation,* Scott, Foresman, Glenview, Ill., 1986.

17. Bartley A. Brennan and Nancy Kubasek, *The Legal Environment of Business,* Macmillan, New York, 1988; David P. Twomey, *Equal Employment Opportunity Law,* South-Western, Cincinnati, Ohio, 1990.

18. William B. Werther, Jr., and Keith Davis, *Personnel Management and Human Resources,* 3d ed., McGraw-Hill, New York, 1989.

19. Randall S. Schuler and Vandra L. Huber, *Personnel and Human Resource Management,* 4th ed., West, St. Paul, Minn., 1990.

20. Wayne F. Cascio, *Managing Human Resources,* 2d ed., McGraw-Hill, New York, 1989.

21. Joel Dreyfuss, "Get Ready for the New Work Force," *Fortune,* Apr. 23, 1990, pp. 165–181.

22. Daniel C. Feldman, "Reconceptualizing the Nature and Consequences of Part-Time Work," *Academy of Management Review,* vol. 15, 1990, pp. 103–112; Jolie Solomon and Gilbert Fuchsberg, "Great Number of Older Americans Seen Ready to Work," *The Wall Street Journal,* Jan. 26, 1990, p. B1.

23. William B. Werther, Jr., and Keith Davis, *Personnel Management and Human Resources,* 3d ed., McGraw-Hill, New York, 1989; Randall S. Schuler and Vandra L. Huber, *Personnel and Human Resource Management,* 4th ed., West, St. Paul, Minn., 1990.

24. Benjamin Schneider and Neal Schmitt, *Staffing Organizations,* 2d ed., Scott, Foresman, Glenview, Ill., 1986.

25. Ibid.

26. Philip G. Swaroff, Lizabeth A. Barclay, and Alan R. Bass, "Recruit-ing Sources: Another Look," *Journal of Applied Psychology,* vol. 70, 1985, pp. 720–728; Benjamin Schneider and Neal Schmitt, *Staffing Organizations,* 2d ed., Scott, Foresman, Glenview, Ill., 1986.

27. Bruce M. Meglino, Angelo S. DeNisi, Stuart A. Youngblood, and Kevin J. Williams, "Effects of Realistic Job Previews: A Comparison Using an Enhancement and a Reduction Preview," *Journal of Applied Psychology,* vol. 73, 1988, pp. 259–266.

28. Steven L. Premack and John P. Wanous, "A Meta-Analysis of Realistic Job Preview Experiments," *Journal of Applied Psychology,* vol. 70, 1985, pp. 706–719.

29. Vida Gulbinas Scarpello and James Ledvinka, *Personnel/Human Resource Management,* PWS-Kent, Boston, 1988; Randall S. Schuler and Vandra L. Huber, *Personnel and Human Resource Management,* 4th ed., West, St. Paul, Minn., 1990.

30. Vida Gulbinas Scarpello and James Ledvinka, *Personnel/Human Resource Management,* PWS-Kent, Boston, 1988; Wayne F. Cascio, *Managing Human Resources,* 2d ed., McGraw-Hill, New York, 1989; Robert D. Gatewood and Hubert S. Feild, *Human Resource Selection,* 2d ed., Dryden, Chicago, 1990.

31. Vida Gulbinas Scarpello and James Ledvinka, *Personnel/Human Resource Management,* PWS-Kent, Boston, 1988.

32. Randall S. Schuler and Vandra L. Huber, *Personnel and Human Resource Management,* 4th ed., West, St. Paul, Minn., 1990.

33. Robert D. Gatewood and Hubert S. Feild, *Human Resource Selection,* 2d ed., Dryden, Chicago, 1990.

34. William B. Werther, Jr., and Keith Davis, *Personnel Management and Human Resources,* 3d ed., McGraw-Hill, New York, 1989; Robert D. Gatewood and Hubert S. Feild, *Human Resource Selection,* 2d ed., Dryden, Chicago, 1990.

35. *Personnel Policies Forum,* Survey No. 146–Recruiting and Selection Procedures, Bureau of National Affairs, Washington, D.C., May 1988.

36. *Personnel Policies Forum,* Survey No. 114, Selection Procedures and

Personnel Records, Bureau of National Affairs, Washington, D.C., September 1976, Milton Hakel, "Employment Interview," in K. Rowland and G. Ferris (eds.), *Personnel Management: New Perspectives*, Allyn and Bacon, Boston, 1982.

37. The material on the types of interviews is based heavily on William B. Werther, Jr., and Keith Davis, *Personnel Management and Human Resources*, 3d ed., McGraw-Hill, New York, 1989.

38. Based on Tom Janz, Lowell Hellervik, and David C. Gilmore, *Behavior Description Interviewing*, Allyn and Bacon, Boston, 1986; James M. Jenks and Brian L. P. Zevnik, "ABCs of Job Interviewing," *Harvard Business Review*, July–August 1989, pp. 38–42; and Robert D. Gatewood and Hubert S. Feild, *Human Resource Selection*, 2d ed., Dryden, Chicago, 1990.

39. This section is based on Robert D. Gatewood and Hubert S. Feild, *Human Resource Selection*, 2d ed., Dryden, Chicago, 1990.

40. Vida Gulbinas Scarpello and James Ledvinka, *Personnel/Human Resource Management*, PWS-Kent, Boston, 1988.

41. Glenn M. McEvoy and Richard W. Beatty, "Assessment Centers and Subordinate Appraisals of Managers: A Seven-Year Examination of Predictive Validity," *Personnel Psychology*, vol. 42, 1989, pp. 37–52.

42. R. L. LoPresto, D. E. Mitcham, and D. E. Ripley, *Reference Checking Handbook*, American Society for Personnel Administration, Alexandria, Va., 1986.

43. Kenneth N. Wexley and Gary P. Latham, *Developing and Training Human Resources in Organizations*, Scott, Foresman, Glenview, Ill., 1981; Douglas T. Hall and James G. Goodale, *Human Resource Management*, Scott, Foresman, Glenview, Ill., 1986.

44. Randall S. Schuler and Vandra L. Huber, *Personnel and Human Resource Management*, 4th ed., West, St. Paul, Minn., 1990.

45. Another interpretation sometimes used is that "training" applies to facilitating learning for lower-level jobs, while "development" is more indicative of a broader learning ori-

entation for higher-level jobs; Wayne F. Cascio, *Managing Human Resources*, 2d ed., McGraw-Hill, New York, 1989.

46. E. B. Fiske, "Booming Corporate Education Efforts Rival College Programs, Study Says," *The New York Times*, Jan. 28, 1985, p. A10.

47. Wayne F. Cascio, *Managing Human Resources*, 2d ed., McGraw-Hill, New York, 1989.

48. Kenneth N. Wexley and Gary P. Latham, *Developing and Training Human Resources in Organizations*, Scott, Foresman, Glenview, Ill., 1981.

49. John P. Campbell, Marvin D. Dunnette, Edward E. Lawler, and Karl E. Weick, *Managerial Behavior, Performance, and Effectiveness*, McGraw-Hill, New York, 1970; Vida Gulbinas Scarpello and James Ledvinka, *Personnel/Human Resource Management*, PWS-Kent, Boston, 1988.

50. D. L. Kilpatrick, "Evaluation of Training," in R. L. Craig and L. R. Bittel (eds.), *Training and Development*, McGraw-Hill, New York, 1967.

51. Vida Gulbinas Scarpello and James Ledvinka, *Personnel/Human Resource Management*, PWS-Kent, Boston, 1988.

52. Arnold H. Wensky and Robin J. Legendre, "Incentive Training at First Service Bank," *Personnel Journal*, April 1989, pp. 102–110.

53. Allan M. Mohrman, Jr., Susan M. Resnick-West, and Edward E. Lawler III, *Designing Performance Appraisal Systems*, Jossey-Bass, San Francisco, 1989.

54. C. A. Peck, *Pay and Performance: The Interaction of Compensation and Performance Appraisal*, Research Bulletin No. 155, Conference Board, New York, 1984.

55. Wayne F. Cascio, *Managing Human Resources*, 2d ed., McGraw-Hill, New York, 1989.

56. H. John Bernardin and Richard W. Beatty, *Performance Appraisal: Assessing Human Behavior at Work*, Kent, Boston, 1984.

57. Frank J. Landy, James L. Farr, Frank E. Saal, and Walter R. Freytag, "Behaviorally Anchored Sales for Rating the Performance of Police Officers," *Journal of Applied Psychology*, vol. 61, 1976, pp. 750–758.

58. Robert Giles and Christine Landauer, "Setting Specific Standards for Appraising Creative Staffs," *Personnel Administrator*, March 1984, pp. 35–47.

59. H. John Bernardin and Richard W. Beatty, *Performance Appraisal: Assessing Human Behavior at Work*, Kent, Boston, 1984; Stephen J. Carroll, Jr., and Craig Eric Schneier, *Performance Appraisal and Review Systems*, Scott, Foresman, Glenview, Ill., 1982.

60. David E. Smith, "Training Programs for Performance Appraisal: A Review," *Academy of Management Review*, vol. 11, 1986, pp. 22–40; David C. Martin and Kathryn M. Bartol, "Training the Raters: A Key to Effective Performance Appraisal," *Public Personnel Management*, vol. 15, 1986, pp. 101–110.

61. H. H. Meyer, "Self-Appraisal of Job Performance," *Personnel Psychology*, vol. 33, 1980, pp. 291–296.

62. David C. Martin, "Performance Appraisal: Improving the Rater's Effectiveness," *Personnel*, August 1986, pp. 28–33.

63. Clinton O. Longenecker, Dennis A. Gioia, and Henry P. Sims, Jr., "Behind the Mask: The Politics of Employee Appraisal," *Academy of Management Executive*, August 1987, pp. 183–193.

64. David C. Martin, Kathryn M. Bartol, and Marvin J. Levine, "The Legal Ramifications of Performance Appraisal," *Employee Relations Law Journal*, Winter 1986–1987, pp. 370–396; David C. Martin and Kathryn M. Bartol, "The Legal Ramifications of Performance Appraisal: An Update," *Employee Relations Law Journal*, Autumn 1991, pp. 257–286.

65. This section is based largely on Robert M. McCaffery, *Employee Benefit Programs*, PWS-Kent, Boston, 1988; Charles H. Fay, *Glossary of Compensation & Benefits Terms*, 2d ed., American Compensation Association, Scottsdale, Ariz., 1989; and George T. Milkovich and Jerry M. Newman, *Compensation*, 3d ed., BPI/Irwin, Homewood, Ill., 1990.

66. Marc J. Wallace, Jr., and Charles H. Fay, *Compensation Theory and Practice*, 2d ed., PWS-Kent, Boston, 1988. Wallace and Fay identify a fourth type of equity, process equity, the extent to which the procedures used in determining and distributing pay are fair. Recent evidence suggests that process equity also influences employees' satisfaction with the compensation that they receive.

67. Richard L. Bunning, "Skill-Based Pay," *Personnel Administrator,* June 1989, pp. 65–68; Henry Tosi and Lisa Tosi, "What Managers Need to Know about Knowledge-Based Pay," *Organizational Dynamics,* Winter 1986, pp. 52–64.

68. Roy Merrills, "How Northern Telecom Competes on Time," *Harvard Business Review,* July–August 1989, pp. 108–114.

69. Henry Tosi and Lisa Tosi, "What Managers Need to Know about Knowledge-Based Pay," *Organizational Dynamics,* Winter 1986, pp. 52–64; R. J. Bullock and Edward E. Lawler, "Gainsharing: A Few Questions, and Fewer Answers," *Human Resource Management,* Spring 1984, pp. 23–40; Christopher S. Miller and Michael H. Schuster, "Gainsharing Plans: A Comparative Analysis," *Organizational Dynamics,* Summer 1987, pp. 44–67.

70. George T. Milkovich and Jerry M. Newman, *Compensation,* 3d ed., BPI/Irwin, Homewood, Ill., 1990.

71. Discussion between Martin Leskowitz, U.S. Chamber of Commerce, and David C. Martin, Aug. 3, 1992.

72. Walter Roessing, "High Marks for Hallmark," *Compass Readings,* March 1990, pp. 32–39.

73. Vida Gulbinas Scarpello and James Ledvinka, *Personnel/Human Resource Management,* PWS-Kent, Boston, 1988.

74. Jeanne M. Brett, "Why Employees Want Unions," *Organizational Dynamics,* Spring 1980, pp. 47–59; Wayne F. Cascio, *Managing Human Resources,* 2d ed., McGraw-Hill, New York, 1989; George T. Milkovich and

John W. Boudreau, *Personnel/Human Resource Management,* 5th ed., Business Publications, Plano, Tex., 1988.

75. The basis for the number of employees belonging to unions changed in 1979 from annual dues-paying members to union members who are employed wage and salary workers; based on information from the U.S. Bureau of Labor Statistics, Industrial Relations Research Division, Washington, D.C., August 1992.

76. Vida Gulbinas Scarpello and James Ledvinka, *Personnel/Human Resource Management,* PWS-Kent, Boston, 1988.

77. This section is based largely on Wayne F. Cascio, *Managing Human Resources,* 2d ed., McGraw-Hill, New York, 1989.

78. Dean Foust, "The UAW vs. Japan: It's Showdown Time in Tennessee," *Business Week,* July 24, 1989, pp. 64–65; Gregory A. Patterson, "The UAW's Chances at Japanese Plants Hinge on Nissan Vote," *The Wall Street Journal,* July 25, 1989, pp. A1, A12; Warren Brown, "UAW Loses Key Battle at Nissan Plant," *The Washington Post,* July 18, 1989, pp. A1, A14; Warren Brown, "Behind the UAW's Defeat in Tennessee," *The Washington Post,* July 30, 1989, p. H3.

79. Frank Swoboda, "Partnership with Union Produces Results," *The Washington Post,* Aug. 2, 1992, p. H4.

80. Information obtained from the National Labor Relations Board Research Department, August 1992.

81. This section is based largely on Ira Michael Shepard, Robert L. Duston, and Karen S. Russell, *Workplace Privacy,* Bureau of National Affairs, Washington, D.C., 1989.

82. Milo Geyelin, "Fired Managers Winning More Lawsuits," *The Wall Street Journal,* Sept. 7, 1989, pp. B1, B2.

83. Randall S. Schuler and Vandra L. Huber, *Personnel and Human Resource Management,* 4th Ed., West, St. Paul, Minn., 1990; Allen I. Fagin and Myron D. Rumeld, "Employer Liability for Sexual Harassment," *Society for Human Resource Management Legal Report,* Fall 1991, pp. 1–4.

84. *Public Health Report,* June 1991, pp. 280–292.

85. H. W. French, "Helping the Addicted Worker," *The New York Times,* Mar. 26, 1987, pp. 29, 34.

86. "Labor Letter," *The Wall Street Journal,* Dec. 2, 1986, p. 1.

87. Judy D. Olian, "Genetic Screening for Employment Purposes," *Personnel Psychology,* vol. 37, 1984, pp. 423–438.

88. Cindy Skrzycki, "Family-Issues Experts See Rising Demand," *The Washington Post,* Jan. 7, 1990, p. H3.

ACKNOWLEDGMENTS

Tables

Table 1: Courtland L. Bovée, Michael H. Mescon, David J. Rachman, and John V. Thill, *Business Today,* 6th ed., McGraw-Hill, Inc., 1990, p. 244. Reproduced by permission of McGraw-Hill, Inc.

Table 3: Charles H. Fay and Marc J. Wallace Jr., *Compensation Theory and Practice,* 2d ed., 1988, p. 214. Reprinted by permission.

Figures

Figure 3: Wayne F. Cascio, *Managing Human Resources,* 2d ed., McGraw-Hill, Inc., 1989, p. 326. Reproduced by permission of McGraw-Hill, Inc.

Figure 4: Wayne F. Cascio, *Managing Human Resources,* 2d ed., McGraw-Hill Book Company, 1989, p. 327. Reproduced by permission of McGraw-Hill, Inc.

CONCLUDING CASE

NUCOR PROSPERS IN TOUGH STEEL INDUSTRY

The Nucor Corporation has gained a reputation for succeeding in an industry where competition is formidable. The company operates so-called minimills, which melt scrap iron to produce basic products such as joists, decking, and steel bars. Through this method, Nucor makes steel very efficiently—at about one-third of its competitors' costs. This has resulted in an annual compounded growth rate of more than 20 percent during the past decade.

Despite Nucor's almost $2 billion in annual sales, company headquarters (located in suburban Charlotte, North Carolina) operates with a small staff of 16 or so. There are only four management levels. The chairman and CEO, F. Kenneth Iverson, and the company's president, Dave Aycock, make up the first level. The second level consists of vice presidents, each of whom is also a general manager of a steel mill, a joist plant, or a division. At the third level are the department heads, who might be managers of melting and casting, sales managers, or division controllers. The fourth level comprises the first-line supervisors. Despite these levels, the company tries hard to eliminate distinctions between management and workers. For example, there are no assigned parking spaces, no executive dining rooms, and no hunting lodges; and everyone in the company travels economy class. Management and workers have the same benefits, such as vacation time and insurance.

A particularly unique aspect of Nucor within the steel industry is the company's incentive pay system. A significant portion of most organization members' pay depends on worker productivity or on company success. For example, in the steel mills, the company identifies groups of 25 to 35 people doing a complete task and puts them on a bonus program. There are typically nine bonus groups. In each case, a standard is set for production. The group then receives extra pay based on the amount it produces above the standard. There is no maximum, and the bonuses are paid weekly so that workers can see the fruits of their efforts quickly. Standards about punctuality and attendance also apply. "If you're late even 5 minutes, you lose your bonus for the day," says Iverson. Lateness of more than 30 minutes or absenteeism for any reason results in a bonus loss for the week (there are four "forgiveness days" available to each worker per year). The bonuses received by groups are normally more than 100 percent above base pay, giving the steelworkers an average annual pay of more than $30,000, with some making more than $40,000. Also, the company has a profit-sharing plan, whereby 10 percent of earnings before taxes are distributed to employee accounts within the plan.

Although pay is higher at Nucor than at its competitors, productivity in terms of tons per employee has been running more than double. This is partly because workers have suggested many innovative ideas. Iverson admits that the Nucor system is not for everyone. When the company starts up a new mill, turnover is usually in the range of 200 percent the first year. After that, turnover is extremely low. Iverson says that the system appeals best to goal-oriented individuals who are willing to work hard.

Nucor has a no-layoff policy. Occasionally, there are reduced workweeks to avoid layoffs. When 3½- or 4-day workweeks are necessary, a worker's pay may be cut by as much as 25 percent. The pay of department heads and officers is cut even more, perhaps as much as 40 and 70 percent, respectively. Iverson calls it Nucor's "Share the Pain" program.

Nucor limits the work force at each of its plants to 500 employees. "We don't feel that a general manager can communicate effectively with employees when you have a group larger than that," says Iverson. Company policy requires that the general manager have dinner with every employee in his or her plant at least once a year, in groups no larger than 50. Most general managers have dinner with employees twice a year. After the first dinner, employees learn that they can speak up. Iverson remembers one incident in particular: "A fellow got up and said, 'You guys are really rotten. You haven't done anything about the parking lot, and they're stealing us blind out there.' Another one stood up and said, 'They stole so much gas out of my car I couldn't even start it when I came off my shift.' A third had a $400 car stereo stolen. We didn't know about any of this, of course. It took us exactly 3 days to fence the parking lot and put up lights. That's the way we work."*

---

* George Gendron, "Steel Man: Ken Iverson," *INC.*, April 1986, pp. 41–48; John Ortman, "Nucor's Ken Iverson on Productivity and Pay," *Personnel Administrator*, October 1986, pp. 46–108; Ruth Simon, "Nucor's Boldest Gamble," *Forbes*, Apr. 3, 1989, pp. 122–124; Jonathan P. Hicks, "Steelmakers' Inferiority Syndrome," *The New York Times*, Aug. 7, 1989, pp. D1, D7; Clare Ansberry, "Steel Industry Is on the Verge of David vs. Goliath Test," *The Wall Street Journal*, Oct. 17, 1989, p. A8; Mary Lord and Dorian Friedman, "Expanding the Recession," *U.S. News & World Report*, Mar. 4, 1991, p. 42; Dana Milbank, "Low Steel Prices May Hold Down Nucor's Earnings," *The Wall Street Journal*, May 1, 1992, p. B7A; and "Minimill Inroads in Sheet Market Rouse Big Steel," *The Wall Street Journal*, Mar. 9, 1992, p. B1.

QUESTIONS FOR
CONCLUDING CASE

1   Explain the components of the
    HRM process evident at Nucor.

2   To what extent does human
    resource management appear to
    be part of strategic
    management at Nucor? Cite
    evidence to support your view.

3   Assess the handling of external,
    internal, and individual equity
    in the compensation system at
    Nucor.

CONCLUDING CASE

STRATEGIC HUMAN RESOURCE PLANNING AT ABB

Asea Brown Boveri (ABB) is a "multidomestic" organization with eight global business segments operating in such diverse areas as power generation, transportation, and financial services. The segments annually generate more than $25 billion in revenues. ABB headquarters is in Zurich, and subordinate companies are located in more than 100 countries. Although the organization has about 215,000 employees, only 170 of them make up the corporate staff. There are about 50 major business areas (BAs) into which the company's various businesses are divided. The BAs, in turn, are grouped into the eight global business segments.

Strategic human resource planning is oriented toward providing the leadership for the major parts of the organization. Most human resources are host-country nationals, giving rise to ABB's preferred designation as a "multidomestic" company. Potential managers are recruited in their home countries. The organization requires that within 24 hours of identifying the need for a new manager, a list of five internal candidates must be on the appropriate business head's desk. Thus the human resource managers need to know their potential leaders well.

Management talent begins to be identified very early in a person's career. A typical job path for individuals identified early in their careers as having the potential to hold the most senior management positions are shown below:

Position	Age
Company president	40
Division manager	37
Production manager	34
Production planning manager	31
Project manager	29
Entry-level position	26

Individuals being prepared for senior management positions are trained in general management tasks by being exposed to multifunctional experiences. As high-potential managers, they can expect transfers across organizational border lines and work assignments on mixed-nationality teams helping to solve problems. Percy Barnevik, the company's CEO, believes that the "global managers" needed for senior management are made, rather than born, and argues that they can best be developed through line experience in several countries. Moreover, ABB insists that all individuals who move to senior management be able to speak fluent English so that they can communicate with one another on a global basis. The corporate human resource function is responsible for ensuring that individuals with the potential to assume senior management positions are both identified and trained.*

QUESTIONS FOR CONCLUDING CASE

1 How might human resource planning be conducted in a multidomestic company like ABB?

2 Discuss the role of the corporate HRM office in identifying and developing senior managers for the organization.

3 How would you proceed if you wanted to be one of the high-potential managers at ABB?

* Speech by Arne Olsson and Richard P. Randazzo, Institute for International Human Resources annual conference, Toronto, Canada, Mar. 30, 1992; Carol Kennedy, "ABB: Model Merger for the New Europe," *Long Range Planning,* vol. 25, 1992, pp. 10–17.

CHAPTER 8

Motivation

GAINING THE EDGE

"ASPIRATIONS" MOTIVATE AT LEVI STRAUSS

Levi Strauss is famous not only for its Levi jeans but also for its longtime commitment to social responsibility and to its employees. The San Francisco–based company was founded in 1850 by the great-great-granduncle of the present chairman and CEO, Robert D. Haas. It is now privately held due to a management-led leveraged buyout completed in 1985. In helping to more clearly focus company values after the buyout, Haas oversaw the development of the Levi Strauss Aspirations Statement.

The initial section of the statement sets a theme of shared values that guide management and the work force as they build their own and the company's future:

> We all want a company that our people are proud of and committed to, where all employees have an opportunity to contribute, learn, grow, and advance based on merit, not politics or background. We want our people to feel respected, treated fairly, listened to, and involved. Above all, we want satisfaction from our accomplishments and friendships, balanced personal and professional lives, and to have fun in our endeavors.

The statement goes on to spell out specific areas where action is necessary to make these shared values and aspirations a reality. For example, the statement calls for valuing a diverse work force, recognizing individual and team contributions, and enforcing stated standards of ethical behavior.

Haas says that the company's strategy in the late 1970s and early 1980s emphasized diversification (such as acquiring new companies and creating new brands). "Our people did what they were asked to do, but the problem was they didn't believe in it," notes Haas. Recently, management has been listening more closely to suppliers, customers, and employees. As a result, Haas says, "We have redefined our business strategy to focus on core products, and we have articulated the values that the company stands for—what we call our Aspirations." The new approach has elicited strong support from employees. The reason, says Haas, is "because it's what they *want* to do."

The Aspirations Statement also emphasizes empowerment, whereby decision making is shifted to the people who are closest to the product and the customer. Haas argues that the traditional, hierarchical command and control approach is no longer effective in today's rapidly changing environment. Such an approach cannot adequately anticipate and respond to shifting customer needs and market changes. Instead, he says, "people have to take responsibility, exercise initiative, be accountable for their own success and for that of the company as a whole." At the same time, the Aspirations Statement gives strong consideration to the needs of the work force in such areas as gaining satisfaction from accomplishments and balancing personal and professional lives.[1,*]

Motivation The force that energizes behavior, gives direction to behavior, and underlies the tendency to persist

By considering the needs of the work force as well as the company, the Aspirations Statement fosters **motivation,** the force that energizes behavior, gives direction to behavior, and underlies the tendency to persist. This definition recognizes that in order to achieve goals, individuals must be sufficiently stimu-

---

lated and energetic, must have a clear focus on what is to be achieved, and must be willing to commit their energy for a long enough period of time to realize their aim.[2] Since the leading function of management involves influencing others to work toward organizational goals, motivation is an important aspect of that function.

In this chapter, we explore the basic nature of motivation and consider a general model of the motivation process. Next, we examine theories of motivation that are based on individual needs, such as the need for achievement. We also look into motivational approaches that emphasize cognitive aspects, focusing on how individuals think about where to direct their efforts and how to evaluate outcomes. We then analyze reinforcement theory, with its emphasis on the power of rewards. Finally, we review a more contemporary extension called social learning theory and consider its implications for promoting innovation.

THE NATURE OF MOTIVATION

Because motivation is an internal force, we cannot measure the motivation of others directly. Instead, we typically infer whether or not other individuals are motivated by watching their behavior. For example, we might conclude that an engineering friend who works late every evening, goes to the office on weekends, and incessantly reads the latest engineering journals is highly motivated to do well. Conversely, we might suspect that an engineering friend who is usually the first one out the door at quitting time, rarely puts in extra hours, and generally spends little time reading up on new developments in the field is not very motivated to excel.

In the end, how successful these two engineers actually are with their respective projects is likely to depend not only on their motivation, as reflected in effort expended, but also on their ability to handle the engineering subject matter. Furthermore, working conditions can affect their performance. Numerous interruptions, extra assignments, or cramped office space may negatively influence performance. On the other hand, a quiet place to work, the help of assistants, and ample support resources, such as equipment, may have a positive effect on project performance. Thus actual performance is likely to be a function of ability, motivation, and working conditions, as shown in Figure 1.[3] As a result, it is important that managers hire individuals who have the ability to do what is required. Then the management challenge is providing working conditions that nurture and support individual motivation to work toward organizational goals.

Management scholars have developed a number of theories that help us understand what motivates people at work. Figure 2 shows the main elements in the motivation process. As the diagram indicates, our inner needs (such as needs for food, companionship, and growth) and cognitions (such as knowledge and thoughts about efforts we might expend and rewards we might receive) lead to various behaviors. Assuming that the behaviors are appropriate to the situation, they may result in rewards. The rewards then help reinforce our behaviors, fulfill our needs, and influence our cognitions about the linkages between our behaviors and possible future rewards. Conversely, lack of rewards may lead to unfulfilled needs, leave behaviors unreinforced, and influence our thinking about

Figure 1 *The relationship between performance and ability, motivation, and working conditions.*

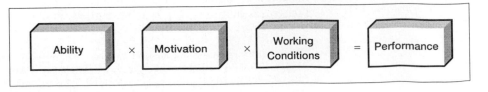

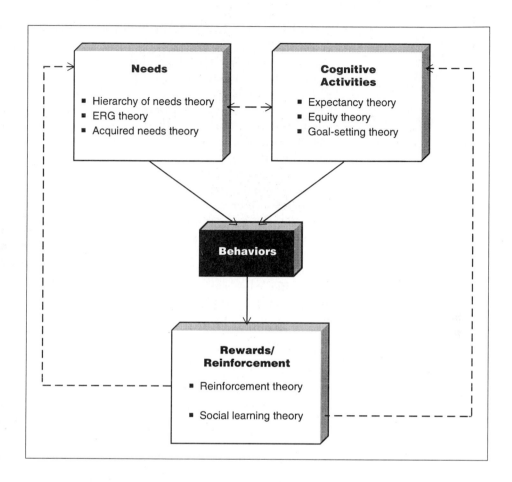

Figure 2 *The motivation process.*

where to expend our efforts in the future. Since motivation is a complex phenomenon, major motivational theories address the various elements in the process (see Figure 2). In order to better understand the implications of these elements for managers, we explore the respective theories in subsequent sections of this chapter, beginning with need theories.

NEED THEORIES

What makes a person such as Linda Wachner, president of Warnaco, Inc., overcome adolescent spinal surgery that left her in a body cast for over a year, tackle the challenge of successfully turning around the ailing U.S. division of Max Factor & Company, and work 14-hour days to eventually reach her lofty position as head of a Fortune 500 apparel conglomerate?[4] What possessed Kemmons Wilson, founder of the Holiday Inns, to start building another hotel chain at age 75?[5] Need theories argue that we behave the way we do because of internal needs we are attempting to fulfill. These theories are sometimes called *content theories* of motivation because they specify *what* motivates individuals (i.e., the content of needs). In this section, we explore three prominent theories that examine what needs individuals are likely to have and how these needs operate as motivators: hierarchy of needs theory, ERG theory, and acquired-needs theory.

Hierarchy of Needs Theory

One of the most widely known theories of motivation is the **hierarchy of needs theory,** developed by psychologist Abraham Maslow and popularized during the

Hierarchy of needs theory A theory (developed by Maslow) that argues that individual needs form a five-level hierarchy

Physiological needs
Survival needs such as food, water, and shelter

Safety needs   Needs that pertain to the desire to feel safe, secure, and free from threats to our existence

Belongingness needs
Needs that involve the desire to affiliate with and be accepted by others

Esteem needs   Needs related to the two-pronged desire to have a positive self-image and to have our contributions valued and appreciated by others

Self-actualization needs
Needs that pertain to the requirement of developing our capabilities and reaching our full potential

early 1960s, which argues that individual needs form a five-level hierarchy (shown in Figure 3). According to this hierarchy, our first need is for survival, so we concentrate on basic **physiological needs,** such as food, water, and shelter, until we feel fairly sure that these needs are covered. Next, we concern ourselves with **safety needs,** which pertain to the desire to feel safe, secure, and free from threats to our existence. Once we feel reasonably safe and secure, we turn our attention to relationships with others in order to fulfill our **belongingness needs,** which involve the desire to affiliate with and be accepted by others. With support from loved ones, we focus on **esteem needs,** which are related to the two-pronged desire to have a positive self-image and to have our contributions valued and appreciated by others. Finally, we reach the highest level, **self-actualization needs,** which pertain to the requirement of developing our capabilities and reaching our full potential. We concern ourselves with such matters as testing our creativity, seeing our innovative ideas translated into reality, pursuing new knowledge, and developing our talents in uncharted directions. Needs at this highest level are never completely fulfilled, because as we work to develop our capabilities, both our potential and our needs for self-actualization grow stronger. Some possible work-related means of fulfilling the various needs in the hierarchy are shown in Figure 3.

Maslow recognized that a need might not have to be completely fulfilled before we start directing our attention to the next level in the hierarchy. At the same time, he argued that once we have essentially fulfilled a need, that need ceases to be a motivator and we begin to feel tension to fulfill needs at the next level.

While Maslow's hierarchy has stimulated thinking about the various needs that individuals have, it has some serious shortcomings. Research suggests that needs may cluster into two or three categories, rather than five. Also, the hierarchy of needs may not be the same for everyone. Entrepreneurs frequently pursue their dreams for years despite the relative deprivation of lower-level needs. Finally, individuals often seem to work on satisfying several needs at once, even though some needs may be more important than others at a given point in time.[6]

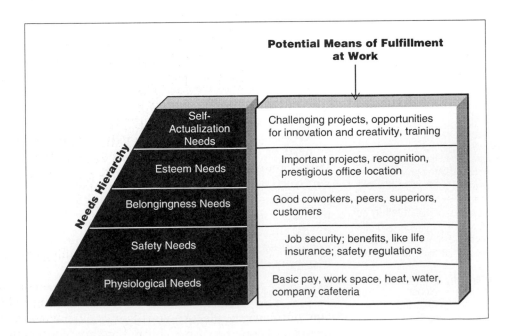

Figure 3   *Maslow's hierarchy of needs.*

ERG Theory

ERG theory An alternative (proposed by Alderfer) to Maslow's hierarchy of needs theory which argues that there are three levels of individual needs

Existence needs Needs that include the various forms of material and physiological desires, such as food and water, as well as such work-related forms as pay, fringe benefits, and physical working conditions

Relatedness needs Needs that address our relationships with significant others, such as families, friendship groups, work groups, and professional groups

Growth needs Needs that impel creativity and innovation, along with the desire to have a productive impact on our surroundings

Satisfaction-progression principle A principle that states that satisfaction of one level of need encourages concern with the next level

Frustration-regression principle A principle that states that if we are *continually* frustrated in our attempts to satisfy a higher-level need, we may cease to be concerned about that need

Because of the criticisms of Maslow's hierarchy of needs theory, motivation researcher Clayton Alderfer proposed an alternative known as **ERG theory**.[7] The name stems from combining Maslow's five levels of needs into three levels: existence, relatedness, and growth. **Existence needs** include physiological desires, such as food and water, and work-related material desires, such as pay, fringe benefits, and physical working conditions. **Relatedness needs** address our relationships with significant others, such as families, friendship groups, work groups, and professional groups. They deal with our desire to be accepted by others, achieve mutual understanding on matters that are important to us, and exercise some influence over those with whom we interact on an ongoing basis. **Growth needs** impel creativity and innovation, along with the desire to have a productive impact on our surroundings.

ERG need levels differ in terms of concreteness, that is, the degree to which their presence or absence can be verified. The existence need level is the most concrete, relating to issues such as the individual's rate of pay and the pleasantness of his or her work surroundings. The growth need level is the least concrete, involving more nebulous issues such as the person's level of creativity, the degree to which the person's capabilities are growing relative to his or her capacity, and the long-term impact of the person's efforts on the organization. According to ERG theory, we generally tend to concentrate first on our most concrete requirements. As existence needs are resolved, we have more energy available for concentrating on relatedness needs. Then, as relatedness needs are somewhat fulfilled, we have the energy and support needed to pursue growth needs. Thus ERG theory incorporates a **satisfaction-progression principle** similar to that of Maslow's hierarchy, since satisfaction of one level of need encourages concern with the next level.

Aside from focusing on three need levels instead of five, ERG theory differs from the hierarchy of needs theory in three significant ways. First, although the general notion of a hierarchy is retained, Alderfer's theory argues that we can be concerned with more than one need category at the same time. Needs at lower levels are not necessarily fairly well satisfied before we concern ourselves with other needs. However, satisfaction of lower-level needs can be helpful in allowing us to devote our attention to higher-level needs. For example, even if a worker has skipped lunch and is extremely hungry, she or he may still be primarily concerned with solving a challenging customer problem. On the other hand, at some point the hunger may interfere with the worker's problem-solving efforts. Second, ERG theory is more flexible, since it acknowledges that some individuals' needs may occur in a different order than that posited by the ERG framework. Inventor Godfrey Hounsfield worked so intensely while developing the CAT scanner at Britain-based EMI, Ltd., that his boss became worried about his health and ordered him to take a vacation.[8] Third, ERG theory incorporates a **frustration-regression principle**. This principle states that if we are *continually* frustrated in our attempts to satisfy a higher-level need, we may cease to be concerned about that need. Instead, we may regress to exhibiting greater concern for a lower-level need that is more concrete and seemingly more within our grasp. For example, an employee may become more concerned with establishing strong relationships with coworkers if continuing efforts to obtain more interesting work are ignored by the boss.

Both Maslow's hierarchy theory and ERG theory are extremely difficult to test because they involve measuring and tracking individuals' changing needs and fulfillment levels over time. So far, the limited research on ERG theory has generally been supportive.[9] If ERG theory is correct in predicting that individuals attempt to fulfill multiple needs at the same time, motivating individuals is likely to require that a variety of means for need fulfillment be offered. Because of the frustration-regression aspect of ERG theory, managers need to be particularly concerned with providing opportunities to satisfy growth needs, lest employees cease to be interested in them. At Levi Strauss, growth issues figure prominently in the Aspirations Statement as the company shifts to increased teamwork in the face of growing global competition. A different, but also challenging, situation exists at Original Copy Centers, Inc. (see the following Case in Point discussion).

CASE IN POINT   ORIGINAL WAYS OF MOTIVATING BEHAVIOR

At Original Copy Centers, Inc., a fast-growing corporate and legal copy service in Cleveland, owners Nancy Vetrone and Robert Bieniek use all the originality they can muster to motivate their more than 145 employees. The workers perform relatively mundane and repetitive tasks, such as operating copy machines or picking up and delivering materials. Noting that the average age of their employees is under 30 and that many are single, Vetrone and Bieniek came up with an unusual, but well-appreciated, employee amenity: a laundry room at work where staff members can wash and dry their clothes. Other amenities include a six-person sauna, locker rooms and showers, a mini-theater, a video library, a game room with a billiards table, an exercise room, company personal computers for employee use, various arcade games, a kitchen, and free coffee. Says Bieniek, "We hope that the Original work environment is as nice or better than their private living conditions, so they'll be in a hurry to get here and they won't be in a hurry to leave."

To afford delivery personnel greater status, these employees are called "corporate couriers" and wear smart, professional-looking uniforms. They seem to view themselves as part of the image of a fast-moving company. Since they are the kingpins in Original's obsessive concern with timely pickups and deliveries, couriers are trained to talk with customers and learn receptionists' names. They have helped develop detailed maps of the inside of every commercial building in Cleveland, a factor that speeds up the almost 300 trips per day made to customer locations. Company employees at all levels (including couriers, receptionists, and production staff) are invited to assist in attracting new customers by staffing the Original booth at trade shows and dispensing "I'm an Original" stickers.

Other methods that ensure growth and loyalty within the Original organization are having employees train on and use personal computers, trusting employees to complete their own time cards, allowing flexible schedules and up to 20 overtime hours per week, and encouraging staff members to come up with new ideas that involve the successful company slogan, "I'm an Original." These efforts to motivate employees appear to be working. Counter to industry trends, turnover at Original is extremely low. Further, members of the staff are generally willing to work extra hours and postpone weekend plans to help out in emergencies. As a result, the firm has earned a reputation for exceptionally fast copy-service turnaround and has experienced rapid growth.[10]   ■ ■ ■

Acquired-needs theory A theory (developed by McClelland) stating that our needs are acquired or learned on the basis of our life experiences

Acquired-Needs Theory

While the hierarchy of needs and ERG theories view certain needs as an inherent part of our makeup, psychologist David C. McClelland offers a different perspective, **acquired-needs theory**. McClelland argues that our needs are acquired or learned on the basis of our life experiences. Although these needs tend to be a product of a variety of conditions to which we are exposed, sometimes even a specific event can profoundly influence our desires. For example, Estee Lauder, the billionaire baroness of the beauty-supply industry, was strongly motivated to succeed by a chance incident that occurred during the depression. While selling her uncle's skin cream in a Manhattan beauty salon, she (then Josephine Esther Mentzer) admired the blouse of the owner and asked where the woman had purchased it. The owner curtly replied that it was an irrelevant question because a salesgirl would never be able to afford such a blouse. Those words fanned the young saleswoman's desire for achievement. "I wouldn't have become Estee Lauder if it hadn't been for her," she says.[11]

For more than three decades, McClelland has mainly studied three needs: achievement, affiliation, and power. He measures these needs using the Thematic Apperception Test (TAT), in which test takers write stories about pictures that are purposely ambiguous. The stories are then scored according to the achievement, affiliation, and power themes that they contain. The assumption is that individuals write about themes that are important to them.[12] For most of us, test results would indicate a blending of the achievement, affiliation, and power needs, rather than a high level of just one of these needs and the absence of the others.

Need for achievement (nAch)
The desire to accomplish challenging tasks and achieve a standard of excellence in one's work

McClelland's initial work centered on the **need for achievement (nAch),** the desire to accomplish challenging tasks and achieve a standard of excellence in one's work. Individuals with a high nAch typically seek competitive situations in which they can achieve results through their own efforts and can receive relatively immediate feedback on how they are doing. They like to pursue moderately difficult goals and take calculated risks. Yet, contrary to what is sometimes believed, high nAchs typically avoid *extremely* difficult goals because of the substantial risk of failure.[13] Since they like problems that require innovative and novel solutions, high-nAch individuals can be a valuable source of creativity and innovative ideas in organizations.[14]

Estimates are that only about 10 percent of the U.S. population has a high nAch. Managers who want to motivate high achievers need to make sure that such individuals have challenging, but reachable, goals that allow relatively immediate feedback about achievement progress. McClelland argues that high-nAch individuals may not be motivated by money per se (because they derive satisfaction mainly from their achievements). Nevertheless, they may still place considerable importance on money as a source of feedback on how they are doing.[15]

Need for affiliation (nAff)
The desire to maintain warm, friendly relationships with others

To a lesser extent, McClelland's work has also addressed the **need for affiliation (nAff),** the desire to maintain warm, friendly relationships with others. High-nAff individuals are particularly likely to gravitate toward professions that involve a large amount of interaction with others, such as health care, teaching, sales, and counseling. To motivate high-nAff individuals, managers need to provide them with a cooperative, supportive work environment in which they can meet both performance expectations and their high affiliation needs by working with others. High-nAff individuals can be particular assets in situations that require a high level of cooperation with and support of others, including clients and customers.[16]

Need for power (nPow) The desire to influence others and control one's environment

Personal power A need for power in which individuals want to dominate others for the sake of demonstrating their ability to wield power

As he studied various needs, McClelland gradually came to view the **need for power (nPow),** the desire to influence others and control one's environment, as a particularly important motivator in organizations. Need for power has two forms, personal and institutional. Individuals with a high need for **personal power** want to dominate others for the sake of demonstrating their ability to wield power. They expect followers to be loyal to them personally rather than to

Institutional power A need for power in which individuals focus on working with others to solve problems and further organizational goals

the organization, a situation that sometimes causes organizational goals to be thwarted. In contrast, individuals with a high need for **institutional power** focus on working with others to solve problems and further organizational goals. Such individuals like getting things done in an organized fashion. They are also willing to sacrifice some of their own self-interests for the good of the organization.[17] Motivating individuals with a high need for institutional power involves giving them opportunities to hold positions that entail organizing the efforts of others.

McClelland has analyzed various needs in terms of their relationship to managerial effectiveness. He originally thought that individuals with a high need for achievement would make the best managers. His subsequent work suggests that, to the contrary, high-nAch individuals tend to concentrate on their own achievements rather than on the development and achievements of others. As a result, high-nAch individuals often make good entrepreneurs because initial success frequently depends largely on individual achievement. They may not, however, make good managers in situations that require working with a number of others and waiting to learn the results of their efforts. Similarly, individuals with a personal-power orientation run into difficulties as managers because they often attempt to use the efforts of others for their own benefit. Critics argue that the demise of E. F. Hutton, the old-line Wall Street brokerage firm that was taken over by the Shearson Lehman brokerage house in the late 1980s, was due largely to the absolute power wielded by CEO Robert Fomon, who headed the firm for 16 years. In addition to hiring and promoting close friends, Fomon apparently personally reviewed the salaries and bonuses of more than 1000 employees, spurned budgets in favor of having employees come to him for resources, spent lavishly on entertainment and perquisites, and made most of the large and small decisions himself.[18] Individuals with a high need for affiliation may also have a managerial weakness, because they tend to concentrate on maintaining good interpersonal relationships rather than achieving goals.[19]

McClelland's work suggests that individuals with a high institutional-power need make the best managers because they are oriented toward coordinating the efforts of others to achieve long-term organizational goals.[20] Thus the need profile of successful managers, at least in competitive environments, appears to include (1) a moderate-to-high need for institutional power, (2) a moderate need for achievement to facilitate individual contributions early in one's career and a desire for the organization to maintain a competitive edge as one moves to higher levels, and (3) at least a minimum need for affiliation to provide sufficient sensitivity for influencing others.

What happens if an individual wants to be a manager but doesn't have the appropriate need profile? McClelland argues that it is possible to develop certain needs in ourselves and others. Through training, McClelland has successfully increased individuals' need for achievement. Subsequently, those who were trained received faster promotions and made more money than those not trained. In this type of training, individuals are exposed to tasks involving the achievement of goals, with the situations becoming more challenging as the individuals increase their ability to handle the tasks. Trainees are also exposed to the behavior of appealing entrepreneurial models. Similar approaches can apparently be used to foster the need for institutional power.[21] Other needs, such as affiliation, may be more difficult to develop through such methods.

Assessing Need Theories

A comparison of the needs identified by the three theories is shown in Figure 4. The theories are generally compatible in pointing to the importance of higher-

Maslow: Hierarchy of Needs Theory	Alderfer: ERG Theory	McClelland: Acquired Needs Theory
Physiological	Existence	
Safety and security	Existence	
Belongingness and love	Relatedness	Need for affiliation
Self-esteem	Growth	Need for achievement
Self-actualization	Growth	Need for power

Figure 4 *Comparison of needs in three theories.*

level needs as a source of motivation. Given the widespread current requirements for innovative ideas, improved quality, and greater capacity to implement needed changes, fostering growth needs is particularly important. Consider, for example, Wal-Mart. The retail chain is expanding so fast that it has become the largest company job creator in the nation, adding over 150,000 employees since 1982. Although Wal-Mart typically hires new workers at only 10 percent above the minimum wage, it retains employees (called "associates") by delegating responsibility and offering scholarships of up to $2500 toward college tuition for those who go to school and work part-time. As a result, approximately 40 percent of Wal-Mart's managers are individuals who began as trainees. This is an unusually high proportion in the turnover-ridden retail business.[22]

COGNITIVE THEORIES

Cognitive theories Theories that attempt to isolate the thinking patterns that we use in deciding whether or not to behave in a certain way

Need theories try to identify the internal desires that influence our behavior, but they do not go very far in explaining the thought processes that are involved. In contrast, **cognitive theories** attempt to isolate the thinking patterns that we use in deciding whether or not to behave in a certain way. Cognitive theories are not necessarily at odds with need theories; rather, they look at motivation from a different perspective. Because they focus on the thought processes associated with motivation, cognitive theories are sometimes called *process theories*. Three major cognitive theories that address work motivation are the expectancy, equity, and goal-setting theories.

Expectancy Theory

Expectancy theory A theory (originally proposed by Vroom) that argues that we consider three main issues before we expend the effort necessary to perform at a given level

The **expectancy theory** of motivation, originally proposed by Victor H. Vroom, argues that we consider three main issues before we expend the effort necessary to perform at a given level. These issues are shown in the circles of Figure 5, which depicts the basic components of expectancy theory.

Effort-performance expectancy Our assessment of the probability that our efforts will lead to the required performance level

EFFORT-PERFORMANCE EXPECTANCY With **effort-performance (E → P) expectancy,** we assess the probability that our efforts will lead to the required performance level. Our assessment may include evaluating our own abilities, as well as considering the adequacy of contextual factors such as the availability of resources. To see how effort-performance expectancy works, imagine that your boss has asked you to consider taking on a major special project. The project

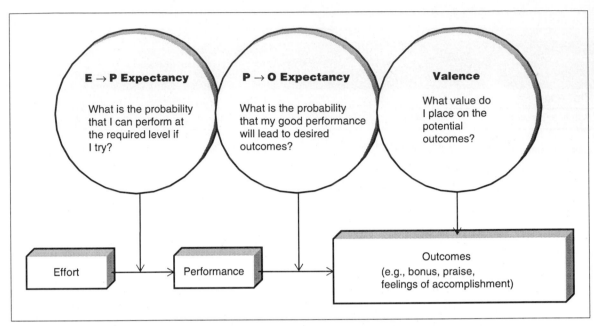

Figure 5 *Basic components of expectancy theory.*

involves designing and implementing a new computerized tracking system for customer complaints to improve individual customer service and find out more quickly about complaint trends. One of the first things you might think about is the probability of your being able to achieve the high level of performance required, given your abilities and the related environmental factors. If you feel that you don't know very much about developing such systems and/or that the availability of resources is inadequate, you might assess the probability of success as low. That is, your E → P expectancy about this particular assignment might be quite low. On the other hand, if you feel that you are well qualified for the project and that the available resources are adequate, you might assess the probability of your efforts' leading to high performance—the E → P expectancy—as quite high. However, assessment of the effort-performance expectancy is only part of your evaluation of the situation.

PERFORMANCE-OUTCOME EXPECTANCY   With **performance-outcome (P → O) expectancy,** we assess the probability that our successful performance will lead to certain outcomes. The major outcomes we consider are potential rewards (such as a bonus, a promotion, or a good feeling of accomplishment), although we are likely to also take into account possible negative results (such as loss of leisure time or family disruption due to putting in extra hours on the job). In your special-project situation, perhaps your boss has a history of giving rewards, such as recognition and bonuses, to individuals who take on special projects. If so, you might assess the P → O expectancy for taking on the project as very high. On the other hand, your past experience with special projects may suggest that the boss sometimes arranges for rewards but other times forgets. If this is the case, you might view the P → O expectancy as medium in strength (perhaps a 50-50 probability of being rewarded). In the worst case, if your boss never rewards extra effort, you might assess the P → O expectancy as virtually zero—at least for rewards available from the boss.

In any given situation, there may be many potential rewards associated with performance. Rewards that are provided by others, such as bonuses, awards, or promotions, are known as **extrinsic rewards.** Rewards that are related to our own internal experiences with successful performance, such as feelings of achieve-

Performance-outcome expectancy   Our assessment of the probability that our successful performance will lead to certain outcomes

Extrinsic rewards   Rewards that are provided by others, such as bonuses, awards, or promotions

Intrinsic rewards Rewards that are related to our own internal experiences with successful performance, such as feelings of achievement, challenge, and growth

ment, challenge, and growth, are known as **intrinsic rewards.** Considering various possible outcomes (both positive and negative), we form an assessment of the probability of our performance's leading to desired outcomes. If our assessment of the P → O expectancy is high, the expectancy will contribute to our motivation. If our assessment is low, the expectancy could have a detrimental effect on our willingness to perform at a high level. Still, we have another motivational component to consider—how important the various outcomes are to us.

Valence Our assessment of the anticipated value of various outcomes or rewards

VALENCE With the **valence** component, we assess the anticipated value of various outcomes. If the available rewards interest us, valence will be high. However, the value of possible negative outcomes, such as the loss of leisure time or the disruption of our family, may offset the value of rewards in a given situation. The available rewards will have a motivating effect only when we attach a high overall valence to the situation. In the special-project example, you might view the prospect of a special bonus from the boss in an extremely positive light. On the other hand, if your rich aunt just left you $3 million, the bonus may be much less important. Still, you may attach a high value to the intrinsic rewards that might result if you develop the innovative project.

COMBINING THE ELEMENTS Expectancy theory argues that in deciding whether or not to put forth effort in a particular direction, we will consider all three elements: E → P expectancy, P → O expectancy, and valence. Research suggests that individuals are likely to make global judgments about each of the three elements in a given situation and then combine the elements according to the general overall formula posited by expectancy theory: (E → P) × (P → O) × valence = motivation.[23] For example, in the special-project situation, suppose that you assess all three elements as relatively high. Chances are that you will be fairly highly motivated to pursue the project: high E → P expectancy × high P → O expectancy × high valence = high motivation. On the other hand, consider the implications of assessing one of the elements as extremely low. For the sake of simplicity, let us assume that you assess the P → O expectancy as virtually zero but the other elements as high. The expectancy theory formula would predict that motivation will be zero: high E → P expectancy × zero P → O expectancy × high valence = zero motivation. An assessment of zero for any of the elements causes the whole equation to equal zero, regardless of the level of the other two elements. This is because you are unlikely to want to pursue the project if you either (1) believe that there is a zero (or an extremely low) probability of being able to perform adequately in the situation, (2) assess a zero (or an extremely low) possibility to the chance that successful performance will lead to certain outcomes, or (3) attach a zero (or an extremely low) valence value to potential outcomes. In more mixed situations, in which none of the elements have extremely low ratings, you will probably compare the situation with alternatives and choose the one that provides the best prospects of leading to outcomes that you value. In the special-project situation, you might try to negotiate with your boss either to improve the prospects of good outcomes or to shift assignments so that you receive a task that offers greater motivational potential.

Expectancy theory was not developed to compare individuals with one another. Rather, it was designed to predict where a given individual might decide to expend effort, given the choices available.[24] For example, the theory has been useful in predicting whether or not individual naval officers would voluntarily decide to retire, foretelling which job a given undergraduate student would choose after graduation, and determining which M.B.A. program a particular college graduate would ultimately select.[25] The theory also helps explain the success of a revolutionary idea at a Ukranian factory (see the following Case in Point discussion).

CASE IN POINT

UKRANIAN FACTORY LEADS MOVE TO PRIVATIZATION

In the early 1980s, the situation was bleak at the Konveyer Industrial Amalgamation. Konveyer manufactures automatic loading machines, conveyor belts, and other "transportation systems" outside of Lvov, a city in what was then the Ukranian region of the Soviet Union. Valentin Vologzhin, a recent plant director, described the state of affairs: "It was bad, really bad. No one wanted to buy our equipment. Our orders were way off. The quality was poor. We couldn't give customers what they needed, so they had to go elsewhere—usually abroad to Italy and France." In addition, the plant was losing large numbers of rubles, necessitating considerable subsidies from Moscow's central financial ministries.

When Vologzhin was brought in as director, he implemented a revolutionary idea, a system known as *aktsiya*, which is comparable to the western concept of corporate ownership. Konveyer was the first Soviet enterprise since Lenin's New Economic Policy in the 1920s to offer workers the opportunity to purchase shares in their organization. Vologzhin was able to convince the Soviet Union's bureaucratic central planners to accept the *aktsiya* idea for two reasons. First, the shares purchased would provide financing for the plant, so it would not need to tap government resources in Moscow. Second, the shares system would give workers a stake in the success of their organization.

Under the plan, which began in the late 1980s, employees could purchase up to 10,000 rubles' worth of shares, which were valued at 50 rubles each. They could sell them back to the plant at any time for the amount of their original purchase price. Thus the shares themselves did not change value, but they were guaranteed by the central financial ministries in the event that Konveyer lost money or went bankrupt. The attraction to workers was the safety of the investment and the relatively high dividend, which was 20 percent for the first year because of vast improvements in quality and production at the plant. More than 80 percent of the workers bought shares in the plan. Now, with the move toward privatization well under way, workers are typically given some shares of stock and have opportunities to purchase others. Of course, under privatization, the value of the stock varies and is tied to the productivity and success of the enterprise.[26] ■ ■ ■

Thus the Konveyer plant has been at the forefront of boosting motivation potential not only by increasing available valences but also by forging a stronger link between performance and outcomes.

EXPANDING EXPECTANCY THEORY If you ask several people whether they would agree that satisfied workers work harder, they are likely to reply in the affirmative. Yet, although the notion seems to have intuitive appeal, research has not always found a strong link between worker satisfaction and performance. To understand why, Lyman W. Porter and Edward E. Lawler III developed the expanded expectancy theory model (shown in Figure 6). According to this model, satisfaction does *not* lead to performance. Rather, the *reverse* is true: performance can (but does not always) lead to satisfaction through the reward process.

To follow this model, let us consider three possible scenarios involving Alissa, Bob, and Christen. In the first scenario, Alissa performs well, receives a bonus from the boss (extrinsic reward), feels good about her achievement (intrinsic reward), and ultimately feels satisfied. In this case, we have high performance and high satisfaction. In the second scenario, Bob performs well and feels good about his achievement (intrinsic reward), but the boss does not even say "good job," much less give him a bonus. As a result, even though Bob feels good

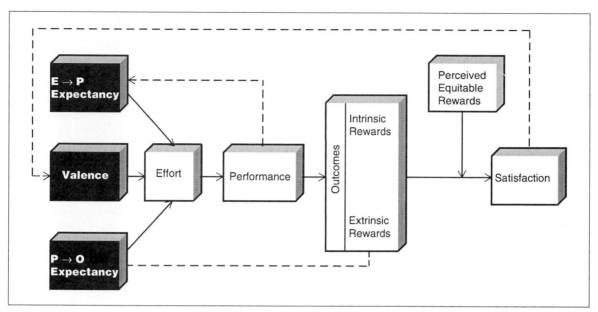

Figure 6 *An expanded model of expectancy theory. (Adapted from David A. Nadler and Edward E. Lawler III, "Motivation: A Diagnostic Approach," in J. Richard Hackman, Edward E. Lawler III, and Lyman W. Porter (eds.),* Perspectives on Behavior in Organizations, *2d ed., McGraw-Hill, New York, 1983, p. 75.)*

about his achievement, he is so annoyed with the boss that his satisfaction level is low. So with Bob we have a case of high performance but low satisfaction because he does not feel that he was adequately rewarded. In our third scenario, Christen does very little work but receives a sizable bonus at the end of the year, which pleases her greatly. With Christen, we have a case of low performance but high satisfaction.

How do we attain the ideal of high performance and high satisfaction? As suggested by the extended model, a crucial element is rewarding high performance (as occurred with Alissa but, unfortunately, not with Bob). Rewarding high performance leads to a high P → O expectancy (see the feedback loop in Figure 6), an important component of motivation. Equally critical, poor performance should *not* be rewarded (as was done in the case of Christen). Rewarding poor performance leads to a low P → O expectancy and ultimately to low subordinate motivation to perform.

This logic underlying expectancy theory is the force behind the recent trend toward basing pay on performance. This is illustrated by a change at the Ford Motor Company. Until the late 1980s, the number of people that a Ford manager supervised was a factor in pay. As a result, managers sometimes concentrated on getting more people to report to them rather than on achieving high performance with the smallest possible staff. The situation has changed with a new merit pay system that ties raises to increases in productivity.[27]

Aside from the issues relating to the P → O expectancy, expectancy theory has other major implications for managers. For one thing, managers should foster a high E → P expectancy in subordinates. They can do this by being very clear about performance expectations; setting challenging, but doable, performance goals; ensuring that employees have the training and resources necessary to reach the required performance levels; and providing encouragement. Managers can also encourage motivation by offering opportunities for rewards (both extrinsic and intrinsic) that have a high valence to employees. As suggested by need theories, valences are likely to differ among employees and are subject to change as some needs are fulfilled and others become paramount.[28] The expanded model of expectancy theory also indicates that managers might not obtain the expected results from their motivational efforts unless employees perceive their outcomes as equitable, an issue specifically addressed by equity theory.

Equity Theory

Faced with growing international competition, General Electric's electric motors division imposed an 11 percent pay cut on its hourly workers and required that they give up scheduled raises. GE next closed 2 of 12 plants, but it guaranteed that the remaining 4500 workers could keep their jobs for at least 3 years. The company then spent $200 million to upgrade equipment and product development. Unfortunately, morale plummeted and so did productivity. Although the company saved $25 million in wages with the pay cuts, GE officials now concede that the cuts were a mistake. They say that they should have pursued other means, such as quality programs and worker teams, to increase productivity and fight international competition. Apparently, the work force perceived the pay cuts as inequitable and responded accordingly.[29] To help explain how we identify and react to situations that we perceive as inequitable, J. Stacy Adams developed equity theory while working for the Behavioral Research Service of GE.[30]

Equity theory A theory that argues that we prefer situations of balance, or equity, which exist when we perceive the ratio of our inputs and outcomes to be equal to the ratio of inputs and outcomes for a comparison other

According to **equity theory,** we prefer situations of balance, or equity, which exist when we perceive the ratio of our inputs and outcomes to be equal to the ratio of inputs and outcomes for a comparison other (or others). The selection of the person or persons with whom we compare ourselves depends on our own view of appropriate comparisons. For example, in considering the equity of a pay raise, a person might compare her or his pay with that of certain coworkers, peers in other units, and/or a friend with similar credentials who works for another company. The inputs we consider in assessing the ratio of our inputs and outcomes relative to the ratios of others may cover a broad range of variables, including educational background, skills, experience, hours worked, and performance results. Outcomes might include such factors as pay, bonuses, praise, parking places, office space, furniture, and work assignments. The inputs and outcomes that we use to assess the equity of a situation are based strictly on our own perceptions of what is relevant.

According to the theory, situations of inequity exist whenever our inputs-outcomes ratio is either less than or greater than the inputs-outcomes ratio of a comparison other. In making equity judgments, we consider equity in *relative* terms (comparison with another) rather than absolute terms (comparison with a set standard). Thus we may feel equitably treated even if we provide high inputs and receive low outcomes as long as the person with whom we compare ourselves also contributes high inputs and receives low outcomes. Likewise, we are likely to feel equitably treated if other people have higher outcomes than we do as long as we perceive their inputs as sufficiently greater than ours to justify the difference. The theory argues that we will feel inequitably treated when we perceive our inputs-outcomes ratio to be greater than that of a comparison other (e.g., when a worker receives a significantly higher pay raise than someone else even though he or she perceives that the inputs of both have been the same). Nevertheless, individuals seem to adjust to such conditions of overreward rather quickly. Therefore, conditions of underreward (in which our inputs-outputs ratio is less than that of a comparison other) have much greater impact on motivation than do conditions of overreward.[31]

The motivational aspect of equity theory is based on its two major premises. First, the theory argues that the perception of inequity creates a tension in us. Second, the tension motivates us to eliminate or reduce the inequity. The greater the perceived inequity, the stronger the tension and the greater our motivation to reduce it.

REDUCING OR ELIMINATING INEQUITY Although the specific actions an individual takes will depend on what appears to be feasible in a given situation, Adams suggests that maintaining one's self-esteem is an important priority. As a result, an individual will probably first attempt to maximize outcomes and to resist personally costly changes in inputs. Changing perceptions about the inputs and outcomes of others or attempting to alter their side of the equation will usually be more palatable than changing perceptions about or actually altering one's own side of the equation. Leaving the situation will probably be done only in cases of high inequity when the other alternatives are not feasible. Finally, an individual will be highly resistant to changing the comparison others, especially if the objects of comparison have stabilized over time.

One particularly interesting study demonstrating the potential impact of inequities traced the performance of 23 major-league baseball players who began the season without contracts. Because of major changes in league contract rules, the researchers speculated that the players would be likely to perceive themselves as underpaid in reference both to others who had signed lucrative contracts and to their own lower compensation as compared with that of the previous year. The prediction that the 23 players would reduce their inputs, one of their few short-term options for reducing the inequity, was confirmed when they logged lower season performance levels for batting average, home runs, and runs batted in.[32]

Adams's equity formulation considered one situation at a given point in time, but recent work has considered inequities that extend over a period of time. The addition of the time perspective helps explain why people sometimes blow up over seemingly small inequities. Residues from previous inequities may pile up until the small incident becomes the "straw that broke the camel's back," and we react strongly.[33]

IMPLICATIONS FOR MANAGERS Equity theory makes several helpful suggestions to supplement the recommendations of expectancy theory. For one thing, managers need to maintain two-way communication with subordinates so that they have some idea of subordinates' equity perceptions. For another, it is important to let subordinates know the "rules" that will govern the allocation of outcomes relative to inputs. This issue is closely related to the expectancy theory recommendation that the relationship between performance and outcomes (performance-outcome expectancy) be made clear to subordinates. Also, since a pattern of inequities over a period of time can build into major difficulties, managers should maintain good communication not only with subordinates but also with superiors, peers, customers, and other individuals associated with the job. In addition, there is growing recognition that employees need to equitably balance the demands of the job against other essentials in their lives if their job motivation is to be sustained. One company that has been at the forefront of social responsibility on children's issues and has helped employees more equitably balance work and family needs is Stride Rite (see the Valuing Ethics box).

Goal-Setting Theory

There are many advantages to establishing goals throughout the organization. In this chapter, we briefly summarize the highlights of goal-setting theory as they apply to motivation. While goal setting was originally viewed as a technique, it is developing into a motivational theory as researchers attempt to better understand the cognitive factors that influence its success. Goal-setting experts Edwin A. Locke and Gary P. Latham argue that goal setting works by directing attention and action, mobilizing effort, increasing persistence, and encouraging

VALUING ETHICS

Stride Rite Helps Employees Be Good Family Members

Stride Rite, based in Cambridge, Massachusetts, is a producer of high-quality children's shoes and is the current parent company for Keds and Sperry Top-Siders. In addition to being well known for its shoes, Stride Rite has the distinction of opening the first corporate day-care center in the United States—more than 20 years ago. Initially, the center was opened to help the community of Roxbury, Massachusetts, where the company was headquartered until the early 1980s. CEO Arnold Hiatt recounts witnessing the decay and urban blight affecting the

neighborhood: "Every time I looked out my window, I saw lots of small children with nothing to do and no place to go." Since the company's business pertained to children, top management decided to do something about the area's needy children by opening a day-care center in some of the firm's empty manufacturing space. Employees were told that they could bring their children to the center also. Eventually, the center was run on a 50-50 basis, with half the children coming from the community and half being the children of employees.

With the move to Cambridge, the company opened a second center. The center has enabled the company to attract very capable

and loyal employees even when the market is tight. For example, one female employee who drives 2 hours each way to work at Stride Rite headquarters told a visitor that the ride is long, but "it's worth it because my child gets quality care and opportunities I couldn't provide otherwise." One unique aspect of the Cambridge center is that it is intergenerational, meaning that the center serves both preschool children and senior citizens. Although only a few employees currently have elderly relatives enrolled in the center, Hiatt and Stride Rite have already taken steps to help employees cope with the growing family issue of elder care.[34]

the development of strategies to achieve the goals. Feedback regarding results is also an essential element in motivating through goal setting.[35]

The success of goal setting in motivating performance depends on establishing goals that have the appropriate attributes, or characteristics. In particular, goals should be specific and measurable, challenging, attainable, relevant to the major work of the organization, and time-limited (i.e., a goal must be accomplished within a defined period of time). At the Intel Corporation, which makes the microprocessor chips that are the "brains" of personal computers, goals have been successfully used to help reduce the time it takes to develop and produce new microprocessors. The reduction—from 64 weeks to less than 52 weeks—is an important accomplishment, given the highly competitive environment within which microprocessor producers operate.[36]

Goal commitment, one's attachment to or determination to reach a goal, is another important element in the goal-setting process. Goal commitment is affected by the major components of expectancy theory: effort-performance expectancy (Can I reach the goal?), performance-outcome expectancy (If I reach it, will I be rewarded?), and valence (Do I value the potential rewards?). Individuals are more likely to be committed to attaining goals when they have high expectations of success in reaching the goals, see strong connections between goal accomplishment and rewards, and value the rewards.[37] Hence expectancy theory and goal-setting theory are largely compatible.[38]

The usefulness of goal setting in enhancing performance has strong research support.[39] As a result, managers are likely to find it a very helpful motivational tool.

Assessing Cognitive Theories

Each of the cognitive theories of motivation offers a different perspective, although the three views are somewhat complementary. Expectancy theory advises managers to help employees develop positive assessments of effort-performance expectancy through such means as training and encouragement. It also highlights the importance of a clear link between performance and outcomes, as well as the need to offer rewards that have a positive valence for employees (clues about valence come from need theories). Goal setting is compatible with expectancy theory in that it can help pinpoint the performance levels associated with effort-performance expectancy and performance-outcome expectancy. Finally, equity issues are a component of the expanded expectancy theory model, indicating the importance of maintaining equity in the motivation process.

REINFORCEMENT THEORY

The reinforcement approach to motivation is almost the antithesis of cognitive theories, since it does not concern itself with the thought processes of the individual as an explanation of behavior. The best-known approach to reinforcement theory, sometimes also called *operant conditioning theory* or *behaviorism,* was pioneered by noted psychologist B. F. Skinner. According to **reinforcement theory,** our behavior can be explained by consequences in the environment and, therefore, it is not necessary to look for cognitive explanations.[40] Instead, the theory relies heavily on a concept called the **law of effect,** which states that behaviors having pleasant or positive consequences are more likely to be repeated and that behaviors having unpleasant or negative consequences are less likely to be repeated.[41]

In the reinforcement process, a stimulus provides a cue for a response or behavior that is then followed by a consequence. If we find the consequence rewarding, we are more likely to repeat the behavior when the stimulus occurs in the future. If we do not find it rewarding, we are less likely to repeat the behavior. For example, assume that you are the manager of a marketing research unit in a consumer-products company. A product manager from another unit asks you for emergency help with market research data (stimulus). You pull some of your people from other priorities and even stay quite late to produce the needed data (behavior). The product manager makes sure that your unit is recognized for its efforts (pleasant consequence). As a result, you will be likely to put extra effort into helping the product manager in the future. On the other hand, if the product manager complains about a minor error (unpleasant consequence) and says nothing about the rest of the data or the extra effort that went into preparing it (less than pleasant consequence), you will be less likely to put the same effort into helping that manager in the future. The use of techniques associated with reinforcement theory is known as **behavior modification.**

Types of Reinforcement

In behavior modification, four types of reinforcement are available to help managers influence behavior: positive reinforcement, negative reinforcement, extinction, and punishment. Positive reinforcement and negative reinforcement are aimed at increasing a behavior, while extinction and punishment focus on decreasing a behavior (see Figure 7). Skinner argued that positive reinforcement and extinction encourage individual growth whereas negative reinforcement and punishment are likely to foster immaturity in individuals and eventually contaminate the entire organization.

POSITIVE REINFORCEMENT Aimed at *increasing* a desired behavior, **positive reinforcement** involves providing a pleasant, rewarding consequence to encour-

Reinforcement theory A theory that argues that our behavior can be explained by consequences in the environment

Law of effect A concept that states that behaviors having pleasant or positive consequences are more likely to be repeated and that behaviors having unpleasant or negative consequences are less likely to be repeated

Behavior modification The use of techniques associated with reinforcement theory

Positive reinforcement A technique, aimed at *increasing* a desired behavior, that involves providing a pleasant, rewarding consequence to encourage that behavior

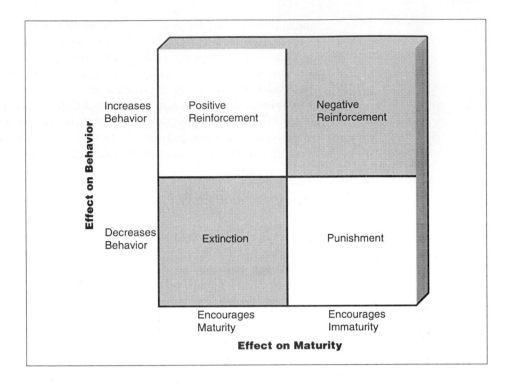

Figure 7 *Types of reinforcement situations according to Skinner.*

age that behavior. The rewarding consequence, such as praise, a raise, or time off, is said to be a positive reinforcer if it leads to repetition of the desired behavior. Since individuals differ in regard to what they find pleasant and rewarding, managers need to monitor the effects of a particular reinforcer to determine whether it is effective in encouraging the desired behavior.

Because individuals frequently do not execute a new behavior exactly as required when they first try it, managers often find it useful to encourage new behaviors through shaping. **Shaping** is the successive rewarding of behaviors that closely approximate the desired response until the actual desired response is made. For example, a manager training a new salesperson may compliment the way that the individual greets customers (if this behavior approximates the desired response). The manager may also suggest questions that the salesperson might ask customers to obtain a better idea of their needs. Then the manager can reward the person's efforts to ask better questions and can make a further suggestion. Through this process the individual's behavior is gradually shaped so that the person becomes a competent salesperson.

NEGATIVE REINFORCEMENT   Like positive reinforcement, negative reinforcement focuses on *increasing* a desired behavior, but it operates in a different way. **Negative reinforcement** involves providing noxious (unpleasant) stimuli so that an individual will engage in the desired behavior in order to stop the noxious stimuli. In other words, the desired behavior is reinforced in a negative way because the individual must engage in the behavior in order to get rid of an unpleasant condition. For example, an engineer may work hard to finish a project on time (desired behavior) in order to stop (consequence) the chief engineer's nagging or yelling (noxious stimuli). With negative reinforcement, either the noxious, or unpleasant, stimuli are actually present or the potential is high that they will occur unless the individual engages in the desired behavior. For instance, the chief engineer may already be nagging about meeting the project deadline; or the chief engineer may not be yelling or nagging yet, but the engi-

Shaping   The successive rewarding of behaviors that closely approximate the desired response until the actual desired response is made

Negative reinforcement   A technique, aimed at *increasing* a desired behavior, that involves providing noxious stimuli so that an individual will engage in the desired behavior in order to stop the noxious stimuli

neer may know from past experience that late projects trigger such behavior. In either case, the negative reinforcement increases the likelihood that the engineer will complete the project on time.

Although negative reinforcement may encourage the desired behavior, it may also make the individual feel negatively toward the person providing the reinforcement. If this is the case, the individual may react by doing only what is required, declining to put in extra time when it might be helpful, or even leaving the organization. Negative reinforcement may also foster immature behavior. For example, it may unwittingly encourage the engineer to complete projects on time only when the boss is in the office.

Extinction A technique that involves withholding previously available positive consequences associated with a behavior in order to *decrease* that behavior

EXTINCTION **Extinction** involves withholding previously available positive consequences associated with a behavior in order to *decrease* that behavior. Suppose that the first few times an employee engages in clowning behavior during a staff meeting, the manager laughs. The laughter might tend to reinforce the clowning to such a point that the behavior becomes disruptive. The employee's clowning behavior would be gradually extinguished if the manager proceeded to refrain from (withhold) laughing in response to it.

Punishment A technique that involves providing negative consequences in order to *decrease* or discourage a behavior

PUNISHMENT **Punishment** involves providing negative consequences in order to *decrease* or discourage a behavior. Examples are criticizing the unwanted behavior whenever it occurs, suspending an individual without pay, denying training opportunities, or withholding resources such as new equipment. Punishment differs from negative reinforcement in at least two important ways. First, punishment aims to decrease or discourage an undesirable behavior, whereas negative reinforcement attempts to increase or encourage a desirable behavior. Second, punishment is usually applied after the individual has engaged in an undesirable behavior. Conversely, negative reinforcement occurs before the individual engages in a desirable behavior. Both punishment and negative reinforcement constitute negative approaches to affecting behavior, approaches that Skinner maintained have long-run detrimental effects on individuals and organizations.

Arguments against the use of punishment are that it can have undesirable side effects (e.g., negative feelings toward the punisher) and that it may eliminate the undesirable behavior only as long as the threat of punishment remains. Also, it does not provide a model of correct behavior. Still, punishment may be necessary under some circumstances, particularly if the undesirable behavior has a serious impact on the organization or endangers others. In such situations, attempts to use extinction to decrease the undesirable behavior might not be practical because immediate action to stop the behavior is necessary. If punishment must be used, it is likely to be most effective if there are recognized company policies that govern the situation; the punishment is given as soon as possible after the undesirable behavior; the punishment is moderate, rather than severe; and it is applied consistently.[42]

Schedules of Reinforcement

Schedules of reinforcement Patterns of rewarding that specify the basis for and timing of positive reinforcement

Reinforcement theory emphasizes using positive reinforcement to encourage desired behaviors. In studying positive reinforcement, researchers have discovered that different patterns of rewarding affect the time required to learn a new behavior and the degree to which the behavior persists. These different patterns, called **schedules of reinforcement**, specify the basis for and timing of positive reinforcement. There are two major types of reinforcement schedules: continuous and partial. With a *continuous* schedule of reinforcement, the desired behavior is rewarded each time it occurs. For example, a manager might praise a worker every time the worker performs a task correctly. This type of reinforcement is very effective during the initial learning process, but it becomes tedious and impractical on an ongoing basis. Further, the desired behavior tends to stop almost immediately (rapid extinction) unless the reinforcement is continued. With a *partial* schedule of reinforcement, the desired behavior is rewarded intermittently rather than each time it occurs. During the initial learning process, the behavior can be rewarded more often to encourage its repetition, and the rewards can become less frequent as time goes on. There are four main types of partial reinforcement schedules: fixed interval, fixed ratio, variable interval, and variable ratio (see Figure 8).

Fixed-interval schedule of reinforcement A pattern in which a reinforcer is administered on a fixed time schedule, assuming that the desired behavior has continued at an appropriate level

FIXED INTERVAL With a **fixed-interval schedule of reinforcement,** a reinforcer is administered on a fixed time schedule, assuming that the desired behavior has continued at an appropriate level. For example, a plant manager might visit a section of the plant every day at approximately the same time and praise efforts being made to increase production quality. A fixed-interval schedule tends to produce an uneven response pattern, with the desired behavior peaking just before the expected reinforcement and then declining somewhat until the next anticipated reinforcement. With this type of schedule, extinction is rapid if the reinforcement is delayed or stopped.

Fixed-ratio schedule of reinforcement A pattern in which a reinforcer is provided after a fixed number of occurrences of the desired behavior

FIXED RATIO With a **fixed-ratio schedule of reinforcement,** a reinforcer is provided after a fixed number of occurrences of the desired behavior, rather than according to a fixed time schedule. For example, special awards for innovative ideas might be given to individuals after they have contributed five implemented ideas. Piecework incentive pay systems, in which workers earn an incentive for producing a specified number of units, are another type of fixed-ratio

Figure 8 *Types of partial reinforcement schedules. (Adapted from Hugh J. Arnold and Daniel C. Feldman,* Organizational Behavior, *McGraw-Hill, New York, 1986, p. 70.)*

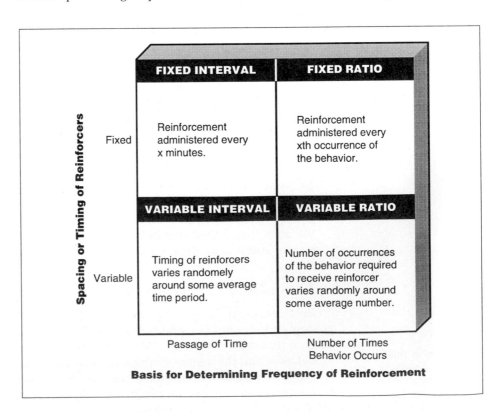

reinforcement. A fixed-ratio schedule tends to elicit a high response rate, but rapid extinction occurs if the reinforcer is discontinued even temporarily.

Variable-interval schedule of reinforcement A pattern in which a reinforcer is administered on a varying, or random, time schedule that *averages* out to a predetermined time frequency

VARIABLE INTERVAL With a **variable-interval schedule of reinforcement**, a reinforcer is administered on a varying, or random, time schedule that *averages* out to a predetermined time frequency. For example, a plant manager might visit a section of the plant to praise good quality an average of five times per week, but at varying times. This type of reinforcement schedule tends to promote a high, steady response rate with slow extinction.

Variable-ratio schedule of reinforcement A pattern in which a reinforcer is provided after a varying, or random, number of occurrences of the desired behavior in such a way that the reinforcement pattern *averages* out to a predetermined ratio of occurrences per reinforcement

VARIABLE RATIO With a **variable-ratio schedule of reinforcement**, a reinforcer is provided after a varying, or random, number of occurrences of the desired behavior (rather than on a varying time schedule) in such a way that the reinforcement pattern *averages* out to a predetermined ratio of occurrences per reinforcement. For example, special awards for innovative ideas might be given to individuals on a ratio average of one award per five innovative ideas (i.e., an award after three ideas one time, after seven ideas another time, etc.). Slot-machine payoff patterns, which provide rewards after a varying number of pulls on the lever, are excellent examples of a variable-ratio schedule. This type of schedule is likely to produce a very high response rate and is the partial reinforcement method with the slowest extinction rate. Variable-ratio reinforcement was used in the McDonald's Monopoly promotion, in which customers were given game pieces that contained stamps corresponding to the properties on a Monopoly game board. Although the odds of winning the top prize of $2 million were very long (1 in 724,214,000), more immediate reinforcement was provided by giving customers the chance to win instant McDonald's food prizes at much better odds (1 in 12), as well the opportunity to collect stamps for possible bigger prizes. The promotion was so successful that it was repeated 2 years in a row.

Using Reinforcement Theory

Researchers have proposed several guidelines to help managers effectively use the reinforcement approach. They advise managers to emphasize positive reinforcement to encourage desired behaviors and to let subordinates know what behaviors will be rewarded. Once desired behaviors have been learned, variable-interval and variable-ratio reinforcement patterns seem to be the most effective approaches to maintaining the behaviors. Finally, if it is necessary to punish, punishment of moderate severity administered quickly and consistently seems to yield the best results.[43] The Union National Bank in Little Rock, Arkansas, has used positive reinforcement principles to increase output in the proof department. Employees there encode machine-readable numbers onto the bottom of checks so that the checks can be credited to the appropriate accounts. As a result of putting up a graph that shows daily production and praising high performers, production increased from 1065 items per hour to 2100 items per hour. With the addition of individual bonuses based on daily output, production rose to 3500 items per hour.[44]

SOCIAL LEARNING THEORY

On the basis of his extensive work on reinforcement theory, noted psychologist Albert Bandura became convinced that the apparent success of the approach could not be explained without taking into account the cognitive, or thinking,

Social learning theory A theory that argues that learning occurs through the continuous reciprocal interaction of our behaviors, various personal factors, and environmental forces

capacity of individuals. Accordingly, he and others developed **social learning theory,** which argues that learning occurs through the continuous interaction of our behaviors, various personal factors, and environmental forces. Individuals influence their environment, which, in turn, affects the ways that they think and behave. In other words, we learn much of our behavior by observing, imitating, and interacting with our social environment. Although social learning theory combines elements of both the cognitive and the reinforcement approaches, it is discussed at this point because it builds on reinforcement theory.

Major Components

Social learning theory argues that three cognitively related processes are particularly important in explaining our behavior: symbolic processes, vicarious learning, and self-control.[45]

Symbolic processes The various ways that we use verbal and imagined symbols to process and store experiences in representational forms that can serve as guides to future behavior

Self-efficacy The belief in one's capabilities to perform a specific task

SYMBOLIC PROCESSES According to social learning theory, we rely heavily on **symbolic processes,** the various ways that we use verbal and imagined symbols to process and store experiences in representational forms (words and images) that can serve as guides to future behavior. Through the use of symbols, we can attempt to solve problems without actually trying all the alternative courses of action. We may also be able to visualize an intriguing vacation spot in the South Pacific even if we have never actually been there. Images of desirable futures allow us to set distant goals and fashion actions that will lead to the accomplishment of those goals. Our symbolic processes incorporate a cognitive element called **self-efficacy,** the belief in one's capabilities to perform a specific task. Although somewhat similar to the effort-performance expectancy component of expectancy theory, self-efficacy is more oriented toward our convictions about our own capacities. It may be useful in explaining the levels of goals that we set, as well as task effort and persistence. For example, one study found that faculty members who feel competent at research and writing tend to produce more articles and books, which, in turn, increases their self-confidence and the likelihood of future productivity. Similar findings have emerged from studies of sales performance among life insurance agents.[46]

Vicarious learning Our ability to learn new behaviors and/or assess their probable consequences by observing others

Modeling Actually observing and attempting to imitate the behaviors of others

VICARIOUS LEARNING **Vicarious learning,** or observational learning, is our ability to learn new behaviors and/or assess their probable consequences by observing others. This concept is important because, contrary to the arguments associated with reinforcement theory, we do not actually have to perform a behavior ourselves to learn about the consequences. The process of observing and attempting to imitate the behaviors of others is called **modeling** (see Figure 9). If you learned to swim or play tennis by imitating the behaviors of others (perhaps a proficient friend or an instructor), you engaged in modeling. Modeling usually takes place in four stages. In the *attention* stage, we select a model for observation, usually because we perceive the model to be skilled and successful, and we pay attention to the relevant aspects of behavior. In the *retention* stage, we retain information about the behavior through mental images and words. In the *repro-*

Figure 9 *The modeling process.*

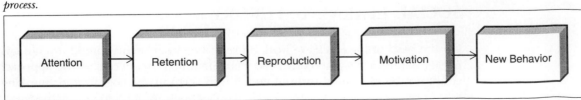

| Attention | → | Retention | → | Reproduction | → | Motivation | → | New Behavior |

duction stage, we attempt to reproduce the behavior, but we may be only partially successful and need to make further adjustment based on feedback. In the *motivation* stage, we are motivated to adopt the model behavior. For this stage to lead to our actual adoption of the behavior, reinforcement must be present, usually from one of three sources. First, our behavior can be reinforced by the consequences in the environment in a manner similar to that noted by reinforcement theory. Second, reinforcement can occur vicariously through our observations of the consequences that have accrued to others engaging in the particular behavior. Third, we can engage in self-reinforcement through the process of self-control.

Self-control Our ability to exercise control over our own behavior by setting standards and providing consequences for our own actions

SELF-CONTROL **Self-control,** or self-regulation, is our ability to exercise control over our own behavior by setting standards and providing consequences (both rewards and punishments) for our own actions. Self-control increases performance when we make our self-rewards conditional on reaching a challenging preset level of performance.[47] For example, we may promise ourselves a 15-minute break if we finish an assignment by a certain time, treat ourselves to something new when we get an A on an exam, or internally congratulate ourselves on a job well done. Since social learning theory recognizes the concept of self-reinforcement, it gives us more credit for control over our own behavior than does reinforcement theory.

Using Social Learning Theory

The social learning theory approach has considerable research support, although investigators have only recently begun to explore fully its implications for organizations.[48] The theory has two major managerial implications beyond those offered by other motivational theories. First, providing positive models appears to greatly accelerate the learning of appropriate behaviors, especially if there are opportunities to try the new behaviors in a supportive setting and obtain feedback. Modeling can be particularly useful for training new workers. Second, the notion of vicarious learning indicates that employees are likely to draw conclusions about prospects for rewards and punishments, not only from their own experiences but also from those of others. One company whose operations reflect social learning theory principles, including modeling and various types of reinforcement, is Domino's Pizza, Inc. (see the following Case in Point discussion).

CASE IN POINT   LEARNING THE DOMINO THEORY

Begun as one small shop in 1960, Domino's Pizza almost went bankrupt before emerging in the late 1980s as the world's largest pizza delivery empire. A large part of Domino's success is attributable to the company's founder, Tom Monaghan. His innovative ideas include the guarantee that Domino's will deliver an ordered pizza within 30 minutes or reduce the price and the use of the "hot box," which ensures that the delivered pizza will taste as if it just came out of the oven. With gross annual sales topping more than $2.5 billion, and over 5000 outlets, the need to train new workers and managers is almost insatiable.

To help meet this challenge, the company has developed a variety of videotapes, most of them aimed at the five basic worker positions in an outlet—phone answerer, pizza maker, oven tender, router, and driver. The videos cover such topics as orientation, image, dough management, pizza making, oven tending and maintenance, delivery, and safe driving. They combine detailed instructions with generous sprinklings of humor to hold the attention of new recruits. On the humorous side, for example, one award-winning video on dough management shows a funeral scene featuring uncooked pizza dough that has "died" before its time. Another, on safe driving, shows a hapless driver gradually turning into a werewolf, consumed by the pressure to deliver pizzas within the 30-minute limit. Managers are trained to show the videos; have individuals perform the various tasks in the desired manner, as clearly illustrated on the videos; and give workers appropriate feedback and reinforcement. The videos are supplemented with numerous well-designed posters that provide further models of desired behaviors. For example, just above the counters where the pizzas are actually made, detailed glossy posters show exactly how a pizza should look at various stages in the process.

To make the grade at Domino's, employees must meet challenging time performance standards. Order takers must answer the telephone within three rings and take an order within 45 seconds; pizza makers are expected to have the ordered pizza made and in the oven within 1 minute; and oven tenders are given 5 seconds to load one pizza while unloading another. Management trainees must be able to meet these same standards, as well as others spelled out in detailed behavioral terms in the performance evaluation system.

Reinforcement comes from pay incentives and a heavy dose of competition based on employee contests within stores for the fastest service and delivery times and the highest sales figures. A powerful and unusual incentive is the prospect that high performers can become store managers within a year and franchisees within 2 years under very generous terms (30 percent of the outlets are company-owned; the rest are franchises). As the number of desirable locations for franchises becomes more limited in the United States and competition grows in the home delivery of pizza, additional motivational strategies may be needed. Other incentives for successful managers currently include company-paid luxury vacations, weekends on the corporate yacht, and the possibility of being awarded a $12,000 Patek Philippe gold watch for beating the company record for weekly store sales.[49] ■ ■ ■

Thus social learning theory and the other motivational theories discussed in this chapter can be important assets in attempting to influence various behaviors in organizations. They are a critical factor in effective leadership.

CHAPTER SUMMARY

Motivation is the force that energizes behavior, gives direction to behavior, and underlies the tendency to persist. Actual performance is a function of ability and working conditions, as well as motivation. Efforts to understand the motivational process have centered on several major elements: needs, cognitive activities, and reward and reinforcement issues.

Need theories argue that we behave the way we do because we have internal needs we are attempting to fulfill. These theories are sometimes called content theories because they focus on what motivates others. Maslow's widely known hierarchy of needs theory argues that our needs form a five-level hierarchy, ranging from physiological to self-actualization needs. ERG theory updates

Maslow's approach by proposing three need levels and including the frustration-regression principle and the satisfaction-progression explanation of movement among need levels. While the hierarchy of needs and ERG theories view certain needs as inherent, McClelland's acquired-needs theory argues that needs are acquired or learned on the basis of our life experiences. His work has focused particularly on needs for achievement, affiliation, and power, as well as on how these needs affect managerial success.

Cognitive theories, sometimes called process theories, attempt to isolate the thinking patterns we use in deciding whether or not to behave in a certain way. Expectancy theory posits that in deciding how much effort to expend in a given direction, we consider three issues: effort-performance expectancy (the probability that our efforts will lead to the required performance level), performance-outcome expectancy (the probability that our successful performance will lead to certain outcomes), and valence (the anticipated value of the various outcomes or rewards). As the expanded model of expectancy theory suggests, managers need to consider all three elements in achieving both high performance and high job satisfaction among employees. Equity theory indicates that we prefer situations of balance, or equity, which occurs when we perceive the ratio of our inputs and outcomes to be equal to the ratio of inputs and outcomes of a comparison other (or others). Goal-setting theory highlights the importance of goal commitment, specific and challenging goals, and feedback. Goal set-

ting works by directing attention and action, mobilizing effort, increasing persistence, and encouraging the development of strategies to achieve the goals.

Reinforcement theory argues that our behavior can be explained by consequences in the environment. The four major types of reinforcement are positive reinforcement, negative reinforcement, extinction, and punishment. Schedules of reinforcement specify the basis for and timing of positive rewards. They include fixed-interval, fixed-ratio, variable-interval, and variable-ratio schedules. Social learning theory argues that learning occurs through the continuous interaction of our behaviors, various personal factors, and environmental forces. Three cognitively related processes are particularly important: symbolic processes, vicarious learning, and self-control.

QUESTIONS FOR DISCUSSION AND REVIEW

1 Briefly describe the concept of motivation and explain the motivation process. Describe a situation that illustrates the idea that performance is a function of ability and working conditions, as well as motivation.

2 Explain the hierarchy of needs theory. Assume that you are the manager of a large fast-food outlet. How could this theory help you motivate the various individuals who work for you?

3 Identify the major differences between ERG theory and the hierarchy of needs theory. Suppose you became the new manager of a work unit. How could ERG theory assist you in assessing how to motivate the members of your new unit?

4 Describe the acquired-needs theory of motivation. Based on McClelland's work on the need for achievement, what are some of the difficulties in attempting to motivate high-nAch individuals in organizations? How could you encourage the need for achievement in others? How might you encourage the need for institutional power?

5 Outline the expectancy theory of motivation. Suppose you are in charge of a group of engineers who are responsible for the completion of various projects. How would you use expectancy theory to motivate them to perform at a high level? How could the

expanded expectancy theory help you keep them motivated?

6 Explain equity theory. In part, equity theory argues that our judgments of equity (or inequity) are based on our own perceptions of situations. What potential difficulties does the perceptual aspect of equity judgments present for managers?

7 Assess the role of goal setting in motivation. Analyze a student group or other organization to which you belong in terms of its goals or lack thereof. To what extent are goals set that are specific and challenging? Is there commitment to the goals? Do these goals improve organizational effectiveness?

8 Explain the four main types of reinforcement. For each one, identify a situation in which you have seen that type used and assess the outcome.

9 Contrast the four major types of partial reinforcement schedules. Provide an example of each type from your own experience.

10 Explain the social learning theory of motivation. Describe an instance in which you obtained important information through vicarious learning. Also describe a situation in which you learned through modeling. To what extent can you identify the steps in the modeling process in your own situation?

DISCUSSION QUESTIONS FOR CHAPTER OPENING CASE

1 How can need theories help provide clues about what is likely to motivate individuals at Levi Strauss?

2 What aspects of expectancy theory are incorporated in the Aspirations Statement? Where are goal-setting theory and equity theory applicable?

3 What evidence exists for the use of various types of reinforcement, vicarious learning, and self-control?

MANAGEMENT EXERCISE: MARKETEER OR ENTREPRENEUR

Lee Brown has been a market planning specialist for the Sweet Tooth Candy Company for the past 2 years. This is her first job following graduation from college, and she is quite pleased with her progress in the organization. She has received three merit raises and expects to be promoted soon to the position of senior market planning specialist. She enjoys her work, and her immediate boss is one of the finest market planners she could ever hope to work with. Her boss gives her autonomy, support, and resources when she needs them. Similarly, he seems to know when she needs help and gives it to her in a way that brings out the best in her. Lee frequently wonders how anyone could be happier than she is with her job and company.

Last week she met Jamie Wilson, one of her former schoolmates, at the local shopping center. Lee recalled that Jamie, an excellent student who majored in human resource management, had accepted a position as a compensation analyst with a local health-care corporation. While catching up on the events of their lives during the previous 2 years, Jamie indicated she had a business proposition that she had been considering for some time but did not believe she could pursue alone. She needed a partner and suggested that Lee be that person.

Her proposition was that child-care centers were desperately needed in their area. The city of approximately 35,000 people had only one small child-care facility, which had a very long waiting list and very high rates. Jamie's research had revealed that three different churches in the area would gladly support additional child-care centers by furnishing their facilities, at little or no cost, provided the centers were managed as separate businesses. Jamie had located a building that could be developed into an excellent child-care center. Jamie reasoned that she and Lee could start the business in one or more of the churches and expand into the building she had found. Financially, the return from operating one child-care center would not quite equal Lee's current total compensation. However, two or more centers would yield a very nice income for both partners. Jamie had determined that appropriate licenses could be obtained in a few weeks and that the financing required to start the business was available at very favorable rates. Other materials and supplies were readily available as well.

Lee was intrigued with this proposition and told Jamie that she wanted a week to think it over. She intends to discuss her interest in this proposition with Jamie tomorrow.

Requirement

Using expectancy theory, indicate the factors that would have an impact on Lee's decision and the strength of her motivation to participate in the proposed child-care business.

REFERENCES

1. Based on Robert Howard, "Values Make the Company: An Interview with Robert Haas," *Harvard Business Review*, September–October 1990, pp. 133–144.

2. Richard M. Steers and Lyman W. Porter (eds.), *Motivation and Work Behavior*, 4th ed., McGraw-Hill, New York, 1987, pp. 5–6.

3. John P. Campbell and Richard D. Prichard, "Motivation Theory in Industrial and Organizational Psychology," in Marvin D. Dunnette (ed.), *Handbook of Industrial and Organizational Psychology*, Rand McNally, Chicago, 1976, pp. 62–130; Terence R. Mitchell, "Motivation: New Directions for Theory, Research, and Practice," in Richard M. Steers and Lyman W. Porter (eds.), *Motivation and Work Behavior*, 4th ed., McGraw-Hill, New York, 1987, pp. 27–40.

4. Reva B. Tooley, "Turning Trials into Triumph," *Working Woman*, January 1987, pp. 66–70; Susan Caminiti, "America's Most Successful Businesswoman," *Fortune*, June 15, 1992, pp. 102–107.

5. Dean Foust, "Innkeepers, Beware: Kemmons Wilson Is Checking In Again," *Business Week*, Feb. 1, 1988, pp. 79–80.

6. Mahmoud A. Wahba and Lawrence G. Bridwell, "Maslow Reconsidered: A Review of Research on the Need Hierarchy Theory," *Organizational Behavior and Human Performance*, vol. 16, 1976, pp. 212–240; Vance F. Mitchell and Pravin Moudgill, "Measurement of Maslow's Need Hierarchy," *Organizational Behavior and Human Performance*, vol. 16, 1976, pp. 334–349.

7. Clayton P. Alderfer, *Existence, Relatedness, and Growth: Human Needs in Organizational Settings*, Free Press, New York, 1972.

8. P. Ranganath Nayak and John M. Ketteringham, *Break-Throughs*, Rawson Associates, New York, 1986.

9. Clayton P. Alderfer, *Existence, Relatedness, and Growth: Human Needs in Organizational Settings*, Free Press, New York, 1972; Benjamin Schneider and Clayton P. Alderfer, "Three Studies of Measures of Need Satisfaction in Organizations," *Administrative Science Quarterly*, vol. 18, 1973, pp. 498–505; Clayton P. Alderfer, Robert E. Kaplan, and Ken K. Smith, "The Effect of Relatedness Need Satisfaction on Relatedness Desires,"

Administrative Science Quarterly, vol. 19, 1974, pp. 507–532; John P. Wanous and Abram Zwany, "A Cross-Sectional Test of Need Hierarchy Theory," *Organizational Behavior and Human Performance*, vol. 18, 1977, pp. 78–97.

10. Robert A. Mamis, "Details, Details," *INC.*, March 1988, pp. 96–98.

11. Jaclyn Fierman, "The Entrepreneurs: The Best of Their Class," *Fortune*, Oct. 12, 1987, p. 144.

12. William D. Spangler, "Validity of Questionnaire and TAT Measures of Need for Achievement: Two Meta-Analyses," *Psychological Bulletin*, vol. 112, 1992, pp. 140–154.

13. David C. McClelland, *Human Motivation*, Scott, Foresman, Glenview, Ill., 1985.

14. Richard M. Steers, "Murray's Manifest Needs Theory," in Richard M. Steers and Lyman W. Porter (eds.), *Motivation and Work Behavior*, 4th ed., McGraw-Hill, New York, 1987, pp. 59–67.

15. David C. McClelland, "Power Is the Great Motivator," *Harvard Business Review*, March–April 1976, pp. 100–110, and *Human Motivation*, Scott, Foresman, Glenview, Ill., 1985.

16. Richard M. Steers, "Murray's Manifest Needs Theory," in Richard M. Steers and Lyman W. Porter (eds.), *Motivation and Work Behavior*, 4th ed., McGraw-Hill, New York, 1987, pp. 59–67.

17. David C. McClelland, "Power Is the Great Motivator," *Harvard Business Review*, March–April 1976, pp. 100–110, and *Human Motivation*, Scott, Foresman, Glenview, Ill., 1985.

18. Brett Duval Fromson, "The Slow Death of E. F. Hutton," *Fortune*, Feb. 29, 1988, pp. 82–87.

19. David C. McClelland, *Human Motivation*, Scott, Foresman, Glenview, Ill., 1985.

20. J. D. W. Andrews, "The Achievement Motive and Advancement in Two Types of Organizations," *Journal of Personality and Social Psychology*, vol. 6, 1967, pp. 163–168; David C. McClelland and Richard E. Boyatzis, "Leadership Motive Pattern and Long-Term Success in Management," *Journal of Applied Psychology*, vol. 67, 1982, pp. 737–743; Richard M. Steers, "Murray's Mani-

fest Needs Theory," in Richard M. Steers and Lyman W. Porter (eds.), *Motivation and Work Behavior*, 4th ed., McGraw-Hill, New York, 1987, pp. 59–67.

21. David C. McClelland, "Achievement Motivation Can Be Developd," *Harvard Business Review*, November–December 1965, pp. 6–25; David C. McClelland and David H. Burnham, "Power Is the Great Motivator," *Harvard Business Review*, March–April 1976, pp. 100–110; John G. Nicholls, "Achievement Motivation: Conceptions of Authority, Subjective Experience, Task Choice, and Performance," *Psychological Review*, July 1984, pp. 328–346; David C. McClelland, *Human Motivation*, Scott, Foresman, Glenview, Ill., 1985, pp. 547–586.

22. Louis S. Richman, "Tomorrow's Jobs: Plentiful, But . . . ," *Fortune*, Apr. 11, 1988, pp. 42–56; Bill Saporito, "A Week Aboard the Wal-Mart Express," *Fortune*, Aug. 24, 1992, pp. 77–84.

23. Barry M. Staw, "Organizational Behavior: A Review and Reformulation of the Field's Outcome Variables," *Annual Review of Psychology*, vol. 35, 1984, pp. 627–666.

24. Craig C. Pinder, *Work Motivation: Theory, Issues, and Applications*, Scott, Foresman, Glenview, Ill., 1984, pp. 144–147; Frank J. Landy and Wendy S. Becker, "Motivation Theory Reconsidered," *Research in Organizational Behavior*, vol. 9, 1987, pp. 1–38.

25. D. F. Parker and L. Dyer, "Expectancy Theory as a Within Person Behavioral Choice Model: An Empirical Test of Some Conceptual and Methodological Refinements," *Organizational Behavior and Human Performance*, vol. 17, 1976, pp. 97–117; H. J. Arnold, "A Test of the Validity of the Multiplicative Hypothesis of Expectancy-Valence Theories of Work Motivation," *Academy of Management Journal*, vol. 24, 1981, pp. 128–141; John P. Wanous, Thomas L. Keon, and Janina C. Latack, "Expectancy Theory and Occupational/Organizational Choices: A Review and Test," *Organizational Behavior and Human Performance*, vol. 32, 1983, pp. 66–86.

26. David Remnick, "Revolutionary Idea for Soviet Workers: Owning Shares," *The Washington Post*, Feb. 5, 1989, p. H3; Karen Pennar, "How Russia Is Slicing Up the State Pie," *Business Week*, July 27, 1992, p. 52.

27. Amanda Bennett, "Salary Rules Aim at New Middle Manager," *The Wall Street Journal*, Apr. 10, 1987, p. 25.

28. David A. Nadler and Edward E. Lawler III, "Motivation: A Diagnostic Approach," in J. Richard Hackman, Edward E. Lawler III, and Lyman W. Porter (eds.), *Perspectives on Behavior in Organizations*, McGraw-Hill, New York, 1983, pp. 67–78.

29. Aaron Bernstein, "GE's Hard Lesson: Pay Cuts Can Backfire," *Business Week*, Aug. 10, 1992, p. 53.

30. J. Stacy Adams, "Inequity in Social Exchange," in L. Berkowitz (ed.), *Advances in Experimental Social Psychology*, vol. 2, Academic, New York, 1965, pp. 267–299.

31. Edwin A. Locke, "The Nature and Causes of Job Satisfaction," in M. Dunnette (ed.), *Handbook of Industrial and Organizational Psychology*, Rand McNally, Chicago, 1976, pp. 1297–1349; Richard T. Mowday, "Equity Theory Predictions of Behavior in Organizations," in Richard M. Steers and Lyman W. Porter (eds.), *Motivation and Work Behavior*, 4th ed., McGraw-Hill, New York, 1987, pp. 89–110.

32. Robert G. Lord and Jeffrey A. Hohenfeld, "Longitudinal Field Assessment of Equity Effects on the Performance of Major League Baseball Players," *Journal of Applied Psychology*, vol. 64, 1979, pp. 19–26. For related studies, see Joseph W. Harder, "Equity Theory versus Expectancy Theory: The Case of Major League Baseball Free Agents," *Journal of Applied Psychology*, vol. 76, 1991, pp. 458–464; and Robert D. Bretz, Jr., and Steven L. Thomas, "Perceived Equity, Motivation, and Final-Offer Arbitration in Major League Baseball," *Journal of Applied Psychology*, vol. 77, 1992, pp. 280–287.

33. Richard A. Cosier and Dan R. Dalton, "Equity Theory and Time: A Reformulation," *Academy of Management Review*, vol. 8, 1983, pp. 311–319.

34. Based on Nan Stone, "Building Corporate Character: An Interview with Stride Rite Chairman Arnold Hiatt," *Harvard Business Review*, March–April 1992, pp. 95–104.

35. Edwin A. Locke and Gary P. Latham, *Goal Setting: A Motivational Technique That Works!* Prentice-Hall, Englewood Cliffs, N.J., 1984; Edwin A. Locke, Karyll N. Shaw, Lise M. Saari, and Gary P. Latham, "Goal Setting and Task Performance: 1969–1980," *Psychological Bulletin*, vol. 90, 1981, pp. 125–152.

36. Richard Brandt, "It Takes More Than a Good Idea," *Business Week*, Innovation 1989 issue, June 16, 1989, p. 123.

37. Edwin A. Locke, Gary P. Latham, and Miriam Erez, "The Determinants of Goal Commitment," working paper, University of Maryland, 1986.

38. Howard Garland, "Relation of Effort Performance Expectancy to Performance in Goal-Setting Experiments," *Journal of Applied Psychology*, vol. 69, 1984, pp. 79–84.

39. Edwin A. Locke, Karyll N. Shaw, Lise M. Saari, and Gary P. Latham, "Goal Setting and Task Performance: 1969–1980," *Psychological Bulletin*, vol. 90, 1981, pp. 125–152.

40. Fred Luthans and Robert Kreitner, *Organizational Behavior Modification*, Scott, Foresman, Glenview, Ill., 1975.

41. This concept was originally articulated by E. L. Thorndike, *Animal Intelligence*, Macmillan, New York, 1911.

42. Richard D. Arvey and John M. Ivancevich, "Punishment in Organizations: A Review, Propositions, and Research Suggestions," *Academy of Management Review*, vol. 5, 1980, pp. 123–132; Janice M. Beyer and Harrison M. Trice, "A Field Study of the Use and Perceived Effects of Discipline in Controlling Work Performance," *Academy of Management Journal*, vol. 27, 1984, pp. 743–764.

43. Janice M. Beyer and Harrison M. Trice, "A Field Study of the Use and Perceived Effects of Discipline in Controlling Work Performance," *Academy of Management Journal*, vol. 27, 1984, pp. 743–764; W. Clay Hamner, "Reinforcement Theory and Contingency Management in Organizational Settings," in Richard M. Steers and Lyman W. Porter (eds.), *Motivation and Work Behavior*, 4th ed., McGraw-Hill, New York, 1987, pp. 139–165.

44. Wayne Dierks and Kathleen McNally, "Incentives You Can Bank On," *Personnel Administrator*, March 1987, pp. 60–65.

45. Albert Bandura, *Social Learning Theory*, Prentice-Hall, Englewood Cliffs, N.J., 1977, and *Social Foundations of Thought and Action: A Social Cognitive Theory*, Prentice-Hall, Englewood Cliffs, N.J., 1986; Robert Krietner and Fred Luthans, "A Social Learning Approach to Behavioral Management: Radical Behaviorists 'Mellowing Out,'" in Richard M. Steers and Lyman W. Porter (eds.), *Motivation and Work Behavior*, 4th ed., McGraw-Hill, New York, 1987, pp. 184–199.

46. J. Barling and R. Beattie, "Self-Efficacy Beliefs and Sales Performance," *Journal of Organizational Behavior Management*, vol. 5, 1983, pp. 41–51; M. Susan Taylor, Edwin A. Locke, Cynthia Lee, and Marilyn Gist, "Type A Behavior and Faculty Research Productivity: What Are the Mechanisms?" *Organizational Behavior and Human Performance*, vol. 34, 1984, pp. 402–418; Marilyn E. Gist, "Self-Efficacy: Implications for Organizational Behavior and Human Resource Management," *Academy of Management Review*, vol. 12, 1987, pp. 472–485.

47. Albert Bandura, *Social Learning Theory*, Prentice-Hall, Englewood Cliffs, N.J., 1977, pp. 128–131.

48. Tim R. V. Davis and Fred Luthans, "A Social Learning Approach to Organizational Behavior," *Academy of Management Review*, vol. 5, 1980, pp. 281–290; Charles C. Manz and Henry P. Sims, Jr., "Vicarious Learning: The Influence of Modeling on Organizational Behavior," *Academy of Management Review*, vol. 6, 1981, pp. 105–113; Martin G. Evans, "Organizational Behavior: The Central Role of Motivation," *Journal of Management*, vol. 12, 1986, pp. 203–222.

49. Based on Aimee Stern, "Domino's: A Unique Concept Pays Off," *Dun's Business Month*, May 1986, pp. 50–51; Dale Feuer, "Training for Fast Times," *Training*, July 1987, pp. 25–30; John Duggleby, "The Domino's Recipe for Making Dough," *Business Week Careers*, February 1988, p. 81; Gregory A. Patterson, "Domino's Founder Monaghan Regains Control by Ousting Four Top Managers," *The Wall Street Journal*, Dec. 9, 1991, p. B6; and Neal Templin, "Monaghan Does an About-Face: It's Time to Sell Part of Domino's," *The Wall Street Journal*, Mar. 2, 1992, p. B1.

ACKNOWLEDGMENTS

Figures

Figure 6: Adapted in part from Edward E. Lawler III and David A. Nadler, "Motivation: A Diagnostic Approach," in J. Richard Hackman, Edward E. Lawler III, and Lyman W. Porter (eds.), *Perspectives and Behavior in Organizations*, 2d ed., McGraw-Hill, Inc., 1983, p. 75. Reprinted by permission of Edward E. Lawler III.

Figure 8: Adapted from Hugh J. Arnold and Daniel C. Feldman, *Organizational Behavior*, McGraw-Hill, Inc., 1986, p. 70. Reproduced with permission of McGraw-Hill, Inc.

CONCLUDING CASE

MAKING VISIBLE CHANGES

In an industry characterized by fragmentation, poor management, and mediocre profits, a Houston-based beauty salon chain called Visible Changes is breaking all the records. Average sales at the chain's 16 salons are triple the industry figure. Sales per customer are almost twice the industry average, and sales of retail products as a percentage of revenues typically beat the industry average by almost a factor of four. In addition, turnover is one-third the industry rate.

When they launched their first salon in 1976, John and Maryanne McCormack envisioned a chain of elegant salons, located in shopping malls, that would provide excellent service to both men and women, require no appointments, attract high-volume business, and make large profits. To make their vision a reality, they would need to motivate their hairdressers to provide better service. This was no small challenge, since hairdressers tended to be recent graduates of hairdressing schools who, with salaries of less than $10,000, were trying to find a better way to make a living.

As a solution, the McCormacks came up with an elaborate incentive plan geared to encouraging their hairdressers to provide excellent service. Hairdressers at Visible Changes receive a 35 percent commission on payments from customers who request them by name, as opposed to 25 percent on payments from regular walk-in customers who make no requests. Further, when they are requested more than 75 percent of the time, they can charge a premium price (about $10 more than the basic fee); for a request rate of 65 percent, there is also an add-on to the basic price. Thus hairdressers who please customers are more likely to be requested and are rewarded for their efforts. Hairdressers can also receive health insurance (an industry rarity) by selling $160 worth of hair-care products per week; for sales beyond that figure, hairdressers receive 15 percent commission. There are also annual bonuses. Once each quarter, each hairdresser is rated on a scale of 1 to 10, with points related to attitude, customer service, and the extent to which individual and salon goals have been met. Individuals who receive all 10 points each quarter are given an additional bonus amounting to 10 percent of their annual commissions. "Superbonuses" are awarded to the most requested hairdressers and the best achievers in product sales. In addition, there is profit sharing, which was recently 15 percent of gross pay for everyone in the company. For one top hairdresser, these incentives added up to more than $60,000, not counting the trips that employees can win under special promotions. On average, Visible Changes hairdressers earn about $33,000 per year, while the national average is about $12,000.

Advanced training sessions in the latest haircutting techniques must be earned by meeting one's goals. Maryanne also makes videotapes showing the latest cutting techniques so that the hairdressers use standardized terminology and follow the same methods. High performers, who are, by definition, also the high earners, are asked to act as role models and share their techniques for success. In addition, the hairdressers compete to be chosen for the "artistic team" that travels throughout the United States and abroad developing and demonstrating new haircuts. The McCormacks work hard to make sure that employees understand the incentive system and the rationale behind each element. The hairdressers often contribute ideas for refining the system. John keeps track of these indicators, as well as information about customer traffic and trends, through a computer system that gives him access to data within seconds.

To increase the level of training received by prospective hairdressers, the McCormacks recently opened Visible Changes University. Tuition is $7000 for the 10-month training program, but the McCormacks say that the quality of the training is much higher than average. John also notes that training haircutters will provide a supply of competent personnel needed for Visible Changes expansion.*

QUESTIONS FOR CONCLUDING CASE

1 Assess the extent to which hairdressers can meet various needs at Visible Changes.
2 Using the cognitive theories of motivation, evaluate the Visible Changes incentive system.
3 Explain how reinforcement and vicarious learning are used at Visible Changes.

* Based on Bruce G. Posner and Bo Burlingham, "The Hottest Entrepreneur in America," *INC.*, January 1988, pp. 44–58; and Pat Rosen, "John McCormack: Haircut King and School Headmaster," *Houston Business Journal*, May 21, 1990, pp. 1, 15–16.

CONCLUDING CASE

AVON'S DIRECT-SALES METHOD SUCCEEDS IN CHINA*

Avon, a U.S. maker of cosmetics and related items, is experiencing noteworthy success in the city of Guangzhou (Canton), capital of Guangdong Province in the People's Republic of China. This success is largely due to the company's method of doing business. Avon recruits representatives who sell the products directly to customers and are paid a commission based on the volume they sell. In Guangzhou, the uniqueness of this incentive system is attracting a cadre of elite sellers, including doctors, engineers, teachers, and computer scientists. In their regular jobs, these professionals normally work for relatively low wages in a Communist system that gives little weight to performance. Becoming an Avon representative offers these individuals an opportunity to earn extra money on the basis of their selling success.

For example, Liang Yungjuan, a pediatrician, is one of Avon's star salespersons. Dr. Liang earns about $120 per month as a pediatrician, but she makes about 10 times that amount as a part-time Avon representative. "Avon has given me confidence in myself," she says. "I'm thinking of quitting my regular job to sell full-time. My son says I love Avon more than I love him."

Most representatives have full-time jobs, often with government agencies. The work norm, though, tends to follow the old Communist rule: "They pretend to pay us, we pretend to work." As a result,

* Andrew Tanzer, "Ding-Dong, Capitalism Calling," *Forbes*, Oct. 14, 1991, pp. 184–186. Reprinted by permission of *Forbes* magazine.

many of the representatives feel justified in spending part of their time at work selling Avon products.

In its representative system, Avon has salaried managers who recruit, train, and manage "franchise dealers." The dealers work to build up a clientele and can earn up to a 30 percent commission on their sales. They can also appoint Avon sales representatives. A dealer then earns about one-third of the 30 percent commissions earned by his or her representatives. Each franchise dealer works with an average of four representatives, resulting in about 25,000 local representatives. Dr. Liang is one such franchise dealer. The top dealers can earn between $2400 and $3000 per month (average per capita income in China is $350 to $400 per year). The typical dealer makes between $60 and $80 per month, which is still a sizable amount by local standards.

Unlike their U.S. counterparts, Avon representatives in China do not ring doorbells looking for sales. That type of cold calling would cause suspicion among potential customers. Instead, the representatives make sales to friends, relatives, neighbors, and coworkers. The major sources of sales, however, are offices, factories, and schools. In these settings, franchise dealers are invited by *danwei*, or work units, to make informal presentations on skin care, makeup, and grooming skills.

Before Avon arrived, cosmetics were available mainly in state-owned department stores, where inventories were unreliable and service was poor. Hence, it seems that there is a pent-up demand for cosmetics in the province. The average Avon product sells for $5, which is more expensive than the cosmetics available in the state-owned store but less expensive than most imported products.

Unlike American women, who tend to favor makeup, Chinese women have a preference for skin-care products.

Avon's success in China did not come easily. During the mid-1980s, company officials spent 5 years attempting to interest government authorities in Beijing in a venture in northern China. "We didn't get anywhere," reports John Novosad, vice president in charge of Pacific operations for Avon. "They didn't understand the concept of direct selling and didn't know how to deal with it."

Eventually, a representative on Avon's international advisory board suggested that the company explore possibilities in Guangdong Province, where capitalism had begun to flourish despite official communism. After a year of negotiating, Avon was able to develop an agreement with province officials. Under the agreement, Avon owns 60 percent of the joint venture; Guangzhou Cosmetics Factory, a local partner, owns 35 percent; and two Hong Kong business associates hold 5 percent. The Avon cosmetics are bottled and packaged at the Guangzhou factory. Meanwhile, Avon is working on expanding into other cities and other provinces.

QUESTIONS FOR CONCLUDING CASE

1 Assess the various motivational needs that underlie the success of Avon in Guangzhou.

2 Use expectancy theory to analyze the likely motivation of Dr. Liang.

3 What role is vicarious learning likely to play in the franchise dealers' success in recruiting and training effective new representatives?

CHAPTER 9

Managerial Communication

STEW LEONARD'S BRAND OF COMMUNICATING

The tone is set when you drive up to Stew Leonard's in Norwalk, Connecticut, billed as the world's largest dairy store. Two cows and a number of goats, hens, and geese grace "The Little Farm," right alongside the 550-car parking lot. A life-size plastic cow stands at the front door. The store's motto is chiseled into the 3-ton granite rock near the door: "Rule 1: The customer is always right! Rule 2: If the customer is ever wrong, reread Rule 1."

Inside, a dairy plant is enclosed in glass so that you can actually see the milk being processed. In one aisle, an employee in a black-and-white cow costume picks up little children and dances with more mature customers, while in another, an employee dressed like a chicken twirls little shoppers around. Above a frozen-food locker, an 8-foot mechanical dog in a Confederate gray uniform sings and plays such favorites as "Dixie" on the banjo. This same spirit of fun can be found throughout the store.

Unique and astoundingly successful, the store began in 1969 when the state of Connecticut decided to build a highway through the family dairy plant. Leonard Sr.'s customers advised him to open a dairy store and offer low prices. Since then, the store has expanded 26 times and now offers 750 carefully chosen items (the average supermarket carries 10,000 to 15,000 items), many bearing a Stew Leonard label.

The store sells immense quantities of the items it stocks. For example, in a given week, customers carry out 5 tons of cookies, 40,000 croissants, 100,000 pounds of chicken, and 25 tons of salad-bar items. Every year, the store's more than 3 million customers generate over $100 million in sales and purchase 10 million quarts of milk, 100 tons of cottage cheese, and 1 million ice-cream cones. On weekends, families come from as far away as Massachusetts, Pennsylvania, Rhode Island, and New York to take advantage of the low prices and experience the carnival-like atmosphere. "This is the funniest place I ever shopped," notes James Ballantoni, a Norwalk resident, who says that he makes sure to partake of the free samples of lemonade, horseradish cheese, gazpacho, cupcakes, nuts, and chocolate cookies.

Leonard's philosophy about running the store stems from an incident involving a customer:

> About a week after opening day, I was standing at the entrance when a customer came up to me and angrily said, "This eggnog is sour." It tasted all right to me, so I said, "You're wrong, it's perfect." Then, to prove the customer *really* was wrong, I said, "We sold over 300 half-gallons of eggnog this week, and you're the only one who's complained." The customer was boiling mad and demanded her money back. I reached into my pocket and gave it to her. She grabbed the money, and as she was heading out the door, the last thing I heard her say was, "I'm never coming back to this store again."
>
> That night, at home, I couldn't get the incident out of my head. As I carefully analyzed it, I realized that I was in the wrong. First, I didn't listen. Second, I contradicted the customer and told her she was wrong. Third, I humiliated her and practically called her a liar by saying 300 other customers had not complained.

Leonard Sr.'s efforts to communicate better with customers now extend to a suggestion box. The box is opened religiously each morning, and its contents are given meticulous attention. Leonard Jr. meets periodically with small groups of customers who volunteer their time to communicate what they like and don't like about what is arguably their favorite place to shop.

Communicating with members of the "team," as the 650 employees are called, also receives a high level of attention from management. Team members help keep each other informed through a monthly newsletter called *Stew's News.* Anyone in the company can write for it or make suggestions to improve it. In a typical issue, as many as 40 names appear on the masthead, a list that changes frequently to reflect the various contributors.

The walls of the store are covered with plaques and framed pictures that highlight the star employees of the month and year. As signals that team members are encouraged to offer new ideas, one can find pictures of such individuals as Henry Gordon, who "eliminated $2300 in motor repairs," and Tony Serrano, who "saved over $6200 by eliminating one dumpster pickup per week."

To further let members of the team know that their efforts to follow S.T.E.W. (Satisfy the customer, Teamwork, Excellence, Wow) are appreciated, management presents them with awards such as gift certificates and $100 dinners. Managers participate in a profit-sharing plan.[1]

As the running of *Stew's News* suggests, good communication in an organization requires the efforts of many individuals. Such efforts are likely to pay off in terms of organizational effectiveness.[2] Although effective communication is critical to all four major management functions, it is particularly vital to the leading function because it provides a necessary conduit for efforts to influence others. In this chapter, we closely examine the nature of managerial communication, including the different types of communication that managers use, managerial communication preferences, and the basic components of the communication process. We consider several important factors that can impede or enhance the way that individuals communicate, and we take a brief look at communication networks involving groups. Finally, we consider various communication channels in organizations, investigate how the use of multiple communication channels can help promote innovation, and explore the growing potential of electronics in facilitating organizational communication.

THE NATURE OF MANAGERIAL COMMUNICATION

Communication The exchange of messages between people for the purpose of achieving common meanings

Communication is the exchange of messages between people for the purpose of achieving common meanings.[3] Unless meanings are shared, managers find it extremely difficult to influence others. For example, in looking back on his efforts to revitalize General Motors, former CEO Roger Smith says that he would make the same decisions again regarding the implementation of major changes to move the company toward global leadership in the twenty-first century. But Smith says that, if he had it to do over again, he would expend much greater time and effort at the beginning of his tenure as CEO communicating his vision for GM to employees. He believes that if he had placed greater emphasis on communicating his vision, employees would have more clearly understood why certain changes were necessary. Then they would have been more willing to support the vision. Instead, Smith says, many GM employees never became committed to helping him implement major changes. As a result, Smith's vision was never realized.[4]

As Smith's predicament illustrates, communication is a critical part of every manager's job. Without effective communication, even the most brilliant strategies and best-laid plans may not be successful.[5]

Types of Communication

In their work, managers use two major types of communication: verbal and nonverbal. Each type plays an important part in the effective transmission of messages within organizations.

Verbal communication The written or oral use of words to communicate

VERBAL COMMUNICATION **Verbal communication** is the written or oral use of words to communicate. Both written and oral communications are pervasive in organizations.

Written communication occurs through a variety of means, such as business letters, office memorandums, reports, résumés, written telephone messages, newsletters, and policy manuals. According to several estimates, the cost of producing a single letter or memo has risen to more than $7, and one estimate places the figure as high as $25 for the average memo.[6] Yet, in one study, more than 80 percent of the managers surveyed judged the quality of the written communications they receive as either fair or poor. They also did not give themselves very high grades, with 55 percent describing their own writing skills as fair or poor.[7]

Despite such shortcomings in writing skills, written communication generally has several advantages over oral communication. It provides a record of the message, can be disseminated widely with a minimum of effort, and allows the sender to think through the intended message carefully. Written communication also has several disadvantages, including the expense of preparation, a relatively impersonal nature, possible misunderstanding by the receiver, and the delay of feedback regarding the effectiveness of the message.[8]

Oral communication, or the spoken word, takes place largely through face-to-face conversation with another individual, meetings with several individuals, and telephone conversations. Oral communication has the advantages of being fast, being generally more personal than written communication, and providing immediate feedback from others involved in the conversation. Among the disadvantages of oral communication are that it can be time-consuming, it can be more difficult to terminate, and additional effort is required to document what is said if a record is necessary.[9]

Given the advantages and disadvantages of written and oral communication, it is not surprising that both types of verbal communication are used by managers. Later in this chapter we give further consideration to managerial preferences for written and oral communication. First, though, we consider another type of communication that is important to managers.

Nonverbal communication Communication by means of elements and behaviors that are not coded into words

NONVERBAL COMMUNICATION **Nonverbal communication** is communication by means of elements and behaviors that are not coded into words. Studies estimate that nonverbal aspects account for between 65 and 93 percent of what is communicated.[10] Interestingly, it is quite difficult to engage in verbal communication without some accompanying form of nonverbal communication. Important categories of nonverbal communication include kinesic behavior, proxemics, paralanguage, and object language.

Kinesic behavior Body movements, such as gestures, facial expressions, eye movements, and posture

Kinesic behavior comprises body movements, such as gestures, facial expressions, eye movements, and posture. In assessing people's feelings about an issue, we often draw conclusions not only from their words but also from their nonverbal behavior, such as their facial expressions.

Proxemics The influence of proximity and space on communication

Proxemics is the influence of proximity and space on communication. For example, some managers arrange their offices so that they have an informal area where people can sit without experiencing the spatial distance and formality created by a big desk. Another example of proxemics, which you have probably

Paralanguage Vocal aspects of communication that relate to how something is said rather than to what is said

Object language The communicative use of material things, including clothing, cosmetics, furniture, and architecture

experienced, is that you are more likely to get to know students whom you happen to sit near in class than students who are sitting in other parts of the room.

Paralanguage consists of vocal aspects of communication that relate to how something is said rather than to what is said. Voice quality, tone of voice, laughing, and yawning are in this category.

Object language is the communicative use of material things, including clothing, cosmetics, furniture, and architecture.[11] If you prepared a job résumé lately, you probably gave some thought to its layout and to the type of paper you wanted it printed on. These are aspects of object language, enabling you to communicate information about yourself beyond that presented by the words on the page. Such nonverbal elements form an important part of the messages that managers communicate.

Managerial Communication Preferences

Managers spend most of their time communicating in one form or another. Studies show that they tend to prefer oral over written communication, largely because oral communication is usually more informal and timely.[12] One detailed study showed that four top managers in four different types of organizations spent almost 74 percent of their working hours communicating orally with others, through informal and formal meetings, telephone calls, and tours of the organization (see Figure 1).[13] The executives spent about 50 percent of that time communicating with subordinates. Most of the remaining contact time was spent with the board of directors, peers, trade organizations, clients, and suppliers. Although the study focused on top-level managers, managers at other levels also lean toward the spoken rather than the written word.[14]

Managers serve as communication centers through several managerial roles (such as monitor, disseminator, and spokesperson). Managers acting in these roles form the basis for the organizations' communication network. If managers

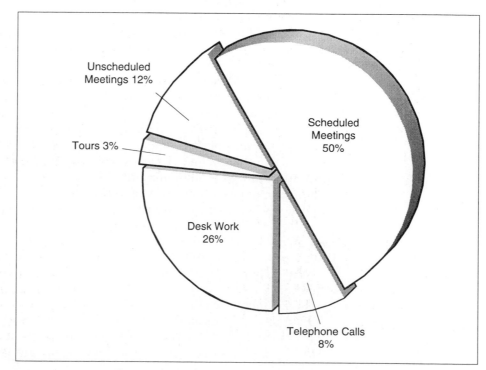

Figure 1 *Proportion of time top managers spent on various activities. (Based on Lance B. Kurke and Howard Aldrich, "Mintzberg Was Right!: A Replication and Extension of* The Nature of Managerial Work," *Management Science, vol. 29, 1983, p. 979.)*

and those with whom they interact do not communicate effectively, the repercussions can be serious, not only for a particular manager's work unit but for the rest of the organization as well. Miscommunications can slow down and even short-circuit communications throughout the organization.

On the other hand, concerted efforts to promote effective communication can be a key ingredient in an organization's success. Recent events at the Scandinavian Airlines System (SAS) help illustrate the importance of both verbal and nonverbal managerial communication (see the following Case in Point discussion).

CASE IN POINT

COMMUNICATION HELPS SAS STAGE TURNAROUND

When Jan Carlzon became the president and chief executive officer of SAS in 1981, the airline was suffering its second consecutive year of serious losses. Within a year, SAS was posting a profit. The turnaround was based on a clear strategy directed at becoming known as "the best airline in the world for the frequent business traveler." In implementing the strategy, SAS spent heavily to upgrade its facilities so that it could better serve business customers. Yet Carlzon recognized that if the airline was really to be the best at serving these travelers, he had to get the employees behind the shift in strategy. In particular, he needed the help of what he calls SAS's "front line," the ticket agents, flight attendants, baggage handlers, and all the others who interact directly with customers.

To help articulate the change in strategy, all 20,000 employees received a little red book entitled *Let's Get in There and Fight*. The book spelled out in concise terms the company's vision and prime goal. Once they understood the vision, the employees began to support the strategy. During that first year, Carlzon spent half his working hours talking with employees and demonstrating his own enthusiasm and involvement in the strategy. He wanted the staff to understand his notion of "moments of truth," by which he meant the average time of 15 seconds during which the customer has contact with an SAS employee. Arguing that those brief moments form the basis of customers' impressions of SAS, Carlzon emphasized that the front line needs to communicate to business customers that SAS is serious about service. One of his favorite stories is about an SAS ticket agent at the Stockholm airport who sent a limousine to retrieve an American businessman's ticket. The customer had left the ticket in his hotel room, checked out, and traveled to the airport. He would have missed his plane had it not been for the quick-thinking agent.

Carlzon, who is known for his capacity to communicate complicated messages in simple, but meaningful, ways, also understands the importance of nonverbal communication. "Leaders should be aware of how far nonverbal communication can go in illustrating the style that others in the organization should follow," he says. He notes, as an example, that SAS passes out magazines and newspapers for customers to read during their flight, but often there are not enough to go around. As a result, when he flies on SAS, the staff sometimes tries to accommodate him first. "Out of the question," he tells the attendants. "I cannot take any myself until I know that all the passengers have gotten what they want!" Thus Carlzon reinforces both verbally and nonverbally (by example) that he really means what it says in the red book.

Furthermore, top management is willing to support the front line. To celebrate the initial turnaround, Carlzon sent every one of the 20,000 employees a gold wristwatch. Since then, his major efforts to communicate with employees have helped SAS earn an international reputation for good service.[15] ■ ■ ■

Basic Components of the Communication Process

A look at the basic components of the communication process helps one appreciate the challenge of effective communication in organizations.[16] These elements are shown in Figure 2.

Sender The initiator of the message

SENDER   The **sender** is the initiator of the message. Messages are usually initiated in response to an outside stimulus, such as a question, a meeting, an interview, a problem, or a report. The stimulus triggers a need or desire for the sender to communicate, or attempt to achieve a common meaning, with an individual or group.

Encoding The process of translating the intended meaning into words and gestures

ENCODING   Before the message exchange can take place, however, the sender must engage in **encoding**, the process of translating the intended meaning into words and gestures. The sender's choice of words and gestures will depend upon such factors as sender encoding skills, assessments of the intended receiver's ability to understand various symbols, judgments regarding the appropriateness of certain symbols, past experience in similar situations, job status, education, and emotional state at the time of the communication attempt.

For example, since Americans often do not speak foreign languages, they frequently fail to recognize that the idioms and regional sayings used in English conversation can cause problems for individuals for whom English is a second language. Hence they do not consider such factors in the encoding process. Jarold Kieffer, chairman of Senior Employment Resources, a not-for-profit organization in Annandale, Virginia, that helps individuals find employment, noticed that puzzled looks sometimes appear on the faces of foreign-born clients. Still, he did not recognize the magnitude of the communication problem until he asked one of his counselors who is Vietnamese to help him move a table. "Give me a hand, will ya?" said Kieffer. The bewildered counselor looked at his hands and exclaimed, "But I need them both." Since then, Kieffer has prepared a pocket-size book of common phrases, such as "foot the bill," "dyed-in-the-wool," and "go fly a kite," to help foreign-born job seekers.[17] Of course, similar problems often occur in international business communications, in which one or more participants may be conversing in other than his or her native language.

Message The encoding-process outcome, which consists of verbal and nonverbal symbols that have been developed to convey meaning to the receiver

MESSAGE   The outcome of the encoding process is a **message** consisting of the verbal (oral or written) and nonverbal symbols that have been developed to

Figure 2   *Basic components of the communication process.*

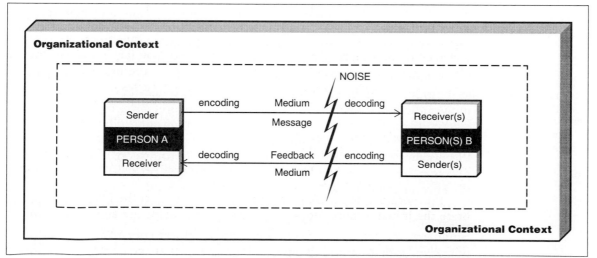

Medium The method used to convey the message to the intended receiver

convey meaning to the receiver. The **medium** is the method used to convey the message to the intended receiver. Examples include written words in a memo, spoken words over the telephone, graphics on a slide, and gestures in face-to-face situations. The sender of a message must consider the appropriateness of the medium. For example, a telephone call may be an effective means of resolving a conflict over a minor item, but a face-to-face meeting may be more appropriate for negotiating a major change in a project.

Receiver The person with whom the message is exchanged

RECEIVER The **receiver** is the person with whom the message is exchanged. If no exchange takes place (i.e., the receiver does not receive the message), there is no communication. There may be one receiver of the message, as in a conversation between two individuals, or many receivers, as in the case of a report sent to various members of the organization. Unintended receivers can also emerge if they overhear a private conversation or read another person's mail.

Decoding The process of translating the symbols into the interpreted message

DECODING When the message is received, the receiver engages in **decoding**, the process of translating the symbols into the interpreted message. When the communication is effective, the sender and the receiver achieve a common meaning. However, the decoding process may result in misunderstandings if the receiver does not decode the message as the sender intended.

Noise Any factor in the communication process that interferes with exchanging messages and achieving common meaning

NOISE **Noise** is any factor in the communication process that interferes with exchanging messages and achieving common meaning. Noise includes, for example, interruptions while the sender is encoding, static on telephone lines as a message is being transmitted, and fatigue on the part of the receiver while he or she is decoding.

Feedback The receiver's basic response to the interpreted message

FEEDBACK **Feedback** is the receiver's basic response to the interpreted message. This response involves a reversal of the communication process so that the receiver becomes the sender and the sender becomes the receiver. Feedback provides preliminary information to the sender about the success of the communication process. Without feedback, managers have difficulty assessing the effectiveness of their communication attempts.

One-way communication The communication that results when the communication process does not allow for feedback

When the communication process does not allow for feedback, it is called **one-way communication.** Memos, newsletters, and announcements are examples of one-way communication—at least when they do not explicitly provide for feedback from those to whom the message is directed. When managers do not incorporate means for immediate feedback into the communication process, they run the risk that the intended message will not be understood by the receiver. With one-way communication, they might not find out about miscommunication until it is too late to correct it.

Two-way communication The communication that results when the communication process explicitly includes feedback

Conversely, when the communication process explicitly includes feedback, as illustrated in Figure 2, it is called **two-way communication.** This type of communication has a better chance of resulting in a reasonably accurate exchange of common meaning. Still, effective two-way communication requires that careful attention be paid to the communication process, particularly if several layers of the organization are involved in the message transmission. Such attention is necessary for two reasons. First, each additional link adds to the possibility that the encoding and decoding processes and/or noise will distort the information. Second, subordinates are often reluctant to provide negative information to upper layers of the hierarchy because they fear that they will be criticized.[18] As a result, managers need to expend considerable effort to obtain accurate information even with two-way communication, as top management at Ashland Oil learned when a serious difficulty turned into a crisis (see the following Case in Point discussion).

CASE IN POINT

ASHLAND OIL FACES A MAJOR CRISIS

When an emergency arose at Ashland Oil, Inc., John R. Hall, the company's CEO, learned firsthand about the perils of information transmission. On a quiet Sunday in January 1988, 1 million gallons of diesel fuel spilled from an Ashland storage tank into the Monongahela River near Pittsburgh. Hall and the company's president spent much of the day in Hall's office (at headquarters in Ashland, Kentucky) talking by speakerphone with colleagues at the accident site and elsewhere. Afterward, Hall believed the situation was under control. He decided against going to the accident scene himself, convinced that his emergency-management team could handle the logistical arrangements. It was still unclear what had caused the leakage.

The next morning, at his regular 3-hour weekly meeting with top executives, Hall devoted only part of the time to discussion of the spill. By midmorning, however, it was clear that he had not obtained sufficient and accurate information about the situation, which was quickly evolving into a crisis. Reporters had been told by the company spokesperson that the storage tank was new and that a permit had been obtained to build it. Now, new information "from several sources" was indicating that the storage tank involved had been recently reconstructed from steel that was 40 years old, that the construction had been done without a permit, and that less testing than usual had been conducted on the tank.

The degenerating situation turned into a major crisis when the arrangements for containing the spill proved inadequate because of unusually strong river currents. There was no contingency plan in place. As a result, the spill formed a 100-mile oil slick and interrupted water supplies for 750,000 Pennsylvania residents, as well as those of many communities in Ohio and West Virginia. By the following morning, Hall was jetting to Pittsburgh to investigate the situation himself and help subordinates deal with the crisis. In retrospect, Hall "would have wanted more accurate information faster," said his vice president and media chief.[19] ■ ■ ■

In addition to the usual communication difficulties, such as encoding, decoding, noise, and the reluctance of subordinates to provide negative information, the stress of the situation likely exacerbated the communication breakdown at Ashland Oil. Factors that influence the way in which particular individuals communicate in organizations probably also played a part.

FACTORS THAT IMPEDE OR ENHANCE INDIVIDUAL COMMUNICATION

You may have experienced the frustration of arriving for a meeting only to find that some of the anticipated participants did not seem to know about it. How is it that some individuals receive a particular communication and others do not? While miscommunications are sometimes due to misdirected mail and lost messages, they often arise from individual factors that can impede or enhance the communication process in organizations. Such factors are perceptual issues, semantics, verbal and nonverbal consistency, and communication skills.

Perceptual Processes

Perception The process that individuals use to acquire and make sense out of information from the environment

Perception is the process that individuals use to acquire and make sense out of information from the environment. The process is complex and involves three main stages. The first stage is *selecting*, the filtering of stimuli that we encounter so that only certain information receives our attention. For example, suppose that a manager taking over a new unit has heard a rumor that a particular individual in the unit has a short temper. If the manager is not careful, this piece of information may cause the manager to pay particular attention to situations in which the person *is* impatient or angry.

The second stage of the perceptual process is *organizing*, the patterning of information from the selection stage. Slowly pronounce each of the following four words:[20]

M-A-C-T-A-V-I-S-H

M-A-C-D-O-N-A-L-D

M-A-C-B-E-T-H

M-A-C-H-I-N-E-R-Y

Like many people, you may have pronounced the last word as "MacHinery." This happens because the previous pattern leads us to expect another word with the same type of pronunciation. This exercise illustrates an interesting characteristic of perception: the tendency to organize information into the patterns that we expect to perceive. In the example of the individual rumored to have a short temper, the manager may begin to organize the selectively perceived behavior into a pattern of incidents in which the individual was angry.

The third stage is *interpreting*, attaching meaning to the information that we have selected and organized. In our example, the manager may, over time, begin to interpret (perhaps unfairly) the organized information as indicating that the person does, indeed, have a short temper.

The perceptions of individuals are affected by a variety of factors such as experiences, needs, personality, culture, and education. As a result, it is very likely that individuals will differ in their perceptions of the very same situations and messages. Several common tendencies to distort perceptions are particularly applicable to managerial communication situations. These tendencies are stereotyping, the halo effect, projection, perceptual defense, and the self-serving bias.[21] Awareness of these perceptual tendencies can help managers avoid the misunderstandings that such distortions often create.

Stereotyping The tendency to attribute characteristics to an individual on the basis of an assessment of the group to which the individual belongs

STEREOTYPING **Stereotyping** is the tendency to attribute characteristics to an individual on the basis of an assessment of the group to which the individual belongs. When a manager engages in stereotyping, two steps occur. First, the manager categorizes the individual as belonging to a group whose members are perceived as sharing certain common characteristics. Second, the manager uses those perceived common characteristics to draw conclusions about the characteristics of the individual, rather than acquiring information about the person's characteristics more directly.

Stereotyping leads to problems when the generalizations do not apply or do not apply equally to all members of the group or when people try to generalize about less specifically related characteristics. In such situations, managers may communicate inappropriate expectations. For example, at American Medical International, Inc., a publicly owned hospital company based in Beverly Hills, California, the president and chief operating officer, Gene Burleson, ran into communication difficulties because of stereotyping. Burleson was addressing a meeting of several hundred employees when one asked why the company did not have any women directors or top executives. Observers reported that Burleson's response implied that women cannot deal with the stress of the executive suite. His reply offended many members of the audience and caused the incident to be reported in *The Wall Street Journal.* Burleson later "admitted he gave a lame and a stupid answer" to the question.[22]

Halo effect The tendency to use a general impression based on one or a few characteristics of an individual to judge other characteristics of that same individual

HALO EFFECT The **halo effect** is the tendency to use a general impression based on one or a few characteristics of an individual to judge other characteristics of that same individual. For example, a manager may use a general impression based on one thing a worker does, such as compiling a well-done or poorly prepared report, to judge the worker's ability in other areas of work, such as handling customers. To avoid the halo effect, interviewers and managers need to make special efforts to collect enough data to make reasonable judgments in all the specific areas that they are trying to evaluate.

Projection The tendency of an individual to assume that others share his or her thoughts, feelings, and characteristics

PROJECTION **Projection** is the tendency of an individual to assume that others share his or her thoughts, feelings, and characteristics. Unfortunately, projection can encourage managers to engage in one-way communication because they assume that they know how their employees feel on various issues. Engaging in two-way communication to learn how other individuals really do feel about various issues can help managers avoid the ill effects of projection.

Perceptual defense The tendency to block out or distort information that one finds threatening or that challenges one's beliefs

PERCEPTUAL DEFENSE **Perceptual defense** is the tendency to block out or distort information that one finds threatening or that challenges one's beliefs.[23] As a result, managers or workers may not be very receptive to certain types of information. This may lead to the "shoot the bearer of bad news" syndrome, in which a person tends to "behead" the bearer of bad news even though the bearer was not the cause of the problem. Thus some managers get angry at employees who provide information about serious problems that cannot be ignored, even though the manager needs to know about them.

Self-serving bias The tendency to perceive oneself as responsible for successes and others as responsible for failures

SELF-SERVING BIAS The **self-serving bias** is the tendency to perceive oneself as responsible for successes and others as responsible for failures.[24] This tendency sets the stage for serious communication problems between managers and their subordinates. For instance, a manager may attribute subordinates' successes to her or his own effective leadership but conclude that failures are due to the subordinates' shortcomings. Subordinates, on the other hand, tend to see successes as resulting from their own hard work and ability and to view failures as stemming from bad luck or factors in the work environment, including areas controlled by their supervisor.[25]

Semantics

Semantic net The network of words and word meanings that a given individual has available for recall

Semantic blocks The blockages or communication difficulties that arise from word choices

Words are symbols; therefore, they do not necessarily have the same meaning for everyone. The study of the meanings and choice of words is called semantics. A **semantic net** is the network of words and word meanings that a given individual has available for recall.[26] Each individual has his or her own semantic net, which overlaps, but does not correspond exactly, with the nets of others. **Semantic blocks** are the blockages or communication difficulties that arise from word choices.[27] Such blocks are commonplace because the various meanings and shades of meanings that individuals attach to words depend on each person's semantic net. Receivers decode words and phrases in conformity with their own semantic networks, which may be very different from those of the senders.[28]

Within organizations, different units can have terminology that has evolved through tradition or is related specifically to the type of work being done. A common cause of semantic blocks is the use of *professional jargon,* language related to a specific profession but unfamiliar to those outside the profession. Such language must be used with care because it can be somewhat bewildering to newcomers, customers, or visitors. Nevertheless, organization-specific language can help build cohesion among employees, reinforce the corporate culture, and, as it does at The Walt Disney Company, support a competitive edge (see the following Case in Point discussion).[29]

CASE IN POINT

AT MANY FIRMS, EMPLOYEES SPEAK A LANGUAGE OF THEIR OWN

A hipo, a Wallenda, and an imagineer order drinks at a bar. They do a little work—edit a violin, non-concur with a wild duck, take care of some bad Mickey—and then ask for the bill. "This is on the mouse," says one of the three. Who picks up the tab?

Organizations often create a language of their own that becomes part of the daily communication among employees. In fact, outsiders may need help translating messages.

For example, a veteran employee at IBM says that a "hipo" (short for "high potential") is an insider designation for an employee who appears to be on the fast track to success. Another IBMer claims that, conversely, an employee perceived as having low potential is known as an "alpo." IBM employees do not disagree with their bosses; instead, they "non-concur." An individual who non-concurs fairly frequently, but does so constructively, is known as a "wild duck." The "wild duck" designation was a favorite of the company's former chairman, Thomas Watson, Jr., who borrowed it from Kierkegaard.

Corporate slang can be particularly prevalent in publishing operations, whose employees frequently have a way with words. At *Newsweek,* top editors are often called "Wallendas," after the famous family of aerialists. The designation is an overt recognition of the editors' job vulnerability. Writers at *Newsweek* speak of the weekly's top national story as the "violin."

In an unusual move, The Walt Disney Company has consciously developed its own corporate jargon to directly support its efforts to have employees think of the Disney theme parks as stages. At orientation and training sessions, employees are taught to say that they are "onstage" when working in the theme park itself and "backstage" when they are in the lower environs, where they cannot be seen by the public. They also learn to refer to coworkers as "cast members." An imagineer is a member of Disney's Imagineering division, an innovative group that is mainly responsible for dreaming up new ideas and figuring out how they can be engineered to work.

Jack Herrman, formerly a Walt Disney World publicist, remembers that his coworkers would label anything positive a "good Mickey" and anything negative (like a cigarette butt on the pavement) a "bad Mickey." When employees take someone to lunch on the Walt Disney World expense account, they say that the meal is "on the mouse." "You're immersed in the jargon they impose upon you as a way of life," Herrman says. Through the use of such language, the company continually reminds organization members of their roles in the production being performed at the theme parks. In this way, Disney uses language to support the company's competitive edge.[30]   ■ ■ ■

Verbal and Nonverbal Consistency

A friend who is about to give a speech may say, "I'm not nervous," as she continuously twists her note cards and shifts from one foot to the other. How do we interpret such a message? When we receive a message, we consider both the verbal and the nonverbal communication elements. There are six major ways that these elements can interrelate. In the first four, the nonverbal communication reinforces the verbal message:

1   *Repeating* the verbal message (e.g., explaining the location of a certain department to a visitor and pointing in the appropriate direction)
2   *Complementing*, or adding to, the verbal message (e.g., having a look of embarrassment when talking to a supervisor about a poor performance issue)
3   *Accenting*, or emphasizing, a verbal message (e.g., pounding the table while stating that quality must be improved)
4   *Regulating* the verbal exchange (e.g., making a head nod, an eye movement, or a shift in position that signals another person to continue speaking or stop speaking)

In the fifth way, the nonverbal message replaces the verbal one:

5   *Substituting* for the verbal message (e.g., using facial expressions or body movements to communicate a message without speaking a word)

In the sixth way, the verbal and nonverbal communication elements combine to send an inconsistent message:

6   *Contradicting* the verbal message (e.g., yelling "I am *not* angry!" or shaking and perspiring heavily before giving a speech while insisting "I'm not nervous")[31]

Evidence suggests that when the verbal and nonverbal elements contradict each other, the receiver is most likely to interpret the nonverbal communication as the true message.[32] This means that managers must pay attention to the nonverbal, as well as the verbal, part of the messages they send. In addition, to gain better insight into the thoughts and feelings of others, managers should scrutinize both the nonverbal and the verbal parts of the messages they receive.

Communication Skills

To be effective communicators in the various settings in which they must function, managers need strong listening skills and feedback skills. These skills are particularly critical because managers spend such a large proportion of their time communicating orally.

LISTENING SKILLS   As the earlier discussion of the communication process suggests, receivers need to expend considerable effort to be sure that they have decoded and interpreted the message that the sender intended. Since managers rely heavily on the information inputs that they receive from oral communication, their listening skills are particularly crucial.[33] Experts on listening often

Active listening The process in which a listener actively participates in attempting to grasp the facts and the feelings being expressed by the speaker

differentiate between listening that is relatively passive, in which the listener follows the general gist of the words being spoken, and listening that is active. **Active listening** is the process in which a listener actively participates in attempting to grasp the facts and the feelings being expressed by the speaker. Actively listening for both the content and the feelings is important in understanding the total meaning of the message.[34] Managers leave themselves at a disadvantage when they are not good listeners. For some guidelines on enhancing your listening skills, see the Practically Speaking discussion, "How to Listen Actively."

FEEDBACK Other interpersonal communication skills that are particularly important for managers center around the issue of feedback, both giving and receiving. Effective feedback has several main characteristics. It focuses on the relevant behaviors or outcomes, rather than on the individual as a person. It deals with specific, observable behavior, rather than generalities. Perceptions, reactions, and opinions are labeled as such, rather than presented as facts. Finally, feedback spells out what individuals can do to improve themselves.[36] Being skilled in giving feedback makes the task of effectively guiding subordinates considerably easier and increases the prospects for mutual success.

In addition to giving feedback, being able to receive feedback is also important. Typically, most individuals have no difficulty receiving positive feedback.

PRACTICALLY SPEAKING

HOW TO LISTEN ACTIVELY

The following guidelines will help you be an active listener:

1 Listen patiently to what the other person has to say, even though you may believe it is wrong or irrelevant. Indicate simple acceptance (not necessarily agreement) by nodding or injecting an occasional "um-hm" or "I see."

2 Try to understand the feeling the person is expressing, as well as the intellectual content. Most of us have difficulty talking clearly about our feelings, so careful attention is required.

3 Restate the person's feeling, briefly but accurately. At this stage, simply serve as a mirror and encourage the other person to continue talking. Occasionally make summary responses, such as "You think you're in a dead-end job" or

"You feel the manager is playing favorites." In doing so, keep your tone neutral and try not to lead the person to your pet conclusions.

4 Allow time for the discussion to continue without interruption, and try to separate the conversation from more official communication of company plans. That is, do not make the conversation any more "authoritative" than it already is by virtue of your position in the organization.

5 Avoid direct questions and arguments about facts; refrain from saying "That's just not so," "Hold on a minute, let's look at the facts," or "Prove it." You may want to review evidence later, but a review is irrelevant to how a person feels now.

6 When the other person does touch on a point you do want to know more about, simply repeat his or her statement as a question. For instance, if the person remarks, "Nobody can

break even on his expense account," you can probe by replying, "You say no one breaks even on expenses?" With this encouragement, he or she will probably expand on the previous statement.

7 Listen for what isn't said— evasions of pertinent points or perhaps too-ready agreement with common clichés. Such omissions may be clues to a bothersome fact the person wishes were not true.

8 If the other person appears to genuinely want your viewpoint, be honest in your reply. But in the listening stage, try to limit the expression of your views, since these may condition or suppress what the other person says.

9 Focus on the content of the message; try not to think about your next statement until the person is finished talking.

10 Don't make judgments until all information has been conveyed.[35]

Receiving feedback that is negative is generally more problematic. Yet the way in which managers and others react to feedback is often a factor influencing how much feedback they receive.[37] When you are receiving negative feedback, it is often helpful to paraphrase what is being said (so that you can check your perceptions), ask for clarification and examples regarding any points that are unclear or with which you disagree, and avoid reacting defensively.[38]

Organizations are learning that it pays to obtain feedback from customers, particularly dissatisfied ones. For example, Roger Nunley, manager of industry and consumer affairs at Coca-Cola USA, says studies indicate that only 1 dissatisfied consumer in 50 complains; the rest switch brands. Yet, when a complaint is redressed, the individual is highly likely to remain a customer. As a result, an increasing number of companies, such as Coca-Cola, American Express, and Procter & Gamble, maintain 800 telephone numbers to encourage customers to voice their complaints.[39]

GROUP COMMUNICATION NETWORKS

Communication network
The pattern of information flow among task group members

When tasks require input from several individuals, managers need to give some thought to the **communication network,** the pattern of information flow among task group members. Considerable research has assessed the impact of different networks on communication and task outcomes. Five major network structures are shown in Figure 3.

Three of these networks are fairly centralized, since most messages must flow through a pivotal person in the network. In the *wheel network,* the most centralized, all messages must flow through the individual at the center of the wheel. In the *chain network,* some members can communicate with more than one member of the network, but the individual in the center of the chain tends to emerge as the controller of the messages. In the *Y network,* the member at the fork of the "Y" usually becomes the central person in the network. The last two networks shown in Figure 3 are more decentralized, since communication flows more freely among the various members. In the *circle network,* each member can

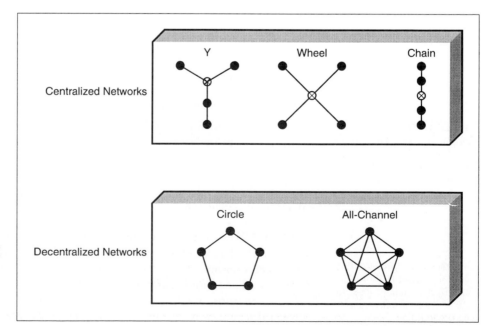

Figure 3 *Group communication networks. (Adapted from Otis W. Baskin and Craig E. Aronoff,* Interpersonal Communication in Organizations, *Scott, Foresman and Company, Glenview, Ill., 1980, p. 77.)*

communicate with the individual on either side. Finally, in the *star network*, the most decentralized, each member can communicate with any other member.

Research indicates that for relatively simple, routine tasks, the centralized networks are usually faster and more accurate. This is because in each of the centralized networks, the individual in the central position (marked with an "x" in Figure 3) tends to become the coordinator, thereby facilitating the completion of routine tasks. In contrast, for more complex tasks, the decentralized networks most often prove to be faster and more accurate, with the star network showing the best performance. With complex tasks, the free exchange of information provided by the circle and the star facilitates the process and encourages creativity.

An intriguing aspect of the research findings is that group morale in the networks studied was higher in the decentralized ones, regardless of the type of task. These results pose somewhat of a dilemma for managers. Centralized networks appear to be the best for achieving accurate performance on simple tasks, particularly when time is an important factor. However, morale may suffer. For more complex tasks, the decentralized networks achieve both high performance and high morale. From a practical point of view, many organizational tasks are likely to fit into the complex category.[40] If tasks are relatively simple and call for more centralized communication networks, managers may be able to improve morale by providing opportunities for subordinates to work on more complex tasks that allow interactions with others in a more decentralized network.

ORGANIZATIONAL COMMUNICATION CHANNELS

An important consideration in assessing organizational communication is the movement of information throughout various parts of the company. When information does not reach the individuals and groups that need it for their work, serious effectiveness and efficiency problems can result. Patterns of organizational communication flow are sometimes referred to as **communication channels** because they represent conduits through which managers and other organization members can send and receive information. In this section, we consider the two major directions of communication flow in organizations: vertical and horizontal. We also examine an informal means of communication flow, the organizational "grapevine." Finally, we consider the implications of communication channel usage for organizational innovation, as well as the growing potential of electronics in facilitating communication in organizations.

Communication channels Patterns of organizational communication flow that represent potential established conduits through which managers and other organization members can send and receive information

Vertical Communication

Vertical communication is communication that involves a message exchange between two or more levels of the organizational hierarchy. Thus vertical communication can involve a manager and a subordinate or can involve several layers of the hierarchy. It can flow in a downward or an upward direction. Studies generally find that managers spend about two-thirds of their communication time engaging in vertical communication.[41]

Vertical communication Communication that involves a message exchange between two or more levels of the organizational hierarchy

DOWNWARD COMMUNICATION When vertical communication flows from a higher level to one or more lower levels in the organization, it is known as **downward communication**. This type of communication can take many forms, such as staff meetings, company policy statements, company newsletters, informational memos, and face-to-face contact. Most downward communication involves information in one of five categories: (1) job instructions related to spe-

Downward communication Vertical communication that flows from a higher level to one or more lower levels in the organization

cific tasks, (2) job rationales explaining the relationship between two or more tasks, (3) procedures and practices of the organization, (4) feedback on individual performance, and (5) efforts to encourage a sense of mission and dedication to the organizational goals.[42]

Downward communication across several levels is prone to considerable distortion. A recent survey of middle managers across the United States indicates that the quality of the information they receive is poor.[43] As illustrated by Figure 4, as much as 80 percent of top management's message may be lost by the time the message reaches five levels below. There are three main reasons for the distortion. First, faulty message transmission may occur because of sender carelessness, poor communication skills, and the difficulty of encoding a message that will be clearly understood by individuals at multiple levels. Second, managers tend to overuse one-way communication, through such means as memos, manuals, and newsletters, leaving little possibility for immediate feedback regarding receiver understanding. Third, some managers may intentionally or unintentionally filter communications by withholding, screening, or manipulating information. Intentional filtering typically occurs when a manager seeks to enhance personal power over subordinates by tightly controlling organizational information.[44]

One way to increase the effectiveness of downward communication is to use multiple channels and repetition. Geneva Steel, located in Provo, Utah, instituted regular meetings for employees and their spouses. It also set up 30-minute cable TV shows, starring Geneva employees, to keep the members of the work force informed about what was happening at the plant and what was expected of them. The plant is now doing well, with both increased quality and increased profits.[45] Another way to make downward communication more effective is to encourage feedback in the form of upward communication.

Upward communication
The vertical flow of communication from a lower level to one or more higher levels in the organization

UPWARD COMMUNICATION When the vertical flow of communication is from a lower level to one or more higher levels in the organization, it is known as **upward communication.** Forms of upward communication include one-to-one meetings with one's immediate superior, staff meetings with superiors, memos and reports, suggestion systems, grievance procedures, and employee attitude

Figure 4 *Levels of understanding as information is transmitted down the organization.*

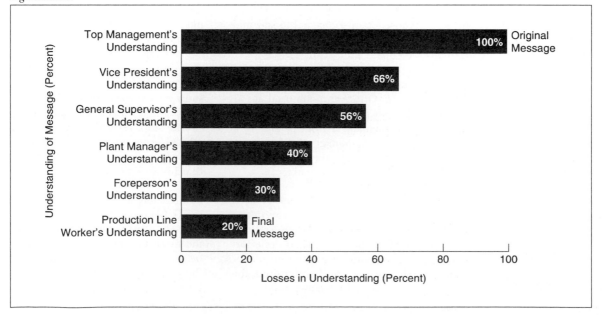

surveys. The information disseminated through upward communication typically pertains to (1) progress of current work projects, (2) serious unsolved problems and situations in which subordinates need help from superiors, (3) new developments arising within or affecting the work unit or organization, (4) suggestions for improvements and innovations, and (5) employee attitudes, morale, and efficiency.[46]

The distortion that characterizes downward communication also plagues upward communication for two main reasons. First, as mentioned previously, information favorable to the sender is very likely to be sent upward, whereas information unfavorable to the sender will probably be blocked, even when it is important to the organization. Subordinates are more likely to filter information when they do not trust their superiors, perceive that their superiors have considerable influence over their careers, and have a strong desire to move up.[47] Second, managers do not expend sufficient effort in encouraging upward communication. In a creative effort to overcome these problems, Robert Darvin, head of Scandinavian Design, Inc., distributes special stationery to every employee at his 21-year-old retail furniture company. The employees include warehouse workers, corporate executives in Natick, Massachusetts, and salespeople in the 70 stores located in the northeastern United States and Hawaii. The stationery is used exclusively for communicating with Darvin, and employees are encouraged to use it to send up bad, as well as good, news.[48] Encouraging upward communication can also be a good means of fostering quality (see the Valuing Quality box).

Horizontal communication Lateral or diagonal message exchange either within work-unit boundaries, involving peers who report to the same supervisor, or across work-unit boundaries, involving individuals who report to different supervisors

Management by wandering around (MBWA) A practice whereby managers frequently tour areas for which they are responsible, talk to various employees, and encourage upward communication

Horizontal Communication

Horizontal communication is lateral or diagonal message exchange either within work-unit boundaries, involving peers who report to the same supervisor, or across work-unit boundaries, involving individuals who report to different supervisors. Horizontal communication can take many forms, including meetings,

---

VALUING QUALITY

Communicating Upward in Turning Detroit Diesel Around

Roger Penske, the former auto racer who is now a transportation tycoon, bought the controlling interest of Detroit Diesel from General Motors in 1988. The firm makes diesel engines used in large trucks, tanks, and similar vehicles. In an address to the employees, he stressed the word "team." He explained that "T" stood for teamwork; "E," for effort; "A," for attitude; and "M," for managing your own business, your job, and your personal life. Penske asked

most senior managers to stay and assist him in changing the company culture.

In the new culture, managers seek information from the work force. One technique used at Detroit Diesel that often helps keep managers from becoming isolated is **management by wandering around (MBWA),** a practice whereby managers frequently tour areas for which they are responsible, talk to various employees, and encourage upward communication.[49] Of course, if the "wandering around" is done for the purpose of finding problems so that people can be punished, the practice will probably build

mistrust and increase managerial isolation.

Every day, at Detroit Diesel, the general manager tours the plant where the 3000 employees work. Individual workers greet him, and he pauses to hear their concerns. At one stop, Jerry Chouinard takes a break from assembling a massive engine to tell the general manager that his area needs more engineering help. He gets the help immediately. Does this system work? Between 1987 and 1991, Detroit Diesel increased its share of the market from 3.2 to 28 percent because of the improved quality of the engines produced by its work force—which now speaks out.[50]

reports, memos, telephone conversations, and face-to-face discussions between individuals. Managers spend about one-third of their communication time in horizontal communication.[51] Horizontal communication usually relates to one or more of the following areas: (1) task coordination, (2) problem solving, (3) information sharing, (4) conflict resolution, and (5) peer support.[52]

Three major factors tend to impede necessary, work-related horizontal communication. First, rivalry among individuals or work units can lead employees to hide information that is potentially damaging to themselves or that may aid others. Second, specialization may cause individuals to be mainly concerned about the work of their own unit and to have little appreciation for the work and communication needs of others. For example, scientists in an R&D unit that is focused on long-term projects may find it difficult to interrupt their work to help with current customer problems identified by the sales department. Third, motivation may be lacking when subordinate horizontal communication is not encouraged or rewarded. Committees, task forces, and matrix structures are common means that managers use to help encourage horizontal communication, particularly across work-unit boundaries. The effective use of horizontal communication in organizations requires that peers doing the communicating across work units keep their respective bosses informed of significant developments. Otherwise, the vertical chain of command would begin to break down, and soon the managers in the hierarchy would not know what is going on.[53]

Informal Communication: The Grapevine

Formal communication
Vertical and horizontal communication that follows paths specified by the official hierarchical organization structure and related task requirements

Informal communication
Communication that takes place without regard to hierarchical or task requirements

Grapevine Another term for *informal communication*

The vertical and horizontal communication patterns that we have just discussed are sometimes referred to as **formal communication** patterns, or channels, because the communication follows paths specified by the official hierarchical organization structure and related task requirements. You might think of formal communication as communication relating to one's *position* in the organization. In contrast, **informal communication,** better known as the **grapevine,** is communication that takes place without regard to hierarchical or task requirements. Informal communication can be thought of as relating to *personal* rather than positional issues.[54] For example, personal relationships unrelated to organizational positions might exist among employees who ride to work in the same car pool, attend the same church, or have children in the same school. Grapevine communications stem largely from such relationships, which may overlap, but frequently do not coincide with, communication requirements associated with the hierarchy and the task.

The term "grapevine" can be traced back to the Civil War, when telegraph lines that were strung from tree to tree in grapevinelike patterns often provided intelligence messages that were garbled.[55] Grapevines exist in virtually all organizations, and grapevine communication patterns are likely to include both vertical and horizontal elements. One classic study investigated four possible configurations for grapevine chains (see Figure 5). In the *single-strand chain,* communication moves serially from person A to B to C and so on. In the *gossip chain,* person A seeks out and communicates with others. When following the *probability chain,* person A spreads the message randomly, as do individuals F and D. In the *cluster chain,* person A tells the message to three selected individuals, and then one of these tells it to three others. According to the study, the cluster chain is the most predominant type. This finding suggests that individuals who are part of grapevines are likely to be selective about the persons to whom they relay information and that only some of those persons will, in turn, pass the information further.[56]

Overall, grapevines tend to be fast, to carry large amounts of information,

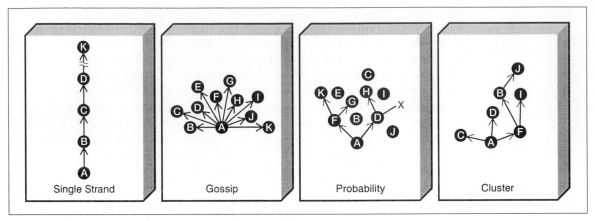

Figure 5 *Types of grapevine chains. (Reprinted from John W. Newstrom and Keith Davis,* Organizational Behavior: Human Behavior at Work, *9th ed., McGraw-Hill, 1993, p. 445.)*

and to produce data that range in accuracy from 50 to 90 percent.[57] Although grapevine communications are often perceived by organization members as being fairly inaccurate, the problem seems to stem largely from misinterpretation when details are incomplete.[58] At the Digital Equipment Corporation (DEC), for example, insufficient explanations precipitated false rumors that ultimately had serious consequences. At the time, Jack Shields, was a senior vice president at DEC and was often mentioned as a possible successor to then-President Kenneth Olson. When Shields did not attend a "state of the company" meeting for top managers, Olson explained the vice president's absence somewhat vaguely. Then a new organization chart of U.S. field operations did not include Shields. As a result, rumors that Shields had been fired started to move through the sales force and soon spread to sources outside the company. The gossip quickly reached Wall Street, raising questions about succession at DEC and causing the company's stock to fall more than a point. Shields, however, had not been fired. At the time of DEC's meeting, he had been attending the annual meeting of a company on whose board of directors he served. His name did not appear on the operations chart because the chart did not extend up to the level of the executive committee, of which he was a member.[59]

Several things can be said about grapevines in organizations. Although not officially put in place or even sanctioned, they are a part of every organization and cannot be abolished. They may sometimes create difficulties when they carry gossip and false rumors, but they have many good aspects if managed properly. The grapevine can be a release mechanism for stress, as many people like to talk to others about their work. Researchers have recently suggested that grapevine gossip, by dwelling on transgressions, may be a valuable aid in communicating organizational rules, values, morals, traditions, and history. Grapevines also give employees reaction time to think through impending changes and thus can facilitate employees' contributions to organizational goals.[60] In addition, they may help foster innovation by enhancing communication among various parts of the organization.

Promoting Innovation: Multiple Communication Channels

Rosabeth Moss Kanter, a researcher on innovation, argues that the use of multiple communication channels is especially critical for innovation.[61] In order to nurture innovative behavior, managers need to emphasize the use of both vertical and horizontal communication channels.

VERTICAL COMMUNICATION Vertical communication can promote innovation in four ways. Managers can use it as a means of

- *Signaling organizational expectations for innovation.* This can be done both through words and through specific actions, such as providing special funds for innovation and giving public recognition for successful innovations.
- *Fostering the upward communication of innovative ideas.* Some innovative companies have "open-door" policies, whereby all levels theoretically have access to any organization member in order to ask questions, present ideas, or even criticize.
- *Encouraging managers in the chain of command to act as sponsors.* Sponsors are needed for funding, protecting, and testing potential innovations in their developmental stages.
- *Facilitating extensive use of horizontal communication channels in the organization.*

HORIZONTAL COMMUNICATION Horizontal communication is critical to the innovation process in four ways. It provides managers with a means of

- *Connecting potential recognizers of opportunities for innovation.* When individuals in various parts of the organization are closely connected through multiple communication channels, they are more likely to be aware of opportunities and problems, which often provide the basis for innovation.
- *Linking different areas of expertise.* The importance of a variety of views is related to Kanter's notion of "kaleidoscopic thinking." The kaleidoscope has multiple elements that form a pattern, but they are not locked in place. Shaking, twisting, or changing the angle provides a new pattern. Similarly, fresh approaches to existing patterns form the basis for innovations.
- *Building coalitions of individuals.* Linking individuals who can help develop innovations and support their implementation is easier when both vertical and horizontal communication channels are active. Innovative companies often use teams with representatives from various functional areas to help with developments that are likely to lead to critical changes. For example, 3M and Honeywell utilize internal conferences and "idea fairs" to connect ideas with those who can use them or develop them into usable innovations. When Linda Bos took over as sales vice president of McKesson Office Products, she instituted monthly sales meetings of district managers to encourage the sharing and generating of innovative ideas.[62]
- *Emphasizing boundary spanning.* Creating roles within the organization that interface with important elements outside the organization can help keep members linked to important sources of environmental information. Encouraging scientists to maintain close ties with their respective fields through association memberships, conferences, and the like, is one means of boundary spanning. Another is maintaining close ties with customers. A study of 500 important industrial innovations found that over three-fourths originated with user suggestions, while only one-fifth developed from technical ideas seeking applications.[63]

Thus efforts at enhancing both vertical and horizontal communication are an important element in encouraging innovation in an organization. Both forms of communication receive special attention from Arthur E. Morrissette, president and founder of Interstate Van Lines, Inc., a $30-million-a-year moving and storage company in Springfield, Virginia. Although Morrissette publishes a newsletter, called *Under the Top Hat,* his main communication media are the training session and the sing-along.

The training sessions, attended by more than 200 employees, are held daily between 7:30 and 8:30 a.m. At the sessions, managers provide information to movers and packers about various business-related issues. Every couple of weeks, there is a sing-along. The sing-along format, which calls for all the employees to meet in the convention hall and mingle, has been designed to discourage employees from thinking of themselves as members of separate groups or camps. The occasions also serve as a forum for Morrissette to emphasize team spirit and to provide recognition for good work and new ideas by distributing individual achievement awards, cash prizes, and points toward performance evaluations. In addition, participants sing patriotic songs, as well as the company anthem:

> Work that you do is more than just a job.
>
> It's important to keep a smile on your face.
>
> You are the one the shipper comes to trust.
>
> You are the image of Interstate.

Evidently, the sing-alongs work: Interstate Van Lines has one of the highest profit ratios in its industry.[64],*

Using Electronics to Facilitate Communication

Electronic advances are providing managers with new methods and channels of communication. Three of the most prominent advances are electronic mail systems, voice mail, and video teleconferencing, and there is growing interest in groupware.

Electronic mail system A mail system that allows high-speed exchange of written messages through the use of computerized text-processing and communication networks

An **electronic mail system** is one that allows high-speed exchange of written messages through the use of computerized text-processing and communication networks. Anyone who has access to a computer terminal can develop and send a written message to anyone else who has a computer mailbox on the network. At the Digital Equipment Corporation, managers indicate that they save about 7 hours per week because their electronic mail system has increased the speed of decision making.[65] At Chemical Bank, managers estimate that their system saves them about 3 hours per week, mainly by eliminating unreturned phone calls and reducing other internal correspondence.[66]

There is also evidence that electronic mail leads to information exchanges among managers who previously did not communicate either by mail or by telephone and that managers receive new types of information through the system.[67] Electronic mail systems not only enhance vertical communication but also can facilitate horizontal communication.[68]

One disadvantage of electronic mail is that it eliminates the nonverbal cues (e.g., facial expressions, body movements, tone of voice) that serve as aids in face-to-face communication. (Of course, regular mail also has far fewer nonverbal cues than does face-to-face message exchange.) Another is that the ease of sending mail electronically can cause individuals to receive excessive amounts of mail that does not interest them.

Voice mail A recording system that provides senders with the opportunity to leave messages for receivers by telephone

An allied form of electronic communication is **voice mail,** a recording system that enables senders to leave messages for receivers by telephone. With voice mail, nonverbal cues such as voice quality and tone of voice are conveyed. Voice mail is particularly useful in imparting short messages that do not require further discussion with the intended receiver.

Video teleconferencing The holding of meetings with individuals in two or more locations by means of closed-circuit television

Another form of electronic communication, **video teleconferencing,** is the holding of meetings with individuals in two or more locations by means of closed-circuit television. Teleconferencing use is growing in Fortune 500 companies.[69] James Treybig, head of Tandem Computers, uses a form of teleconferencing in monthly television broadcasts over the company's in-house TV station. Employees throughout the world can watch the broadcast and call in with questions and comments.[70] Other companies with their own private television networks include J. C. Penney, Ford, Merrill Lynch, and Xerox.[71]

An alternative method being developed to help groups communicate electronically is the use of *groupware,* computer software designed to facilitate meetings. Groupware coordinates simultaneous electronic messages from group members, each of whom sits in front of a computer, and displays them on a special screen at the front of the room that all can see. The messages are anonymous, and most of the communicating is done through the computers. Sometimes no one speaks a word. At Boeing, managers say that the time needed to complete a wide variety of team projects has been cut by an average of 91 percent by using groupware to help team members coordinate their views.[72]

CHAPTER SUMMARY

Effective communication is important in gaining and maintaining the competitive edge in organizations. Communication is the exchange of messages between people for the purpose of achieving common meanings. In their work, managers use two types of communication: verbal (including written and oral) and nonverbal. Managers tend to prefer oral over written communication, spending approximately 75 percent of their working hours communicating orally with others.

The communication process has several basic components: sender, encoding, message, receiver, decoding, noise, and feedback. When communication provides for relatively immediate feedback, it is called two-way communication. Without a feedback provision, it is known as one-way communication.

A number of factors affect individual communication. Perception is susceptible to five major types of distortion: stereotyping, the halo effect, projection, perceptual defense, and the self-serving bias. Semantic blocks sometimes occur because the various meanings and shades of meanings that individuals attach to words depend on each person's semantic net. The consistency of verbal and nonverbal communication elements can reinforce a message in various ways. When the elements contradict each other, the receiver is most likely to interpret the nonverbal communication as the true message. Individual communication is facilitated by the development of skills in such areas as listening, giving feedback, and receiving feedback.

When tasks require input from several individuals, managers need to give some thought to the communication network among task group members. Centralized networks are the wheel, chain, and Y; decentralized networks are the circle and the star. For relatively simple, routine tasks, centralized networks tend to be faster and more accurate. When tasks are more complex, decentralized networks are likely to be faster and more accurate.

Managers need to be concerned with the flow of information among the various parts of the organization. Formal communication in organizations follows channels specified by the official hierarchical organization structure and related task requirements. It flows in two main directions, vertical and horizontal. When vertical communication flows from a higher level to one or more lower levels, it is known as downward communication. When it moves from a lower level to one or more higher levels, it is known as upward communication. Horizontal communication is lateral message exchange. Informal communication, better known as the grapevine, takes place without regard to hierarchical or task requirements or organizational position. In order to nurture innovative behavior in an organization, managers need to emphasize the use of both vertical (upward and downward) and horizontal communication channels. Electronic mail systems, voice mail, and teleconferencing systems are examples of the new communication aids that are being made available to managers through advances in electronics.

QUESTIONS FOR DISCUSSION AND REVIEW

1 Explain the major types of communication that managers use, and discuss managerial communication preferences. For an organization with which you are familiar, identify examples of each type.

Classify the nonverbal communication examples in terms of kinesic behavior, proxemics, paralanguage, and object language.

2 Outline the basic components of the communication process. Identify these components in a conversation that you witness.

3 Delineate several common tendencies to distort perceptions. Give an example of how each could adversely affect communication.

4 Explain the notion of semantic blocks. List some words that are used at your university that might cause semantic blocks to outsiders who are unfamiliar with the terminology.

5 Explain how nonverbal communication can reinforce or substitute for a verbal message and how it can contradict a verbal message. Give examples.

6 Outline the major types of centralized and decentralized group communication networks. Explain the conditions under which centralized and decentralized networks are likely to result in the best performance. Evaluate how well suited they appear to be for the situations involved.

7 Differentiate between vertical and horizontal communication. Identify the major methods used in your college or university for downward communication from chief administrators to students and for upward communication from students to chief administrators. What mechanisms exist for horizontal communication among students?

8 Assess the organizational implications of the grapevine. What evidence points to the existence of a student grapevine in your department at your college or university?

9 Explain how vertical and horizontal communication channels can be used to foster innovation in an organization. How can communication be used to promote innovation in a campus organization to which you belong?

10 How can managers use electronic mail systems and video teleconferencing to advantage in communicating? What potential problems exist with each?

DISCUSSION QUESTIONS FOR CHAPTER OPENING CASE

1 Identify the vertical communication methods, both downward and upward, used at Stew Leonard's.

2 What methods are used to provide horizontal communication?

3 Would you characterize the management at Stew Leonard's as attempting to foster innovation? What evidence exists for your view?

MANAGEMENT EXERCISE: A QUESTION OF INFERENCES

 Read the story presented below, and indicate whether you believe the statements that follow the story are true (T), false (F), or unknown(?). Then get together with a group designated by your instructor, and determine as a group whether each statement is true, false, or unknown.

Haney Test of Uncritical Inferences (1992)

The Story*

A businessman had just turned off the lights in the store when a man appeared and demanded money. The owner opened a cash register. The contents of the cash register were scooped up, and the man sped away. A member of the police force was notified promptly.

Statements about the Story

1 A man appeared after the owner had turned off his store lights.   T F ?

2 The robber was a *man*.   T F ?

3 The man who appeared did not demand money.   T F ?

4 The man who opened the cash register was the owner.   T F ?

5 The store owner scooped up the contents of the cash register and ran away.   T F ?

6 Someone opened a cash register.   T F ?

7 After the man who demanded the money scooped up the contents of the cash register, he ran away.   T F ?

8 While the cash register contained money, the story does *not* state *how much*.   T F ?

9 The robber demanded money of the owner.   T F ?

10 A businessman had just turned off the lights when a man appeared in the store.   T F ?

11 It was broad daylight when the man appeared.   T F ?

12 The man who appeared opened the cash register.   T F ?

| 13 | No one demanded money. | T F ? | 15 | The following events occurred: someone demanded money; a cash register was opened; its contents were scooped up; and a man dashed out of the store. | T F ? |

13 No one demanded money.   T F ?

14 The story concerns a series of events in which only three persons are referred to: the owner of the store, a man who demanded money, and a member of the police force.   T F ?

15 The following events occurred: someone demanded money; a cash register was opened; its contents were scooped up; and a man dashed out of the store.   T F ?

*The story and statements are a portion of the "Uncritical Inference Test," copyrighted 1955, 1964, 1979, 1992 by William V. Haney. The full-length test is available for educational purposes from Haney Associates, 2453 Cardinal Lane, Wilmette, IL 60091. "Haney Test of Uncritical Inferences," reprinted with permission from *Communication and Interpersonal Relations,* 6th ed. by William V. Haney (Homewood, IL: Richard D. Irwin, Inc., 1992), pp. 232–233.

REFERENCES

1. Based on Nelson W. Aldrich, Jr., "Lines of Communication," *INC.,* June 1986, pp. 140–144; Joanne Kaufman, "In the Moo: Shopping at Stew Leonard's," *The Wall Street Journal,* Sept. 17, 1987, p. 32; and Stew Leonard, "Love That Customer!" *Management Review,* October 1987, pp. 36–39.

2. Gerald M. Goldhaber, *Organizational Communication,* 4th ed., Brown, Dubuque, Iowa, 1986, pp. 4–33.

3. O. W. Baskin and Craig E. Aronoff, *Interpersonal Communication in Organizations,* Scott, Foresman, Santa Monica, Calif., 1980, p. 4.

4. Roger Smith, " 'The U.S. Must Do as GM Has Done,' " *Fortune,* Feb. 13, 1989, pp. 70–73.

5. J. Thomas and P. Sireno, "Assessing Management Competency Needs," *Training and Development Journal,* vol. 34, 1980, pp. 47–51; H. W. Hildebrant, F. A. Bon, E. L. Miller, and A. W. Swinyard, "An Executive Appraisal of Courses Which Best Prepare One for General Management," *The Journal of Business Communication,* Winter 1982, pp. 5–15.

6. Robert R. Max, "Wording It Correctly," *Training and Development Journal,* March 1985, pp. 50–51; Joy Van Skiver, quoted in Neil Chesanow, "Quick, Take This Memo," *The Washington Post,* Sept. 7, 1987, p. C5.

7. Walter Kiechel III, "The Big Presentation," *Fortune,* July 26, 1982, pp. 98–100.

8. Phillip V. Lewis, *Organizational Communication: The Essence of Effective Management,* 2d ed., Prentice-Hall, Englewood Cliffs, N.J., 1980, p. 11.

9. Ibid.

10. R. Birdwhistell, *Kenesics and Context,* University of Pennsylvania, Philadelphia, 1970; A. Mehrabian, *Silent Messages,* Wadsworth, Belmont, Calif., 1972.

11. Otis W. Baskin and Craig E. Aronoff, *Interpersonal Communication in Organizations,* Scott, Foresman, Santa Monica, Calif., 1980.

12. Henry Mintzberg, *The Nature of Managerial Work,* Prentice-Hall, Englewood Cliffs, N.J., 1973; Lance B. Kurke and Howard E. Alrich, "Mintzberg Was Right! A Replication and Extension of the Nature of Managerial Work," *Management Science,* vol. 29, 1983, pp. 975–984.

13 Larry L. Smeltzer and Gail L. Fann, "Comparison of Managerial Communication Patterns in Small, Entrepreneurial Organizations and Large, Mature Organizations," *Group and Organization Studies,* vol. 14, 1989, pp. 198–215. Also see Henry Mintzberg, *The Nature of Managerial Work,* Prentice-Hall, Englewood Cliffs, N.J., 1973.

14. Phillip V. Lewis, *Organizational Communication: The Essence of Effective Management,* 2d ed., Prentice-Hall, Englewood Cliffs, N.J., 1980; Larry R. Smeltzer and Gail L. Fann, "Comparison of Managerial Communication Patterns in Small, Entrepreneurial Organizations and Large, Mature Organizations," *Group and Organization Studies,* vol. 14, 1989, pp. 198–215.

15. Jan Carlzon, *Moments of Truth,* Ballinger, Cambridge, Mass, 1987; Amanda Bennett, "SAS's 'Nice Guy' Aiming to Finish First," *The Wall Street Journal,* Mar. 2, 1989, p. B12; Jonathan Kapstein, "Can SAS Keep Flying with the Big Birds?" *Business Week,* Nov. 27, 1989, pp. 142–146.

16. For a discussion of different theoretical perspectives on communication, see Kathleen J. Krone, Fredric M. Jablin, and Linda L. Putnam, "Communication Theory and Organizational Communication: Multiple Perspectives," in Fredric M. Jablin, Linda L. Putnam, Karlene H. Roberts, and Lyman W. Porter (eds.), *Handbook of Organizational Communication: An Interdisciplinary Perspective,* Sage, Newbury Park, Calif., 1987, pp. 18–40.

17. Don Oldenburg, "What Do You Say?" *The Washington Post,* Aug. 23, 1989, p. C5.

18. Charles A. O'Reilly III and Karlene H. Roberts, "Information Filtration in Organizations: Three Experiments," *Organizational Behavior and Human Performance,* vol. 11, 1974, pp. 253–265; Robert E. Kaplan, Wilfred H. Drath, and Joan R. Kofodimos, "Power and Getting Criticism," *Center for Creative Leadership Issues and Observations,* August 1984, pp. 1–6.

19. Based on Clare Ansberry, "Oil Spill in the Midwest Provides Case Study in Crisis Management," *The Wall Street Journal,* Jan. 8, 1988, p. 21.

20. Fred Luthans, *Organizational Behavior,* 5th ed., McGraw-Hill, New York, 1989.

21. Judith R. Gordon, *A Diagnostic Approach to Organizational Behavior,* 2d ed., Allyn and Bacon, Boston, 1987; Fred Luthans, *Organizational Behavior,* 5th ed., McGraw-Hill, New York, 1989.

22. William Mathewson, "Shop Talk," *The Wall Street Journal,* Sept. 30, 1988, p. 29.

23. Fred Luthans, *Organizational Behavior*, 5th ed., McGraw-Hill, New York, 1989.

24. Henry L. Tosi, John R. Rizzo, and Stephen J. Carroll, *Managing Organizational Behavior*, Pitman, Marshfield, Mass., 1986; Gary Johns, *Organizational Behavior*, 2d ed., Scott, Foresman, Glenview, Ill., 1987.

25. C. S. Carver, E. DeGregoria, and R. Gillis, "Field-Study Evidence of an Attribution among Two Categories of Observers," *Personality and Social Psychology Bulletin*, vol. 6, 1980, pp. 44–50; D. G. Myers, *Social Psychology*, McGraw-Hill, New York, 1983.

26. Phillip V. Lewis, *Organizational Communication: The Essence of Effective Management*, 2d ed., Prentice-Hall, Englewood Cliffs, N.J., 1980, p. 54.

27. Mary Munter, *Business Communication: Strategy and Skill*, Prentice-Hall, Englewood Cliffs, N.J., 1987, p. 15.

28. Stephen R. Axley, "Managerial and Organizational Communication in Terms of the Conduit Metaphor," *Academy of Management Review*, vol. 9, 1984, pp. 428–437.

29. Ernest G. Bormann, "Symbolic Convergence: Organizational Communication and Culture," in Linda Putnam and Michael E. Pacanowsky (eds.), *Communication and Organizations: An Interpretive Approach*, Sage, Beverly Hills, Calif., 1983, pp. 99–122.

30. Based on Michael W. Miller, "At Many Firms, Employees Speak a Language That's All Their Own," *The Wall Street Journal*, Dec. 29, 1987, p. 17.

31. Mark Knapp, *Nonverbal Communication in Human Interaction*, Holt, New York, 1972; Phillip V. Lewis, *Organizational Communication: The Essence of Effective Management*, 2d ed., Prentice-Hall, Englewood Cliffs, N.J., 1980.

32. M. A. Hayes, "Nonverbal Communication: Expression without Word," in R. C. Huseman, C. M. Logue, and D. L. Freshley (eds.), *Readings in Interpersonal and Organizational Communication*, Holbrook, Boston, 1973; Otis W. Baskin and Craig E. Aronoff, *Interpersonal Communication in Organizations*, Goodyear, Santa Monica, Calif., 1980.

33. Marilyn H. Lewis and N. L. Reinsch, Jr., "Listening in Organizational Environments," *Journal of Business Communication*, Summer 1988, pp. 49–67.

34. Judith Gordon, "Learn How to Listen," *Fortune*, Aug. 17, 1987, pp. 107–108.

35. Reprinted from Judith R. Gordon, *A Diagnostic Approach to Organizational Behavior*, 2d ed., Allyn and Bacon, Boston, 1987, p. 230.

36. Robert E. Kaplan, Wilfred H. Drath, and Joan R. Kofodimos, "Power and Getting Criticism," *Center for Creative Leadership Issues and Observations*, August 1984, pp. 1–8.

37. Ibid.

38. "Essentials of Feedback," *A Seven-Day Leadership Development Course*, Center for Creative Leadership, Greensboro, N.C., 1976, pp. 77–78, as cited in Phillip V. Lewis, *Organizational Communication: The Essence of Effective Management*, 2d ed., Prentice-Hall, Englewood Cliffs, N.J., 1980, pp. 157–158.

39. Patricia Sellers, "How to Handle Customers' Gripes," *Fortune*, Oct. 24, 1988, pp. 88–100.

40. Marvin E. Shaw, *Group Dynamics: The Psychology of Small Group Behavior*, McGraw-Hill, New York, 1981, pp. 150–157.

41. Lyman W. Porter and Karlene Roberts, "Communication in Organizations," in Marvin D. Dunnette (ed.), *Handbook of Industrial and Organization Psychology*, Rand McNally, Chicago, 1976, pp. 1553–1589.

42. David Katz and Robert Kahn, *The Social Psychology of Organizations*, Wiley, New York, 1966.

43. Jules Harcourt, Virginia Richerson, and Mark Wattier, "A National Study of Middle Managers' Assessment of Organizational Communication Quality," *Journal of Business Communication*, vol. 28, 1991, pp. 348–365.

44. Otis W. Baskin and Craig E. Aronoff, *Interpersonal Communication in Organizations*, Scott, Foresman, Santa Monica, Calif., 1980, pp. 92–93; Phillip V. Lewis, *Organizational Communication: The Essence of Effective Management*, 2d ed., Prentice-Hall, Englewood Cliffs, N.J., 1980, pp. 62–63.

45. Clare Ansberry, "Utah's Geneva Steel, Once Called Hopeless, Is Racking Up Profits," *The Wall Street Journal*, Nov. 20, 1991, p. A1.

46. Earl Planty and William Machaver, "Upward Communications: A Project in Executive Development," *Personnel*, vol. 28, 1952, pp. 304–318; J. R. Cranwell, "How to Have a Well-Informed Boss," *Supervisory Management*, May 1969, pp. 5–6; Gerald M. Goldhaber, *Organizational Communication*, 4th ed., Brown, Dubuque, Iowa, 1986, pp. 170–173.

47. Charles A. O'Reilly III and Karlene H. Roberts, "Information Filtration in Organizations: Three Experiments," *Organizational Behavior and Human Performance*, vol. 11, 1974, pp. 253–265.

48. Nelson W. Aldrich, Jr., "Lines of Communication," *INC.*, June 1986, pp. 140–144.

49. T. J. Peters and R. H. Waterman, *In Search of Excellence: Lessons from America's Best-Run Companies*, Harper & Row, New York, 1982; Peter R. Monge, Lynda White Rothman, Eric M. Eisenberg, Katherine I. Miller, and Kenneth K. Kirste, "The Dynamics of Organizational Proximity," *Management Science*, vol. 31, 1985, pp. 1129–1141.

50. Joseph B. White, "How Detroit Diesel, Out from under GM, Turned Around Fast," *The Wall Street Journal*, Aug. 16, 1991, p. A1.

51. Lyman W. Porter and Karlene Roberts, "Communication in Organizations," in Marvin D. Dunnette (ed.), *Handbook of Industrial and Organization Psychology*, Rand McNally, Chicago, 1976, pp. 1553–1589.

52. R. Wayne Pace, *Organizational Communication: Foundations for Human Resource Development*, Prentice-Hall, Englewood Cliffs, N.J., 1983, pp. 53–54.

53. Gerald M. Goldhaber, *Organizational Communication*, 4th ed., Brown, Dubuque, Iowa, 1986, pp. 174–175.

54. R. Wayne Pace, *Organizational Communication: Foundations for Human Resource Development*, Prentice-Hall, Englewood Cliffs, N.J., 1983, pp. 56–57.

55. Keith Davis, *Human Behavior at Work*, McGraw-Hill, New York, 1972.

56. Keith Davis, "Management

Communication and the Grapevine," in Stewart Ferguson and Sherry Devereaux Ferguson (eds.), *Intercom: Readings in Organizational Communication,* Hayden, Rochelle Park, N.J., 1980, pp. 55–66.

57. S. Friedman, "Where Employees Go for Information: Some Surprises," *Administrative Management,* vol. 42, 1981, pp. 72–73; Gerald M. Goldhaber, *Organizational Communication,* 4th ed., Brown, Dubuque, Iowa, 1986, pp. 176–177; Alan Zaremba, "Working with the Organizational Grapevine," *Personnel Journal,* July 1988, pp. 38–42.

58. R. Wayne Pace, *Organizational Communication: Foundations for Human Resource Development,* Prentice-Hall, Englewood Cliffs, N.J., 1983, pp. 57–58.

59. "Out of Sight, Not Out of Mind," *The Wall Street Journal,* June 20, 1989, p. B1.

60. J. G. March and G. Sevon, "Gossip, Information, and Decision Making," in L. S. Sproull and P. D. Larkey (eds.), *Advances in Information Processing in Organizations,* vol. 1, JAI, Greenwich, Conn., 1984, pp. 95–107; Karl E. Weick and Larry D. Browning, "Argument and Narration in Organizational Communication," *Journal of Management,* vol. 12, 1986, pp. 243–259; Jitendra Mishra, "Managing the Grapevine," *Public Personnel Management,* Summer 1990, pp. 213–228.

61. This section relies heavily on Rosabeth Moss Kanter, "When a Thousand Flowers Bloom: Structural, Collective, and Social Conditions for Innovation in Organizations," *Research in Organizational Behavior,* vol. 10, 1988, pp. 169–211.

62. Leslie Brennan, "McKesson Takes to Meeting Monthly," *S&MM* (Sales and Marketing Management), July 1986, pp. 102 ff.

63. D. G. Marquis and S. Myers, *Successful Industrial Innovations,* National Science Foundation, Washington, D.C., 1969.

64. Based on Nelson W. Aldrich, Jr., "Lines of Communication," *INC.,* June 1986, pp. 140–144.

65. Albert B. Crawford, "Corporate Electronic Mail—A Communication-Intensive Application of Information Technology," *MIS Quarterly,* vol. 6, 1982, pp. 1–14.

66. Edward H. Nyce and Richard Groppa, "Electronic Mail at MHT," *Management Technology,* May 1983, pp. 65–72.

67. R. E. Rice and D. Case, "Electronic Message Systems in the University: A Description of Use and Utility," *Journal of Communication,* vol. 33, 1983, pp. 131–152; Lee Sproull and Sara Kiesler, "Reducing Social Context Cues: Electronic Mail in Organizational Communication," *Management Science,* vol. 32, 1986, 1492–1512.

68. Richard C. Huseman and Edward W. Miles, "Organizational Communication in the Information Age: Implications of Computer-Based Systems," *Journal of Management,* vol. 14, 1988, pp. 181–204.

69. Susan Hellweg, Kevin Freiberg, and Anthony Smith, "The Pervasiveness and Impact of Electronic Communication Technologies in Organizations: A Survey of Major American Corporations," paper presented at a meeting of the Speech Communication Association, Chicago, 1984.

70. Nelson W. Aldrich, Jr., "Lines of Communication," *INC.,* June 1986, p. 140.

71. Fleming Meeks, "Live from Dallas," *Forbes,* Dec. 26, 1988, pp. 112–113.

72. David Kirkpatrick, "Here Comes the Payoff from PCs," *Fortune,* Mar. 23, 1992, pp. 93–102; Jim Bartino, "At These Shouting Matches, No One Says a Word," *Business Week,* June 11, 1992, p. 78.

ACKNOWLEDGMENTS

Figures

Figure 1: Reprinted by permission of Howard Aldrich and Lance B. Kurke, "Mintzberg Was Right! A Replication and Extension of *The Nature of Managerial Work,*" *Management Science,* vol. 29, no. 8, August 1983, p. 979. Copyright © 1983, The Institute of Management Sciences, 290 Westminster Street, Providence, R.I. 02903.

Figure 3: Group communication networks. Adapted from Craig E. Aronoff and Otis W. Baskin, *Interpersonal Communication in Organizations,* Scott, Foresman and Company, Glenview, Ill., 1980, p. 77. Reprinted by permission of Otis W. Baskin.

Figure 4: Adapted in part from Phillip V. Lewis, *Organizational Communication: The Essence of Effective Management,* 3d ed., © 1987, pp. 9, 35, 139. Adapted by permission of Prentice-Hall, Inc., Englewood Cliffs, N.J. Adapted in part from Edward E. Scannel, *Communication for Leadership,* McGraw-Hill Book Company, 1970. Adapted by permission of the author.

Figure 5: John W. Newstrom and Keith Davis, *Human Behavior at Work: Organizational Behavior,* 9th ed., McGraw-Hill, Inc., 1993, p. 445.

CONCLUDING CASE

CHAIRMAN'S COST-CUTTING HUMOR AT BEAR, STEARNS*

Even before cost cutting replaced scandal dodging as the latest game on Wall Street, one firm kept a sharp eye on its bottom line—thanks mainly to advice from the revered Haimchinkel Malintz Anaynikal, a reclusive philosopher of budgetary restraint.

The fictional Anaynikal resides in the fertile imagination of Alan C. (Ace) Greenberg, chairman and chief executive of Bear, Stearns & Company, a noted Wall Street investment firm. "I have no further comment about him," Greenberg said when asked to supply details of Anaynikal's biography. "If other firms found out about him, there might be big trouble."

Through a series of memos distributed to employees at Bear, Stearns, Greenberg and Anaynikal have worked overtime to slash costs.

The company's memos typically contain nuggets of Anaynikal's instructive—and diverting—wisdom. What follows, in chronological order, are excerpts from a few of these memos.

FR: Alan C. Greenberg

June 19

The month of May is history, but it looks like we did get 10 runs in the first inning. I frankly cannot remember any time in the past where we ever broke even in the month of May, much less made money.

Haimchinkel Malintz dropped down, saw the figures and made some

---

*Steve Coll and David A. Vise, "Chairman's Cost-Cutting Humor," *The Washington Post*, Oct. 18, 1987, pp. H1, H20. Copyright © 1987 The Washington Post. Reprinted with permission.

---

suggestions. . . . He pointed out to me that the tendency is to cut expenses when things are tough and how stupid that line of reasoning is. When things are good you should be even more careful of expenses. . . . The partners of this firm must continue to work together and learn to overlook petty differences. We are all expendable and I hope that your Executive Committee does not have to prove that to any of us.

August 9

I was just shown the results for our first quarter. They were excellent. When mortals go through a prosperous period, it seems to be human nature for expenses to balloon. We are going to be the exception. I have just informed the purchasing department that they should no longer purchase paper clips. All of us receive documents every day with paper clips on them. If we save these paper clips, we will not only have enough for our own use, but we will also in a short time be awash in the little critters. Periodically, we will collect excess paper clips and sell them. . . .

In addition to the paper clip caper, we also are going to cut down on ordering the blue envelopes used for interoffice mail. These envelopes can be used over and over again. You have probably guessed by now that these thoughts are not original. They came from one of Haimchinkel Molonitz [sic] Anaynikal's earlier works. His thoughts have not exactly steered us wrong so far. Let's stick with his theories till he lets us down.

August 15

Thank you, thank you, thank you! The response to the memo on paper clips and envelopes has been overwhelming. It seems that we already have an excess of paper clips. . . . If we can save paper clips from incoming mail, we can save rubber bands, and my hope is that we can become awash in those little stretchies also. Obviously, if we can handle the rubber band challenge, I have something even bigger in mind.

September 10

We have been supplying everyone with memo pads. These pads have, at the top, our logo and also a person's name and telephone number. This is conceptually wrong. We are in a person-to-person business. It would be much warmer if the sender of a note signed it with his name and telephone number along with some sweet words, such as "I love you" or "I need more business to feed my family."

. . . . Haimchinkel Malintz Anaynikal just informed me that this superior way of communicating will save us $45,000 a year.

August 29 (the next year)

Because we are rolling along, it is essential that we review the fundamentals of Haimchinkel Malintz Anaynikal. . . . Do not get conceited or cocky. . . . Check on the people that answer telephones. Are they courteous? . . . Return all calls as soon as possible. . . . Watch expenses—like a hawk. Now is the time to cut out fat! The rest of the world cuts expenses when business turns sour. With your help, we will be different, smarter and richer.

August 21 (the following year)

I would like to announce at this time a freeze on expenses and carelessness. We probably throw away millions every year with stupidities and slop. In fact, I have seen more slop in the last three weeks than in the previous six month. Stop it now.

Haimchinkel Malintz Anaynikal is really something. . . . He hates slop even more than I do. In fact, he pointed out to me where our stock could be if we ran a neat, tight shop. I am tired of cleaning up poo-poos. The next associate of mine that does something "un-neat" is going to have a little meeting with me and I will not be the usual charming, sweet, understanding, pleasant, entertaining, affable, yokel from Oklahoma.

QUESTIONS FOR CONCLUDING CASE

1 Compare the Anaynikal memos with other communication options. Do you feel that the memos effectively communicate the importance of cost cutting?

2 Evaluate the Anaynikal memos in terms of the basic components of the communication process.

3 To what extent do the memos encourage vertical (upward and downward) and horizontal communication? Give evidence to support your answer.

CONCLUDING CASE

CITICORP VIES TO BECOME FIRST TRULY GLOBAL BANK

Ever since John S. Reed took over as chairman and CEO in 1984, Citicorp, the largest bank in the United States, has been working to become the world's first truly global bank. To that end, Citicorp has built one of the most sophisticated computerized communication networks in the world. With assets of over $230 billion, Citicorp seeks to become an international star in both consumer and corporate banking.

On the consumer banking side, Citicorp has been extremely successful. Throughout the world, the bank has more than 35 million outstanding charge and credit cards. There are more than 700 Citicorp branches in Europe, and Asian accounts are climbing beyond the 5 million mark. Citicorp is attracting new business because of its 24-hour telephone banking and its ability to offer customers the convenience of using the Citicorp automated teller card from Singapore to New York to Paris.

In researching the requirements to build a global consumer banking presence, Citicorp executives found that consumer banking needs around the world tend to be more similar than different. It also found that consumer attitudes about finance tend to be related more to the way individuals are raised, their education, and their values than to their nationality. As a result, Citibank has concentrated on offering similar services linked throughout the world to achieve global economies of scale.

"To make it work, you need three things," says Reed: "a shared vision and common vocabulary around the world, an organization than can translate global scale into local advantage, and the capacity to transfer local innovations around the world." Citicorp has standardized such services as branch banking, home mortgages, and auto loans, regardless of location. This approach reflects the shared vision of making it easy for consumers to buy things (including stocks and investments).

Reed refers to spreading local innovations around the world as "success transfer." He says that you establish the "demand for sharing ideas with a strong and consistent drive from the top." At first, several top executives helped orchestrate the process by flying around the world and urging people to share. Highlighting successes has also encouraged others to adapt and to try new things themselves. Reed says that Citicorp also holds many meetings organized by function or lines of business. For instance, Citicorp might bring all its credit card people together to tell "war stories— what works in Australia, what's working in Germany." In the auto loans area, a global conference might consider issues such as revenues, expenses, and write-offs. Successful practices would then be incorporated globally.

Citicorp has been experiencing much greater difficulty building a truly global presence within the corporate banking sector. The most important element within this sector is Citicorp's JENA business, a complex organization that handles lending, trading, and high-level deals within the interlinked economies of Japan, Europe, and North America. Whereas Citicorp's consumer bank business can be standardized to a large extent, the JENA operations cannot. There are no common products that can be sold to a wide range of customers, so the business is more customized. Moreover, it is intensely competitive and depends heavily on building unique relationships with various corporations, who may then come to Citicorp for their financial needs.

To facilitate a global perspective in JENA, Citicorp has recently developed a structure around approximately 50 units called "activity centers." Centers specialize in such activities as trading on foreign exchanges, serving the financial requirements of specialized sets of customers, handling pension funds, or dealing with mergers and acquisitions. Although the activity centers are carefully defined areas of specialization, they must frequently collaborate with one another in serving customers. As a result, Citicorp is attempting to build the heads of the 50 activity centers into a team. Several levels of hierarchy have been eliminated, and the 50 heads report to the JENA sector executive. Eight coordinators help the sector executive by facilitating the handling of the most complex situations, in which multiple activity centers are involved. Also, the 50 center heads are brought together periodically to help enhance trust and teamwork.*

* Noel Tichy and Ram Charan, "Citicorp Faces the World: An Interview with John Reed," *Harvard Business Review,* November–December 1990, pp. 1135–1144; Pete Engardio, "For Citibank, There's No Place Like Asia," *Business Week,* Mar. 30, 1992, pp. 66–69.

QUESTIONS FOR CONCLUDING CASE

1 Using the diagram of the basic components of the communication process (Figure 2), analyze likely communication challenges associated with conducting a global consumer banking business.

2 Use the basic components of the communication process to assess the difficulties of building a global corporate banking sector. How do the challenges differ from those in the consumer banking sector?

3 Evaluate Citicorp's use of various communication channels to facilitate communication and promote innovation.

CHAPTER 10

Managing Groups

GAINING THE EDGE

TEAMWORK PAYS OFF AT MONSANTO

Managers at the Monsanto chemical and nylon complex just east of Pensacola, Florida, have successfully challenged the traditional belief that an employee's main job is to follow orders. Monsanto employees working in teams are expected to make decisions related to such major issues as hiring, purchasing, job assignments, and production.

The team strategy began by necessity. In the mid-1980s the factory, in which Monsanto had invested $1 billion over the course of three decades, was beginning to lose money. In an attempt to control costs, unprofitable operations were cut, and almost one-third of the jobs were eliminated. More than half of the first-level supervisors took early retirement. Instead of naming new supervisors to fill some of the vacant positions, the remaining managers realized that the situation presented an ideal opportunity for switching to the self-managing team concept. They cut the layers of management from seven to four. Then they organized employees into teams of 10 to 12 persons.

Today, teams perform many of the functions previously executed by managers. For example, teams decide the mix of chemicals going into the production of nylon yarn. They are empowered to—and have—shut down production lines for reasons of quality or safety. Recently, during a thunderstorm, the appropriate team decided to switch to Monsanto's generators immediately, instead of waiting to see if the electric power would be knocked out by the storm. The move saved hundreds of thousands of dollars by avoiding a shutdown when the local power was subsequently interrupted for several hours. When machines or equipment need repair, teams go directly to the maintenance shop or to suppliers to obtain the necessary assistance. Teams interview prospective employees and rank them in order of qualifications for the job. Managers pay close attention to team hiring recommendations. No one has ever been hired without being recommended by a team.

The team approach has led to a rapid turnaround. Instead of losses, the factory is now achieving its best levels of safety and production ever. As a result, plans are being made to pay all regular employees a salary, thereby eliminating hourly wages. Programs are also being developed to share profits with teams on the basis of their performance. In addition, the teams are working so well that another layer of management will soon be eliminated.

Despite the successes at the Pensacola plant, there are still areas where team performance can improve. In some cases, teams have not communicated well enough with one another. In others, teams have done little to appraise and improve themselves on an ongoing basis. Some jobs have kept employees too busy to confer regularly with team members. In addition, some employees have hesitated to push improvements until team members are compensated fairly for their achievements. Some team members have also been reluctant to take charge in areas where they are capable of providing leadership.

Still, the results have been so positive that Monsanto is studying the possibility of duplicating the team concept in its plants throughout the world.[1]

By implementing the team strategy, Monsanto recognizes that individuals working effectively in groups can often be a powerful competitive force. However, to take advantage of the power of groups, managers must have a solid understanding of group behavior—often referred to as group dynamics—

because of the ongoing interchanges that characterize groups. Managers also need to be aware of their own potential to influence groups as part of the leading function.

In this chapter, we examine some basic group characteristics, including types of work groups, the development of informal groups, and the operation of groups. Next, we investigate inputs and processes that affect group outcomes. We also explore how task forces and teams can be used to foster innovation. Finally, we analyze how conflict within and between groups can be managed, addressing possibilities for both reducing and stimulating conflict.

FOUNDATIONS OF WORK GROUPS

What Is a Group?

Group Two or more interdependent individuals who interact and influence each other in collective pursuit of a common goal

A **group** is two or more interdependent individuals who interact and influence each other in collective pursuit of a common goal.[2] This definition helps differentiate a group from a mere gathering of individuals. Several strangers who happen to leave by the same door at the theater or who can be found studying in the reference section of a library do not constitute a group. In neither case are those individuals interdependent, nor do they interact and influence one another in collectively attempting to achieve a shared goal. Likewise, groups differ from organizations because the latter involve systematic efforts (through the use of the four major management functions and a formal structure), as well as the production of goods or services. Groups typically do not engage in systematic efforts to the same extent as organizations and may or may not produce goods or services.

Although groups have always been a central part of organizations, they are gaining increasing attention as potentially important organizational assets. Organizations that are making more extensive use of groups range from mammoth General Motors to much smaller Castite, a Cleveland firm that employs 17 people and is just approaching its first $1 million in annual sales. At Castite, when an order for a new part comes in, President Joan Lamson has a salesperson, a quality assurance person, and a production worker meet together. They determine exactly what the customer wants, how to get the job done in the best possible way, and how to maximize quality. Castite, which uses an epoxylike resin to fill the tiny holes that are left by gas bubbles in molten metal as it is cast, has customers that include the "Big Three" automakers.[3]

Types of Work Groups

A number of different types of groups exist in the workplace. They can be classified into two main categories: formal and informal. These categories and several subcategories are shown in Figure 1.

Formal group A group officially created by an organization for a specific purpose

Command, or **functional, group** A formal group consisting of a manager and all the subordinates who report to that manager

FORMAL GROUPS A **formal group** is a group officially created by an organization for a specific purpose. There are two major types of formal groups: command and task.

A **command,** or **functional, group** is a formal group consisting of a manager and all the subordinates who report to that manager. Each identifiable work unit (manager and subordinates) in an organization is considered to be a command group. For example, if you stay in a large Marriott hotel, your room will be cleaned by one of several housekeepers who report to an area housekeeping

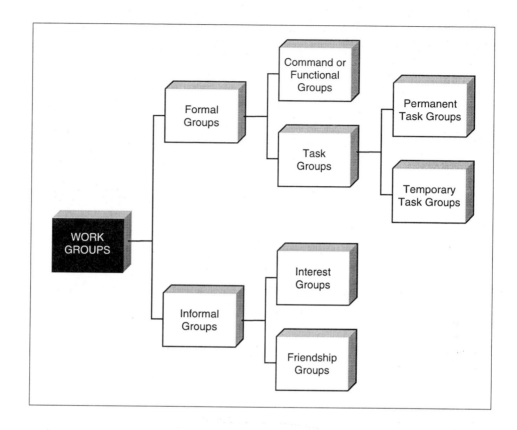

Figure 1   *Types of work groups.*

supervisor, making up one command group. If you attend a luncheon, the individuals who wait on the tables report to a catering supervisor, forming part of another command group. Each supervisor reports to a respective higher-level manager and belongs to that higher-level command group. In this way, each supervisor forms a linking pin between a lower-level and a higher-level group. A **linking pin** is an individual who provides a means of coordination between command groups at two different levels by fulfilling a supervisory role in the lower-level group and a subordinate role in the higher-level group (see Figure 2). Thus organizations are made up of command, or functional, groups arranged in pyramidal fashion, with linking pins tying them together.

A **task group** is a formal group created for a specific purpose that supplements or replaces work normally done by command groups. Task groups can be either relatively permanent or temporary. A *permanent* task group, often called a **standing committee** or *team*, is charged with handling recurring matters in a narrowly defined subject area over an indefinite, but generally lengthy, period of time. An example is the Quality Improvement Team of Hazleton Laboratories America, Inc., a high-level permanent task group charged with facilitating quality improvement efforts across various units of the biotechnology firm. A *temporary* task group is created to deal with a specific issue within a specific time frame. For example, as part of its Profitability Improvement program, Heinz USA frequently organizes temporary teams of managers from different departments to seek out and prioritize projects that can lead to major cost savings.[4] Temporary task groups are often called *ad hoc committees, task forces,* and *project groups* or *teams.*[5] Names vary somewhat across organizations, so it may be necessary to ask about time frames to establish whether a particular task group is relatively permanent or temporary. We discuss task forces and teams in greater detail later in this chapter.

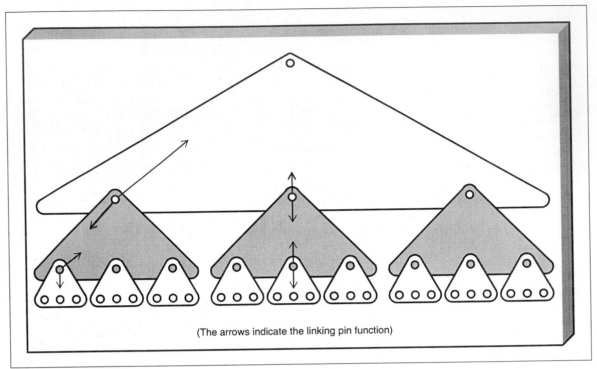

(The arrows indicate the linking pin function)

Figure 2 *The linking-pin concept. (Reprinted from Rensis Likert,* New Patterns of Management, *McGraw-Hill, New York, 1961, p. 113.)*

Informal group A group that is established by employees, rather than by the organization, to serve group members' interests or social needs

Interest group An informal group created to facilitate employee pursuits of common concern

Friendship group An informal group that evolves primarily to meet employee social needs

INFORMAL GROUPS An **informal group** is a group that is established by employees, rather than by the organization, to serve group members' interests or social needs. Such groups may or may not also further the goals of the organization. Sometimes, an informal group has the same members as does a formal group, as when members of a work group begin to have lunch together. Other times, an informal group is made up of only some members of one or more formal groups (see Figure 3). There are two major types of informal groups: interest and friendship.

An **interest group** is an informal group created to facilitate employee pursuits of common concern. The types of interests that spawn informal groups can be wide-ranging, such as a radical new technology that may not be practical for the company to pursue at the time (but which a group of engineers investigate informally), a sport (e.g., volleyball), or a desire to influence the company to alter some policy. Interest groups can benefit the organization, but they can also create difficulties, R. R. Donnelly & Sons, one of the four companies that print over 1 million copies of *Business Week* each week, found it necessary to fire several employees who allegedly conspired to sell early copies of the magazine to stockbrokers. The brokers wanted early access to the "Inside Wall Street" column so that they could use the information to buy stocks before it became public knowledge and demand pushed prices up.[6]

A **friendship group** is an informal group that evolves primarily to meet employee social needs. Such groups typically stem from mutual attraction, often based on common characteristics, such as similar work, backgrounds, and/or values. Members of a friendship group may eat lunch together frequently, attend plays, play golf, or engage in other friendship-related social activities. Friendship groups can benefit an organization by enhancing the flow of information and reinforcing the willingness of employees to work together cooperatively. They can be detrimental, however, when employees place social concerns above im-

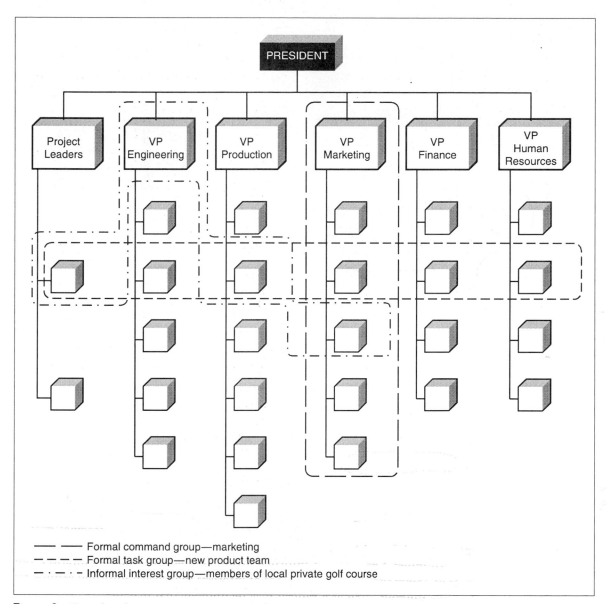

— — — Formal command group—marketing
- - - - Formal task group—new product team
- · — · - Informal interest group—members of local private golf course

Figure 3 *Formal and informal groups in an organization.*

portant work goals or when friends have a serious falling out. Thus managers need to understand informal groups because of their potential for influencing organizational effectiveness.

How Informal Groups Develop

Work by sociologist George Homans helps explain how informal groups often arise from the dynamics of formal groups.[7] When a formal group is established, certain behaviors and sentiments are required of its members (see Figure 4). *Required activities* are the behaviors necessary to perform job tasks. *Required interactions* are the dealings with others that are specified as part of the job. *Required sentiments* are the views and attitudes that are necessary to do the job. Also involved are *given sentiments,* the nonrequired attitudes and values that individuals inevitably bring to their jobs.

For example, when Federal Express was a fledgling company in the early 1970s, there were some basic, but limited, requirements that its employees were

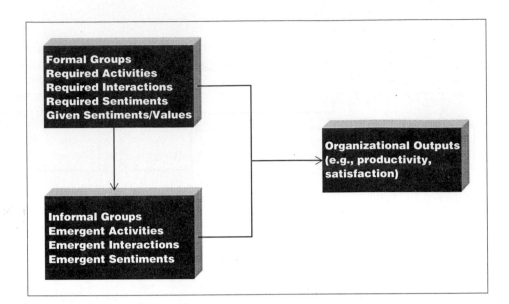

Figure 4 *The informal-group emergence process.*

expected to meet. Couriers were expected to pick up packages on time, get them to the airport, look clean and professional, and keep their trucks washed (required activities). They were also expected to interact with customers when they picked up and dropped off packages, as well as to cooperate with Federal Express pilots, plane loaders, and other company employees at airports (required interactions). Finally, they were supposed to be courteous and respectful to customers (required sentiments). No doubt, the couriers also held feelings about a variety of issues, such as the way the organization was run, other employees, sports, and politics (given sentiments and values).[8]

During this period, the company was operating on the edge of financial disaster. Skeptics were certain the endeavor would fail. As the couriers in their formal groups performed their required behaviors, other behaviors, interactions, and sentiments began to emerge. According to Homans, *emergent activities* are actions that either supplant or supplement required behaviors. Similarly, *emergent interactions* and *emergent sentiments* are actions that either supplant or supplement required interactions and sentiments. These emergent activities, interaction and sentiments are associated with informal groups.

In the Federal Express case, the couriers began to form a strong, informal camaraderie with the pilots, plane loaders, and others involved with their packages. For example, stories abound about couriers who were so dedicated to getting their packages picked up and delivered that they did things like pawning watches to buy gasoline (emergent activities). They bent over backward to make sure that they built not only good but outstanding relationships with customers (emergent interactions), prompting customers to make notations on Federal Express customer surveys such as "Say hello to Ginny in Wichita for me." One observer likened the informal team spirit that arose to that of bomber crews in movies about World War II (emergent sentiments). For Federal Express, the emergence of informal groups led to emergent activities, interactions, and sentiments that supplemented those required and were a major factor in the survival of the company.[9] Informal groups may have positive, minimal, or negative effects on the achievement of organizational goals. For example, emergent sentiments can lead to emergent activities that interfere with required activities.

Most organizations have many formal and informal groups. While formal groups generally spawn informal ones, sometimes the process works in reverse, as when a group of friends starts a business together.

Inputs
Processes
Outcomes

How Work Groups Operate

A number of factors affect the way that groups operate and their ultimate effectiveness. In analyzing these factors, it is useful to think of groups as systems that use inputs, engage in various processes, or transformations, and produce outcomes. Figure 5 lists several general factors that are important in understanding the interactions and outcomes of groups. These factors are organized under the input, process, and outcome categories.

WORK GROUP INPUTS

In order for groups to operate, they must have certain basic inputs. Some of the major inputs that affect groups are the composition of the group, the roles that members play, and the size of the group.

1. Work Group Composition

The composition of a work group has a strong bearing on a group's ultimate success. Two especially important compositional factors are the characteristics of members and the reasons that members are attracted to a particular group.

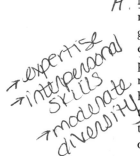

→ expertise
→ interpersonal skills
→ moderate diversity

A. MEMBER CHARACTERISTICS Group expert J. Richard Hackman argues that managers need to consider three main issues when selecting members for work groups.[10] For one thing, individual group members need to have task-relevant expertise.[11] Another consideration is that group members need to have appropriate interpersonal skills. Finally, for tasks that involve at least some challenge, a moderate degree of diversity in the makeup of a group is useful. If a group is too homogeneous, members may get along well but lack enough differing perspectives to generate new ideas. On the other hand, if a group is too heterogeneous, the advantages of the breadth of talent may be lost because the group may have difficulty coordinating the diverse efforts.[12]

B. ATTRACTION TO THE GROUP Another factor to consider in composing a group is potential members' attraction to the group. While employees are not always able to choose the groups in which they work, they often have some discretion in the matter, particularly for certain types of task groups, such as task forces and committees.

Why do individuals join or agree to participate in groups?[13] Some may be attracted to or like other members of the group. Others may enjoy the activities of the group—perhaps a committee is exploring new ideas in a technical area of interest. Still others may value the goals or purposes of the group. For example, Michael J. Daly left a $45,000 accounting job with Manufacturers Hanover Bank to join the Peace Corps in the Dominican Republic for $200 per month plus

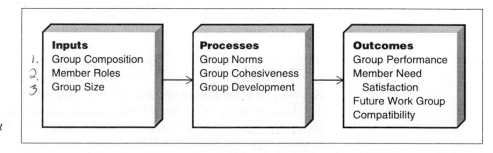

Inputs	Processes	Outcomes
1. Group Composition	Group Norms	Group Performance
2. Member Roles	Group Cohesiveness	Member Need
3. Group Size	Group Development	Satisfaction
		Future Work Group
		Compatibility

Figure 5 *Factors that affect work group behavior.*

room and board. There, Daly taught peasant-owned financial cooperatives how to operate at a profit and compete with local banks.[14] People also join groups because groups help meet individuals' needs for affiliation. According to McClelland's acquired-needs theory of motivation, such needs may be higher in some individuals than others, but we are all likely to have at least some need for affiliation. Finally, individuals may join a group because the group can be instrumental in achieving a goal outside the group (e.g., joining a fraternity to facilitate meeting members of sororities or vice versa). Individuals may join groups for any or all of these reasons.

Member Roles

Why are we likely to expect that the designated chair of a committee will call the meeting to order, a group member from the finance department will provide relevant financial expertise, and the designated secretary will take notes? One reason is that each of these individuals is fulfilling a **role,** a set of behaviors expected of an individual who occupies a particular position in a group. When operating in a work group, individuals typically fulfill several roles. For example, a person may be acting in the role of an expert in a given area, the role of a representative of a particular command group, and the role of a member of the work force interested in the implications of the matter under discussion.

In addition, the fact that an individual is a member of a group brings with it other roles. Some expectations are set initially, particularly if supervisors are in charge or leaders have been named. Others develop as the group operates and members take on various roles that differentiate them from others in the group. Common member roles in groups fit into three categories: group task roles, group maintenance roles, and self-oriented roles.[15]

Role A set of behaviors expected of an individual who occupies a particular position in a group

Group task roles help a group develop and accomplish its goals. Among these roles are the following:

■ *Initiator-contributor:* Proposes goals, suggests ways of approaching tasks, and recommends procedures for approaching a problem or task
■ *Information seeker:* Asks for information, viewpoints, and suggestions about the problem or task
■ *Information giver:* Offers information, viewpoints, and suggestions about the problem or task
■ *Coordinator:* Clarifies and synthesizes various ideas in an effort to tie together the work of the members
■ *Orienter:* Summarizes, points to departures from goals, and raises questions about discussion direction
■ *Energizer:* Stimulates the group to higher levels of work and better quality

Group task roles Roles that help a group develop and accomplish its goals

Group maintenance roles Roles that do not directly address a task itself but, instead, help foster group unity, positive interpersonal relations among group members, and development of the ability of members to work effectively together

Group maintenance roles do not directly address a task itself but, instead, help foster group unity, positive interpersonal relations among group members, and development of the ability of members to work effectively together. Group maintenance roles include the following:

■ *Encourager:* Expresses warmth and friendliness toward group members, encourages them, and acknowledges their contributions
■ *Harmonizer:* Mediates disagreements between other members and attempts to help reconcile differences
■ *Gatekeeper:* Tries to keep lines of communication open and promotes the participation of all group members

■ *Standard setter:* Suggests standards for the way in which the group will operate and checks whether members are satisfied with the functioning of the group
■ *Group observer:* Watches the internal operations of the group and provides feedback about how participants are doing and how they might be able to function better
■ *Follower:* Goes along with the group and is friendly but relatively passive

Self-oriented roles Roles that are related to the personal needs of group members and often negatively influence the effectiveness of a group

Self-oriented roles are related to the personal needs of group members and often negatively influence the effectiveness of a group. These roles include the following:

■ *Aggressor:* Deflates the contributions of others by attacking their ideas, ridiculing their feelings, and displaying excessive competitiveness
■ *Blocker:* Tends to be negative, stubborn, and resistive of new ideas, sometimes in order to force the group to readdress a viewpoint that it has already dealt with
■ *Recognition seeker:* Seeks attention, boasts about accomplishments and capabilities, and works to prevent being placed in an inferior position in the group
■ *Dominator:* Tries to assert control and manipulates the group or certain group members through such methods as flattering, giving orders, or interrupting others

Group leaders often assume many of the task roles. In addition, the leaders may use some maintenance roles to facilitate group progress. Often, however, it is difficult for a leader to engage in all the necessary task and maintenance behaviors without some help from others in the group. In leaderless groups (those with no appointed leader), the individuals most likely to emerge as leaders (be perceived by others as leaders) are active participants who adopt task roles.[16]

Informal leader An individual, other than the formal leader, who emerges from a group, has major influence, and is perceived by group members as a leader

Even when a group has a formally designated leader, one or more informal leaders may develop. An **informal leader** is an individual, other than the formal leader, who emerges from a group, has major influence, and is perceived by group members as a leader. Although some group members may attempt to exercise informal leadership regardless of the formal leader's behavior, informal leaders are most likely to emerge when the formal leader has difficulty facilitating group progress.[17] In addition to roles, another important group input factor is group size.

Group Size

Research on small groups provides some interesting insights into the effects of group size. One thrust has considered how different numbers of members affect interactions, while another has investigated how group size affects performance.[18]

SIZE AND GROUP INTERACTIONS The number of individuals in a group influences how the members interact. With two-person groups, or dyads, there are no other members to help resolve differences. Yet, if one leaves the group, the task may not be able to be completed. As a result, dyads often follow one of two patterns. Either the two members are extremely polite and attempt to avoid disagreements or they disagree frequently, causing relations to be somewhat strained. Adding a third person often does not resolve the interaction difficulties because there is a tendency for the group to split into a "two-against-one" situation. Groups with four or six members are susceptible to deadlocks because the groups can easily split into factions of equal size.

On the other hand, midsize groups of five—or possibly seven—members have several advantages, at least in terms of making decisions or completing tasks that require multiple interactions. For one thing, deadlocks cannot occur, because of the odd number of members. For another, the groups are large enough to generate many different ideas but small enough to allow various members to participate fully in the group.

As groups grow beyond seven—and particularly beyond eleven or twelve—it becomes more difficult for all members to participate actively. As a result, the interaction tends to become more centralized, with a few individuals taking more active roles relative to the other members. Disagreements may occur more easily and group satisfaction may decline unless the members put a good deal of effort into group maintenance roles. Sometimes, because of the way in which the work must be done or the number of viewpoints that must be included, large-size groups are necessary. However, interactions in large groups are fairly lengthy when complex issues are involved.[19] In an effort to be responsive to competitive pressures, Procter & Gamble revamped its highest-ranking group, the administrative committee. Traditionally, the 40-member committee met every Tuesday morning to approve all significant promotions and spending plans. In its place, a 20-member executive committee now meets weekly to review only extremely important issues, pushing other decisions down to lower levels in the organization for handling. The change was made because the difficulty of engaging in meaningful dialogue in such a large group bogged down the whole decision-making process.[20]

SIZE AND PERFORMANCE What impact does size have on group performance? This is not an easy question to answer because the effects of size depend to some degree on the nature of the task. For example, the effects might be different in a group whose members work somewhat independently (such as waiters in a restaurant) and in one whose members must coordinate their efforts closely (such as a rescue team). Generally, though, the impact of size on group performance is shaped like an inverted "U" (see Figure 6).[21] Thus, as managers initially add workers to a group, performance goes up; but after a certain point, the added impact of more workers begins to level off performance, and it may even go down.

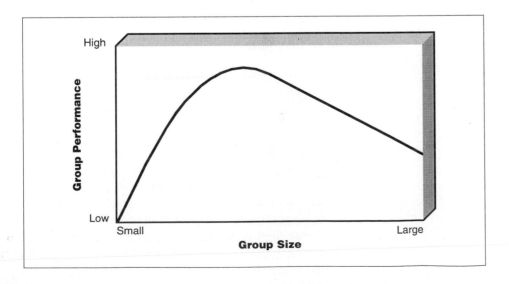

Figure 6 *Effects of group size on performance.*

Size & Performance

Social loafing The tendency of individuals to expend less effort when working in groups than when working alone

Free riders Individuals who engage in social loafing, thus benefiting from the work of the group without bearing their proportional share of the costs involved

Why does performance stop rising and even possibly decline as group size increases? One reason is **social loafing,** the tendency of individuals to expend less effort when working in groups than when working alone.[22] The effects can snowball if others in the group detect the social loafing and consequently reduce their own efforts.[23] Individuals who engage in social loafing are often called **free riders** because they benefit from the work of the group without bearing their proportional share of the costs involved.[24] As a result, social loafing is sometimes called *free riding*.

Managers can take several steps to reduce the likelihood of social loafing. Assigning just enough people to do the work is one prime step. Others are having each group member do different tasks, making each individual's work visible in some way, providing for individual feedback, and making rewards contingent on individual, as well as group, performance. Finally, since social loafing is less likely to occur when the group is committed to the task, managers should try to design interesting, challenging tasks or select group members who are likely to be committed to particular tasks.[25] Challenging tasks, small work groups, and a committed work force are all factors that have helped boost company success at Brazil's Semco (see the Case in Point discussion).

CASE IN POINT

GROUPS MAKE A DIFFERENCE AT BRAZIL'S SEMCO

In 1980, when Richard Semler joined Semco, founded by his father 27 years earlier, the company had about 100 employees, manufactured hydraulic pumps for ships, produced about $4 million in revenues, and tottered on the edge of bankruptcy. For the next 2 years, top managers constantly sought bank loans and fought off rumors that the company was about to sink. They also traveled four continents seeking the seven license agreements that enabled the company to reduce its cyclical marine business to 60 percent of total sales.

Today, Semco has five factories, which produce a range of sophisticated products, including marine pumps, digital scanners, commercial dishwashers, truck filters, and mixing equipment for substances ranging from bubble gum to rocket fuel. Customers include Alcoa, Saab, and General Motors. Semco is frequently cited in the press as one of the best companies in Brazil for which to work.

The company's survival and ultimate success is due largely to a major change in its management approach. Semco shifted toward an emphasis on three fundamental values—democracy, information, and profit sharing. These values ultimately led to reliance on work groups as a primary mechanism for managing the company.

After some experimentation, Semco found that the optimal number for an effective production unit is about 150 people per factory. In the spirit of democracy and worker involvement, work teams of about 10 employees each were given major responsibility for outcomes associated with their areas. Initially, costs rose because of duplicated effort and lost economies of scale. Within a year, though, sales doubled, inventory dropped from 126 to 46 days, eight new products appeared that had been tied up in R&D for 2 years, and the product rejection rate at inspection dropped from 33 to 1 percent. Increased productivity enabled the company to reduce the work force by 32 percent through attrition and offers of early retirement.

At Semco, once the members of a group agree on a monthly production schedule, they meet it. In one situation, a group determined that it could make 220 meat slicers. As the end of the month approached, everything was completed except for motors that had not yet arrived, despite repeated phone calls to the supplier. Finally, two employees went to the supplier's plant, talked to the supplier, and got delivery on the last day of the month. Then everyone stayed until 4:45 the next morning in order to finish production of the meat slicers on time.

Several factors have contributed to the success of Semco's system. One is that everyone in the company has access to important information. Each employee gets a balance sheet, a profit-and-loss analysis, and a cash-flow statement for his or her division every month. All workers voluntarily attend monthly classes so that they can learn to read and understand the numbers. Although top-level managers are strict about meeting the financial targets, workers have wide latitude in determining the necessary actions and carrying them out. Another factor in the company's success is that the workers share in profits. Twice a year, employees receive 23 percent of the after-tax profits for their division. Employees vote on how to disburse the funds, which are usually distributed equally. Semco doesn't bother to advertise job openings because word of mouth brings 300 applications for every open position.[26]   ■ ■ ■

The success at Semco is also due to the effective interactions of group members, a subject we take up next.

WORK GROUP PROCESSES

Why do some groups seem to accomplish very little, while others with similar inputs achieve a great deal? In part, the answer lies in *group processes*, the dynamic, inner workings of groups as they operate over a period of time. As members of a group go about their work, some of their energy must be allocated to developing and operating the group itself. This energy is, in essence, diverted from the task. Therefore, it is sometimes called process loss, since it represents a loss of energy that could have been devoted to the task.[27] Some process loss is inevitable, given the interdependence that is characteristic of groups.

Even with process loss, there are possibilities of tremendous gains from the combined force, or synergy, of group members.[28] **Positive synergy** occurs when the combined gains from group interaction (as opposed to individuals operating alone) are greater than group process losses. When there is positive synergy, the whole (the total effect of the group) is greater than the sum of its parts (the tasks the members could accomplish individually). For instance, Procter & Gamble's premium diaper, Luvs Deluxe, made it to market in half the usual 18 months because of a multidisciplinary team that cut through departmental barriers.[29] **Negative synergy** occurs when group process losses are greater than any gains achieved from combining the forces of group members. If you have ever enlisted the help of a group that proved to be so ineffective that you felt you could have done the job faster yourself, then you have witnessed negative synergy. Scientific Computer Systems, founded to develop a machine that could run the software for high-speed Cray computers more slowly, and also more cheaply, experienced the difficulties of negative synergy. Development of the new machine ran into severe problems when the company had its software specialists work out of Wilsonville, Oregon, and its hardware experts operate in San Diego. The coordination difficulties, aggravated by the geographic separation, slowed completion by many months and greatly increased costs.[30] We next discuss three of the major group process factors that affect group synergy and effectiveness: norms, cohesiveness, and group development.

Positive synergy   The force that results when the combined gains from group interaction are greater than group process losses

Negative synergy   The force that results when group process losses are greater than any gains achieved from combining the forces of group members

1.) Group Norms

Norms Expected behaviors sanctioned by a group that regulate and foster uniformity in member behaviors

Norms are expected behaviors sanctioned by a group that regulate and foster uniformity in member behaviors.[31] Therefore, for a behavior to fit into the norm category, there must be some recognition among group members that the behavior is generally expected for membership in the group.

Work groups do not try to regulate all behavior through norms. Instead, they attempt to develop and enforce norms that are related mainly to certain central issues.[32] For example, groups often develop norms about the issue of production processes. Such norms typically pertain to standards of quality and quantity, as well as how to get the job done. Informal social arrangements are another common issue about which norms are apt to arise. That is, groups often establish norms regarding when and where to have lunch; what type of social function, if any, to have when someone leaves; and how much socializing to do both at and outside of work. Finally, work groups frequently have norms about the allocation of resources, including materials, equipment, the assigned work area (e.g., near a window), and pay.

Norms typically develop through one of the following four mechanisms: explicit statements, critical events, primacy, and carryover behaviors.[33]

A.) **EXPLICIT STATEMENTS** *Explicit statements* made by supervisors and coworkers can provide important information about the expectations of various group members. Such statements provide a particularly good opportunity for the supervisor to influence the norms of the group. Supervisory statements may be especially important when a new group is formed or when a new person is added to a group. Recognizing the potential power of explicit statements, Thomas Tyrrell, CEO of 5-year-old American Steel & Wire in Cuyahoga Heights, Ohio, has every new employee come to his office for a get-acquainted chat. He also visits each of the company's three plants for 1 day every month to let workers know how business is going and what they can do to cut costs.[34]

B.) **CRITICAL EVENTS** In any group, there can be *critical events* in the group's history that set precedents for the future. Tyrrell's efforts at American Steel & Wire are aided by the fact that the company's three plants were acquired from USX, including the Cuyahoga works, which had been shut down for 2 years because of a labor dispute. The difficult competitive position of the plants and the past labor dispute have encouraged cooperation among employees within the plant.

C.) **PRIMACY** *Primacy* as a source of norms is the tendency for the first behavior pattern that emerges in a group to establish group expectations from that point on. To get new workers to take responsibility for their actions, Tyrrell insists that all new hires invest at least $100 cash in company stock on their first day of work, despite the fact that many are steelworkers who have been unemployed for a significant period of time. He wants the new workers to develop a norm of concern for the welfare of the company right from the start. The plants shut down for the annual stockholders' meeting, and the company also has a profit-sharing plan.

D.) **CARRYOVER BEHAVIORS** Many norms are *carryover behaviors* from other groups and perhaps other organizations. When group members share similar past experiences (such as working on similar committees in the company), the establishment of norms progresses quickly. Otherwise, norms may evolve more slowly.[35] Tyrrell wants to encourage more worker involvement in figuring out ways to cut costs and improve operations, but he has found that it is difficult to break down the old norms and taboos that discourage workers from speaking out when they feel that something should be changed.

Group Cohesiveness

Group cohesiveness The degree to which members are attracted to a group, are motivated to remain in the group, and are mutually influenced by one another

Another factor related to group process is **group cohesiveness,** the degree to which members are attracted to a group, motivated to remain in the group, and influenced by one another. We take a look at some of the consequences of group cohesiveness before exploring more specifically its determinants.[36]

CONSEQUENCES OF GROUP COHESIVENESS The degree of cohesiveness in a group can have important positive consequences for communication and job satisfaction. Members of relatively cohesive groups tend to communicate more frequently and be more sensitive to one another, and they are generally better able to gauge the feelings of other members of the group. Members of highly cohesive groups are apt to feel more satisfied with their jobs than are members of groups that are not very cohesive.[37] This is evident at Cleveland Track Materials, a maker of rail joints used by railroads to lay and repair track. The company has achieved success by training workers in several skills so that work groups can react quickly to the varying product specifications of customers. Welding supervisor Willie Smith says, "This is the best job I've ever had. All the guys—black, white—we're like a family. Everyone is important."[38] Although there are some negative possibilities (such as excessive amounts of communication among group members), the communication and job satisfaction consequences of group cohesiveness are generally positive from an organizational point of view.

Group cohesiveness also tends to influence the degree of hostility and aggression that one group exhibits toward another. Whether the impact is an organizational asset or liability depends largely on where the group's energy is directed. For example, cohesiveness may be helpful when it leads to friendly competition among groups that do the same type of work but do not depend upon each other to get the work done. Aggressiveness as a by-product of group cohesiveness can also energize a group to fight outside competition. On the other hand, among groups that depend on one another to reach organizational goals, hostility or aggression usually leads to a lack of cooperation and related dysfunctional consequences, such as missing deadlines, raising costs, and frustrating customers.

Another area affected by group cohesiveness is performance, since performance levels of group members tend to be more *similar* in highly cohesive groups. This is because members of such groups tend to avoid either letting the group down by underperforming or showing up other group members by performing at a significantly higher level.

The impact of cohesiveness on the actual *level* of performance in a group, however, depends not only on the group's degree of cohesiveness but also on its existing performance norms. This relationship is shown in Figure 7. When group cohesiveness is high, group performance tends to be either high or low, depending on performance norms. Groups perform at their *highest* level when group cohesion and performance norms are both high, thus encouraging all group members to perform at the same high level. In contrast, when group cohesion is high but performance norms are low, group performance tends to be at its *lowest* level.[39] Here, the high group cohesion bolsters adherence to the low performance norms. The effects can be seen in an illustration provided by former M.B.A. student Glen Huston, whose summer-job experience involved a highly

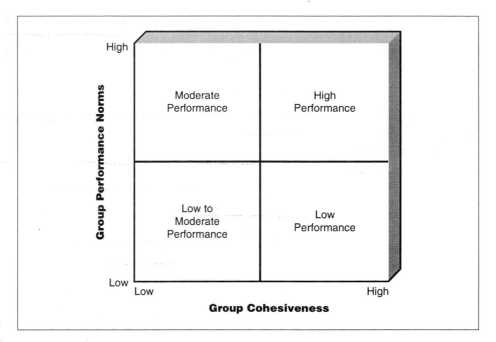

Figure 7 *Effects of cohesiveness and performance norms on group performance.*

cohesive lawn-care crew with low performance norms. As he was diligently raking grass clippings on his first day of work, members of the crew, and even the crew leader, told him to slow down because they would all get tired if they worked at that pace. Then the crew leader showed him how to use a handkerchief to mop his brow while leaning on his rake so that it would look like he had been working strenuously and just stopped to wipe off the resulting perspiration. The handkerchief routine was for use if one got caught standing around when the supervisor drove up on periodic checks of the various work crews.

On the other hand, when group cohesiveness itself is low, performance levels tend to be more mixed regardless of performance norms. This is because there tends to be more variability in performance levels when group cohesiveness is low. Therefore, even when performance norms are high, it is likely that not everyone will adhere closely to the high norms and, thus, that moderate group performance will result. Similarly, mixed adherence to low performance norms results in low to moderate group performance.

Group cohesiveness can also affect a group's willingness to innovate and change. Changes will be more difficult to implement when they are opposed by a highly cohesive group, but they can be greatly facilitated when they have the strong backing of such a group.

DETERMINANTS OF GROUP COHESIVENESS A number of factors have a positive effect on group cohesiveness. For example, similar attitudes and values make it easier for individuals to communicate, find common ground, and develop mutual understandings. External threats, such as fierce outside competition or challenges to survival, can provide a compelling reason for a group to pull together into a cohesive unit. Similarly, outstanding successes often create strong positive feelings about group membership and establish linkages among group members. The difficulty encountered in joining a group can build a common bond based on such factors as high standards (college), sacrifice (the Peace Corps), or difficult training (the Green Berets). Finally, group size can be a factor. Cohesiveness is much easier to attain when groups are relatively small, and it becomes much more difficult to achieve and maintain as groups grow larger. At Patagonia, Inc., a mail-order company well known for its expensive, high-performance outdoor clothing, positive norms about quality and innovation, as well as high cohesiveness among employees, have been important factors in the company's success. While the founder spends about half the year traveling the world, employees maintain his vision of producing high-quality, durable clothing that can be worn during such activities as scaling Kilimanjaro or sailing the Atlantic in a one-person boat. Group cohesion is aided by the fact that employees are encouraged to engage in outdoor activities on company time, as long as their work is done.[40]

Group Development

New groups are constantly being formed in organizations. They may be created as formal groups, such as new work units, committees, and task forces, or may arise as informal interest or friendship groups. Even existing groups are often in a state of flux as current members leave and new members are added. Such comings and goings affect the inner workings of groups.

A number of researchers argue that groups go through developmental stages that are relatively predictable. Understanding these stages can help managers both participate more effectively in groups and assist groups for which they have managerial responsibility. One of the best-known approaches to analyzing group development, proposed by group researcher Bruce W. Tuckman, holds that there are five major stages: forming, storming, norming, performing, and adjourning (see Figure 8).[41] New groups may progress through these phases, but

Figure 8 *Stages of group development.*

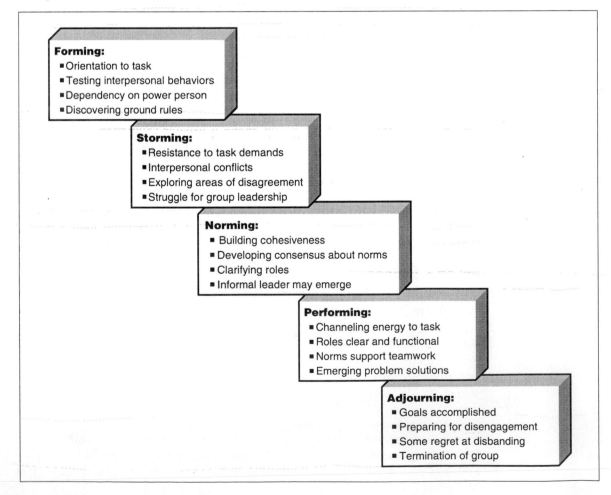

Forming:
- Orientation to task
- Testing interpersonal behaviors
- Dependency on power person
- Discovering ground rules

Storming:
- Resistance to task demands
- Interpersonal conflicts
- Exploring areas of disagreement
- Struggle for group leadership

Norming:
- Building cohesiveness
- Developing consensus about norms
- Clarifying roles
- Informal leader may emerge

Performing:
- Channeling energy to task
- Roles clear and functional
- Norms support teamwork
- Emerging problem solutions

Adjourning:
- Goals accomplished
- Preparing for disengagement
- Some regret at disbanding
- Termination of group

if there are changes in group membership, the development of the group may regress to an earlier stage—at least temporarily.

Forming A stage in which group members attempt to assess the ground rules that will apply to a task and to group interaction

STAGE 1: FORMING In the **forming** stage of group development, group members attempt to assess the ground rules that will apply to a task and to group interaction. At this point, members seek basic information about the task, make a preliminary evaluation of how the group might interact to accomplish it, and begin to test the extent to which their input will be valued. Some members may try out the acceptability of various interpersonal behaviors, such as engaging in small talk, making jokes, being sarcastic, or leaving the meeting to make telephone calls. Often, because of the uncertainty associated with forming, members may initially depend on a powerful person, if one is present, or on existing norms, if they are commonly known. Because of the need to make sense of the ground rules, groups at the forming stage often require some time to get acquainted with the task and with each other before attempting to proceed in earnest with task responsibilities.

Storming A stage in which group members frequently experience conflict with one another as they locate and attempt to resolve differences of opinion regarding key issues

STAGE 2: STORMING During the **storming** stage, group members frequently experience conflict with one another as they locate and attempt to resolve differences of opinion regarding key issues. The issues in contention might revolve around task requirements and possible resistance to them. Another common area of conflict centers on interpersonal relations—how various group members relate to one another. Often, at this stage, there is a struggle among members for leadership of the group if a leader has not been appointed. Listening and attempting to find mutually acceptable resolutions of major issues are important approaches during this period. Otherwise, the group is not likely to operate effectively; it may not progress beyond this stage, and it may even disband.

Norming A stage in which group members begin to build group cohesion, as well as develop a consensus about norms for performing a task and relating to one another

STAGE 3: NORMING In the **norming** stage, group members begin to build group cohesion, as well as develop a consensus about norms for performing a task and relating to one another. The idiosyncrasies of individual members are generally accepted, and members start to identify with the group. Member roles also become clearer, and the group shows a greater willingness to engage in mutual problem solving. If there is no appointed leader or the appointed leader is weak, an informal leader may emerge. At this stage, clarifying norms and roles, building cohesiveness, and attempting to use the resources of the group to solve problems are particularly important. In order to help a newly formed multicultural team progress smoothly through the early stages of group development, and particularly through the norming stage, British Petroleum held a special 2-day conference (see the Valuing Diversity box).

Performing A stage in which energy is channeled toward a task and in which norms support teamwork

STAGE 4: PERFORMING The **performing** stage is the period in which energy is channeled toward a task and in which norms support teamwork. Solutions from the problem solving of the previous stage begin to emerge. The roles of group members become clearer and more functional as the group works to achieve positive synergy and group goals. Not all groups reach this stage of development. Those that do are likely to be effective as long as they devote their energies to the task and work to maintain good group relationships.

Adjourning A stage in which group members prepare for disengagement as the group nears successful completion of its goals

STAGE 5: ADJOURNING During the **adjourning** stage, group members prepare for disengagement as the group nears the successful completion of its goals. While members may be pleased with completing their tasks, they may also feel some regret at the imminent disbanding of the group. The adjourning stage applies more frequently to temporary task groups, such as committees, task

VALUING DIVERSITY

Multicultural Teamworking at British Petroleum

British Petroleum (BP) decided to establish the Finance Europe Centre in Brussels to help its associate companies in European countries handle their financial needs. Rob Ruijter, a Hollander who had worked for BP in several countries, was appointed team leader and center manager. Other members of the team were chosen from BP finance centers throughout the world, resulting in a team of 40 professionals representing 13 different nationalities.

From the start, the aim was to consciously implement multicultural teamworking. This meant that the team members had to become aware of each other's different cultural orientations. They also needed to develop into a productive group. Ruijter soon recognized that, given the diversity, some initial support for the group development process would be desirable. Accordingly, the team planned a 2-day event that had several objectives:

- To make team members aware of the cultural differences and their impact on organizational structure, management style, decision making, and interpersonal behavior
- To aid team members in recognizing their different roles, preferences, and strengths, and understanding how these could complement one another
- To devise methods of communicating with each other
- To institute a set of ground rules for maintaining team effectiveness
- To create a shared vision for the team

In the course of the 2-day discussion, team members exchanged information about cultural differences in how they approach their work. For example, the group learned that a French executive will tend to assume that the authority to make decisions comes as "a right of office and a privilege of rank" and will operate accordingly. In contrast, in the United Kingdom, the Netherlands, and Scandinavia, leaders expect their decisions to be challenged, discussed, or even made by the group. In France, it is customary to shake hands with everyone in your work group each morning as a show of friendliness, whereas U.S. managers regard shaking hands as a formal sign of politeness. German team members normally do not expect to be greeted by their first names, even by people who know them well, and Scandinavians expect to be called by their last name only.

In part of the exercise, the team developed an initial set of norms, or "ground rules." These included "Do not prejudge people, functions, cultures; create a climate where people are not embarrassed to ask; give and ask for feedback; and draw on the strengths of the other person."

A year later the team reviewed its progress. Overall, the team was performing well, further norms were being established, and the operation was meeting the needs of BP.[42]

forces, or teams of limited duration. With ongoing or permanent formal groups, adjournments apply less frequently. However, reorganizations and related phenomena such as takeovers and mergers can bring about the adjourning stage of a group.

DO ALL GROUPS HAVE THESE STAGES? The five stages of group development apply mainly to newly formed, relatively unstructured groups. They are less likely to appear in groups with members who work frequently together or in those with fairly well established operating methods or ground rules.[43]

One important forum for group development is meetings. According to a survey, senior executives spend an average of 23 hours per week in meetings, while middle managers attend meetings about 11 hours per week.[44] Many other organization members are likely to be in meetings several hours per week. Meetings are frequently criticized because they are often not run well or do not achieve useful results.[45] One way of facilitating group development in meetings is by giving careful attention to how the meetings are conducted. Meetings are more productive when they are well organized and operate with appropriate ground rules. To learn more about running effective meetings, see the Practically Speaking discussion, "How to Lead a Meeting."

PRACTICALLY SPEAKING

HOW TO LEAD A MEETING

There are three major phases in leading a meeting: preparation, meeting in progress, and follow-up.

PREPARATION

Preparation is a key element in conducting an effective meeting. The following steps are involved:

Make sure the meeting is necessary. According to one estimate, it costs about $100 per hour, including overhead, to have a manager attend a meeting. Therefore, a 2-hour meeting attended by 10 managers can quickly add up to $2000. Colleagues will appreciate not having to attend meetings about routine matters that could be handled with a memo.

Define the meeting's objectives. An objective might be to involve others in a decision, coordinate major activities, or discuss important information. It is helpful to orient attendees by briefly describing each objective either in the memo announcing the meeting or on the agenda. Be specific when stating objectives. For example, "Decide between using sales reps or an in-house sales force" is much more helpful than "Discuss sales."

Identify participants. Try to limit participation to those who are the decision makers, have needed expertise, and/or are affected by the outcome. As noted earlier, a group of five to seven is an ideal number for interaction, but sometimes meetings must be larger to involve all the necessary participants. If the group gets too large however, the meeting will be more difficult to handle.

Prepare an agenda. When there is time, circulate the agenda early and obtain feedback. The agenda should be a short list of the main topics to be discussed. It helps key participants focus on what preparations they need to make for the meeting and also assists in ensuring that the important topics are covered. Send the final agenda out 2 or 3 days in advance.

Distribute needed background information. Consider what information participants will need to review in advance, and send it out with the final agenda. Avoid sending out huge reports that participants are unlikely to read. A better strategy is to send a summary and note that the full report is available if needed.

MEETING IN PROGRESS

Good preparation helps the meeting progress more smoothly. Actually running the meeting involves these five steps:

1. *Review the agenda.* Start on time, and review the agenda and major objectives. The review helps focus participants on why they are there and what outcomes are needed. It often helps to print the agenda on a blackboard or flip chart for easy reference.

2. *Get reports from individuals with preassigned tasks.* This should be done as early as feasible, although it may be necessary to wait for a particular agenda item to ask for a report or presentation. Getting reports as early as possible ensures that presenters have adequate time and provides recognition for their premeeting work. It also provides some of the necessary background information for other parts of the agenda.

3. *Encourage participant input.* Group effectiveness and member satisfaction are likely to be greater when all the members are able to provide input in their areas of expertise. A meeting leader should ensure that the meeting is not dominated by one faction or a few members. If someone speaks excessively, the leader might say something like "Well, Joan, let me see if I understand what you are saying." Then, after summarizing, the leader might follow with "Perhaps others have views on this issue." If an individual has said little, the leader might say, "Jim, we haven't heard from you yet. What are your views?"

4. *Keep the meeting on track.* If the discussion wanders, refer to a point someone made just before the digression to get the discussion back on track. If an issue is raised that cannot be resolved because of insufficient information, ask someone to check into it and report back.

5. *Summarize and review assignments.* Summarize what has been agreed upon or accomplished in the meeting. Also, review what each person has agreed to do and make sure that deadlines are set. Review plans for the next meeting if that is appropriate. End the meeting on time.

FOLLOW-UP

The meeting leader should follow up on the meeting:

Send out a memo summarizing the meeting. The memo should summarize the main things that were accomplished, and it should specify the actions that each person agreed to take and the deadlines that were set.

Follow up on assignments where appropriate. This involves checking with the various individuals about their progress, usually in preparation for a subsequent meeting.

Meeting leadership takes practice. It is usually a good idea for individuals to chair small, lower-level meetings early in their careers to gain experience.[46]

PROMOTING INNOVATION: USING TASK FORCES AND TEAMS

Groups are used in many contexts in which organizations can benefit from the experience and ideas of two or more individuals. Increasingly, their efforts are being tapped when creativity and innovation are important to organizational success. In this section, we investigate some current special uses of teams.

Task Forces

Task force A temporary task group usually formed to make recommendations on a specific issue

Ad hoc committee Another term for *task force*

[handwritten: 1) deal with problems identified by others 2.) Makes recommendations]

A **task force** is a temporary task group usually formed to make recommendations on a specific issue.[47] It is sometimes called an **ad hoc committee** or a *temporary committee*.[48] Because they deal with issues that typically involve several parts of the organization, task forces are often composed of individuals from the main command groups affected by a given issue. These individuals are usually needed to provide the necessary expertise, to furnish information about the needs of their command groups, and to help develop innovative ideas for solving problems or taking advantage of opportunities. Because task forces promote interaction among individuals from diverse departments, these groups are particularly well suited to fostering creativity and innovation.

Teams

Team A temporary or an ongoing task group whose members are charged with working together to identify problems, form a consensus about what should be done, and implement necessary actions in relation to a particular task or organizational area

[handwritten: 1.) identify problems 2) reach concensus + act upon it.]

A **team** is either a temporary or an ongoing task group whose members are charged with working together to identify problems, form a consensus about what should be done, and implement necessary actions in relation to a particular task or organizational area. Two major characteristics distinguish a team from a task force. First, team members typically identify problems in a given area (rather than deal with them after they have been identified by others). Second, they not only reach a consensus about what should be done but actually implement the decisions as a team (rather than make recommendations that are then implemented by others). Of course, team members (unless they are top-level managers) usually keep their superiors informed, as necessary. Also, they are likely to need their superiors' agreement on decisions that have major implications for others and the organization.

Teams are often, but not always, task groups made up of individuals who cross command groups. Temporary teams handle a specific project to completion, whereas permanent teams have ongoing responsibilities in a given area. Teams sometimes have a fluid membership consisting of individuals who join when their expertise is needed and leave when their work is done.

In a recent structural change, Amgen, the Thousand Oaks, California, biotechnology firm, reorganized by assigning all employees except its senior management to product development teams or task forces. The move was aimed at preserving Amgen's small-company atmosphere, which had played a role in the company's successful and rapid growth. Teams and task forces support the entrepreneurial spirit desired at Amgen.[49] The use of teams has been highly successful in such organizations as Monsanto, General Motors, and many Japanese companies. As a result, teams are gaining increasing attention, particularly as means of fostering innovation, increasing quality, and facilitating successful implementation of changes.[50] Two types of teams that are of particular current importance are entrepreneurial teams and self-managing teams.

Entrepreneurial team A group of individuals with diverse expertise and backgrounds who are brought together to develop and implement innovative ideas aimed at creating new products or services or significantly improving existing ones

ENTREPRENEURIAL TEAMS An **entrepreneurial team** is a group of individuals with diverse expertise and backgrounds who are brought together to develop and implement innovative ideas aimed at creating new products or services or significantly improving existing ones.[51] Entrepreneurial teams focus on new business either by pioneering completely different types of endeavors or by devising novel products and services that are congruent with existing lines of business. For example, an entrepreneurial team at the Ford Motor Company was responsible for the introduction of the very successful Taurus and its companion car, the Mercury Sable (see the following Case in Point discussion).

CASE IN POINT

Entrepreneurial Team Example

TEAM TAURUS SCORES BIG*

During the dark recession days of 1980, Ford Motor Company executives found themselves facing not only a slowed economy but also the toughest foreign-car competition they had ever encountered. "It was painfully obvious that we weren't competitive with the rest of the world in quality," says John A. Manoogian, Ford's chief of quality during that period. Company members decided to fight back. Their basic strategy involved using some of their competitors' methods, such as thoroughly studying the competition, making quality a top priority, and changing the organization of the firm's developmental efforts.

In a major step, Ford departed from the traditional approach to new car development. Normally, the company followed a sequential 5-year process to launch a new automobile. Product planners would start with a basic concept. Next, a design team would develop the look. The designers' work would go to engineering for specifications and then go on to manufacturing and suppliers for process design. Each step in the sequence was done with little ongoing communcation with the other parties.

This time, the company put an unprecedented $3 billion behind a new group, dubbed Team Taurus. With the team approach, representatives from all the affected units—planning, design, engineering, and manufacturing—worked together. The team had the overall final responsibility of developing the vehicle. With appropriate representatives on the team, issues could be resolved early. For example, manufacturing suggested design changes that made it easier to build in quality during manufacturing.

Some of the investigative work was done by special subteams. For instance, a five-member group had the job of developing comfortable, easy-to-use seats. In the course of their work, the group members took seats from 12 different cars, put them in Crown Victorias, and conducted 100,000 miles of driving tests using a variety of different drivers who indicated what they liked and didn't like.

In a major departure from traditional modes of operation, the team asked assembly-line workers for advice during the design phase and was flooded with helpful ideas. Worker suggestions led to changes such as reducing the parts in a door panel from eight to two for easier handling and ensuring that all the bolts had the same-size head to eliminate the need for different wrenches. "In the past we hired people for their arms and their legs," says Manoogian. "But we weren't smart enough to make use of their brains." In another unusual move, supplier ideas were also tapped during the design stage, and long-term contracts were signed with suppliers so that they had a strong stake in the new car development.

The success of the Taurus and Sable has sold Ford on the team idea for new car development. Teams also have been a significant factor in the strong sales of

* Russell Mitchell, "How Ford Hit the Bull's Eye with Taurus," *Business Week,* June 30, 1986, pp. 69–70.

the new Lincoln Continental and Thunderbird automobiles. While the team approach has been a strong success, there is more work ahead for Ford teams in achieving their goals for high quality.[52] ■ ■ ■

Self-managing team A work group given responsibility for a task area without day-to-day supervision and with authority to influence and control both group membership and behavior

Autonomous work group Another name for *self-managing team*

SELF-MANAGING TEAMS A **self-managing team** is a work group given responsibility for a task area without day-to-day supervision and with authority to influence and control both group membership and behavior.[53] Another name for a self-managing team is an **autonomous work group.** A famous example of the use of such groups is the system at A. B. Volvo's automobile plant in Kamar, Sweden. There, autonomous work teams of about 20 workers each are responsible for putting together entire units of cars, such as the electric system or the engine. The cars move about the plant on a separate computer-controlled carrier. Each worker usually performs a series of tasks over several minutes, rather than a single task over a few seconds as is typical of U.S. automobile assembly lines. In addition, workers on a team are taught several jobs to build in variety and to enable them to cover for sick or vacationing team members. After some initial efforts to fine-tune the system, the autonomous work group approach has proved successful. During the last decade or so, it has helped Volvo reduce the labor hours that go into making a car by 40 percent, increase inventory turnover from 9 times per year to 22, and cut the number of defects by 40 percent. The company has recently built a new plant at Uddevalla, where work teams will complete an even greater variety of tasks.[54]

A number of companies in the United States are experimenting with self-managing teams.[55] One of the most prominent examples is the NUMMI project, a joint venture of General Motors and the Toyota Motor Corporation, whose teams build automobiles in Fremont, California. A self-managing team approach is also used at Digital Equipment Corporation's Enfield, Connecticut, facility. Compared with DEC's traditional plants, Enfield builds products 40 percent faster, uses fewer workers, maintains lower inventories, has double to triple the quality, and generates lower turnover.[56]

MANAGING CONFLICT

Conflict A perceived difference between two or more parties that results in mutual opposition

Of course, the positive results with task forces and teams do not occur without some conflict. In organizations, conflicts within and between groups are common. By **conflict** we mean a perceived difference between two or more parties that results in mutual opposition.[57]

While conflict is often considered to be a negative factor, it can have constructive, as well as destructive, consequences. Some of the destructive prospects are well known. For example, conflict can cause individuals or groups to become hostile, withhold information and resources, and interfere with each other's efforts. It can delay projects, drive up costs, and cause valued employees to leave. On the constructive side, conflict can highlight problems and the need for solutions. It can also promote change as parties work to resolve problems. In addition, conflict can enhance morale and cohesion as group members deal with areas of concern and frustration. Finally, conflict can stimulate interest, creativity, and innovation by encouraging new ideas.[58]

As a result, some conflict in an organization is important, but too much can have a detrimental effect on organizational performance (see Figure 9). Conflict levels that are very low may indicate that problems are being hidden and new ideas stifled. For instance, a major factor in the famous failed Edsel project of the Ford Motor Company was the fact that subordinates withheld information be-

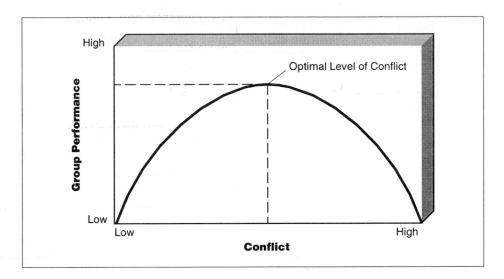

Figure 9 *Effects of conflict on group performance.*

cause conflict was discouraged and because they felt that managers were already committed to the project.[59] In contrast, too much conflict may indicate that excessive amounts of energy are aimed at dissension and opposition. Accordingly, managers need to understand the causes of conflict, know how to reduce or resolve conflict, and also be able to stimulate it in a positive way when appropriate.

Causes of Conflict

A number of factors contribute to conflict.[60] Several of the most important are discussed below.

TASK INTERDEPENDENCE Two types of task interdependence are particularly prone to conflict. One is *sequential interdependence,* in which one individual or work unit is heavily dependent on another. For example, waiters are generally more reliant on cooks than the reverse because waiters must depend on cooks to furnish good meals in a timely manner. The second form of task interdependence is *reciprocal interdependence,* in which individuals or work units are mutually-interdependent. For instance, purchasing agents want engineers to provide detailed generic specifications so that they can negotiate lower costs from suppliers. At the same time, engineers need to obtain materials of the proper quality on a timely basis, so they may find it more convenient to specify a brand name.[61]

SCARCE RESOURCES Possibilities for conflict expand when there are limited resources, such as office space, equipment, training, human resources, operating funds, and pay allocations.[62] For example, if two groups require the same facilities, each may feel that its needs are more important and neither may be willing to compromise.

GOAL INCOMPATIBILITY Out of necessity, organization members frequently pursue goals that are somewhat different from one another, setting the stage for potential conflicts. For example, sales personnel may find it easier to battle the competition by promising quick deliveries, while people in manufacturing may find that small production runs on short notice interfere with their cost-cutting efforts.

COMMUNICATION FAILURES Breakdowns in communication due to distortions or lack of communication often lead to conflicts.

INDIVIDUAL DIFFERENCES Differences in personality, experience, and values make frequent conflicts likely. For example, personality conflicts with Robert A. Schoellhorn, former chairman of Abbott Laboratories, led three potential successors to leave the company, causing concern among board members about who would succeed to the chairperson's position. Critics say Schoellhorn, who was ultimately ousted by the board, was intolerant of dissent and undermined executives who built power of their own.[63]

POORLY DESIGNED REWARD SYSTEMS Reward systems can unwittingly lead to destructive conflict when they reward competition in situations that require cooperation for success.[64] For instance, at Solar Press, Inc., based in Napier, Illinois, a bonus system that rewarded team production also undermined cooperation when sequential dependence was needed among teams. Solar switched to a bonus system tied to company results, and so far it seems to be an improvement.[65]

Reducing and Resolving Conflict

Managers can use a number of different approaches to reduce or resolve conflict.[66] Such efforts are typically aimed at minimizing the destructive impact of conflict.

CHANGING SITUATIONAL FACTORS One obvious way to reduce conflict is to change the factors in the situation that are causing the problem. For example, a manager might increase the resources available, reorganize to reduce interdependence, redesign reward systems (as Solar Press did), or take steps to improve communication systems. Unfortunately, these solutions may not always be feasible or may be extremely expensive.

APPEAL TO SUPERORDINATE GOALS If the situations causing excessive conflict are difficult to change, managers are sometimes able to refocus the individuals or groups on **superordinate goals,** major common goals that require the support and effort of all parties. Examples are ensuring the survival of the organization and beating highly visible competition. The success of appeals to superordinate goals depends heavily on identifying goals that are sufficiently important to all parties. For instance, word of a serious defect in factory floor sweepers shipped to Japan and Toyota's announcement of a competing product in 1979 united the various elements of the Tennant Company in a lifesaving push for quality. Today, the Minneapolis-based company has approximately 60 percent of the North American market and 40 percent of the world market for floor maintenance equipment, such as sweepers and scrubbers.[67]

USE AN INTERPERSONAL CONFLICT-HANDLING MODE Aside from situational changes and appeals to superordinate goals, interpersonal modes are another means of handling conflict. Managers have five major interpersonal modes that they can use to attempt to resolve conflicts in which they are involved:[68]

■ **Avoidance** involves ignoring or suppressing a conflict in the hope that it will either go away or not become too disruptive.

Superordinate goals Major common goals that require the support and effort of all parties

Avoidance A conflict-handling mode that involves ignoring or suppressing a conflict in the hope that it will either go away or not become too disruptive

Accommodation A conflict-handling mode that focuses on solving conflicts by allowing the desires of the other party to prevail

Competition A conflict-handling mode that involves attempting to win a conflict at the other party's expense

Compromise A conflict-handling mode that aims to solve conflict issues by having each party give up some desired outcomes in order to get other desired outcomes

Collaboration A conflict-handling mode that strives to resolve conflicts by devising solutions that allow both parties to achieve their desired outcomes

■ **Accommodation** focuses on solving conflicts by allowing the desires of the other party to prevail. Essentially, the manager voluntarily lets the other party have his or her way rather than continue the conflcit.

■ **Competition** involves attempting to win a conflict at the other party's expense. In other words, one party wins and the other loses.

■ **Compromise** aims to solve conflict issues by having each party give up some desired outcomes in order to get other desired outcomes. Compromise often involves bargaining by the conflicting parties and generally requires a situation that offers both parties the chance to be in a better position or at least in no worse position after the conflict is resolved. With compromise each person wins some major issues and loses others.

■ **Collaboration** strives to resolve conflicts by devising solutions that allow both parties to achieve their desired outcomes. In other words, the solution is such that both parties win at least their major issues. Collaboration frequently involves considerable creativity in developing solutions that suit the needs of both parties in the conflict.

Although collaboration is often an advantageous way to handle conflict because both sides are likely to be satisfied, circumstances frequently call for the use of the other approaches as well. Table 1 summarizes situations in which each of the conflict-handling modes might apply, as reported by 28 chief executives.

Stimulating Conflict

Since too little conflict can lead to apathy, lethargy, and low performance, managers sometimes need to stimulate conflict. Obviously, conflict stimulation should be initiated in as positive a way as possible—and with caution, to prevent the conflict from reaching a destructive level that outweighs its advantages. There are several prime means of increasing constructive conflict.[69] Adding individuals with more diverse backgrounds to a group is one means. Another is communicating information that will prompt organization members to engage in constructive dialogue about the potential need for change. Still another means is encouraging internal competition.[70] Of course, in stimulating conflict, managers must have mechanisms in place to monitor the situation and maintain control.

CHAPTER SUMMARY

Work groups are becoming an increasingly important competitive factor in organizations. There are two major types of work groups, formal and informal. Formal groups include command, or functional, groups and task groups. Informal groups include interest and friendship groups. Required aspects of formal groups lead to the emergent behaviors, interactions, and sentiments associated with informal groups.

A useful way to analyze groups is to view them as systems that use inputs, engage in various processes or transformations, and produce outcomes. Important group inputs are group composition, particularly member characteristics and reasons for attraction to the group; member roles, including group task roles, group maintenance roles, and self-oriented roles; and group size.

Hopefully, work group processes result in positive synergy. Important factors influencing group processes are group norms, group cohesiveness, and group development. Group norms stem from explicit statements by supervisors and coworkers, critical events in a group's history, primacy, and carryover behaviors. A number of factors contribute to group cohesiveness. Cohesion, in turn, has important consequences for group communication, satisfaction, performance, hostility and aggression toward other groups, and a group's willingness to innovate and change. New groups typically go through five stages of development: forming, storming, norming, performing, and adjourning. Because of the widespread presence of groups, managers spend a considerable amount of their time in meetings. Therefore, it is important for managers to know how to lead a meeting effec-

TABLE 1	Situations in Which to Use the Five Conflict-Handling Modes, as Reported by Chief Executives		
Conflict Mode	**Situation**	**Conflict Mode**	**Situation**

 COMPETING

1. When quick, decisive action is vital—e.g., emergencies
2. On important issues where unpopular actions need implementation—e.g., cost cutting, enforcing unpopular rules, discipline
3. On issues vital to company welfare when you know you're right
4. Against people who take advantage of noncompetitive behavior

 COLLABORATING

1. To find an integrative solution when both sets of concerns are too important to be compromised
2. When your objective is to learn
3. To merge insights from people with different perspectives
4. To gain commitment by incorporating concerns into a consensus
5. To work through feelings which have interfered with a relationship

 COMPROMISING

1. When goals are important, but not worth the effort or potential disruption of more assertive modes
2. When opponents with equal power are committed to mutually exclusive goals
3. To achieve temporary settlements to complex issues
4. To arrive at expedient solutions under time pressure
5. As a backup when collaboration or competition is unsuccessful

 AVOIDING

1. When an issue is trivial, or more important issues are pressing
2. When you perceive no chance of satisfying your concerns
3. When potential disruption outweighs the benefits of resolution
4. To let people cool down and regain perspective
5. When gathering information supersedes immediate decision
6. When others can resolve the conflict more effectively
7. When issues seem tangential or symptomatic of other issues

ACCOMMODATING

1. When you find you are wrong—to allow a better position to be heard, to learn, and to show your reasonableness
2. When issues are more important to others than yourself—to satisfy others and maintain cooperation
3. To build social credits for later issues
4. To minimize loss when you are outmatched and losing
5. When harmony and stability are especially important
6. To allow subordinates to develop by learning from mistakes

Source: Reprinted from Kenneth W. Thomas, "Toward Multi-Dimensional Values in Teaching: The Example of Conflict Behaviors," *Academy of Management Review*, vol. 2, 1977, p. 487.

tively. Important outcomes to consider in evaluating the effectiveness of groups are group performance, member need satisfaction, and future work group compatibility.

Some of the major mechanisms that organizations use to tap the creativity and innovative capacity of groups include task forces, or ad hoc committees, and teams, particularly entrepreneurial and self-managing teams.

Managing conflict is also an important managerial skill related to groups. Causes of conflict include task interdependence, scarce resources, goal incompatibility, communication failures, individual differences, and poorly designed reward systems. Methods of reducing or resolving conflict include changing situational factors, appealing to superordinate goals, and using interpersonal conflict-handling modes. In addition, managers may need to stimulate conflict in order to encourage creativity and innovation.

QUESTIONS FOR DISCUSSION AND REVIEW

1 Outline the major types of work groups. Identify several work groups at your college or university. Classify them according to work group type.

2 Explain how informal groups develop in organizations. Choose an organization with which you are familiar and identify two informal groups. Trace how the informal groups came about.

3 Using a systems perspective, identify the main factors that influence the way that groups in organizations operate. Evaluate the effectiveness of a work group with which you are familiar.

4 Explain the basic inputs that groups require to operate. Analyze the inputs of a work group that you think runs effectively. What are the member characteristics that help it operate successfully? What attracts the various members to the group? What roles do members play? How does the number of members affect the group interaction?

5 Explain the significance of norms and cohesiveness in group functioning. Think of a group to which you belong. What are four important norms in the

group? How did they develop? Assess the level of group cohesiveness and its consequences.

6 Explain how groups develop. Trace the development of a group in which you have participated.

7 Differentiate among task forces and teams. Explain how each can be used to promote innovation. Identify examples of task forces and teams in the business section of your local paper, *The Wall Street Journal*, and/or magazines such as *Business Week* and *Fortune*.

8 Explain why self-managing teams have been so successful. If you were a manager, why would you like or not like to have them in your organization?

9 Explain the causes of conflict in organizations. Describe an organizational conflict situation of which you are aware and trace its causes.

10 Describe several ways to reduce or resolve conflict and to stimulate conflict. Think of a conflict situation that you have witnessed in a group. What approaches could you take to reduce or resolve the conflict?

DISCUSSION QUESTIONS FOR CHAPTER OPENING CASE

1 What input factors appear to be helping to make teams successful at Monsanto?

2 How has the group development process worked at Monsanto, and what remains to be done?

3 If you were the local manager, how rapidly would you proceed with implementing the remaining actions? Why?

REFERENCES

1. Barnaby J. Feder, "At Monsanto, Teamwork Works," *The New York Times*, June 25, 1991, p. D1.

2. Based on Marvin E. Shaw, *Group Dynamics: The Psychology of Small Group Behavior*, 3d ed., McGraw-Hill, New York, 1981; and Clayton P. Alderfer, "An Intergroup Perspective on Group Dynamics," in Jay W. Lorsch (ed.), *Handbook of Organizational Behavior*, Prentice-Hall, Englewood Cliffs, N.J., 1987.

3. Myron Magnet, "The Resurrection of the Rust Belt," *Fortune*, Aug. 15, 1988, pp. 40–48.

4. Bill Saporito, "Heinz Pushes to Be the Low Cost Producer," *Fortune*, June 24, 1985, pp. 44–54.

5. Ernest Stech and Sharon A. Ratliffe, *Effective Group Communication: How to Get Action by Working in Groups*,

National Textbook, Lincolnwood, Ill., 1985.

6. Chris Welles and James R. Norman, "The Case of the Purloined Magazines," *Business Week*, Aug. 15, 1988, pp. 40–44.

7. George Homans, *The Human Group*, Harcourt, Brace, New York, 1950.

8. P. Ranganath Nayak and John M. Ketteringham, *Break-Throughs*, Rawson Associates, New York, 1986.

9. Ibid; see also Robert A. Sigafoos, *Absolutely Positively Overnight!* St. Luke's Press, Memphis, Tenn., 1988.

10. J. Richard Hackman, "The Design of Work Teams," in Jay W. Lorsch (ed.), *Handbook of Organizational Behavior*, Prentice-Hall, Englewood Cliffs, N.J., 1987, pp. 315–342.

11. Preston C. Bottger and Philip W.

Yetton, "Improving Group Performance by Training in Individual Problem Solving," *Journal of Applied Psychology*, vol. 72, 1987, pp. 651–657.

12. Paul S. Goodman, Elizabeth C. Ravlin, and Linda Argote, "Current Thinking about Groups: Setting the Stage for New Ideas," in Paul S. Goodman and Associates (eds.), *Designing Effective Work Groups*, Jossey-Bass, San Francisco, 1986, pp. 1–33.

13. Marvin E. Shaw, *Group Dynamics: The Psychology of Small Group Behavior*, 3d ed., McGraw-Hill, New York, 1981.

14. Pete Engardio, "The Peace Corps' New Frontier," *Business Week*, Aug. 22, 1988, pp. 62–63.

15. This section is based largely on Kenneth Benne and P. H. Sheats, "Functional Roles of Group Mem-

bers," *Journal of Social Issues*, vol. 4, 1948, pp. 41–49; and Seth Allcorn, "What Makes Groups Tick," *Personnel*, September 1985, pp. 52–58.

16. Bernard M. Bass, *Stogdill's Handbook of Leadership*, Free Press, New York, 1981.

17. William B. Eddy, *The Manager and the Working Group*, Praeger, New York, 1985.

18. This section is based on Fremont A. Shull, Jr., Andre L. Delbecq, and L. L. Cummings, *Organizational Decision Making*, McGraw-Hill, New York, 1970; and Marvin E. Shaw, *Group Dynamics: The Psychology of Small Group Behavior*, 3d ed., McGraw-Hill, New York, 1981.

19. William J. Altier, "SMR Forum: Task Forces—An Effective Management Tool," *Sloan Management Review*, Spring 1986, pp. 69–76.

20. Zachary Schiller, "The Marketing Revolution at Procter & Gamble," *Business Week*, July 25, 1988, pp. 72–76.

21. L. L. Cummings, George P. Huber, and Eugene Arendt, "Effects of Size and Spatial Arrangements on Group Decision Making," *Academy of Management Journal*, vol. 17, 1974, pp. 460–475; George E. Manners, Jr., "Another Look at Group Size, Group Problem Solving, and Member Consensus," *Academy of Management Journal*, vol. 18, 1975, pp. 715–724; Paul S. Goodman, Elizabeth C. Ravlin, and Linda Argote, "Current Thinking about Groups: Setting the Stage for New Ideas," in Paul S. Goodman and Associates (eds.), *Designing Effective Work Groups*, Jossey-Bass, San Francisco, 1986, pp. 1–33.

22. Richard Z. Gooding and John A. Wagner III, "A Meta-Analytic Review of the Relationship between Size and Performance: The Productivity and Efficiency of Organizations and Their Subunits," *Administrative Science Quarterly*, vol. 30, 1985, pp. 462–481; Jeffrey M. Jackson and Stephen G. Harkins, "Equity in Effort: An Explanation of the Social Loafing Effect," *Journal of Personality and Social Psychology*, vol. 49, 1985, pp. 1199–1206; Bibb Latane, "Responsibility and Effort in Organizations," in Paul S. Goodman and Associates (eds.), *Designing Effective*

Work Groups, Jossey-Bass, San Francisco, 1986, pp. 277–304.

23. Jeffrey M. Jackson and Stephen G. Harkins, "Equity in Effort: An Explanation of the Social Loafing Effect," *Journal of Personality and Social Psychology*, vol. 49, 1985, pp. 1199–1206.

24. Robert Alabanese and David D. Van Fleet, "Rational Behavior in Groups: The Free-Riding Tendency," *Academy of Management Review*, vol. 10, 1985, pp. 244–255.

25. Ibid.; Jeffrey M. Jackson and Stephen G. Harkins, "Equity in Effort: An Explanation of the Social Loafing Effect," *Journal of Personality and Social Psychology*, vol. 49, 1985, pp. 1199–1206; Stephen J. Zaccaro, "Social Loafing: The Role of Task Attractiveness," *Personality and Social Psychology Bulletin*, vol. 10, 1984, pp. 99–106.

26. Based on Ricardo Semler, "Managing without Managers," *Harvard Business Review*, September–October 1989, pp. 76–84.

27. I. D. Steiner, *Group Process and Productivity*, Academic, New York, 1972.

28. The discussion of synergy is based on J. Richard Hackman, "The Design of Work Teams," in Jay W. Lorsch (ed.), *Handbook of Organizational Behavior*, Prentice-Hall, Englewood Cliffs, N.J., 1987.

29. Bill Saparito, "Luv That Market," *Fortune*, Aug. 3, 1987, p. 56.

30. Patrick E. Cole, "SCS May Have Defeated Its Worst Enemy—Itself," *Business Week*, June 27, 1988, p. 88D.

31. Paul S. Goodman, Elizabeth Ravlin, and Marshall Schminke, "Understanding Groups in Organizations," *Research in Organizational Behavior*, vol. 9, 1987, pp. 121–173.

32. Ibid.

33. Daniel C. Feldman, "The Development and Enforcement of Group Norms," *Academy of Management Review*, vol. 9, 1984, pp. 47–53.

34. The information regarding American Steel & Wire in this section is from Myron Magnet, "The Resurrection of the Rust Belt," *Fortune*, Aug. 15, 1988, pp. 40–48.

35. Kenneth Bettenhausen and J. Keith Murnighan, "The Emergence of Norms in Competitive Decision-

Making Groups," *Administrative Science Quarterly*, vol. 30, 1985, pp. 350–372.

36. This section relies heavily on Hugh J. Arnold and Daniel C. Feldman, *Organizational Behavior*, McGraw-Hill, New York, 1986; and H. Joseph Reitz, *Behavior in Organizations*, 3d ed., Irwin, Homewood, Ill., 1987. See also A. V. Lott and B. E. Lott, "Group Cohesiveness as Interpersonal Attraction: A Review of Relationships with Antecedent and Consequent Variables," *Psychological Bulletin*, vol. 64, 1965, pp. 259–302; and Nancy J. Evans and Paul A. Jarvis, "Group Cohesion: A Review and Reevaluation," *Small Group Behavior*, vol. 11, 1980, pp. 359–370.

37. Gregory H. Dobbins and Stephen J. Zaccaro, "The Effects of Group Cohesion and Leader Behavior on Subordinate Satisfaction," *Group and Organizational Studies*, vol. 11, 1986, pp. 203–219.

38. Myron Magnet, "The Resurrection of the Rust Belt," *Fortune*, Aug. 15, 1988, pp. 40–48.

39. Stanley Seashore, *Group Cohesiveness in the Industrial Work Group*, Institute for Social Research, Ann Arbor, Mich., 1954; Ralph M. Stogdill, "Group Productivity, Drive, and Cohesiveness," *Organizational Behavior and Human Performance*, vol. 8, 1972, pp. 26–43.

40. Paul B. Brown, "The Anti-Marketers," *INC.*, March 1988, pp. 62–72; Fleming Meeks, "The Man Is the Message," *Forbes*, Apr. 17, 1989, pp. 148–152.

41. Bruce W. Tuckman, "Developmental Sequence in Small Groups," *Psychological Bulletin*, vol. 63, 1965, pp. 384–399; Bruce W. Tuckman and Mary Ann C. Jensen, "Stages of Small-Group Development Revisited," *Group and Organization Studies*, vol. 2, 1977, pp. 419–427.

42. Rosemary Neale and Richard Mindel, "Rigging Up Multicultural Teamworking," *Personnel Management*, January 1992, pp. 36–39.

43. John A. Seeger, "No Innate Phases in Group Problem Solving," *Academy of Management Review*, vol. 8, 1983, pp. 683–689.

44. Study by Wharton Center for Applied Research, cited in Carol

Hymowitz, "A Survival Guide to the Office Meeting," *The Wall Street Journal,* June 21, 1988, p. 41.

45. Helen B. Schwartzman, "The Meeting as a Neglected Social Form in Organizational Studies," *Research in Organizational Behavior,* vol. 8, 1986, pp. 233–258.

46. Based on Anthony Jay, "How to Run a Meeting," *Harvard Business Review,* March–April 1976, pp. 120–134; George Huber, *Managerial Decision Making,* Scott, Foresman, Glenview, Ill., 1980; David A. Whetten and Kim S. Cameron, *Developing Management Skills,* Scott, Foresman, Glenview, Ill., 1984; and Julie Bailey, "The Fine Art of Leading a Meeting," *Working Woman,* August 1987, pp. 68–70, 103.

47. William J. Altier, "SMR Forum: Task Forces—An Effective Management Tool," *Sloan Management Review,* Spring 1986, pp. 69–75.

48. Ernest Stech and Sharon A. Ratliffe, *Effective Group Communication: How to Get Action by Working in Groups,* National Textbook, Lincolnwood, Ill., 1985; Walter Kiechel III, "The Art of the Corporate Task Force," *Fortune,* Jan. 29, 1991, pp. 104–105.

49. Andrew Erdman, "How to Keep That Family Feeling," *Fortune,* Apr. 6, 1992, pp. 95–96.

50. Rober B. Reich, "Entrepreneurship Reconsidered: The Team as Hero," *Harvard Business Review,* May–June 1987, pp. 77–83.

51. Jerome M. Rosow, *World of Work Report,* cited in Jeffrey P. Davidson, "A Way to Work in Concert," *Management World,* March 1986, pp. 9–12.

52. Russell Mitchell, "How Ford Hit the Bull's-Eye with Taurus," *Business Week,* June 30, 1986, pp. 69–70.

53. Jerome M. Rosow, *World of Work Report,* cited in Jeffrey P. Davidson, "A Way to Work in Concert," *Management World,* March 1986, pp. 9–12.

54. Steve Lohr, "Manufacturing Cars the Volvo Way," *The New York Times,* June 23, 1987, pp. D1, D5.

55. Brian Dumaine, "Who Needs a Boss?" *Fortune,* May 7, 1990, pp. 52–60.

56. Barbara Anne Solomon, "A Plant That Proves That Team Management Works," *Personnel,* June 1985, pp. 6–8; Patricia Galagan, "Work Teams That Work," *Training and Development Journal,* November 1986, pp. 33–35.

57. Steven P. Robbins, *Managing Organizational Conflict: A Nontraditional Approach,* Prentice-Hall, Englewood Cliffs, N.J., 1974.

58. Dean Tjosvold, "Making Conflict Productive," *Personnel Administrator,* June 1984, pp. 121–130.

59. Ibid.

60. This section is based largely on Richard E. Walton and John M. Dutton, "The Management of Interdepartmental Conflict: A Model and Review," *Administrative Science Quarterly,* March 1969, pp. 73–84; and Stephen P. Robbins, *Organizational Theory: The Structure and Design of Organizations,* Prentice-Hall, Englewood Cliffs, N.J., 1983.

61. George Strauss, "Work Flow Frictions, Interfunctional Rivalry, and Professionalism: A Case Study of Purchasing Agents," *Human Organization,* vol. 23, 1964, pp. 137–149.

62. Noah E. Friedkin and Michael J. Simpson, "Effect of Competition on Members' Identification with Their Subunits," *Administrative Science Quarterly,* vol. 30, 1985, pp. 377–394.

63. Julia Flynn Siler, "The Slippery Ladder at Abbott Labs," *Business Week,* Oct. 30, 1989, pp. 136–137; Jeff Bailey, "Ousted Chairman of Abbott Accuses Company in Filing," *The Wall Street Journal,* June 6, 1990, p. A6.

64. Alfie Kohn, *No Contest: The Case against Competition,* Houghton Mifflin, Boston, 1986; Alfie Kohn, "It's Hard to Get Left Out of a Pair," *Psychology Today,* October 1987, pp. 53–57.

65. Bruce G. Posner, "If at First You Don't Succeed," *INC.,* May 1989, pp. 132–134.

66. This section is based on Stephen P. Robbins, *Organizational Theory: The Structure and Design of Organizations,* Prentice-Hall, Englewood Cliffs, N.J., 1983.

67. Christopher Knowlton, "Making It Right the First Time," *Fortune,* Mar. 28, 1988, p. 48.

68. Kenneth W. Thomas, "Toward Multi-Dimensional Values in Teaching: The Example of Conflict Behaviors," *Academy of Management Review,* vol. 2, 1977, pp. 484–490; H. Joseph Reitz, *Behavior in Organizations,* 3d ed., Irwin, Homewood, Ill., 1987.

69. Stephen P. Robbins, *Organizational Theory: The Structure and Design of Organizations,* Prentice-Hall, Englewood Cliffs, N.J., 1983.

70. Tom Peters, "Letter to the Editor," *INC.,* April 1988, pp. 80–82.

ACKNOWLEDGMENTS

Table

Table 1: Kenneth W. Thomas, "Toward Multi-Dimensional Values in Teaching: The Example of Conflict Behaviors," *Academy of Management Review,* vol. 2, 1977, p. 487.

Figure

Figure 2: Rensis Likert, *New Patterns of Management,* McGraw-Hill, Inc., 1961, p. 113. Reproduced by permission of McGraw-Hill, Inc.

CONCLUDING CASE

BEN & JERRY'S THRIVES ON COMPANY SPIRIT

Known for its rich ice cream generously laced with tasty tidbits and for its black-and-white cow logo, Ben & Jerry's Homemade, Inc., began simply enough as an ice cream parlor in a renovated gas station. When it opened in 1978 in Burlington, Vermont, it was a social experiment. Cofounders Ben Cohen and Jerry Greenfield wanted to demonstrate that their business could operate differently from many others. They believed that it could be unconventional, share its prosperity with employees, interact responsibly with the community, and still do well from a business standpoint. In fact, they intended to sell the business as soon as it was established and they had proved their point.

But things didn't turn out quite as they planned. Happily, the ice cream was an instant success. The magnitude of the business success, though, caused philosophical problems for Ben and Jerry. Jerry even left the company for 3 years. Ben put the company up for sale until another entrepreneur persuaded him to use the profits for social change.

As the company grew, Ben and Jerry worked hard to foster fun, charity, goodwill toward coworkers, and the feeling of a small, close-knit group. The company founded Ben & Jerry's Foundation, Inc., which receives 7.5 percent of the company's pretax income and spends it on various social causes. Ben & Jerry's has a 5-to-1 salary ratio, whereby the highest salaries paid cannot equal more than five times the lowest. Even Ben and Jerry have salaries that abide by the ratio. For example, each received only $83,000 in salary in 1991. The same year, the company had revenues in excess of $97 million and profits of $3.7 million. This provision has meant that some upper-level managers from other companies had to take pay cuts when they came to work for Ben & Jerry's. It has also sometimes made it difficult to recruit managers.

In the process of making ice cream, the company tries to be a model employer. Among its programs are hiring the handicapped; providing for free therapy sessions, including drug and alcohol counseling for any worker; and taking employees on all-company trips to see baseball and hockey games. As a result, dedication to the company runs high among the workers.

The rapid growth of the company has sometimes led to crises. On one occasion, a new machine to automatically fill pints did not work and production fell behind. Everyone—including Ben and Jerry—worked the production line to fill orders. Some workers made dinner for the rest of the staff, and pizzas were ordered. As always, the group spirit came through.

The group spirit that characterizes the company is further reflected in the monthly staff meetings, which all the approximately 400 employees are invited to attend. The meetings, held in the receiving bay of the Waterbury plant, usually begin at 8 a.m. on a Friday with fresh coffee and donuts for all. Looking in on one of these occasions, an observer sees more than 150 managers and workers sitting on folding chairs. Most are wearing jeans. Ben is absent, but Jerry is there. Jerry begins with some routine reports. He talks of Ben's effort to open an ice cream parlor in Moscow, with profits earmarked for east-west exchange programs. He gives the latest on another of Ben's ideas, the plan to refurbish and maintain a New York City subway station for a year, a project that has run into considerable bureaucracy, as well as transit authority debate.

Since his return to the company, Jerry has been attempting to serve as keeper of Ben & Jerry's spiritual soul (his title is "Minister of Joy"). At the staff meeting, he talks about joy and proposes a joy committee charged with putting more joy into the workday. No one laughs. He asks if anyone is interested. The group applauds as hands go up.

In the old days, Ben kept himself informed through the monthly staff meetings. Employees would break into small groups and provide input on solutions to problems. Lately, the meetings are characterized by one-way communication from Ben and other managers. Recently, Ben attempted to institute the old format by posing the question: "What are the most pressing problems confronting us?" One manager who spent a night helping Ben categorize the responses said, "It was like having this 8-ton dump truck back up and dump its load over you." The message to Ben was that the employees were beginning to feel left out. They wanted to know where the company was heading and what the company wanted to be.*

* Based on Erik Larson, "Forever Young," *INC.*, July 1988, pp. 50–62; N. R. Kleinfield, "Wntd: C.F.O. with 'Flair for Funk,'" *The New York Times*, Mar. 26, 1989, p. D5; Joe Queenan, "Purveying Yuppie Porn," *Forbes*, Nov. 13, 1989, pp. 60–64; Howard Kurtz, "Ben & Jerry: Premium Ice Cream Sprinkled with Liberal Ideology," *The Washington Post*, Nov. 29, 1989, p. A3; Maxine Lipner, "Ben & Jerry's: Sweet Ethics Evince Social Awareness," *COMPASS Readings*, July 1991, pp. 22–30; and Fleming Meeks, "We All Scream for Rice and Beans," *Forbes*, Mar. 30, 1992, p. 20.

QUESTIONS FOR
CONCLUDING CASE

1   What group norms are evident
    at Ben & Jerry's?

2   What factors have contributed
    to the development of high
    cohesiveness among Ben &
    Jerry's employees? What is your
    prognosis for the future?

3   What could Ben and Jerry do in
    attempting to preserve some of
    the positive aspects of group
    dynamics at Ben & Jerry's?

CONCLUDING CASE

PERPETUAL-LEARNING TEAMS OPERATE GE FACTORY IN PUERTO RICO

At the new GE factory in Bayamón, Puerto Rico, the organization structure is extremely flat. There are only three layers: the factory manager, 15 salaried "advisers," and 172 hourly workers. The factory produces arresters, which are surge protectors that guard power stations and transmission lines against lightning strikes.

At Bayamón, every hourly worker is on a team consisting of about 10 employees. Each team "owns" a part of the process, such as assembly, shipping, or receiving. Since the members of each team work in different areas of the plant, they represent operations that provide input to or receive output from the part of the process owned by the team. Team members meet weekly to discuss various issues. A salaried adviser attends the meeting as a resource person, answering questions when queried by members of the team.

What is particularly unique about the Bayamón factory is the institutionalized perpetual learning. Hourly employees change jobs every 6 months, rotating through the four main work areas. In this way, workers learn how their jobs affect every other operation in the plant. To encourage the continual learning, the firm pays workers for their skill, knowledge, and business performance. After each 6-month rotation they receive a 25-cent-an-hour raise. They can then select a "major," such as machine maintenance or quality control, and double their pay. They can receive additional pay by passing courses in English, business practices, and the like. Further, perfect attendance and plantwide performance can result in bonuses of $225 or more each quarter. Promotions and layoffs are decided by skill level, not seniority. This is to motivate the employees to higher skill levels.

After only a year and a half of operation, the work force is 20 percent more productive than its nearest company equivalent in General Electric. The prediction is that productivity will continue to rise at least 20 percent in the next year.*

QUESTIONS FOR CONCLUDING CASE

1 What is the role of groups at the factory in Bayamón, Puerto Rico?
2 Explain how group norms are being established at the factory.
3 When the factory reaches the "performing stage," what changes may take place?

* Rahul Jacob, "The Search for the Organization of Tomorrow," *Fortune*, May 18, 1992, pp. 93–94.

CHAPTER 11

Managerial
Control
Methods

GAINING THE EDGE

USAA PLACES A PREMIUM ON HIGH-QUALITY SERVICE

When it comes to stellar service, few organizations can equal the United Services Automobile Association (USAA). The San Antonio–based company is the fifth-largest insurer of privately owned automobiles and homes in the United States and is increasingly making inroads in the financial services area. Member-owned USAA has 2.2 million customers, most of whom are active or retired military officers and their dependents. Almost 95 percent of active-duty military officers are USAA members. By law, the company's financial services must be offered to the general public.

USAA was started in 1922 by Army officers who experienced difficulty obtaining auto insurance because they were perceived as poor risks. By the time Robert F. McDermott, a former pilot and retired Air Force brigadier general, took over as CEO in the late 1960s, the company had a good reputation for offering low-cost insurance and paying claims. Service, however, was abysmal—particularly in the promptness category. There was paper everywhere, including files, correspondence, and claims relating to the 650,000 members at the time. In fact, so much paperwork was habitually lost that the company typically had between 200 and 300 college students on the payroll who worked each night searching the desks of the 3000 employees for missing files.

To help improve service, McDermott quickly steered the company toward the use of new technology. A new computer system soon slashed the time required to process a new automobile policy from 13 days to 3. Since then, USAA has pioneered the use of imaging systems that store documents on optical disks. In the property and casualty division, for example, the system scans 40,000 pages of mail per day. As a result, a USAA representative can instantly call up correspondence and other parts of a customer's file on a computer screen. Because the company depends on direct mail and advertising instead of outside agents, almost 90 percent of its business is conducted by telephone. An 800 number is provided for customers.

McDermott also broke down barriers between departments and decentralized operations. Policy writing and service, two main divisions that barely communicated with each other, were reorganized into five groups. Each group served one-fifth of the members. Once the groups began to compete with each other in offering the best service, USAA was never the same again.

The company's strategy for high-quality service includes the process of empowering employees. One aspect of this process involves providing employees with increased knowledge. USAA has 75 classrooms, more than 200 full-time instructors, and a training and education budget of $19 million. Service representatives receive at least 16 weeks of training before they begin answering customer telephone calls. That way, they are prepared to answer most questions, even those that involve less common situations. A strong tuition reimbursement program, as well as night college classes offered on the premises, encourage employees to obtain degrees and work toward various certifications in the insurance industry. Another aspect of the empowering process entails giving service representatives considerable authority so that they can handle situations without checking with supervisors.

The Family of Measures (FOM) program is used to keep the work force focused on continual improvement of service quality. For example, service representatives are scored on the quality of phone calls. The scoring is done by auditors who periodically monitor the telephone lines. The representatives are also rated on the number of transactions per hour. "What we're trying to have is a teaching and coaching tool. We're not looking to find fault," says Gerald L. Gass, director of quality measurement and improvement. An FOM for each work unit is developed by a representative group of employees who determine which aspects of the job are most important to track. They ask questions such as "Is the activity under our control? Does it involve some form of data that we can collect? Can we easily analyze the results?" The group then votes on the measures to be used and passes the recommendations to managers, who may make some adjustments before implementing the measures. In addition, an independent team of 14 organizational experts continually evaluates the company, one division at a time, with an eye to areas where innovations and continual improvements can be made.

To help retain its well-trained work force, USAA typically promotes from within. Every year, about 45 percent of employees are promoted and about 50 percent change jobs within the company. The movement broadens employee experience, encourages flexibility, fosters innovation, and enriches jobs. To help employees meet child-care and other personal needs, USAA has an arrangement whereby 70 percent of the work force works a 38-hour, 4-day workweek. The company is located on a 286-acre campus that offers subsidized cafeterias and a health club. The turnover rate of about 7 percent is half the industry average.

USAA has increased the assets that it owns and manages from $200 million to more than $20 billion since McDermott took over the helm. In noting that USAA profits are among the highest in the insurance industry, McDermott says, "But service comes first."[1]

When McDermott became CEO, he quickly recognized that a key element in the future success of USAA would be the ability to offer excellent service. As one part of his effort, he instituted a variety of controls, particularly in the area of quality control, to ensure that excellent service would be achieved. In this chapter, we focus on specific methods that managers use to maintain control in organizations. Although many control systems must be custom-designed, most organizations share a common need for certain systems. Accordingly, we first describe the general nature of six major control systems that organizations are apt to require to some degree. Throughout the remainder of the chapter, we explore four of these systems in greater depth. In considering quality control systems, we examine the prospects of promoting innovation through the use of quality improvement teams and benchmarking.

MAJOR CONTROL SYSTEMS

If you decided to investigate the major control systems in prominent business organizations such as IBM, RJR Nabisco, or American Express, you would likely find the systems shown in Figure 1.[2] Since the purpose of control systems is to increase the probability of meeting organizational goals and standards, managers use these systems to boost their prospects for success. For example, financial control systems help managers keep track of important overall money matters, such as whether the organization is making a profit or taking on too much debt. Budgetary control systems assist managers by giving them quantitative tools for monitoring how closely the revenues and costs of various organizational activities match what has been planned. Quality control systems provide a means of assessing the quality of products and services, an increasingly important competitive

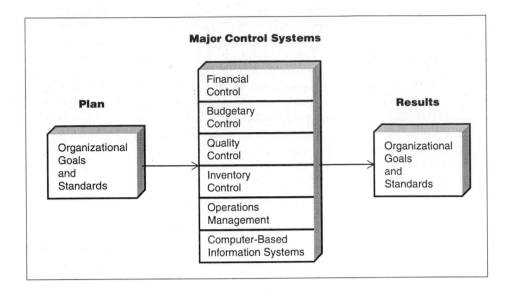

Figure 1 *Major organizational control systems.*

issue. Inventory control systems offer a way to ensure that necessary inputs are available when needed and that the costs involved are kept at a minimum. Operations management involves controlling the processes associated with actually producing a product or service. Finally, computer-based information systems are used to develop sophisticated systems geared toward maintaining better control over information and related functions.

For the remainder of this chapter, we concentrate on financial, budgetary, quality, and inventory control systems. Before considering each one individually, we explore how these systems differ in terms of the level of management to which they are mainly oriented and their timing emphasis.

Managerial Level

Control systems tend to differ somewhat in the degree to which they are used by different managerial levels (see Figure 2). For example, financial control systems are a primary control mechanism used by top-level management because such systems relate mainly to the overall financial health of the organization. However, middle managers also have an interest in monitoring financial matters as

Figure 2 *Major control systems by managerial level and timing.*

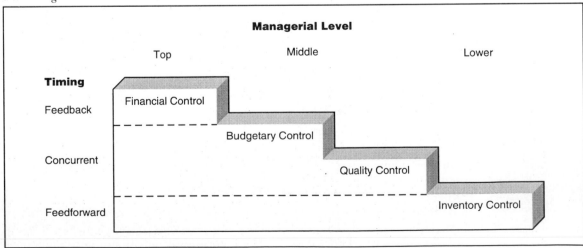

they affect their particular specialized area. On the other hand, middle and lower-level managers make the main use of budgetary controls, since it is typically their job to run organizational activities so that various budgets are met. Still, top management may monitor overall budget performance, as well as major deviations from what is expected. When it comes to quality, related control is mainly the responsibility of lower-level managers, since they are the ones who work primarily at the operational level, where product and service quality is directly affected. Middle and top managers may also be interested in trends in quality, but they are less involved in the hands-on issues. Finally, inventory control rests largely with lower-level and middle managers, although upper management may use some indexes to evaluate costs.

Timing Emphasis

Major control systems also lean toward different emphases on timing. Timing relates to the degree to which controls take place before (feedforward), during (concurrent), or after (feedback) the transformation process that produces a product or service. Financial control systems tend to constitute feedback control because the data are usually evaluated at the end of particular reporting periods. Although it is too late at that point to make changes that will affect the particular data, the information is useful in planning changes that can affect future organizational performance and results. In contrast, budgetary control often has more of a concurrent focus, since it can be used to regulate ongoing activities so that planned budget levels are met. For example, budgets may be checked during expenditure decisions. To the degree that budgets are considered only at the end of particular periods, budgetary control moves closer to being a form of feedback control. At the same time, quality control is increasingly used as concurrent control, since checks are often made during the actual production or service process to be sure that quality standards are being met. If checks are not made until after production, when materials must be scrapped or rejected if they are faulty, quality control fits into the feedback category. Finally, inventory control is mainly oriented toward feedforward control, because it is geared to ensuring that materials and products will be available when needed. In the remaining sections of this chapter, we consider these major control systems in greater detail.

FINANCIAL CONTROL

Suppose that you are a top manager at a giant organization such as RJR Nabisco. What types of financial controls could you use? In this section, we review some of the more common financial control techniques, including the use of financial statements, ratio analysis, and comparative financial analysis. We also consider how managers can avoid some of the major pitfalls associated with financial controls.

Financial Statements

Financial statement A summary of a major aspect of an organization's financial status

A **financial statement** is a summary of a major aspect of an organization's financial status. The information contained in such statements is essential in maintaining financial control over organizations. Two basic types of financial statements that are typically used by business organizations are the balance sheet and the income statement.[3] Financial statements are typically prepared at the end of reporting periods, such as quarterly and annually, although the widespread availability of computers is facilitating more frequent preparation.

Balance sheet A financial statement that depicts an organization's assets and claims against those assets at a given point in time

BALANCE SHEET A **balance sheet** is a financial statement that depicts an organization's assets and claims against those assets at a given point in time.[4] A balance sheet for The Limited, Inc., is shown in Table 1. You may find it helpful to think of a balance sheet as a financial "snapshot" that is made up of two main sections. The top half shows current assets, and the bottom half documents existing claims against assets.[5]

Assets, the resources that an organization controls, fall into two main categories: current and fixed. *Current assets* consist of cash and other assets that are usually converted to cash or are used within 1 year. (Examples are marketable securities, such as U.S. Treasury bills or money market mutual funds that can be

---

TABLE 1

THE LIMITED, INC.

Comparative Balance Sheet
January 28, 1989 and February 3, 1990
(in thousands of dollars)

	1990	1989
ASSETS		
Current assets:		
Cash and equivalents	$ 21,734	$ 15,276
Accounts receivable	596,171	531,461
Inventories	482,136	407,006
Other	63,703	69,851
Total current assets	$1,163,744	$1,023,594
Fixed assets:		
Property and equipment, net	1,172,688	1,066,646
Other assets	82,054	55,266
Total assets	$2,418,486	$2,145,506
LIABILITIES AND SHAREHOLDERS' EQUITY		
Current liabilities:		
Accounts payable	$ 175,319	$ 189,184
Accrued expenses	239,921	189,579
Income taxes	62,980	77,192
Total current liabilities	$ 478,220	$ 455,955
Long-term debt	445,674	517,952
Other long-term liabilities	39,280	26,499
Deferred income taxes	214,858	198,893
Total liabilities	$1,178,032	$1,199,299
Shareholders' equity:		
Common stock	$ 94,863	$ 94,863
Paid-in capital	196,232	203,693
Retained earnings	1,168,842	879,386
Less treasury stock at cost	(219,483)	(231,735)
Total shareholders' equity	$1,240,454	$ 946,207
Total liabilities and shareholders' equity	$2,418,486	$2,145,506

Source: From Robert K. Eskew and Daniel L. Jensen, *Financial Accounting,* 4th ed., McGraw-Hill, New York, 1992, p. 686.

converted to cash within a relatively short period; accounts receivable, which are sales on credit for which payment has not yet been received; and inventory. *Fixed assets* are assets that have a useful life that exceeds 1 year (such as property, buildings, and equipment). In the case of The Limited, the balance sheet indicates that the company has $1.16 billion in current assets and $1.17 billion in fixed assets, such as property and equipment, including other miscellaneous assets. Total assets are $2.4 billion.

The bottom half of the balance sheet, devoted to claims, includes both liabilities and shareholders' equity. *Liabilities* are claims by nonowners against company assets (in other words, debts owed to nonowners, such as banks). Liabilities also fall into two categories: current and long-term. *Current liabilities* are accounts that are typically paid within 1 year (such as accounts payable—current bills the company must pay—and short-term loans). *Long-term liabilities* are debts usually paid over a period that exceeds 1 year (such as bonds). The Limited, Inc. has $478 million in current liabilities and $700 million in long-term liabilities, for a total of $1.18 billion in liabilities.

Shareholders' equity represents claims by owners against the assets. As you might expect, shareholders' equity is equal to the company's assets minus liabilities. Shareholders' equity is, in essence, the organization's net worth. It is represented on the balance sheet by stock and retained earnings (funds accumulated from the profits of the organization). In the case of The Limited, shareholders' equity is equal to $1.2 billion. Since shareholders' equity equals assets minus liabilities, by placing the assets ($2.4 billion) on the top and the liabilities and shareholders' equity ($1.18 billion plus $1.24 billion, for a total of $2.4 billion) on the bottom, the balance sheet "balances." By using a comparative balance sheet, which shows figures from one year to the next (as in Table 1), it is possible to track trends in the growth of assets, the state of liabilities, and current net worth.

Income statement A financial statement that summarizes the financial results of company operations over a specified time period, such as a quarter or a year

INCOME STATEMENT The balance sheet focuses on the overall financial worth of the organization at a specific point in time. In contrast, an **income statement** is a financial statement that summarizes the financial results of company operations over a specified time period, such as a quarter or a year. An income statement shows revenues and expenses. *Revenues* are the assets derived from selling goods and services. *Expenses* are the costs incurred in producing the revenue (such as cost of goods sold, operating expenses, interest expense, and taxes). The difference between revenues and expenses represents the profits or losses over a given period of time and is often referred to as the *bottom line*.

As with balance sheets, income statements for different periods of time are frequently compared. A comparative income statement for The Limited, Inc., is shown in Table 2. The statement indicates that net income (revenues minus expenses) is about $347 million, up from about $245 million the previous year.

Ratio Analysis

Ratio analysis The process of determining and evaluating financial ratios

In assessing the significance of various financial data, managers often engage in **ratio analysis,** the process of determining and evaluating financial ratios.[6] A *ratio* is an index that measures one variable relative to another, and it is usually expressed as a percentage or a rate. The notion of a ratio will become clearer as we consider specific examples below. Ratios are meaningful only when compared with other information. Since they are often compared with industry data, ratios help managers understand their company's performance relative to that of competitors and are often used to track performance over time. Four types of financial ratios are particularly important to managerial control: liquidity, asset man-

TABLE 2

THE LIMITED, INC.

Income Statement
For the Years Ended December 31, 1988 and 1989
(in thousands of dollars)

	1989	1988
Net sales	$4,647,916	$4,070,777
Cost of goods sold, occupancy & buying costs	3,201,281	2,856,074
Gross income	$1,446,635	$1,214,703
General, administrative & store operating expenses	821,381	747,285
Operating income	625,254	467,418
Interest expense	(58,059)	(63,418)
Other income (expenses), net	6,731	(7,864)
Income before taxes	$ 573,926	$ 396,136
Provision for income taxes	227,000	151,000
Net income	$ 346,926	$ 245,136

Source: From Robert K. Eskew and Daniel L. Jensen, *Financial Accounting,* 4th ed., McGraw-Hill,
New York, 1992, p. 684.

Liquidity ratios Financial ratios that measure the degree to which an organization's current assets are adequate to pay current liabilities (current debt obligations)

agement, debt management, and profitability. Formulas and end-of-the-year data for The Limited for the four types of ratios are shown in Table 3.

LIQUIDITY RATIOS **Liquidity ratios** are financial ratios that measure the degree to which an organization's current assets are adequate to pay current liabilities (current debt obligations). A major liquidity ratio is the *current ratio,* which

TABLE 3 — Ratio Analysis for The Limited, Inc. (dollar amounts in thousands)

Ratio	Formula	Calculation		1989	1988
LIQUIDITY RATIOS					
Current ratio	$\dfrac{\text{Current assets}}{\text{Current liabilities}}$ =	$\dfrac{\$1,163,744}{\$478,220}$	=	2.43x	2.24x
ASSET MANAGEMENT RATIOS					
Inventory turnover	$\dfrac{\text{Cost of goods sold}}{\text{Inventory}}$ =	$\dfrac{\$3,201,281}{\$444,571}$	=	7.20x	7.51x
DEBT MANAGEMENT RATIOS					
Debt ratio	$\dfrac{\text{Total liabilities}}{\text{Total assets}}$ =	$\dfrac{\$478,220}{\$1,163,744}$	=	41.09%	44.54%
PROFITABILITY RATIOS					
Net profit margin	$\dfrac{\text{Net income}}{\text{Net sales}}$ =	$\dfrac{\$346,926}{\$4,647,916}$	=	7.5%	6.0%
Return on investment	$\dfrac{\text{Net income}}{\text{Total assets}}$ =	$\dfrac{\$381,994}{\$2,281,996}$	=	16.7%	14.0%

Source: From Robert K. Eskew and Daniel L. Jensen, *Financial Accounting,* 4th ed., McGraw-Hill, New York, 1992, pp. 686–700.

measures a company's ability to meet the claims of short-term creditors by using only current assets. The current ratio shown in Table 3 indicates that The Limited has $2.43 in current assets for every dollar in current.liabilities.

Asset management ratios
Financial ratios that measure how effectively an organization manages its assets

ASSET MANAGEMENT RATIOS **Asset management ratios** (sometimes called *activity ratios*) measure how effectively an organization manages its assets. One of the most used asset management ratios is inventory turnover.

Inventory turnover helps measure how well an organization manages its inventory. Low inventory turnover may point to either excess or obsolete inventory. High inventory turnover generally signals effective handling of inventory relative to selling patterns, because less money is tied up in inventory that is waiting to be sold. It is, of course, possible to have an inventory turnover ratio that is too high. This would be the case if significant sales are lost because items ordered by potential customers are out of stock. The Limited's turnover rate of 7.20 is above average for the industry.

Debt management ratios
Financial ratios that assess the extent to which an organization uses debt to finance investments, as well as the degree to which it is able to meet its long-term obligations

DEBT MANAGEMENT RATIOS **Debt management ratios** (often called *leverage ratios*) assess the extent to which an organization uses debt to finance investments, as well as the degree to which it is able to meet its long-term obligations. The more an organization uses debt to finance its needs, the more it must commit funds to pay interest and repay principal. As debts increase, so does the risk that the organization may not be able to pay its debts and may end up in bankruptcy. Thus one of the most important ratios is the *debt ratio,* which measures the percentage of total assets financed by debt (including current liabilities). The higher the percentage, the more the organization's assets are furnished by creditors rather than owners. The Limited's debt ratio of 41.09 percent (shown in Table 3) indicates that creditors have supplied about 41 cents of every dollar in assets. The Limited's debt ratio is probably reasonable for the industry. If a company's debt ratio becomes higher than average, future creditors may require a higher rate of return on their money because of the additional risk associated with the high debt ratio.

Profitability ratios Financial ratios that help measure management's ability to control expenses and earn profits through the use of organizational resources.

PROFITABILITY RATIOS **Profitability ratios** help measure management's ability to control expenses and earn profits through the use of organizational resources.[7] Two commonly used profitability ratios are net profit margin and return on investment.

The *net profit margin* indicates the percentage of each sales dollar that is left after deducting all expenses. In the case of The Limited, the net profit margin (shown in Table 3) is 7.5 percent. According to this figure, The Limited earns about 7½ cents on every dollar of sales.

The *return on investment,* or ROI (also called *return on assets*), measures the overall effectiveness of management in generating profits from its total investment in assets. The ROI for The Limited (shown in Table 3) is 16.7 percent. To raise it even higher, the company may want to consider either increasing sales relative to costs or reducing costs relative to sales.

Top managers in most major companies, including RJR Nabisco, make strong use of financial controls (see the following Case in Point discussion).

CASE IN POINT

GIANT RJR NABISCO GOES BY THE NUMBERS

Many of the brand names of RJR Nabisco, such as Oreo, Ritz, Premium, Planters, Life Savers, Camel, Winston, and Salem, are familiar to consumers in the United States and various other parts of the world. The company became RJR Nabisco in

1985, when R. J. Reynolds bought Nabisco Brands for $4.9 million. At the time, R. J. Reynolds was noted for its southern, genteel, methodical, take-care-of-the-people style of operating, while Nabisco Brands was regarded as a risk-taking, freewheeling, decentralized organization. The purchase has produced a blend of both styles at RJR Nabisco, although the company tends more toward the Nabisco Brands approach. For example, it requires few approvals to get jobs done, has few policies to which one must conform, and rewards managers well for good performance. To maintain control over the organization, yet allow managers considerable latitude in running their particular specialized areas, top management relies heavily on financial controls.

In fact, since the two companies were joined, RJR Nabisco has been literally run by the book when it comes to financial control. Each of the 173 unit managers prepares a report that is forwarded up the chain. The reports are then assembled into books for senior executives at various levels. Each division president gets a green book that depicts information concerning that division. Each member of the board of directors gets a blue book that includes a corporate summary. The chief executive officer gets a red book that outlines the problem areas in each reporting unit. The reports track such financial statement items as receivables, inventories, and working capital—all of which are considered critical indicators of the state of the business. Reportedly, newcomers have not looked forward to the reports, particularly the one to the CEO, because "it says nothing nice about no one."

With the takeover of RJR Nabisco by the leveraged-buyout firm Kohlberg Kravis Roberts in 1989, top management has more reason than ever to keep a close eye on the financial picture. Management has had to find ways to pay off the $25 billion debt associated with the takeover. So far, almost half the debt has been paid, but at heavy cost to the company's businesses. For example, price hikes on its Nabisco cookies and crackers helped retail stores' private-label brands gain a foothold during the recent recession. The company is fighting back with new products and smaller packages for the drugstore and convenience store market. RJR also faces difficulties in the tobacco business, its traditional cash cow, in part because of the growing public concern about the health hazards of tobacco.[8]   ■ ■ ■

Comparative Financial Analysis

Financial statements and ratios are more meaningful when managers can compare the data against some standard. Managers are expected to explain significant variances (positive and negative) from standards so that top-level managers can better understand why the variances are occurring and their implications. The three major standards that managers most often use to compare data are management goals, historical standards, and industry standards.

Management financial goals are frequently set during the planning process. Then they become standards against which actual achievements are compared during the control process. In the case of The Limited, top management usually sets goals for the year and then compares company performance with those goals.

In contrast to management goals, which project future standards, *historical financial standards* are financial data from past years' statements or ratios that are used as a basis for comparing the current year's financial performance. The balance sheet and income statement for The Limited, as well as the chart of the company's financial ratios, illustrate uses of historical standards since they include data from the previous year for comparison.

Another method of comparison is the use of *industry financial standards,* financial data based on averages for the industry. Financial ratios for a variety of industries are published by several sources, including Robert Morris Associates and Dun & Bradstreet.[9]

Financial data provide managers with major indicators about the overall direction of the organization. For example, Rupert Murdoch, who runs his Australia-based News Corporation, Ltd., from New York, makes heavy use of financial data to maintain control over his media holdings on four continents. Among the data he receives are weekly reports with itemized profit and loss figures for every single business, "whether it be from Perth, in western Australia, or in London or in San Antonio. Those figures," he says, "are what keeps us up to date." Modern communication systems and computers enable Murdoch to receive timely information from all over the world.[10] Still, while financial information helps identify problem areas, managers must investigate beyond the numbers to determine the causes of the data's results before taking action.

Avoiding Financial Control Pitfalls

While financial controls can be extremely helpful to top management, there are six primary pitfalls that can short-circuit their usefulness (see Table 4).[11] One pitfall is relying on standard financial controls without tailoring them to the specific needs of the organization. For example, concentrating too much on the financial numbers helped blind Xerox's management to the coming intense competition from Japanese copy-machine makers. A second pitfall is failing to link the controls to the strategic planning process. Controls should help increase the prospects of realizing goals rather than constitute ends in themselves. A third potential problem is instituting controls that send mixed messages to managers. For example, it is sometimes difficult to maximize both return on investment and sales growth at the same time, because sales growth may involve spending extra money in the present to reap more sales in the future (thus lowering ROI in the short run). At Corning Glass Works, both the long-term and the short-term implications are considered in setting financial goals for the company's businesses. A fourth problem is allowing financial controls to stifle innovation and creativity by making it difficult to get financial backing for new ideas. During the mid-1970s, product development at Xerox, from inception to implementation, required more than 100 sign-offs before a proposal reached top management. A fifth pitfall is failing to meet subunit needs by forcing the same financial controls on various subunits and businesses that may be very different. Finally, when systems are too sophisticated, just providing information to the system can use up excessive managerial time. Reginald Jones, the previous chief at General Electric, used his financial background to change the company from being chronically short of cash to having tremendous financial strength. Unfortunately, the financial reporting got out of hand. The present chief financial officer, Dennis Dammerman, recounts that he had to stop computers in one GE

TABLE 4	**Six Potential Financial Control Pitfalls**

1. Failing to tailor financial controls to the specific requirements of the organization
2. Neglecting to link financial controls to the strategic planning process
3. Instituting controls that send mixed messages about desired behaviors
4. Allowing financial controls to stifle innovation and creativity
5. Forcing the same financial controls on various subunits that have different control requirements
6. Implementing financial controls that are too sophisticated for organizational needs

business from producing seven daily reports, one of which was 12 feet high and contained sales data on hundreds of thousands of items, accurate to the penny.[12]

BUDGETARY CONTROL

Budgeting The process of stating in quantitative terms, usually dollars, planned organizational activities for a given period of time

While financial controls are a major tool of top management, budgetary controls are a mainstay for middle managers. Lower-level managers also use budgets to help track progress in their own units. **Budgeting** is the process of stating in quantitative terms, usually dollars, planned organizational activities for a given period of time. Budgets, the quantitative statements prepared through the budgeting process, may include such figures as projected income, expenditures, and profits. Budgets are useful because they provide a means of translating diverse activities and outcomes into a common measure, such as dollars.

Budgets are typically prepared for the organization as a whole, as well as for various subunits (such as divisions and departments). For budgetary purposes, organizations define subunits as responsibility centers.

Responsibility Centers

Responsibility center A subunit headed by a manager who is responsible for achieving one or more goals

A **responsibility center** is a subunit headed by a manager who is responsible for achieving one or more goals.[13] In fact, organizations can be thought of as forming a hierarchy of responsibility centers, ranging from small subunits at the bottom to large ones at the top. For example, the local AT&T phone store and the marketing division of AT&T are responsibility centers at different levels of the organization. There are five main types of responsibility centers: standard cost centers, discretionary expense centers, revenue centers, profit centers, and investment centers. The particular designation that a unit receives for budgetary purposes depends on how much control the unit has over the major elements, such as revenues and expenses, that contribute to profits and return on investment.

Standard cost center A responsibility center whose budgetary performance depends on achieving its goals by operating within standard cost constraints

STANDARD COST CENTERS A **standard cost center** is a responsibility center whose budgetary performance depends on achieving its goals by operating within standard cost constraints. Because standard costs are often determined by using engineering methods, this type of center is also called an *engineered expense center*. With a standard cost center, managers face the challenge of controlling input costs (e.g., labor, raw materials) so that the costs do not exceed predetermined standards. For example, at RJR Nabisco, the bakery operations have standard costs for cracker production that are based on such factors as ingredients, expected breakage rates of between 5 and 7 percent, and an 8 percent "giveaway" rate (the overweight amount in an average package of Nabisco crackers).[14] Therefore, one measure of the efficiency of baking operations is the unit's ability to turn out the required number of boxes of crackers at a given level of quality within specified cost constraints. A standard cost center is appropriate only if (1) standards for costs involved in producing a product or service can be estimated with reasonable accuracy and (2) the unit cannot be held directly responsible for profit levels because it does not have significant control over other expenses and/or revenues.

Discretionary expense center A responsibility center whose budgetary performance is based on achieving its goals by operating within predetermined expense constraints set through managerial judgment or discretion

DISCRETIONARY EXPENSE CENTERS A **discretionary expense center** is a responsibility center whose budgetary performance is based on achieving its goals by operating within predetermined expense constraints set through managerial judgment or discretion. Discretionary expense centers are commonly departments such as research and development, public relations, human resources, and legal units, in which it is difficult to determine standard costs or to measure the direct profit impact of the unit's efforts.

Revenue center A responsibility center whose budgetary performance is measured primarily by its ability to generate a specified level of revenue

REVENUE CENTERS A **revenue center** is a responsibility center whose budgetary performance is measured primarily by its ability to generate a specified level of revenue. Prime examples of revenue centers are sales and marketing divisions, which are typically evaluated on the sales (and thus revenues) that they generate in relation to the level of resources that they are allocated. For example, Nabisco's cookies are delivered directly to supermarkets and other outlets by combination driver-salespersons, who are part of revenue centers. They can influence revenues but have little control over the costs of the products they handle.[15] Revenue centers are used when the unit in question is responsible for revenues but does not have control over all the costs associated with a product or service, which makes it difficult to hold the unit responsible for profit levels.

Profit center A responsibility center whose budgetary performance is measured by the difference between revenues and costs—in other words, profits

PROFIT CENTERS A **profit center** is a responsibility center whose budgetary performance is measured by the difference between revenues and costs—in other words, profits. Profit centers are appropriate only when the organizational unit in question has significant control over both costs and revenues, since these are the elements that ultimately affect profit levels. At RJR Nabisco, large divisions, such as Reynolds Tobacco USA, are considered profit centers because they have major control over both costs and revenues.[16] Organizations as a whole are also considered to be profit centers.

Investment center A responsibility center whose budgetary performance is based on return on investment

INVESTMENT CENTERS An **investment center** is a responsibility center whose budgetary performance is based on return on investment. The ROI ratio, discussed earlier in this chapter, entails not only revenues and costs but also the assets involved in producing a profit. Thus investment centers motivate managers to concern themselves with making good decisions about investments in facilities and other assets. Of course, this type of center works best if the unit has at least some control over investment decisions, as well as over both revenues and expenses. For example, at General Electric, businesses such as its aircraft engine, broadcasting (NBC), and major appliance divisions are operated as investment centers.[17]

USES OF RESPONSIBILITY CENTERS The uses of responsibility centers depend to a great extent on the type of organization structure involved.[18] Standard cost centers, discretionary expense centers, and revenue centers are more often used with functional organization designs and with the functional units in a matrix design. Thus manufacturing or production units are likely to be treated as standard cost centers, while accounting, finance, and human resources are usually designated as discretionary expense centers. Sales or marketing units are normally considered to be revenue centers.

In contrast, with a divisional organization design, it is possible to use profit centers because the large divisions in such a structure usually have control over both the expenses and the revenues associated with profits. Of course, within divisions, various departments may operate as other types of responsibility centers. Major companies that operate their divisions as separate and autonomous businesses often use investment centers for budgetary purposes. At Hanson PLC, a British-based conglomerate, businesses are run as investment centers, although managers of operating units must obtain permission from superiors for all significant capital investments (see the following Case in Point discussion).

CASE IN POINT

BUDGETS ARE SACRED AT HANSON PLC

At budget time, Hanson managers from all over the world go to Iselin, New Jersey, or London to present their cost and revenue projections for the forth-coming year to the senior management of Hanson PLC. This sprawling transatlantic conglomerate has products ranging from Jacuzzi whirlpool baths and Smith Corona typewriters to bricks and cement. Hanson has grown to be Britain's seventh-largest business empire by following a simple formula: Buy undervalued companies with poor management in mature industries, and then improve the management practices. In the process, Hanson typically sells off some businesses of the acquired companies and keeps others, particularly low-technology businesses that do not require continual major capital expenditures. For more than 20 years, Hanson has posted record profits. Its earnings per share have frequently been as high as 38 percent annually, although they have been somewhat lower recently.

Hanson has a reputation for granting a great deal of autonomy to local managers, yet the company maintains control through budgets. At Hanson, budgets are considered sacred. For each business, "it's a promise from the operating CEO to us," says one senior vice president. In the United States alone, some 150 Hanson investment centers file monthly and quarterly reports to their Iselin headquarters. The reports, a little more than a yard high when stacked up, are generally considered to be the company bible. Several group vice presidents and their controllers review the reports, which show how pretax profits and other financial data compare with budget projections. One expectation is that Hanson managers will produce a pretax payback on investment in 3 years. For meeting their return on investment targets, the managers are rewarded well with bonuses that can be as much as 60 percent of base pay.

At Hanson, capital expenditures are very closely controlled. Every capital investment of $1000 or more must be approved by headquarters. Such requests occasion close perusal by company accountants. If a manager argues that an investment in more efficient machinery will reduce labor costs, the manager must furnish the names of employees who will be cut from the payroll as a result. Critics argue that such tight control discourages managers from requesting capital investments that may be important for future earnings. Still, the Hanson brand of budgetary control has produced a number of successes. For example, Smith Corona was operating in the red under SCM but flourished with Hanson, allowing Hanson to sell some of SCM's assets at premium prices.[19] ■ ■ ■

Types of Budgets

To maintain budgetary control, organizations usually have a master budget that includes a number of other budgets that together summarize the planned activities of the organization. Two major types of budgets that are typically included in the master budget are operating budgets and capital expenditures budgets.[20]

Operating budget A statement that presents the financial plan for each responsibility center during the budget period and reflects operating activities involving revenues and expenses

OPERATING BUDGETS An **operating budget** is a statement that presents the financial plan for each responsibility center during the budget period and reflects operating activities involving revenues and expenses.[21] The overall operating budget allows management to assess the resulting profit levels after taking into consideration the anticipated revenues and expenses across the responsibility centers.[22] If profits are too small, managers can plan actions that will raise revenues (such as conducting marketing promotions to increase sales) and/or reduce expenses (such as cutting proposed expenditures for travel or delaying the purchase of nonessential equipment).

Capital expenditures budget
A plan for the acquisition or divestiture of major fixed assets, such as land, buildings, or equipment

CAPITAL EXPENDITURES BUDGETS　A **capital expenditures budget** is a plan for the acquisition or divestiture of major fixed assets, such as land, buildings, or equipment. Acquisitions of such assets are often referred to as *capital investments*. Since capital investments must be paid for over a long period of time and companies often borrow to cover the investments, they represent important organizational decisions. As a result, top-level managers are usually heavily involved, and the decision process often includes the board of directors. During the 1970s, many companies in energy-related businesses made heavy capital investments on the premise that oil prices would continue to rise in the 1980s. When prices plunged instead, many of these companies experienced acute difficulties because they did not have sufficient revenue to pay the long-term obligations associated with their capital investments.[23]

Impacts of the Budgeting Process

Depending on how they are used, budgets can have either positive or negative effects on managerial behavior in organizations. On the positive side, budgets can help keep managers informed about organizational activities and enhance coordination across various units. They can also provide standards against which managers' efforts will be evaluated, and they can offer a means of making adjustments when corrective action is needed. Yet budgets can also have negative effects, particularly if they are used in a rigid manner and managers have concerns about fair treatment. Poorly run budgetary processes sometimes produce negative managerial behaviors. These include politicking to increase budget allocations, overstating needs so that allocations will be increased, and abandoning potential innovations because the fight for resources is too formidable.[24]

QUALITY CONTROL

While budgetary control and financial control are typically given considerable emphasis in most organizations, the issue of quality control is currently receiving greater attention than it did in the past. This is largely because a number of companies based in Japan and elsewhere are making serious inroads into U.S. and global markets by offering products and services of superior quality. As a result, in a Gallup poll, top executives of major U.S. companies rated improvements in service quality and product quality as the most critical challenges currently facing their companies.[25]

Quality　The totality of features and characteristics of a product or service that bear on its ability to satisfy stated or implied needs

Although quality has been defined in many ways, the American Society for Quality Control offers this standard definition: **Quality** is the totality of features and characteristics of a product or service that bear on its ability to satisfy stated or implied needs.[26] This definition recognizes that quality can involve every aspect of a product or service, that quality affects the ability of a product or service to satisfy needs, and that customer needs for quality may not always be explicitly stated. The Malcolm Baldrige National Quality award created by Congress in 1987 is the most prestigious recognition of quality in the United States. The award is given annually to U.S. companies in manufacturing, service, and small-business categories that represent the best in quality management. (For one such company, see the Valuing Quality box.) In examining the issue of quality and the need for quality control, we explore the strategic implications of

VALUING QUALITY

Federal Express Absolutely Positively Controls Quality

When Federal Express won the Malcolm Baldridge National Quality award in 1990, it was the first service company to do so. Since its inception in 1973, FedEx has become the domestic leader in guaranteed overnight delivery, primarily on the basis of its philosophy, "People, Service, and Profit." FedEx continues to expand its vision of quality. Efforts in this direction include refining its measure of customer satisfaction—a critical element in its reputation for excellent service. Now, FedEx's

performance is measured each day on 12 service quality indicators, known as SQIs. The SQIs encompass service missteps and are weighted according to their likelihood of resulting in customer dissatisfaction. For example, a late delivery on the right day is given 1 point, while a lost package or a damaged package each receives 10 points.

The SQIs are measured by a variety of information systems and human analysis. The computerized tracking system COSMOS, which collects package data worldwide on a daily basis, measures the indices "Right Day Late" and "Wrong Day Late." Such measurement is possible because as packages

change hands in the delivery process, each package's bar code is scanned. Couriers have hand-held computers, called SuperTrackers, which they use to scan packages and record related information. Even if a package is only a minute late, COSMOS will record a late delivery point. Each day the SQI score is televised to every Federal Express location. The rating helps keep employees focused on the goal of 100 percent customer satisfaction. Quality action teams throughout FedEx work to solve the causes of service problems. They also work to invent innovative ways to improve service still further so that packages "absolutely positively" arrive on time.[27]

quality, the concept of total quality control, quality improvement teams, benchmarking, and statistical aids to quality management.

Strategic Implications of Quality

Quality expert David A. Garvin argues that quality can be used in a strategic way to compete effectively.[28] Choosing an appropriate quality strategy, though, depends on thoroughly understanding the important dimensions of quality. Therefore, we explore these dimensions before considering the issue of how to compete through quality.

EIGHT DIMENSIONS   From a strategic point of view, there are eight dimensions of quality that are important.

Performance involves a product's primary operating characteristics. For an automobile, performance would include acceleration, braking, handling, and fuel usage. In service industries, such as fast-food restaurants, airlines, or hotels, performance is apt to mean prompt service.[29]

Features are supplements to the basic functioning characteristics of the product or service. Examples include complimentary newspapers for hotel guests, extra options on autofocus cameras, or stereo tape decks in automobiles.

Reliability addresses the probability of a product's not working properly or breaking down altogether within a specific period. Since a significant period of usage is typically involved in assessing reliability, this quality dimension does not apply as readily to products and services that are used immediately. Reliability is becoming increasingly important, particularly for major items such as home appliances. It was a significant factor when General Electric introduced its new SpaceCenter 27 refrigerator. The appliance, with crushed-ice and cold-water dispensers on the door, had a revolutionary new rotary compressor that provided the cooling. Unfortunately, some of the new compressors failed, particularly in warm-weather states such as Florida. While working to resolve the bugs in its rotary compressor, GE switched back to the standard reciprocating compressor used by the competition, and it replaced compressors in refrigerators already sold. The company took these expensive steps because it did not want to ruin its carefully cultivated reputation for quality.[30]

Conformance refers to the degree to which a product's design or operating characteristics conform to preestablished standards. Typically, products and services are developed with some standards or specifications in mind. Conformance to specifications was an issue when the Michigan-based Van Dresser Corporation showed Toyota engineers a prototype part designed for use in the automaker's Kentucky plant. One Toyota engineer got "down on his hands and knees measuring the gap" between the automobile's steel door frame and the interior panel by Dresser. The engineer said, "Look, the gap is a millimeter too wide." Van Dresser retooled the mold that produced the panel.[31]

Durability is a measure of how much use a person gets from a product before it deteriorates or breaks down to such a point that replacement makes more sense than continual repair. For instance, durability for major home appliances varies widely, ranging from 5.8 to 18 years for washing machines and from 6 to 17 years for vacuum cleaners.[32]

Serviceability refers to the promptness, courtesy, proficiency, and ease of repair. In a Florida Power & Light (FP&L) Company push for quality, the utility has developed a number of unique computer programs, one of which geographically groups customer complaints about blackouts. After comparing the location of the customers against service routes, the computer system automatically figures out whether the problem is a downed line, disabled transformer, or blown household fuse. The system has helped FP&L cut the average duration of blackouts from 70 minutes to 48.[33]

Aesthetics refers to how a product looks, feels, sounds, tastes, or smells—all subjective issues highly dependent on personal judgment and preference. Recognizing the importance of aesthetics, Herman Miller, Inc., an office-furniture maker, places a great deal of emphasis on ensuring that its products are artistically attractive and functional.[34]

Perceived quality refers to individuals' subjective assessments of product or service quality. Such assessments may be based on incomplete information, but often it is perceptions that count with customers. For this reason, Honda, which produces cars in Marysville, Ohio, and Sony, which makes television sets in San Diego, have been reticent about noting that their products are "made in America." Ironically, they fear that their U.S. products will be perceived as lower in quality than counterparts made in Japan.[35]

COMPETING ON QUALITY   While some dimensions of quality reinforce one another, others do not. For example, adding more features will often reduce reliability, while aesthetics sometimes interferes with durability. As a result, organizations do not usually attempt to compete on exceptionally high quality on all eight dimensions simultaneously. In fact, competing on all the dimensions is generally not possible without charging very high prices. For example, a few products that probably do rank high on all eight dimensions, such as Cross pens, Rolex watches, and Rolls Royce automobiles, cost premium prices.

Consequently, companies must often make trade-offs among the quality dimensions. For example, Cray Research, a manufacturer of high-speed supercomputers, had to accept the fact that building its computers for maximum speed (a gain in performance) meant that the machines would likely fail every month or so (a sacrifice of reliability). Similarly, Japanese automobile manufacturers marketing in the United States often highlight the reliability (low repair rates) and conformance (good fits of parts and smooth finishes) of their cars, while deemphasizing the limited options in the features category.

In pursuing quality as a competitive advantage, then, most companies choose a quality niche rather than attempt to emphasize all eight dimensions simultaneously. Not surprisingly, it is critical to select a quality niche that customers consider important. After deregulation, AT&T assumed that customers equated expensive features with quality in telephones, but durability and reliability proved to be more important.[36] Of course, another crucial issue is actually delivering the intended level of quality, once it has been decided upon.

Total Quality Management

Total quality management (TQM) A quality control approach that emphasizes organizationwide commitment, integration of quality improvement efforts with organizational goals, and inclusion of quality as a factor in performance appraisals

To improve quality, a number of organizations, such as Xerox and Corning, are adopting a stance known as total quality management. **Total quality management (TQM)** is a quality control approach that emphasizes organizationwide commitment, integration of quality improvement efforts with organizational goals, and inclusion of quality as a factor in performance appraisals.[37] In essence, it highlights collective responsibility for the quality of products and services. It also encourages individuals in different, but related, departments (such as product design and manufacturing) to work together to improve quality.

Total quality management represents a change in the way quality is perceived. Traditionally, quality has been viewed in terms of the degree of deviation from standards that is deemed allowable for products and services. Speaking of U.S. suppliers, Osamu Nobuto, president of Mazda Motor Manufacturing, the U.S. unit of the Mazda Motor Corporation, complains, "It often seems that if something is 90 percent right, there is a tendency to believe that further improvement is either unnecessary or not worth the extra effort."[38] In contrast, the total quality management approach is aimed at achieving **zero defects,** a quality mentality in which the work force strives to make a product or service conform exactly to desired standards.[39]

Zero defects A quality mentality in which the work force strives to make a product or service conform exactly to desired standards

Although Japanese companies are generally credited with pioneering total quality management, the roots of the concept actually originated in the United States. American quality management expert W. Edwards Deming developed ideas on statistical methods for improving quality, but he took his concepts to Japan in the late 1940s after they were ignored in the United States. He also promoted the concept of involving employees and various units throughout the organization in the quality effort, and he set forth 14 management points that portray his overall philosophy. His ideas were embraced by Japanese companies, eager to rebuild after World War II. In fact, his contributions were so well appreciated that the Japanese established the Deming prize, a coveted annual award for excellence in quality management. In the 1950s, another American quality expert, J. M. Juran, also helped Japanese companies develop their total quality management efforts.[40] For some ideas about how to improve quality in organizations, see the Practically Speaking discussion, "Deming's 14 Points on How to Improve Quality."

An important aspect of TQM is its emphasis on the cost of quality, the cost of not doing things right the first time.[42] According to one estimate, the typical U.S. factory spends between 20 and 25 percent of its operating budget on finding and fixing mistakes.[43] Quality experts argue that if just some of these funds were spent on prevention, the number of mistakes that require fixing (and the associated costs) could be substantially lowered. This has been the case at Dow Chemical USA, which credits its 5-year quality improvement effort with saving $100 million in operating costs.[44] Similarly, total quality efforts have produced a 60 percent reduction in scrap and rework at Harley-Davidson, a 69 percent cut-

PRACTICALLY SPEAKING

DEMING'S 14 POINTS ON HOW TO IMPROVE QUALITY*

In the course of his work, W. Edwards Deming developed 14 management points that summarize what he believes managers, especially at the upper levels, must do to produce high-quality products:

1   Create and publish to all employees a statement of the aims and purposes of the

* Reprinted from *Out of the Crisis* by W. Edwards Deming, by permission of M.I.T. and W. Edwards Deming. Published by M.I.T., Center for Advanced Engineering Study, Cambridge, Mass. 02139. Copyright © 1986 by W. Edwards Deming.

company or other organization. The management must demonstrate constantly their commitment to this statement.

2   Learn the new philosophy, top management and everybody.

3   Understand the purpose of inspection, for improvement of processes and reduction of cost.

4   End the practice of awarding business on the basis of price tag alone.

5   Improve constantly and forever the system of production and service.

6   Institute training.

7   Teach and institute leadership.

8   Drive out fear. Create trust. Create a climate for innovation.

9   Optimize toward the aims and purposes of the company the efforts of teams, groups, staff areas.

10 Eliminate exhortations for the work force.

11 (a) Eliminate numerical quotas for production. Instead, learn and institute methods for improvement.
(b) Eliminate M. B. O. Instead, learn the capabilities of processes, and how to improve them.

12 Remove barriers that rob people of pride of workmanship.

13 Encourage education and self-improvement for everyone.

14 Take action to accomplish the transformation.[41]

---

back in customer returns at Westinghouse's semiconductor division, and savings of more than $52 million in 60 days at AT&T (by eliminating errors in service documents).[45] A total quality effort has also paid off handsomely for Spectrum Control, Inc. (see the following Case in Point discussion).

CASE IN POINT   UPGRADING QUALITY AT SPECTRUM CONTROL, INC.

When Thomas L. Venable, president and chairman of Spectrum Control, Inc., announced with fanfare a new companywide commitment to quality, Ed Leofsky, a process engineer at the company's Fairview, Pennsylvania, electromagnetic division, knew it was time to act. Each week, Leofsky's division solders terminals to about 75,000 tubular ceramic capacitors that are manufactured at Spectrum's material science division in nearby Saegertown. The capacitors are then used in one of the company's primary products, electronic filters.

Unfortunately, for the previous 12 years Leofsky had faced a chronic problem: for unknown reasons, the solder often would not stick. When that happened, all sorts of unusual steps had to be taken, such as inspecting each soldering point with a microscope. Leofsky's efforts to get a vice president at Saegertown interested in solving the problem got nowhere. Just as the quality program was being announced, the soldering problem grew worse. The reject rate jumped from 3 to 32 percent. Leofsky wrote a letter to the vice president at Saegertown, with copies to everyone he could think of who could help.

The letter got people's attention, including concern from Venable himself. Venable and others in top management had become seriously concerned about quality because of two events: a Japanese company had purchased a major competitor, and Spectrum's principal customers, such as Hewlett-Packard and IBM, had announced that they were adopting a zero-defects approach. In addition, Spectrum's sales and marketing personnel were complaining that the company was not very good at meeting delivery dates. Recognizing that these problems were related to the overall lack of a quality orientation, senior management began reviewing quality programs, attending training programs, and adapting materials to fit the Spectrum situation. Next, all employees were taught how to work toward error-free performance.

Leofsky's letter was the first major test of the quality commitment. Laboratory tests showed that surface contaminants were the problem, but finding the sources was tough. Just as one was identified and eliminated, another would appear. Solving the problem took capital, people, and time resources that would have been unthinkable in the past. Soon other victories also began to occur. Meanwhile, overall sales returns and related allowances on Spectrum products plummeted 75 percent, saving more than $767,000 annually. Spectrum's growing reputation for quality recently helped the company gain new Canadian business when several of a competitor's products failed to meet the quality standard set by the Canadian government.[46]   ■ ■ ■

Savings such as those attained by Spectrum Control add significantly to profit levels. Quality efforts typically make use of several important tools that we consider in the next two sections: quality improvement teams and benchmarking, and statistical aids to quality management.

Quality improvement teams
Small groups of employees who work on solving specific problems related to quality and productivity, often with stated targets for improvement

Benchmarking The process of identifying the best practices and approaches by comparing productivity in specific areas within one's own company with the productivity of other organizations both within and outside the country

Promoting Innovation: Quality Improvement Teams and Benchmarking

Quality improvement teams and benchmarking are commonly used by organizations engaging in total quality management. Although the two can be used independently, benchmarking tends to be conducted by quality improvement teams.

Quality improvement teams are small groups of employees who work on solving specific problems related to quality and productivity, often with stated targets for improvement. Typically, membership in these teams is mandatory, because the teams frequently consist of individuals who are responsible for the work areas that are the target of quality improvement efforts. Of course, if a number of alternative individuals are qualified to work on a problem, team membership may be voluntary. Problems to be addressed may be identified by management as well as workers, and the groups often set specific improvement goals and compete with one another.[47] Quality improvement teams are proving to be highly successful at tracking down the causes of poor quality and productivity, as well as taking remedial action. For example, Monsanto formed a quality improvement team when Ford Motor reported trouble with Saflex, a Monsanto material used to make laminated windshields. The material's dimensions were changing by the time the Saflex was delivered to Ford. Within 2 months, the quality improvement team traced the trouble to packaging, designed a new prototype, tested it, and implemented a new packaging process that eliminated Ford's complaints.[48]

Benchmarking is the process of identifying the best practices and approaches by comparing productivity in specific areas within one's own company with the productivity of other organizations both within and outside the industry.[49] Benchmarking became a commonly used technique only recently as companies with major quality management efforts adopted the approach. Such companies include AT&T, Du Pont, Ford Motor, IBM, Eastman Kodak, Milliken, and

Motorola. Xerox is generally credited with the first use of benchmarking by a U.S. company. In 1979, a team of Xerox line managers went to Japan to study the productivity of Japanese photocopy manufacturers. The manufacturers had been selling midsize copiers in the United States for $9600 each, which was substantially less than Xerox's production costs. At first, Xerox management had assumed that the Japanese companies were "dumping"—that is, selling the machines for substantially less than cost to undermine Xerox's market position. However, the benchmark team made the shocking discovery that the Japanese companies could build higher-quality machines for substantially less than could Xerox. (Much of the information was provided by Xerox's own joint venture, Fuji-Xerox, which knew the competition well.) The benchmark study marked the beginning of Xerox's recovery and dedication to TQM. Xerox then began to benchmark other companies, even those outside its industry that had expertise that could be of help. For example, a Xerox team studied L. L. Bean, the venerable catalog operation, to learn more about fulfilling orders quickly and accurately. Other companies are now following suit in pursuing benchmarking as a means of enhancing quality and productivity.[50]

Thus a number of companies have been benefiting from TQM efforts, such as quality improvement teams and benchmarking. However, a recent study indicates that other companies have expended considerable time and effort on TQM without major results. Part of the reason for poor results may be that organizations implementing total quality efforts sometimes attempt to do too much too quickly. According to the study, it may be best to concentrate on a few changes that really make a difference and then build on the successes in these areas rather than initiate major changes on many fronts at once.[51]

Statistical Aids to Quality Management

A mainstay of quality management in production environments is the use of statistical techniques that facilitate the tracing of quality difficulties. Two statistical approaches are most common: acceptance sampling and statistical process control.[52]

Acceptance sampling is a statistical technique that involves evaluating random samples from a group, or "lot," of produced materials to determine whether the lot meets acceptable quality levels. An **acceptable quality level (AQL)** is a predetermined standard against which the random samples are compared. If a certain number of the samples fall below the AQL, the entire lot will be rejected. Since this type of procedure is typically done after production is completed, it normally represents feedback control. On the other hand, acceptance sampling can be a method of feedforward control if it is used to determine whether incoming components from suppliers meet standards for inputs to a production process.

Statistical process control is a statistical technique that uses periodic random samples taken during actual production to determine whether acceptable quality levels are being met or production should be stopped for remedial action. In contrast to acceptance sampling, statistical process control assesses quality during production so that problems can be resolved before materials are completed. Since the emphasis is on prevention of poor-quality output during the actual process, this approach represents concurrent control. Because most production processes produce some variations, statistical process control uses statistical tests to determine when variations fall outside a narrow range around the acceptable quality level. Such variations signal systematic fluctuations attributable to some malfunction in the production process.

Acceptance sampling A statistical technique that involves evaluating random samples from a group, or "lot," of produced materials to determine whether the lot meets acceptable quality levels

Acceptable quality level (AQL) A predetermined standard against which random samples of produced materials are compared in acceptance sampling

Statistical process control A statistical technique that uses periodic random samples taken during actual production to determine whether acceptable quality levels are being met or production should be stopped for remedial action

INVENTORY CONTROL

Inventory A stock of materials that are used to facilitate production or to satisfy customer demand

Raw materials inventory The stock of parts, ingredients, and other basic inputs to a production or service process

Work-in-process inventory The stock of items currently being transformed into a final product or service

Finished-goods inventory The stock of items that have been produced and are awaiting sale or transit to a customer

Another major type of control system found in most organizations is inventory control. **Inventory** is a stock of materials that are used to facilitate production or to satisfy customer demand. There are three major types of inventory: raw materials, work in process, and finished goods.[53]

Raw materials inventory is the stock of parts, ingredients, and other basic inputs to a production or service process. For example, McDonald's raw materials inventory includes hamburgers, cheese slices, buns, potatoes, and soft-drink syrup. The raw materials inventory at a bicycle factory includes such items as chains, sprockets, handlebars, and seats.

Work-in-process inventory is the stock of items currently being transformed into a final product or service. For McDonald's, work-in-process inventory includes the hamburgers being assembled, the salads being made, and the syrup and soda water being mixed to make a soft drink. A bicycle frame with only the handlebars and seat attached would be work-in-process at a bicycle factory.

Finished-goods inventory is the stock of items that have been produced and are awaiting sale or transit to a customer. At McDonald's, finished-goods inventory includes the hamburgers waiting on the warmer and the salads in the refrigerated case. Bicycles constitute the finished-goods inventory at a bicycle factory. Organizations that provide services, rather than products, such as hospitals, beauty salons, or accounting firms, do not have finished-goods inventory, since they are not able to stockpile finished goods (e.g., kidney operations, haircuts, and audits).

Significance of Inventory

Inventory serves several major purposes in organizations.[54] For one thing, it helps deal with uncertainties in supply and demand. For example, having extra raw materials inventory may preclude shortages that hold up a production process. Having extra finished-goods inventory makes it possible to serve customers better. Inventory also facilitates more economic purchases, since materials are sometimes less expensive when purchased in large amounts at one time. Finally, inventory may be a useful means of dealing with anticipated changes in demand or supply, such as seasonal fluctuations or an expected shortage. However, caution must be exercised in predicting changes. During the late 1980s, Apple Computer, Inc., paid high prices to stockpile memory chips worth hundreds of millions of dollars because the company anticipated a continued chip shortage. Instead, the shortage eased and chip prices fell. When Apple tried to raise computer prices to cover the costs of its high-priced chips, sales fell and quarterly profits plunged almost 43 percent.[55]

Item cost The price of an inventory item itself

Ordering cost The expenses involved in placing an order (such as paperwork, postage, and time)

Carrying, or holding, cost The expenses associated with keeping an item on hand (such as storage, insurance, pilferage, breakage)

Stockout cost The economic consequences of running out of stock (such as loss of customer goodwill and possibly sales)

Costs of Inventory

Inventory is important to organizations because it represents considerable costs. For one thing, there is **item cost,** the price of an inventory item itself (the cost of the handlebars or seats). Then there is the **ordering cost,** the expenses involved in placing an order (such as paperwork, postage, and time). There is also the **carrying,** or **holding, cost,** the expenses associated with keeping an item on hand (such as storage, insurance, pilferage, breakage). Finally, there is **stockout cost,** the economic consequences of running out of stock. Stockout costs include the loss of customer goodwill and possibly sales because an item requested by customers is not available. When Compaq Computer Corporation launched its new low-cost ProLinea personal computers in 1992, they proved to be so popular that the company could not keep up with the demand. A 3-month backlog resulted, giving competitors opportunities to strike back.[56] Inventory control aims to minimize the costs of inventory (including considerations of stockout costs). One approach to minimizing such costs is the use of an inventory method called the economic order quantity.

Economic Order Quantity

Economic order quantity (EOQ) An inventory control method developed to minimize ordering plus holding costs, while avoiding stockout costs

The **economic order quantity (EOQ)** is an inventory control method developed to minimize ordering plus holding costs, while avoiding stockout costs. The method involves an equation that includes annual demand (D), ordering costs (O), and holding costs (H). Assume that a bicycle manufacturer estimates a total annual demand of 1470 bicycle frames for use in the manufacturing process, ordering costs of \$10 per order, and holding costs of \$6 per unit per year. Substituting these estimates into the equation indicates that the economic order quantity is 70 bicycle frames:

$$\text{EOQ} = \frac{2DO}{H} \text{ (square root)} = \frac{2(1470)(10)}{6} = 70$$

Reorder point (ROP) The inventory level at which a new order should be placed

The EOQ equation helps managers decide how much to order, but they also need to know the **reorder point (ROP)**, the inventory level at which a new order should be placed. To determine the reorder point, managers estimate *lead time* (L), the time between placing an order and receiving it. In the case of the bicycle manufacturer, the lead time for obtaining frames from a nearby producer is 7 days. In the equation for ROP, lead time is multiplied by average daily demand (annual demand ÷ 365 days). Conceptually, the bicycle frames should be ordered when there are just enough frames to keep making bicycles until the new frames come in. Substituting the data for the bicycle manufacturer into the ROP equation indicates that an order should be placed when the stock of bicycle frames reaches 29:

$$\text{ROP} = (L)\frac{D}{365} = (7)\frac{1470}{365} = 28.19, \text{ or } 29 \text{ (rounded)}$$

The EOQ inventory control system, which requires continuous monitoring of inventories, is depicted in Figure 3. Although the approach assumes that demand and unit costs are constant, in many cases demand may vary substantially and suppliers may offer quantity discounts and special promotions. Still, the EOQ often gives a useful approximation. In using the EOQ, an organization will often add some slack to the system in the form of *fluctuation*, or *safety, stock*. This is extra inventory kept on hand in case of unforeseen contingencies such as quality problems or reorder delays.[57] On the other hand, a number of U.S. companies are taking a completely different approach to inventory control by emulating the ''just-in-time'' method pioneered in Japan.

Just-in-Time Inventory Control

Just-in-time (JIT) inventory control An approach to inventory control that emphasizes having materials arrive just as they are needed in the production process

Just-in-time (JIT) inventory control is an approach to inventory control that emphasizes having materials arrive just as they are needed in the production process.[58] The JIT approach to inventory is actually part of the broader JIT philosophy of manufacturing. According to this philosophy, organizations should attempt to eliminate all sources of waste, including any activities that do

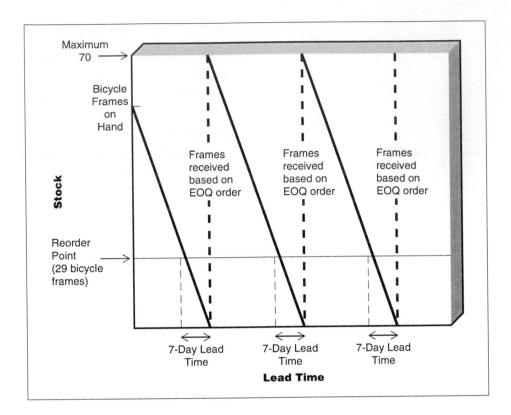

Figure 3 *EOQ inventory control system.*

not add value, by focusing on having the right part at the right place at exactly the right time. Thus applying the JIT concept to inventory means having materials arrive only as required, rather than holding backup parts in inventory for a period of time. This approach enables an organization to minimize holding costs and to save space that is usually taken up by inventory waiting in the production area.

The JIT philosophy was popularized by the Toyota Motor Company in Japan during the mid-1970s and was transferred to the United States at Kawasaki's Lincoln, Nebraska, plant around 1980. One report indicates that a Japanese plant designed to produce 1000 cars per day requires 1 million square feet and a just-in-time inventory of $150 per car. In contrast, a U.S. car manufacturer producing the same number of cars per day but not using a just-in-time system requires 2 million square feet and a conventional inventory of $775 per car.[59] With such potential savings, it is not surprising that the JIT inventory approach has been adopted to some degree by most of the Fortune 1000 largest industrial companies.[60] In its focus on eliminating waste, the JIT philosophy also calls for utilizing the full capabilities of workers, giving them greater responsibilities for the production process, and involving them in continual efforts at improving the production process.

Kanban A simple parts-movement system that depends on cards and containers to pull parts from one work center to another

For handling inventory, the JIT approach uses a subsystem called **Kanban** (Japanese for "card" or "signal"), a simple parts-movement system that depends on cards and containers to pull parts from one work center to another. With the Kanban system, workstations along the production process produce only enough to fill the containers that they are given. They begin producing again only when they receive a card and an empty container from the next workstation, indicating that more parts will be needed shortly. If the process stops because of machine breakdowns or quality problems, all the workstations involved in the process produce only until their containers are full and then they stop.

With a JIT system, high quality is a vital necessity. Since materials are either delivered by suppliers or made in various internal work centers just before they will be used, the items must be perfect. Otherwise, not only is there waste, but the production process itself must be halted because there is no significant amount of inventory to cover mistakes. Because of the high need for coordination and control, JIT inventory systems often help forge close relationships between suppliers and customers. In the case of Polycom Hunstman, Inc., and GM's Harrison radiator division in Lockport, New York, the relationship is exceptionally close—just 1500 feet, to be exact. After GM invited suppliers to move closer to its Harrison plant, Polycom built a new plant right next door so that a pneumatic conveying system could connect the two plants, thereby eliminating shipping costs. Now, when the GM plant begins to run low on the plastic compounds that Polycom supplies, a computer-based control system automatically begins sending materials from Polycom's facility to the Harrison plant.[61] Of course, it takes time to install a JIT system, and the system is dependent on near-perfect coordination. For example, a recent walkout at GM's metal-stamping plant in Lordstown, Ohio, quickly idled more than 32,500 workers at a number of other GM plants that depend on just-in-time parts fabricated at Lordstown.[62]

CHAPTER SUMMARY

Among the major control systems used in organizations are financial control, budgetary control, quality control, and inventory control. These systems vary in the degree to which they are used at different managerial levels, ranging from financial controls, which are used more at the top, to inventory controls, which are used more at the lower levels. Timing also varies, with financial control representing mainly feedback control, budgetary and quality control being more concurrent, and inventory control often matching feedforward timing.

Financial controls consist mainly of financial statements, ratio analysis, and comparative financial analysis. The primary financial statements are the balance sheet and the income statement. The major types of ratios used in financial control are liquidity, asset management, debt management, and profitability ratios. Financial statements and ratios can be assessed through the use of comparative financial analysis based on management financial goals, historical financial standards, or industry financial standards. Managers need to guard against major pitfalls associated with financial controls.

Budgetary control requires that various organizational units be designated as responsibility centers, such as standard cost centers, discretionary expense centers, revenue centers, profit centers, and investment centers. The specific designation depends mainly on the type of organization structure involved. Two major types of budgets are operating budgets and capital expenditures budgets. Depending on how they are used, budgets can have either positive or negative effects on managerial behavior in organizations.

Quality control has strategic implications that are related to the eight dimensions of quality: performance, features, reliability, conformance, durability, serviceability, aesthetics, and perceived quality. Organizations usually find it difficult to compete on all dimensions simultaneously and must make trade-offs. To improve quality, a number of organizations are adopting a quality stance known as total quality management. The approach is aimed at achieving zero defects, a quality mentality in which the work force strives to make a product or service conform exactly to desired standards. Quality efforts typically make use of quality improvement teams and benchmarking, as well as statistical aids to quality management.

Inventory control serves a number of important purposes in organizations and involves several significant costs. Two major inventory control methods are the economic order quantity and just-in-time inventory control.

QUESTIONS FOR DISCUSSION AND REVIEW

1 How do major control systems differ in their emphasis on timing control? In what ways might the timing of these control systems be altered?

2 Identify and briefly explain the main types of financial statements and financial ratios used by organizations. Suppose that your friend asks you to help res-

cue a motorcycle factory that is losing money. How would you use the various financial analyses to help assess the situation?

3   There are a number of potential pitfalls associated with financial controls. Could any of these pitfalls occur at Hanson PLC (see the Case in Point)?

4   Explain each type of responsibility center, and show the connection with organization structure. Identify the type of responsibility center in which you or a friend works. Give reasons for your classification of the center's type.

5   Contrast operating budgets and capital expenditures budgets. How can budgets be used so that they have positive, rather than negative, effects on managerial behavior?

6   Describe the eight dimensions of quality. Choose an item that you recently purchased, and rate your pur-

chase on each of the dimensions. What dimension was most important in your decision to purchase the item you did instead of a competitor's item?

7   Explain the total quality management approach. Why might employee involvement teams be useful with such an approach?

8   Describe the concept of benchmarking. How can you use benchmarking to learn about your worth in the job market?

9   Contrast acceptance sampling and statistical process control. From the point of view of a consumer, how would you like to see these quality control aids used by the companies whose products you buy?

10 Compare and contrast the economic order quantity and just-in-time approaches to inventory control. Why do you think that so many companies are attempting to make greater use of the JIT approach?

DISCUSSION QUESTIONS FOR CHAPTER OPENING CASE

1   In what ways does USAA probably use financial and budgetary control techniques to help meet its service and profit goals?

2   Although it is a service, in what ways does USAA use the dimensions of quality to compete? To what extent is benchmarking in evidence at the company?

3   Assess the quality improvement efforts at USAA in terms of Deming's 14 points on how to improve quality.

MANAGEMENT EXERCISE: MEETING WATER BED DEMAND

 A recent announcement from your state health department has proclaimed that water beds are very good for people with minor back pains. This has resulted in an extremely high demand for the water beds your firm produces. Although this is very good news, as the operating manager of the firm, you are concerned that your firm's ability to produce may be impeded by several considerations. You review these:

Market share: The firm currently has about 12 percent of the local market. You recognize that you will need to increase productivity 5 percent just to maintain the current market position. However, to reach your goal of a 5 percent increase in market share, you must further step up productivity.

Capacity: You believe that you have the plant capacity to expand productivity to 6500 water beds annually. The firm now produces and sells 5000 water beds annually. The increase in market share, for both maintaining the current position and achieving your stated goal, will require 5500 water beds per year.

Inventory: You have storage capacity for raw materials for 450 water beds per month, and your work-in-process inventory is normally 470 beds per month. The finished-goods inventory is usually 8 percent of monthly production.

Quality: Inspections conducted after the water beds are made typically result in about 10 percent of them being rejected because of quality problems. Only about 50 percent of these can be repaired; the others must be scrapped.

Human resources: You have the skilled employees required to support increased production but will need additional unskilled workers. There are many potential employees in the local labor market.

Tomorrow you must tell the president of the firm whether or not you can meet the projected production schedule. If you need to make some modifications in your procedures to meet the projected schedule, these changes should be included in your discussion with the president. What are you going to tell the president tomorrow morning?

REFERENCES

1. Wendy Zellner, "USAA: Premium Treatment," *Business Week,* Oct. 25, 1991, p. 124; Thomas Teal, "Service Comes First: An Interview with USAA's Robert F. McDermott," *Harvard Business Review,* September–October 1991, pp. 117–127.

2. Eric G. Flamholtz, "Accounting, Budgeting and Control Systems in Their Organizational Context: Theoretical and Empirical Perspectives," *Accounting, Organizations and Society,* vol. 8, 1983, pp. 253–269; Robert N. Anthony, John Dearden, and Norton M. Bedford, *Management Control Systems,* 5th ed., Irwin, Homewood, Ill., 1984; Everett E. Adam, Jr., and Ronald J. Ebert, *Production and Operations Management,* 3d ed., Prentice-Hall, Englewood Cliffs, N.J., 1986.

3. John J. Pringle and Robert S. Harris, *Essentials of Managerial Finance,* 2d ed., Scott, Foresman, Glenview, Ill., 1987. For a discussion of financial statements for not-for-profit organizations, see Robert N. Anthony, "Making Sense of Nonbusiness Accounting," *Harvard Business Review,* May–June 1980, pp. 83–93.

4. George E. Pinches, *Essentials for Financial Management,* 3d ed., Harper & Row, New York, 1990.

5. Examples involving The Limited are based on information from Robert K. Eskew and Daniel L. Jensen, *Financial Accounting,* 4th ed., McGraw-Hill, New York, 1992, pp. 684–700.

6. Jerry A. Viscione and Gordon S. Roberts, *Contemporary Financial Management,* Merrill, Columbus, Ohio, 1987.

7. Ibid.

8. Based on Bill Saporito, "The Tough Cookie at RJR Nabisco," *Fortune,* July 18, 1988, pp. 32–46; Scott Ticer, "The Boss at RJR Likes to Keep 'Em Guessing," *Business Week,* May 23, 1988, pp. 175–182; Peter Waldman, "New RJR Chief Faces a Daunting Challenge at Debt-Heavy Firm," *The Wall Street Journal,* Mar. 14, 1989, pp. A1, A19; Bryan Burrough and John Helyar, "Secret Scenes from the RJR Wars," *The Wall Street Journal,* Jan. 4, 1990, pp. B1, B4–B5; "RJR Can't Seem to Find a Spot in the Shade," *Business Week,* July 20, 1992, pp. 70–71; and Suein L. Hwang, "Healthy Eating, Premium Private Labels Take a Bite Out of Nabisco's Cookie Sales," *The Wall Street Journal,* July 13, 1992, pp. B1, B4.

9. The major sources are *Annual Statement Studies,* Robert Morris Associates, Philadelphia; *Key Business Ratios,* Dun & Bradstreet, New York; *Almanac of Business and Industrial Financial Ratios,* Prentice-Hall, Englewood Cliffs, N.J.; *Quarterly Financial Report for Manufacturing Corporations,* Federal Trade Commission and Securities and Exchange Commission, Washington, D.C.; and data from various trade associations.

10. David S. Vise, "The World According to Rupert Murdoch," *The Washington Post,* Aug. 14, 1988; Chris Welles, "Even Rupert Murdoch Has His Limits," *Business Week,* Oct. 2, 1989, pp. 34–35.

11. Scott S. Cowen and J. Kendall Middaugh II, "Designing an Effective Financial Planning and Control System," *Long Range Planning,* vol. 21, 1988, pp. 83–92.

12. Stratford P. Sherman, "Inside the Mind of Jack Welch," *Fortune,* Mar. 27, 1988, pp. 39–50.

13. This section is based heavily on Joseph A. Maciariello, *Management Control Systems,* Prentice-Hall, Englewood Cliffs, N.J., 1984.

14. Peter Waldman, "New RJR Chief Faces a Daunting Challenge at Debt-Heavy Firm," *The Wall Street Journal,* Mar. 14, 1989, pp. A1, A19.

15. Bill Saporito, "The Tough Cookie at RJR Nabisco," *Fortune,* July 18, 1988, pp. 32–46.

16. Ibid.

17. Stratford P. Sherman, "Inside the Mind of Jack Welch," *Fortune,* Mar. 27, 1989, pp. 39–50.

18. Joseph A. Maciariello, *Management Control Systems,* Prentice-Hall, Englewood Cliffs, N.J., 1984.

19. Based on John A. Burne, "Hanson: The Dangers of Living by Takeover Alone," *Business Week,* Aug. 15, 1988, pp. 62–64. See also Sir Gordon White, "How I Turned $3,000 into $10 Billion," *Fortune,* Nov. 7, 1988, pp. 80–89; and James R. Norman, "Don't Rush Us," *Forbes,* Oct. 14, 1991, pp. 116–118.

20. Walter B. Meigs and Robert F. Meigs, *Accounting: The Basis for Business Decisions,* 7th ed., McGraw-Hill, New York, 1987.

21. Joseph A. Maciariello, *Management Control Systems,* Prentice-Hall, Englewood Cliffs, N.J., 1984; H. Kent Baker, *Financial Management,* Harcourt Brace Jovanovich, San Diego, Calif., 1987.

22. Robert N. Anthony, John Dearden, and Norton M. Bedford, *Management Control Systems,* 5th ed., Irwin, Homewood, Ill., 1984.

23. Jerry A. Viscione and Gordon S. Roberts, *Contemporary Financial Management,* Merrill, Columbus, Ohio, 1987. For a thorough discussion of the capital budgeting process and its relationship to decision support systems, see Lawrence A. Gordon and George E. Pinches, *Improving Capital Budgeting: A Decision Support System Approach,* Addison-Wesley, Reading, Mass., 1984.

24. V. Bruce Irvine, "Budgeting: Functional Analysis and Behavioral Implications," *Cost and Management,* March–April 1970, pp. 6–16; Henry L. Tosi, Jr., "The Human Effects of Budgeting Systems on Management," *MSU Business Topics,* Autumn 1974, pp. 53–63.

25. Cindy Skrzycki, "Making Quality a Priority," *The Washington Post,* Oct. 11, 1987, p. K1.

26. Note to Principles of Management Textbook Authors, provided by the American Society for Quality Control, Milwaukee, 1987.

27. Based on Patricia A. Galagan, "Training Delivers Results to Federal Express," *Training & Development,* December 1991, pp. 27–33; and Patricia L. Panchak, "How to Implement a Quality Management Initiative," *Modern Office Technology,* February 1992, pp. 27–31.

28. David A. Garvin, "Competing on the Eight Dimensions of Quality,"

Harvard Business Review, November–December 1987, pp. 101–109.

29. G. M. Hostage, "Quality Control in a Service Business," *Harvard Business Review,* July–August 1975, pp. 98–106; William A. Sherden, "Gaining the Service Quality Advantage," *Journal of Business Strategy,* March–April 1988, pp. 45–48.

30. Zachary Schiller, "The Refrigerator That Has GE Feeling the Heat," *Business Week,* Apr. 25, 1988, p. 65; Ira C. Magaziner and Mark Patinkin, "Cold Competition: GE Wages the Refrigerator War," *Harvard Business Review,* March–April 1989, pp. 114–124; Thomas F. O'Boyle, "GE Refrigerator Woes Illustrate the Hazards in Changing a Product," *The Wall Street Journal,* May 7, 1990, pp. A1, A5.

31. Joseph B. White, "U.S. Car-Parts Firms Form Japanese Ties," *The Wall Street Journal,* Apr. 12, 1988, p. 6.

32. Roger B. Yepsen, Jr. (ed.), *The Durability Factor,* Rodale, Emmaus, Penn., 1982, cited in David A. Garvin, "Competing on the Eight Dimensions of Quality," *Harvard Business Review,* November–December 1987, pp. 101–109.

33. Antonio N. Fins, "A Utility That's All Charged Up over Quality," *Business Week,* Feb. 13, 1989, pp. 94A–94D.

34. Kenneth Labich, "Hot Company, Warm Culture," *Fortune,* Feb. 27, 1989, pp. 74–78.

35. David A. Garvin, "Competing on the Eight Dimensions of Quality," *Harvard Business Review,* November–December, 1987, pp. 101–109.

36. Ibid.

37. Otis Port, "The Push for Quality," *Business Week,* June 8, 1987, pp. 130–135; Roger G. Schroeder, *Operations Management,* 3d ed., McGraw-Hill, New York, 1989.

38. Joseph B. White, "U.S. Car-Parts Firms Form Japanese Ties," *The Wall Street Journal,* Apr. 12, 1988, p. 6.

39. Roger G. Schroeder, *Operations Management,* 3d ed., McGraw-Hill, New York, 1989.

40. David A. Garvin, "Competing on the Eight Dimensions of Quality," *Harvard Business Review,* November–December 1987, pp. 101–109. See also J. M. Juran, *Juran on Planning for Quality,* Free Press, New York, 1988.

41. Adapted from W. Edwards Deming, *Out of the Crisis,* M.I.T., Center for Advanced Engineering Study, Cambridge, Mass., 1986.

42. Joseph G. Monks, *Operations Management,* 3d ed., McGraw-Hill, New York, 1987.

43. Otis Port, "The Push for Quality," *Business Week,* June 8, 1987, pp. 130–136.

44. Ellen Goldbaum, "How Quality Programs Win Respect and Get Results," *Chemical Week,* Oct. 5, 1988, pp. 30–33.

45. James Houghton, "For Better Quality, Listen to the Workers," *The New York Times,* Forum, Oct. 18, 1987, section 3, p. 3. For more examples, see Joel Dreyfus, "Victories in the Quality Crusade," *Fortune,* Oct. 10, 1988, pp. 80–88.

46. Based on Craig R. Waters, "Quality Begins at Home," *INC.,* August 1985, pp. 68–71; and Daniel Bates, "Spectrum Gets a Break, Moves to Capture Greater Market Share," *Pittsburgh Business Times & Journal,* Sept. 2, 1991, p. 11.

47. Beverly Geber, "Quality Circles: The Second Generation," *Training,* December 1986, pp. 54–61.

48. Ellen Goldbaum, "How Quality Programs Win Respect—And Get Results," *Chemical Week,* Oct. 5, 1988, pp. 30–33.

49. Jonathan D. Weatherly, "Dare to Compare for Better Productivity," *HR Magazine,* September 1992, pp. 42–46.

50. Jeremy Main, "How to Steal the Best Ideas Around," *Fortune,* Oct. 19, 1992, pp. 102–106.

51. Gilbert Fuchsberg, "Total Quality Is Termed Only Partial Success," *The Wall Street Journal,* Oct. 1, 1992, pp. B1, B9. See also Michael S. Leibman, "Getting Results from TQM,"
HR Magazine, September 1992, pp. 34–38.

52. Roger G. Schroeder, *Operations Management,* 3d ed., McGraw-Hill, New York, 1989.

53. This discussion is based largely on ibid.

54. Ibid.

55. Brenton R. Schlender, "Apple Slips as Result of Hoarding Chips," *The Wall Street Journal,* Jan. 30, 1989, p. A6.

56. Catherine Arnst and Stephanie Anderson Forest, "Compaq: How It Made Its Impressive Move Out of the Doldrums," *Business Week,* Nov. 2, 1992, pp. 146–151.

57. Dennis W. McLeavey and Seetharama L. Narasimhan, *Production Planning and Inventory Control,* Allyn and Bacon, Boston, 1985.

58. This discussion is based largely on Roger G. Schroeder, *Operations Management,* 3d ed., McGraw-Hill, New York, 1989.

59. Charles G. Burck, "Can Detroit Catch Up?" *Fortune,* Feb. 8, 1982, pp. 34–39.

60. Richard J. Schonberger, "An Assessment of Just-in-Time Implementation," in *Readings in Zero Inventory* (APICS 27th Annual International Conference proceedings, Las Vegas, Oct. 9–12, 1984), p. 57.

61. Martha E. Mangelsdorf, "Beyond Just-in-Time," *INC.,* February 1989, p. 21.

62. Jacqueline Mitchell and Neal Templin, "GM Idles Plant in Oklahoma; Talks Heat Up," *The Wall Street Journal,* Sept. 3, 1992, p. A3.

ACKNOWLEDGMENTS

Tables

Table 1, 2, 3: Adapted from *Financial Accounting,* 4th ed., by Robert K. Eskew and Daniel L. Jensen. Copyright 1992 by McGraw-Hill, Inc. Reprinted by permission.

CONCLUDING CASE

POOR QUALITY LEADS TO FINANCIAL PROBLEMS FOR REGINA

The Regina Company, one of America's largest makers of vacuum cleaners, recently had severe problems with the quality of its products. The market response to this lack of quality caused financial problems for the company.

In late 1988 Regina began having return rates as high as 30 to 50 percent on some of its Housekeeper and Housekeeper Plus models. These lines were sold primarily through discount stores. Further, Regina's Stutz vacuum cleaner, an upgraded version sold in specialty stores, was introduced in 1988 with many quality problems. The specific problems identified for the Housekeeper and Housekeeper Plus lines were associated with faulty belts and weak suction. In the Stutz, the agitator was melting and making a loud noise, the foot pedals were breaking, and the steel-encased motor (which had been advertised as the power source for the vacuum cleaner) had been replaced with a less desirable, less reliable motor.

As a result of these problems, the Dayton Hudson Corporation dropped one line. Target Stores discontinued Regina's Housekeeper Plus 500 line after reporting that "at least half of those sold were returned." At K mart, which accounts for about a quarter of the Housekeeper 1000 sales, 1 out of every 5 machines sold was returned. To help service customer complaints, Regina set up an 800 telephone number for customers to contact the firm directly.

It should be noted that the Hoover Company and the Eureka Corporation, both leaders in the vacuum cleaner industry, reported return rates for their machines of less than 1 percent. They further indicated that they would have cause for alarm if the return rate reached 3 percent.

The many returns caused Regina's shareholders to question the 1988 fiscal earnings report. Furthermore, both inventories and accounts receivable doubled during the 1988 fiscal year. At the end of that period, Regina's chairman and 40 percent stockholder resigned. His resignation was closely followed by a company announcement stating that the financial results reported for the 1988 fiscal year were materially incorrect and had been withdrawn. This announcement brought a suit from shareholders who had bought Regina stock on the basis of the 1988 earnings report. It also prompted an audit of the 1988 results and a request to another accounting organization to work on Regina's business and accounting controls. In addition, both the Securities and Exchange Commission and the National Association of Securities Dealers began investigating the company's affairs. Regina filed for bankruptcy protection under Chapter 11 of the Federal Bankruptcy Code in 1989. A few months later, it agreed to be acquired by a unit of Electrolux, a vacuum cleaner and water-purification company based in Marietta, Georgia.

Under Electrolux, Regina shut down production while engineers worked to solve the problems inherent in the Housekeeper and Housekeeper Plus vacuums, particularly the suction difficulties. In September 1990, Electrolux and Regina decided to separate the two companies again. Since then, Regina has been regaining market share with its Housekeeper Upright line. The vacuums are popular because they carry on-board tools and offer the capability of cleaning above the floor. Competitors have been copying the on-board tools concept originally pioneered by Regina.*

QUESTIONS FOR CONCLUDING CASE

1 What type of controls would you have established to preclude the major returns experienced by Regina?
2 How would you have controlled the finished-goods inventory to avoid its growing to twice the size that it was in the previous year?
3 What actions would you have taken to reduce Regina's accounts receivable?

* Andrea Rothman, "High Return Rate for Regina Vacuums May Have Added to Financial Problems," *The Wall Street Journal,* Sept. 29, 1988, p. 4, and "Judge's Opinion Says Regina Had Product Problems," *The Wall Street Journal,* Oct. 5, 1988, p. 5; Terry Troy, "From Sweeping to Suction," *The Weekly Home Furnishings Newspaper,* Nov. 25, 1991, p. 1, and "Carpet Bombing the Mass Market," *The Weekly Home Furnishings Newspaper,* Aug. 3, 1992, p. 48.

CONCLUDING CASE

SAMSONITE CANADA TAKES CONTROL

During the late 1980s, Samsonite Canada, Inc., began to question its prospects for survival. The market for Canadian luggage was maturing, and the 17 percent tariff on imported luggage was to be phased out by the end of the 1990s. Moreover, Samsonite Canada, based in Stratford, Ontario, had recently lost a contract for making plastic parts for a European toy company. (The parts were made with the same injection-molding equipment used in the manufacture of hard luggage.) Until this point, the company's balance sheet had always shown a reasonable profit. Profits in the future looked less certain.

Although management had always suspected that its luggage manufacturing costs were high relative to those of its Denver-based U.S. parent, an investigation showed the situation to be worse than anticipated. Comparative indicators pointed to costs that were 50 to 70 percent higher than those in Denver. Company officials concluded that if the firm was to remain in operation, they would need to both cut costs and find ways to expand business.

As a result, Samsonite Canada initiated a rejuvenation program in 1991. The company received both financial and expert assistance from a Canadian federal agency, Employment and Immigration of Canada. The agency helped establish and chair a steering committee with equal representation from employees and management. The steering committee manages the ongoing process of change. Because of the focus on teams, as well as employee empowerment, continuous improvement, and training, the new program was called SPIRIT (Samsonite's Purpose Is Resulting In Teamwork). In regard to financial help, the agency provided half of the $392,000 cost for the first 2 years of the program. The company also received support from its Denver parent, which allowed the subsidiary to remain in business and encouraged its efforts to turn things around.

During the first year of the program, the company met its goal of cutting costs by half a million dollars. The cost cutting has continued at a brisk pace as employees have been offering many cost-saving ideas.

Many of the ideas have come from teams created to focus on continuous improvement. The teams, which meet on a weekly or biweekly basis, look for cost-cutting ideas in their work areas. They also consider ways to improve products and enhance service. For example, many teams send questionnaires to obtain feedback from customers about changes that are needed.

One initial problem was that the employees were accustomed to taking orders rather than taking the initiative to solve problems. To help employees learn appropriate skills and adapt to the required new culture, the company brought in a training program developed by the Canadian Manufacturers' Association with the help of the Canadian federal government. During a 6-month period, every employee, including management, received some or all components of the training program. The training focused on leadership and continuous improvement.

One result was the reorganization of the production area into work cells, where teams of workers collaborated with engineering to determine the best ways to lay out their work areas for manufacture and assembly of products. Because of these efforts, production runs more smoothly, a JIT inventory approach has been adopted, and materials are handled more efficiently. Quality control has also improved. The new work cell arrangements are 60 to 70 percent on their way to eliminating the need for quality inspectors. Instead, the workers themselves will take responsibility for maintaining quality at a sufficient level. Moreover, profit margins are up, and the streamlined work cells have freed up space that the company is now leasing to other businesses.

The push for higher quality has had another benefit. Samsonite Canada decided to pursue further business with FAG Bearings Limited, a major supplier for the Ford Motor Company. Samsonite had done a small amount of business with FAG Bearings in the past, but now it wanted to become the firm's single source for molding automotive strut bearings. FAG Bearings required the entire Samsonite Canada company to submit to a quality audit, not just the molding department. Samsonite Canada has also been working to shift some of its luggage expertise toward making other types of specialty containers. To that end, it has established its own research and development department. Already, specialty products account for 25 percent of gross sales.

Continuous improvements, even minor ones, made a big difference at Samsonite Canada.*

---

* Ken, "Taking Up the Gauntlet," *London Business Monthly Magazine,* Sept., 1992, p. 7.

QUESTIONS FOR CONCLUDING CASE

1 What role did financial controls play in helping Samsonite identify the need for change?

2 To what extent does Samsonite Canada appear to have initiated total quality management? How did the role of the Canadian federal government differ from what might be expected in the United States?

3 Explain how quality improvement teams operated in the Samsonite environment. What evidence exists that benchmarking was done?

CHAPTER 12

Entrepreneurship and Small Business

GAINING THE EDGE

PHIL ROMANO KEEPS SCORING ENTREPRENEURIAL SUCCESSES

Phil Romano is perhaps best known for one of his most intriguing creations, Fuddruckers, the upscale hamburger chain that he founded in 1979. When developing a new venture, Romano typically starts with a "concept," a basic idea about what he wants to do. He then thinks about it, talks with others, and puts the concept on paper. Next, he is likely to get help from experts, such as architects and market researchers. If conditions look favorable, he usually puts together a business plan that includes a detailed description of the concept and related business issues. The business plan is particularly helpful during the process of lining up financing for the new venture.

In creating Fuddruckers, for example, Romano built his concept around freshness and quality. By the time Fuddruckers had gone public and developed into a $25 million company with restaurants in 19 states and Canada, Romano had already trained his successor as CEO. After selling a large part of his interest in Fuddruckers, Romano left the business in January 1985 to create more new ventures.

Actually, Fuddruckers was the twelfth new venture that Romano had started. Within a year of leaving Fuddruckers, Romano started two new businesses, a restaurant named Stix and a fashionable men's clothing store named Baroni. Both subsequently failed, costing Phil Romano almost $1.5 million. Undaunted by these relatively rare setbacks, he started DocuCon, an organization that specializes in setting up systems that convert paper files to automated retrieval systems. DocuCon is growing into a multi-million-dollar business.

In 1988, Romano's Macaroni Grill opened and won the Silver Spoon award as the best restaurant in San Antonio. Featuring some Romano family recipes, the restaurant specialized in fresh vegetables, grilled meats, gourmet pizzas, and other northern Italian fare. In December 1989, Phil Romano sold the popular restaurant and concept to Dallas-based Chili's, Inc., for a reported $4.5 million. Chili's has been building several more Macaroni Grills in such cities as Dallas, Chicago, Houston, Kansas City, Tulsa, Orlando, and Miami. Phil Romano has been retained as a consultant to assist in ensuring the success of the new chain.

Romano also started Texas Tortilla Bakery, Inc., with an initial site in New York City's Greenwich Village. The Tex-Mex restaurant serves soft tacos made with a new machine developed by Romano. This venture features an open-style kitchen. Tacos are produced right in front of the customer and sold by the bucket. They come with a choice of fillings and can be eaten at tables or stands outside the bakery.

In 1992, Romano opened another restaurant in San Antonio as a joint venture with Brinker International. Called Nachomama's, this "funky" Mexican concept is indicative of the Romano philosophy that restaurants should be fun. Barrels of produce and peppers flank the entryway. Empty tomato cans are strung up as light fixtures, billboards cover the ceiling, and rotisserie chickens line the wall of a visible kitchen. Tortilla chips are served in hubcaps, and the servers wear tuxedos. To date, this concept, like Romano's others, has been quite appealing to the public.

Romano's advice to potential entrepreneurs is straightforward. Find an industry you really like, search out the problems in the industry, and create solutions.[1]

If there are heroes and heroines in American business in recent years, they are entrepreneurs like Phil Romano. Entrepreneurs create new organizations, provide innovative services and products, pique our imagination, and stimulate the economy. The insights into Phil Romano's world help us better understand entrepreneurs and the phenomenon called entrepreneurship. An understanding of entrepreneurship is particularly important for aspiring managers because 99 percent of the businesses in the United States are small businesses, most of which have been created by entrepreneurs. Most likely, many of you who read this book will become entrepreneurs or operate one of the small businesses that result from entrepreneurial activities. Some businesses created by entrepreneurs quickly become relatively large businesses. Most, though, spend a significant period of time as relatively small businesses, assuming that they survive beyond the initial start-up period. In this chapter, we explore the nature of entrepreneurship, including the role of innovation in entrepreneurial endeavors. We investigate the factors that influence the entrepreneurship phenomenon. We also analyze the development approaches that entrepreneurs and small-business owners can pursue, and we discuss the main preparations necessary to operate a small business. Finally, we consider some of the principal issues involved in the ongoing management of small businesses.

THE NATURE OF ENTREPRENEURSHIP

What is entrepreneurship? In this section, we explore the meaning of the term, consider the importance of innovation in assessments of entrepreneurial opportunities, and examine some of the major economic and social contributions of entrepreneurship.

Defining Entrepreneurship

Entrepreneurship The creation of new entreprise

Entrepreneurship is the creation of new enterprise.[2] Although one could conceivably engage in entrepreneurship geared toward establishing a new not-for-profit organization (such as an association or a cultural center), most entrepreneurship activities involve profit-oriented businesses. Accordingly, this chapter focuses on entrepreneurship aimed at profit making.

Entrepreneur An individual who creates a new enterprise

On the basis of our definition of entrepreneurship, an **entrepreneur** is an individual who creates a new enterprise. Many of today's familiar product names were born in enterprises created by entrepreneurs. Some examples include Brooks Brothers apparel (Henry Sands Brooks), Gerber baby food (Dan Gerber), Gucci loafers (Guccio Gucci), Barbie dolls (Barbara Handler), Wurlitzer instruments (Rudolph Wurlitzer), Calvin Klein jeans (Calvin Klein), Hummel figurines (Berta Hummel), Post cereals (Charles W. Post), and Heinz ketchup (Henry J. Heinz).[3] When an enterprise is in the process of being created by an entrepreneur, it is often referred to as a **new venture.**

New venture An enterprise that is in the process of being created by an entrepreneur

New ventures typically fall into the category of "small businesses," a classification that is itself somewhat difficult to define. The U.S. Chamber of Commerce suggests that businesses employing fewer than 500 persons are small. Others sometimes use a figure of fewer than 100 persons. With either figure, small businesses would still constitute 99 percent of all U.S. businesses.[4] Another criterion that is often used to identify a small business is independent ownership. In other words, the business is not a subsidiary of a larger organization. Accordingly, we consider a *small business* to be an independently owned business that employs fewer than 500 persons. For the most part, we use the terms "entrepreneurship" and "entrepreneur" in conjunction with creating new ventures. We use "small business" or "small-business owner" when the discussion applies more generally. In some cases, we may refer to both small businesses and new ventures (or owners and entrepreneurs) to make clear that the discussion applies to both. So far, researchers have experienced difficulty determining precisely when the creation phase attributable to entrepreneurship ends.

Promoting Innovation: Assessing Entrepreneurial Opportunities

In his book *Innovation and Entrepreneurship,* noted management consultant and writer Peter Drucker observes, "Innovation is the specific tool of entrepreneurs, the means by which they exploit change as an opportunity for a different business or a different service."[5] Essentially, it is difficult to be an entrepreneur without engaging in at least some innovation, since merely duplicating what is already being done will usually attract insufficient customers.[6] The innovation dilemma related to entrepreneurship is illustrated in Table 1.

As shown in the table, opportunity conditions vary according to the degree of innovation. The probable conditions associated with a particular innovation level can be assessed in terms of risk, evaluation, and profit potential. *Risk* is the probability of the venture's failing. *Evaluation* is the ease of estimating the significance and feasibility of a new venture idea. *Profit potential* is the likely level of return or compensation to the entrepreneur for taking on the risk of developing an idea into an actual business venture. As the table indicates, if a new venture is very much like the competition (a copycat), its significance and feasibility are easy to evaluate (since others are already doing it). Unfortunately, such a venture involves high risk because there is little to attract customers, and thus its profit potential is low. As new venture ideas become somewhat more innovative, the risk goes down because there is something new to offer the customer. As ideas become more innovative, though, the significance and feasibility become more difficult to evaluate and the risk increases. As innovation and risk both increase, so does profit potential because of the possibility of being able to offer a highly desirable unique product or service. At the invention end of the spectrum, the entrepreneur is often not the actual inventor of a product or service but, rather, is the one who recognizes the commercial applications. In any event, innovation is an important part of the entrepreneurial process, because without it the prospects of success are extremely low.

TABLE 1	Opportunity Conditions Associated with New Venture Innovation				
	LEVELS OF INNOVATION				
Opportunity Conditions	**New Invention**	**Highly Innovative**	**Moderately Innovative**	**Slightly Innovative**	**Copycat**
Risks	Very high	High	Moderate	Moderate to low	Very high
Evaluation	Very difficult	Difficult	Somewhat difficult	Easy	Easy
Profit potential	Very high	High	High to moderate	Moderate to low	Low to nil

Source: Reprinted from John G. Burch, *Entrepreneurship,* Wiley, New York, 1986, p. 72.

Economic and Social Contributions of Entrepreneurship

Entrepreneurship has been receiving increasing attention from both scholars and the popular press. This focus reflects the growing recognition of the substantial economic and social contributions of entrepreneurship and the small businesses it spawns. In this section, we consider major contributions associated with entrepreneurship in the areas of economic growth, innovation, employment opportunities, and career alternatives for women and minorities.

ECONOMIC GROWTH Entrepreneurship leads to the creation of many new businesses that help fuel economic growth. Since there is no central source of data on new company formations, accurate numbers are impossible to obtain. However, according to one report, more than 2,694,859 new companies were formed between 1987 and 1990.[7] Of course, many of these new ventures fail. While statistics vary, as many as 50 to 70 percent of new businesses fail or merge with other organizations within their first 5 years.[8] Nevertheless, there is little doubt that new ventures make a significant contribution to economic expansion.[9]

INNOVATION As might be anticipated given the innovation requirements for successful entrepreneurship that were just discussed, entrepreneurs have introduced many new products and services that have changed the way we live. Henry Ford's automobile, Joyce Hall's Hallmark greeting cards, Isaac Singer's sewing machine, and King Gillette's razors are just a few examples.[10] Evidence suggests that compared with larger, more established firms, new ventures produce a disproportionately large share of product and process innovations.[11]

EMPLOYMENT OPPORTUNITIES New ventures and small businesses provide the majority of new job opportunities in the United States.[12] The economic impact of small-business job growth is likely to be the greatest during times of economic slowdown, when larger companies are cutting back.[13] During such reductions, many individuals whose jobs are eliminated find employment with small businesses.

OPPORTUNITIES FOR WOMEN AND MINORITIES Entrepreneurship offers an alternative avenue into business for women and minorities. One major attraction is the possibility of avoiding patterns of discrimination. In established organizations, women and minorities may often be channeled to relatively lower-level and poorly paid positions. Another attraction is the prospect of material independence and the ability to control the outcomes of one's own efforts.[14] Finally, some government agencies, at the federal, state, and local levels, have been encouraging businesses owned by minorities and women. They have established programs whereby such businesses are favored in the awarding of some government contracts.

Between 1988 and 1992, the number of women-owned sole proprietorships (a legal form of business with one owner) increased from 2,535,240 to 4,610,951.[15] Although the percentage of businesses started and operated by women is relatively small (estimates range from 4.6 to 5.7 percent), women are making significant inroads.[16] Minorities are also starting more new businesses. For instance, even though blacks presently own less than 2 percent of U.S. businesses, the number of black-owned businesses is rising rapidly.[17] One example of the new entrepreneurs is Lillian Lincoln, the daughter of a Virginia subsistence farmer. She attended segregated schools before managing to earn a Harvard M.B.A. Since then, she has founded Centennial One, a successful company based in Crofton, Maryland, that provides cleaning and pest-control services to major corporations, such as IBM and Westinghouse. As she notes, "Where I have to go can't be as rough climbing as where I've been."[18]

FACTORS INFLUENCING ENTREPRENEURSHIP

What makes someone like Lillian Lincoln create a successful new business? To find the answer, researchers have explored several different avenues. They have focused on characteristics of the entrepreneur, theorizing that there may be some special traits involved. They have also begun to examine more closely the life-path circumstances of individuals that might influence them to become entrepreneurs. In addition, researchers have considered the possibility that certain environmental factors might encourage entrepreneurship. Finally, they have examined perceptions of the desirability and feasibility of becoming an entrepreneur, which also appear to affect the decision to engage in entrepreneurship.[19] These factors are shown in Figure 1 and discussed in detail below.

Personal Characteristics

One fascinating question surrounding entrepreneurship is whether entrepreneurs have personality traits and background experiences that set them apart from others. A number of studies have addressed this issue.[20]

PERSONALITY CHARACTERISTICS Given the variety of businesses that entrepreneurs have created, identifying characteristics that entrepreneurs have in common is a formidable task. So far, the search for personality characteristics has yielded only a few results that may be helpful in separating potential entrepreneurs from the general population, but the traits that have surfaced are also often indicative of managers.

Psychologist David C. McClelland, who is the chief architect of acquired-needs theory, has argued that entrepreneurs tend to have a *high need for achievement* (nAch). Such individuals gravitate toward situations in which they can achieve results through their own efforts, pursue moderately difficult goals, and receive relatively immediate feedback on how they are doing.[21]

While evidence suggests that entrepreneurs do have a relatively high need for achievement, it also indicates that high nAch, by itself, does not single out

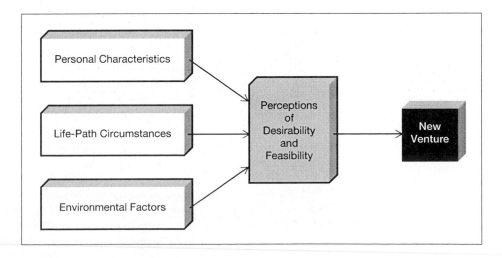

Figure 1 *Factors influencing entrepreneurship.*

entrepreneurs. High nAch can be found among salespeople, professionals, and managers as well. Most likely, high nAch is an important ingredient in entrepreneurial success, just as it is a useful trait in other occupations that involve taking personal responsibility in order to reach significant achievements.

Another characteristic that has been found in entrepreneurs is an *internal locus of control*. Individuals with an internal locus of control tend to feel that they control their fate largely through their own efforts. (In contrast, individuals with an external locus of control view their fate as mainly determined by outside forces and luck.) Again, though, an internal locus of control often characterizes managers as well as entrepreneurs.

One characteristic that does seem to separate entrepreneurs from managers is a *high tolerance for ambiguity,* an ability to continue to function effectively and persist even when situations are highly uncertain. Since entrepreneurship involves starting new organizations, a great deal of uncertainty is frequently involved. Managers often have fairly high levels of tolerance for ambiguity, but not as high as those of entrepreneurs.[22]

BACKGROUND CHARACTERISTICS   A variety of studies have attempted to isolate important background characteristics of entrepreneurs. Much of the focus has been on the areas of childhood family environment, education, age, and work history.[23]

Inquiries into the *childhood family environment* of entrepreneurs have considered issues such as birth order and occupations of parents. One recurring question is whether entrepreneurs tend to be the firstborn or only children in the family. The basic idea is that such children are likely to gain a greater share of their parents' time, leading to an increased self-confidence that may fuel entrepreneurship. Although some studies have found a firstborn or only-child effect, others have not, leaving the theory in doubt.[24]

On the other hand, there is considerable evidence that entrepreneurs tend to have self-employed fathers. They often also have self-employed mothers or parents who jointly own (or owned) a business.[25] Apparently, having one or both parents as business owners provides a salient role model for potential entrepreneurs.

Another focus of inquiry has been the level of entrepreneurs' *education*. Usually, entrepreneurs tend to be better-educated than the general population, although they may be less well educated than individuals who pursue managerial careers, particularly in large organizations. Within the entrepreneurial ranks there is wide variation in educational attainment, with some entrepreneurs lacking high school diplomas and others having graduate degrees.[26] Female entrepreneurs are particularly likely to have college degrees.[27]

Age has been another variable of interest in explaining entrepreneurial activity. Although individuals are more likely to become entrepreneurs between the ages of 25 and 40, some do so across a wider span—more like 22 to 55. Individuals can become entrepreneurs before age 22, but such endeavors are less likely because these individuals do not have the education, experience, and financial resources needed to create new ventures. By the mid-50s, reduced energy and physical problems can impede some, though certainly not all, would-be entrepreneurs. For example, the late Ray Kroc founded McDonald's when he was over 50.[28]

Not surprisingly, there is evidence that *work history* and related experience is an important factor in initiating a new enterprise. Several studies indicate that in new ventures at least one of the company founders had previously worked in the same industry as the new business. Moreover, creating new ventures seems to

Corridor principle A principle which states that the process of beginning a new venture helps entrepreneurs visualize other opportunities that they could not envision or take advantage of until they started the initial venture

become easier after the first one, giving rise to the corridor principle. The **corridor principle** states that the process of beginning a new venture helps entrepreneurs visualize other opportunities that they could not envision or take advantage of until they started the initial venture.[29] For example, Phil Romano developed ideas for several other businesses after he created Fuddruckers. Of course, individuals who begin their entrepreneurial careers at the lower end of the age scale may be better able to exploit the corridor principle because of their potentially longer entrepreneurial career.

All in all, there do appear to be a few characteristics that separate entrepreneurs from the general population and even, in some cases, from managers. Yet personal characteristics are relatively weak predictors of entrepreneurship. What distinguishes those who make the decision to become entrepreneurs from those who do not? Some further clues come from recent efforts to study the life-path circumstances of entrepreneurs.

Life-Path Circumstances

Several types of life-path, or individual, circumstances seem to increase the probability that an individual will become an entrepreneur. The four major types of circumstances are unsatisfactory work environment, negative displacement, career transition points, and the presence of positive-pull influencers.[30]

UNSATISFACTORY WORK ENVIRONMENT An unsatisfactory work environment is a job situation characterized by circumstances that impel the worker to think about leaving and starting a new venture. One common factor is strong dissatisfaction with either the work itself or some other aspect of the work environment, such as supervision. Another is an employer's refusal to recognize the value of an innovative idea.[31] For example, H. Ross Perot tried to get IBM to adopt his idea of selling customers computer software services along with the company's hardware. When IBM refused to support his idea, he quit and started Electronic Data Services. The company netted him close to a billion dollars when he sold his final holdings in 1984, 22 years after founding it.[32]

NEGATIVE DISPLACEMENT Negative displacement, or disruption, occurs when circumstances in a person's life situation cause the person to make major changes in lifestyle. Factors in this category include being fired, getting a divorce, becoming widowed, reaching middle age, or emigrating from another country. For instance, negative displacement precipitated a very different lifestyle for brother and sister Marty and Helen Shih when they came to Los Angeles from Taiwan in 1979. At the time, they had $500 between them to start a new business. The pair opened a flower shop because they felt that their English language skills were not sufficient to land good corporate jobs, despite their strong educational backgrounds. Today, they operate as Shih's Flowers, Inc. They own nine shops (the downtown store alone grosses $1 million per year), and the business is still growing.[33]

CAREER TRANSITIONS Career transition points are circumstances in which an individual is moving between one type of career-related activity and another. Such points are completing studies or a degree, being discharged from military service, finishing a major project, or having children leave home. For example, Nancy Barocci was at a transition point when she returned to Wilmette, Illinois, with her husband and children after several years in Europe. She had been studying Italian food and wines and now wanted to put her learning to good use. So, in 1980, she opened an Italian restaurant that was an immediate hit. She has since moved the original Convito Italiano to a larger location and opened a second, even larger and equally successful, Convito in Chicago.[34]

POSITIVE-PULL INFLUENCERS Positive-pull influencers are individuals, such as mentors, investors, customers, or potential partners, who urge an individual to start a business. For instance, Scott McNealy, co-founder and chief executive of Sun Microsystems, Inc., got involved in starting the company when his former Stanford roommate, Vinod Khosia, approached him with the idea. The pair teamed up with two other Stanford M.B.A.s in 1982 and have built the company into a billion-dollar player in the field of engineering workstations.[35] The pull notion is unlike the other life-path changes discussed above, since they involve circumstances that push individuals toward the entrepreneurial life. Individuals in push situations must either take action or suffer negative consequences. While life-path circumstances can be an impetus for entrepreneurship, real and perceived environmental conditions favoring new businesses are also an ingredient.

Favorable Environmental Conditions

A number of environmental conditions appear to influence entrepreneurs. Generally, they deal with the basic prerequisites of running a business, such as adequate financing, a technically skilled labor force, accessibility of suppliers, accessibility of customers or new markets, availability of land or facilities, accessibility of transportation, and availability of supporting services. Other, more indirect conditions provide support as well, such as the presence of experienced entrepreneurs and incubator organizations, government influences, proximity of universities, attitude of the area's population, and living conditions.

One factor mentioned above that requires further explanation is the notion of an incubator. An **incubator** is an organization whose purpose is to nurture new ventures in their very early stages by providing space (usually at a site housing other new ventures as well), stimulation, support, and a variety of basic services, often at reduced fees. The idea is to help the new ventures during their first 2 or 3 years or so, until they have grown enough to "hatch" and join the normal business world.[36] Although there were only about 50 incubators in the United States in 1984, the number had grown to more than 600 by 1992, according to figures from the National Business Incubation Association.[37]

Incubator An organization whose purpose is to nurture new ventures in their very early stages by providing space (usually at a site housing other new ventures as well), stimulation, support, and a variety of basic services, often at reduced fees

Perceptions of Desirability and Feasibility

Even when personal characteristics, life-path circumstances, and/or environmental conditions are either pushing or pulling individuals toward entrepreneurship, such individuals are still unlikely to take action unless another element is present: they must perceive entrepreneurship as both desirable and feasible.[38]

Some factors that influence desirability are related to the personal characteristics mentioned earlier, such as family members who have owned their own businesses and/or who encourage independence. Others are related mainly to life-path circumstances, such as the presence of positive-pull influencers. These may be peers who have created new ventures, teachers (especially in courses on entrepreneurship) who point out the potential for success, and supportive colleagues in the organization that the individual worked for before initiating the new venture.

Even with perceived desirability, would-be entrepreneurs must also make an assessment of the feasibility of creating a new enterprise. While personal characteristics and life-path circumstances play a part, environmental conditions are an important aspect of feasibility assessments. Thus perceptions of feasibility are influenced by seeing oneself as having the necessary background, the presence of successful role models, the availability of advice from knowledgeable others, and the availability of financial support. For example, after graduating from college and moving to Hong Kong, Katha Diddel began to perceive that she, too, could start her own business (see the following Case in Point discussion).

CASE IN POINT

KATHA DIDDEL LAUNCHES HER HOME COLLECTION

When Katha Diddel graduated from college in 1979, she went directly to mainland China seeking a job in which she could use her 6 years of intensive language training in Mandarin Chinese. After a few short-term jobs as an interpreter, she landed a position in the China trade division of the Associated Merchandising Corporation (AMC) in Hong Kong. She worked as a merchandiser and market guide for American retailers who wanted to meet Chinese suppliers on the mainland. This position enabled her to build a network of business contacts at a time when China was beginning to show interest in exporting products to U.S. markets. In the process, she slowly put together a business plan to fulfill her dream of having a business of her own—a company that would market exquisite Chinese embroidery in the United States.

Diddel traveled around the country visiting dozens of tiny villages and remote islands before finally finding what she was looking for in an old factory in a mountain community. There she located workers doing lovely embroidery in patterns that earlier generations had learned from European missionaries. Unfortunately, the workers were using "garish" colors and cheap polyester fabric. She proposed that the workers embroider fine linens, and her plan was accepted by the plant managers. Afterward, she stayed to supervise the learning process by, for example, picking out the thread colors and showing the artisans where to put the designs on the fabric.

Having developed the products, Diddel now needed to find interested importers in the United States. In New York, she made numerous calls to importers listed in the telephone book, went to trade shows and collected names of potential customers, advertised in trade journals, and sent out over 1000 letters to prospects. "The process took a very long time," she says, "It was not the most pleasant period of my life." Nevertheless, she was ultimately successful. To finance her operation, she obtained a $5000 loan from a Hong Kong bank. She also worked out an arrangement with her importers that guaranteed immediate payment for products received.

With the pieces in place, Diddel launched Twin Panda, Inc., in 1981, just when the U.S. home-furnishings market was expanding rapidly. From 1981 to 1986, sales boomed. Then, suddenly, she began to notice signs of trouble. Diddel says that competitors, taking note of her success, went to her sources and set up rival contracts for imitations using cheaper materials that allowed them to undercut her prices. Since copyright laws in China are weak, Diddel decided to fight the low-cost approach of her competitors by means of a differentiation strategy. She focused on top-of-the-line, hand-worked products and a greater variety of designs. As part of the implementation process, Diddel went to China and renegotiated contracts for higher volumes in return for guaranteed protection of her designs. She has also renamed her product line the Katha Diddel Home Collection, to denote that the products are created by a designer. The change has been accompanied by new catalogs, new promotional strategies, and new advertising. Her expanding product line recently included baby-bed linens that were an instant hit.[39]   ■ ■ ■

Because of the current interest in entrepreneurs like Katha Diddel, our emphasis here has been on factors that influence individuals to create new ventures. Of course, creating a new organization is not the only way to engage in small-business ownership. There are alternative approaches.

DECIDING ON A DEVELOPMENT APPROACH

One major aspect of both entrepreneurship and small-business ownership is determining which development path to pursue.[40] There are three general approaches: starting a new firm, buying an existing business, or purchasing a franchise.

Starting a New Firm

Start-up A type of new firm or venture started from scratch by an entrepreneur

A new firm started from scratch by an entrepreneur is often referred to as a **start-up**. A study of 106 entrepreneurs offers clues about the types of new firms, or start-ups, that one might create.[41] On the basis of interviews with their reasonably representative sample of entrepreneurs, the researchers identified the following reasons why these individuals started new firms:

Escaping to something new: In starting a new firm, the entrepreneur in this category is attempting to escape from his or her previous type of job, which the individual feels did not offer prospects for sufficient rewards in terms of salary, challenging work, promotion opportunities, or other factors.

Putting the deal together: The individual in this category aims to bundle the different aspects of the business (such as suppliers, wholesale and retail channels, and customers) into a "deal," from which each participant will gain.

Rolling over skills and contacts: Before establishing the new firm, the individual in this category worked in a position that involved technical skills and expertise closely related to those needed in the new enterprise. The venture offers goods and services that rely on the owner's professional expertise and are most often generic services (e.g., auditing or advertising).

Leveraging expertise: The individual is one of the top people in his or her technical field. The entrepreneur brings in partners to help start the firm. The venture enters an established market and competes through flexibility in adapting to customer needs, which is based on the entrepreneur's keen awareness of environmental changes.

Forming an aggressive service: The entrepreneur creates an aggressive service-oriented firm, usually a consulting firm in a highly specialized area.

Pursuing the unique idea: The venture develops because of an idea for a product or service that is not being offered. The product or service is not technically sophisticated or difficult to produce.

Organizing methodically: The entrepreneur in this category uses extensive planning both to acquire the skills and to perform the tasks required in the new venture. The products or services are similar to those of competitors, but the firm provides a new twist, usually either a slightly different way to produce the product or service or a slightly different customer to whom to sell.

One entrepreneur who has parlayed a knack for new twists into a British company that now has annual revenues of more than $1 billion is Alan Michael Sugar (see the following Case in Point discussion).

CASE IN POINT

EUROPE'S MOST SUCCESSFUL NEW ENTREPRENEUR

Alan Michael Sugar was born in 1947 and grew up in London's working-class East End, where his achievement orientation exhibited itself early. He would take various odd jobs, such as photographing neighbors on Sunday outings and rising at the crack of dawn to stock grocery shelves. In this way, Sugar was earning more than his father by the time Sugar left school at 16. Soon after, he started his own business by renting a van and using it as a base from which to sell car-radio antennas. In 1968, he started Amstrad (for "Alan Michael Sugar Trading"), a wholesale distributor of cassette players, speakers, and other electronic gear for cars. By 1978, Sugar had his first major success, a stackable stereo unit priced for the ordinary consumer. Sales were impressive enough to enable him to get Amstrad listed on the London stock exchange 2 years later, and he immediately acquired a net worth of $8 million.

Sugar's basic strategy is offering established technology at prices so low that specialty markets are immediately transformed into mass markets—a phenomenon that stock market analysts have dubbed "the Amstrad effect." For example, when Amstrad introduced its first word-processing computer in 1985, British industry experts figured that it would sell about 50,000 units per year. Sugar set the price of the unit about equal to the price of a good electronic typewriter and soon was selling 50,000 per month. A year later, Amstrad became the first European company to offer a low-priced IBM personal computer clone. The price was set at below $600, or less than half the price of equivalent machines from other sources. As a result, Amstrad more than doubled the British PC market before pushing into France and Spain. Now Amstrad tops everyone but IBM in European sales of personal computers.

In another move, Amstrad has been selling satellite dishes for use in conjunction with British Sky Broadcasting, a European satellite TV network. By offering the dishes for about one-half the price of similar dishes based on a different technology, the dishes quickly became Amstrad's most important product line. Once again, the Amstrad effect was in action. Such moves have transformed Sugar's original wholesale distributor into an electronics giant in less than two decades. In keeping with his low-cost emphasis, Sugar continues to work from Amstrad's spartan headquarters overlooking the railroad tracks in a commuter town by the name of Brentwood. The future will be tougher for Amstrad, as many of its major electronic products face maturing markets.[42]

■ ■ ■

Buying an Existing Business

The second major approach to developing a new venture is purchasing an existing business. This can also apply to acquiring and managing a small business. Entrepreneurs typically acquire an existing business when they believe that they can quickly change its direction in a fairly substantial way so that it will grow in major new areas. Often the organization may be faltering. For example, in 1988, a group of entrepreneurs purchased Cuisinarts, Inc., the company that pioneered the food processor, after it failed to capitalize on its name in developing new products. Unfortunately, the entrepreneurs were not experienced in the small-kitchen-appliance business and 1 year later were forced to file for bankruptcy protection themselves.[43] In contrast, prospective small-business owners tend to purchase an existing business with the idea of retaining the business in basically the same form, although it may possibly need to be managed more effectively (especially if it was doing poorly). In the long run, of course, small-business owners may make substantial changes.

Several of the major considerations that go into purchasing an existing business are shown in Figure 2. It is usually imperative to obtain professional help, particularly from a lawyer (to review such matters as current contracts with suppliers and to set up an acquisition agreement) and an accountant (to audit the financial records and help determine a purchase price).[44]

Purchasing a Franchise

The third major approach to developing a small business is purchasing a franchise. (The study of entrepreneurs discussed earlier did not cover franchises.) A **franchise** is a continuing arrangement between a franchiser and a franchisee in which the franchiser's knowledge, image, manufacturing or service expertise,

Franchise A continuing arrangement between a franchiser and a franchisee in which the franchiser's knowledge, image, manufacturing or service expertise, and marketing techniques are made available to the franchisee in return for the payment of various fees or royalties and conformity to standard operating procedures

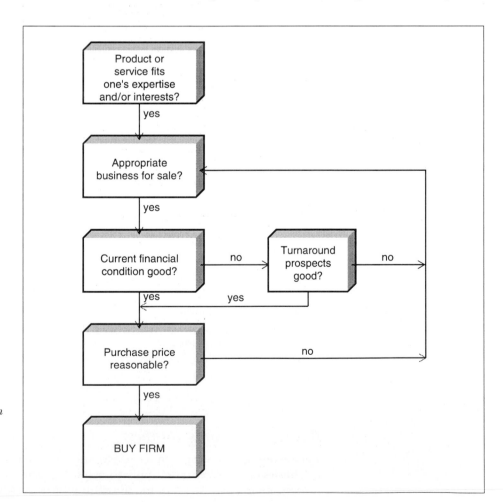

Figure 2 *Considerations in purchasing an existing business. (Adapted from Nicholas C. Siropolis,* Small Business Management. *Houghton Mifflin, Boston, 1990, p. 103.)*

Franchiser A manufacturer or sole distributor of a trademarked product or service who typically has considerable experience in the line of business being franchised

Franchisee An individual who purchases a franchise and, in the process, is given an opportunity to enter a new business, hopefully with an enhanced chance of success

and marketing techniques are made available to the franchisee in return for the payment of various fees or royalties and conformity to standard operating procedures.[45] A **franchiser** is usually a manufacturer or sole distributor of a trademarked product or service who typically has considerable experience in the line of business being franchised. A **franchisee** is an individual who purchases a franchise and, in the process, is given an opportunity to enter a new business, hopefully with an enhanced chance of success.[46] When one mentions franchises, fast-food operations, such as McDonald's, often come to mind.

Franchises are normally considered to be small businesses but not new ventures, since the creation process is largely controlled by the franchiser, rather than the franchisee. In fact, some writers do not include most franchise arrangements in the small-business category. Instead, they view franchises as appendages of larger organizations.[47]

The primary advantage of a franchise is that the franchisee gains access to the proven business methods, established reputation, training, and assistance of the franchiser, so the new venture risk is minimized. On the other hand, there are a number of disadvantages. These include a lack of independence in regard to making major modifications, the considerable difficulty involved in canceling franchise contracts, the likelihood of continual monitoring by the franchiser, and the substantial expense that may be involved in establishing a franchise with a well-known company.[48] Nevertheless, for individuals who lack expertise in a viable business specialty, a franchise may be the answer. (Table 2 lists a number of recommended franchises for the 1990s.)

PREPARING TO OPERATE A SMALL BUSINESS

Regardless of which development path an individual decides to pursue, there are major preparations involved in starting a small business. Important steps include developing a business plan, obtaining the necessary resources, and selecting an appropriate site for the business.

Developing a Business Plan

Business plan A document written by the prospective owner or entrepreneur that details the nature of the business, the product or service, the customers, the competition, the production and marketing methods, the management, the financing, and other significant aspects of the proposed business venture

Most small-business and entrepreneurship experts strongly recommend the development of a business plan. A **business plan** is a document written by the prospective owner or entrepreneur that details the nature of the business, the product or service, the customers, the competition, the production and marketing methods, the management, the financing, and other significant aspects of the proposed business venture.[49]

A well-prepared business plan can take 200 to 400 hours or even more to complete, depending on the complexity of the business contemplated, the strength of the competition, the number of different parties involved, and the number of other factors that must be considered.[50] For an outline of the major steps involved in developing a business plan, see the Practically Speaking discussion, "Steps in Developing a Business Plan."

A business plan serves several important purposes.[52] First, it helps prospective owners and entrepreneurs carefully think through every aspect of their proposed endeavor. Since the plan requires writing down information about such aspects as the risks involved, financing requirements, and intended markets, prospective owners and entrepreneurs are forced to think concretely about such matters.

Second, a business plan helps prospective owners and entrepreneurs obtain financing. For example, the U.S. Small Business Administration (SBA) requires

TABLE 2	10 Top Franchises for the 1990s*		
Franchise/Line of Business	Initial Cash Investment†	Total Start-Up Costs‡	Comments
Alphagraphics Printshops, Tucson Printing and copying	$70,000	$250,000– $300,000	Chain stays competitive by providing the latest technology and offering self-service. It prefers franchisees with management experience.
Decorating Den Systems, Bethesda, Md. Home decorating products and services	$6,900– $18,900	$14,900– $30,900	These are low-overhead operations selling custom draperies and furnishings. You don't need decorating experience; they'll train you.
Dunhill Personnel System, Woodbury, N.Y. Employment services	$10,000– $12,000	$50,000– $120,000	A respected 40-year-old name in executive recruitment and temporary personnel. Continued corporate downsizing will increase the demand for such services.
Everything Yogurt, Staten Island, N.Y. Health-food restaurant	$56,000	$175,000– $225,000	Chain is capitalizing on the public's growing appetite for salads, soups, and yogurt drinks.
Jani-King International, Dallas Commercial cleaning	$2,850– $6,000	$5,000– $25,000	A low-cost, strong-performing franchise in a stable industry.
Jazzercise, Carlsbad, Calif. Fitness	$650	$2,000– $3,000	Initial investment is low, partly because it doesn't include facility leasing and equipment is minimal.
McDonald's, Oak Brook, Ill. Fast food	$66,000– $244,000	$610,000 (average)	Its powerhouse reputation will keep it growing, albeit more slowly in a fast-food market. Expect a long wait for a franchise, and be prepared for a turndown.
Merry Maids, Omaha Residential cleaning	$18,500	$28,500– $33,500	More and more two-career families are hooked on residential cleaning services
Petland, Chillicothe, Ohio Pet store	$40,000– $80,000	$180,000– $400,000	Franchisees are always installed in high-traffic shopping centers, and outlets offer a wide range of merchandise. Result: even higher traffic.
Precision Tune, Sterling, Va. Automotive services	$20,000	$146,620– $163,620	A relatively recessionproof industry.

*Established franchisors that promise to have continued growth in the 1990s.
†The amount of cash you must put up.
‡Can include cash and financing. Some franchisors charge annual royalties and marketing and advertising fees.
Source: Adapted from Derek E. Dingle, "Franchising's Fast Track to Freedom," *Money Extra,* 1990, p. 40.

that a business plan accompany applications for the agency's small-business loan program. Most private investors will not even consider financing a venture without seeing a well-thought-out plan. For example, Phil Romano uses business plans to help obtain outside funding for his various ventures. Obtaining significant funding from banks will also involve submitting a business plan. Even short-run loans may be easier to negotiate when an entrepreneur can demonstrate that a new business venture is progressing according to plan.

Third, a business plan provides a basis for measuring plan progress. Some experts argue that planning is particularly important for new ventures because of their inherent instability. A business plan can help establish milestones for periodic reviews, during which assumptions and accomplishments can be compared. Careful monitoring increases the likelihood of identifying significant deviations

PRACTICALLY SPEAKING

STEPS IN DEVELOPING A BUSINESS PLAN

The steps below will give you a good idea of what is involved in putting together a business plan. The timetable for developing the plan will depend on the complexity of the situation and your own time schedule.

1   Make commitment to go into business for yourself.
2   Analyze your strengths and weaknesses, paying special attention to your business experience, business education, and desires. Then answer this question:
    Why should I be in business for myself?
3   Choose the product or service that best fits your strengths and desires. Then answer these questions:
    What need will my product or service fill?
    What is unique about my product or service? How do I know it is unique?
    What will my product or service do for customers? What will it not do? What should it do later that it does not now do?
4   Research the market for your product or service to find answers to such questions as these:
    Who are my customers? Where are they? What is their average income? How do they buy? At what price? In what quantities? When do they buy? When will they use my product or service? Where will they use it? Why will they buy it? Who are my competitors? Where are they? How strong are they?

What is the total market potential? Is it growing?
5   Forecast your share of market, if possible. Then forecast your sales revenues over a 3-year period, broken down as follows:
    First year—monthly
    Second year—quarterly
    Third year—yearly
    Next, answer this question:
    Why do I believe my sales revenue forecast is realistic?
6   Choose a site for your business. Then answer this question:
    Why do I prefer this site to other possible sites?
7   *This step applies only to entrepreneurs who plan to go into manufacturing.* Develop your production plan, answering these questions:
    How big should my plant be?
    How should my production process be laid out?
    What equipment will I need?
    In what size?
    How will I control the waste, quality, and inventory of my product?
8   Develop your marketing plan, answering such questions as these:
    How am I going to create customers? At what price? By what kinds of advertising and sales promotion? Through personal selling? How?
9   Develop your organizational plan, answering this question:
    What kinds of skills and talents will I need to make my business grow?
    Draw up an organization chart that spells out who does what, who has what authority, and who reports to whom.

10 Develop your legal plan, focusing on whether to form a sole proprietorship, a partnership, or a corporation, and then explain your choice.
11 Develop your accounting plan, explaining the kinds of records and reports you need and how you will use them.
12 Develop your insurance plan, answering this question:
    What kinds of insurance will I need to protect my venture against possible loss from unforeseen events?
13 Develop a computer plan, spelling out the ways that computer services may help you plan and control your business.
14 Develop your financial plan by preparing these statements:
    A 3-year cash budget. Show how much cash you will need before opening for business and how much cash you expect will flow in and out of your business, broken down as follows:
    First year—monthly
    Second year—quarterly
    Third year—yearly
    An income statement for the first year only.
    Balance sheets for the beginning and end of the first year.
    A profit graph (break-even chart), showing when you will begin to make a profit.
    Then determine how you will finance your business and where you expect to raise money.
15 Write a cover letter summarizing your business plan, stressing its purpose and its promise.[51]

from the plan and making modifications before the frail new venture is forced out of business.[53]

Fourth, business plans often help prospective owners and entrepreneurs establish credibility with others. For example, potential employees may need to be convinced that they are joining an organization with a strong chance of success. Suppliers may be more willing to extend a line of credit when the business plan appears sound. Major customers may be more inclined to place orders when there are convincing arguments that the new venture or small business will be able to deliver the necessary products or services.

Obtaining Resources

Two of the most important resources typically needed in starting a new firm or acquiring an existing small business are financing and human resources. Each plays a crucial role.

FINANCING   New ventures, even small ones, require funds to operate. Moreover, most of their revenues in the early years must be plowed back into the business to fuel growth. There are many sources of financing for entrepreneurs and prospective small-business owners. The most common are personal savings and loans from family and friends, as well as loans from banks. For example, Katha Diddel started her business with a $5000 loan from a Hong Kong bank. Phil Romano has initiated several businesses with loans from banks, money borrowed from friends, loans from the U.S. Small Business Administration, and funds from stock sold to private investors, as well as with his own funds. Potential sources of funding for entrepreneurs and prospective small-business owners are shown in Table 3.

One of the major issues associated with securing funding is the amount of equity (or ownership of the firm) and potential control an entrepreneur or prospective small-business owner must relinquish to obtain the necessary financing. There are two major types of funding available.[54] The first is **debt capital,** financing that involves a loan to be repaid, usually with interest. Typically, part of the loan arrangement involves putting up some asset (such as a car, a house, or machinery) as collateral in case the firm is not able to repay the debt. Banks are the major source of debt capital to new ventures and small businesses, although some debt capital is available through other sources, such as the Small Business Administration.

The second major type of funding is **equity capital,** financing which usually requires that the investor be given some form of ownership in the venture. The investor shares in the profits and in any proceeds from the sale of assets in proportion to the equity held. For example, Phil Romano gave up 48 percent of his equity in Fuddruckers to obtain the $150,000 that he needed to start the business. When he later sold the company, the investors were entitled to 48 percent of the proceeds. Because of the success of the venture, a $15,000 investment in Fuddruckers was worth about $3.5 million 3 years later. One study of entrepreneurs showed that the overall equity relinquished by their firms in order to obtain capital during the early stages averaged 45.1 percent.[55]

New venture capital has recently been playing a major role in the creation of start-up companies in eastern Europe. In one such case, Jan Bednarek, the general manager of Wistom, a state-owned synthetic fibers company in Poland, has used some of the profits from the company to furnish seed money for 18 start-up companies. His goal is to create enough jobs and pump enough profits into the local economy of Tomaszow Mazowiecki (a town of 70,000 people, located 60 miles southwest of Warsaw) to enable him to close his antiquated synthetic fibers

Debt capital   A type of financing that involves a loan to be repaid, usually with interest

Equity capital   A type of financing which usually requires that the investor be given some form of ownership in the venture

TABLE 3	Potential Sources of Funding New Ventures and Small Businesses

Wealthy individuals: Go to these individuals either directly or through a third party. These people normally prefer common stock and secured loans, expect a substantial ownership stake in the company, and like to keep tabs on their investment.

Venture capitalists: These institutional risk takers are normally located through CPAs, attorneys, and bankers. They usually have formulas for evaluating a business, tend to specialize in certain types of businesses, and prefer strong minority positions. They often structure deals with both equity and debt characteristics.

Small Business Administration: The SBA has a variety of loan programs for small businesses that cannot borrow from conventional vendors on reasonable terms. There are normally limits on the amount of money available, but the interest rates are slightly lower than those on regular commercial loans.

Commercial banks: Banks generally require security and guarantees before making start-up loans and sometimes impose other restrictions on the borrower. A borrower can expect to pay the prime rate plus 1 to 4 points.

Business development corporations: BDCs are privately owned corporations chartered by about half the states to make loans to small businesses. They can develop creative financing packages, and their loans are generally guaranteed by the SBA.

State venture-capital funds: About half the states have programs which provide venture-capital funds. Most make loans, and some provide equity capital. Information about these sources of funding can normally be obtained from the local state economic or industrial development office.

Shares sold by the entrepreneur or small-business owner: To attract outside investors, some entrepreneurs and small-business owners sell shares at private or public offerings. Such offerings are very technical and require expert legal help to conform to the federal securities laws and appropriate state laws.

Source: Adapted from *Changing Times,* September 1985, pp. 38–43. [Also reprinted in "How to Bankroll Your Future," in Clifford M. Baumback and Joseph Mancuso (eds.), *Entrepreneurship and Venture Management,* Prentice-Hall, Englewood Cliffs, N.J., 1987, pp. 188–189.]

plant. Wistom invests in new ventures for an agreed-upon amount of stock. In one case, a new venture began by designing and producing improved lighting fixtures for the Wistom factory. Another start-up, which specializes in factory automation and industrial processing equipment, is housed in the Wistom facility. It is currently making $20,000 per month in profits, and Bednarek is looking forward to the time when its employees can buy out Wistom's stake in the company.[56]

In the United States, new ventures typically use a combination of debt and equity capital. Debt capital tends to be used for short-time financing (funds needed for a year or less) to pay for such things as monthly expenses, advertising, special sales from suppliers, and unforeseen emergencies. For the longer range, both long-term debt capital (funds for 1 to 5 years or more) and equity capital are often used to finance basic start-up costs, the purchase or replacement of equipment, expansions, and other major expenditures. Small businesses that are aiming for relatively moderate growth frequently use mainly debt capital, with the owners retaining most or all of the equity.

HUMAN RESOURCES Although many new ventures are initiated by entrepreneurs, others have multiple founders who are often referred to as a venture team. **A venture team** is a group of two or more individuals who band together for the purpose of creating a new venture. Ideally, venture-team members complement one another's skills, thus strengthening the prospects of the new ven-

Venture team A group of two or more individuals who band together for the purpose of creating a new venture

ture. Mutual trust and strong commitment to the start-up are also essential ingredients. Potential venture-team members need to explore their mutual expectations carefully, since a breakup of the team early in the venture can have a serious detrimental effect on the success of the endeavor.[57]

Of course, new ventures and small businesses typically require the help of others besides entrepreneurs or owners. In fact, a poll of small-business owners showed that their most difficult problem is finding competent workers and then motivating them to perform.[58] Since each employee in a small business represents a large percentage of the work force, a given individual's contribution can be particularly significant to the success of the organization. Thus entrepreneurs and small-business owners need to use good selection processes to find individuals who will be strong assets as the organization grows. For example, Leo Imperiali, the founder of the Tile World chain of tile stores, hired many workers who were inexperienced but showed a willingness to learn and an enthusiasm for the venture. As the venture grew, Imperiali generally followed a policy of good training and hiring from within. As a result, he had the human resources needed to support his expansion plans.[59]

Selecting an Appropriate Site

Choosing a location for a business is typically an important decision. For instance, a fast-food restaurant depends in large part on having potential customers pass by. On the other hand, a general contracting operation that relies heavily on advertising to reach customers will not be as directly affected by its location. In selecting an appropriate business site, entrepreneurs and small-business owners usually take into consideration major factors such as the community, the trade area, lease or buy trade-offs, zoning or licensing requirements, and cost per square foot.[60]

COMMUNITY The community in which an entrepreneur or small-business owner chooses to operate is often a matter of personal choice. Some may prefer a specific geographic location, such as the northwest; others may wish to operate in a small town; while still others will opt for a large metropolitan area. Some local governments offer benefits and incentives to businesses willing to locate in their areas.

TRADE AREA Usually, location decisions also involve identifying a *trade area,* the geographic area that contains the firm's prospective customers. Determining a trade area includes deciding who the customers will be and learning about their buying habits. For example, a study of food-store purchases in a major city found that close to 70 percent of the customers shopped at stores within one to five blocks of their homes. For suburban locations, the majority of customers lived within 3 miles of the stores, although some traveled as far as 5 miles. In rural locations, most of the customers lived a 10-minute drive away, with the trade area extending as far as a 20-minute drive.

LEASE OR BUY New businesses typically lease facilities, sometimes with an option to buy. This is partly because financing sources are normally reluctant to provide funds for the purchase of physical facilities when a firm has no established track record. As the business develops, small-business owners tend to purchase facilities.

ZONING AND LICENSING Zoning laws can sometimes have a bearing on the location of new ventures and small businesses. For example, many types of businesses, such as light manufacturing or automobile sales, are usually not permitted in residential areas. Moreover, licenses are frequently required in many jurisdictions in order to operate certain types of businesses, such as restaurants, dry cleaners, gas stations, liquor stores, and bars. For these reasons, a thorough investigation into zoning and licensing requirements is usually conducted early in the site selection process.

COST PER SQUARE FOOT   Rental or lease costs will vary and can be substantial for a new venture or other small business. Commercial property is usually rented or leased on a cost-per-square-foot basis. These costs are normally determined by location, condition of property, services furnished, and availability of parking for both employees and customers. Sometimes, starting a business in an incubator can greatly reduce such costs, although the location of the incubator may not be suitable in many cases.

MANAGING A SMALL BUSINESS

As new ventures begin to take shape and other small businesses engage in commerce, they must be managed. In this section we consider the growth stages of small businesses as they emerge and develop, the transition from entrepreneurship to intrapreneurship, and some special issues and problems associated with entrepreneurship and small-business management.

Stages of Small-Business Growth

While some researchers have examined the growth stages of organizations, others have explored the stages of small-business growth in order to better understand the very early life of organizations.[61] According to one analysis, small-business growth consists of five major stages, as shown in Figure 3.

STAGE I: EXISTENCE   In the existence stage, the small business is just getting started. The main problems it faces are attracting customers and delivering the products and services required. Critical questions are whether or not sufficient customers can be lined up, whether the production process can actually fulfill the needs of customers, and whether there are sufficient funds to cover the emerging start-up costs. Companies at this stage are struggling for their existence. Many times, customers or adequate production capabilities do not materialize before funds run out. If that happens, the new venture collapses or perhaps is sold for asset value.

STAGE II: SURVIVAL   In the survival stage, the problem changes from concern for mere existence to concern for revenues relative to expenses. Two issues are critical at this point: Can the company break even and make enough profit to repair and replace assets, and can it generate enough funds to finance the growth necessary for eventually earning a good return on assets and labor? The main concern at this stage is survival, and the owner still makes most of the important decisions concerning the organization. Some organizations may remain at this level for a long time, barely making ends meet, until the owner gives up or retires. Others may grow in size and begin to earn a reasonable profit, thereby moving to the next stage.

STAGE III: SUCCESS   At the success stage, the owner faces a major decision. Should the owner stabilize at a profitable level that can be used to support his or

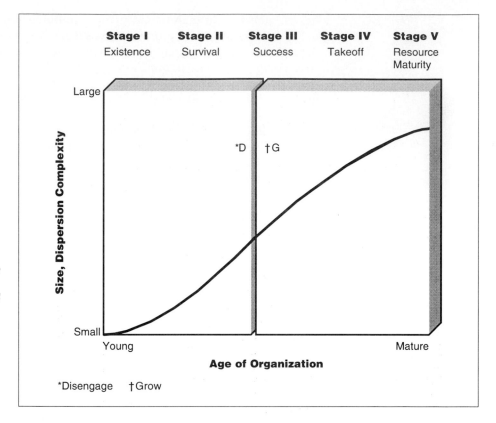

Figure 3 *Stages of new venture growth. (Reprinted by permission of* Harvard Business Review. *An exhibit from "The Five Stages of Business Growth," by Neil C. Churchill and Virginia L. Lewis, May–June 1983. Copyright © 1983 by the President and Fellows of Harvard College; all rights reserved.)*

her other interests (success-disengagement substage) or build on the accomplishments so far and go for further growth (success-growth substage)?

In *substage III-D* (disengagement), the company has good economic health and earns average or above-average profits. If it does not adapt to environmental changes, the organization may go under or revert to the survival stage.

In *substage III-G* (growth), the owner pulls together the cash and borrowing power of the company to invest in significant further growth. Important tasks are managing the business so that it continues to be profitable and developing managers to handle the expansion. Strategic planning becomes critical, and the owner is involved in all phases of the business. If successful, the company moves to the next stage. If not, it may be able to shift to III-D. Otherwise, it may slide back to the survival stage or be sold.

STAGE IV: TAKEOFF In the takeoff stage, the key problems are how rapidly to grow and how to finance the growth. One critical issue is whether the owner is willing to delegate responsibilities to others in order to handle the growing enterprise. Another is whether the cash flow will be sufficient. Both operational planning and strategic planning are extremely important. Entrepreneurs, and some small-business owners, often do not have the breadth of managerial skills and experience that is needed to handle a company at this stage. In some cases, entrepreneurs recognize their shortcomings and move aside so that professional managers can steer the company.

One company in which entrepreneurs successfully turned the operation of an organization over to professional managers is BDM International, headquartered in McLean, Virginia. The high-technology consulting firm was founded in 1959 by three physicists. It was awarded its first major contract by the U.S. Army in 1960. A president was promoted from within in 1972. The founders remained major shareholders and advisers to the organization. The company had \$8.1 million in contract awards and 434 employees in 1972. By 1991 its annual contract awards totaled \$297 million, and the company employed 2200 people.[62]

If efforts at this stage are unsuccessful, a company may fold or revert to one of its former stages. One company that ran into difficulty attempting to move from substage III-G (success-growth) to stage IV (takeoff) is J. Bildner & Sons (see the following Case in Point discussion).

CASE IN POINT   JAMES BILDNER'S SPECTACULAR RISE AND FALL

When James Bildner opened his first upscale grocery store in 1984, it was greeted with rave reviews. Bildner and his company, J. Bildner & Sons, Inc., were even featured in a *Newsweek* cover story on yuppies. Within 3 years, the company had 21 stores, more than 2000 employees, and sales approaching \$50 million. Yet 1 year later, the company was in proceedings under Chapter 11 of the Federal Bankruptcy Code, with debts exceeding assets by about \$30 million. The number of stores had shrunk to six, and the work force had been cut to 250 members. How could a business that started up so well turn so sour?

The first J. Bildner & Sons was located in an ornate Boston building dating back to 1865. It stayed open long hours, took phone orders, allowed credit cards, and offered free delivery. In fact, delivery people would even pick up a customer's dry cleaning on the way and shop at other stores for items that Bildner's didn't have. Bildner's itself was well stocked with an enticing array of selections, including such delights as hot red-pepper fettucine and salmon-spinach, prepared in Bildner's own kitchens.

The store was extremely popular from the day it opened. Since its success relied on a concept, rather than a patentable product, Bildner was concerned that competitors would attempt to establish similar stores. Accordingly, he opened five more stores in the Boston area in 1985. The following year, he opened eight more, including locations in Atlanta and in Birmingham.

In September 1986, the company sold stock to the public at \$13 per share in order to raise \$15 million for further expansion. Shortly thereafter, Bildner's had a store in New York City, as well as leases for seven additional stores in New York. Leases were also signed for nine other stores in such cities as Philadelphia; Chicago; and Fairfax, Virginia. The expansion had reached a feverish pace.

By the following summer, though, trouble signs were appearing. That's when the company closed its Birmingham store and its first two New York stores. By July 1988, Bildner's had filed for bankruptcy protection.

In sorting out what went wrong, some observers say that the company's executives didn't do enough planning before expanding. For example, the company expected costs in New York to be about 10 percent higher than in Boston, but they were actually 40 percent more. Construction problems and an attempt to unionize the New York stores delayed openings and drove up costs. In addition, company executives underestimated the competition in New York, where Bildner's offerings were not as unique as those in Boston. Furthermore, the expansion into some other cities involved locating outlets in department stores, a concept far different from the original Bildner's site.

The company's management also found it difficult to make the transition from a small number of stores with a local orientation to a larger company in multiple cities. Top managers became so absorbed in the expansion that they soon began to lose touch with what was going on in individual stores. Financial controls were fairly loose, so the company's good cash position faded quickly.

Still, the struggling company has managed to emerge from bankruptcy. Now Bildner is working hard with the remaining Boston-area stores to bring them back into line with his original concept.[63] ■ ■ ■

Unfortunately, James Bildner was not able to effectively navigate his company from the success-growth stage to takeoff. Had he been successful, J. Bildner & Sons would have been ready to move on to the next stage, resource maturity.

STAGE V: RESOURCE MATURITY At this stage, the company needs to consolidate and control the financial gains resulting from rapid growth, but it must also attempt to retain the spirit that brought it this far. However, growing size may cause **ossification,** a condition characterized by lack of innovation and avoidance of risk (which may be in marked contrast to the company's orientation in its early days). Eventually, depending on how quickly the environment changes, ossification can lead to decline, perhaps even back to the survival stage or to the end of the business. At this stage, the company must begin aggressive steps to encourage innovation. Here the emphasis shifts from entrepreneurship to intrapreneurship.

Ossification A condition that is characterized by lack of innovation and avoidance of risk

Entrepreneurship versus Intrapreneurship

We have discussed many means of fostering innovation in the Promoting Innovation sections throughout this book. When a company reaches the resource maturity stage, its need for the initial momentum of entrepreneurship is replaced by a strong need for intrapreneurship. *Intrapreneurship* is the practice of innovating by developing new products, processes, or services while one is part of an organization. Entrepreneurship, as we have seen, also involves innovating, but the innovations are carried out by creating a new organization.

Major Issues and Problems

New ventures and small businesses can bring considerable satisfaction in terms of both accomplishments and financial remuneration. On the other hand, such endeavors involve several relatively unique issues and problems.

BANKRUPTCY AND FAILURE PROSPECTS As we saw with J. Bildner & Sons, small businesses do not always progress smoothly. In fact, the odds of failure are quite high. When things do go wrong and a company fails, what are the major reasons? As shown by one study of 570 businesses that went bankrupt, the causes cited by business owners are not always the same as those cited by their creditors. While business owners cite business depression, insufficient capital, and competition as major causes of their bankruptcies, their creditors blame inefficient management first, and then go on to cite business depression and insufficient capital as other causes. Still, the study's data do cast some doubt on the explanations frequently given by small-business owners and managers to the effect that the blame necessarily lies mainly with outside factors.

ETHICAL ISSUES Some experts believe that small businesses are particularly vulnerable to unethical practices. Reasons include the weak financial condition of many small firms, the temptation to offer bribes in order to lure business away from larger competitors, and the relatively small number of checks and balances usually in place in small firms. Other experts argue that small businesses have an advantage in regard to maintaining ethical standards, since their small size enables the owner to detect unethical practices within the firm.[64] Moreover, entrepreneurs who are particularly successful financially can often spearhead ethical actions (see the Valuing Ethics box).

FAMILY-LIFE STRESSES Both small-business owners and entrepreneurs often work grueling hours, frequently neglecting their families in the process. One survey found that entrepreneurs commonly work 60 to 70 hours per week and sometimes more during the early years of establishing their businesses. Although some managers, particularly top-level executives of large corporations, also work long hours, small-business owners face added pressure because of the high odds of failure associated with young small ventures. In one case, business pressures led entrepreneur Carl R. Zwerner and his wife of 19 years to obtain a divorce. Zwerner, who runs Glass, Inc., a glass-importing firm in Miami, later donated $500,000 to Georgia State University for a professorship in family-run businesses, with strong emphasis on the conflict between family and business.[66]

DARK SIDE OF ENTREPRENEURSHIP One researcher writes of the "dark side of entrepreneurship," alluding to the creative energy of entrepreneurs that can, at the same time, be a destructive force in building a company. For example, their bias toward action sometimes causes entrepreneurs to act without thinking. Moreover, they often find it very difficult to take directions from others, and they frequently have high needs for control that make it hard for them to delegate responsibility.[67]

NEED FOR OUTSIDE ASSISTANCE Entrepreneurs and small-business owners often do not recognize the need to seek outside assistance from local agencies, such as a state-sponsored small-business development center, or from other advisers. Yet small firms that receive such assistance tend to perform better than

VALUING ETHICS

"Hat King" Helps Poor People

If you have ever worn a baseball-type cap bearing the logo of your favorite major league team, chances are that the cap was made by South Korea's Young An Hat Company. Founded by Sung Hak Baik, the company is the world's largest hat manufacturer, producing about 60 million hats per year. Many of them are licensed sports-team caps that are sold in 20 countries, including the United States.

Baik took an unlikely path in becoming a hat maker. Born in North Korea, he was accidently transported to South Korea when a refugee boat on which he was selling candy sailed off, separating him from his family. The 10-year-old Baik made his way to a U.S. military base, where he was befriended by a G.I. fighting in the Korean war. After working in a hat factory, he struck out on his own and eventually began exporting hats. He says that he gained entry to the U.S. market with the aid of hat distributors who helped him learn marketing and imported his high-quality hats.

Baik contributes 10 to 30 percent of his profits each year to charity. In fact, he will not take his company public because he is concerned that doing so would limit the amount of profits that he can donate. Among other things, he has provided money for scholarships for more than 5000 poor students in Korea, the United States, and Costa Rica. He also purchased the 50-acre site of the G.I. camp where he spent the Korean war and turned it into a complex that includes an orphanage, medical clinic, church, vocational school, and homes for the handicapped and elderly, as well as two hat factories. Baik has similar complexes planned for several developing countries. "I have to repay God for saving my life and giving me a big chance to make a profit," he says.[65]

those that do not. The best results are usually achieved when the assistance also addresses strategic management issues, which are likely to be somewhat neglected by small businesses.[68]

CHAPTER SUMMARY

Entrepreneurship is the creation of new enterprise, and it involves innovation. Three criteria that can be used to evaluate the entrepreneurial opportunity conditions associated with different degrees of innovation are risk, evaluation, and profit potential. Entrepreneurship has been the subject of increasing research and public interest because of important contributions made by new ventures and related small businesses in the areas of economic growth, innovation, employment opportunities, and alternatives for women and minorities.

A number of factors influence the decision of whether to engage in entrepreneurship. Entrepreneurs tend to have a few personality, background, and other characteristics in common, but these same characteristics are often also associated with managers and individuals in other occupations. Certain life-path circumstances seem to increase the probability that an individual will become an entrepreneur: unsatisfactory work environment, negative displacement, career transition points, and the presence of positive-pull influencers. Favorable environmental conditions and positive perceptions of desirability and feasibility can also influence individuals to become entrepreneurs.

In considering which development path to pursue, entrepreneurs and prospective small-business owners have three main choices. Entrepreneurs most often start

a new firm, although they may sometimes acquire an existing firm and quickly make major changes in its direction. Other small-business owners may acquire existing businesses and retain their basic direction. Alternatively, they may purchase a franchise.

Most experts on small business and entrepreneurship strongly recommend that individuals preparing to start a business develop a business plan. Two of the most important resources needed in starting a new firm are adequate financing and human resources. A number of major factors must be considered when selecting an appropriate site for a business, including the community, the trade area, lease or buy trade-offs, zoning or licensing requirements, and cost per square foot.

The process of managing and developing new ventures and small businesses comprises five major stages of growth: existence, survival, success (including disengagement or growth substages), takeoff, and resource maturity. As businesses reach the resource maturity stage, the emphasis needs to shift from entrepreneurship to intrapreneurship. Entrepreneurs and owners face several particularly important issues and problems in managing their small businesses. These include high bankruptcy and failure prospects, ethical issues, family-life stresses, behaviors of entrepreneurs that can undermine a growing organization, and the need for outside help.

QUESTIONS FOR DISCUSSION AND REVIEW

1 Define entrepreneurship. What difficulties might you have in attempting to use this definition to separate entrepreneurship from managing a small business?

2 Outline three criteria that can be used to assess the probable opportunity conditions associated with different degrees of new venture innovation. Use the criteria to evaluate the opportunity conditions inherent in two recent new ventures in your geographic area.

3 Explain the major economic and social contributions of new ventures and other small businesses. Identify specific situations in your geographic area in which entrepreneurship and small-business ownership have made such contributions.

4 What personality traits and other personal characteristics would you use to identify potential entrepreneurs? What advantages and disadvantages exist in using this approach to determine who should receive a loan for a new venture?

5 Explain other important factors that can influence an individual to become an entrepreneur. To what

extent could these factors be used to encourage entrepreneurship among one's friends and associates?

6 What major options exist in deciding on a development approach for a new venture? If you were considering a new venture, which would you prefer and why? What are some advantages and disadvantages of purchasing an existing small business or a franchise?

7 Explain the main purposes of a business plan. Why is a well-constructed business plan an important factor in obtaining outside financing and other resources for a new venture?

8 Enumerate several major considerations involved in selecting an appropriate site for a new business. Use these considerations to evaluate the sites of two small businesses in your geographic area.

9 Outline the principal stages in new venture growth. Explain how the J. Bildner & Sons new venture (see the Case in Point) got off track.

10 Identify three common pitfalls associated with entrepreneurship. What could be done to minimize these pitfalls?

DISCUSSION QUESTIONS FOR CHAPTER OPENING CASE

1 What factors probably influence Phil Romano to continually start new ventures?

2 Considering the discussion of new firms, how would you classify Romano's various enterprises?

3 What entrepreneurial process does Romano follow? What role do you think this process plays in his various successes? How do you account for his failures?

MANAGEMENT EXERCISE: AN ENTREPRENEURIAL OPPORTUNITY

 You have been working as an appliance salesperson at a local store for 3 years. This is your first job after graduating from college, and you took it for several reasons: You wanted to see how a small business is organized and operates, and you wanted some practical, hands-on small-business experience. You were also looking for a niche in which you could eventually set up your own business. Finally, the business is located in an area where you thought you might want to set up a business in the future. You believe your experience in this job has been very valuable.

Yesterday, while you were talking to the owner, he confided that he had long dreamed of setting up a kitchen design and appliance shop in an affluent area on the other side of town. The population of the area is expanding and is expected to continue to do so for the next two decades. The shop would be oriented toward dual-career couples who share some cooking chores, and it would focus on kitchen atmosphere, as well as utility.

The owner said that he would be willing to finance such a start-up but could not actually take charge of setting it up himself because of family obligations. He wondered if you knew anyone who would be interested in developing such a project for a large chunk of equity.

You are surprised to learn of his interest in the kitchen design and appliance shop and are definitely interested in the opportunity yourself. The next day, you indicate your interest to the owner, who tells you how much financing he could make available and what equity he would expect in return. His proposal seems fair to you, and you talk it over with several people whom you trust. You are convinced that you could be successful in this type of business, but must study it further.

You recognize that you will need much more information before deciding whether or not to take on this entrepreneurial endeavor. Describe the information you will need and the decisions you should make before involving yourself in this start-up.

REFERENCES

1. Sherrie Brammall, "Romano Unveils His Macaroni Masterpiece," *San Antonio Business Journal,* June 13–19, 1988, pp. 1, 16–17; Charles Boisseau, "Execs Go Back to the Future after Fuddruckers Success," *San Antonio Light,* May 10, 1987, pp. E1, E5; "Fuddruckers: A New Generation of Fast Food," *Restaurant Hospitality,* December 1984, pp. 45–50; Sherrie Brammall, "Romano Focuses on Restaurant Financing," *San Antonio Business Journal,* June 6–12, 1988, pp. 1, 2, 12, 21; Tom Richman, "Love 'Em and Leave 'Em," *INC.,* May 1986, pp. 124–130; Chuck McCollough, "Starting Anew Ends Boredom," *San Antonio Sunday Express-News,* Feb. 9, 1986, pp. 1K, 10K; Charles Boisseau, "Unlikely Duo Gets Going at DocuCon," *San Antonio Light,* May 13, 1989, pp. C1, C4, C5; "Stock to Go," *INC.,* July 1989,

p. 17; interview with David C. Martin, Mar. 18, 1989; Tracey Taylor Woodward, "Mangia, Amigos! Chili's Acquired Italian Dinnerhouse," *Restaurant News,* Dec. 11, 1989, pp. 1, 77; Marj Charlier, "Romano Varies Menu to Cook Up Another Restaurant," *The Wall Street Journal,* Apr. 11, 1990, p. B2; Robin Lee Allen, "Romano, Brinker Unveil 'Funky' Mexican Concept," *Nation's Restaurant News,* May 11, 1992, p. 1; Enlightened Epicure, "Nachomana's—Romano's Still on a Roll," *San Antonio Express-News,* Apr. 24, 1992, p. 1D.
2. Murray B. Low and Ian C. MacMillan, "Entrepreneurship: Past Research and Future Challenges," *Journal of Management,* vol. 14, 1988, pp. 139–161. The meaning of this term is somewhat controversial; see Max S. Wortman, Jr., "Entrepreneurship: An Integrating Typology and Evalua-

tion of the Empirical Research in the Field," *Journal of Management,* vol. 13, 1987, pp. 259–279; William B. Gartner, "'Who Is an Entrepreneur?' Is the Wrong Question," *American Journal of Small Business,* Spring 1988, pp. 11–39.
3. Joseph J. Fucini and Suzy Fucini, *Entrepreneurs,* Hall, Boston, 1985.
4. *The State of Small Business—1985: A Report to the President,* GPO, Washington, D.C., 1985; Charles R. Kuehl and Peggy A. Lambing, *Small Business,* 2d ed., Dryden, Chicago, 1990.
5. Peter F. Drucker, *Innovation and Entrepreneurship,* Harper & Row, New York, 1985, p. 19.
6. John G. Burch, *Entrepreneurship,* Wiley, New York, 1986.
7. *The State of Small Business—1988: A Report to the President,* GPO, Washington, D.C., 1988, p. 22.
8. For a compilation of some recent

statistics relating to failure rates, see Barbara J. Bird, *Entrepreneurial Behavior*, Scott, Foresman, Glenview, Ill., 1989.

9. John Case, "The Disciples of David Birch," *INC.*, January 1989, pp. 39–45.

10. Joseph J. Fucini and Suzy Fucini, *Entrepreneurs*, Hall, Boston, 1985, p. 240.

11. Howard Aldrich and Ellen R. Auster, "Even Dwarfs Started Small: Liabilities of Age and Size and Their Strategic Implications," *Research in Organizational Behavior*, vol. 8, 1986, pp. 165–198.

12. David L. Birch, *The Job Generation Process*, M.I.T. Program on Neighborhood and Regional Change, Cambridge, Mass., 1979.

13. John Case, "The Disciples of David Birch," *INC.*, January 1989, pp. 39–45; Gene Koretz, "Small Businesses Tend to Stay Pint-Size," *Business Week*, July 31, 1989, p. 20.

14. Lois A. Stevenson, "Against All Odds: The Entrepreneurship of Women," *Journal of Small Business Management*, October 1986, pp. 30–36.

15. *The State of Small Business—1989: A Report to the President*, GPO, Washington, D.C., 1989.

16. Donald D. Bowen and Robert D. Hisrich, "The Female Entrepreneur: A Career Development Perspective," *Academy of Management Review*, vol. 11, 1986, pp. 393–407.

17. Robert D. Hisrich and Candida Bruch, "Characteristics of the Minority Entrepreneur," *Journal of Small Business Management*, October 1986, pp. 1–8; U.S. Department of Commerce, *Statistical Abstract of the United States*, GPO, Washington, D.C., 1989.

18. Janice Castro, "She Calls All the Shots," *Time*, July 4, 1988, pp. 54–57.

19. Andrew H. Van de Ven, Roger Hudson, and Dean M. Schroeder, "Designing New Business Startups: Entrepreneurial, Organizational, and Ecological Considerations," *Journal of Management*, vol. 10, 1984, pp. 87–107; William B. Gartner, "A Conceptual Framework for Describing the Phenomenon of New Venture Creation," *Academy of Manage-*

ment Review, vol. 10, 1985, pp. 696–706; Albert Shapero and Lisa Sokol, "The Social Dimensions of Entrepreneurship," in Calvin A. Kent, Donald L. Sexton, and Karl H. Vesper (eds.), *Encyclopedia of Entrepreneurship*, Prentice-Hall, Englewood Cliffs, N.J., 1982, pp. 72–90; Robert D. Hisrich and Michael P. Peters, *Entrepreneurship*, BPI/Irwin, Homewood, Ill., 1989.

20. This section relies extensively on Murray B. Low and Ian C. MacMillan, "Entrepreneurship: Past Research and Future Challenges," *Journal of Management*, vol. 14, 1988, pp. 139–161; Robert H. Brockhaus, Sr., and Pamela S. Horwitz, "The Psychology of the Entrepreneur," in Donald L. Sexton and Raymond W. Smilor, *The Art and Science of Entrepreneurship*, Ballinger, Cambridge, Mass., 1986, pp. 25–48; Robert H. Brockhaus, Sr., "The Psychology of the Entrepreneur," in Calvin A. Kent, Donald L. Sexton, and Karl H. Vesper (eds.), *Encyclopedia of Entrepreneurship*, Prentice-Hall, Englewood Cliffs, N.J., 1982; and Yvon Gasse, "Elaboration on the Psychology of the Entrepreneur," in ibid.

21. David C. McClelland, *Human Motivation*, Scott, Foresman, Glenview, Ill., 1985.

22. Bernard M. Bass, *Stogdill's Handbook of Leadership*, Free Press, New York, 1981; D. L. Sexton and N. Bowman, "The Entrepreneur: A Capable Executive and More," *Journal of Business Venturing*, vol. 1, 1985, pp. 129–140.

23. This section relies heavily on Yvon Gasse, "Elaboration on the Psychology of the Entrepreneur," in Calvin A. Kent, Donald L. Sexton, and Karl H. Vesper (eds.), *Encyclopedia of Entrepreneurship*, Prentice-Hall, Englewood Cliffs, N.J., 1982; and Robert D. Hisrich and Michael P. Peters, *Entrepreneurship*, BPI/Irwin, Homewood, Ill., 1989.

24. Robert D. Hisrich and Candida G. Bruch, "The Woman Entrepreneur: Management Skills and Business Problems," *Journal of Small Business Management*, vol. 22, 1984, pp. 30–37.

25. A. C. Cooper and W. C.

Dunkelberg, "Entrepreneurial Research: Old Questions, New Answers, and Methodological Issues," *American Journal of Small Business*, Winter 1987, pp. 1–20.

26. Ibid.

27. Donald D. Bowen and Robert D. Hisrich, "The Female Entrepreneur: A Career Development Perspective," *Academy of Management Review*, vol. 11, 1986, pp. 393–407.

28. Jeffry A. Timmons, Leonard E. Smollen, and Alexander L. M. Dingee, Jr., *New Venture Creation*, 2d ed., Irwin, Homewood, Ill., 1985.

29. Robert Ronstadt, "The Corridor Principle," *Journal of Business Venturing*, vol. 3, 1988, pp. 31–40.

30. Albert Shapero and Lisa Sokol, "The Social Dimensions of Entrepreneurship," in Calvin A. Kent, Donald L. Sexton, and Karl H. Vesper (eds.), *Encyclopedia of Entrepreneurship*, Prentice-Hall, Englewood Cliffs, N.J., 1982, pp. 72–90. This section also relies heavily on Robert D. Hisrich and Michael P. Peters, *Entrepreneurship*, BPI/Irwin, Homewood, Ill., 1989.

31. Robert H. Brockhaus, Sr., "The Psychology of the Entrepreneur," in Calvin A. Kent, Donald L. Sexton, and Karl H. Vesper (eds.), *Encyclopedia of Entrepreneurship*, Prentice-Hall, Englewood Cliffs, N.J., 1982.

32. Bo Burlingham and Curtis Hartman, "Cowboy Capitalist," *INC.*, January 1989, pp. 54–69.

33. David J. Jefferson, "Land of Opportunity," *The Wall Street Journal*, June 10, 1988, p. R29.

34. Denie S. Weil, "Doing Business in the Burbs," *Working Woman*, August 1989, pp. 58–66.

35. Mark Lewyn, "Scott McNealy," *USA Today*, Jan. 19, 1988, p. 7B.

36. Barbara J. Bird, *Entrepreneurial Behavior*, Scott, Foresman, Glenview, Ill., 1989.

37. Martha T. Moore, "Fledgling Firms Learn to Fly in Incubators," *USA Today*, May 8, 1989, p. 3E.

38. Albert Shapero and Lisa Sokol, "The Social Dimensions of Entrepreneurship," in Calvin A. Kent, Donald L. Sexton, and Karl H. Vesper (eds.), *Encyclopedia of Entrepreneurship*, Prentice-Hall, Englewood

Cliffs, N.J., 1982, pp. 72–90; Robert Hisrich and Michael P. Peters, *Entrepreneurship*, BPI/Irwin, Homewood, Ill., 1989.

39. Based on Elizabeth A. Conlin and Louise Washer, "They Tried to Steal My Business. . . ." *Working Woman*, October 1988, pp. 43–46; and Kimberly Pfaff, "Luxury Orientation," *Weekly Home Furnishings Newspaper*, Dec. 23, 1991, p. 33.

40. Robert D. Hisrich and Michael P. Peters, *Entrepreneurship*, BPI/Irwin, Homewood, Ill., 1989.

41. William B. Gartner, Terrence R. Mitchell, and Karl H. Vespers, "A Taxonomy of New Business Ventures," *Journal of Business Venturing*, vol. 4, 1989, pp. 169–186.

42. Based on Richard I. Kirkland, Jr., "Pile 'Em High and Sell 'Em Cheap," *Fortune*, Aug. 29, 1988, pp. 91–92; and Richard Evans, "Alan Sugar Shoots for the Stars," *International Management*, March 1989, pp. 42–44; John Jay, Amstrad to Stun with £75m Loss, *Sunday Telegraph*, Aug. 23, 1992, p. 27.

43. Lena H. Sun, "Cuisinart's Finances Dicey; It Seeks Bankruptcy Protection," *The Washington Post*, Aug. 4, 1989, p. D1.

44. Nicholas C. Siropolis, *Small Business Management*, 4th ed., Houghton Mifflin, Boston, 1990.

45. Ibid.; D. D. Seltz, *The Complete Handbook of Franchising*, Addison-Wesley, Reading, Mass., 1982.

46. Robert D. Hisrich and Michael P. Peters, *Entrepreneurship*, BPI/Irwin, Homewood, Ill., 1989.

47. Nicholas C. Siropolis, *Small Business Management*, 4th ed., Houghton Mifflin, Boston, 1990.

48. Derek T. Dingle, "Franchising's Fast Track to Freedom," *Money Extra*, 1990, p. 40.

49. John G. Burch, *Entrepreneurship*, Wiley, New York, 1986.

50. Carson R. Kennedy, "Thinking of Opening Your Own Business? Be Prepared," *Business Horizons*, September–October 1985, pp. 38–42.

51. Adapted from Nicholas C. Siropolis, *Small Business Management*, 4th ed., Houghton Mifflin, Boston, 1990, pp. 164–165.

52. Jeffry A. Timmons, Leonard E. Smollen, and Alexander L. M. Dingee, Jr., *New Venture Creation*, 2d ed., Irwin, Homewood, Ill., 1985; John G. Burch, *Entrepreneurship*, Wiley, New York, 1986.

53. Zenas Block and Ian C. MacMillan, "Milestones for Successful Venture Planning," *Harvard Business Review*, September–October 1985, pp. 184–190.

54. This section relies heavily on Jeffry A. Timmons, Leonard E. Smollen, and Alexander L. M. Dingee, Jr., *New Venture Creation*, 2d ed., Irwin, Homewood, Ill., 1985; and Robert D. Hisrich and Michael P. Peters, *Entrepreneurship*, BPI/Irwin, Homewood, Ill., 1989.

55. Albert V. Bruno and Tyzoon T. Tyebjee, "The Entrepreneur's Search for Capital," *Journal of Business Venturing*, vol. 1, 1985, pp. 61–74.

56. Steven Greenhouse, "In Poland, a Small Capitalist Miracle," *The New York Times*, Dec. 19, 1989, pp. D1, D13.

57. Jeffry A. Timmons, Leonard E. Smollen, and Alexander L. M. Dingee, Jr., *New Venture Creation*, 2d ed., Irwin, Homewood, Ill., 1985.

58. Robert D. Gatewood and Hubert S. Field, "A Personnel Selection Program for Small Business," *Journal of Small Business Management*, October 1987, pp. 16–25.

59. Thomas F. Jones, *Entrepreneurism*, Donald L. Fine, Inc., New York, 1987.

60. This section is based on Charles R. Kuehl and Peggy A. Lambing, *Small Business*, 2d ed., Dryden, Chicago, 1990.

61. Neil C. Churchill and Virginia L. Lewis, "The Five Stages of Small Business Growth," *Harvard Business Review*, May–June 1983, pp. 30–50.

62. Information obtained from the Government Relations Office, BDM International, McLean, Va., Jan. 2, 1990, and BDM 1991 Annual Report.

63. Buck Brown, "James Bildner's Spectacular Rise and Fall," *The Wall Street Journal*, Oct. 24, 1988, p. B1; Thomas Vannah, "Rebuilding a Business," *New England Business*, June 1990, p. 21.

64. Charles R. Kuehl and Peggy A. Lambing, *Small Business*, 2d ed., Dryden, Chicago, 1990. See also Justin G. Longnecker, Joseph A. McKinney, and Carlos W. Moore, "Ethics in Small Business," *Journal of Small Business Management*, January 1989, pp. 27–31.

65. Andrew Tanzer, "The 60 Million Hats of Sung Hak Baik," *Forbes*, Oct. 14, 1991, pp. 72–74.

66. Mark Robichaux, "Business First, Family Second," *The Wall Street Journal*, May 12, 1989, p. B1.

67. Manfred F. R. Kets de Vries, "The Dark Side of Entrepreneurship," *Harvard Business Review*, November–December 1985, pp. 160–167.

68. Richard B. Robinson, Jr., "The Importance of Outsiders in Small Firm Planning and Performance," *Academy of Management Journal*, vol. 25, 1982, pp. 80–93; James J. Chrisman and John Leslie, "Strategic Administrative, and Operating Problems: The Impact of Outsiders on Small Firm Performance," *Entrepreneurship Theory and Practice*, Spring 1989, pp. 37–51.

ACKNOWLEDGMENTS

Tables
Table 1: John G. Burch, *Entrepreneurship*, p. 72. Copyright © 1986 by John Wiley & Sons, Inc. Reprinted by permission of John Wiley & Sons, Inc.
Table 2: Derek E. Dingle, reprinted from the *Money* Extra 1990 Issue of *Money* magazine by special permission. Copyright © 1990 Time Inc.
Table 3: Adapted with permission from the September 1985 issue of *Changing Times Magazine*. Copyright © 1985 The Kiplinger Washington Editors, Inc.

Figures
Figure 2: Nicholas C. Siropolis, *Small Business Management*, 4th ed. Copyright © 1990 by Houghton Mifflin Company. Adapted with permission.
Figure 3: Modified and reprinted by permission of *Harvard Business Review*. An exhibit from "The Five Stages of Business Growth," by Neil C. Churchill and Virginia L. Lewis (May/June 1983). Copyright © 1983 by the President and Fellows of Harvard College; all rights reserved.

CONCLUDING CASE

BARBARA GROGAN BEATS OUT BIG-NAME COMPETITION*

At 35, Barbara Grogan was out of work and ending a 12-year marriage. For the first time in her life, she faced the problem of how to pay the mortgage and feed her two children. In figuring out what to do, Grogan chose a relatively unusual niche in the construction industry—millwrighting. Her company, Denver-based Western Industrial Contractors, Inc. (WIC), moves and installs mammoth industrial equipment. Millwrighting involves projects such as hanging a four-story theater screen, installing a freestanding stack of storage cubicles eight stories high where the maximum vertical variance cannot exceed an eighth of an inch, and guiding a 100-ton cooling system into a plant with a crane that comes within one-sixteenth of an inch of the building's main support.

Grogan had heard of millwrighting during a 9-month period when she served as general manager of her husband's crane- and truck-rental company, but she didn't know much about the business. Millwrighting requires huge equipment, such as cranes up to 20 stories high, trucks that are as big as railroad cars, and intricate machinery that must be synchronized perfectly to get the job done.

To compete with the other 4600 millwrighting contractors nationwide, Grogan works hard to get customers and then tries to keep them through outstanding service. "Once I get the clients, I service their socks off," says Grogan. "The client has to win for

us to win." For example, Grogan recently received a call at 6 a.m. from a client at a cement factory where a kiln had been knocked out of service by an explosion. The client was losing thousands of dollars every hour that the kiln was out of commission. Grogan had a staff of 12 at the site by 9 a.m. and had shifts work around the clock for 4 days to repair the kiln. Nevertheless, Grogan charged only her usual fees. She says that she does not like to take advantage of clients when they have troubles. She prefers establishing long-term relationships, which is one reason for her company's success. Recent annual sales exceeded $5 million.

When she began in 1982, Grogan had $50,000 in capital and a limited knowledge of cranes. She went into partnership with a man who had 15 years' experience as a millwright. At the time, the Denver economy was experiencing the beginnings of an economic decline linked to problems in the energy industry. As a result, many construction companies were abandoning union contracting. In a contrary move, Grogan allied herself with the millwright's union. "My business is so specialized," she says. "When you are installing a Mylar press and it can have a vertical variance of only one ten-thousandth of an inch every 80 feet, you need people who know what they are doing." By being a union contractor, Grogan can get the skilled help she needs.

Start-up was difficult. Her initial business plan was sketchy, and people were skeptical. However, when she began interviewing insurance companies to determine insurance needs, she found two people who were receptive and helped her make connections with bankers and a CPA. At this point, she was ready for customers and began making calls. Most of her contact attempts were rebuffed, but

she managed to talk with an engineer who had worked in her grandfather's firm. He introduced her to others, and she finally got a contract to install equipment in a bakery.

Her major breakthrough came after she was in business for 8 months and was running out of money. She bid on a contract from the Manville Corporation to disassemble a pipe-manufacturing plant in Florida, ship it to Malaysia, and reassemble it. Although her own experience was meager, she highlighted the credentials of her employees and won the bid for the 5-month job. Successful completion of this project gave her credibility.

One of her efforts led to a small contract with United Airlines to modify an odd-size conveyor belt at Denver's airport. United was impressed with WIC's service orientation. A series of other contracts with United finally led to a major contract to install an underground baggage-sorting system at Chicago's O'Hare International Airport. The project involved 3 miles of conveyor belts and took 1 year to complete. WIC also does millwrighting for other large firms, including AT&T, Ralston Purina, Nabisco Brands, IBM, and ITT.

Grogan has been able to finance growth from sales, leaving the company in a sound financial position with very little debt. She now employs more than 80 people, has moved her firm into its own new 7000-square-foot building, and recently served as the chair of the Greater Denver Chamber of Commerce.†

---

* Sharon Nelton, excerpted by permission, *Nation's Business*, May 1992. Copyright © 1992, U.S. Chamber of Commerce.

† Based on Barbara Wright, "How to Beat Out Big-Name Competition," *Working Woman*, May 1988, pp. 55–57; and Sharon Nelton, "When Failure Is Not an Option; Making a New Company Work," *Nation's Business*, May 1992, p. 20.

QUESTIONS FOR
CONCLUDING CASE

1 Why did Grogan decide to become an entrepreneur?

2 Assess the process Grogan followed in setting up business.

3 At what stage of the small-business growth cycle would you place WIC? What factors led to Grogan's success, and how did she enhance her company's success? What dilemmas does she now face in terms of the small-business growth cycle?

CONCLUDING CASE

AN ENTREPRENEUR'S GLOBAL STRATEGY

Li Ka-shing is the richest man in Hong Kong, a billionaire several times over. He came from very humble beginnings. Following the premature death of his father, the 14-year-old Li began working 16 hours each day, selling plastic belts and watchbands to dealers so he could support his mother and two younger siblings. At 20, he became general manager of a small company, but 2 years later he started his own company making plastic combs and soap boxes. He then added plastic flowers to his inventory during the 1950s, when they were popular, and made a fortune exporting them to Europe and America.

Li next launched into real estate development. His method of attracting investors in his real estate ventures is unique. He shops for undervalued assets. For example, he acquired 204 acres of waterfront land in Vancouver in 1988, for the equivalent of $637,000 an acre. (Recently, he sold a 14-acre slice of that property for $2.38 million an acre.) He then sells the investors parts of the to-be-finished product, such as a block of apartments, before he starts construction. Thus the investors cover the costs of construction of his projects.

He is involved in many businesses. His public companies in Hong Kong include: Hutchison Telecom, a mobile phone company that operates in Asia and Europe; drugstores and supermarkets in Hong Kong, China, and Singapore; container ports in Hong Kong and Felixstowe, England; 49 percent of Husky Oil; and joint ventures with Lockheed (for aircraft maintenance in Guangzhou, China) and Procter & Gamble (for making shampoo and face lotion in south China). His personal investments include 49 percent of a building located at 60 Broad Street, New York City; 46 percent of Husky Oil; and 9 percent of Canadian Imperial Bank of Commerce. He recently sold most of his holdings in STAR TV, which broadcasts to 38 countries in Asia and the Mideast, for a handsome profit.

Li is expanding internationally in several areas. He is now negotiating with Chinese officials to develop a container port in Shanghai. He recently sold 400 condos, in just 3 days, in the first two high-rise apartment buildings started in the Vancouver area. He is negotiating with AT&T to buy up to 40 percent of his Hutchison Telecom (for a sum reported to be in excess of $500 million). He also has been negotiating with the Beijing Tourism Bureau to set up a joint venture in which two major Beijing hotels would be updated and made into more luxurious facilities. At the same time, he is building apartments and homes in the Beijing suburbs. One project will involve 42 buildings with more than ten stories, 23 buildings with fewer than six stories. The complex will include a shopping center, a cultural center, and several schools.

Li has two sons whom he is encouraging to be entrepreneurs.

He recently appointed his 29-year-old elder son, Victor Li, as deputy chairman of the Cheung Kong group, the major company in the family's property empire. His 27-year-old son, Richard Li, is slated to head Hutchinson Whampoa, a major family conglomerate. Li has given his two sons some advice which might be helpful to all who wish to be successful entrepreneurs: always treat partners fairly, seek and use the advice of experts, work very hard, treat people with respect, and keep your word.*

QUESTIONS FOR CONCLUDING CASE

1 How would you describe Li Ka-shing's personal characteristics?
2 What life-path circumstances could have influenced Li Ka-shing's decision to be an entrepreneur?
3 Explain how Li Ka-shing moved through the stages of starting a small business, enlarging, and finally establishing a global empire.

* Louis Kraar, "A Billionaire's Global Strategy," *Fortune*, July 13, 1992, pp. 106–109, Kennie Chu, "Li Signs $2.8b Deal to Build Beijing Homes," *South China Morning Post*, January 9, 1994, p. 1; Catherine Ong, "Li Ka-shing Names Elder Son as Cheung Kong's Deputy Chairman," *Business Times*, January 14, 1994, p. 22; Paul Blustein, "In Hong Kong, The Son Also Rises, and Rises," *The Washington Post*, January 16, 1994, p. H1; "Li Ka-Shing Views Tie-Ups with State-Run Hotels in Beijing," *Business Times*, March 15, 1994, p. 9.

CHAPTER 13

The Role
of Services
in an
Economy

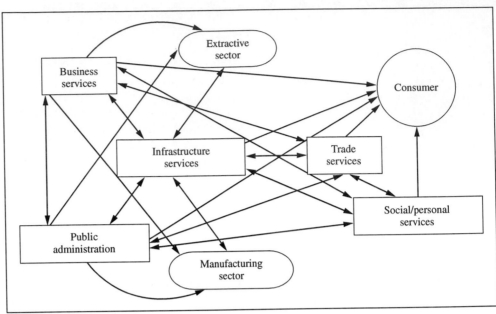

Figure 1. *Interactive model of an economy.*
(After Dorothy I. Riddle, *Service-Led Growth,* Praeger, New York, 1986, p. 27.)

Services lie at the very hub of economic activity in any society. Writing about the role of the service sector in world development, Dorothy Riddle formulated the economic model shown in Figure 1. This model shows the flow of activity among the three principal sectors of the economy: extractive (mining and farming), manufacturing, and service, which is divided into five subgroups. All activity eventually leads to the consumer. Examples of services in each of the five subgroups are:

Business services.   Consulting, finance, banking

Trade services.   Retailing, maintenance, repair

Infrastructure services.   Communications, transportation

Social/personal services.   Restaurants, health care

Public administration.   Education, government

Infrastructure services, such as transportation and communications, are the essential links between all sectors of the economy, including the final consumer. In a complex economy, both infrastructure and trade services function as intermediaries between the extractive and manufacturing sectors and as the channel of distribution to the final consumer. Infrastructure services are a prerequisite for an economy to become industrialized; therefore, no advanced society can be without these services.

In an industrialized economy, specialized firms can supply business services to manufacturing firms more cheaply and efficiently than manufacturing firms can supply these services for themselves. Thus, more and more often we find advertising, consulting, financing, testing, and other business functions being provided for the manufacturing sector by service firms.

Except for basic subsistence living, where individual households are self-sufficient, service activities are absolutely necessary for the economy to function and to enhance the quality of life. Consider, for example, the importance of a banking industry to transfer funds and a transportation industry to move food products to areas that cannot produce them. Moreover, a wide variety of social and personal services, such as restaurants, lodging, cleaning, and child care, have been created to move former household functions into the economy.

Public administration plays a critical role in providing a stable environment for investment and economic growth. Services such as public education, health care, well-maintained roads, safe drinking water, clean air, and public safety are necessary for any nation's economy to survive and people to prosper.

Thus, it is imperative to recognize that services are not peripheral activities but rather integral parts of society. They are central to a functioning and healthy economy and lie at the heart of that economy. The service sector not only facilitates but also makes possible the goods-producing activities of the extractive and manufacturing sectors. Services are the crucial force for today's change toward a global economy.

CHAPTER PREVIEW

We begin with a discussion of economic evolution, finding that modern industrialized economies are dominated by employment in the service sector industries. This represents a natural evolution of economies from preindustrial to industrial and, finally, to postindustrial societies. The economic activity of a society determines the nature of how its people live and how the standard of living is measured. The nature of the service sector is explored in terms of employment opportunities, contributions to economic stability, and sources of economic leadership. Finally, the role of the service manager is discussed in terms of innovation, opportunities for new services based on demographic trends, and the many managerial challenges in an expanding service economy.

ECONOMIC EVOLUTION

In the early 1900s, only three of every ten workers in the United States were employed in the services sector. The remaining workers were active in agriculture and industry. By 1950, employment in services accounted for 50 percent of the workforce. Today, services employ about eight out of every ten workers. During the past 90 years, we have witnessed a major evolution in our society from being predominantly manufacturing-based to being predominantly service-based.

Economists studying economic growth are not surprised by these events. Colin Clark argues that as nations become industrialized, there is an inevitable shift of employment from one sector of the economy to another.[1] As productivity increases in one sector, the labor force moves into another. This observation, known as the *Clark-Fisher hypothesis*, leads to a classification of economies by noting the activity of the majority of the workforce.

Table 1 describes five stages of economic activity. Many economists, including Clark, limited their analyses to only three stages, of which the tertiary stage was simply services. We have taken the suggestion of Nelson N. Foote and Paul K. Hatt and subdivided the service stage into three categories.[2]

Today, an overwhelming number of countries are still in a primary stage of development. These economies are based on extracting natural resources from the land. Their productivity is low, and income is subject to fluctuations based on the

---

[1]Colin Clark, *The Conditions of Economic Progress,* 3d ed., The Macmillan Co., London, 1957.
[2]N. N. Foote and P. K. Hatt, "Social Mobility and Economic Advancement," *American Economic Review,* May 1953, pp. 364–378.

TABLE 1   Stages of Economic Activity

Primary (Extractive) Agriculture Mining Fishing Forestry	*Quaternary* (Trade and Commerce Services) Transportation Retailing Communication Finance and insurance Real estate Government
Secondary (Goods-Producing) Manufacturing Processing	*Quinary* (Refining and Extending Human Capacities) Health Education Research Recreation Arts
Tertiary (Domestic Services) Restaurants and hotels Barber and beauty shops Laundry and dry cleaning Maintenance and repair	

prices of commodities such as sugar and copper. In much of Africa and parts of Asia, more than 70 percent of the labor force is engaged in extractive activities.

Based on the work activity of their populations, however, many of the so-called advanced industrial nations would be better described as service economies. Table 2 is a partial list of industrialized countries ranked in order of the percentage of those employed in service-producing jobs. This table contains some surprises, such as finding Canada and Australia (known for their mining industries) high on the list. Several observations can be made: global economic development is progressing in unanticipated directions, successful industrial economies are built on a strong service sector, and just as it has in manufacturing, competition in services will become global. In fact, many of the largest commercial banks in the world at present are owned by the Japanese. Trade in services remains a challenge, however, because many countries erect barriers to protect domestic firms. For example, India and Mexico, among others, prohibit the sale of insurance by foreign companies.

TABLE 2   Percent Employment in Service Jobs for Selected Industrialized Nations, 1980–1993

Country	1980	1987	1993
Canada	67.2	70.8	74.8
United States	67.1	71.0	74.3
Australia	64.7	69.7	71.8
Belgium	64.3	70.1	70.7
Israel	63.3	66.0	68.0
France	56.9	63.6	66.4
Finland	52.2	60.1	65.9
Italy	48.7	57.7	60.2
Japan	54.5	58.1	59.9
United Kingdom	60.4	67.7	NA

NA—Not available.

Source: 1993 Statistical Yearbook, Department of International Economic and Social Affairs Statistical Office, United Nations, New York, 1993, pp. 236–242.

As Figure 2 shows, the service sector now accounts for more than three-fourths of total employment in the United States, which continues a trend that began more than a century ago. Therefore, based on employment figures, the United States can no longer be characterized as an industrial society; instead, it is a postindustrial, or service, society.

STAGES OF ECONOMIC DEVELOPMENT

Describing where our society has been, its current condition, and its most likely future is the task of social historians. Daniel Bell, a professor of sociology at Harvard University, has written extensively on this topic, and the material that follows is based on his work.[3] To place the concept of a postindustrial society in perspective, we must compare its features with those of preindustrial and industrial societies.

Preindustrial Society

The condition of most of the world's population today is one of subsistence, or a *preindustrial society*. Life is characterized as a game against nature. Working with muscle power and tradition, the labor force is engaged in agriculture, mining, and fish-

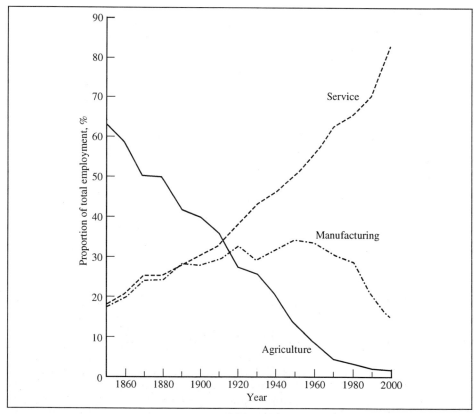

Figure 2. *Trends in U.S employment by sector, 1850–2000.*
(From U.S. Department of Commerce, Bureau of the Census, *Historical Statistics of the United States,* 1975, p. 137, and U.S. Department of Commerce, Bureau of the Census, *Statistical Abstract of the U.S.,* 1995, p. 417.)

[3]Daniel Bell, *The Coming of Post-Industrial Society: A Venture in Social Forecasting,* Basic Books, Inc., New York, 1973.

ing. Life is conditioned by the elements, such as the weather, the quality of the soil, and the availability of water. The rhythm of life is shaped by nature, and the pace of work varies with the seasons. Productivity is low and bears little evidence of technology. Social life revolves around the extended household, and this combination of low productivity and large population results in high rates of underemployment (workers not fully utilized). Many seek positions in services, but of the personal or household variety. Preindustrial societies are agrarian and structured around tradition, routine, and authority.

Industrial Society

The predominant activity in an *industrial society* is the production of goods. The focus of attention is on making more with less. Energy and machines multiply the output per labor-hour and structure the nature of work. Division of labor is the operational "law" that creates routine tasks and the notion of the semiskilled worker. Work is accomplished in the artificial environment of the factory, and people tend the machines. Life becomes a game that is played against a fabricated nature—a world of cities, factories, and tenements. The rhythm of life is machine-paced and dominated by rigid working hours and time clocks.

An industrial society is a world of schedules and acute awareness of the value of time. The standard of living becomes measured by the quantity of goods, but note that the complexity of coordinating the production and distribution of goods results in the creation of large bureaucratic and hierarchic organizations. These organizations are designed with certain roles for their members, and their operation tends to be impersonal, with persons treated as things. The individual is the unit of social life in a society that is considered to be the sum total of all the individual decisions being made in the marketplace. Of course, the unrelenting pressure of industrial life is softened by the countervailing force of labor unions.

Postindustrial Society

While an industrial society defines the standard of living by the quantity of goods, the *postindustrial society* is concerned with the quality of life, as measured by services such as health, education, and recreation. The central figure is the professional person, because rather than energy or physical strength, information is the key resource. Life now is a game played among persons. Social life becomes more difficult, because political claims and social rights multiply. Society becomes aware that the independent actions of individuals can combine to create havoc for everyone, as seen in traffic congestion and environmental pollution. The community rather than the individual becomes the social unit.

Bell suggests that the transformation from an industrial to a postindustrial society occurs in many ways. First, there is a natural development of services, such as transportation and utilities, to support industrial development. As labor-saving devices are introduced into the production process, more workers engage in non-manufacturing activities, such as maintenance and repair. Second, growth of the population and mass consumption of goods increase wholesale and retail trade, along with banking, real estate, and insurance. Third, as income increases, the proportion spent on the necessities of food and home decreases, and the remainder creates a demand for durables and then for services.

Ernst Engel, a Prussian statistician of the nineteenth century, observed that as family incomes increase, the percentage spent on food and durables drops while consumption of services that reflect a desire for a more enriched life increases correspondingly. This phenomenon is analogous to the Maslow hierarchy of needs, which says that once the basic requirements of food and shelter are satisfied, people seek physical goods and, finally, personal development. However, a necessary condition for the "good life" is health and education. In our attempts to eliminate disease and increase the span of life, health services become a critical feature of modern society.

Higher education becomes the condition for entry into a postindustrial society, which requires professional and technical skills of its population. Also, claims for more services and social justice lead to a growth in government. Concerns for environmental protection require government intervention and illustrate the interdependent and even global character of postindustrial problems. Table 3 summarizes the features that characterize the preindustrial, industrial, and postindustrial stages of economic development.

NATURE OF THE SERVICE SECTOR

For many people, *service* is synonymous with *servitude* and brings to mind workers flipping hamburgers and waiting on tables. However, the service sector that has grown significantly over the past 30 years cannot be accurately described as being composed only of low-wage or low-skill jobs in department stores and fast-food restaurants. Instead, as Table 4 shows, the fastest-growing jobs within the service sector are in finance, insurance, real estate, miscellaneous services (e.g., health, education, professional services), and retail trade. Note that job areas whose growth rates were less than the rate of increase in total jobs (i.e., less than 31.8 percent) lost market share, even though they showed gains in their absolute numbers. The exceptions are in mining and manufacturing, which lost in absolute numbers and thus showed negative growth rates. This trend should accelerate with the end of the cold war and the subsequent downsizing of the military and defense industry.

Changes in the pattern of employment will have implications on where and how people live, on educational requirements, and, consequently, on the kinds of organizations that will be important to that society. Industrialization created the need for the semiskilled worker who could be trained in a few weeks to perform the routine machine-tending tasks. The subsequent growth in the service sector has caused a shift to white-collar occupations. In the United States, the year 1956 was a turning point. For the first time in the history of industrial society, the number of white-collar workers exceeded the number of blue-collar workers, and the gap has been widening since then. The most interesting growth has been in the managerial and professional-technical fields, which are jobs that require a college education. Figure 3 shows the shift in employment from an industrial society of machine operators to a postindustrial society of professional and technical workers.

Today, service industries are the source of economic leadership. During the past 30 years, more than 44 million new jobs have been created in the service sector to absorb the influx of women into the workforce and to provide an alternative to the lack of job opportunities in manufacturing. The service industries now account for approximately 70 percent of the national income in the United States. Given that there is a limit to how many cars a consumer can use and how much one can eat and drink, this should not be surprising. The appetite for services, however, especially innovative ones, is insatiable. Among the services presently in demand are those that reflect an aging population, such as geriatric health care, and others that reflect a two-income family, such as day care.

The growth of the service sector has produced a less cyclic national economy. During the past four recessions in the United States, employment by service indus-

TABLE 3   Comparison of Societies

Society				Features			
	Game	Predominant Activity	Use of Human Labor	Unit of Social Life	Standard of Living Measure	Structure	Technology
Preindustrial	Against nature	Agriculture, mining	Raw muscle power	Extended household	Subsistence	Routine, traditional, authoritative	Simple hand tools
Industrial	Against fabricated nature	Goods production	Machine tending	Individual	Quantity of goods	Bureaucratic, hierarchic	Machines
Postindustrial	Among persons	Services	Artistic, creative, intellectual	Community	Quality of life in terms of health, education, recreation	Interdependent, global	Information

TABLE 4   Rate of Growth of U.S. Jobs, January 1982–April 1996

	Nonfarm Jobs Jan. 82, in 1000's	Nonfarm Jobs Jan. 82, %	Nonfarm Jobs April 96, in 1000's	Nonfarm Jobs April 96, %	Growth of Nonfarm Jobs, %
Service-producing					
Finance, insurance, real estate	5341	6.0	7060	6.0	32.2
Miscellaneous services	19,036	21.3	33,642	28.5	76.7
State and local government	13,098	14.6	16,600	14.0	26.7
Wholesale trade	5296	5.9	6444	5.5	21.7
Retail trade	15,161	16.9	21,100	17.9	39.2
Transportation and utilities	5082	5.7	6262	5.3	23.2
Federal government	2739	3.1	2775	2.3	16.6
Total	65,753	73.5	93,883	79.5	
Goods-producing					
Construction	3905	4.4	5378	4.6	37.7
Mining	1127	1.3	574	0.5	−49.1
Manufacturing	18,781	21.0	18,187	15.4	−3.2
Total	23,813	26.7	24,139	20.5	
Total jobs	89,566		118,022	Percent increase	31.8

Source: Economic Indicators, prepared for the Joint Economic Committee by the Council of Economic Advisors, U.S. Government Printing Office, June 1996, p. 14.

tries has actually increased, while jobs in manufacturing have been lost. This suggests that consumers are willing to postpone the purchase of products but will not sacrifice essential services like education, telephone, banking, health care, and public services such as fire and police protection.

Several reasons can explain the recession-resistant nature of services. First, by their nature, services cannot be inventoried, as is the case for products. Because consumption and production occur simultaneously for services, the demand for them is more stable than that for manufactured goods. When the economy falters, many services continue to survive. Hospitals keep busy as usual, and, while commissions may drop in real estate, insurance, and security businesses, employees need not be laid off.

Second, during a recession, both consumers and business firms defer capital expenditures and instead fix up and make do with existing equipment. Thus, service jobs in maintenance and repair are created.

ROLE OF THE SERVICE MANAGER

Successful growth of the service sector will depend on innovation and skilled management that will promote an ethic of continuous improvement in both quality and productivity.

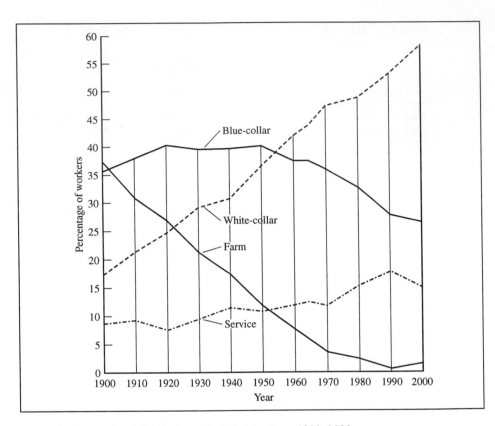

Figure 3. *Occupational distribution of the U.S. labor force, 1900–2000.*
(From U.S. Department of Commerce, Bureau of Census, Statistical Abstract of the U.S.,
1995.)

Innovation

The product development model that is driven by technology and engineering
could be called a *push theory of innovation.* A concept for a new product germinates
in the laboratory with a new scientific discovery that becomes a solution looking for
a problem. The 3M experience with Post-it notes® is one example of this innovation
process. The laboratory discovery was a poor adhesive, which found a creative use
as a glue for notes to be attached temporarily to objects without leaving a mark when
removed.

Information technology provides many examples of the push theory of service
innovation. The growth of the World Wide Web as a place of commerce is changing the delivery of services. People can browse the Internet for every imaginable
product or service from around the world. In fact, to stay competitive, many businesses may soon be required to offer new cost-effective and convenient services for
customers who have home computers equipped with modems.

For services, the Cash Management Account introduced by Merrill Lynch is an
example of the *pull theory of innovation.* During the period of high interest rates in
the 1980s, a need arose to finance short-term corporate cash flows, and individual
investors were interested in obtaining an interest rate that was higher than those
currently available on passbook bank deposits.

The French Revolution provides another view of service formation, this time
based on changing demographics. Before the revolution, only two restaurants were
in existence in Paris; shortly afterward, there were more than 500. The dispossessed

nobility had been forced to give up their private chefs, who found that opening their own restaurants was a logical solution to their unemployment.

For a manufacturing firm, product innovation is often driven by engineering-based research, but in service firms, software engineers and programmers are the technocrats who develop new innovations. Customers interact directly in the service process; therefore, the focus on meeting customer needs drives service innovation and explains why marketing plays such a central role in service management.

The introduction of a new technology, however, does have an ancillary effect on service innovation. For example, the VCR has spawned a video rental business and created a renewed demand for old movies. Thus, the creation of an innovative service enterprise has many sources.

Service innovation also can arise from exploiting information available from other activities. For example, records of sales by auto parts stores can be used to identify frequent failure areas in particular models of cars. This information has value both for the manufacturer, who can accomplish engineering changes, and for the retailer, who can diagnose customer problems. In addition, the creative use of information can be a source of new services, or it can add value to existing services. For example, an annual summary statement of transactions furnished by one's financial institution has added value at income tax time.

Service innovators face a difficult problem in testing their service ideas. The process of product development includes building a laboratory prototype for testing before full-scale production is initiated. New services are seldom tested before they are launched in the marketplace, however, which provides a partial explanation for the observed high failure rate of service innovations, particularly in retailing and restaurants. At present, new service concepts usually must prove themselves in the field instead of in a "laboratory" setting. Methods to simulate service delivery systems before their introduction must be developed. One example of an effort in this direction is provided by Burger King, which acquired a warehouse in Miami to enclose a replica of its standard outlet. This mock restaurant was used to simulate changes in layout that would be required for the introduction of new features such as drive-through window service and a breakfast menu. The marketing concept of a "focus group," consisting of customers selected to review service proposals in a roundtable discussion, is another means of evaluating new service ideas. The difficulty in service prototyping is the need to evaluate the service delivery system in operation where technology, service providers, and customers are integrated.

Social Trends

Three social trends will have a major influence on services: the aging of the U.S. population, the growth of two-income families, and the increase in the number of single people. As the baby boom generation matures, the percentage of older people in America will increase greatly. Currently, 6.2 million Americans are older than 80 years old. By the year 2000, this figure is projected to be 8 million, and by the year 2010, the number will be 21.1 million.[4] This aging of the population will create opportunities for retired people to take part-time work, in part because of fewer young people entering the workforce. In the future, companies facing a labor shortage may be forced to hire retired workers, at least on a temporary or part-time basis, and this trend is already apparent. For example, The Travelers' Insurance Company has developed a Retirement Job Bank of its retired employees that is used as a source

---

[4]Susan B. Garland, "The Graying of America Spawns a New Crisis," *BusinessWeek*, Aug. 17, 1987, pp. 60–62.

of skilled labor to fill in during peak work times, absences, and vacations.[5] Also, elderly people are living longer and have more active lives, with consequent demands on health care, public transportation, and leisure services.

The two-income family is fast replacing the traditional family of the 1950s, which consisted of a husband, a housewife, and two children. The new two-income family unit has created demands for services such as day care, preschool, and "eating out" services. For two-income families, time is at a premium, and they are willing to pay for services that give them more free time. As a result, many new services have been created that focus exclusively on saving time for these individuals. Examples include home delivery services and personal shopping services for everything from gifts to clothing. Increased disposable income from two wage earners also may translate into increased demands for leisure, entertainment, and tourism services.

The number of single people in America is growing, and this trend is expected to continue.[6] Recreational sports and other group-oriented activities will be in demand, because they will offer the opportunity to meet other single people. Home food delivery services that now offer pizza may find a market for the delivery of gourmet meals to single people.

All of these social trends support the notion that the home will become a sanctuary for people in the future, and that sanctuary will be supported by a communication system bringing video and electronic messages from the global community into the living room.

Management Challenges

Complacency in the management of service industries, inattention to quality, disregard for customer concerns, and exclusive attention to short-term financial orientation all threaten to undermine the service sector of the economy. It is important to realize that under the pressures just mentioned, the service sector could become as vulnerable to foreign competition as the manufacturing sector has. The following discussion of the competitive challenges in services is based in part on a classic article by James Brian Quinn and Christopher E. Gagnon, in which they caution the reader that services could follow manufacturing into decline.[7]

Quinn and Gagnon point out that the economic trends in services are undeniable, and that they are similar to the recent experience in manufacturing. Since the early 1980s, the net positive trade balances in services have fallen steadily. For example, a serious loss of market share has been experienced in international airline travel as the once powerful carriers, Pan Am and TWA, declared bankruptcy in the face of foreign competitors that upgraded their fleets and emphasized quality of service.

Purely domestic services are not immune to foreign competition, either. Direct foreign investment in the U.S. service sector is substantial. Many famous names in services, such as 20th Century Fox, Stouffer's Hotels and Restaurants, Marshall Field, and Giant Foods, are now foreign-owned. In California, Japanese banks are changing the nature of competition and winning accounts by taking a much longer view in making business loans to new ventures at very competitive interest rates.

The nature of competition in services also is changing, because the forces of deregulation and new technologies have restructured service industries in recent

[5]Harold E. Johnson, "Older Workers Help Meet Employment Needs," *Personnel Journal*, May 1988, pp. 100–105.

[6]Edward Cornish, "The Coming of the Singles Society," *The Futurist*, July–August 1987, p. 2.

[7]J. B. Quinn and C. E. Gagnon, "Will Services Follow Manufacturing into Decline?" *Harvard Business Review*, November–December 1986, pp. 95–103.

years. Deregulation has caused significant restructuring in the domestic airline industry, with successful new regional carriers appearing (e.g., Southwest and Alaska) and old giants declaring bankruptcy (e.g., Eastern and Braniff). New route networks have formed around the hub-and-spoke concept to provide service in a more cost-effective manner. The use of computer reservation systems has allowed airlines to provide a variety of competitive fares based on preselling seats at a discount; thus, they can ensure high-load factors and profitable operations. Service managers need to understand these new competitive dimensions to take advantage of opportunities to improve service quality and performance, thereby creating barriers to the entry of foreign and domestic competitors. Competing on the traditional dimensions of quality, price, and availability will always be important, but consider the following additional dimensions based on the use of information technologies, which are the source of the value added by service firms.

ECONOMIES OF SCALE *Economies of scale* are realized when fixed costs in new technology are allocated over increased volume; the result is reduced cost per transaction. For example, automation of the securities trading process changed the entire structure of the industry and made possible the handling of daily volumes in the millions of shares. The old system of transferring shares from seller to buyer manually has been replaced by an electronic clearinghouse. Without using a central electronic depository, Wall Street could not function as an efficient securities marketplace. New and expensive medical technologies, such as the CAT or MRI scanners, have resulted in regional treatment centers and the concentration of medical services at these large hospitals. Thus, we find that the introduction of capital-intensive technologies has resulted in the concentration of services and aggregation of demand.

ECONOMIES OF SCOPE *Economies of scope,* a new and somewhat controversial concept, describes the benefits that are realized when entirely new service products move through established distribution networks with little added cost. For example, once the communications and information-handling technologies are in place, a much wider set of services can be distributed to a more diffuse customer base at low marginal costs. In addition, this information technology base can offer strategic benefits through more rapid product introduction and faster response to competitors' moves. Insurance companies that automated their back-office operations in the 1960s to improve billing and collections found themselves with a competitive advantage during the interest rate explosion of the 1980s. Companies had to alter their products rapidly to attract interest-sensitive new customers and to avoid the losses from current customers borrowing against their policies at low interest rates. Only those companies with the flexibility of computer information systems could design and deploy their products quickly enough to obtain a competitive edge. Some companies added new computer-intensive financial services such as cash management accounts to attract funds. A very common example of economies of scope can be found at any local convenience store that has added self-service gasoline and microwave meal service to its original grocery stocks.

COMPLEXITY Since deregulation, the domestic airline industry has witnessed an everchanging fare structure so complex that fares can no longer be published in flight schedules. Computerized reservations systems allow airlines to analyze the status of flights and customer buying behavior in such detail that they can optimize margins on each type of demand and meet competitors' responses. The ability to monitor hundreds of flights and make seat allocation decisions on an hourly basis is accomplished with significant computer support and software algorithms. This special use of computer information to manage perishable capacity and to maximize revenues is called *yield management.*

Sophisticated use of information systems to manage complexity also can be found in retail stores. Bar-code scanners give instant feedback on sales and inventory movements, which results in a better match of inventory to customers' needs. This information has enabled major chains to customize the stock featured at their stores so that they can accommodate regional preferences and compete better with small specialty shops.

BOUNDARY CROSSING Competition among services once thought to be in different industries is now becoming commonplace. Some of the most striking examples are found in the financial services. Today, many consumers use their banks and brokers almost interchangeably, because neither is seriously restricted in its scope of operations. Banks, insurance companies, and brokerage houses offer a similar range of financial products and services and now compete in one market, without the traditional boundaries. As noted earlier, convenience stores now compete with fast-food restaurants as well as with service stations, and even manufacturing firms such as GM and Ford have entered the service arena by offering financing services to auto buyers. The ability of auto manufacturers to finance the sales of their cars has allowed them to offer loans at reduced interest rates as an incentive to buy their products. In fact, at present, General Motors Acceptance Corporation is the nation's largest single holder of consumer debt. Thus, we can readily see that competition in services can come from any quarter.

INTERNATIONAL COMPETITIVENESS The worldwide service trade is growing with the help of cheaper and more flexible transportation and communication capabilities. During the 1960s, only 7 percent of the U.S. economy was exposed to foreign competition. Today, that figure is greater than 75 percent, and it is still climbing. With the world heading toward a single economy, or "global village," this trend toward greater international competition is expected to continue for both manufacturing and service firms.[8] For example, the purchase of Flying Tigers by Federal Express has enabled it to guarantee delivery anywhere in the world in two days; as a result, it joins DHL and others for a share in the growing business of global package delivery. Geographic distance is no longer a barrier between nations, and the challenges of ethnic diversity in the domestic market are multiplied by the difficulties of delivering a service in an international market with different cultural and language barriers.

SUMMARY

We have discovered that the modern industrial economies are dominated by employment in the service sector. Just as farming jobs migrated to manufacturing in the nineteenth century under the driving force of labor-saving technology, manufacturing jobs in due time migrated to services. Chapter 14 will conclude our discussion of the role of services in our new society and prepare us for developing new managerial skills by arguing that the distinctive characteristics of services require an approach to management significantly different from that found in manufacturing.

[8]John Greenwald, "Down and Down the Dollar Goes," *Time,* Sept. 7, 1992, pp. 36–37.

KEY TERMS AND DEFINITIONS

Clark-Fisher hypothesis a classification of economies according to the activity of the majority of the workforce.

Economies of scale allocation of the fixed costs of technology over an increased volume of sales (e.g., airline reservation system).

Economies of scope movement of new service products through established distribution networks (e.g., convenience stores adding self-serve gasoline pumps).

Industrial society a society dominated by factory work in mass-production industries.

Postindustrial society a service society in which people are engaged in information, intellectual, or creative-intensive activities.

Preindustrial society an agrarian society structured around farming and subsistence living.

Pull theory of innovation service innovations that are driven by customer needs.

Push theory of innovation product innovations that originate in scientific laboratories.

TOPICS FOR DISCUSSION

- Illustrate how a person's lifestyle is influenced by the type of work that he or she does. For example, contrast a farmer, a factory worker, and a schoolteacher.
- Is it possible for an economy to be based entirely on services?
- Speculate on the nature of the society that may evolve after the postindustrial society.

- What would be the impact on the service industry of the emerging social trend called *voluntary simplicity* (i.e., people choosing to spend less time working to enjoy life more)?
- Comment on the role that marketing plays in the service innovation process.

SERVICE BENCHMARK

IN THE 1990s THE NEW JOBS ARE IN SERVICES AND MANY ARE HIGH PAYING!

More and more, Americans are serving each other. There has been a net increase of roughly 11 million jobs since the recession ended in early 1991, and almost all of the new ones are in industries that provide one kind of service or another. The fastest growth took place in business services, a catch-all category that includes everything from accountants and data processors to janitors and temporary workers; leisure services, from blackjack dealers to amusement park operators; and social services, like welfare workers. The industries that lost jobs at the greatest rate include clothing and textile manufacturing, oil and gas extraction and coal mining. Some fast-growing industries pay extraordinarily well: annual earnings at brokerage firms average more than $96,000. But some of the biggest gainers pay well below average: many providers of social welfare services work for nonprofit agencies and earn little more than those they try to help. All in all, the gap has widened between those at the top of the job ladder and those at the bottom. Researchers at the Bureau of Labor Statistics have found that the largest gains in job growth in recent years took place in the highest-paying job categories; relatively low-paying industries and occupations have also grown, but at a slower pace. Employment has actually shrunk among job categories in the middle range.

Source: "The New Jobs: A Growing Number Are Good Ones," Judith H. Dobrzynski, *The New York Times,* July 21, 1996, p. 10

Winners and Losers, Industry by Industry
(Industries ranked by how quickly they added or lost jobs from the first quarter of 1991 to the first quarter of 1996. Top 25 and bottom 25.)

	Total Jobs in First Quarter 1996 in 1000s	Avg. Annual Growth Rate, %	Avg. Annual Earnings in 1993, $
Business services	7,009	6.7	22,499
Leisure	1,505	6.2	21,018
Nonbanking financial institutions	496	5.7	NA
Social services	2,370	5.6	15,326
Brokerage	531	4.9	96,497
Local transit	439	4.7	20,496
Transportation services	430	4.4	31,617
Motion pictures	516	4.4	31,692
Agricultural services	599	4.2	NA
Museum and zoos	83	4.0	19,514
Auto repair and parking	1,059	3.6	20,430
Furniture stores	950	3.4	21,208
Building materials stores	883	3.3	22,914
Health services	9,463	3.3	34,200
Trucking and warehousing	1,879	3.2	27,289
Engineering and management	2,849	3.1	33,709
Special trade contractors	3,334	3.1	26,443
Education	1,982	3.0	20,088
Eating and drinking places	7,419	2.8	11,920
Misc. services	44	2.5	NA
Auto dealers and service stations	2,234	2.2	25,433
Rubber and plastics	962	2.2	33,103
Air transportation	828	2.2	43,093
Lumber products	754	2.1	27,713
State and local government	16,584	1.5	28,859
Legal services	926	0.3	61,224
Stone, clay, and glass	535	0.2	33,566
Food products	1,674	0.1	32,369
Paper products	682	0.1	42,178
Printing and publishing	1,532	−0.3	32,515
Primary metal industries	708	−0.7	47,020
Textile mills	642	−0.8	24,897
Chemicals	1,026	−0.9	56,289
Apparel and accessory stores	1,100	−1.1	13,971
Utility services	905	−1.2	55,722
Federal government	2,781	−1.2	NA
Transportation equipment	1,747	−1.2	NA
Banks and savings institutions	2,022	−1.7	35,252
Metal mining	51	−2.3	56,964
Petroleum and coal	140	−2.4	67,996
Railroads	234	−2.7	55,707
Apparel and textile	868	−2.8	19,225
Tobacco	41	−3.4	55,983
Instruments	831	−3.4	45,795
Leather	99	−4.8	22,664
Oil and gas extraction	312	−5.0	36,011
Pipelines	14	−5.9	54,011
Coal mining	101	−6.4	62,044

Sources: Regional Financial Associates, Bureau of Labor Statistics, as reprinted in *The New York Times*, July 21, 1996, p. 10.

SELECTED BIBLIOGRAPHY

BELL, DANIEL: *The Coming of Post-Industrial Society: A Venture in Social Forecasting,* Basic Books, Inc., New York, 1973.

COOK, JAMES: "You Mean We've Been Speaking Prose All These Years?" *Forbes,* April 11, 1983, pp. 143–149.

DAVIS, STANLEY M.: *Future Perfect,* Addison-Wesley, Reading, Mass., 1987.

FUCHS, VICTOR R.: *The Service Economy,* National Bureau of Economic Research, New York, 1968.

GERSHUNG, J. I.: *After Industrial Society,* The Macmillan Co., New York, 1978.

GERSUNY, C., and W. ROSENGREN: *The Service Society,* Schenkman Publishing Co., Cambridge, Mass., 1973.

GINZBERG, E., and G. VOJTA: "The Service Sector of the U.S. Economy," *Scientific American,* vol. 244, no. 3, March 1981, pp. 48–55.

GUILE, BRUCE E., and JAMES B. QUINN (ed.): *Managing Innovation: Cases from the Service Industries,* National Academy Press, Washington, D.C., 1988.

———: *Technology in Services: Policies for Growth, Trade, and Employment,* National Academy Press, Washington, D.C., 1988.

HESKETT, J. L.: "Lessons in the Service Sector," *Harvard Business Review,* March–April 1987, pp. 118–126.

———: *Managing in the Service Economy,* Harvard Business School Press, Boston, 1986.

———, W. E. SASSER, JR., and C. W. L. HART: *Service Breakthroughs,* Free Press, New York, 1990.

HIRSCHHORN, L.: "The Post-Industrial Economy: Labour, Skills and the New Mode of Production," *The Service Industries Journal,* vol. 8, no. 1, 1988, pp. 19–38.

JOHNSTON, R.: "Service Industries: Improving Competitive Performance," *The Service Industries Journal,* vol. 8, no. 2, 1988, pp. 202–211.

KULONDA, D. J., and W. H. MOATES, JR.: "Operations Supervisors in Manufacturing and Service Sectors in the United States: Are They Different?" *International Journal of Operations and Production Management,* vol. 6, no. 2, 1986, pp. 21–35.

LEWIS, R.: *The New Service Society,* Longman, New York, 1973.

LOVELOCK, C. H.: "Business Schools Owe Students Better Service," *Managing Services,* Prentice-Hall, Englewood Cliffs, N.J., 1988, pp. 22–24.

———, and R. K. SHELP: "The Service Economy Gets No Respect," *Managing Services,* Prentice-Hall, Englewood Cliffs, N.J., 1988, pp. 1–5.

QUINN, J. B., and C. E. GAGNON: "Will Services Follow Manufacturing into Decline?" *Harvard Business Review,* November–December 1986, pp. 95–103.

RIDDLE, D. I.: *Service-Led Growth,* Praeger, New York, 1986.

RIFKIN, JEREMY: *The End of Work: The Decline of the Global Labor Force and the Dawn of the Post-Market Era,* Tarcher/Putnam, New York, 1995.

TOFFLER, ALVIN: *The Third Wave,* William Morrow and Co., Inc., New York, 1980.

CHAPTER 14

The Nature of Services

In this chapter, we explore the distinctive features of services. The service environment is sufficiently unique to allow us to question the direct application of traditional manufacturing-based techniques to services without some modification, although many approaches are analogous. Ignoring the differences between manufacturing and service requirements will lead to failure, but more importantly, recognition of the special features of services will provide insights for enlightened and innovative management. Advances in service management cannot occur without an appreciation of the service system environment.

The distinction between a *product* and a *service* is difficult to make, because the purchase of a product is accompanied by some facilitating service (e.g., installation) and the purchase of a service often includes facilitating goods (e.g., food at a restaurant). Each purchase includes a bundle of goods and services in varying proportions, as shown in Table 1.

Services have a clear *front-office* (e.g., bank-teller interaction with a customer) and *back-office* (e.g., a bank's check-clearing operations) dichotomy in their operations, so we would be foolish to ignore the substantial opportunities for applying manufacturing techniques to the isolated back-office operations. These opportunities will be explored in Chapter 16, in which we consider the design of the service delivery system.

CHAPTER PREVIEW

The chapter begins with a classification of services based on the degree of customer interaction or customization and the degree of labor intensiveness. This classification allows us to focus on managerial issues that are found across similar service industries. An appreciation of the nature of services begins with the realization that a service is a package of explicit and implicit benefits performed within a supporting facility and using facilitating goods. These multiple dimensions of a service are central to the design and control of a service delivery system. The distinctive characteristics of service operations are discussed, and the implications for management are noted.

On the basis of these characteristics, the role of the service manager is viewed from an open-system perspective. That is, the service manager must deal with an environment in which the customers are present in the delivery system. This contrasts with manufacturing operations that are isolated or "buffered" from the customer by an inventory of finished goods. Thus, manufacturing traditionally has op-

TABLE 1   Proportion of Goods and Services in Typical Purchase Bundle

Goods					Services			
100%	75	50	25	0	25	50	75	100%

```
I ......... Self-service gasoline.......................... I
     I ........... Personal computer...................... I
        I ............. Office copier ................................. I
           I .............. Fast-food restaurant .................. I
              I ............... Gourmet restaurant ................... I
                 I .............. Auto repair ............................. I
                    I ............ Airline flight ............................. I
                       I .................... Haircut ................................ I
```

Source: Adapted from W. E. Sasser, R. P. Olsen, and D. D. Wyckoff, *Management of Service Operations*, Allyn and Bacon, Boston, 1978, p. 11.

erated as a cost center, focusing on process efficiency. Service managers, who often operate as profit centers, must be concerned with both efficient and effective delivery of services.

SERVICE CLASSIFICATION

Concepts of service management should be applicable to all service organizations. For example, hospital administrators could learn something about their own business from the restaurant and hotel trade. Professional services such as consulting, law, and medicine have special problems, because the professional is trained to provide a specific clinical service (to use a medical example) but is not knowledgeable in business management. Thus, professional service firms offer attractive career opportunities for many college graduates.

A service classification scheme can help to organize our discussion of service management and break down the industry barriers to shared learning. As suggested, hospitals can learn about housekeeping from hotels. Less obviously, dry-cleaning establishments can learn from banks—cleaners can adapt the convenience of night deposits enjoyed by banking customers by providing laundry bags and after-hours drop-off boxes. For professional firms, scheduling a consulting engagement is similar to planning a legal defense or preparing a medical team for open heart surgery.

To demonstrate that management problems are common across service industries, Roger Schmenner proposed the *service process matrix* in Figure 1. In this matrix, services are classified across two dimensions that significantly affect the character of the service delivery process. The horizontal dimension measures the degree of labor intensity, which is defined as the ratio of labor cost to capital cost. Thus, capital-intensive services such as airlines and hospitals are found in the upper row because of their considerable investment in plant and equipment relative to labor costs. Labor-intensive services such as schools and legal assistance are found in the bottom row because their labor costs are high relative to their capital requirements.

The vertical dimension measures the degree of customer interaction and customization, which is a marketing variable that describes the ability of the customer

Figure 1 *The service process matrix.*
(From "How Can Service Businesses Survive and Prosper?" by Roger W. Schmenner, *Sloan Management Review,* vol. 27, no. 3, Spring 1986, p. 25, by permission of publisher. Copyright 1986 by the Sloan Management Review Association. All rights reserved.)

Degree of Labor Intensity	**Degree of Interaction and Customization**	
	Low	High
Low	*Service factory:* • Airlines • Trucking • Hotels • Resorts and recreation	*Service shop:* • Hospitals • Auto repair • Other repair services
High	*Mass service:* • Retailing • Wholesaling • Schools • Retail aspects of commercial banking	*Professional service:* • Doctors • Lawyers • Accountants • Architects

to affect personally the nature of the service being delivered. Little interaction between customer and service provider is needed when the service is standardized rather than customized. For example, a meal at McDonald's, which is assembled from prepared items, is low in customization and served with little interaction occurring between the customer and the service providers. In contrast, a doctor and patient must interact fully in the diagnostic and treatment phases to achieve satisfactory results. Patients also expect to be treated as individuals and wish to receive medical care that is customized to their particular needs. It is important to note, however, that the interaction resulting from high customization creates potential problems for management of the service delivery process.

The four quadrants of the service process matrix have been given names, as defined by the two dimensions, to describe the nature of the services illustrated. *Service factories* provide a standardized service with high capital investment, much like a line-flow manufacturing plant.[1] *Service shops* permit more service customization, but they do so in a high-capital environment. Customers of a *mass service* will receive an undifferentiated service in a labor-intensive environment, but those seeking a *professional service* will be given individual attention by highly trained specialists.

Managers of services in any category, whether service factory, service shop, mass service, or professional service, share similar challenges, as noted in Figure 2. Services with high capital requirements (i.e., low labor intensity), such as airlines and hospitals, require close monitoring of technological advances to remain competitive. This high capital investment also requires managers to schedule demand to maintain utilization of the equipment. Alternatively, managers of highly labor-intensive services, such as medical or legal professionals, must concentrate on personnel matters. The degree of customization affects the ability to control the quality of the service being delivered and the perception of the service by the customer.

THE SERVICE PACKAGE

Service managers have difficulty identifying their product. This problem is partly a result of the intangible nature of services, but it is the presence of the customer in the process that creates a concern for the total service experience. Consider the following examples. For a sit-down restaurant, atmosphere is just as important as the meal, because many diners regard the occasion as a way to get together with friends. A customer's opinion of a bank can be formed quickly on the basis of a teller's cheerfulness or length of the waiting line.

The *service package* is defined as a bundle of goods and services that is provided in some environment. This bundle consists of the following four features:

1. *Supporting facility.* The physical resources that must be in place before a service can be offered. Examples are a golf course, a ski lift, a hospital, and an airplane.

2. *Facilitating goods.* The material purchased or consumed by the buyer, or the items provided by the customer. Examples are golf clubs, skis, food items, replacement auto parts, legal documents, and medical supplies.

3. *Explicit services.* The benefits that are readily observable by the senses and that consist of the essential or intrinsic features of the service. Examples are the ab-

---

[1]This concept of a service operated like a manufacturing factory is different from the more recent realization by manufacturing firms that operating a factory more like a service can achieve a competitive advantage. *See* R. B. Chase and D. A. Garvin, "The Service Factory," *Harvard Business Review*, vol. 67, no. 4, July/August 1989, pp. 61–69.

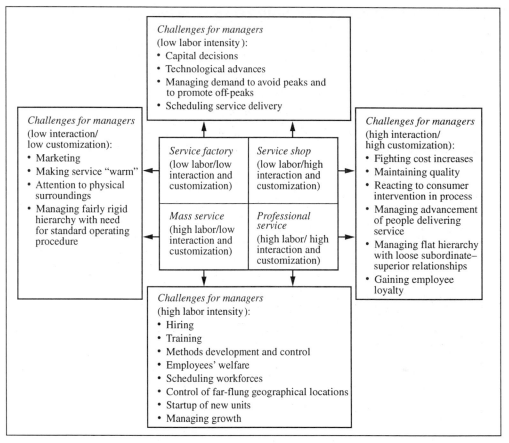

Figure 2 *Challenges for service managers.*
(From "How Can Service Businesses Survive and Prosper?" by Roger W. Schmenner, *Sloan Management Review,* vol. 27, no. 3, Spring 1986, p. 27, by permission of publisher. Copyright 1986 by the Sloan Management Review Association. All rights reserved.)

sence of pain after a tooth is repaired, a smooth-running automobile after a tune-up, and the response time of a fire department.

4. *Implicit services.* Psychological benefits that the customer may sense only vaguely, or the extrinsic features of the service. Examples are the status of a degree from an Ivy League school, the privacy of a loan office, and worry-free auto repair.

All these features are experienced by the customer and form the basis of his or her perception of the service. It is important that the service manager offer a total experience for the customer that is consistent with the desired service package. Take, for example, a budget hotel. The supporting facility is a concrete-block building with austere furnishings. Facilitating goods are reduced to the minimum of soap and paper. The explicit service is a comfortable bed in a clean room, and implicit services might include a friendly desk clerk and the security of a well-lighted parking area. Deviations from this service package, such as adding bellhops, would destroy the bargain image. Table 2 lists criteria (with examples) for evaluating the service package.

The importance of facilitating goods in the service package can be used to classify services across a continuum from pure services to various degrees of mixed services. For example, psychiatric counseling with no facilitating goods would be considered a "pure" service. Automobile maintenance usually requires more facilitating goods than a haircut does.

TABLE 2   Criteria for Evaluating the Service Package

SUPPORTING FACILITY

1. *Location*
   Is it accessible by public transportation?
   Is it centrally located?
2. *Interior decorating*
   Is the proper mood established?
   Quality and coordination of furniture.
3. *Supporting equipment*
   Does the dentist use a mechanical or air drill?
   What type and age of aircraft does the charter airline use?

4. *Architectural appropriateness*
   Renaissance architecture for university campus.
   Unique recognizable feature of a blue tile roof.
   Massive granite facade of downtown bank.
5. *Facility layout*
   Is there a natural flow of traffic?
   Are adequate waiting areas provided?
   Is there unnecessary travel or backtracking?

FACILITATING GOODS

1. *Consistency*
   Crispness of french fries.
   Portion control.
2. *Quantity*
   Small, medium, or large drink.

3. *Selection*
   Variety of replacement mufflers.
   Number of menu items.
   Rental skis available.

EXPLICIT SERVICES

1. *Training of service personnel*
   Is the auto mechanic certified by the National Institute for Automotive Service Excellence (NIASE)?
   To what extent are paraprofessionals used?
   Are the physicians board certified?
2. *Comprehensiveness*
   Discount broker compared with full service.
   General hospital compared with clinic.

3. *Consistency*
   Airline's on-time record.
   Professional Standards Review Organization (PSRO) for doctors.
4. *Availability*
   24-hour ATM service.
   Is there a web site?
   Is there a toll-free number?

IMPLICIT SERVICES

1. *Attitude of service*
   Cheerful flight attendant.
   Police officer issuing traffic citation with tact.
   Surly service person in restaurant.
2. *Atmosphere*
   Restaurant decor.
   Music in a bar.
   Sense of confusion rather than order.
3. *Waiting*
   Joining a drive-in banking queue.
   Being placed on hold.
   Enjoying a martini in the restaurant bar.

4. *Status*
   College degree from Ivy League school.
   Box seats at sports event.
5. *Sense of well-being*
   Large commercial aircraft.
   Well-lighted parking lot.
6. *Privacy and security*
   Attorney advising client in private office.
   Magnetic key card for hotel room.
7. *Convenience*
   Use of appointments.
   Free parking.

Making general statements about service management is difficult when there are such variations in the nature of services. However, an appreciation of the unique features of the service environment is important for understanding the challenges facing service managers.

DISTINCTIVE CHARACTERISTICS OF SERVICE OPERATIONS

In services, a distinction must be made between *inputs* and *resources*. For services, inputs are the customers themselves, and resources are the facilitating goods, employee labor, and capital at the command of the service manager. Thus, to function, the service system must interact with the customers as participants in the service process. Because customers typically arrive at their own discretion and with unique demands on the service system, matching service capacity with demand is a challenge.

For some services, such as banking, however, the focus of activity is on processing information instead of people. In these situations, information technology, such as electronic funds transfer, can be substituted for physically depositing a payroll check; thus, the presence of the customer at the bank is unnecessary. Such exceptions will be noted as we discuss the distinctive characteristics of service operations. It should be noted here that many of the unique characteristics of services, such as customer participation and perishability, are interrelated.

The Customer as a Participant in the Service Process

The presence of the customer as a participant in the service process requires an attention to facility design that is not found in traditional manufacturing operations. That automobiles are made in a hot, dirty, noisy factory is of no concern to the eventual buyers, because they first see the product in the pleasant surroundings of a dealer's showroom. The presence of the customer on-site requires attention to the physical surroundings of the service facility that is not necessary for the factory. For the customer, service is an experience occurring in the environment of the service facility, and the quality of service is enhanced if the service facility is designed from the customer's perspective. Attention to interior decorating, furnishings, layout, noise, and even color can influence the customer's perception of the service. Compare the feelings invoked by picturing yourself in a stereotypical bus station with those produced by imagining yourself in an airline terminal. Of course, passengers are not allowed in the terminal's back office (e.g., the luggage-handling area), which is operated in a factory-like environment. However, some innovative services have opened the back office to public scrutiny to promote confidence in the service (e.g., some restaurants provide a view into the kitchen, some auto repair bays can be observed through windows in the waiting area).

An important consideration in providing a service is the realization that the customer can play an active part in the process. A few examples will illustrate that the knowledge, experience, motivation, and even honesty of the customer all directly affect the performance of the service system:

1. The popularity of supermarkets and discount stores is predicated on the idea that customers are willing to assume an active role in the retailing process.

2. The accuracy of a patient's medical record can greatly influence the effectiveness of the attending physician.

3. The education of a student is determined largely by the student's own effort and contributions.

This strategy is best illustrated by the fast-food restaurants that have significantly reduced the typical number of serving and cleaning personnel. The customer not only places the order directly from a limited menu but also is expected to clear the table after the meal. Naturally, the customer expects faster service and less expensive meals to compensate for these inputs, but the service provider benefits in many subtle ways. First, there are fewer personnel who require supervision and such things as fringe benefits. Second, and more importantly, the customer provides the labor just at the moment it is required; thus, service capacity varies more directly with demand rather than being fixed by the size of the employed staff. The customer acts like a temporary employee, arriving just when needed to perform duties to augment the work of the service staff.

This strategy has received great acceptance in a society, such as the United States, where self-reliance is valued. Instead of being a passive buyer, the customer becomes a contributor to the gross national product.

Taking the customer out of the process, however, is becoming a common practice. Consider retail banking, in which customers are encouraged to use telephone or computer transactions, direct deposit, and automatic-debit bill paying instead of actually traveling to the bank. Moreover, the advent of Internet commerce gives new meaning to the phrase "window shopping."

Simultaneous Production and Consumption of Services

The fact that services are created and consumed simultaneously and, thus, cannot be stored is a critical feature in the management of services. This inability to inventory services precludes using the traditional manufacturing strategy of relying on inventory as a buffer to absorb fluctuations in demand. An inventory of finished goods serves as a convenient system boundary for a manufacturer, separating the internal operations of planning and control from the external environment. Thus, the manufacturing facility can be operated at a constant level of output that is most efficient. The factory is operated as a *closed system,* with inventory decoupling the productive system from customer demand. Services, however, operate as *open systems,* with the full impact of demand variations being transmitted to the system.

Inventory also can be used to decouple the stages in a manufacturing process. For services, the decoupling is achieved through customer waiting. Inventory control is a major issue in manufacturing operations, whereas in services, the corresponding problem is customer waiting, or "queuing." The problems of selecting service capacity, facility utilization, and use of idle time all are balanced against customer waiting time.

The simultaneous production and consumption in services also eliminates many opportunities for quality-control intervention. A product can be inspected before delivery, but services must rely on other measures to ensure the quality of services delivered.

Time-Perishable Capacity

A service is a perishable commodity. Consider an empty airline seat, an unoccupied hospital or hotel room, or an hour without a patient in the day of a dentist. In each case, a lost opportunity has occurred. Because a service cannot be stored, it is lost forever when not used. The full utilization of service capacity becomes a management challenge, because customer demand exhibits considerable variation and building inventory to absorb these fluctuations is not an option.

Consumer demand for services typically exhibits very cyclic behavior over short periods of time, with considerable variation between the peaks and valleys. The custom of eating lunch between noon and 1 PM places a burden on restaurants to accommodate the noon rush. The practice of day-end mailing by businesses contributes to the fact that 60 percent of all letters are received at the post office between 4 and 8 PM.[2] The demand for emergency medical service in Los Angeles was found to vary from a low of 0.5 calls per hour at 6 AM to a peak of 3.5 calls per hour at 6 PM.[3] This peak-to-valley ratio of 7 to 1 also was true for fire alarms during an average day in New York City.[4]

For recreational and transportation services, seasonal variation in demand creates surges in activity. As many students know, flights home are often booked months in advance of spring break and the Christmas holiday.

Faced with variable demand and a perishable capacity to provide the service, the manager has three basic options:

1. Smooth demand by:
   a. Using reservations or appointments.
   b. Using price incentives (e.g., giving telephone discounts for evening and weekend calls).
   c. Demarketing peak times (e.g., advertising to shop early and avoid the Christmas rush).

2. Adjust service capacity by:
   a. Using part-time help during peak hours.
   b. Scheduling work shifts to vary workforce needs according to demand (e.g., telephone companies staff their operators to match call demand).
   c. Increasing the customer self-service content of the service.

3. Allow customers to wait.

The last option can be viewed as a passive contribution to the service process that carries the risk of losing a dissatisfied customer to a competitor. By waiting, the customer permits greater utilization of service capacity. The airlines explicitly recognize this by offering standby passengers a reduced price for their tickets.

Site Selection Dictated by Location of Customers

In manufacturing, products are shipped from the manufacturer to the wholesaler to the retailer, but in services, the customer and provider must physically meet for a service to be performed. Either the customer comes to the service facility (e.g., restaurant), or the service provider goes to the customer (e.g., ambulance service). Of course, there are exceptions, such as buying stock by phone or modem and taking university courses via teleconferencing. In fact, because of advances in information technology such as the Internet, opportunities for innovation in service systems abound (e.g., Federal Express allows its customers to track their packages using a Web site).

Travel time and costs are reflected in the economics of site selection (e.g., in the case of Domino's Pizza). The result is that many small service centers are located close to prospective consumers. Of course, the tradeoff is between the fixed cost of the facility and the travel costs of the customers. The more expensive the facility, the larger or more densely populated the market area must be. For example, many a major-league baseball team has had trouble surviving in a medium-sized city.

[2]R. C. Cohen, R. McBridge, R. Thornton, and T. White, *Letter Mail System Performance Design: An Analytical Method for Evaluating Candidate Mechanization*, Report R-168, Institute for Defense Analysis, Washington, D.C., 1970.

[3]James A. Fitzsimmons, "The Use of Spectral Analysis to Validate Planning Models," *Socio-Economic Planning Sciences*, vol. 8, no. 3, June 1974, pp. 123–128.

[4]E. H. Blum, *Urban Fire Protection: Studies of the New York City Fire Department*, R-681, New York City Rand Institute, New York, January 1971.

The resulting small size of operation and the multisite locations of some services create several challenges.

LIMITED-SCALE ECONOMIES For services in which physical travel by the customer is necessary (e.g., restaurants), the immediate geographic market area limits the effective size of operations and removes the opportunity to gain economies of scale. However, some services such as franchised food firms have centralized many of their common functions (e.g., purchasing, advertising, and food preparation) to achieve these economies. Faced with a limited market area, some firms such as convenience stores have turned to an economy of scope strategy by offering a wide range of services from self-service gasoline to microwave meals.

CONTROL OF DECENTRALIZED SERVICES Unlike manufacturing, services are performed in the field, not in the controlled environment of a factory. For example, fast-food restaurants maintain service consistency across multiple locations through a standardized delivery process. In this case, the standardization may be achieved by designing special equipment (e.g., a french-fry scoop that measures the portion) or by offering a limited service (e.g., only burgers, fries, and shakes). More sophisticated services such as management consulting must rely on extensive training, licensing, and peer review.

For services that travel to the customer (e.g., telephone installations, delivery services, and maintenance and repair services), the problems of routing, dispatching, and scheduling become important. These aspects are examined in the supplement to Chapter 16, Vehicle Routing.

Labor Intensiveness

In most service organizations, labor is the key resource that determines the effectiveness of the organization. For these organizations, technological obsolescence is not fully accommodated by investments in new equipment; it is the skills of the labor force that age as new knowledge makes current skills obsolete. In an expanding organization, recruitment provides an avenue to acquiring this new knowledge. In a slow-growth or stable organization, however, the only successful strategy may be continuous retraining. The problem of aging labor skills is particularly acute in the professional service organization, in which extensive formal education is a prerequisite to employment.

The interaction between customer and employee in services creates the possibility of a more complete human work experience. In services, work activity generally is oriented toward people rather than toward things. There are exceptions, however, for services that process information (e.g., communications) or customers' property (e.g., brokerage services). In the limited customer-contact service industries, we now see a dramatic reduction in the level of labor intensiveness through the introduction of information technology.

Even the introduction of automation may strengthen personalization by eliminating the relatively routine impersonal tasks, thereby permitting increased personal attention to the remaining work. At the same time, personal attention creates opportunities for variability in the service that is provided. This is not inherently bad, however, unless customers perceive a significant variation in quality. A customer expects to be treated fairly and to be given the same service that others receive. The development of standards and of employee training in proper procedures is the key to ensuring consistency in the service provided. It is rather impractical to monitor the output of each employee, except via customer complaints.

The direct customer–employee contact has implications for service (industrial) relations as well. Auto workers with grievances against the firm have been known to sabotage the product on the assembly line. Presumably, the final inspection will ensure that any such cars are corrected before delivery. A disgruntled service employee, however, can do irreparable harm to the organization, because the employee is the firm's sole contact with customers. Therefore, the service manager must be concerned about the employees' attitudes as well as their performance. J. Willard Marriott, founder of the Marriott Hotel chain, has said, "In the service business you can't make happy guests with unhappy employees."[5] Through training and genuine concern for employee welfare, the organizational goals can be internalized.

Intangibility

Services are ideas and concepts; products are things. Therefore, it follows that service innovations are not patentable. To secure the benefits of a novel service concept, the firm must expand extremely rapidly and preempt any competitors. Franchising has been the vehicle to secure market areas and establish a brand name. Franchising allows the parent firm to sell its idea to a local entrepreneur, thus preserving capital while retaining control and reducing risk.

The intangible nature of services also presents a problem for customers. When buying a product, the customer is able to see it, feel it, and test its performance before purchase. For a service, however, the customer must rely on the reputation of the service firm. In many service areas, the government has intervened to guarantee acceptable service performances. Through the use of registration, licensing, and regulation, the government can assure consumers that the training and test performance of some service providers meet certain standards. Thus, we find that public construction plans must be approved by a registered professional engineer, a doctor must be licensed to practice medicine, and the telephone company is a regulated utility. In its efforts to "protect" the consumer, however, the government may be stifling innovation, raising barriers to entry, and generally reducing competition.

Difficulty in Measuring Output

Measuring the output of a service organization is a frustrating task for several reasons. Counting the number of customers served is seldom useful because it does not account for the uniqueness of the service that is performed. The problem of measurement is further complicated by the fact that not-for-profit service systems (e.g., universities, governments, and some hospitals) do not have a single criterion, such as maximizing profit, on which to base an evaluation of their performance. More importantly, can a system's performance be evaluated on the basis of output alone when this assumes a homogeneous input of service demands? A more definitive evaluation of service performance is a measure of the change in each customer from the input to the output state, a process known as *transactional analysis*. For example, consulting services and market research often involve providing clients with access to appropriate information and showing them how it relates to their situations, which is a very customized activity.

[5] G. M. Hostage, "Quality Control in a Service Business," *Harvard Business Review*, vol. 53, no. 4, July–August 1975, pp. 98–106.

AN OPEN-SYSTEMS VIEW OF SERVICES

Service organizations are sufficiently unique in their character to require special management approaches that go beyond the simple adaptation of the management techniques found in manufacturing a product. The distinctive characteristics suggest enlarging the system view to include the customer as a participant in the service process. As Figure 3 shows, the customer is viewed as an input that is transformed by the service process into an output with some degree of satisfaction.

The role of the service operations manager includes the functions of both production and marketing in an open system with the customer as a participant. The traditional manufacturing separation of the production and marketing functions, with finished-goods inventory as the interface, is neither possible nor appropriate in services. Marketing performs two important functions in daily-service operations: 1) educating the consumer to play a role as an active participant in the service process and 2) "smoothing" demand to match service capacity. This marketing activity must be coordinated with scheduling staff levels and with both controlling and evaluating the delivery process. By necessity, the operations and marketing functions are integrated for service organizations.

For services, *the process is the product.* The presence of the customer in the service process negates the closed-system perspective that is taken in manufacturing. Techniques to control operations in an isolated factory producing a tangible good are inadequate for services. No longer is the process machine-paced and the output easily measured for compliance with specifications. Instead, customers arrive with different demands on the service; thus, multiple measures of performance are necessary. Service employees interact directly with the customer, with little opportunity for management intervention. This requires extensive training and empowerment of employees to act appropriately in the absence of direct supervision.

Figure 3 *Open-systems view of service operations.*

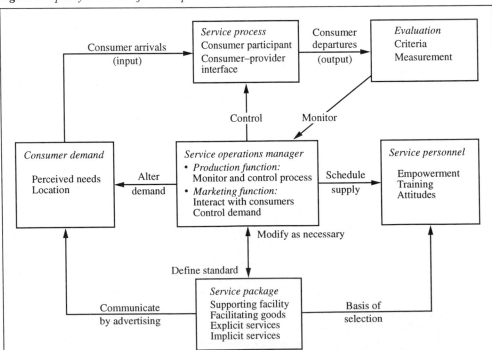

Further, customer impressions of service quality are based on the total service experience, not just on the explicit service that is performed. A concern for employee attitudes and training becomes a necessity to ensure that the implicit service is also appreciated by the customer. When viewed from the customer's perspective, the entire service process raises concerns ranging from the aesthetic design of the facility to pleasant diversions in waiting areas.

An open-system concept of services also allows one to view the customer as a co-producer. Permitting the customer to participate actively in the service process (e.g., providing a salad bar at a restaurant) can increase productivity, which in turn can create a competitive edge.

SUMMARY

The management of an open system requires techniques and sensitivities different from those of a closed system. Service managers are faced with nonroutine operations in which only indirect control is possible. In services, it is the human element that is central to effective operations. For example, the unavoidable interaction between service provider and consumer is a source of great opportunity, as in direct selling. However, this interaction seldom can be fully controlled; thus, service quality may suffer. For this reason, the attitude and appearance of personnel in service organizations are important considerations. For services, the presence of the customer in the process materially alters what is viewed as the product. The unique characteristics of intangibility, perishability, and simultaneous provision and consumption introduce special challenges for service management. In many respects, the service manager adopts a style of management that incorporates the functions of marketing and operations.

Next we will examine strategic service issues, beginning in Chapter 15 with the formulation of a strategic service concept. We also will discover insights from a strategic classification system, discuss generic competitive service strategies, and conclude with a look at how customers are won in the marketplace.

KEY TERMS AND DEFINITIONS

Explicit services the essential or intrinsic features readily observable by the senses (e.g., on-time departure, quality of meal).

Facilitating goods material purchased or consumed by the buyer, or items provided by the customer (e.g., food, golf clubs).

Implicit services psychologic benefits or extrinsic features the customer may sense only vaguely (e.g., security of a well-lighted parking lot, privacy of a loan office).

Service process matrix a classification of services based on the degree of interaction and customization and the degree of labor intensity that results in four categories: service factory, service shop, mass service, and professional service.

Supporting facility the physical resources that must be in place before a service can be offered (e.g., golf course, hospital building, airplane).

The service package a description of a service based on four components: supporting facility, facilitating goods, explicit service, and implicit service.

Time-perishable capacity a service that is not used during some period of time and, therefore, is lost forever (e.g., an empty seat on an airplane).

TOPICS FOR DISCUSSION

- What are some possible measures of performance for a fire department? For a fast-food restaurant?
- Comment on why hospitals, given that they are so labor-intensive, are classified as a service shop in Figure 1.
- Select a service with which you are familiar, and identify the seven "distinctive characteristics of service operations" that it has.

- What factors are important for a manager to consider when attempting to enhance a service organization's image?
- What contributions to the management of professional service firms can a business school graduate provide?

SERVICE BENCHMARK

TO COMPETE BETTER, LOOK FAR AFIELD

How can companies best compete? One excellent and relatively under-used way is to seek creative insights in industries far afield from their own.

Of course, in a time of fierce global competition businesses are hardly unaware of the need to improve performance. Many have relentlessly cut costs through downsizing and other strategies, for instance. Others have scrutinized similar companies in their quest for innovative processes, technologies, and products.

But cost-cutting has its limits. And so does seeking inspiration only within one's own field. For example, many commercial real estate companies assumed during the last recession that once the economy picked up so would their business. Failing to look beyond their own realm, they could not see that more and more businesses were opting for portable and "at home" offices.

Enter the quest for creative ideas from beyond a company's own industry—from those normally unexplored regions that business strategists call "outside the box."

When Southwest Airlines wanted to improve the turnaround of its aircraft at airports, for instance, it could have examined the practices of other airlines' maintenance workers. Instead, the company went to the Indianapolis 500 to watch pit crews fuel and service race cars. The airline recognized that pit crews perform the same functions airplane maintenance crews do, just in a different industry and at a much faster speed. The observations gave Southwest new ideas about equipment fittings, materials management, teamwork, and speed that, in part, enabled the airline to cut its turnaround time by 50 percent.

Or consider Granite Rock. This company wanted to improve the way it loaded gravel into trucks in its yards. Before the gravel could be loaded, drivers had to leave their trucks and fill out paperwork to indicate how much gravel they needed. But, by observing automatic teller machines in banks, Granite Rock was able to revise this expensive and time-consuming procedure. Now, the truck drivers plug their "bank" cards into a machine so they do not have to leave the truck in order to make their requests for gravel.

Focusing on processes is the key to finding useful insights in apparently unrelated places. From a process standpoint, all companies do the same things—sell to customers, buy from suppliers, hire employees.

Understanding this broad connection, a major gas utility examined how Federal Express delivers packages overnight—and discovered ways to speed the delivery of its own product, fuel. Similarly, a major telecommunications company improved its billing system by visiting a package delivery concern. The telephone company recognized that the shipper's tracking of cargo was analogous to its tracking of invoices.

The lesson for businesses? Look for insights in apparently unrelated fields. An enterprise hoping to improve its production processes, for example, might do well to examine Domino's Pizza—a company that completes its order entry, manufacturing, distribution, billing, and collection processes in 30 minutes. But the enterprise should perform this inquiry quickly. For, day by day, the global marketplace is growing more and more competitive.

Skeptical about "outside the box" thinking? Just recall Isaac Newton. The famous scientist gained his greatest insight into gravity not from learned, ancient treatises but from an apparently unlikely source: an apple.

Source: Robert Hiebeler, "To Compete Better, Look Far Afield," *The New York Times*, September 18, 1994, p. 11.

CONCLUDING CASE

VILLAGE VOLVO

Village Volvo is the "new kid in town." It represents an effort by two former authorized Volvo dealer mechanics to provide quality repair service on out-of-warranty Volvos at a reasonable cost. On the basis of their 22 combined years of training and experience with the local Volvo dealer, they have earned a respected reputation and a following of satisfied customers, which make an independent service operation feasible. Village Volvo occupies a new Butler building (i.e., a prefabricated metal structure) that has four work bays in addition to an office, waiting area, and storage room.

The owners feel they have designed their operation to provide clients with a custom car care service that is unavailable at the local dealer. They have set aside specific times each week when clients may drive in for quick, routine services such as tune-ups and oil changes, but they encourage clients to schedule appointments for the diagnosis and repair of specific problems.

At the time of the appointment, the mechanic who will be working on the vehicle and the client discuss the problems the client has noticed. On occasion, the mechanic may take a short test drive with the client to be certain that both understand the area of concern.

Another source of information for the mechanic is the Custom Care Vehicle Dossier (CCVD). Village Volvo maintains a continuing file on each vehicle it services. This history can help the mechanic to diagnose problems and also provides a convenient record if a vehicle is returned for warranty service on an earlier repair. The owners are considering use of the CCVD as a way of "reminding" customers that routine maintenance procedures may be due.

After the mechanic has made a preliminary diagnosis, the service manager gives the vehicle owner an estimate of the cost and the approximate time when the repair will be completed if no unexpected problems arise. Company policy states that the owner will be consulted before any work other than the agreed-on job is done. Although the customer may speak with the mechanic during the repair process, the service manager is the main point of contact. It is the service manager's responsibility to be sure the customer understands the preliminary diagnosis, to advise the customer of any unexpected problems and costs, and to notify the customer when the vehicle is ready for pickup.

Village Volvo has no provisions for alternate transportation for customers at this time. A shuttle service two or three times a day is being considered, because the owners think their suburban location may deter some clients. The waiting room is equipped with a television set, comfortable chairs, coffee, a soft-drink vending machine, magazines, and the local newspaper. This facility is used almost exclusively by clients who come during the "drop-in" times (3 to 5 PM Wednesdays and 8 to 10 AM Thursdays) for quick, routine jobs such as tune-ups and buyer checks of used cars.

The owner-mechanics do no repairs between 7 and 8 AM and 5 and 6 PM, because these are heavy customer contact hours. They believe it is just as important to discuss with the client the repairs that have been done as it is to discuss what problems exist before that work is done. As repairs are made the owner-mechanic notes any other problems that might need attention in the future (e.g., fan and alternator belts show some wear and may need to be replaced in about 6000 miles). These notes are

brought to the customer's attention at pickup time and also are recorded in the CCVD for future use, perhaps in the form of a reminder postcard to the owner.

All small worn-out parts that have been replaced are put in a clean box inside the car. More cumbersome replaced parts are identified and set aside for the client's inspection. Care is taken throughout the repair process to keep the car clean, and the inside is vacuumed as a courtesy before pickup. After the repairs are finished, the vehicle is taken for a short test drive. Then it is parked, ready for pickup.

The Village Volvo owners see their responsibility as extending beyond immediate service to their clients. The owners have developed a network of other service providers who assist in recycling used parts and waste products and to whom they can refer clients for work that is not part of Village Volvo's services (e.g., body work, alignments, and reupholstering). The owners also are considering the possibility of offering a minicourse one Saturday morning each month to teach clients what they can do to attain their 200,000-mile Volvo medals.

QUESTIONS

1 Describe Village Volvo's service package.
2 How are the distinctive characteristics of a service firm illustrated by Village Volvo?
3 How could Village Volvo manage its back office (i.e., repair operations) like a factory?
4 How can Village Volvo differentiate itself from Volvo dealers?

SELECTED BIBLIOGRAPHY

COLLIER, DAVID A.: "Managing a Service Firm: A Different Management Game," *National Productivity Review,* Winter 1983–1984, pp. 36–45.

KILLEYA, J. C., and C. G. ARMISTEAD: "The Transfer of Concepts and Techniques between Manufacturing and Service Systems," *International Journal of Operations and Production Management,* vol. 3, no. 3, 1983, pp. 22–28.

MORRIS, B., and R. JOHNSTON: "Dealing with Inherent Variability: The Difference between Manufacturing and Service?" *International Journal of Operations and Production Management,* vol. 7, no. 4, 1986, pp. 13–22.

RIDDLE, D. I.: *Service-Led Growth,* Praeger, New York, 1986.

SASSER, W. E., R. P. OLSEN, and D. D. WYCKOFF: *Management of Service Operations,* Allyn and Bacon, Inc., Boston, 1978.

SCHMENNER, ROGER W.: "How Can Service Businesses Survive and Prosper?" *Sloan Management Review,* vol. 27, no. 3, Spring 1986, pp. 21–32.

CHAPTER 15

Service
Strategy

Most service firms compete in an economic environment that generally consists of a large number of small- and medium-sized firms, many of them privately owned. Of course, large service firms such as major airlines and hospitals also exist. In this type of economic environment, no firm has a significant market share; thus, no firm can dominate the industry (with the exception of government services, cable TV, and utilities). Since the deregulation of various industries in the 1980s, however, there has been some service industry consolidation, particularly with airlines and financial institutions. In any event, a thorough understanding of the competitive dimensions and limitations of the industry is necessary before a firm can begin to formulate its service strategy.

CHAPTER PREVIEW

The diversity of firms in the service sector makes generalizations concerning strategy difficult. Five schemes are presented, however, to classify services in ways that provide strategic insight and transcend narrow industry boundaries. These schemes can be used to think about the choices being made to position the service in relation to its competitors. *Positioning* is a marketing term that is used to describe the process of establishing and maintaining a distinctive place in the market.

Three generic strategies are successful in formulating methods that allow a firm to outperform competitors. The strategies of overall cost leadership, differentiation, and market focus are approaches that both manufacturing and service firms have adopted in various ways to gain a competitive advantage. With each of these strategies, however, management must not lose sight of the fact that only a focus on customers and satisfying their needs will result in a loyal customer base.

Winning customers in the marketplace means competing on several dimensions. Customers base their purchase decisions on many variables, including price, convenience, reputation, and safety. The importance of a particular variable to a firm's success depends on the competitive marketplace and the preferences of individual customers.

This chapter begins with a discussion of the strategic service concept, which contains all elements in the design of a competitive service. The service concept is divided into four structural elements: delivery system, facility design, location, and capacity planning. It also is divided into four managerial elements: service encounter, quality, managing capacity and demand, and information. These eight elements represent the competitive dimensions of a service firm.

THE STRATEGIC SERVICE CONCEPT

Chapter 14, The Nature of Services, introduced the idea of a *service package*, which contained four elements—supporting facility, facilitating goods, explicit service, and implicit service—as a way to describe an existing service or a vision of a new service. In this chapter, this service vision will be translated into a strategically focused *service concept* or *design* that contains eight dimensions.

Consider a building, which begins in the mind's eye of the architect and is translated onto paper in the form of engineering drawings for all the building's systems: foundation, structural, plumbing, and electrical. An analog to this design process is the strategic service concept with the system elements outlined here. These elements must be engineered to create a consistent service offering that achieves the strategic objectives. The service concept becomes a blueprint that communicates to customers and employees alike what service they should expect to give and to receive. These system elements are:

Structural

Delivery system. Front and back office, automation, customer participation.

Facility design. Size, aesthetics, layout.

Location. Customer demographics, single or multiple sites, competition, site characteristics.

Capacity planning. Managing queues, number of servers, accommodating average or peak demand.

Managerial:

Service encounter. Service culture, motivation, selection and training, employment empowerment.

Quality. Measurement, monitoring, methods, expectations versus perceptions, service guarantee.

Managing capacity and demand. Strategies for altering demand and controlling supply, queue management.

Information. Competitive resource, data collection.

A successful hospital located in Toronto, Canada, that performs only inguinal hernia operations will be used to illustrate how each element of the service concept contributes to the strategic mission. Shouldice Hospital is privately owned and uses a special operating procedure to correct inguinal hernias that has resulted in an excellent reputation. Its success is measured by the recurrence rate, which is twelve times lower than that of its competitors.[1]

The structural elements of Shouldice's service concept that support its strategy to target customers suffering from inguinal hernias are:

- *Delivery system.* A hallmark of the Shouldice approach is patient participation in all aspects of the process. For example, patients shave themselves before the operation, walk from the operating table to the recovery area, and are encouraged the evening after surgery to discuss the experience with new patients to alleviate their preoperative fears.
- *Facility design.* The facility is intentionally designed to encourage exercise and rapid recovery within four days, which is approximately one-half the time at traditional hospitals. Hospital rooms are devoid of amenities, and patients must walk to lounges, showers, and the cafeteria. The extensive hospital grounds are landscaped to encourage strolling, and the interior is carpeted and decorated to avoid any typical hospital "associations."
- *Location.* Being located in a large metropolitan community with excellent air service gives Shouldice access to a worldwide market. The large local population also provides a source of patients who can be scheduled on short notice to fill any canceled bookings.
- *Capacity planning.* Because hernia operations are elective procedures, patients can be scheduled in batches to fill the operating time available; thus, capacity is utilized to its maximum. This ease in scheduling operations allows Shouldice to operate like a fully occupied hotel; thus, the supporting activities, such as housekeeping and food service, also can be fully employed.

---

[1]Harvard Business School case, Shouldice Hospital Limited, ICCH no. 9-683-068, 1983, p. 3.

The managerial elements of the Shouldice service concept also support the strategy of delivering a quality medical procedure:

- *Service encounter.* All employees are trained to help counsel patients and encourage them to achieve a rapid recovery. A service culture fostering a family-type atmosphere is reinforced by communal dining for both workers and patients.
- *Quality.* The most important quality feature is the adherence of all physicians to the Shouldice method of hernia repair, which results in the low recurrence rate of inguinal hernias among these patients. In addition, patients with difficulties are referred back to the doctor who performed the procedure. Perceived quality is enhanced by the Shouldice experience, which is more like a short holiday than a typical hospital stay.
- *Managing capacity and demand.* Patients are screened by means of a mail-in questionnaire and are admitted by reservation only. Thus, the patient demand in terms of timing and appropriateness can be controlled effectively. As mentioned, walk-in patients or local residents on a waiting list are used to fill vacancies created by canceled reservations; thus, full use of hospital capacity is ensured.
- *Information.* A unique feature of the Shouldice service is the annual alumni reunion, which represents a continuing relationship of the hospital with its patients. Keeping information on patients allows Shouldice to build a loyal customer base, which is an effective word-of-mouth advertising medium. Providing free annual check-ups also allows Shouldice to build a unique data base on its procedure.

CLASSIFYING SERVICES FOR STRATEGIC INSIGHTS[2]

A general discussion of service strategy is complicated by the diversity of service firms in the economy and their differing customer relationships. However, strategic insights that transcend industry boundaries are needed to avoid the myopic view, which is prevalent among service managers, that concepts do not translate from one industry to another. For example, competitive strategies used by banking services could find an application in laundry services, because both deal with a customer's property. The new laundry drop-off and pick-up service available at commuter rail stations is similar in concept to bank automatic teller machines in supermarkets. The following classification schemes developed by Christopher Lovelock provide us with an appreciation of possible strategic dimensions that transcend industry boundaries.

Nature of the Service Act

As Figure 1 shows, the service act can be considered across two dimensions: who or what is the direct recipient of the service, and the tangible nature of the service. This creates four possible classifications: 1) tangible actions directed to the customer, such as passenger transportation and personal care; 2) tangible actions directed at the customer's possessions, such as laundry cleaning and janitorial services; 3) intangible actions directed at the customer's intellect such as entertainment; and 4) intangible actions performed on customer's assets, such as financial services.

[2]Adapted from Christopher H. Lovelock, "Classifying Services to Gain Strategic Marketing Insights," *Journal of Marketing*, vol. 47, Summer 1983, pp. 9–200.

Figure 1 *Understanding the nature of the service act.*
(Reprinted with permission of the American Marketing Association: Christopher H. Lovelock, "Classifying Services to Gain Strategic Marketing Insights," *Journal of Marketing*, vol. 47, Summer 1983, p. 12.)

Nature of the Service Act	Direct Recipient of the Service	
	People	Things
Tangible actions	*Services directed at people's bodies:* Health care Passenger transportation Beauty salons Exercise clinics Restaurants Haircutting	*Services directed at goods and other physical possessions:* Freight transportation Industrial equipment repair and maintenance Janitorial services Laundry and dry cleaning Landscaping/lawn care Veterinary care
Intangible actions	*Services directed at people's minds:* Education Broadcasting Information services Theaters Museums	*Services directed at intangible assets:* Banking Legal services Accounting Securities Insurance

This classification scheme raises questions about the traditional way in which services have been delivered. For example, does the customer need to be present physically throughout the service, only to initiate or terminate the transaction, or not at all? If customers must be present, then they must travel to the service facility and become part of the process, or the server must travel to the customer (e.g., ambulance service). This has significant implications for facility design and employee interaction, because the impressions that are made on the customer will influence his or her perceptions of the service. In addition, questions are raised concerning the impact of facility location and business hours on customer convenience. It is not surprising that retail banks have embraced ATMs and other electronic communication alternatives to personal interaction.

Thinking creatively about the nature of the service may identify more convenient forms of delivery or even a product that can substitute for the service. For example, videotapes of lectures and CD recordings of concerts represent a convenient substitute for physical attendance, and they also serve as permanent library records of the events.

Relationship with Customers

Service firms have the opportunity to build long-term relationships, because customers conduct their transactions directly with the service provider, most often in person. In contrast, manufacturers traditionally have been isolated from the eventual end user by a distribution channel consisting of some combination of distributors, wholesalers, and/or retailers. Figure 2 contrasts the nature of the customer's "membership" with the nature of the service delivery. The value to the firm of customer membership is captured in this figure; however, a number of changes have occurred since it was first published in 1983. For example, car rental firms and major hotel chains have joined airlines in offering discounts through frequent flyer programs. In addition, some private toll highways offer annual passes, which can be attached to one's car. These passes electronically trigger a debit so that the driver need not stop to pay a toll.

Figure 2. *Relationships with customers.*
(Reprinted with permission of the American Marketing Association: Christopher H. Lovelock, "Classifying Services to Gain Strategic Marketing Insights," *Journal of Marketing*, vol. 47, Summer 1983, p. 13.)

Nature of Service Delivery	Type of Relationship between Service Organization and Its Customers	
	"Membership" relationship	No formal relationship
Continuous delivery of service	Insurance Telephone subscription College enrollment Banking American Automobile Association	Radio station Police protection Lighthouse Public highway
Discrete transactions	Long-distance phone calls Theater series subscription Commuter ticket or transit pass Sam's Wholesale Club Egghead computer software	Car rental Mail service Toll highway Pay phone Movie theater Public transportation Restaurant

Knowing your customers is a significant competitive advantage for a service organization. Having a data base of customers' names and addresses and their use of the service permits targeted marketing and individual treatment of customers. Customers benefit from membership because of the convenience of annual fixed fees and the knowledge that they are valued customers who will receive occasional perks (e.g., frequent flyer awards).

Customization and Judgment

Because services are created as they are consumed and the customer is often a participant in the process, an opportunity exists to tailor a service to the needs of the customer. Figure 3 shows that customization proceeds along two dimensions: either

Extent to Which Customer Contact Personnel Exercise Judgment in Meeting Individual Customer Needs	Extent to Which Service Characteristics Are Customized	
	High	Low
High	Professional services Surgery Taxi service Beautician Plumber Education (tutorials) Gourmet restaurant	Education (large classes) Preventive health programs College food service
Low	Telephone service Hotel services Retail banking (excl. major loans) Family restaurant	Public transportation Routine appliance repair Movie theater Spectator sports Fast-food restaurant

Figure 3. *Customization and judgment in service delivery.*
(Reprinted with permission of the American Marketing Association: Christopher H. Lovelock, "Classifying Services to Gain Strategic Marketing Insights," *Journal of Marketing*, vol. 47, Summer 1983, p. 15.)

the character of the service permits customization, or the service personnel have the discretion to modify the service.

Selecting the quadrant of Figure 3 in which to position a service is a strategic choice. For example, traditional movie theaters offer only one screen; thus, they are appropriately located in the low-low quadrant. Most new movie theaters, however, are built with multiple screens, allowing some degree of customization. Among fast-food restaurants, Burger King advertises "Have it your way," permitting some customization of its "Whopper." Within a particular industry, every quadrant could be occupied by different segments of that industry, as illustrated by the various types of food service operations in Figure 3. A strategic choice of offering more customization and allowing service personnel to exercise judgment, however, has implications for the service delivery system.

Nature of Demand and Supply

As noted in Chapter 14, the time perishability of service capacity creates a challenge for service managers, because these managers lack the option of producing and storing inventory for future sale. Even so, the extent of demand-and-supply imbalances varies across service industries, as shown in Figure 4.

To determine the most appropriate strategy in each case, it is necessary to consider the following questions:

1. What is the nature of the demand fluctuation? Does it have a predictable cycle (e.g., daily meal demand at a fast-food restaurant) that can be anticipated?

2. What are the underlying causes of these fluctuations in demand? If the causes are customer habits or preference, could marketing produce a change?

3. What opportunities exist to change the level of capacity or supply? Can part-time workers be hired during peak hours?

Extent to Which Supply Is Constrained	Extent of Demand Fluctuation over Time	
	Wide	Narrow
Peak demand can usually be met without a major delay	Electricity Natural gas Telephone Hospital maternity unit Police and fire emergencies	Insurance Legal services Banking Laundry and dry cleaning
Peak demand regularly exceeds capacity	Accounting and tax preparation Passenger transportation Hotels and motels Restaurants Theaters	Services similar to those above but with insufficient capacity for their base level of business

Figure 4. *What is the nature of demand for the service relative to supply?*
(Reprinted with permission of the American Marketing Association: Christopher H. Lovelock, "Classifying Services to Gain Strategic Marketing Insights," *Journal of Marketing*, vol. 47, Summer 1983, p. 17.)

Method of Service Delivery

As Figure 5 shows, the method of service delivery has both a geographic component and a level-of-customer-interaction component.

Services with multiple sites have significant management implications for ensuring quality and consistency in the service offering. With advances in electronic communications, arm's-length transactions are becoming more common, because they offer customer convenience and efficient service delivery. For example, use of personal computers and modems allows businesses to customize their services and to decrease the amount of physical interaction between the customer and a human service provider. The strategic implications of the design of a service delivery system and its effect on the interaction between customer and service organization are discussed in Chapter 16.

The classification schemes described earlier are useful in suggesting strategic alternatives and avoiding industry myopia. Before a service strategy can be formulated, however, an understanding of the competitive nature of the industry is necessary.

UNDERSTANDING THE COMPETITIVE ENVIRONMENT OF SERVICES

In general, service firms compete in a difficult economic environment, and there are many reasons for this difficulty:

- *Relatively low overall entry barriers.* Service innovations are not patentable, and in most cases, services are not capital-intensive. Thus, innovations can easily be copied by competitors. However, other types of entry barriers exist, such as locating a resort hotel on the best beach of an island (e.g., the Club Med location on Moorea in French Polynesia).
- *Minimal opportunities for economies of scale.* Recall from Chapter 14 that because of the simultaneous production and consumption of services, the customer must travel to the service facility or the service must travel to the customer. The necessity of physical travel limits the market area and results in small-scale outlets. Franchised firms can realize some economies of scale by sharing purchasing or advertising costs; in other instances, electronic communications can be substituted for physical travel (e.g., ordering from L.L. Bean by telephone).
- *Erratic sales fluctuations.* Service demand varies as a function of the time of day and the day of the week (and sometimes seasonally), with random arrivals. Can

Figure 5. *Method of service delivery.*
(Reprinted with permission of the American Marketing Association: Christopher H. Lovelock, "Classifying Services to Gain Strategic Marketing Insights," *Journal of Marketing*, vol. 47, Summer 1983, p. 18.)

Nature of Interaction between Customer and Service Organization	Availability of Service Outlets	
	Single site	Multiple site
Customer goes to service organization	Theater Barbershop	Bus service Fast-food chain
Service organization comes to customer	Lawn care service Pest control service Taxi	Mail delivery AAA emergency repairs
Customer and service organization transact at arm's length (mail or electronic communications)	Credit card company Local TV station	Broadcast network Telephone company

you think of some exceptions?

- *No advantage of size in dealing with buyers or suppliers.* The small size of many service firms places them at a disadvantage in bargaining with powerful buyers or suppliers. Many exceptions should come to mind, however, such as McDonald's buying beef and Marriott buying mattresses.
- *Product substitution.* Product innovations can be a substitute for services (e.g., the home pregnancy test). Thus, service firms must not only watch other service competitors but also anticipate potential product innovations that might make their services obsolete.
- *Customer loyalty.* Established firms using personalized services create a loyal customer base, which becomes a barrier to entry by new services. For example, a hospital supply firm may place its own ordering computer terminals at its customers' sites. These terminals then facilitate the placement of new orders to the extent that competitors are effectively excluded.
- *Exit barriers.* Marginal service firms may continue to operate despite low, or even nonexistent, profits. For example, a privately held firm may have employment of family members rather than maximizing profit as its goal. Other service firms, such as antique stores or scuba diving shops, have a hobby or romantic appeal that provides their owners with enough job satisfaction to offset low financial compensation. Thus, profit-motivated competitors would find it difficult to drive these privately held firms from the market.

For any particular service industry, there are firms that have overcome these competitive difficulties and prospered. For example, McDonald's has achieved a dominant position in the fast-food industry by overcoming many of the difficulties listed here. New entrants, however, must develop a service strategy that will address the important competitive features of their respective industries. Three generic strategies have been successful in providing a competitive advantage, and illustrations of how service firms have used these strategies will be our next topic.

COMPETITIVE SERVICE STRATEGIES[3]

Michael Porter has argued persuasively that three generic competitive strategies exist: overall cost leadership, differentiation, and focus.[4] Each strategy will be described in turn, with examples of how service firms use them to outperform their competition.

Overall Cost Leadership

An overall cost leadership strategy requires efficient-scale facilities, tight cost and overhead control, and often innovative technology as well. Having a low-cost position provides a defense against competition, because less efficient competitors will suffer first from competitive pressures. Implementing a low-cost strategy usually requires high capital investment in state-of-the-art equipment, aggressive pricing, and start-up losses to build market share. A cost leadership strategy sometimes can revolutionize an industry, as illustrated by the success of McDonald's, Wal-Mart, and Fed-

[3]Adapted from James L. Heskett, "Positioning in Competitive Service Strategies," *Managing in the Service Economy,* Harvard Business School Press, Boston, 1986.
[4]Michael E. Porter, "Generic Competitive Strategies," *Competitive Strategy,* Free Press, New York, 1980.

eral Express. Moreover, service firms have been able to achieve low-cost leadership using a variety of approaches.

SEEKING OUT LOW-COST CUSTOMERS Some customers cost less to serve than others, and they can be targeted by the service provider. For example, the United Services Automobile Association (USAA) occupies a preeminent position among automobile insurers because it serves only military officers, a group that presents a lower-than-average risk of problems requiring compensation. This group also entails lower cost because its members, who are relatively nomadic, are willing to do business by telephone or mail and are accustomed to doing so. Consequently, the USAA is able to conduct all of its business transactions by phone and mail, eliminating any need for the expensive sales force employed by traditional insurers. Another example of this strategy is provided by low-cost retailers such as Sam's Wholesale Club and Price Club, which target customers who are willing to buy in quantity, do without frills, and serve themselves.

STANDARDIZING A CUSTOM SERVICE Typically, income tax preparation is considered to be a customized service. H. & R. Block, however, has been successful in serving customers nationwide when only routine tax preparation is required. Also, storefront legal services and family health care centers are attractive means of delivering routine professional services at low cost. The key word here is *routine*.

REDUCING THE PERSONAL ELEMENT IN SERVICE DELIVERY The potentially high-risk strategy of reducing the personal element in service delivery can be accepted by customers if increased convenience results. For example, convenient access to ATMs has weaned customers from personal interaction with live tellers and, consequently, has reduced transaction costs for banks.

REDUCING NETWORK COSTS Unusual start-up costs are encountered by service firms that require a network to knit together providers and customers. Electric utilities, which have substantial fixed costs in transmission lines, provide the most obvious example. Federal Express conceived a unique approach to reducing network costs by using a "hub-and-spoke" network. By locating a hub in Memphis with state-of-the-art sorting technology, the overnight air-package carrier was able to serve the United States with no direct routes between the cities that it served. Each time a new city is added to the network, Federal Express only needs to add one more route to and from the hub instead of adding routes between all the cities served. The efficiency of the hub-and-spoke network strategy has not been lost on passenger airline operators, either.

TAKING SERVICE OPERATIONS OFF-LINE Many services, such as haircutting and passenger transportation, are inherently "on-line," because they can only be performed with the customer present. For services in which the customer need not be present, the service transaction can be "decoupled," with some content performed "off-line." For example, a shoe repair service could locate dispersed kiosks for customer drop-off/pick-up, thus consolidating orders for delivery to an off-site repair factory, which could even be located off-shore. Performing services off-line represents significant cost savings because of economies of scale from consolidation, low-cost facility location (e.g., American Airlines has one of its 800-number reservations centers located in the Caribbean), and absence of the customer in the system. In short, the decoupled service operation is run like a factory.

Differentiation

The essence of the *differentiation* strategy lies in creating a service that is perceived as being unique. Approaches to differentiation can take many forms: brand image (e.g., McDonald's golden arches), technology (e.g., Sprint's fiberoptics network), features (e.g., American Express's complete travel services), customer service (e.g., Nordstrom's reputation among department stores), dealer network (e.g., Century 21's nationwide real estate presence), and other dimensions. A differentiation strategy does not ignore costs, but its primary thrust lies in creating customer loyalty. As illustrated here, differentiation to enhance the service often is achieved at some cost that the targeted customer is willing to pay.

MAKING THE INTANGIBLE TANGIBLE By their very nature, services often are intangible and leave the customer with no physical reminder of the purchase. Recognizing the need to remind customers of their stay, many hotels now provide complimentary toiletry items with the hotel name prominently affixed. The Hartford Steam Boiler Inspection and Insurance Company writes insurance on industrial power plants, but this company has enhanced its service to include regular inspections and recommendations to managers for avoiding potential problems.

CUSTOMIZING THE STANDARD PRODUCT Providing a customized touch may endear a firm to its customers at very little cost. A hotel operator who is able to address a guest by name can make an impression that translates into repeat business. Hair salons have added many personalizing features (e.g., personal stylist, juice bar, relaxed surroundings, mood music) to differentiate themselves from barbershops. Burger King's efforts to promote a made-to-order policy is an attempt to differentiate itself from McDonald's classic make-to-stock approach to fast-food service.

REDUCING PERCEIVED RISK Lack of information about the purchase of a service creates a sense of risk-taking for many customers. Lacking knowledge or self-confidence about services such as auto repair, customers will seek out providers who take the extra time to explain the work to be done, present a clean and organized facility, and guarantee their work (e.g., Village Volvo). Customers often see the "peace of mind" that is engendered when this trusting relationship develops as being worth the extra expense.

GIVING ATTENTION TO PERSONNEL TRAINING Investment in personnel development and training that results in enhanced service quality is a competitive advantage that is difficult to replicate. Firms that lead their industries are known among competitors for the quality of their training programs. In some cases, these firms have established college-like training centers (e.g., Arthur Andersen's facility in St. Charles, Illinois; McDonald's Hamburger University near Chicago).

CONTROLLING QUALITY Delivering a consistent level of service quality at multiple sites with a labor-intensive system is a significant challenge. Firms have approached this problem in a variety of ways, including personnel training, explicit procedures, technology, limits on the scope of the service, direct supervision, and peer pressure, among others. For example, to ensure consistency, the Magic Pan chain of restaurants designed a foolproof machine to produce its famous crêpes. The question of service quality is further complicated by the potential gap between customer expectations and experiences. Influencing customer quality expectations thus becomes an issue.

Focus

The *focus* strategy is built around the idea of serving a particular target market very well by addressing the customers' specific needs. The market segment could be a particular buyer group (e.g., USAA and military officers), service (e.g., Shouldice Hospital and patients with inguinal hernias, Motel 6 and budget travelers, Federal Express and people who need guaranteed overnight package delivery), or geographic region (e.g., Wal-Mart and rural retail buyers, Southwest Airlines and other regional airlines). The focus strategy rests on the premise that the firm can serve its narrow target market more effectively and/or efficiently than other firms trying to serve a broad market. As a result, the firm achieves differentiation in its narrow target market by meeting customer needs better and/or by lowering costs.

Davidow and Uttal argue how important customer selection is to achieving a successful focus strategy.[5] They relate how one bank in Palo Alto, California, targets wealthy individuals and discourages others by policies such as closing an account after two checks have bounced. Davidow and Uttal's three-step approach to focus includes segmenting the market to design core services, classifying customers according to the value they place on service, and setting expectations slightly below perceived performance.

The focus strategy thus is the application of overall cost leadership and/or differentiation to a particular market segment. The relationship of the three generic strategies to market position is shown in Figure 6. We conclude this chapter with discussions of winning customers in the marketplace.

WINNING CUSTOMERS IN THE MARKETPLACE

Depending on the competition and personal needs, customers select a service provider using criteria listed here. This list is not intended to be complete, because the very addition of a new dimension by a firm represents an attempt to engage in a strategy of differentiation. For example, initiation of the frequent flyer program "AAdvantage" by American Airlines was an attempt to add the dimension of customer loyalty to competition among airlines.

- *Availability.* How accessible is the service? The use of ATMs by banks has created 24-hour availability of some banking services (i.e., service beyond the tra-

Figure 6. *Market position of generic strategies.*
(Adapted with the permission of The Free Press, a Division of Macmillan, Inc., from *Competitive Strategy: Techniques for Analyzing Industries and Competitors* by Michael E. Porter. Copyright © 1980 by The Free Press.)

Target	Strategic Advantage	
	Low cost	Uniqueness
Entire market	Overall cost leadership	Differentiation
Market segment	Focus	

---

[5]W. H. Davidow and B. Uttal, "Service Companies: Focus or Falter," *Harvard Business Review,* July/August 1989, pp. 77–85.

ditional "banker's hours"). Use of 800-numbers by many service firms facilitates access after normal working hours.

- *Convenience.* The location of the service defines convenience for customers who must travel to that service. Gasoline stations, fast-food restaurants, and dry cleaners are examples of services that must select locations on busy streets if they are to succeed.
- *Dependability.* How reliable is the service? For example, once the exterminator is gone, how soon do the bugs return? A major complaint regarding automobile repair services is the failure to fix the problem on the first visit. For airlines, on-time performance is a statistic collected by the FAA.
- *Personalization.* Are you treated as an individual? For example, hotels have discovered that repeat customers respond to being greeted by their name. The degree of customization allowed in providing the service, no matter how slight, can be viewed as more personalized service.
- *Price.* Competing on price is not as effective in services as it is with products, because it often is difficult to compare the costs of services objectively. It may be easy to compare costs in the delivery of routine services such as an oil change, but in professional services, competition on price might be considered counterproductive because price often is viewed as being a surrogate for quality.
- *Quality.* Service quality is a function of the relationship between a customer's prior expectations of the service and his or her perception of the service experience both during and after the fact. Unlike product quality, service quality is judged by both the process of service delivery and the outcome of the service.
- *Reputation.* The uncertainty that is associated with the selection of a service provider often is resolved by talking with others about their experiences before a decision is made. Unlike a product, a poor service experience cannot be exchanged or returned for a different model. Positive word-of-mouth is the most effective form of advertising.
- *Safety.* Well-being and security are important considerations, because in many services, such as air travel and medicine, the customers are putting their lives in the hands of the service provider.
- *Speed.* How long must I wait for service? For emergency services such as fire and police protection, response time is the major criterion of performance. In other services, waiting sometimes may be considered a tradeoff for receiving more personalized services, such as reduced rates.

Writing about manufacturing strategy, Terry Hill used the term *order-winning criteria* to refer to competitive dimensions that sell products.[6] He further suggested that some criteria could be called *qualifiers,* because the presence of these dimensions is necessary for a product to enter the marketplace. Finally, Hill said that some qualifiers could be considered *order-losing sensitive.*

We will use a similar logic and the service criteria listed earlier to describe the service purchase decision. The purchase decision sequence begins with qualifying potential service firms (e.g., must the doctor be on my PPO list?), followed by making a final selection from this subset of service firms using a service winner (e.g., which of the PPO doctors has the best reputation?). After the initial service experience, a return will be based on whether a "service loser" has occurred (e.g., the doctor was cold and impersonal).

---

[6]Terry Hill, *Manufacturing Strategy,* Irwin, Homewood, Ill., 1989, pp. 36–46.

Qualifiers

Before a service firm can be taken seriously as a competitor in the market, it must attain a certain level for each service-competitive dimension, as defined by the other market players. For example, in airline service, we would name safety, as defined by the air-worthiness of the aircraft and by the rating of the pilots, as an obvious qualifier. In a mature market such as fast foods, established competitors may define a level of quality, such as cleanliness, that new entrants must at least match to be viable contenders. For fast food, a dimension that once was a service winner, such as a drive-in window, over time could become a qualifier, because some customers will not stop otherwise.

Service Winners

Service winners are dimensions such as price, convenience, or reputation that are used by a customer to make a choice among competitors. Depending on the needs of the customer at the time of the purchase, the service winner may vary. For example, seeking a restaurant for lunch may be based on convenience, but a dinner date could be influenced by reputation. Note that a service winner can become an industry qualifier (e.g., ATM use by banks).

Service Losers

Failure to deliver at or above the expected level for a competitive dimension can result in a dissatisfied customer who is lost forever. For various reasons, the dimensions of dependability, personalization, and speed are particularly vulnerable to becoming *service losers*. Some examples might be failure of an auto dealer to repair a mechanical problem (i.e., dependability), rude treatment by a doctor (i.e., personalization), or failure of an overnight service to deliver a package on time (i.e., speed).

SUMMARY

The topic of service strategy began with a number of schemes to classify service industries to gain insights into possible strategic opportunities that transcend industry boundaries. We looked at the strategic service concept as a blueprint for implementing the service. Our discussion then turned to the economic nature of competition in the service sector. The fragmented nature of service industries populated with many small- to medium-sized firms suggests a rich environment for the budding entrepreneur.

The three generic competitive strategies of overall cost leadership, differentiation, and focus were used to outline examples of creative service strategies. Because of the transferability of concepts among service firms, strategies that are successful in one industry may find application in firms seeking a competitive advantage in another service industry.

Next, we looked at several dimensions of service competition and examined the concepts of service winners, qualifiers, and losers as competitive criteria. The application of the service concept to Shouldice Hospital illustrated how all eight elements support the service strategy.

KEY TERMS AND DEFINITIONS

Differentiation a competitive strategy that creates a service that is perceived as being unique.

Focus a competitive strategy built around the concept of serving a particular target market very well by addressing the customers' specific needs.

Overall cost leadership a competitive strategy based on efficient operations, cost control, and innovative technology.

Qualifiers criteria used by a customer to create a subset of service firms meeting minimum performance requirements.

Service losers criteria representing failure to deliver a service at or above the expected level, resulting in a dissatisfied customer who is lost forever.

Service winners criteria used by a customer to make the final purchase decision among competitors that have been previously qualified.

Strategic service concept eight elements that define the service to be offered that are in turn grouped into structural and managerial categories.

TOPICS FOR DISCUSSION

- What are the characteristics of services that will be affected most by the emerging electronic and communication technologies?
- When does collecting information through service membership become an invasion of privacy?
- What are some management problems that are associated with allowing service employees to exercise judgment in meeting customer needs?
- What are the implications of the growing use of personal computers for the customization of services and elimination of human service interactions?

- Give examples of service firms that use both the strategy of focus and differentiation and the strategy of focus and overall cost leadership.
- Apply the strategic service concept to a service of your choice, and illustrate how all eight elements support the service strategy.

SERVICE BENCHMARK

CENTRAL MARKET SHUNS CONVENTIONAL WISDOM AND BIG-NAME PRODUCTS

Central Market's opening in January prompted some friendly wagering among food-industry heavyweights who were left out in the cold.

The odds favored Frito-Lay's snacks appearing in the store, a specialty and fresh food supermarket, by the end of the summer. Other wagers bet that Coca-Cola and Budweiser trucks would pull up to the market's loading docks within six months. Now all bets are off.

Shunning big-name product lines is one reason why Central Market has caught the attention of the nation's $279.4 billion supermarket industry. The market—which within a year has become a flagship of the 225 Texas stores owned by parent-company H.E.B. Food Stores—has made it a practice to defy many of the standards that the country's 30,000 supermarkets embrace.

Although most supermarkets subscribe to the notion that customers want one-stop shopping, Central Market has proved that food alone sells well.

At Central Market, which carries virtually nothing except food, the average shopper spends $30 at the checkout counter, said Central Market general manager John Campbell. The national industry average, which also includes spending on general merchandise and health and beauty products, is $18.11, according to the Washington, D.C.-based Food Marketing Institute. The lower industry average results from shoppers who dash in for a few items, such as diapers or mascara, and then check out through the 10-items-or-fewer express lanes, Campbell said. "Here, they do serious shopping," he said.

Central Market also looks different from traditional stores. Its layout forces customers to walk through serpentine sections instead of straight aisles. It also houses a cooking school. There are 250 kinds of mustard, dozens of olive oils, and jams from all over the world on its shelves.

While at least half of the nation's 3.2 million supermarket workers are part-time employees, 90 percent of Central Market's 400 workers are full-time employees who receive health benefits, paid vacation time, tuition reimbursements and profit-sharing. It's an expensive staffing decision that Campbell says pays off by generating greater enthusiasm and product knowledge among workers, two factors that he says are vital to building customer satisfaction.

At Central Market at least 20 percent of the store's sales come from its roomy produce section which eats up almost a third of the store's 60,000 square feet of sales space. The section, kept at 65 degrees, stocks on any given day as many as 450 kinds of fruits and vegetables.

Seventy-five feet of refrigerator space displays fresh fish, while the 68-foot meat counter sells more than 100 types of meat, game, and poultry. The cheese department offers 600 varieties.

In all, about two-thirds of the store's floor space is stocked with perishables. And each day, a truck from a local food bank comes by to take away the items that have failed Central Market's freshness guidelines.

Although the market risks losing money if too many of its meats and fruits aren't sold quickly, those items have higher profit margins than dry groceries. The margins for perishables are larger because those items are priced higher to make up for losses, refrigeration costs, and the increased labor expenses that result from product displays.

"The more sales you can move to perishable, the better, because the amount you can charge for Coke, Pepsi or Tide is tight," said Kevin Coupe, executive editor of *Progressive Grocer* trade magazine in Stamford, Conn.

H.E.B. began discussing the Central Market concept in the mid 1980s when its market studies found that customers were increasingly interested in home cooking, nutrition, and better-tasting foods.

"With Central Market, we were trying to get ahead of what we see as a definite trend and one that we feel will only continue to grow," Ozmun said.

Source: Adapted from Diana Dworin, "Central Market proves it can thrive even as it shuns conventional wisdom and big-name products," ©*Austin American Statesman*, October 2, 1994, p. H1.

CONCLUDING CASE

AMERICA WEST AIRLINES

America West Airlines was established in Phoenix as an employee-owned organization serving ten cities in the southwestern United States with a fleet of new Boeing 737 aircraft. Since then, it has grown to include 60 cities and extended its range westward to Hawaii and eastward to Boston.

This neophyte company showed remarkable daring by entering an arena where the majors, American Airlines and Delta Air Lines, already were firmly entrenched and where Southwest Airlines was digging in. Even more daring—some would say foolhardy—was the timing: deregulation was threatening to swallow up small airlines faster than they could refuel their planes.

America West, however, came into the game prepared with a skilled and creative management team, well-trained support personnel, and an effective inside pitch. Obviously, the fledgling company did not have the resources to provide the nationwide, much less the worldwide, coverage that American and Delta provided. Its smaller region, however, allowed it to do something the majors could not: America West established a major hub in Phoenix and offered more flights per day at lower cost between its cities than the two larger competitors could. In many cases, America West offered direct routing and, consequently, relatively short flight times between destinations. "Burdened" with serving everywhere from Tallahassee to Seattle, American and Delta were able to schedule flights between America West destinations, but with longer layovers and at premium prices because they were major carriers. For example, consider travel from Austin, Texas, to

Los Angeles. America West has four flights scheduled each day, with each taking approximately 4.5 hours and requiring one layover of 30 minutes in Phoenix, and its least expensive fare is $238. American Airlines offers eight flights each day, with each lasting at least 5 hours, but the traveler has a 60-minute layover in Dallas and spends $298 for American's least expensive flight.

When America West passengers have a layover, it is almost always at the Phoenix hub. (America West has a "sub-hub" in Las Vegas, where layovers usually are overnight, an appeal not lost on many travelers.) Consequently, America West's "accommodations" at the Phoenix airport are as comfortable as one could hope for in a place that hosts such a large number of people each day. The waiting areas are spacious, with banks of well-padded seats placed farther apart than in most airports. Television monitors are mounted in several places throughout the facility, and because the concessions are run by nationally known fast-food franchises, the traveler has ample reason to "feel at home."

Southwest Airlines presented a competitive challenge somewhat different from that of American and Delta. Southwest was serving the same general region as America West and also was offering frequent, low-cost flights but with older Boeing 737 aircraft. Thus, it would seem that these two airlines were meeting head to head and might be destined to "flight"-to-the-finish of one of them.

Southwest established its hub at Love Field in Dallas, thereby offering its passengers easier access both to and from the city, which is especially attractive to commuters. (Landing at Love Field does, however, present a problem for those

who must make connections in the Dallas–Fort Worth International Terminal.) Southwest began as the "fun airline," the one with female attendants in hot pants and snappy commercials on television. Since then, however, it has met the competitive challenge by offering its frequent, low-cost, no-frills service. It generally has just two fares, peak and off-peak, and there is no need to call at 1 AM "to see if fares have changed in the past ten hours." Reservations for flights can be made by phone, but they must be paid for either through a travel agent or in person at the airport desk. There are no preassigned seats; seating is handled on a first-come, first-served basis according to a numbered boarding pass that is handed to the passenger at check-in time. On-board amenities usually are limited to free soft drinks, juice, and peanuts. Prepackaged cookies and crackers with cheese or peanut butter are available on long flights, and alcoholic beverages are available for a price. Except for short commuter flights, routing frequently involves several lengthy layovers, and it is not always possible to check baggage clear through to one's destination.

Thus far, America West has managed to meet Southwest's challenge in a variety of ways. With America West, the traveler can make reservations and pay for them with a credit card by telephone, a very real convenience for many people. Preassigned seating also can be done by telephone, and, in contrast to Southwest's ticketing policy, travel agents can ticket passengers using the SABRE reservation system. On-board amenities include complimentary copies of *USA Today* and *The Wall Street Journal,* free beverages and peanuts, and on longer trips, an uncooked snack such as a sandwich, salad, cheese, fruit, and dessert. Baggage can be checked on all flights.

Clearly, America West's strategies have kept it in the game, although in recent times it has been struggling with some financial problems.

QUESTIONS

1 What generic competitive strategy has America West chosen to use in entering the air passenger market? What are the dangers of this strategy?

2 Identify the service winners, qualifiers, and service losers in America West's market.

3 How has America West addressed the eight elements in its strategic service concept?

4 Marketing analysts use market position maps to display visually the customers' perceptions of a firm in relation to its competitors regarding two attributes. Prepare a market position map for America West comparing it with American, Delta, and Southwest using the differentiation attributes of "cabin service" and "preflight service." You will need to define the endpoints on each scale to anchor the relative positioning of the airlines along the attribute (e.g., one extreme for cabin service is no amenities). The actual position is subjective, because no precise measurements are available.

SELECTED BIBLIOGRAPHY

DAVIDOW, W. H., and B. UTTAL: "Service Companies: Focus or Falter," *Harvard Business Review,* July–August 1989, pp. 77–85.

HESKETT, JAMES L.: *Managing in the Service Economy,* Harvard Business School Press, Boston, 1986.

HILL, TERRY: *Manufacturing Strategy,* 2nd ed., Irwin, Homewood, Ill., 1994.

LOVELOCK, CHRISTOPHER H.: "Classifying Services to Gain Strategic Marketing Insights," *Journal of Marketing,* vol. 47, Summer 1983, pp. 9–20.

———: *Services Marketing,* Prentice-Hall, Englewood Cliffs, N.J., 1984.

PORTER, MICHAEL E.: *Competitive Strategy,* Free Press, New York, 1980.

ROTH, A. V., and M. VAN DER VELDE: "Operations as Marketing: The Key to Effective Service Delivery Systems," Boston University Press, Boston, 1989.

SHOSTACK, LYNN G.: "Service Positioning through Structural Change," *Journal of Marketing,* January 1987, pp. 34–43.

THOMAS, DAN R. E.: "Strategy Is Different in Service Business," *Harvard Business Review,* July–August 1978, pp. 158–165.

ZEITHAML, VALARIE A.: "How Consumer Evaluation Processes Differ between Goods and Services," in James H. Donnelly and William R. George (eds.), *Marketing of Services,* American Marketing Association, Chicago, 1984.

———, A. PARASURAMAN, and L. L. BERRY: "Problems and Strategies in Services Marketing," *Journal of Marketing,* Spring 1985, pp. 33–46.

CHAPTER 16

The Service Delivery System

Designing a service delivery system is a creative process. It begins with a service concept and strategy to provide a service with features that differentiate it from the competition. The various alternatives for achieving these objectives must be identified and analyzed before any decisions can be made. Designing a service system involves issues such as location, facility design and layout for effective customer and work flow, procedures and job definitions for service providers, measures to ensure quality, extent of customer involvement, equipment selection, and adequate service capacity. The design process is never finished; once the service becomes operational, modifications in the delivery system are introduced as conditions warrant.

For an example of innovative service system design, consider Federal Express. The concept of guaranteed overnight air-freight delivery of packages and letters was the subject of a college term paper by the company's founder, Frederick W. Smith. As the story is told, the term paper received a C because the idea was so preposterous, but the business now is a model for the industry.

Traditionally, air freight has been slow and unreliable, an ancillary service provided by airlines that primarily are interested in passenger service. The genius of Smith, an electrical engineer, was in recognizing the analogy between freight transport and an electrical network connecting many outlets through a junction box. From this insight was born the "hub-and-spoke" network of Federal Express, with Memphis serving as the hub and sorting center for all packages. Arriving at night from cities throughout the United States, planes would unload their packages and wait approximately 2 hours before returning to their home cities with packages ready for delivery the next morning. Thus, a package from Los Angeles destined for San Diego would travel from Los Angeles to Memphis on one plane, then from Memphis to San Diego on another. With the exception of severe weather grounding an aircraft or a sorting error, the network design guaranteed that a package would reach its destination overnight. Thus, the design of the service delivery system itself contained the strategic advantage that differentiated Federal Express from the existing air-freight competitors. Today, Federal Express has expanded to several hubs (e.g., Newark and Los Angeles) and uses trucks to transport packages between nearby large urban centers (e.g., Boston and New York).

CHAPTER PREVIEW

Our discussion begins with the concept of *blueprinting*, which is an effective technique to describe the service delivery process in visual form. Using a *line of visibility*, we will differentiate between the front- and back-office portions of the service delivery system. The front office is where customer contact occurs, with concern for ambiance and effectiveness (e.g., a bank lobby) being necessary. The back office is hidden from the customer and often operated as a factory for efficiency (e.g., the check-sorting operations of a bank).

The analysis of structural alternatives in the system design will be considered in the context of the strategic objectives. Linking the concepts of production efficiency and sales opportunity will illustrate the necessity of integrating marketing and operations in service management.

Following a taxonomy for service process design, four generic approaches for viewing service system design—the production-line approach, customer as coproducer, customer contact, and information empowerment—are presented. Each approach advocates a particular philosophy, and the features of these approaches will be examined. A chapter supplement treats the problem of vehicle routing that occurs when a service makes deliveries to customer locations.

SERVICE BLUEPRINTING[1]

Developing a new service based on the subjective ideas contained in the service concept can lead to costly trial-and-error efforts to translate the concept into reality. When developing a building, the design is captured on architectural drawings called *blueprints,* because the reproduction is printed on special paper, creating blue lines. These blueprints show what the product should look like and all the specifications needed for its manufacture. G. Lynn Shostack has proposed that a service delivery system also can be captured in a visual diagram (i.e., a *service blueprint*) and used in a similar manner for the design of services.

As we explore the blueprint for a bank installment lending operation shown in Figure 1, many uses for this diagram will become apparent. First, the blueprint is a map or flowchart (called a *process chart* in manufacturing) of all transactions constituting the service delivery process. Some activities are processing information, others are interactions with customers, and still others are decision points. The decision points are shown as diamonds to highlight these important steps, such as providing protocols to avoid mistakes, for special consideration. Studying the blueprint could suggest opportunities for improvement and also the need for further definition of

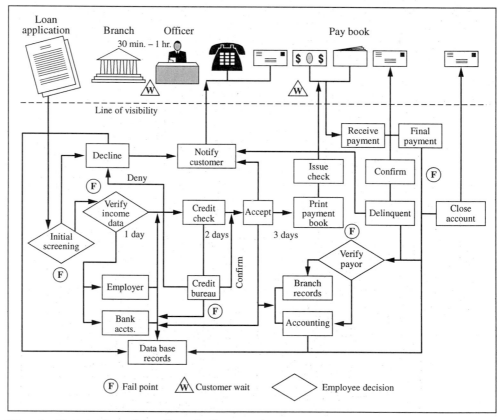

Figure 1. *Blueprint for bank installment lending operation.*
(Reprinted with permission of the American Marketing Association: G. Lynn Shostack, "Service Positioning through Structural Change," *Journal of Marketing*, vol. 51, January 1987, p. 36.)

[1]Adapted from G. Lynn Shostack, "Designing Services That Deliver," *Harvard Business Review*, January–February 1984, pp. 133–139.

certain processes (e.g., the step "Print payment book" contains many activities, such as printing booklet, preparing check, and addressing and mailing envelope).

The *line of visibility* separates activities of the front office, where customers obtain tangible evidence of the service, from those of the back office, which is out of the customers' view. The high- and low-contact parts of the service delivery process are kept physically separate, but they remain linked by communications. This separation highlights the need to give special attention to operations above the line of visibility, where customer perceptions of the services' effectiveness are formed. The physical setting, decor, employees' interpersonal skills, and even printed material all make a statement about the service. Designing an efficient process is the goal of the back office, but the back-office operations have an indirect effect on the customer because of delays and errors.

The blueprinting exercise also gives managers the opportunity to identify potential *fail points* (F) and to design "foolproof" (*poka-yoke* is the term borrowed from Japan) procedures to avoid their occurrence, thus ensuring the delivery of high-quality service. In the installment lending example, several verification points are included in the back-office activities. At these locations, *poka-yoke* devices such as check lists could be used to avoid errors. An automatic *poka-yoke* system could verify the mailing address by checking the compatibility of the city, state, and zip code as given by the customer with the U.S. Zip Code Registry.

For critical operations that are performance determinants of the service, we find that *standard execution times* are displayed. Some execution times will be represented as a range to account for the discretion necessary in some transactions (e.g., 30 minutes to 1 hour to apply for a loan). These standard times also will be useful in making capacity decisions and in setting expectations (e.g., loan check received 6 days after the application is approved).

Triangles are used to identify places in the process where customer waiting can be anticipated. Thus, customers who are waiting to see a loan officer will need a pleasant and adequate seating area with amenities such as coffee and reading material. The subject of managing queues is discussed in Chapter 17, Managing Queues. Separating the activity of preparing the payment book from issuing the loan check could significantly reduce the time a customer must wait for that check.

In summary, a blueprint is a precise definition of the service delivery system that allows management to test the service concept on paper before any final commitments are made. The blueprint also facilitates problem solving and creative thinking by identifying potential points of failure and highlighting opportunities to enhance customers' perceptions of the service.

STRATEGIC POSITIONING THROUGH PROCESS STRUCTURE

Preparing the service blueprint is the first step in developing a service process structure that will position a firm in the competitive market. Decisions still remain on the degree of complexity and divergence desired in the service. G. Lynn Shostack defined these concepts and used them to show how a service firm can position itself on the basis of process structure.[2]

The steps and sequences in the process captured by the service blueprint and measured by the number and intricacy of the steps represent the *degree of complexity*

---

[2]G. Lynn Shostack, "Service Positioning through Structural Change," *Journal of Marketing*, vol. 51, January 1987, pp. 34–43.

of the service delivery structure. For example, preparation of a take-out order at a fast-food restaurant is less complex than preparation of a gourmet dinner at a fine French restaurant. The amount of discretion or freedom permitted the server to customize the service is the *degree of divergence* that is allowed at each service process step. For example, the activities of an attorney, as contrasted with those of a paralegal, are highly divergent, because interaction with the client requires judgment, discretion, and situational adaptation.

The two dimensions of complexity and divergence, for example, allow us to create a market-positioning chart for the financial services industry, as shown in Figure 2. In all service industries, we can see movement in every direction of the process structure chart as firms position themselves in relation to their competitors.

Firms like H. & R. Block have sought high-volume, middle-class taxpayers by creating a *low-divergence* tax service for those seeking help in preparing standard tax returns. With low divergence, the service can be provided with narrowly skilled employees performing routine tasks, and the result is consistent quality at reduced cost.

A hair-styling salon for men represents a *high-divergence* strategy reshaping the traditional barbering industry. High divergence is characterized as a niche strategy that seeks out customers who are willing to pay extra for the personalization.

Narrowing the scope of a service by specializing is a focused strategy that results in *low complexity*. Retailing recently has seen an explosion of specialty shops selling only one product, such as ice cream, cookies, or coffee. For such a strategy to succeed, the service or product must be perceived as being unique or of very high quality.

To gain greater market penetration or maximize the revenue from each customer, a strategy of adding more services can be initiated, thereby creating a structure with *high complexity*. For example, supermarkets have evolved into superstores through the addition of banking services, pharmacies, flower shops, books, video rentals, and food preparation.

Repositioning need not be limited to changes in only one dimension of the process structure (i.e., level of divergence or complexity). For a family restaurant seeking a strategy combining changes in levels of both complexity and divergence, consider Table 1.

Figure 2. *Structural positioning of financial services.*

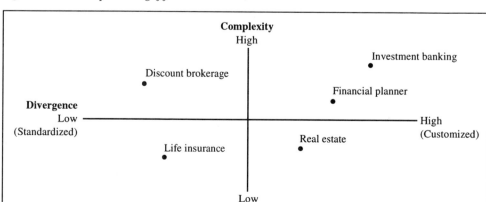

TAXONOMY FOR SERVICE PROCESS DESIGN

Service processes can be classified using the concept of divergence, the object toward which the service activity is directed, and the degree of customer contact. In Table 2, services are broadly divided into low divergence (i.e., standardized service) and high divergence (i.e., customized service). Within these two categories, the object of the service process is identified as goods, information, or people. The degree of customer contact ranges from no contact to indirect contact to direct contact (and is divided further into self-service and personal interaction with the service worker).

Degree of Divergence

A standardized service (i.e., low divergence) is designed for high volumes with a narrowly defined and focused service. The tasks are routine and require a workforce with relatively low levels of technical skills. Because of the repetitive nature of the service, opportunities to substitute automation for labor abound (e.g., use of vending machines, automatic car wash). Reducing the discretion of service workers is one approach to achieving consistent service quality, but one that also has possible negative consequences. These concepts will later be referred to as the *production-line approach* to service design.

For customized services (i.e., high divergence), more flexibility and judgment are required to perform the service tasks. In addition, more information is exchanged between the customer and the service worker. These characteristics of customized services require high levels of technical and analytic skills, because the service process is unprogrammed and not well defined (e.g., counseling, landscaping). To achieve customer satisfaction, decision making is delegated to service workers who can perform their tasks with some autonomy and discretion (i.e., the workers are empowered).

TABLE 1 Structural Alternatives for a Family Restaurant

Lower Complexity/Divergence	Current Process	Higher Complexity/Divergence
No reservations	Take reservation	Specific table selection
Self-seating, menu on blackboard	Seat guests, give menus	Recite menu, describe entrees and specials
Eliminate	Serve water and bread	Assortment of hot breads and hors d'oeuvres
Customer fills out form	Take orders	At table, taken personally by maitre d'
	Prepare orders:	
Pre-prepared, no choice	Salad (4 choices)	Individually prepared at table
Limit to 4 choices	Entree (15 choices)	Expand to 20 choices: add flaming dishes, bone fish at table, prepare sauces at table
Sundae bar, self-service	Dessert (6 choices)	Expand to 12 choices
Coffee, tea, milk only	Beverage (6 choices)	Add exotic coffees, wine list, liqueurs
Serve salad and entree together, bill and beverage together	Serve orders	Separate-course service, sherbet between courses, handgrind pepper
Cash only, pay when leaving	Collect payment	Choice of payment, including house accounts; serve mints

Source: Reprinted with permission of the American Marketing Association: G. Lynn Shostack, "Service Positioning through Structural Change," *Journal of Marketing*, vol. 51, January 1987, p. 41.

TABLE 2 Taxonomy of Service Processes

	Low Divergence (standardized service)			High Divergence (customized service)		
	Processing of goods	Processing of information or images	Processing of people	Processing of goods	Processing of information or images	Processing of people
No customer contact	Dry cleaning Restocking a vending machine	Check processing Billing for a credit card		Auto repair Tailoring a suit	Computer programming Designing a building	
Indirect customer contact		Ordering groceries from a home computer Phone-based account balance verification			Supervision of a landing by an air controller Bidding at a TV auction	
Direct customer contact — No customer-service worker interaction (self-service)	Operating a vending machine Assembling premade furniture	Withdrawing cash from an automatic bank teller Taking pictures in a photo booth	Operating an elevator Riding an escalator	Sampling food at a buffet dinner Bagging of groceries	Documenting medical history at a clinic Searching for information in a library	Driving a rental car Using a health club facility
Direct customer contact — Customer-service worker interaction	Food serving in a restaurant Car washing	Giving a lecture Handling routine bank transactions	Providing public transportation Providing mass vaccination	Home carpet cleaning Landscaping service	Portrait painting Counseling	Haircutting Performing a surgical operation

Source: Reprinted with permission from Urban Wemmerlov, "A Taxonomy for Service Process and Its Implications for System Design," *International Journal of Service Industry Management,* vol. 1, no. 3, 1990, p. 29.

Object of the Service Process

When goods are processed, a distinction must be made between goods that belong to the customer and goods that are provided by the service firm (i.e., *facilitating goods*). For services such as dry cleaning or auto repair, the service is performed on the property of the customer; in this case, the property must be secured from damage or loss. Other services such as restaurants supply facilitating goods as a significant part of the service package. Therefore, appropriate stock levels and the quality of these facilitating goods become a concern, as illustrated by McDonald's attention to the purchase of food items.

Processing information (i.e., receiving, handling, and manipulating data) occurs in all service systems. In some cases, this is a back-office activity, such as check processing at a bank. For other services, the information is communicated indirectly by electronic means, as with telephone-based account balance verification. Service workers in these situations may spend hours before a video screen performing routine tasks, and motivation becomes a challenge. There are services such as counseling, however, in which information is processed through direct interactions between the customer and the service worker. For highly skilled employees in these services, the challenge of dealing with unstructured problems is important to job satisfaction.

Processing people involves physical changes (e.g., a haircut or a surgical operation) or geographic changes (e.g., a bus ride or a car rental). Because of the "high-touch" nature of these services, workers must possess interpersonal as well as technical skills. Attention also must be paid to service facility design and location, because the customer is physically present in the system.

Type of Customer Contact

Customer contact with the service delivery system can occur in three basic ways. First, the customer can be physically present and interact directly with the service providers in the creation of the service. In this instance, the customer has full sensory awareness of the service surroundings. Second, the contact may be indirect and occur via electronic media from the customer's home or office. Third, some service activities can be performed with no customer contact at all. Banking provides an example where all three options occur: making an application for an automobile loan requires an interview with a loan officer, payment on the loan can be accomplished by the electronic transfer of funds, and the financial record keeping for the loan is conducted in a back office of the bank.

Direct customer contact is subdivided into two categories: no interaction with service workers (i.e., self-service), and customer interaction with service workers. Self-service often is particularly attractive, because customers provide the necessary labor at the necessary time. Many cost-effective applications of technology in services, such as direct dialing and automatic teller machines, have relied on a market segment of customers who are willing to learn how to interact with machines. When customers desire direct interaction with service providers, all the issues addressed earlier concerning the processing of people (i.e., training in interpersonal skills and facility issues of location, layout, and design) become important to ensure a successful service experience. When customers are in the service process physically, additional management problems (e.g., managing queues to avoid creating a negative image) arise. The topic of customer waiting is discussed in Chapter 17.

Service processes with indirect customer contact or with no customer contact need not be constrained by issues that arise from the physical presence of the customer in the system. Because the customer is decoupled from the service delivery system, a more manufacturing type of approach can be taken. Decisions regarding site location, facility design, work scheduling, and training of employees all can be driven by efficiency considerations. In fact, the no-customer-contact and goods-processing combination creates a category that normally is thought of in manufacturing. For example, dry cleaning is a batch process, and auto repair is a job shop.

This taxonomy of service processes presents a way to organize the various types of processes that are encountered in service systems and helps us to understand the design and management of services. This taxonomy also serves as a strategic positioning map for service processes and, thus, as an aid in the design or redesign of service systems.

GENERIC APPROACHES TO SERVICE SYSTEM DESIGN

In Chapter 14, we defined the service package as a bundle of attributes that a customer experiences. This bundle consists of four features: supporting facility, facilitating goods, explicit services, and implicit services. With a well-designed service system, these features are harmoniously coordinated in light of the desired service package. Consequently, the definition of the service package is key to designing the service system itself. This design can be approached in several ways.

At one extreme, we can deliver services through a *production-line approach*. With this approach, routine services are provided in a controlled environment to ensure consistent quality and efficiency of operation. Another approach is to encourage active customer participation in the process. Allowing the customer to take an active role in the service process can result in many benefits to both the consumer and provider. An intermediate approach divides the service into high- and low-customer-contact operations. This allows the low-contact operations to be designed as a technical core that is isolated from the customer.

It should be noted that combinations of these approaches also can be used. For example, banks isolate their check-processing operation, use self-serve automated tellers, and provide personalized loan service.

Production-Line Approach

We tend to see service as something personal: it is performed by individuals directly for other individuals. This humanistic perception can be overly constraining, however, and therefore can impede development of an innovative service system design. For example, we sometimes might benefit from a more technocratic service delivery system. Manufacturing systems are designed with control of the process in mind. The output often is machine-paced, and jobs are designed with explicit tasks to be performed. Special tools and machines are supplied to increase worker productivity. A service taking this production-line approach could gain a competitive advantage with a cost leadership strategy.

McDonald's provides the quintessential example of this manufacturing-in-the-field approach to service.[3] Raw materials (e.g., hamburger patties) are measured and prepackaged off-site, leaving the employees with no discretion as to size, quality, or consistency. In addition, storage facilities are designed expressly for the predetermined mix of products. No extra space is available for foods and beverages that are not called for in the service.

---

[3]Theodore Levitt, "Production-Line Approach to Service," *Harvard Business Review*, September–October 1972, pp. 41–52.

The production of french fries illustrates attention to design detail. The fries come precut, partially cooked, and frozen. The fryer is sized to cook a correct quantity of fries. This is an amount that will be not so large as to create an inventory of soggy fries or so small as to require making new batches very frequently. The fryer is emptied into a wide, flat tray near the service counter. This setup prevents fries from an overfilled bag from dropping to the floor, which would result in wasted food and an unclean environment. A special wide-mouthed scoop with a funnel in the handle is used to ensure a consistent measure of french fries. The thoughtful design ensures that employees never soil their hands or the fries, that the floor remains clean, and that the quantity is controlled. Further, a generous-looking portion of fries is delivered to the customer by a speedy, efficient, and cheerful employee.

This entire system is engineered from beginning to end, from prepackaged hamburgers to highly visible trash cans that encourage customers to clear their table. Every detail is accounted for through careful planning and design. The production-line approach to service system design attempts to translate a successful manufacturing concept into the service sector, and several features contribute to its success.

LIMITED DISCRETIONARY ACTION OF PERSONNEL A worker on an automobile assembly line is given well-defined tasks to perform along with the tools to accomplish them. Employees with discretion and latitude might produce a more personalized car, but uniformity from one car to the next would be lost. Standardization and quality (defined as consistency in meeting specifications) are the hallmarks of a production line. For standardized routine services, consistency in service performance would be valued by customers. For example, specialized services like muffler replacement and pest control are advertised as having the same high-quality service at any franchised outlet. Thus, the customer can expect identical service at any location of a particular franchise operation (e.g., one Big Mac is as desirable as another), just as one product from a manufacturer is indistinguishable from another. If more personalized service is desired, however, the concept of employee empowerment becomes appropriate.

DIVISION OF LABOR The production-line approach suggests that the total job be broken down into groups of simple tasks. Task grouping permits the specialization of labor skills (e.g., not everyone at McDonald's needs to be a cook). Further, the division of labor allows one to pay only for the skill that is required to perform the task. Of course, this raises the criticism of many service jobs as being minimum-wage, dead-end, and low-skill employment. Consider, for example, a new concept in health care called the *automated multiphasic testing laboratory*. Patients are processed through a fixed sequence of medical tests, which are part of the diagnostic work-up. Tests are performed by medical technicians using sophisticated equipment. Because the entire process is divided into routine tasks, the examination can be accomplished without an expensive physician.

SUBSTITUTION OF TECHNOLOGY FOR PEOPLE The systematic substitution of equipment for people has been the source of progress in manufacturing. This approach also can be used in services, as seen by the acceptance of automated teller machines in lieu of bank tellers. A great deal can be accomplished by means of the "soft" technology of systems, however. Consider, for example, the use of mirrors placed in an airplane galley. This benign device provides a reminder and an opportunity for flight attendants to maintain a pleasant appearance in an unobtrusive manner. Another example is the greeting card display that has a built-in inventory replenishment and reordering feature; when the stock gets low, a colored card appears to signal a reorder. Using a laptop computer, insurance agents can personalize their recommendations and illustrate the accumulation of cash values.

SERVICE STANDARDIZATION The limited menu at McDonald's guarantees a fast hamburger. Limiting service options creates opportunities for predictability and preplanning; the service becomes a routine process with well-defined tasks and an orderly flow of customers. Standardization also helps to provide uniformity in service quality, because the process is easier to control. Franchise services take advantage of standardization to build national organizations and thus overcome the problem of demand being limited only to the immediate region around a service location.

Customer as Coproducer

For most service systems, the customer is present when the service is being performed. Instead of being a passive bystander, the customer represents productive labor just at the moment it is needed, and opportunities exist for increasing productivity by shifting some of the service activities onto the customer (i.e., making the customer a *coproducer*). Further, customer participation can increase the degree of customization. For example, Pizza Hut's lunch buffet permits customers to make their own salads and select pizza-by-the-slice while the cooks work continuously at restocking only the pizzas that are selling rather than at filling individual orders. Thus, involving the customer in the service process can support a competitive strategy of cost leadership with some customization if it is focused on customers who are interested in serving themselves.

Depending on the degree of customer involvement, a spectrum of service delivery systems, from self-service to complete dependence on a service provider, is possible. For example, consider the services of a real estate agent. A homeowner has the option of selling the home personally as well as of staying away from any involvement by engaging a real estate agent for a significant commission. An intermediate alternative is the "Gallery of Homes" approach. For a flat fee (e.g., $500), the homeowner lists the home with the Gallery. Home buyers visiting the Gallery are interviewed concerning their needs and are shown pictures and descriptions of homes that might be of interest. Appointments for visits with homeowners are made, and an itinerary is developed. The buyers provide their own transportation, the homeowners show their own homes, and the Gallery agent conducts the final closing and arranges financing, as usual. Productivity gains are achieved by a division of labor. The real estate agent concentrates on duties requiring special training and expertise, while the homeowner and buyer share the remaining activities.

The following features illustrate some of the contributions that customers can make in the delivery of services.

SUBSTITUTION OF CUSTOMER LABOR FOR PROVIDER LABOR The increasing minimum wage has hastened the substitution of customer labor for personalized services. Fewer hotel bellhops are seen today, and more salad bars are being used in restaurants. Airlines are encouraging passengers to use carry-on luggage. Technology also has helped to facilitate customer participation. Consider, for example, the use of automated teller machines at banks and of long-distance direct dialing. The modern customer has become a coproducer, receiving benefits for his or her labor in the form of lower-cost services. Interestingly, a segment of the customer population actually appreciates the control aspects of self-service. For example, the popularity of salad bars is a result of allowing the customer to individualize his or her salad in terms of quantity and items selected. Finally, coproduction addresses the problem of matching supply with demand in services, because the customer brings the extra service capacity at the time when it is needed.

SMOOTHING SERVICE DEMAND Service capacity is a time-perishable commodity. For example, in a medical setting, it is more appropriate to measure capacity in terms of physician-hours rather than in terms of the number of doctors on staff. This approach emphasizes the permanent loss to the service provider of capacity whenever the server is idle through lack of customer demand. The nature of demand for a service, however, is one of pronounced variation by the hour of the day (e.g., restaurants), the day of the week (e.g., theaters), or the season of the year (e.g., ski resorts). If variations in demand can be smoothed, the required service capacity will be reduced, and fuller, more uniform utilization of capacity can be realized. The result is improved service productivity.

To implement a demand-smoothing strategy, customers must participate, adjusting the timing of their demand to match the availability of the service. Typical means of accomplishing this are appointments and reservations; in compensation, customers expect to avoid waiting for the service. Customers also may be induced to acquire the service during off-peak hours by price incentives (e.g., reduced telephone rates after 5 PM, or midweek discounts on lift tickets at ski resorts).

If attempts to smooth demand fail, high utilization of capacity still may be accomplished by requiring customers to wait for service. Thus, customer waiting contributes to productivity by permitting greater utilization of capacity. Perhaps a sign such as the following should be posted in waiting areas: "Your waiting allows us to offer bargain prices!"

We would expect customers to be compensated for this input to the service process through lower prices, but what about "free" or prepaid government service? In this situation, waiting is a surrogate for the price that otherwise might be charged the user. The results are a rationing of the limited public service among users and high utilization of capacity. Using customers' waiting time as an input to the service process, however, may be criticized on the grounds that individual customers value their time differently.

The customer may need to be "trained" to assume a new, and perhaps more independent, role as an active participant in the service process. This educational role for the provider is a new concept in services. Traditionally, the service provider has kept the consumer ignorant and, thus, dependent on the server.

As services become more specialized, the customer also must assume a diagnostic role. For example, does the loud noise under my car need the attention of AAMCO (i.e., transmission) or Midas (i.e., muffler)? Further, an informed customer also may provide a quality-control check, which has been particularly lacking in the professional services. Thus, increased service productivity may depend on an informed and self-reliant customer.

Customer Contact Approach

The manufacture of products is conducted in a controlled environment. The process design is totally focused on creating a continuous and efficient conversion of inputs into products without consumer involvement. Using inventory, the production process is decoupled from variations in customer demand and, thus, can be scheduled to operate at full capacity.

How can service managers design their operations to achieve the efficiencies of manufacturing when customers participate in the process? Richard B. Chase has argued persuasively that service delivery systems can be separated into high- and low-contact customer operations.[4] The low-contact, or back-office, operation is run as a plant, where all the production management concepts and automation technology are brought to bear. This separation of activities can result in a customer perception of personalized service while in fact achieving economies of scale through volume processing.

The success of this approach depends on the required amount of customer contact in the creation of the service, and on the ability to isolate a technical core of low-contact operations. In our taxonomy of service processes, this approach to service design would seem to be most appropriate for the processing-of-goods category (e.g., dry cleaning, where the service is performed on the customer's property).

DEGREE OF CUSTOMER CONTACT *Customer contact* refers to the physical presence of the customer in the system. The degree of customer contact can be measured by the percentage of time that the customer is in the system relative to the total service time. In high-contact services, the customer determines the timing of demand and the nature of the service by direct participation in the process. The perceived quality of service is determined to a large extent by the customer's experience. Consumers have no direct influence on the production process of low-contact systems, however, because they are not present. Even if a service falls into the high-contact category, it still may be possible to seal off some operations to be run as a factory. For example, the maintenance operations of a public transportation system and the laundry of a hospital are plants within a service system.

SEPARATION OF HIGH- AND LOW-CONTACT OPERATIONS When service systems are separated into high- and low-contact operations, each area can be designed separately to achieve improved performance. Different considerations in the design of the high- and low-contact operations are listed in Table 3. Note that high-contact operations require employees with excellent interpersonal skills. The service tasks and activity levels in these operations are uncertain, because customers dictate the timing of demand and, to some extent, the service itself. Note also that low-contact operations can be physically separated from customer contact operations; however, there is some need for communication across the line of visibility to track progress of customer orders or property (e.g., shoes dropped off at a kiosk for repair at a distant factory). The advantage of separation occurs because these back-office operations can be scheduled like a factory to obtain high utilization of capacity.

Airlines have used this approach effectively in their operations. Airport reservation clerks and flight attendants wear uniforms designed in Paris and attend training sessions on the proper way to serve passengers. Baggage handlers seldom are seen, and aircraft maintenance is performed at a distant depot and run like a factory.

SALES OPPORTUNITY AND SERVICE DELIVERY OPTIONS The commonly held view that organizations are information-processing systems is evident when considering information content requirements as a variable in designing service tasks. The service design matrix developed by Richard B. Chase, which is shown in Figure 3, illustrates the relationship between production efficiency and sales opportunity as a function of service delivery options.[5]

---

[4]Richard B. Chase, "Where Does the Customer Fit in a Service Operation?" *Harvard Business Review,* November–December 1978, pp. 137–142.
[5]R. B. Chase and N. J. Aquilano, "A Matrix for Linking Marketing and Production Variables in Service System Design," *Production and Operations Management,* 6th ed., Irwin, Homewood, Ill., 1992.

TABLE 3   Major Design Considerations for High- and Low-Contact Operations

Design Considerations	High-Contact Operation	Low-Contact Operation
Facility location	Operations must be near the customer.	Operations may be placed near supply, transportation, or labor.
Facility layout	Facility should accommodate the customer's physical and psychological needs and expectations.	Facility should enhance production.
Product design	Environment as well as the physical product define the nature of the service.	Customer is not in the service environment.
Process design	Stages of production process have a direct, immediate effect on the customer.	Customer is not involved in the majority of processing steps.
Scheduling	Customer is in the production schedule and must be accommodated.	Customer is concerned mainly with completion dates.
Production planning	Orders cannot be stored, so smoothing production flow will result in loss of business.	Both backlogging and production smoothing are possible.
Worker skills	Direct workforce makes up a major part of the service product and so must be able to interact well with the public.	Direct workforce need only have technical skills.
Quality control	Quality standards often are in the eye of the beholder and hence variable.	Quality standards generally are measurable and hence fixed.
Time standards	Service time depends on customer needs, and therefore time standards are inherently loose.	Work is performed on customer surrogates (e.g., forms), and time standards can be tight.
Wage payment	Variable output requires time-based wage systems.	"Fixable" output permits output-based wage systems.
Capacity planning	To avoid lost sales, capacity must be set to match peak demand.	Storable output permits setting capacity at some average demand level.
Forecasting	Forecasts are short-term and time-oriented.	Forecasts are long-term and output-oriented.

Service delivery options are ordered from left to right by increasing richness of information transfer. As discussed earlier, production efficiency is related to the degree of customer contact with the core service operations. Sales opportunity is a measure of the probability of making add-on sales and increasing the revenue that is generated from each customer. This matrix permits the explicit consideration of the tradeoffs made between marketing and production considerations when selecting the service delivery option.

We should not conclude that only one service delivery option must be selected. In order not to eliminate certain market segments, multiple channels of service should be considered. For example, gas stations have both full- and self-service pumps, and most banks still have live in addition to automated tellers.

Information Empowerment

Forget the "Age of Aquarius"—this is the age of information, and like it or not, we are all a part of it. Information technology (IT) is no longer just for computer "nerds." IT touches all of us everyday. The breakfast cereal on your table represents more than puffs, flakes, or shreds of grain. You can safely assume that three funny-looking little guys named Snap, Crackle, and Pop are not actually responsible for processing and packaging your rice, nor does a little sprite cavort around putting two scoops of raisins in each box of Raisin Bran. IT can be seen all the way from the rice paddy or wheat field, where it helps to manage the planting,

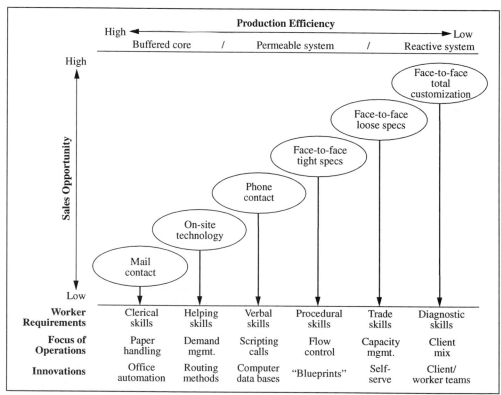

Figure 3. *Sales opportunity and service system design.*
(Reprinted with permission from R. B. Chase and N. J. Aquilano, "A Matrix for Linking Marketing and Production Variables in Service System Design," *Production and Operations Management,* 6th ed., Richard D. Irwin, Inc., Homewood, Ill., 1992, p. 123.)

propagating, harvesting, and transportation of the grain, to the processing and packaging facility to your market and even to your table (e.g., those traffic lights you passed between market and home are operated by an information-based technology). Essential services such as fire and police protection demand the use of IT, and the electricity and running water in our homes are brought to us by IT. In fact, IT is such a fundamental part of daily life throughout the entire world that the challenge is to find some aspect not touched by it.

Certainly, no service today could survive without the use of IT, and successful managers will see that IT offers much more than simply a convenient way to maintain records. Indeed, one of its most important functions is to empower both employees and customers.

EMPLOYEE EMPOWERMENT The earliest use of IT was in record keeping. A business might have had a computerized data base of customer names and addresses, and perhaps another data base of the names and addresses for suppliers of essential goods and services. These various data bases made it a little easier to keep the shareholders—and the IRS—happy. They made record keeping a little faster and a little more accurate, but secretaries still just entered data, procurement clerks just ordered supplies or services, front-line service people smiled a lot, and production-floor workers still went about their routine duties. Top management held the task of juggling these diverse activities.

The development of *relational data bases*, however, changed everything. Relational, or integrated, data bases meant that information from all aspects of an operation could be used by anybody. A production manager could look at sales numbers and know immediately how much production to schedule in the next work period. A production-floor or front-line service worker could call for necessary supplies from inventory and even initiate an order for replacement inventory without having to go through the procurement office. The day of the empowered employee had arrived.

Of course, computers were the key to maintaining these data bases. The machines were powerful tools for keeping track of names and numbers, but when they began "talking to each other," another revolution was in store. Now employees of one organization could interact with each other across functional boundaries, and even with those in other organizations in "real time" and without the need to be together physically. This means, for example, that when a Delta flight is canceled, a Delta agent can book the stranded passengers not only on other Delta flights but also on those of other carriers from his or her computer terminal. It no longer is necessary for the agent or the passengers to scurry frantically from one airline counter to another in search of an available seat.

CUSTOMER EMPOWERMENT In the previous discussion, we looked at how computers and IT empower employees, which translates into better service for customers. Customers, too, can be directly empowered by IT. The Internet, which links people together around the entire world, is one example of a very powerful tool. Customers no longer are dependent entirely on local service providers. A person with a medical question can search the world for answers, and we can shop around the world. Do you have a "sick" Mazda that defies the best of local mechanics? Just get on the Internet and ask the folks at http://www.inslab.uky.edu/MailingLists/mazda-list.html to suggest solutions.

IT provides customers with other ways of taking an active part in the service process. For example, we can go to FedEx's home page, enter the airbill number of a package sent through FedEx, and find out exactly where the package is at that moment. If it has been delivered, we can find out who signed for it. We also can make our own travel reservations on-line and get information about our destination, which can enhance our trip immeasurably.

Our daily lives surely will be affected more and more by IT, and the impact will be measured in days and weeks rather than in years. Right now, customers in many supermarkets can speed up their checkout time by weighing and labeling their own produce. In some cases, the customer takes a sticky, bar-coded label from a dispenser over the cucumbers, and the integrated scale/checkout register automatically weighs the produce, reads the bar code, and prices the purchase. In other cases, the customer places lemons on a scale in the produce department. A sign over the lemons gives an item number, which the buyer enters on a number pad on the scale, and the scale spits out a sticky label with the total cost. Some scales are extremely user-friendly and have labeled buttons for different items so that the customer does not have to remember the code number from the item's bin to the scale. Very soon, many of us will be engaging in a "total" shopping experience: in addition to weighing and pricing our own produce, we will be scanning all our supermarket purchases ourselves, scanning our credit card, and bagging our groceries, too. (Some may think that's carrying customer empowerment too far!)

SUMMARY

We found that a service delivery system design can be captured in a visual diagram called a *service blueprint*. The line of visibility in this diagram introduced the concept of a front- and back-office partition of the service system. Competitive positioning of the service delivery system was accomplished using the dimensions of complexity and divergence to measure structural differentiation. We also looked at classifying services according to the concept of divergence, the object of the service, and the degree of customer contact. Four generic approaches to the design of service delivery systems were considered: production-line approach, customer participation, customer contact, and information empowerment. These approaches and their combinations provide many opportunities for innovative designs.

KEY TERMS AND DEFINITIONS

Coproducer the productive role a customer can play in the service delivery process.

Complexity a dimension of service process structure that measures the number and intricacy of steps in the process.

Customer contact a measure of the physical presence of the customer in the system as a percentage of the total service time.

Divergence a dimension of service process structure that measures the degree of customization or decision making permitted of service employees.

Line of visibility a line drawn on the service blueprint showing separation of front-office from back-office activities.

Production-line approach a service design analogous to that in a manufacturing system with tight control, use of low-skilled labor, and the offering of a standard service.

Service blueprint a diagram of the service process showing activities, flows, fail points, customer waits, and a line of visibility.

TOPICS FOR DISCUSSION

■ Shostack's "line of visibility" on a service blueprint divides the service into front-office and back-office operations. How can this be useful to managers?

■ Select a service and prepare a "blueprint" identifying fail points, decision points, customer wait points, and the line of visibility.

■ What are the limits to the production-line approach to service?

■ Give an example of a service in which isolation of the technical core would be inappropriate.

■ What are some drawbacks of increased customer participation in the service process?

■ What ethical issues are involved in the promotion of sales opportunities in a service transaction?

SERVICE BENCHMARK

PACBELL'S EXPERIMENT

The project, now called Infotel, was born in September 1991, when San Francisco-based PacBell sent a dozen managers to the Double Tree Inn in Santa Ana, Calif. Their familiar mission: think up ways to increase productivity.

Their leader, John Lewis, then general manager of PacBell's Los Angeles staff, wondered why the company was using traditional methods if it really wanted a quantum leap. Puzzling over the problem in the shower that first morning, he had an idea: He would "fire" his colleagues (and himself) and, unbeknownst to his bosses, change the agenda. He asked them to pretend that they had just inherited a phone company from "Uncle Herman" and found that the old man hadn't left enough money to buy a new computer system. Otherwise, they could invent a whole new phone company.

For the first few days, the participants got nowhere. They were simply too tangled in the PacBell culture, speaking in corporate acronyms and thinking old thoughts. So, Mr. Lewis imposed 25-cent fines for each peep of PacBell lingo. "We had lots of cocktails" with the proceeds, he says.

Then, changes came more easily. During "I wish" sessions, the managers offered ideas beginning with those words, as in: "I wish the first person who answered . . . the phone could solve my problem." That drill developed ideas for, among other things, changing office procedures so individual workers could perform many tasks quickly. Such an office could be set up, the managers thought, if they could invent software giving workers instant access to numerous databases.

A REALITY TEST

After some four weeks of brainstorming, Mr. Lewis told his boss, Marty A. Kaplan, PacBell's executive vice president for reengineering, that the group wanted to create and run a real Infotel within the phone company. Mr. Kaplan agreed, and Infotel spent the next year developing a business plan—despite the doubts of other senior managers. The group chose Santa Clarita as the site because it is small—its population is 30,000—but has a mix of business and residential accounts. For staffing, Infotel asked the Communications Workers of America for four union volunteers, who would bring along their old work but handle it with Infotel's new procedures, plus their own innovations.

Most of Infotel's cost savings come from small changes. Because of one software glitch, for instance, PacBell computers couldn't automatically process requests for voice mail from customers served by a certain kind of phone switch. Every day, the computers across the state kicked out hundreds of orders, and employees had to spend about 10 minutes processing each one.

Sandy Coash, an Infotel worker, identified the problem and told Mr. Lewis, to whom she wouldn't normally have had access. Within three months, PacBell software engineers fixed the problem for the whole state—and eliminated all that work. That and other software fixes allowed Infotel's four union workers to cut out 85% of the work they had brought with them from their old jobs, Mr. Lewis says.

There were many other changes. A new software program for repair workers' portable computers gives them all the information they need to fix a line; no longer do they have to call other PacBell employees for help. The computers also dispatch them to their next assignment; now they don't have to call in for those, either. Cellular telephones in their vans allow them to make phone calls on the road instead of pulling over at gas stations.

And that is just the beginning. Infotel has yet to implement its crowning achievement, a software program that should make customer-service computers as easy to use as a cash register at McDonald's. Once it's in place, workers will be able to point and click at a menu of orders when a customer calls, filling the order in minutes. The same workers will have remote access to switches and also will be able to perform tests on lines.

Currently, when a customer calls regular PacBell offices to start phone service, the worker who answers must type in the name, address, billing information and how the person wants to be listed in the directory. Then the worker fumbles through heavy manuals to look up corresponding computer codes for the whole order and type in the codes—sometimes making mistakes. The process takes an average of 22 minutes. A customer who also wants to report trouble on a line must transfer to a different department and talk to at least two more people.

PacBell's customers in Santa Clarita are getting better service. They can now get new features such as call-waiting in seconds, instead of hours. And repair workers have developed a sixth sense. When Cindy Pascoe's daughter shorted out a phone line by knocking over a fish tank, a repairman arrived even before she knew the line was dead. "It was wonderful!" the department-store saleswoman exclaims.

Since the Infotel group didn't have enough money to buy a new, easy-to-use computer system, they jerry-rigged the one they had by writing a new software program. So far, the software has taken more than a year and more than $10 million to develop, but that is small change compared with the $4 billion Mr. Lewis estimates as the cost of replacing all of PacBell's current computers.

The bottom line: company-wide adoption of Infotel innovations, combined with other reengineering efforts, will allow PacBell to serve its existing customers with 10,000 fewer workers. Mr. Lewis is a bit sensitive about linking Infotel's success to the job cuts, which were to be completed by 1997. Infotel "is not laying them off. Competition is laying them off," he argues. Mr. Kaplan agrees: "We didn't say we're going to reengineer the business to cut 10,000 people. We said we've got to take a lot of costs out . . . and improve service."

A crucial question is how many well-paying jobs destroyed by technology will be offset by well-paying jobs created by technology. And many are being created. United Parcel Service of America Inc., for example, now has 3,000 information-technology employees, up from 90 in 1983. At many companies, more technicians will be needed to service computer networks, and more programmers to write software.

For at least a few years, however, technology-driven layoffs seem likely to dwarf new high-tech jobs. Many layoff victims will have to settle for the low-paying or part-time positions that are dominating recent job growth, because they generally aren't the ones who will get the new high-paying jobs. A telephone operator isn't qualified to install wireless communications equipment, for example. The danger is that America's workforce could evolve into an elite minority of highly paid "knowledge workers" and frustrated masses of the underemployed or unemployed.

Already, many workers are aware that technology cuts two ways. Riding in an Infotel van, Steve Symach, a repairman, marvels at how technology has made his job easier. But he realizes it could cost him his job—before he plans to retire, in 12 years. "If the result of us being efficient is me being laid off," the silver-haired 18-year phone company veteran says, "I hate to say it, but I guess that's progress."

Source: Reprinted with permission from Joan E. Rigdon, "Retooling Lives: Technological Gains Are Cutting Costs, and Jobs, in Services," *The Wall Street Journal,* February 24, 1994, p. A5. Reprinted by permission of *The Wall Street Journal,* 1994, Dow Jones & Company, Inc. All rights reserved worldwide.

CONCLUDING CASE

100 YEN SUSHI HOUSE[6]

Sang M. Lee tells of a meeting with two Japanese businessmen in Tokyo to plan a joint U.S.–Japanese conference to explore U.S. and Japanese management systems. As lunchtime drew near, his hosts told him with much delight that they wished to show him the "most productive operation in Japan."

Lee describes the occasion: "They took me to a sushi shop, the famous 100 Yen Sushi House, in the Shinzuku area of Tokyo. Sushi is the most popular snack in Japan. It is a simple dish, vinegared rice wrapped in different things, such as dried seaweed, raw tuna, raw salmon, raw red snapper, cooked shrimp, octopus, fried egg, etc. Sushi is usually prepared so that each piece will be about the right size to be put into the mouth with chopsticks. Arranging the sushi in an appetizing and aesthetic way with pickled ginger is almost an art in itself.

"The 100 Yen Sushi House is no ordinary sushi restaurant. It is the ultimate showcase of Japanese productivity. As we entered the shop, there was a chorus of 'Iratsai,' a welcome from everyone working in the shop—cooks, waitresses, the owner, and the owner's children. The house features an ellipsoid-shaped serving area in the middle of the room, where inside three or four cooks were busily preparing sushi. Perhaps 30 stools surrounded the serving area. We took seats at the counters and were promptly served with a cup of 'Mis-oshiru,' which is a bean paste soup, a pair of chopsticks, a cup of green tea, a tiny plate to make our own sauce, and a small china piece to hold the chopsticks. So far, the service was average for any sushi house. Then, I noticed something special. There was a conveyor belt going around the ellipsoid service area, like a toy train track. On it I saw a train of plates of sushi. You can find any kind of sushi that you can think of—from the cheapest seaweed or octopus kind to the expensive raw salmon or shrimp dishes. The price is uniform, however, 100 yen per plate. On closer examination, while my eyes were racing to keep up with the speed of the traveling plates, I found that a cheap seaweed plate had four pieces, while the more expensive raw salmon dish had only two pieces. I sat down and looked around at the other customers at the counters. They were all enjoying their sushi and slurping their soup while reading newspapers or magazines.

"I saw a man with eight plates all stacked up neatly. As he got up to leave, the cashier looked over and said, '800 yen, please.' The cashier had no cash register, since she can simply count the number of plates and then multiply by 100 yen. As the customer was leaving, once again we heard a chorus of 'Arigato Gosaimas' (thank you) from all the workers."

Lee continues his observations of the sushi house operations: "In the 100 Yen Sushi House, Professor Tamura [one of his hosts] explained to me how efficient this family-owned restaurant is. The owner usually has a superordinate organizational purpose such as customer service, a contribution to society, or the well-being of the community. Furthermore, the organizational purpose is achieved through a long-term effort by all the members of the organization, who are considered 'family.'

"The owner's daily operation is based on a careful analysis of information. The owner has a complete summary of demand information about different types of sushi plates, and thus he knows exactly how many of each type of sushi plates he should prepare and when. Furthermore, the whole operation is based on the repetitive manufacturing principle with appropriate 'just-in-time' and quality control systems. For example, the store has a very limited refrigerator capacity (we could see several whole fish or octopus in the glassed chambers right in front of our counter). Thus, the store uses the 'just-in-time' inventory control system. Instead of increasing the refrigeration capacity by purchasing new refrigeration systems, the company has an agreement with the fish vendor to deliver fresh fish several times a day so that materials arrive 'just-in-time' to be used for sushi making. Therefore, the inventory cost is minimum.

". . . In the 100 Yen Sushi House, workers and their equipment are positioned so close that sushi making is passed on hand to hand rather than as independent operations. The absence of walls of inventory allows the owner and workers to be involved in the total operation, from greeting the customer to serving what is ordered. Their tasks are tightly interrelated and everyone rushes to a problem spot to prevent the cascading effect of the problem throughout the work process.

"The 100 Yen Sushi House is a labor-intensive operation, which is based mostly on simplicity and common sense rather than high

[6]Reprinted with permission from Sang M. Lee, "Japanese Management and the 100 Yen Sushi House," *Operations Management Review,* Winter 1983, pp. 46–48.

technology, contrary to American perceptions. I was very impressed. As I finished my fifth plate, I saw the same octopus sushi plate going around for about the thirtieth time. Perhaps I had discovered the pitfall of the system. So I asked the owner how he takes care of the sanitary problems when a sushi plate goes around all day long, until an unfortunate customer eats it and perhaps gets food poisoning. He bowed with an apologetic smile and said, 'Well, sir, we never let our sushi plates go unsold longer than about 30 minutes.' Then he scratched his head and said, 'Whenever one of our employees takes a break, he or she can take off unsold plates of sushi and either eat them or throw them away. We are very serious about our sushi quality.' "

QUESTIONS

1 Prepare a service blueprint for the 100 Yen Sushi House operation.

2 What features of the 100 Yen Sushi House service delivery system differentiate it from the competition, and what competitive advantages do they offer?

3 How has the 100 Yen Sushi House incorporated the just-in-time system into its operation?

4 Suggest other services that could adopt the 100 Yen Sushi House service delivery concepts.

CONCLUDING CASE

COMMUTER CLEANING—A NEW VENTURE PROPOSAL[7]

The service vision of Commuter Cleaning is to provide dry cleaning services for individuals with careers or other responsibilities that make it difficult for them to find the time to go to traditional dry cleaners. The company's goals are to provide a high-quality dry cleaning service that is both reliable and convenient.

The targeted market consists of office workers who live in the suburbs of large metropolitan areas. The service will be marketed primarily to single men and women as well as dual-career couples, because this segment of the population has the greatest need for a quality dry cleaning service but does not have the time to go to the traditional dry cleaners. The targeted cities are those surrounded by suburbs from which many people commute via mass transit.

The facilities where customers will drop-off and pick-up their dry cleaning will be located at sites where commuters meet their trains or buses into the downtown area (i.e., park-and-ride locations and commuter train stations). For each city, it will be necessary to determine who owns these transit stations and how land can be rented from the owner. In some locations, facilities where space could be rented already exist. In other locations, there may not be any existing facilities, and the pick-up and drop-off booths will need to be built.

The facilities for laundry pick-up and drop-off need not be large. The building or room at the station need only be large enough to accommodate racks for hanging the finished dry cleaning.

[7]Prepared by Mara Segal under the supervision of Professor James A. Fitzsimmons.

Initially, it may be necessary to restrict the service to laundering business-wear shirts, because these are the easiest of all clothing articles to clean and also will allow the operations to be simplified. Typically, a man or woman will need a clean shirt for each workday, so a large demand exists. One drawback would be the diminished customer convenience, because dry cleaning of garments would necessitate a separate trip to a traditional dry cleaner. If dry cleaning were outsourced, however, it would be possible to offer full-service cleaning very quickly, because a plant and equipment need not be purchased.

A decision also needs to be made about providing same-day or next-day service. One factor in this decision will be whether competitors in the area offer same-day service. These cleaners represent a serious threat only if they open early enough and close late enough to be convenient and accessible to customers. Most important, same-day service should be provided only where it is feasible to deliver on this promise consistently.

All advertisements will include a phone number that potential customers can call to inquire about the service. When a customer calls, he or she can request the service. That same day, the customer will be able to pick up a Commuter Cleaning laundry bag with the customer's name and account number on it and a membership card that is coded with the account number.

The delivery system will be a hub-and-spoke system, similar to the one that FedEx uses for package handling. Customers will have the convenience of dropping off their laundry at numerous neighborhood commuter stations. All dry cleaning will be picked up and delivered to one central plant, and once the shirts are clean, they will be returned to the customer's drop-off point. Same-day service is possible with pick-ups be-

ginning at 8:00 AM and returns completed by 5:00 PM.

The customer will place the dirty shirts in the bag at home and simply leave the bag at the station on the way to work. The station worker will attach a color-coded label on the bag to identify the location where the shirts were dropped off so that they can be returned to the same station. A laundry pick-up route will be established to bring bags from each location to the central cleaning plant. Once the bag reaches the central plant, the items will be counted and the number entered into the billing data base. After the shirts have been cleaned, they will be put on hangers with the customer's laundry bag attached. The cleaned shirts will be segregated according to the location to which they need to be returned and then placed on a truck in reverse order of the delivery route. The customer will provide the station worker with his or her membership card, which will be used to identify and retrieve the customer's clothing and bag. Because all customers will be billed monthly, the time to pick up the laundry should be expedited and waiting lines avoided.

Initially, cleaning will be outsourced to a large dry cleaner with excess capacity. A favorable rate should be negotiated because of the predictable volume, convenience of aggregating the demand into one batch, and performing the pick-up and delivery service. Contracting for the cleaning will reduce the initial capital investment required to build a plant and buy equipment, and it also will provide for the business to build a customer base that would support a dedicated cleaning plant. Further, contracting will limit the financial risk exposure if the concept fails. If the cleaning is outsourced, there will be no need to hire and manage a workforce to perform the cleaning; therefore, management can focus on building a customer base instead of supervising back-office activities. Also, with contract cleaning, it is more feasible to offer dry cleaning services in addition to laundering business shirts.

In the long run, however, contract cleaning may limit the potential profitability, expose the business to quality problems, and prevent the opportunity to focus cleaning plant operations around the pick-up-and-delivery concept. Ideally, once Commuter Cleaning has built a large client base and has access to significant capital, all cleaning will be done internally.

Most of the hiring will be targeted to area college students. Initially, two shifts of workers will be needed for the transit station facilities but just one van driver at any given time. As business expands, additional vans will be acquired and additional drivers hired. The first shift of drop-off station workers will begin at 6:00 AM and finish at 9:00 AM, at which time the van driver will transport the items from the drop-off sites to the cleaning site. The number of drivers needed and the hours they work will depend on how many pick-up and drop-off sites exist, their proximity to each other, the cleaning plant location, and the ability to develop efficient routing schedules. The second shift of drivers will deliver the cleaning from the plant to the transit stations from about 3:30 to 5:00 PM. The second shift of transit-site workers will begin at 5:00 PM and end when the last train or bus arrives, usually about 8:30 PM. Once cleaning is done internally, it will be possible to have plant employees also pick up the laundry and deliver it to the stations each day. This will allow Commuter Cleaning to hire some full-time workers, and it also will bring the back-office workers closer to the customers so that they can be more aware of problems and customer needs.

College students will be the best candidates for workers, because their schedules vary and classes usually are held in the middle of the day, from about 10 AM to 3 PM. Also, depending on course loads, some students may only have time to work 3 hours a day, while others may choose to work both the first and second shifts. The starting salary will be set slightly above the wage for typical part-time service jobs available to college students to discourage turnover.

When Commuter Cleaning is first introduced into a city, additional temporary workers will be needed to manage the customer inquiries for initiating the service. The week before introduction of the service, representatives will be at the station facilities to answer questions and perform the paperwork necessary to initiate service for interested customers. Because all advertisements will include the customer service number, it will be necessary to have additional representatives manning the phones to handle the inquiries. All employees will have the title "customer service representative" to stress the function of their jobs. These workers will be encouraged to get to know their customers and reach a first-name basis with them.

When customers initiate service, they will be encouraged to open an account for monthly billing rather than to pay each time that items are picked up. At this time, the customer service representative will collect all the necessary information, including name, address, phone number, location from where they commute, and credit card number. If a customer desires, the amount owed will be charged to the credit card each month. This is the most desirable form of payment, because it is efficient and involves no worry of delayed payments. This method also is becoming more common, and people generally now are comfortable having their credit card billed automatically. Each month, statements will be sent to all customers with transactions to verify the bill and request payment from those who do not use a credit card. If a customer is late in paying, a customer service representative will call and ask if he or she would like to begin paying with a credit card. Repeatedly delinquent customers will be required to pay at the time of pick-up, a stipulation that will be included in the customer's initial agreement for service. The customer service representatives will be responsible for answering all customer inquiries, including the initiation of new service, and one customer service representative will be responsible for customer billings. Each day, the laundry delivered to the plant will be entered into a data base that accumulates each customer's transactions for the month.

A smooth demand throughout the week is desirable to create a stable work load; however, actions likely will be needed to control fluctuations in demand and to avoid imbalances in the work load. One method of controlling demand is through price specials and promotions. Offering a discount on certain days of the week is common practice for dry cleaners, and one approach would be to offer special prices to different customer segments to entice them to bring in their laundry on a certain day. For example, Friday may be the busiest day of the week and Monday and Tuesday the slowest. In this case, the customer base could be divided (e.g., alphabetically) and each segment offered a discount price on a particular day. Other ideas include providing a complimentary cup of coffee to anyone bringing in laundry on Monday. These promotions can be implemented once demand fluctuations are observed. Attention also must be given to holidays, which may create temporary surges or lulls in business.

QUESTIONS

1 Prepare a service blueprint for Commuter Cleaning.
2 What generic approach to service system design is illustrated by Commuter Cleaning, and what competitive advantages does this design offer?
3 Using the data in Table 4, calculate a break-even price per shirt if monthly demand is expected to be 20,000 shirts and

the contract with a cleaning plant stipulates a charge of $.50 per shirt.
4 Critique the business concept, and make suggestions for improvement.

TABLE 4 Commuter Cleaning Economic Analysis

Expense Item	Monthly Amount, $	Assumptions
Transit station rent	2,400	7 locations at $400 each
Delivery van	500	1 minivan (includes lease payment and insurance)
Station customer service representatives	5,544	7 locations, 2 shifts averaging 3 hours per shift at $6 per hour
Driver	528	1 driver, 2 shifts averaging 2 hours per shift at $6 per hour
Fuel	165	30 miles per shift at 12 mpg and $1.50 per gallon
Business insurance	100	
Office customer service representatives	4,000	2 office workers, each paid $24,000 a year
Laundry bags	167	Cost of 1,000 laundry bags at $2, each amortized over one year
Total Monthly Expenses	13,404	22-day month

SELECTED BIBLIOGRAPHY

BARTHOLDI, J. J. III, L. K. PLATZMAN, R. L. COLLINS, and W. H. WARDEN III: "A Minimal Technology Routing System for Meals on Wheels," *Interfaces,* vol. 13, no. 3, June 1983, pp. 1–8.

CHASE, RICHARD B.: "Where Does the Customer Fit in a Service Operation?" *Harvard Business Review,* November–December 1978, pp. 137–142.

———: "The Customer Contact Approach to Services: Theoretical Bases and Practical Extensions," *Operations Research,* vol. 29, no. 4, July–August 1981, pp. 698–706.

———, and N. J. AQUILANO: "A Matrix for Linking Marketing and Production Variables in Service System Design," *Production and Operations Management,* 6th ed., Irwin, Homewood, Ill., 1992.

———, G. B. NORTHCRAFT, and G. WOLF: "Designing High-Contact Service Systems: Application to Branches of a Savings and Loan," *Decision Sciences,* vol. 15, no. 4, 1984, pp. 542–556.

———, and D. A. TANSIK: "The Customer Contact Model for Organization Design," *Management Science,* vol. 29, no. 9, 1983, pp. 1037–1050.

COOK, T., and R. RUSSELL: "A Simulation and Statistical Analysis of Stochastic Vehicle Routing with Timing Constraints," *Decision Sciences,* vol. 9, no. 4, October 1978, pp. 673–687.

FITZSIMMONS, JAMES A.: "Consumer Participation and Productivity in Service Operations," *Interfaces,* vol. 15, no. 3, 1985, pp. 60–67.

HESKETT, J. L.: "Operating Strategy: Barriers to Entry," *Managing in the Service Economy,* Harvard Business School Press, Boston, 1986.

HILL, ARTHUR V.: "An Experimental Comparison of Dispatching Rules for Field Service Support," *Decision Sciences,* vol. 23, no. 1, January–February 1992, pp. 235–249.

———, V. A. MABERT, and D. W. MONTGOMERY: "A Decision Support System for the Courier Vehicle Scheduling Problem," *Omega,* vol. 16, no. 4, July 1988, pp. 333–345.

JOHNSTON, B., and B. MORRIS: "Monitoring Control in Service Operations," *International Journal of Operations and Production Management,* vol. 5, no. 1, 1985, pp. 32–38.

LEE, SANG M.: "Japanese Management and the 100 Yen Sushi House," *Operations Management Review,* Winter 1983, pp. 45–48.

LELE, M. M.: "How Service Needs Influence Product Strategy," *Sloan Management Review,* Fall 1986, pp. 63–70.

LEVITT, THEODORE: "Production-Line Approach to Service," *Harvard Business Review,* September–October 1972, pp. 41–52.

———: "The Industrialization of Service," *Harvard Business Review,* September–October 1976, pp. 63–74.

LOVELOCK, C. H., and R. F. YOUNG: "Look to Customers to Increase Productivity," *Harvard Business Review,* May–June 1979, pp. 168–178.

MILLS, P. K., R. B. CHASE, and N. MARGULIES: "Motivating the Client/Employee System as a Service Production Strategy," *Academy of Management Review,* vol. 8, no. 2, 1983, pp. 301–310.

ORLOFF, C. S.: "Routing a Fleet of M-Vehicles to/from a Central Facility," *Networks,* vol. 4, 1974, pp. 147–162.

RUSSELL, ROBERT: "An Effective Heuristic for the M-Tour Traveling Salesman Problem with Some Side Conditions," *Operations Research,* vol. 25, no. 3, May–June 1977, pp. 517–525.

SCHMENNER, ROGER: "How Can Service Business Survive and Prosper?" *Sloan Management Review,* Spring 1986, pp. 21–32.

SHOSTACK, G. L.: "Designing Services That Deliver," *Harvard Business Review,* January–February 1984, pp. 133–139.

———: "Service Positioning through Structural Change," *Journal of Marketing,* vol. 51, January 1987, pp. 34–43.

———: "How to Design a Service," *European Journal of Marketing,* vol. 16, no. 1, 1982, pp. 49–63.

SUPPLEMENT:

THE SERVICE DELIVERY SYSTEM: VEHICLE ROUTING

Delivery of some services requires travel to the customer's location. In these cases, a method to develop vehicle routes quickly that minimize time and distance traveled becomes an important consideration in service design. An algorithm to perform this task will be developed and illustrated here.

On a typical Saturday, a college student may need to accomplish several tasks: work out at the gym, do some research in the library, go to the laundromat, and stop at a food market. Assuming no constraints on when these tasks may be done, the student faces no great obstacle in developing an itinerary that will require the least amount of time and distance traveled. The solution is straightforward and can be formulated in one's head.

Many services likewise must develop itineraries, but in these cases, the solutions may not be as obvious as the college student's. Examples range from Federal Express's ground transportation pick-up and delivery routes to bread deliveries at your local supermarket to a telephone repair person's route each day. Clearly, these cases require a useful tool to determine acceptable routing and scheduling without a great deal of hassle.

Enter G. Clarke and J. W. Wright, who in the 1960s developed the Clarke-Wright (C-W) algorithm to schedule vehicles operating from a central depot and serving several outlying points.[8] In practice, the C-W algorithm is applied to a problem through a series of iterations until an acceptable solution is obtained. Practical applications of the algorithm may not necessarily be optimal, but the short amount of time and the ease with which it can be applied to problems that are not elementary and straightforward make it an extremely useful tool. The logic of this algorithm, which involves a savings concept, serves as the basis for the more sophisticated techniques available in many commercial software programs.

The C-W savings concept considers the savings that can be realized by linking pairs of "delivery" points in a system that is composed of a central depot serving the outlying sites. As a very simple example, consider Bridgette's Bagel Bakery. Bridgette bakes her bagels during downtime at her brother Bernie's Beaucoup Bistro. Then she must transport her bagels to two sidewalk concession stands that are run by her sisters, Bernadette and Louise. Each stand is located 5 miles

from the Bistro, but the stands themselves are 6 miles apart. The layout may be represented graphically as follows:

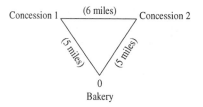

In this situation, the C-W algorithm first looks at the cost of driving from the bakery to one concession and back to the bakery, and then driving to the second concession and back to the bakery. Therefore, the total cost is equal to the sum of the costs (in miles) of driving from 0 to 1 and returning ($2C_{01}$) and driving from 0 to 2 and returning ($2C_{02}$), or

$$\text{Total cost} = 2C_{01} + 2C_{02}$$

Bridgette's total cost for following this route is 2×5 (miles) $+ 2 \times 5$ (miles), or 20 miles.

The C-W algorithm next considers the savings that can be realized by driving from the bakery to one concession, then to the second concession, and finally back to the bakery. This route saves Bridgette the cost of one trip from concession 1 back to the bakery and of one trip from the bakery to concession 2, but it adds the cost of the trip from concession 1 to concession 2. The net savings, S_{ij}, gained by linking any two locations i and j into the same route is expressed as

$$S_{ij} = C_{0i} + C_{0j} - C_{ij}$$

Bridgette would realize a net savings of 4 miles from linking the two concessions by creating one trip from the bakery to concession 1 and then traveling to concession 2 and returning to the bakery.

$$\begin{aligned} S_{12} &= C_{01} + C_{02} - C_{12} \\ &= 5 + 5 - 6 \\ &= 4 \end{aligned}$$

[8]G. Clarke and J. W. Wright, "Scheduling of Vehicles from a Central Depot to a Number of Delivery Points," *Operations Research*, vol. 12, no. 4, July–August 1964, pp. 568–581.

Admittedly, this example can be solved easily by inspection, and it does not require a sophisticated heuristic. Even so, it does serve as a convenient illustration of the savings concept that forms the basis of the C-W algorithm.

USING THE C-W ALGORITHM UNCONSTRAINED

Application of the C-W algorithm to a less obvious situation proceeds through five steps, which will be described as we put them to work helping Bridgette, who is expanding her bagel service to four concessions in outlying areas. The distances related to each of these concessions and the bakery are given in Exhibit 1.

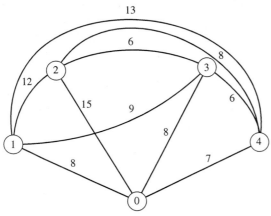

Exhibit 1. *Network of bakery and four concessions with distances in miles.*

1. *Construct a shortest-distance half-matrix (i.e., the matrix will contain the shortest distance between each pair of sites, including the starting location). A half-matrix is sufficient for this use, because travel distance or time is the same in both directions.* The shortest-distance half-matrix for Bridgette's bakery and the four outlying concessions is shown in Exhibit 2. (*Note:* For very large problems, the shortest distances may not be obvious. In these cases, computer software to make these calculations is available.)

		Concessions			
		1	2	3	4
Bakery	0	8	15	8	7
	1		12	9	13
Concessions	2			6	8
	3				6

Exhibit 2. *Shortest-distance half-matrix: miles between bakery and concessions.*

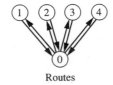

Routes

2. *Develop an initial allocation of one round-trip to each destination.* Note in the diagram below that each concession is linked to the bakery by double lines with directional arrows. Four round-trips are represented.

3. *Calculate the net savings for each pair of outlying locations, and enter them in a net savings half-matrix.* These net savings for each pair of outlying locations are calculated using the equation for S_{ij}, just as we did in Bridgette's initial problem. In this example, the net savings from linking concessions 1 and 2 is $8 + 15 - 12 = 11$. Similar calculations are made for each of the other possible pairs, and the values then are entered into a net savings half-matrix, as shown in Exhibit 3.

		Concessions			
		1	2	3	4
Bakery	0	...	...	...	...
	1		11	7	2
Concessions	2			17	14
	3				9

Exhibit 3. *Net savings between all concession pairs.*

4. *Enter values for a special trip indicator T into appropriate cells of the net savings half-matrix.* Our net savings calculation for linking each pair is based on how much is saved relative to the cost of the vehicle making a round-trip to each member of the pair. We will add to our net savings half-matrix the indicator T, which will show if two locations in question—for example, i and j or 0 (which represents the point of origin) and j—are directly linked. T may have one of three values, as given below:

   a. $T = 2$ when a vehicle travels from the point of origin (Bridgette's bakery in our example) to location j (concession 1, 2, 3, or 4 in our example) and then returns. This is designated as $T_{0j} = 2$ and will appear only in the first row of the half-matrix. The appropriate value of T is entered into the net savings half-matrix and circled to distinguish it from the savings value. Remember, $T = 2$ indicates a *round-trip*.

   b. $T = 1$ when a vehicle travels *one way directly* between two locations i and j. This is designated as $T_{ij} = 1$ and can appear anywhere in the half-matrix. Remember, $T = 1$ indicates a *one-way trip*.

   c. $T = 0$ when a vehicle does *not* travel *directly* between two particular locations i and j. Accordingly, this is designated as $T_{ij} = 0$. Remember, $T = 0$ indicates that *no trip* is made between that pair of locations.

By convention, the $T = 0$ value is not entered; a cell without a T value of 1 or 2 noted in the matrix is understood to have a $T = 0$. It is important to recognize that for each location x, the sum of the T values in column x plus the sum of the T values in row x must equal 2 (i.e., a vehicle must arrive and depart for every location served).

Exhibit 4a shows Bridgette's net savings half-matrix for her four new concessions, with the appropriate T value of 2

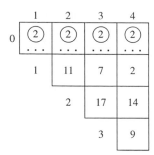

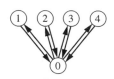

Routes

Routes: First trip: 0–1–0
Second trip: 0–2–0
Third trip: 0–3–0
Fourth trip: 0–4–0

Exhibit 4a. *Initial solution.*

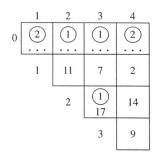

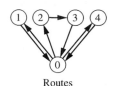

Routes

Routes: First trip: 0–1–0
Second trip: 0–2–3–0
Third trip: 0–4–0

Exhibit 4b. *First iteration.*

listed in the cells representing round-trips between the bakery and each concession location. Note that the directional lines on the graphical depiction of this initial solution indicate a round-trip to each location.

5. *Identify the cell in the net savings half-matrix that contains the maximum net savings.* If the maximum net savings occurs in cell *(i, j)* in the half-matrix, then locations *i* and *j* can be linked if, and only if, the following conditions are met:
   a. T_{0i} and T_{0j} must be greater than zero.
   b. Locations *i* and *j* are not already on the same route or loop.
   c. Linking locations *i* and *j* does not violate any system constraints, which will be discussed later.

If all three conditions *are* met, set $T_{ij} = 1$. In Bridgette's case, cell (2, 3) has the highest net savings (i.e., 17). T_{02} and T_{03} are each greater than zero, locations 2 and 3 are not already on the same route, and at present, there are no constraints to linking locations 2 and 3. Thus, all conditions are met, and we may enter a *T* value of 1 in cell (2, 3), as shown in Exhibit 4*b*. This $T_{23} = 1$ in the cell indicates a *one-way trip* between concessions 2 and 3. At the same time that we have established the one-way trip between locations 2 and 3, we have eliminated a one-way trip from location 2 back to the bakery (0) and another one-way trip from the bakery to location 3. Therefore, it is necessary to reduce the *T* = 2 values in cells (0, 2) and (0, 3) to *T* = 1 in each. Exhibit 4*b* shows the appropriate *T* values for this new iteration, and the graphical depiction indicates the three new one-way routes.

If any one of the conditions—5*a*, 5*b*, or 5*c*—is not met, then identify the cell with the next highest savings, and repeat step 5. If necessary, repeat this inspection until you have identified the cell with the highest savings that satisfies all three conditions, and set its *T* value equal to 1 (remember to reduce the appropriate *T* = 2 or *T* = 1 values in row 0). If no cell meets the conditions, then the algorithm ends. (The algorithm also ends when all locations are linked together on a single route, which we will discover as we proceed with Bridgette's problem.)

This first application of the C-W algorithm has saved Bridgette 17 miles, but still more savings can be realized by subjecting her data to another iteration of step 5. Looking again at Exhibit 4*b*, we can identify cell (2, 4) as having the

next highest net savings value (i.e., 14). T_{02} and T_{04} are each greater than zero, locations 2 and 4 are not on the same route at present, and there are no constraints against having locations 2 and 4 on the same route. Therefore, we can link these two locations. Enter *T* = 1 in cell (2, 4), and reduce each of the *T* values in cells (0, 2) and (0, 4) by one trip, as shown in Exhibit 4*c*. Note in the graphical depiction that the trips from the bakery to concession 2 and from concession 4 back to the bakery have been eliminated, thus requiring an adjustment of the directional arrows.

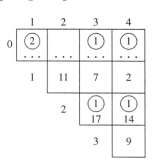

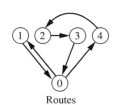

Routes

Routes: First trip: 0–1–0
Second trip:
0–4–2–3–0

Exhibit 4c. *Second iteration.*

Is further improvement possible? The next highest net savings is 11, found in cell (1, 2). In this situation, T_{01} is greater than zero, but T_{02} is not. Therefore, linking these two locations would violate condition 5*a*. Moving on, cell (3, 4) has the next highest net savings. The T_{03} and T_{04} values are each greater than zero, but concessions 3 and 4 are already on the same route, which violates condition 5*b*. Therefore, we must look at the next highest net savings, which is 7, in cell (1, 3). Here, T_{01} and T_{03} are each greater than zero, concessions 1 and 3 are not already on the same route, and no constraints exist. Therefore, we may link these two locations. We enter *T* = 1 in cell (1, 3) and reduce the *T* values in cells (0, 1) and (0, 3) by 1 each, as shown in Exhibit 4*d*. We have removed one trip between the bakery and concession 1 and one trip from concession 3 to the bakery. The directional arrows suggest that a counterclockwise route be used, but our assumption of equal time or distance traveling in either direction would permit the final route to be traversed in either direction.

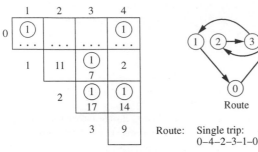

Exhibit 4d. *Final solution.*

Route: Single trip: 0–4–2–3–1–0

USING THE C-W ALGORITHM WITH CONSTRAINTS

Suppose that business booms and Bridgette decides to supply four new franchise operations, and that these franchises are located according to the schematic shown in Exhibit 5. Unfortunately, Bridgette cannot carry enough bagels in her Blue Bagel Beamer to supply all the new locations on a single route such as the one we constructed in the previous section. Each franchise requires 500 bagels per day, and she can transport a maximum of 1000 bagels per trip. How can we use the C-W algorithm to solve Bridgette's problem? In general, the introduction of a constraint such as Bridgette's capacity limit or a delivery-time window does not alter the method of applying the algorithm. We need only account for the constraint so it does not violate step 5c.

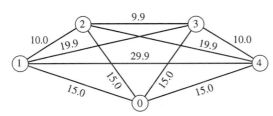

Exhibit 5. *Network representation of a single bakery and four concessions.*

In the present example, our first step again is to construct a shortest-distance half-matrix containing the distance between each pair of locations, as shown in Exhibit 6. Next, we construct the net savings half-matrix and enter the appropriate $T = 2$ values for the initial solution, as shown in Exhibit 7a. (Note that we have not included graphical depictions of the individual trips and their directional arrows

	1	2	3	4
Bakery 0	15.0	15.0	15.0	15.0
1		10.0	19.9	29.9
2			9.9	19.9
3				10.0

Exhibit 6. *Shortest-distance half-matrix: miles between pairs of locations.*

in this example, although some readers may find it helpful to add such sketches.)

Note that cell (2, 3) has the largest net savings and satisfies all the conditions under step 5 of the C-W algorithm. Therefore, we can link locations 2 and 3. Enter the $T = 1$ value in cell (2, 3), and reduce the T values in cells (0, 2) and (0, 3) to 1, as shown in Exhibit 7b.

	1	2	3	4
Bakery 0	② ···	② ···	② ···	② ···
1		20.0	10.1	0.1
2			20.1	10.1
3				20.0

Routes: First trip: 0–1–0
Second trip: 0–2–0
Third trip: 0–3–0
Fourth trip: 0–4–0

Exhibit 7a. *Initial solution.*

	1	2	3	4
Bakery 0	② ···	① ···	① ···	② ···
1		20.0	10.1	0.1
2			① 20.1	10.1
3				20.0

Routes: First trip: 0–1–0
Second trip: 0–2–3–0
Third trip: 0–4–0

Exhibit 7b. *First iteration.*

The route just established from the bakery to franchise 2 to franchise 3 and back to the bakery (0–2–3–0) cannot have any more links added, because additional links would exceed Bridgette's capacity (a violation of condition 5c). Therefore, we must eliminate the following links: (1, 2), (1, 3), (2, 4), and (3, 4). The only link that remains possible is between locations 1 and 4. Adding the $T = 1$ value to cell (1, 4) and reducing the T values in cells (0, 1) and (0, 4) yields the final solution, as shown in Exhibit 7c.

	1	2	3	4
Bakery 0	① ···	① ···	① ···	① ···
1		20.0	10.1	① 0.1
2			① 20.1	10.1
3				20.0

Routes: First trip: 0–2–3–0
Second trip: 0–1–4–0

Exhibit 7c. *Final solution.*

Exhibit 8 shows the final routes that we constructed. The total mileage to be driven is 99.8; however, Exhibit 9 shows an alternate route devised from inspection that does the job in only 80 miles! As noted earlier, the C-W algorithm does not guarantee an optimal solution every time. In fact,

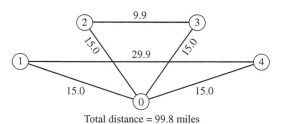

Total distance = 99.8 miles

Exhibit 8. *Final routes developed.*

in this simple case, the solution with the algorithm is approximately 25 percent poorer than the optimal solution. In general, however, the algorithm is highly effective, yielding very acceptable results, that, when combined with its simplicity of use, make it a very useful tool for developing vehicle routes.

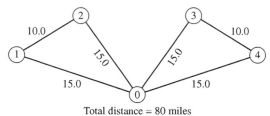

Total distance = 80 miles

Exhibit 9. *Optimal solution.*

USE OF A "MINIMAL TECHNOLOGY ROUTING SYSTEM"

Bartholdi et al. have reported using a very clever, manual method for routing vehicles that deliver Meals on Wheels (MOW) for Senior Citizens Services, Inc., in Atlanta, Georgia.[9] This program involved delivering a very large number of lunches to people located in a widely dispersed pattern within the city. This alone could daunt the most intrepid vehicle scheduler, but consider an added complication: the clientele being served were incapacitated, mostly by age and/or illness, which resulted in a high turnover of clients and, accordingly, in routes that had to be changed. Moreover, the sponsoring organization did not have the funding for sophisticated computers or skilled people to operate

them. In fact, at the time of this study, one person was responsible for all administrative aspects of the program.

So, MOW needed a way of routing and scheduling that could accommodate the following constraints:

1. A large and frequently changing clientele made necessary the ability to add and remove both clients and locations easily.
2. It was necessary to allot the delivery work equally, because meals were delivered by four drivers who were paid by the hour and each was anxious to have his or her fair share of the work.
3. The program had to be utilized without computer support.
4. The program had to be utilized by an "unskilled" scheduler.

Very simply, the solution was first to assign each location on a grid of the Atlanta city map a Θ (theta) value. This part was done by the researchers using a traveling-salesperson heuristic based on a "space-filling curve" concept. The resulting Θ map would form a reference sheet for the MOW manager to use in scheduling the routes and vehicles. Next, two Rolodex cards were made for each client; the client's cards contained his or her name and address and the Θ value of that address. One card was inserted in one Rolodex alphabetically, and the other was filed in a second Rolodex according to increasing values of Θ.

Using the system was an exercise in elegance and simplicity. First, the Θ file, which was organized according to Θ location, was manually divided into four relatively equal parts, and each part was assigned to one delivery person. Accommodating changes in clientele was equally easy. As a person was removed from the service, his or her card was pulled from the alphabetical file, the Θ value was noted, and the corresponding card was pulled from the Θ file. This automatically updated the route. Similarly, when a client was added to the service, his or her cards were added to the files, and again, the routing was automatically updated. In practice, this system proved to work exceedingly well.

Obviously, many methods exist to facilitate vehicle routing and scheduling, and it would not be possible to explore each and every one in this space. We have, however, looked at one of the most widely used methods, the Clarke-Wright algorithm, and at another method that is charming in its simplicity and usefulness.

[9]Adapted from J. J. Bartholdi III, L. K. Platzman, R. L. Collins, and W. H. Warden III, "A Minimal Technology Routing System for Meals on Wheels," *Interfaces*, vol. 13, no. 3, June 1983, pp. 1–8.

SOLVED PROBLEMS

1. Unconstrained Route

Problem Statement

A cable TV installer has the new accounts shown on the map below to visit today for hook-up. Her office is located at node 0 with distances shown in miles between all places she must visit. What route will minimize her total distance traveled to visit each account and return to the office at the end of her workday?

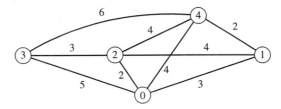

Solution

Step 1: Prepare shortest distance matrix

	1	2	3	4
0	3	2	5	4
1		4	7	2
2			3	4
3				6

Step 2: Prepare savings matrix using the expression $S_{ij} = C_{0i} + C_{0j} - C_{ij}$

	1	2	3	4
0	...	...	...	...
1		1	1	5
2			4	2
3				3

Step 3: Look for the largest savings (5), and connect accounts 1 and 4, creating the routes shown below:

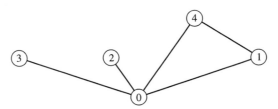

Step 4: Look for the next largest savings (4), and connect accounts 2 and 3, creating the routes shown below:

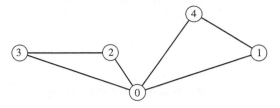

Step 5: Look for the next largest savings (3), and connect accounts 3 and 4, creating the final single route shown below with total travel distance of 16 miles:

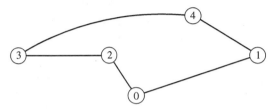

2. Route Constrained by Time Window

Problem Statement

For the cable TV installer, assume that the even-numbered accounts (2, 4) must be accomplished in the morning and the odd-numbered accounts (1, 3) in the afternoon.

Solution

Step 1: Using the savings matrix above, connect accounts 2 and 4, creating the route shown below. If more than two accounts had existed, we would find the largest savings and proceed to build a route with even-numbered accounts.

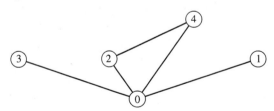

Step 2: Look for the largest savings (5), and connect accounts 1 and 4, creating the routes shown below:

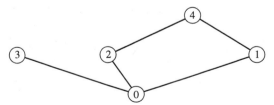

Step 3: Connect accounts 3 and 1, creating the final single route with total distance of 20 miles shown below. Note that accounts 3 and 2 could not be connected, because the resulting route would leave accounts 2 and 4 in the middle of a route violating the time window.

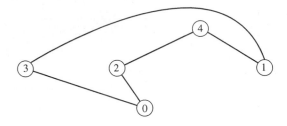

EXERCISES

1. For the following net savings matrix, find the recommended route.

	1	2	3	4
0	...	...	...	...
1		3	2	5
2			7	9
3				8

2. For the following net savings matrix, find the recommended route.

	1	2	3	4
0	...	...	...	...
1		2	4	3
2			5	7
3				2

3. The *New York Times* delivery service has customers at four apartments in the northwest part of town. Recommend an efficient route given the shortest-distance matrix in miles below for travel from the distribution center to and between the apartments.

	1	2	3	4
0	6	7	9	8
1		12	13	12
2			8	9
3				14

4. A florist has received orders to deliver flowers to four office buildings. The matrix below contains the shortest distance in miles between the florist's shop and the offices. Construct a net savings matrix, and recommend a route to minimize the distance traveled.

	1	2	3	4
0	6	6	9	8
1		7	11	12
2			5	9
3				10

5. The Lone Star Beer distributor makes deliveries to four taverns from a central warehouse, as shown in the figure below. Distances are given in miles.
   a. Construct a shortest-route matrix for travel between all pairs of locations.
   b. Construct a net savings matrix.
   c. Recommend a delivery route to minimize the distance traveled.

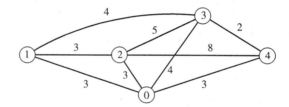

6. A university is planning to serve four off-campus apartments with a shuttle bus service. Given the net savings matrix below, recommend a bus route that minimizes the distance traveled.

	1	2	3	4
0	...	...	...	...
1	9	14	2	
2		16	7	
3			11	

7. Wal-Mart has five distribution centers and one central warehouse. Below are the distances between all nodes (0 = warehouse). Construct the net savings matrix for this problem, and determine a route to minimize the distance traveled to serve all five distribution centers.

0-1	10 mi	1-2	7 mi	2-4	20 mi
0-2	10 mi	1-3	16 mi	2-5	19 mi
0-3	14 mi	1-4	13 mi	3-4	6 mi
0-4	12 mi	1-5	8 mi	3-5	18 mi
0-5	13 mi	2-3	5 mi	4-5	6 mi

8. The city refuse collection department uses a fleet of small trucks that collect trash around the city and make periodic deliveries to four staging sites. Currently, two dump trucks transport the trash from these staging sites to an incinerator. One truck is assigned to service sites 1 and 2 and the other to sites 3 and 4. The network in the figure below gives the miles between the staging sites and the incinerator, which is shown as node 0.

    a. What is the cost per day to operate this two-truck system if gasoline is $1.50 per gallon and the trucks average 5 miles per gallon and make 10 trips to each staging site per day? Truck drivers are paid $80 per day.

    b. A proposal has been made to purchase one large diesel truck with enough capacity to visit all four staging sites during one trip. What should be its route to minimize the distance traveled?

    c. If diesel fuel costs $1 per gallon and the truck averages 10 miles per gallon, determine the daily savings in operating costs.

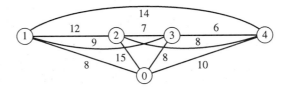

Case: The Daley Monthly Car Pool[10]

Alice Daley, owner and publisher of the local periodical *The Daley Monthly,* has a staff of six writers. Currently, employees drive in each morning from their homes, as shown in the figure below:

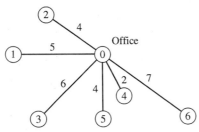

    Because of increasing gasoline prices, however, the employees have approached Ms. Daley with a suggestion to use the company's nine-passenger van for a car pool. In considering this idea, Ms. Daley collected the additional data shown below on mileage between all pairs of employee locations.

1-2	2 mi	2-3	5 mi	3-5	5 mi
1-3	4 mi	2-4	6 mi	3-6	10 mi
1-4	6 mi	2-5	7 mi	4-5	3 mi
1-5	6 mi	2-6	11 mi	4-6	5 mi
1-6	12 mi	3-4	6 mi	5-6	5 mi

An alternative to using the company van is using an economy car. A compact car can hold only three passengers, however, so it would require two trips. Even so, the average of 26 miles per gallon for the compact compared with 12 miles per gallon for the van makes this option worth considering, particularly when gasoline is averaging 90 cents per gallon.

    One final consideration is traffic congestion. The average possible speed is 30 miles per hour before 8 AM and 15 miles per hour between 8 and 9 AM.

QUESTIONS

1 What is the total cost of gasoline per day under the current arrangement of employees driving their own cars? Assume that fuel economy is 10 miles per gallon.

2 Find the least costly route for a car pool using the nine-passenger van. What would be the cost of gasoline per day for this arrangement?

3 What time would the van need to leave the office to return with all employees by 8 AM? By 9 AM?

4 If the employee living at location 6 offered to keep the van overnight, how is the route changed? To use the C-W algorithm, what must we now consider to be the origin?

5 If the compact car were used, what routes would you recommend to minimize the gasoline expense? What would the daily cost of gasoline be for this proposal?

---

[10]Prepared by Roland Bressler and Raymond Matthews under the supervision of James A. Fitzsimmons.

6 At what time would the compact car need to leave the office to begin its pick-ups to be finished by 8 AM? By 9 AM?

7 Would your routes be modified if the employees living at locations 2 and 5 volunteered to use their compact cars and left from home to begin pick-ups?

8 What advantages and disadvantages are there to starting work at 8 AM?

Case: Airport Services, Inc.[11]

Airport Services, Inc., is planning to implement a remote shuttle service among five terminals and the Port Welkin Airport. Mr. Kelly Mist has been given the task of developing the route and service schedules for the proposed operation to be used in the franchise application to the Port Welkin City Council. Mrs. Janet Rush, Mr. Mist's supervisor, asks him to create schedules with low operating costs for each round trip. Mrs. Rush states that with the locations currently in mind for terminal sites, Airport Services may have to run five buses, one between each terminal and the airport. She is hopeful, however, that fewer buses can be used.

ASSIGNMENTS

1. Mr. Mist is given the following information on which his analysis must be based:

Average operating cost: $0.455 per kilometer

Average operating speed: 60 kilometers per hour

Average layover time per stop: 9 minutes

From a city map, he develops a distance matrix for all proposed service locations, designating the airport as site 0. All distances are given in kilometers.

	1	2	3	4	5
0	10	4	5	5	7
1		7	11	15	6
2			8	9	8
3				6	4
4					9

Using the Clarke-Wright algorithm, recommend the best routing schedule under Mrs. Rush's least-cost objective.

2. Mrs. Rush's initial reaction to Mr. Mist's work is very favorable; however, she has just been informed by the mayor that Port Welkin will require each bus to have a round-trip time (to and from the airport) of 40 minutes or less, excluding the loading and unloading time at the airport only. Although Mrs. Rush realizes that this will offer the shuttle users faster service, she is sure that it will cost the company more money.

Develop a new routing schedule that will meet this new time constraint yet still keep Airport Services's costs low.

3. The Port Welkin City Council awarded Airport Services a shuttle franchise on the basis of Mr. Mist's latest routing plan, and Mrs. Rush feels that initiation of the service has gone about as well as could be expected. Mr. Mist informs her that they are experiencing a recurring shortage of capacity at terminal 3; that is, there are more people boarding the bus than there are seats available. Mrs. Rush decides to seek a solution that meets the franchise conditions but does not require people to stand or use any more vehicles, even though the operating costs may rise slightly. Mr. Mist has analyzed the normal average boarding and alighting volumes at each remote terminal, as shown below. Also, he knows that Airport Services is using 48-passenger vehicles, which usually are full when leaving the airport on a multistop route.

Develop a routing schedule that will incorporate the additional capacity constraint. How does this final solution compare with the previous two solutions regarding operating costs and round-trip time?

Terminal	Avg. No. Boarding	Avg. No. Alighting
1	28	30
2	20	18
3	18	14
4	21	26
5	30	32

[11]Prepared by James Vance under the supervision of James A. Fitzsimmons.

CHAPTER 17

Managing Queues

The management of queues at Burger King represents an evolving process of refinement. When these stores first opened, a "conventional" lineup was used that required customers to arrange themselves in single file behind a single cash register, where orders were taken. Assemblers prepared the orders and presented them to customers at the far end of the counter. This conventional style of line-up often is called the "snake," as mentioned in the following *Wall Street Journal* article.[1]

Louis Kane hates snakes.

The restaurant executive means the single lines that feed customers one at a time to a group of cashiers. He thinks snakes are much too "institutional." Besides, he says, he would rather try to guess which line will move the fastest. But surveys show that customers prefer snakes to multiple lines because they hate "getting stuck behind some guy ordering nine cappuccinos, each with something different on top," says Mr. Kane, co-chairman of the Boston-based Au Bon Pain soup-and-sandwich chain.

The customers have won. Over the past couple of years, Au Bon Pain has instituted snakes at every restaurant that has enough room. But the debate lives on. "We talk about this a great deal," Mr. Kane says.

The issue is queues. Experts suggest that no aspect of customer service is more important than the wait in line to be served. The act of waiting—either in person or on the phone—"has a disproportionately high impact" on customers, says David Maister, a Boston consultant who has studied the psychology of waiting. "The wait can destroy an otherwise perfect service experience."

A customer waiting in line is potentially a lost customer. According to one study, up to 27 percent of customers who can't get through on the telephone will either buy elsewhere or skip the transaction altogether, says Rudy Oetting, a senior partner at Oetting & Co., a New York company that consults on telephone use. Adds Russell James, an official at Avis Rent a Car Inc.: "You can't be out-lined by a competitor or you will lose business."

Today's customers are also more demanding than ever. "The dramatic difference between 1980 and 1990 can be described in one word: speed," says N. Powell Taylor, manager of GE Answer Center, a General Electric Co. operation that fields three million calls a year. "People expect quicker answers. No one has the time any more."

In the past few years particularly, many companies have stepped up efforts to shorten waits—or at least make them more tolerable. Here are some of the methods they are trying:

Animate

Some contend that a wait isn't a wait if it's fun. At Macy's in New York now, the line to see Santa Claus wends its way through displays of dancing teddy bears, elves, and electric trains. "It's part of the adventure of going to see Santa Claus," says Jean McFaddin, a vice president at the big department store, where 300,000 people see Santa in 30 days.

At Disneyland and Walt Disney World, the waits—which can be up to 90 minutes long—are planned along with the attractions themselves. Visitors waiting for rides that board continuously pass animated displays that are designed to be viewed as people walk along. Waits for theater shows include such attractions as singers and handicraft displays aimed at audiences that will be waiting in one place as long as 30 minutes. Indeed, the waits themselves are called "preshows." Says Norman Doerges, executive vice president of Disneyland, "that's what makes the time pass, is the entertainment."

At the Omni Park Central Hotel in New York, when a line exceeds six people, assistant managers are dispatched to the hotel restaurant to bring out orange

[1]Reprinted with permission. Amanda Bennett, "Their Business Is on the Line," *The Wall Street Journal,* Dec. 7, 1990, p. B1. Reprinted by permission of *The Wall Street Journal,* 1989, Dow Jones & Company, Inc. All Rights Reserved Worldwide.

and grapefruit juice to serve to the people in line. "We are trying to tell the guest 'we know you are here,' " says Philip Georgas, general manager and regional vice president.

Still, not all diversions are suitable. Many callers don't like listening to recordings while they're on hold. GE plays its corporate theme for customers while they wait, but it draws the line at playing recorded advertising. "We tend to stay away from commercials," says Mr. Taylor, because of the fear that customers will think company employees "are probably sitting there doing nothing," making customers wait so they will have to listen to the commercials.

Discriminate

"The key thing is not just moving people out of the line," says Mr. James at Avis. "The key is who you move out of the line." For the past two years, high-volume renters at Avis have been able to sign a permanent rental agreement in advance and be driven directly to their cars when they arrive at many Avis locations. Somewhat less-frequent renters check in at a kiosk near the car park. Other car rental concerns are offering similar preferential services.

Such service is increasingly common in the travel, banking, and credit-card industries. But "one needs a great deal of creativity in this area" lest less-favored customers be offended, says Mr. Maister. "Those businesses that want to serve priority customers faster are best advised to do it out of sight of the regular customers." He cites some airlines that locate first-class check-in counters away from the economy counters. "You don't want to rub the noses of the economy passengers in it."

Automate

While assembly-line techniques can accelerate manufacturing operations, they often slow the delivery of services. When callers must speak to several different people to get a complete answer, "crew interference" sets in, says Warren Blanding, editor of *Customer Service Newsletter* in Silver Spring, Md. "The most efficient way to do a job is to have one person do it."

So Employers Health Insurance, Green Bay, Wis., has assembled a complex computer data base of scripts that employees can read to customers on the telephone. The employee keys in the caller's name, location and type of health insurance question. The computer then pops up a question-and-answer format that can be read verbatim.

"We know that 75 percent of the calls we get in are standard questions," says Sterling L. Phaklides, an assistant vice president in the claims division. "Because people are sticking to the scripts, they are giving up-to-date information" without consulting technicians, he says. But callers who ask questions that aren't covered in the scripts can be referred to specialists at any point. "It does save telephone time," the official says. The claims area handles 3,700 calls a day; only about 1 percent of callers hang up before they are connected—which is better than average, he says.

Obfuscate

Mr. Maister says the perceived wait is often more important than the actual wait. In a paper on the psychology of waiting, he notes that some restaurants deliberately announce longer waiting times, thus pleasing customers when the wait is actually shorter. At Disneyland in Anaheim, Calif., lines snake around corners, Mr. Maister says. Thus people focus more on how fast the line is moving than on how long the line is.

Disneyland says its aim isn't to deceive. It posts waiting times at the start of each line. "A big danger in disguising a line is that people don't know what they are getting into," says Mr. Doerges. "If you do it without proper preparation, people get frustrated."

Still, some think that even that information will be too depressing. Technology is available that will announce a caller's place in line, but Penny Rhode, vice president, customer service, at First Gibralter Bank in Dallas, chose not to use it. "I felt like . . . focusing on the positive, rather than perhaps saying that there are fourteen callers ahead of you."

Under First Gibralter's system, after 1½ minutes a phone voice offers the caller the option of continuing to wait or leaving a message. Since it started the system in October, the bank has averaged about 100 messages a day out of between 3,000 and 3,200 calls.

Dissatisfaction with the slowness of a single-line arrangement led Burger King to try the "hospitality" line-up, in which cash registers are evenly spaced along the counter and customers select a line (in effect betting on which of several will move the fastest). In this arrangement, the cashier who takes an order also assembles the order. Although the hospitality line-up proves to be very flexible in meeting peak-period demand, it does tend to be more labor-intensive than the conventional line-up. Consequently, Burger King made yet another change, this time to what is called a "multiconventional" lineup, which is a hybrid of both earlier systems. The restaurant returned to a single line, but a new cash register now allows up to six orders to be recorded at the same time. Assemblers prepare the orders and distribute them at the end of the counter. Returning to a single line has guaranteed fairness, because customers are served in the order of their arrival. In addition, customers have enough time to make their meal selection without slowing the entire order-taking process.

Burger King's concern with reducing customer waiting time represents a trend toward providing faster service. In many cases, speed of delivery is viewed as a competitive advantage in the marketplace. For example, many hotels today will total your bill and slide it under your room door during the last night of your stay, thereby achieving "zero waiting time" at the check-out counter.

Fluctuations in demand for service are difficult to cope with, because the consumption and production of services occur simultaneously. Customers typically arrive at random and place immediate demands on the available service. If service capacity is fully utilized at the time of his or her arrival, then the customer is expected to wait patiently in line. Varying arrival rates and service time requirements result in the formation of queues (i.e., lines of customers waiting their turn for service). The management of queues is a continuing challenge for service managers.

CHAPTER PREVIEW

Our understanding of waiting lines begins with a definition of queuing systems and the inevitability of waiting, and then the implications of asking people to wait are studied further from a psychological perspective. We shall discover that the perception of waiting often is more important to the consumer than the actual time spent waiting, suggesting that innovative ways should be found to reduce the negative aspects of waiting. The economic value of waiting as a cost for the provider and currency for the consumer also is considered. Finally, the essential features of a service system are discussed in terms of a schematic queuing model, and queuing terminology is defined.

QUEUING SYSTEMS

A *queue* is a line of waiting customers who require service from one or more servers. The queue need not be a physical line of individuals in front of a server, however. It might be students sitting at computer terminals that are scattered around a college campus, or a person being placed on "hold" by a telephone operator. Servers typically are considered to be individual stations where customers receive service. The stereotypical queue—people waiting in a formal line for service—is seen at the check-out counters of a supermarket and the teller windows in a bank, yet queuing systems occur in a variety of forms. Consider the following variations:

1. Servers need not be limited to serving one customer at a time. Transportation systems such as buses, airplanes, and elevators are bulk services.

2. The consumer need not always travel to the service facility; in some systems, the server actually comes to the consumer. This approach is illustrated by urban services such as fire and police protection as well as by ambulance service.

3. The service may consist of stages of queues in a series or of a more complex network of queues. For example, consider the haunted-house attraction at amusement parks like Disneyland, where queues are staged in sequence so that visitors can be processed in batches and entertained during the waiting periods (e.g., first outside on the walk, then in the vestibule, and finally on the ride itself).

In any service system, a queue forms whenever current demand exceeds the existing capacity to serve. This occurs when servers are so busy that arriving consumers cannot receive immediate service. Such a situation is bound to occur in any system for which arrivals occur at varying times and service times also vary.

THE INEVITABILITY OF WAITING

As Figure 1 shows, waiting is part of everyone's life, and it can involve an incredible amount of time. For example, a typical day might include waiting at several stoplights, waiting for someone to answer the telephone, waiting for your meal to be served, waiting for the elevator, waiting to be checked out at the supermarket—the list goes on and on.

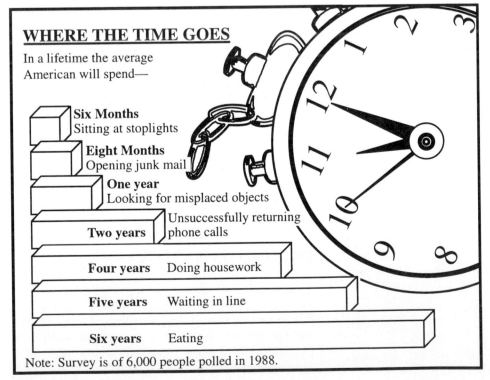

Figure 1. *Where the time goes.*
Source: Copyright, 1989, *U.S. News & World Report,* January 30, 1989, p. 81.

In the old Soviet Union and even the newly independent countries that have formed since its break-up, we find dramatic examples of the role that queuing can play in people's daily lives. A noted Russian scholar, Hedrick Smith, observed that the queue in that country is a national pastime:

> Personally, I have known of people who stood in line 90 minutes to buy four pineapples, three hours for a two-minute roller coaster ride, three and a half hours to buy three large heads of cabbage only to find the cabbages were gone as they approached the front of the line, eighteen hours to sign up to purchase a rug at some later date, all through a freezing December night to register on a list for buying a car, and then waiting eighteen more months for actual delivery, and terribly lucky at that. Lines can run from a few yards long to half a block to nearly a mile, and usually they move at an excruciating creep.[2]

He also found that there was a matter of line etiquette. Line jumping by serious shoppers was accepted for ordinary items but not for scarce ones. Smith observed:

> "People know from experience that things actually run out while they are standing in line," advised one young [woman]. "So if the line is for something really good and you leave it for very long, people get very upset. They fly off the handle and curse you and try to keep you from getting back in when you return. It's up to the person behind you to defend your place in line. So it's serious business asking someone to hold your place. They take on a moral obligation not only to let you in front of them later on but to defend you. You have to be stubborn yourself and stand your ground in spite of the insults and the stares. And when you get to the front of the line, if the sales clerks are not limiting the amount, you can hear people, maybe six or eight places back, shouting at you not to take so much, that you are a person with no scruples or that you have no consideration for other people. It can be rather unpleasant."[3]

Since Smith made his observations, perestroika has brought about many changes in the former Soviet Union, but it has yet to affect the queues that still are so much a part of daily life in that region. The Russian queuing experience is far more severe than that found in the United States; however, in any service system, waiting is bound to occur. A complete absence of waiting only would be possible in a situation where consumers are asked to arrive at fixed intervals and service times are deterministic (e.g., a psychiatrist schedules patients every hour for 50-minute sessions). Later, we will demonstrate that waiting is caused by both the fluctuations in arrival rates and the variability in service times. Thus, as long as service times vary, delays can be encountered even when arrivals are scheduled by appointment. This is a common experience for patients waiting in a physician's office. Waiting also occurs at fast-food restaurants, where the variability of service times has been reduced by offering a short menu but customers arrive at random. Therefore, waiting is inevitable, and service operations managers must consider how customers in queue are to be treated.

THE PSYCHOLOGY OF WAITING[4]

If, as noted above, waiting is such an integral and ordinary part of our lives, why does it cause us so much grief? David H. Maister offers some interesting perspectives on this subject.

[2]Hedrick Smith, *The Russians,* Quadrangle Press, New York, 1975, pp. 64–65.
[3]Ibid., p. 67.
[4]Adapted from David H. Maister, "The Psychology of Waiting Lines," in J. A. Czepiel, M. R. Solomon, and C. F. Surprenant (eds.), *The Service Encounter,* Lexington Press, Lexington, Mass., 1985, pp. 113–123.

He suggests two "Laws of Service." The first deals with the customer's expectations versus his or her perceptions. If a customer receives better service than he or she expects, then the customer departs a happy, satisfied person, and the service may benefit from a trickle-down effect (i.e., the happy customer will tell friends about the good service). Note, however, that the trickle-down effect can work both ways: a service can earn a bad reputation in the same manner (and create more interesting stories for the customer to pass along).

Maister's second law states that it is hard to play "catch-up ball." By this, he means that first impressions can influence the rest of the service experience; thus, a service that requires its customers to wait would be advised to make that period a pleasant experience. To do the "impossible"—to make waiting at least tolerable and, at best, pleasant and productive—a creative and competitive service management must consider the following aspects of the psychology of waiting.

That Old Empty Feeling

Just as "nature abhors a vacuum," people dislike "empty time." Empty, or unoccupied, time feels awful. It keeps us from other productive activities; frequently is physically uncomfortable; makes us feel powerless and at the mercy of servers, whom we may perceive as uncaring about us; and, perhaps worst of all, seems to last forever. The challenge to the service organization is obvious: fill this time in a positive way. It may require no more than comfortable chairs and a fresh coat of paint to cheer up the environment. Furnishings in a waiting area can affect indirectly the perception of waiting. The fixed, bench-like seating in bus and rail terminals discourages conversation. The light, movable table-and-chair arrangement of a European sidewalk cafe brings people together and provides opportunities for socializing. In another situation, a music recording may be enough to occupy a telephone caller who is on hold and, at the same time, reassure the caller that he or she has not been disconnected.

Perhaps the strategy most widely noted in the literature is that of installing mirrors near elevators. Hotels, for example, record fewer complaints about excessive waits for elevators that are surrounded by mirrors. The mirrors allow people to occupy their time by checking their grooming and surreptitiously observing others who are waiting.

Services often can make waiting times productive as well as pleasurable. Instead of treating the telephone caller mentioned above to the strains of Mozart or Madonna, the service can air some commercials. Such a practice involves risk, however, because some people resent being subjected to this tactic when they are being held captive. At The Olive Garden restaurants, diners who are waiting for tables can spend their time in the bar, which benefits the restaurant with added sales, or can wait in the lobby and watch a chef prepare fresh pastas, which certainly stimulates appetites. No need to play "catch-up ball" here. Each diner reaches the table happily anticipating an agreeable experience rather than sourly grumbling, "It's about time!"

Services that consist of several stages, such as one might find at a diagnostic clinic, can conceal waiting by asking people to walk between successive stages. There are innumerable other ways to fill time: reading matter, television monitors, live entertainment, posters, artwork, toys to occupy children, and cookies and pots of coffee. The diversions are limited only by management's imagination and desire to serve the customer effectively.

A Foot in the Door

As noted above, some diversions merely fill time so that waiting doesn't seem so long, and others also can provide the service organization with some ancillary benefits. Happy customers are more likely than unhappy customers to be profitable customers. Another aspect of diversions is important, however.

Maister points out that "service-related" diversions themselves, such as handing out menus to waiting diners or medical history forms (and paper cups) to waiting patients, "convey a sense that service has started." One's level of anxiety subsides considerably once service has started. In fact, people generally can tolerate longer waits, within reason, if they feel service has begun better than they can tolerate such waits if service has not even started. Another view is that customers become dissatisfied more quickly with an initial wait than with subsequent waits after the service has begun.

The Light at the End of the Tunnel

There are many anxieties at work before service begins. Have I been forgotten? Did you get my order? This line doesn't seem to be moving; will I ever get served? If I run to the rest room, will I lose my turn? When will the plumber get here? Will the plumber get here at all? Whether rational or not, anxieties may be the single biggest factor influencing the waiting customer.

Managers must recognize these anxieties and develop strategies to alleviate them. In some cases, this may be a simple matter of having an employee acknowledge the customer's presence. At other times, telling the customer how long he or she will have to wait is sufficient reassurance that the wait at some point will end. Signs can serve this purpose as well. As you approach the Port Aransas, Texas, ferry landing, for example, you see signs posted along the road noting the number of minutes you have left to wait if you are stopped in line at that point.

When appropriate, scheduling appointments is one strategy to reduce waiting time, but it is not foolproof. Unforeseen events might interfere, or prior appointments may require more time than expected. If the appointed time comes and goes, the anxiety of not knowing how long the wait will be sets in—along with some measure of irritation at the "insult" of being stood up. A simple explanation and apology for the delays, however, usually will go a long way in reestablishing goodwill.

Excuse Me, but I Was Next

Uncertain and unexplained waits create anxieties and, as noted above, occasionally some resentment in customers. The moment a customer sees a later arrival being served first, however, anxiety about how long the wait will be is transformed into anger about the unfairness of it all. This can lead to a testy—if not explosive—situation, and the service provider is just as likely as the usurper to be the target of the anger.

A simple strategy for avoiding violations of the first-come, first-served (FCFS) queuing policy is the take-a-number arrangement. For example, customers entering a meat market take a number from a dispenser and wait for it to be called. The number currently being served may be displayed so that the new customer can see how long the wait will be. With this simple measure, management has relieved the customer's anxiety over the length of the wait—and the possibility of being treated unfairly. As an ancillary benefit, it also encourages "impulse buying" through allowing the customer to wander about the shop instead of needing to protect a place in line. As equitable as it is, however, this system is not totally free from producing anxiety; it does require the customer to stay alert for the numbers being called or risk losing his or her place in line.

Another simple strategy for fostering FCFS service when there are multiple servers is use of a single queue. Banks, post offices, and airline check-in counters commonly employ this technique. A customer who enters one of these facilities joins the back of the line; the first person in line is served by the next available server. Anxiety is relieved, because there is no fear that later arrivals will "slip" ahead of their rightful place.[5] Often, customers who have been "guaranteed" their place in this way will relax and enjoy a few pleasantries with others in the line. Note that such camaraderie also occupies the customer's empty time and makes the waiting time seem shorter. Queue configurations are examined in more detail later in this chapter.

Not all services lend themselves to such a straightforward prioritization, however. Police service is one example; for obvious reasons, an officer on the way to a call about a "noisy dog next door" will change priorities when told to respond to a "robbery-in-progress." In this case, the dispatcher can ameliorate the "noisy-dog" caller's wait anxiety by explaining the department's response policy and providing the caller with a reasonable expectation of when an officer will arrive.

Other services may wish to give preferential treatment to special customers. Consider the express check-in for "high rollers" at Las Vegas hotels, or for first-class passengers at airline check-in counters. Keep in mind, however, that such special "perks" also can engender irritation among the unfavored who are standing in long lines nearby. A management sensitive to the concerns of all its customers will take measures to avoid an image of obvious discrimination. In the example just mentioned, one solution might be to "conceal" the preferential treatment by locating it in an area that is separate from the regular service line.

They Also Serve, Who Sit and Wait

Management must remember that one of the most important parts of its service package is attention to the needs of its customers during the waiting process. The customer who is subjected to unnecessary anxiety or aggravation during this period likely will be a demanding and difficult customer—or, worse, a former customer.

THE ECONOMICS OF WAITING

The economic cost of waiting can be viewed from two perspectives. For a firm, the cost of keeping an employee (i.e., an internal customer) waiting may be measured by unproductive wages. For external customers, the cost of waiting is the forgone alternative use of that time. Added to this are the costs of boredom, anxiety, and other psychological distresses.

In a competitive market, excessive waiting—or even the expectation of long waits—can lead to lost sales. How often have you driven by a filling station, observed many cars lined up at the pumps, and then decided not to stop? One strategy to avoid lost sales is to conceal the queue from arriving customers. In the case of restaurants, this often is achieved by diverting people into the bar, a tactic that frequently results in increased sales. Amusement parks such as Disneyland require people to

---

[5]For a discussion of slips and skips, see Richard C. Larson, "Perspectives on Queues: Social Justice and the Psychology of Queuing," *Operations Research*, vol. 35, no. 6, November–December 1987, pp. 895–905.

pay for their tickets outside the park, where they are unable to observe the waiting lines inside. Casinos "snake" the waiting line for nightclub acts through the slot-machine area both to hide its true length and to foster impulsive gambling.

The consumer can be considered a resource with the potential to participate in the service process. For example, a patient who is waiting for a doctor can be asked to complete a medical history record and thereby save valuable physician time (i.e., service capacity). The waiting period also can be used to educate the person about good health habits, which can be achieved by making health publications or film-strips available. As another example, restaurants are quite innovative in their approaches to engaging the customer directly in providing the service. After giving your order to a waiter in many restaurants, you are asked to go to the salad bar and prepare your own salad, which you eat while the cook prepares your meal.

Consumer waiting may be viewed as a contribution to productivity by permitting greater utilization of limited capacity. The situation of customers waiting in line for a service is analogous to the work-in-process inventory for a manufacturing firm. The service firm actually is inventorying customers to increase the overall efficiency of the process. In service systems, higher utilization of facilities is purchased at the price of customer waiting. Prominent examples can be found in public services such as post offices, medical clinics, and welfare offices, where high utilization is achieved with long queues.

Yoram Barzel reports the following event to illustrate the economic value of waiting[6]:

> On June 14, 1972, the United States of America Bank (of Chicago) launched an anniversary sale. The commodity on sale was money, and each of the first 35 persons could "buy" a $100 bill for $80 in cash. Those farther down the queue could each obtain similar but declining bonuses: the next 50 could gain $10 each; 75, $4 each; 100, $2 each; and the following 100, $1 each. Each of the next 100 persons could get a $2 bill for $1.60 and, finally, 800 (subsequently, it seems, expanded to 1800) persons could gain $0.50 each. The expected waiting time in such an unusual event was unpredictable; on the other hand, it was easy to assess the money value of the commodity being distributed.
>
> First in line were four brothers aged 16, 17, 19, and 24. Because the smallest was 6´2˝, their priority was assured. "I figured," said Carl, the youngest brother, "that we spent 17 hours to make a $20 profit. That's about $1.29 an hour."
>
> "You can make better than that washing dishes," added another of the brothers. Had they been better informed they could have waited less time. The 35th person to join the line arrived around midnight, had to wait just 9 hours, and was the last to earn $20—$2.22 per hour. To confirm her right, she made a list of all those ahead of her in the line.
>
> "Why am I here?" she asked. "Well, that $20 is the same as a day's pay to me. And I don't even have to declare it on my income tax. It's a gift, isn't it?"

The experience described above demonstrates that those in line considered their waiting time as the cost of securing a "free" good. While waiting can have a number of economic interpretations, its true cost is always difficult to determine. For this reason, the tradeoff between the cost of waiting and the cost of providing service seldom is made explicit, yet service providers must consider the physical, behavioral, and economic aspects of the consumer waiting experience in their decision making.

---

[6]Yoram Barzel, "A Theory of Rationing by Waiting," *The Journal of Law and Economics,* vol. 17, no. 1, April 1974, p. 74.

ESSENTIAL FEATURES OF QUEUING SYSTEMS

Figure 2 depicts the essential features of queuing systems. These are: 1) calling population, 2) arrival process, 3) queue configuration, 4) queue discipline, and 5) service process.

Services obtain customers from a *calling population*. The rate at which they arrive is determined by the *arrival process*. If servers are idle, then the customer is immediately attended; otherwise, the customer is diverted to a queue, which can have various configurations. At this point, some customers may *balk* when confronted with a long or slow-moving waiting line and seek service elsewhere. Other customers, after joining the queue, may consider the delay to be intolerable, and so they *renege,* which means that they leave the line before service is rendered. When a server does become available, a customer then is selected from the queue, and service begins. The policy governing the selection is known as the *queue discipline.* The service facility may consist of no servers (i.e., self-service), one or more servers, or complex arrangements of servers in series or in parallel. After the service has been rendered, the customer departs the facility. At that time, the customer may either rejoin the calling population for future return or exit with no intention of returning.

We shall now discuss in more detail each of these five essential features of queuing systems.

Calling Population

The calling population need not be homogeneous; it may consist of several subpopulations. For example, arrivals at an outpatient clinic can be divided into walk-in patients, patients with appointments, and emergency patients. Each class of patient will place different demands on services, but more important, the waiting expectations of each will differ significantly.

In some queuing systems, the source of calls may be limited to a finite number of people. For example, consider the demands on an office copier by a staff of three secretaries. In this case, the probability of future arrivals depends on the number of persons who currently are in the system seeking service. For instance, the probability of a future arrival becomes zero once the third secretary joins the copier queue. Unless the population is quite small, however, an assumption of independent arrivals or infinite population usually suffices. Figure 3 shows a classification of the calling population.

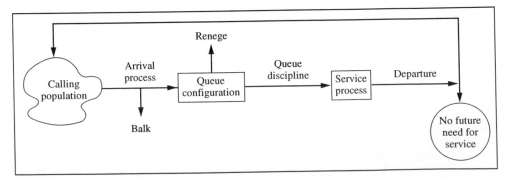

Figure 2. *Queuing system schematic.*

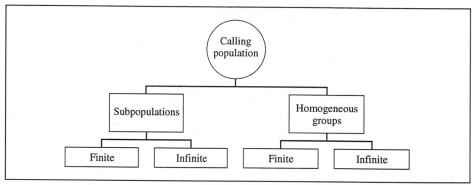

Figure 3. *Classification of calling population.*

Arrival Process

Any analysis of a service system must begin with a complete understanding of the temporal and spatial distribution of the demand for that service. Typically, data are collected by recording the actual times of arrivals. These data then are used to calculate interarrival times. Many empirical studies indicate that the distribution of interarrival times will be exponential, and the shape of the curve in Figure 4 is typical of the exponential distribution. Note the high frequency at the origin and the long tail that tapers off to the right. The exponential distribution also can be recognized by noting that both the mean and the standard deviation are theoretically equal ($\mu = 2.4$ and $\sigma = 2.6$ for Figure 4).

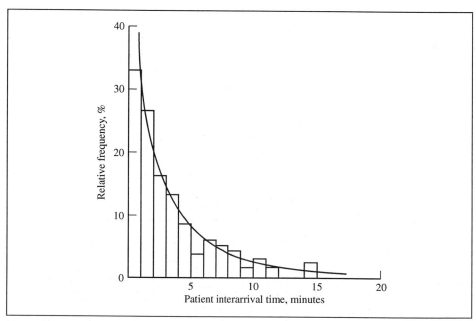

Figure 4. *Distribution of patient interarrival times for a university health clinic.*
(E. J. Rising, R. Baron, and B. Averill, "A Systems Analysis of a University Health-Service Outpatient Clinic." Reprinted with permission from *Operations Research*, vol. 21, no. 5, Sept.–Oct. 1973, p. 1038, Operations Research Society of America. No further reproduction permitted without the consent of the copyright owner.)

The exponential distribution has a continuous probability density function of the form

$$f(t) = \lambda e^{-\lambda t} \qquad\qquad t \geq 0 \tag{1}$$

where λ = average arrival rate within a given interval of time
(e.g., minutes, hours, days),
t = time between arrivals,
e = base of natural logarithms (2.718 . . .),
mean = $1/\lambda$, and
variance = $1/\lambda^2$.

The cumulative distribution function is:

$$F(t) = 1 - e^{-\lambda t} \qquad\qquad t \geq 0 \tag{2}$$

Equation (2) gives the probability that the time between arrivals will be t or less. Note that λ is the inverse of the mean time between arrivals. Thus, for Figure 4, the mean time between arrivals is 2.4 minutes, which implies that λ is $1/2.4 = 0.4167$ arrival per minute (i.e., an average rate of 25 patients per hour). Substituting 0.4167 for λ, the exponential distribution for the data displayed in Figure 4 is:

$$f(t) = 0.4167 e^{-0.4167t} \qquad\qquad t \geq 0 \tag{3}$$

$$F(t) = 1 - e^{-0.4167t} \qquad\qquad t \geq 0 \tag{4}$$

Equation (4) now can be used to find the probability that if a patient has already arrived, another will arrive in the next 5 minutes. We simply substitute 5 for t, and so

$$\begin{aligned}
F(5) &= 1 - e^{-0.4167(5)} \\
&= 1 - 0.124 \\
&= 0.876
\end{aligned}$$

Thus, there is an 87.6 percent chance that another patient will arrive in the next 5-minute interval. Test this phenomenon the next time you are waiting in a physician's office

Another distribution, known as the *Poisson distribution*, has a unique relationship to the exponential distribution. The Poisson distribution is a discrete probability function of the form

$$f(n) = \frac{(\lambda t)^n e^{-\lambda t}}{n!} \qquad\qquad n = 0, 1, 2, 3, \ldots \tag{5}$$

where λ = average arrival rate within a given interval of time
(e.g., minutes, hours, days),
t = number of time periods of interest (usually $t = 1$),
n = number of arrivals ($0, 1, 2, \ldots$),
e = base of natural logarithms (2.718 . . .),
mean = λt, and
variance = λt.

The Poisson distribution gives the probability of n arrivals during the time interval t. For the data of Figure 4, substituting for $\lambda = 25$, an equivalent description of the arrival process is

$$f(n) = \frac{(25)^n e^{-25}}{n!} \qquad n = 0, 1, 2, 3, \ldots \tag{6}$$

This gives the probability of 0, 1, 2, . . . patients arriving during any 1-hour interval. Note that we have taken the option of converting $\lambda = 0.4167$ arrival per minute to $\lambda = 25$ arrivals per hour. Equation (6) can be used to calculate the interesting probability that no patients will arrive during a 1-hour interval by substituting 0 for n as shown below:

$$f(0) = \frac{(25)^0 e^{-25}}{0!}$$
$$= e^{-25}$$
$$= 1.4 \times 10^{-11} \text{ which is a very small probability.}$$

Figure 5 shows the relationship between the Poisson distribution (i.e., arrivals per hour) and the exponential distribution (i.e., minutes between arrivals). As can be seen, they represent alternative views of the same process. Thus, an exponential distribution of interarrival times with a mean of 2.4 minutes is equivalent to a Poisson distribution of number of arrivals per hour with a mean of 25 (i.e., 60/2.4).

Service demand data often are collected automatically (e.g., by trip wires on highways), and the number of arrivals over a period of time is divided by the number of time intervals to arrive at an average rate per unit of time. The demand rate during the unit of time should be stationary with respect to time (i.e., lambda [λ] is a constant); otherwise, the underlying fluctuations in demand rate as a function of time will not be accounted for. This dynamic feature of demand is illustrated in Figure 6 for hours in a day, in Figure 7 for days of the week, and in Figure 8 for months of the year.

Variation in demand intensity directly affects the requirements for service capacity. When possible, service capacity is adjusted to match changes in demand, perhaps by varying the staffing levels. Another strategy is to smooth demand by asking customers to make appointments or reservations. Differential pricing is used by the telephone company to encourage callers to use off-peak hours, and movie theaters provide ticket discounts for patrons arriving before 6 PM. Smoothing demand and adjusting supply are important topics. Figure 9 presents a classification of arrival processes.

Figure 5. *Poisson and exponential equivalence.*

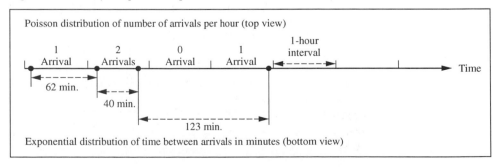

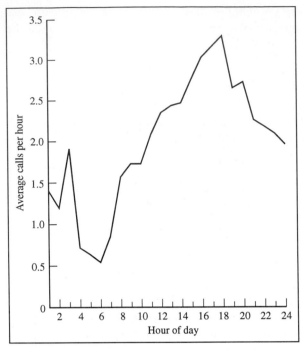

Figure 6. *Ambulance calls by hour of day.*
(Reprinted with permission from James A. Fitzsimmons,
"The Use of Spectral Analysis to Validate Planning
Models," *Socio-Economic Planning*, vol. 8, no. 3, June 1974,
p. 127. Copyright © 1974, Pergamon Press Ltd.)

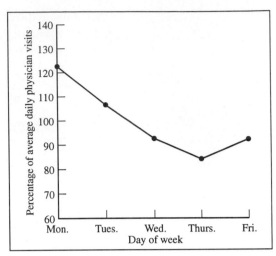

Figure 7. *Patient arrivals at health clinic by day of week.*
(E. J. Rising, R. Baron, and B. Averill, "A Systems
Analysis of a University Health-Service Outpatient
Clinic." Reprinted with permission from *Operations
Research*, vol. 21, no. 5, Sept.–Oct. 1973, p. 1035,
Operations Research Society of America. No
further reproduction permitted without the
consent of the copyright owner.)

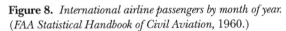

Figure 8. *International airline passengers by month of year.*
(*FAA Statistical Handbook of Civil Aviation*, 1960.)

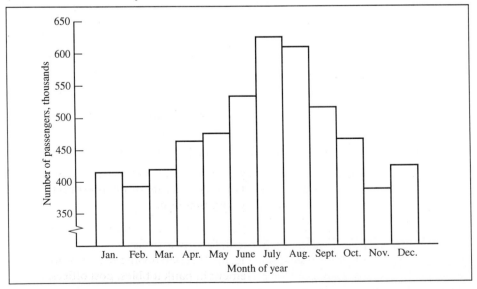

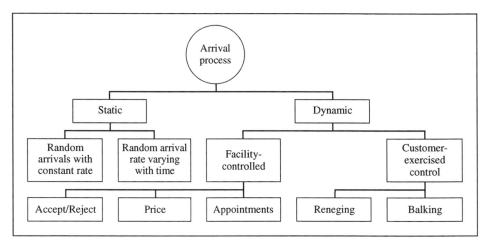

Figure 9. *Classification of arrival processes.*

Our discussion has focused on the frequency of demand as a function of time, but the spatial distribution of demand also may vary. This is particularly true of emergency ambulance demand in an urban area, which has a spatial shift in demand resulting from the temporary movements of population from residential areas to commercial and industrial areas during working hours.

Queue Configuration

Queue configuration refers to the number of queues, their locations, their spatial requirements, and their effects on customer behavior. Figure 10 illustrates three alternative waiting configurations for a service, such as a bank, a post office, or an airline counter, where multiple servers are available.

For the multiple-queue alternative shown in Figure 10*a*, the arriving customer must decide which queue to join. The decision need not be irrevocable, however, because one may switch to the end of another line. This line-switching activity is called *jockeying*. In any event, watching the line next to you moving faster than your own is a source of aggravation, but the multiple-queue configuration does have the following advantages:

1. The service provided can be differentiated. The use of express lanes in supermarkets is an example. Shoppers with small demands on service can be isolated and processed quickly, thereby avoiding long waits for little service.

2. Division of labor is possible. For example, drive-in banks assign the more experienced teller to the commercial lane.

3. The customer has the option of selecting a particular server of preference.

4. Balking behavior may be deterred. When arriving customers see a long, single queue snaked in front of a service, they often interpret this as evidence of a long wait and decide not to join that line.

Figure 10*b* depicts the common arrangement of brass posts with red velvet ropes strung between them, forcing arrivals to join one sinuous queue. Whenever a server becomes available, the first person in line moves over to the service counter. This is a popular arrangement in bank lobbies, post offices, and amusement parks. Its advantages are:

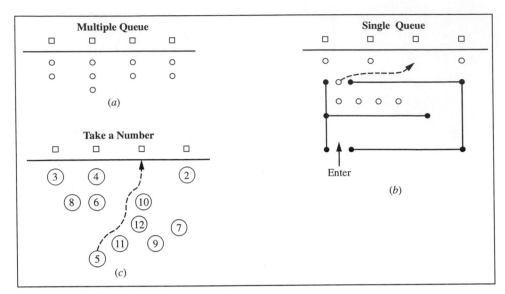

Figure 10. *Alternative waiting-area configurations.*

1. The arrangement guarantees fairness by ensuring that a first-come, first-served rule (FCFS) applies to all arrivals.

2. There is a single queue; thus, no anxiety is associated with waiting to see if one selected the fastest line.

3. With only one entrance at the rear of the queue, the problem of cutting-in is resolved and reneging made difficult.

4. Privacy is enhanced, because the transaction is conducted with no one standing immediately behind the person being served.

5. This arrangement is more efficient in terms of reducing the average time that customers spend waiting in line.

Figure 10c illustrates a variation on the single queue in which the arriving customer takes a number to indicate his or her place in line. When using such numbers to indicate positions in a queue, there is no need for a formal line. Customers are free to wander about, strike up a conversation, relax in a chair, or pursue some other diversion. Unfortunately, as noted earlier, customers must remain alert to hear their numbers being called or risk missing their turns for service. Bakeries make subtle use of the "take-a-number" system to increase impulse sales. Customers who are given the chance to browse among the tantalizing pastries often find that they purchase more than just the loaf of fresh bread for which they came.

If the waiting area is inadequate to accommodate all customers desiring service, then they are turned away. This condition is referred to as a *finite queue*. Restaurants with limited parking may experience this problem to a certain extent. A public parking garage is a classic example, because once the last stall is taken future arrivals are rejected with the word *FULL* until a car is retrieved.

Finally, concealment of the waiting line itself may deter customers from balking. Amusement parks often process waiting customers by stages. The first stage is a line outside the concession entrance, the second is the wait in an inside vestibule area, and the final stage is the wait for an empty vehicle to convey a party through the attraction. Figure 11 shows a classification of queue configurations.

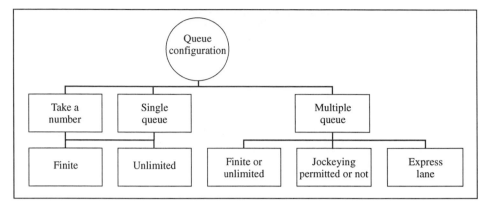

Figure 11. *Classification of queue configurations.*

Queue Discipline

The *queue discipline* is a policy established by management to select the next customer from the queue for service. The most popular service discipline is the first-come, first-served (FCFS) rule. This represents an egalitarian approach to serving waiting customers, because all customers are treated alike. The rule is considered to be static, because no information other than position in line is used to identify the next customer for service.

Dynamic queue disciplines are based on some attribute of the customer or status of the waiting line. For example, computer installations typically give first priority to waiting jobs with very short processing times. This shortest-processing-time (SPT) rule has the important feature of minimizing the average time that a customer spends in the system.[7] This rule is seldom used in its pure form, however, because jobs with long operation times would continually be set aside for more recent arrivals with shorter times. By selecting next the job with the shortest service time, excessive delays result for jobs with long service times. Typically, arrivals are placed in priority classes on the basis of some attribute, and the FCFS rule is used within each class. An example is the express check-out counter at supermarkets, where orders of ten or fewer items are processed. This allows large stores to segment their customers and, thereby, compete with the neighborhood convenience stores that provide prompt service. In a medical setting, the procedure known as *triage* is used to give priority to those who would benefit most from immediate treatment.

The most responsive queue discipline is the preemptive priority rule. Under this rule, the service currently in process for a person is interrupted to serve a newly arrived customer with higher priority. This rule usually is reserved for emergency services, such as fire or ambulance service. An ambulance that is on the way to a hospital to pick up a patient for routine transfer will interrupt this mission to respond to a suspected-cardiac-arrest call.

The queue discipline can have an important effect on the likelihood that a waiting customer will renege. For this reason, information on the expected waiting time might be made available to the arriving customer, and updated periodically for each waiting customer. This information usually is available to computer-center users who are interested in the status of their jobs waiting in queue to be processed.

[7]R. W. Conway, W. L. Maxwell, and L. W. Miller, *Theory of Scheduling*, Addison-Wesley Publishing Company, Reading, Mass., 1967, p. 27.

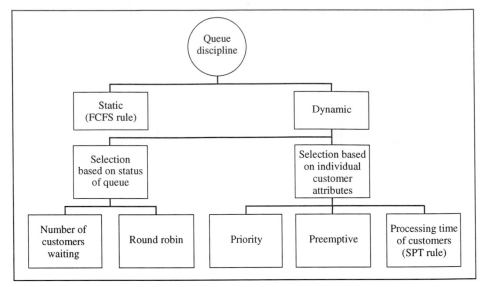

Figure 12. *Classification of queue disciplines.*

Some fast-food chains (e.g., Wendy's) take a more direct approach to avoid customer reneging. When long lines begin to form, a service person begins to take orders while customers are waiting in line. Taking this idea further is the concept of round-robin service as used by time-shared computer systems. In these systems, a customer is given partial service, and then the server moves on to the next waiting customer. Thus, customers alternate between waiting and being served. Figure 12 shows a classification of queue disciplines.

Service Process

The distribution of service times, arrangement of servers, management policies, and server behavior all contribute to service performance. Figure 13 contains histograms of several service time distributions in an outpatient clinic, and as the figure shows, the distribution of service times may be of any form. Conceivably, the service time could be a constant, such as the time to process a car through an automated car wash; however, when the service is brief and simple to perform (e.g., preparing orders at a fast-food restaurant, collecting tolls at a bridge, or checking out items at a supermarket), the distribution of service times frequently is exponential (*see* Figure 4). The histogram for second-service times, Figure 13*c*, most closely approximates an exponential distribution. The second-service times represent those brief encounters in which, for example, the physician prescribes a medication or goes over your test results with you. The distribution of service times is a reflection of the variations in customer needs and server performances.

Table 1 illustrates the variety of service facility arrangements that are possible. With servers in parallel, management gains flexibility in meeting the variations in demand for service. Management can vary the service capacity effectively by opening and closing service lines to meet changes in demand. At a bank, additional teller windows are opened when the length of queues becomes excessive. Cross-training employees also adds to this flexibility. For example, at supermarkets, stockers often are used as cashiers when lines become long at the check-out counters. A final advantage of parallel servers is that they provide redundancy in case of equipment failures.

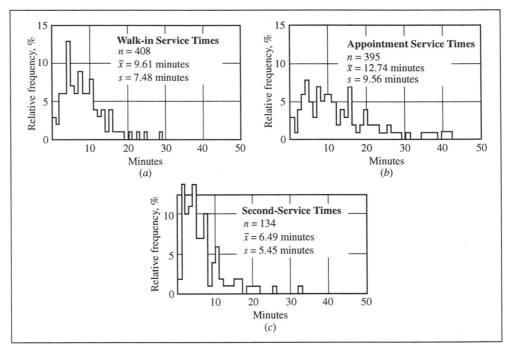

Figure 13. *Histograms of outpatient-clinic service times.*
(E. J. Rising, R. Baron, and B. Averill, "A Systems Analysis of a University Health-Service Outpatient Clinic." Reprinted with permission from *Operations Research*, vol. 21, no. 5, Sept.–Oct. 1973, p. 1039, Operations Research Society of America. No further reproduction permitted without the consent of the copyright owner.)

The behavior of service personnel toward customers is critical to the success of the organization. Under the pressure of long waiting lines, a server may speed up and spend less time with each customer; unfortunately, a gracious and leisurely manner then becomes curt and impersonal. Sustained pressure to hurry may increase the rate of customer processing, but it also sacrifices quality. This behavior on the part of a pressured server also can have a detrimental effect on other servers in the system. For example, a busy emergency telephone operator may dispatch yet another patrol car before properly screening the call for its critical nature; in this situation, the operator should have spent more time than usual to ensure that the limited resources of patrol cars were being dispatched to the most critical cases. Figure 14 suggests a classification of service processes.

TABLE 1   Service Facility Arrangements

Service Facility	Server Arrangement
Parking lot	Self-service
Cafeteria	Servers in series
Toll booths	Servers in parallel
Supermarket	Self-serve, first stage; parallel servers, second stage
Hospital	Many service centers in parallel and series, not all used by each patient

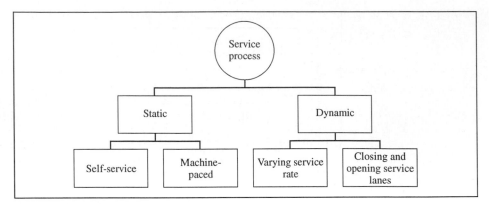

Figure 14. *Classification of service processes.*

SUMMARY

An understanding of the queuing phenomenon is necessary before creative approaches to the management of service systems can be considered. An appreciation of the behavioral implications of keeping customers waiting reveals that the perception of waiting often is more important than the actual delay. Waiting also has economic implications for both the service firm and its customers.

A schematic queuing model identified the essential features of queuing systems: calling population, arrival process, queue configuration, queue discipline, and service process. An understanding of each feature provides insights and identifies management options for improving customer service.

KEY TERMS AND DEFINITIONS

Balk occurs when an arriving customer sees a long queue and decides not to seek service.

Calling population source of service customers from a market area.

Exponential distribution the continuous distribution that describes the time between arrivals or service times.

Jockeying the practice of customers in a multiple queue system leaving one queue to join another.

Poisson distribution the discrete distribution that describes random arrivals or departures from a busy server per time interval (e.g., hour).

Queue discipline a rule for selecting the next customer in line to be served (e.g., FCFS).

Reneging occurs when a customer in queue departs before obtaining service.

TOPICS FOR DISCUSSION

■ Suggest some strategies for controlling the variability in service times.

■ Suggest diversions that could make waiting less painful.

■ Select a bad and good waiting experience, and contrast the situations with respect to the aesthetics of the surroundings, diversions, people waiting, and attitude of servers.

■ Suggest ways that service management can influence the arrival times of customers.

■ When the line becomes long at some fast-food restaurants, an employee will walk along the line taking orders. What are the benefits of this policy?

SERVICE BENCHMARK

CONQUERING THOSE KILLER QUEUES

Five o'clock at a Grand Union market in Greenwich Village. One line swelled to five people, then fell back to three. Another hit four, whereupon the woman at the end maneuvered her cart to the next lane just in time to beat out a less dexterous man. Two express lanes stayed steady at two or three deep. It was pretty much what the computer said should happen. Supermarkets have found from research that customers will put up with a line of seven people before getting fed up enough to leave, so many use computers to schedule cashiers.

Grand Union tries to keep lines at no more than three. At its 300-store chain, it has determined three peak periods: 8:30 to 10 AM, 11:30 to 1 PM, and 4:30 to 7 PM. To deal with these bursts, Grand Union, like some others in the business, relies heavily on part-timers. As many as 65 percent of its cashiers are elderly, housewives, or high school students who work four hours a day.

Additional help has come from electronic scanners, which Grand Union has installed in about half its stores. All large stores also have at least one express checkout. In May, Grand Union opened a 65,000-square-foot expanse in Kingston, N.Y. It boasts 20 checkouts, six of them express lanes. Two of them are a new concept being tested: the super-express lane, which takes six items or less and only cash. "Our goal is to get people through the cash registers in about five to seven minutes," the Grand Union spokesman said. "That's what we assume is tolerable."

One way to take some of the sting out of waiting is to entertain customers. Since 1959, the Manhattan Savings Bank has offered live entertainment during the frenzied noontime hours. In 13 branches, a pianist performs and one branch has an organ player (Willard Denton, the former Chemical chairman who dreamed up the idea, liked organs, though present management thinks they are a trifle loud for a bank). Occasionally, to make line-waiting even more wonderful, Manhattan Savings has scheduled events such as a fancy-cat exhibit, a purebred dog show, and a boat show.

Because of all this, Manhattan Savings believes customers endure long waits better than those who go to banks where the only music is the person in front of you grinding his teeth. "At very hectic times, we get very few complaints," said Jean Madsen, a senior vice president.

At hotels and office buildings, mirrors affixed to elevator doors make people less maniacal during waits. Instead of deciding whom to kill, they can comb their hair. A study done by Russel Ackoff showed that hotels that had mirrors received far less grumbling about elevator delays than ones without mirrors.

Just telling people how long they have to wait often cheers them up. Disneyland is sensitive to waiting, since the line for a hot attraction like Star Tours can run to 1,800 people. Like many amusement parks, Disney employs entertainment for waiters, but it is also big on feedback. At various spots along lines, signs give estimated delays from those points. Queuing experts say nothing is worse than the blind waiting familiar to people at bus stops, who don't know if the next bus is one minute or 15 minutes away. Disney's feedback permits parents to weigh odd options: Is it wiser to wait 25 minutes for Mr. Toad's Wild Ride or 30 minutes for Dumbo?

There are lots more tricks to be tried. The Port Authority of New York and New Jersey once figured out that the best way to move cars through the Holland Tunnel was to have stoplights space the cars into clusters of 14. When PATH train fares rose to $1 from 75 cents, the Port Authority found that lines moved quickest when quarters-only machines collected fares.

Peter Kolesar, a professor of operations research at the Columbia University Business School, thinks there ought to be more efforts to shift demand by altering pricing. Some rail lines, for example, charge less for off-peak trains and restaurants offer early-bird discounts.

During a whimsical moment, Dick Larson speculated that if the average American waited half an hour a day in one line or another, then the population expended 37 billion hours a year in lines. It strikes him, he said, that businesses ought to consider merchandising products to idle waiters to take their minds off pulling out their hair. "Like those flower peddlers outside tunnels and bridges," he said. "They're very shrewd."

Source: N. R. Kleinfield, "Conquering Those Killer Queues," *The New York Times*, September 25, 1988, p. 1.

CONCLUDING CASE

THRIFTY CAR RENTAL

Thrifty Car Rental has become one of the U.S. southwest's major rental agencies, even though it competes with several national firms. It definitely is the largest regional company, with offices and outlets in 19 cities and five states, and it primarily operates off-site from the airport terminals of those major cities. Thrifty's rental fleet consists almost entirely of fuel-efficient compact and subcompact automobiles. Its clientele utilizes these vehicles for tourism and business purposes, obtaining service at any location with or without prior arrangements. Thrifty does lose customers on occasion when the desired vehicles are unavailable at a given location, but this "stockout" situation occurs less than 10 percent of the time.

The service counter where customers are processed by Thrifty's personnel has a simple design. In the "old days," it varied only in the number of cubbyholes that keep various forms within easy reach of the servers. Today, the cubbies and forms have given way to computer terminals for more streamlined service. The number of servers varies with the size of the local market and the level of demand at specific times. In smaller markets, Thrifty may need three people at one time behind the counter, but in the largest markets, this number could be as high as eight when demand is heaviest. Usually, these peak-demand times reflect the airport's inbound-outbound flight schedule; as they occur, one or more attendants may deal exclusively with clients who have made prior arrangements to pick up a vehicle or with those who are returning vehi-

cles. When this situation exists, these attendants hang appropriate messages above their chosen stations to indicate their special service functions to clientele. Because the speed of customer service is an important factor in maintaining Thrifty's competitive edge, management and service personnel have worked very hard to ensure that each client is processed without unnecessary delay.

Another important factor in Thrifty's competitive stance is the ability to turn incoming vehicles around and quickly prepare them for new clients. The following steps are necessary to process a vehicle from incoming delivery to outgoing delivery: 1) confirmation of odometer reading, 2) refueling and confirmation of fuel charge, 3) visual damage inspection, 4) priority assessment, 5) interior cleaning, 6) maintenance assessment, 7) maintenance and checkout, 8) exterior cleaning and polishing, 9) refueling and lot storage, and 10) delivery to customer.

When a client returns a vehicle to any location, one of Thrifty's crew will confirm the odometer reading, drive about 200 meters to the service lot, and confirm any fuel charge necessary to refill the car's tank. In some cases, the crew member may be able to process all this information on a hand-held computer, and the customer can be on her or his way without having to queue up in the office. In less streamlined locations, the crew member will relay the information to all attendants immediately so that the client may complete payment inside and be released as soon as possible. (If the crew member notices any interior or exterior damage to the vehicle, the attendant will notify the man-

ager on duty; the client must clarify his or her responsibility in the circumstances and may be delayed while this is occurring.) After the damage-inspection step, the fleet supervisor assigns a priority status to incoming cars on the basis of the company's known (i.e., certain) demand and reserve policy (for walk-up clients): high-priority treatment for cars that are needed within the next 6-hour period, and normal treatment for everything else. High-priority vehicles get preferential treatment for servicing.

After the vehicle's interior is cleaned thoroughly and sprayed with a mild air freshener, a mechanic examines the vehicle's maintenance record, gives the vehicle a test drive, and notes on a form any maintenance actions he or she deems necessary. Thrifty has certain policies covering periodic normal maintenance, such as oil and filter changes, tire rotation and balancing, lubrication, coolant replacement, and engine tune-ups. Major special maintenance actions, such as brake repair, transmission repair or adjustment, or air-conditioning and heating repair, are performed as needed.

Typically, a garage in Thrifty's system has a standard side-by-side, three-bay design: two bays always are used for normal maintenance, and the third is used for either normal or special maintenance. About 20 percent of the time is spent on special maintenance in this third bay. In general, Thrifty uses a team of five mechanics for its garages: one master mechanic (who is the garage manager), two journeymen mechanics, and two apprentices. The apprentices who are responsible for all normal maintenance tasks except the engine tune-up are stationed to service every vehicle in each outside bay, and alternate on vehicles in the middle bay. The journeyman mechanics are responsible for all other maintenance, and they also alternate on servicing vehicles in the middle bay.

After servicing, the vehicle is moved outside to the car wash area, and a team of two people washes, rinses, and buffs the exterior to en-sure a good appearance. Because part of the rinse cycle contains a wax-type liquid compound, the vehicle usually does not require a time-consuming wax job. From this point, the vehicle's fuel tank again is topped off, and the vehicle is placed in the lot for storage. When the vehicle is called for by an attendant, a driver will take it to the rental area for the client.

ASSIGNMENT

On the basis of your experience and the description of Thrifty's operations, describe the five essential features of the queuing systems at the customer counter, the garage, and the car wash.

CONCLUDING CASE

EYE'LL BE SEEING YOU[8]

Mrs. F arrives 15 minutes early for a 1:30 PM appointment with her Austin, Texas, ophthalmologist, Dr. X. The waiting room is empty, and all the prior names on the sign-in sheet are crossed out. The receptionist looks up but does not acknowledge her presence. Mrs. F, unaware of the drama about to unfold, happily anticipates that she may not have to wait long beyond her scheduled time and settles into a chair to read the book she has brought with her. Large windows completely surround three sides of the waiting room. The receptionist sits behind a large opening in the remaining wall. Attractive artwork decorates the available wall space, and trailing plants rest on a shelf above the receptionist's opening. It is an appealing, comfortable waiting room.

At 1:25 PM, another patient, Jack, arrives. Mrs. F knows his name must be Jack, because the receptionist addresses him by first name and the two share some light-hearted pleasantries. Jack takes a seat and starts looking through a magazine.

At 1:40 PM, a very agitated woman enters and approaches the receptionist. She explains that she is very sorry she missed her 1 o'clock appointment and asks if it would be possible for Dr. X to see her anyway. The receptionist replies very coldly, "You're wrong. Your appointment was for 11."

"But I have 1 o'clock written down!" responds the patient, whose agitation now has changed to distress. "Well, you're wrong."

"Oh dear, is there any way I can be worked in?" pleads the patient.

"We'll see. Sit down."

Mrs. F and her two "companions" wait until 1:50 PM, when staff person number 2 (SP2) opens the door between the waiting room and the hallway leading to the various treatment areas. She summons Jack, and they laugh together as she leads him to the back. Mrs. F thinks to herself, "I was here first, but maybe he just arrived late for an earlier appointment," then goes back to her book. Five minutes later, Ms. SP2 appears at the door and summons the distressed patient. At this point, Mrs. F walks to the back area (she's a long-time patient and knows the territory), seeks out Ms. SP2, and says, "I wonder if I've been forgotten. I was here before those two people who have just been taken in ahead of me."

Ms. SP2 replies very brusquely, "Your file's been pulled. Go sit down."

Once again occupying an empty waiting room, Mrs. F returns to her reading. At 2:15 PM (no patient has yet emerged from a treatment area), Ms. SP2 finally summons Mrs. F and takes her to room 1, where she uses two instruments to make some preliminary measurements of Mrs. F's eyes. This is standard procedure in Dr. X's practice. Also standard is measuring the patient's present eyeglass prescription on a third instrument in room 1. Mrs. F extends her eyeglasses to Ms. SP2, but Ms. SP2 brushes past her and says curtly, "This way." Mrs. F then is led to a seat in the "dilating area," although no drops have been put in her eyes to start dilation.

The light in the dilating area is dimmed to protect dilating eyes, but Mrs. F is able to continue reading her book. No one else is seated in the dilating area. At 2:45 PM, Ms. SP2

reappears, says "this way" (a woman of very few words, our Ms. SP2), and marches off to examining room 3. "Wait here," she commands, leaving Mrs. F to seat herself in the darkened room.

Mrs. F can hear Dr. X and Jack laughing in the next examining room. At 2:55 PM, she hears the two men say good-bye and leave the room. Mrs. F expects Dr. X to enter her room shortly. At 3:15 PM, however, when he still has not appeared, she walks forward and interrupts Ms. SP2, the receptionist, the bookkeeper, and Ms. SP3, who are socializing. "Excuse me, but have I been forgotten?" she asks.

Ms. SP2 turns her head from her companions and replies, "No, he's in the line. Go sit down."

Mrs. F wonders what that means but returns to her assigned place. She is here, after all, for a particular visual problem, not just for a routine check-up.

All good things, however, including Mrs. F's patience and endurance of abusive treatment, eventually end. At 4:00 PM, Mrs. F does some marching of her own—to the front desk, where she announces to the assembled Mss. SP1 through SP4 that she has been waiting since 1:30 PM, that she has been sitting in the back for 2½ hours, and that not once during that time has one member of the staff come to let her know what the problem is, how much longer she can expect to wait, or, indeed, that she has not been forgotten. She adds that she will wait no longer, and she feels forced to seek the services of a physician who chooses to deliver health care. There are several patients seated in the waiting room at the time.

[8]This case, sad to say, is true in its entirety. The names of the physician and his staff have been omitted, not to protect them but because such treatment of patients is so pervasive in the U.S. health care system that it serves no purpose to identify them. We offer the case for two reasons: first, because it is so wonderfully instructive regarding important material in this chapter; and second, because we wish to point out that customers and providers must work together in our emerging service society. Service providers must be sensitive to the needs of customers, and customers must demand and reward good service.

There is an epilogue to this case. Mrs. F went directly home and wrote the following letter to Dr. X informing him of the treatment she had (not) received at his office and stating that she and her family would seek care elsewhere:

_____
_____
January 5, 1989
_____, M.D.
Austin, Texas

Dear Dr. _____:

It is with very real regret that I am transferring our eye care to another physician, and I want you to know the reason for my decision.

It is 4:22 PM, and I have just returned home from a 1:30 PM appointment with(out) you. The appointment was made because I had received an adverse report from Seton Hospital's recent home vision test. I was kept waiting in the dila-

tion area and in examining room 3 for more than two-and-one-half hours, during which time not one single member of your staff gave me any explanation for the delay or assured me I had not been forgotten. When I finally asked if I were forgotten, I was treated with a very bad attitude ("how dare I even ask!") and still was given no reason for the delay or any estimate of how much longer I would have to wait. Consequently, I left without seeing you.

As I stated above, I make this change with very real regret, because I value your expertise and the treatment you personally have given the four of us during these past many years. But I will not tolerate the callous treatment of your staff.

Sincerely yours,

Mrs. _____

QUESTIONS

1 In this chapter, we referred to Maister's First and Second Laws of Service. How do they relate to this case?

2 What features of a good waiting process are evident in Dr. X's practice? List the shortcomings that you see.

3 Do you think that Mrs. F is typical of most people waiting for a service? How so? How not?

4 If Dr. X were concerned with keeping the F family as patients, how could he have responded to Mrs. F's letter? Write a letter on Dr. X's behalf to Mrs. F.

5 How could Dr. X prevent such incidents in the future?

6 List constructive ways in which customers can respond when services fall seriously short of their requirements or expectations.

SELECTED BIBLIOGRAPHY

BARZEL, YORAM: "A Theory of Rationing by Waiting," *The Journal of Law and Economics,* vol. 17, no. 1, April 1974, pp. 73–94.

DAVIS, MARK M., and M. J. MAGGARD: "An Analysis of Customer Satisfaction with Waiting Times in a Two-Stage Service Process," *Journal of Operations Management,* vol. 9, no. 3, August 1990, pp. 324–334.

KATZ, K. L., B. M. LARSON, and R. C. LARSON: "Prescription for the Waiting-in-Line Blues: Entertain, Enlighten, and Engage," *Sloan Management Review,* vol. 32, no. 2, Winter 1991, pp. 44–53.

LARSON, RICHARD C.: "Perspectives on Queues: Social Justice and the Psychology of Queuing," *Operations Research,* vol. 35, no. 6, November–December 1987, pp. 895–905.

———: "There's More to a Line Than Its Wait," *Technology Review,* July 1988, pp. 61–67.

MAISTER, D. H.: "The Psychology of Waiting Lines," in J. A. Czepiel, M. R. Solomon, and C. F. Surprenant (eds.), *The Service Encounter,* Lexington Press, Lexington, Mass., 1985, pp. 113–123.

RISING, E. J., R. BARON, and B. AVERILL: "A Systems Analysis of a University Health-Service Outpatient Clinic," *Operations Research,* September 1973, pp. 1030–1047.

SCHWARTZ, BARRY: *Queuing and Waiting,* University of Chicago Press, Chicago, 1975.

SMITH, HEDRICK: *The Russians,* Quadrangle Press, New York, 1975.

TAYLOR, SHIRLEY: "Waiting for Service: The Relationship Between Delays and Evaluations of Services," *Journal of Marketing,* vol. 58, April 1994, pp. 56–69.

CHAPTER 18

Operations Management: Managing Quality, Efficiency, and Responsiveness to Customers

A CASE IN CONTRAST

TWO PRODUCTION SYSTEMS AT FEDERAL-MOGUL

In the mid-1980s when Federal-Mogul (www.federal-mogul.com), an auto-parts manufacturer in Lancaster, Pennsylvania, was getting hammered by low-cost Japanese competitors, managers resolved to reduce operating costs. Brief visits to a few Japanese plants led Federal-Mogul managers to suspect that the major source of their Japanese competitors' cost advantage was the sophisticated computers, robots, and other automated equipment they used. Accordingly, in 1987 the company reorganized its auto-parts plant with state-of-the art automation, including robots, overhead conveyer belts to carry semifinished parts along the production line, and automated guided vehicles (carts that are guided by signals from underground wires and haul parts from one workstation to another). Several sophisticated production-line computers controlled this automated system.

The results of this reorganization were not what Federal-Mogul's managers hoped for.[1] The automated plant turned out parts faster than before, but managers found that the plant could not switch quickly from producing one type of part to another. To switch from making a small clutch bearing to a large one, for example, required many time-consuming changes, ranging from readjusting the parts' "feeding system" to realigning the mechanisms that held the parts in place while they were being machined.

In a business where a plant that is not running is losing money, this lack of flexibility made it difficult for Federal-Mogul to produce a wide range of parts at a reasonable cost. Indeed, to cover the fixed costs of setting up the equipment for a production run, managers found that they had to produce parts in batches ranging from 5,000 to 10,000 units, even if a customer wanted only 250. Surplus parts then had to be stored in a warehouse until a customer desired them, and this storage was extremely costly. To make matters worse, automobile companies were increasing the number of car models they made and consequently were demanding from suppliers such as Federal-Mogul a wider range of parts in smaller quantities.

Managers at Federal-Mogul found that the plant could not respond quickly and cost-effectively to customer demands; it lacked the required flexibility. Thus, instead of gaining on Japanese competitors, Federal-Mogul fell farther behind.

Faced with a deteriorating situation, in 1993 Federal-Mogul once more reorganized its Lancaster auto-parts plant. This time, manufacturing flexibility was the goal uppermost in the minds of the company's managers. Out went the robots, most production-line computers, the overhead conveyer belts, and the automated guided vehicles. In their place, managers created a modular production assembly line that could be changed or retooled quickly to produce different parts. Now, when a switch is made from assembling, say, a washer ring for the steering column of a car to a ring for a pickup truck, workers simply wheel away sections of the modular assembly line and replace them with sections geared for the next product. The parts needed to alter the production line are kept in bins within easy reach of workers.

The reengineered plant, which assembles 1,800 different parts, now produces three times as many different varieties as before in the same amount of time. And because it can switch from producing one part to another very quickly, it produces only what its customers immediately need and has eliminated the need for a warehouse to store excess inventory. It now can make cost-effective parts in batches ranging from 250 to 500 units instead of the 5,000 to 10,000 previously needed to break even. Federal-Mogul managers have found that the change from a high-tech automated factory to a low-tech factory has simultaneously increased their organization's flexibility and lowered its costs.

OVERVIEW

The "Case in Contrast" describes the response of auto-parts maker Federal-Mogul to low-cost Japanese competition. Federal-Mogul first built a state-of-the art automated factory. However, setting up the computer-controlled machinery for a production run took so long that Federal-Mogul was unable to provide its customers with the products they wanted at a reasonable cost. Seeing high equipment setup times translate into low responsiveness to customers and low efficiency, Federal-Mogul reorganized again, bringing in a low-tech, modular production assembly line that allowed the organization to improve performance and achieve its goals.

To achieve superior quality, efficiency, responsiveness to customers, and innovation——the four building blocks of competitive advantage ——managers at all levels in an organization must adopt state-of-the-art management techniques and practices that give them more control over an organization's activities. In this chapter we focus on the operations management techniques that managers can use to control and increase the quality of an organization's products, the efficiency of production, and the organization's responsiveness to customers. By the end of this chapter, you will understand the vital role operations management plays in building competitive advantage and creating a high-performing organization. In the next chapter we examine techniques that managers can use to enhance innovation and manage the product development process.

OPERATIONS MANAGEMENT AND COMPETITIVE ADVANTAGE

Operations management the management of any aspect of the production system that transforms inputs into finished goods and services.

Production system the system that an organization uses to acquire inputs, convert the inputs into outputs, and dispose of the outputs.

Operations manager a manager who is responsible for managing an organization's production system and for determining where operating improvements might be made.

Operations management is the management of any aspect of the production system that transforms inputs into finished goods and services. A **production system** is the system that an organization uses to acquire inputs, convert the inputs into outputs, and dispose of the outputs (goods or services). **Operations managers** are managers who are responsible for managing an organization's production system. They do whatever it takes to transform inputs into outputs. Their job is to manage the three stages of production——acquisition of inputs, control of conversion processes, and disposal of goods and services——and to determine where operating improvements might be made in order to increase quality, efficiency, and responsiveness to customers and so give an organization a competitive advantage (see Figure 1).

Quality refers to goods and services that are reliable, dependable, and satisfying in the sense that they do the job they were designed for, and do it well, so that they give customers what they want.[2] *Efficiency* refers to the amount of inputs required to produce a given output. *Responsiveness to customers* refers to actions taken to be responsive to the demands and needs of customers. Operations managers are responsible for ensuring that an organization has sufficient supplies of high-quality, low-cost inputs, and they are responsible for designing a production system that creates high-quality, low-cost products that customers are willing to buy.

Notice that achieving superior efficiency and quality is part of attaining superior responsiveness to customers. Customers want value for money, and an organiza-

Figure 1 *The Purpose of Operations Management*

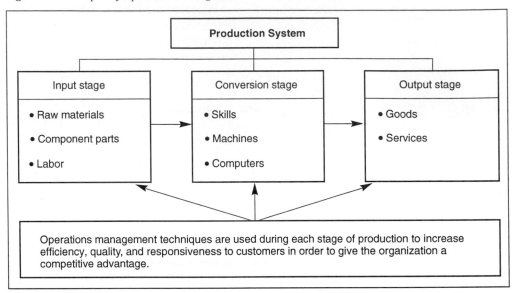

Operations management techniques are used during each stage of production to increase efficiency, quality, and responsiveness to customers in order to give the organization a competitive advantage.

tion whose efficient production system creates high-quality, low-cost products is best able to deliver this value. For this reason, we first discuss how operations managers can design the production system to increase responsiveness to customers.

IMPROVING RESPONSIVENESS TO CUSTOMERS

Organizations produce outputs—goods or services—that are consumed by customers. All organizations, profit seeking or not-for-profit, have customers. Without customers, most organizations would cease to exist. If Federal-Mogul lost the business of its customers Chrysler, Ford, and General Motors, it would go bankrupt. The customers of a business school are students, the businesses that hire the school's graduates, and society at large, which benefits from an educated and informed population. If a business school failed to attract student applicants—perhaps because employers were no longer hiring the school's graduates—it too could no longer function and would have to close its doors.

Because customers are vital to the survival of most organizations, it is important for managers to correctly identify customers and promote organizational strategies that respond to customer needs. This is why management writers recommend that organizations define their business in terms of the customer needs they are satisfying, not the type of products they are producing.[3] The credo of pharmaceutical company Johnson & Johnson, for example, begins, "We believe our first responsibility is to the doctors, nurses and patients, to mothers and fathers and all others who use our products and services."[4] In other words, through the credo Johnson & Johnson's managers emphasize their commitment to exemplary customer service. In contrast, in the 1980s, Digital Equipment Corporation (DEC) defined its business as producing high-powered mainframe computers. When the dramatic shift away from mainframe computers to personal computers occurred in the 1980s, DEC found itself unprepared and almost went bankrupt after suffering over $2.5 billion in losses. Had DEC's managers defined its business as "satisfying customer needs for computing solutions" (a customer-oriented definition) as opposed to "producing powerful computers" (a product-oriented definition), they might have recognized the shift in consumer demand and begun producing personal computers earlier.

What Do Customers Want?

Given that satisfying customer demands is central to the survival of an organization, an important question is, What do customers want? To specify exactly what they want is not possible because their wants vary from industry to industry. However, it is possible to identify some universal product attributes that most customers in most industries want. Generally, other things being equal, most customers prefer each of these:

1. A lower price to a higher price
2. Higher-quality products to low-quality products
3. Quick service to slow service (They will always prefer good after-sales service and support to poor after-sales support.)
4. Products with many features to products with few features (They will prefer a personal computer with a CD-ROM drive, lots of memory, and a powerful microprocessor to one without these features.)
5. Products that are, as far as possible, customized or tailored to their unique needs

Of course, the problem is that other things are not equal. For example, providing higher quality, quick service, and after-sales service and support, products with many features, and products that are customized raises costs and thus the price that must be charged to cover costs.[5] So customers' demands for these attributes typically conflict with their demands for lower price. Accordingly, customers must make a trade-off between price and preferred attributes, and so must managers. This price/attribute trade-off is illustrated in Figure 2.

Desired attributes of a product—such as high quality, service, speed, after-sales support, features, and customization—are plotted on the horizontal axis; price is plotted on the vertical axis; and the solid line shows the price/attribute relationship—that is, the combination of price and attributes an organization can offer and still make a profit. As the figure illustrates, the higher the price the customer is willing to pay for a product, the more desired attributes the customer is able to get. Or, in other words, the more desired

Figure 2 *The Price/Attribute Relationship*

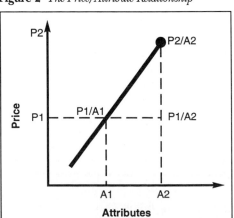

attributes that an organization builds into its products, the higher is the price that the organization has to charge to cover its costs. At price P1 managers can offer a product with A1 attributes. If managers offer a product with A2 attributes at price P1, they will lose money because the price is too low to cover costs. A product with A2 attributes needs a price of P2 to be profitable for the organization. Thus, the nature of the organization's production system limits how responsive managers can be to customers.

Given the limits imposed on managers by their existing production system, what do the managers of the customer-responsive organization try to do? They try to push the price/attribute curve to the right (toward the vertical dotted line) by developing new or improved production systems that are able to deliver either more desired product attributes for the same price or the same product attributes for a lower price.[6]

Figure 3 shows the price/attribute curves for Federal-Mogul in 1987, when the automated production system was put in place, and in 1993, when the low-tech modular system was installed. By accommodating customer demands for greater product customization and speedy delivery, the flexible modular system lowered operating costs so much that it allowed Federal-Mogul to offer *more* product attributes than previously—at a lower price to customers. The shift from an automated to a flexible production system increased Federal-Mogul's responsiveness to customers on two fronts—lower cost and more attributes—and did so without imposing higher costs on Federal-Mogul.

Designing Production Systems that Are Responsive to Customers

Because satisfying customers is so important, managers try to design production systems that can produce the outputs that have the attributes customers desire. The attributes of an organization's outputs—their quality, cost, and features—are determined by the organization's production system.[7] As we saw in the "Case in Contrast," for example, the need to respond to customer demands for competitively priced small batches of different products drove Federal-Mogul managers to dismantle the automated system of production and replace it with a more flexible modular layout. The imperative of satisfying cus-

Figure 3 *Federal-Mogul's Price/Attribute Relationship in 1987 and 1993*

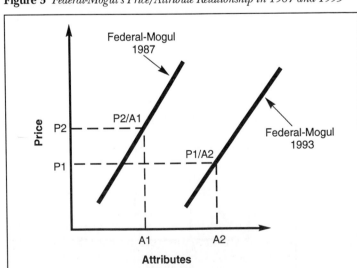

tomer needs shaped Federal-Mogul's production system. When managers focus on being responsive to their customers, and not just on producing a product, they see new ways to reduce costs and increase quality.

Since the ability of an organization to satisfy the demands of its customers derives from its production system, managers need to devote considerable attention to constantly improving production systems. Managers' desire to attract customers by shifting the price/attribute line to the right explains their adoption of many new operations management techniques in recent years—such as total quality management, flexible manufacturing systems, and just-in-time inventory, discussed in detail later in this chapter.

The total quality management movement, for example, is concerned with designing production systems that produce high-quality outputs, thereby satisfying customer demands for product quality. The redesign of Motorola's semiconductor production system resulted in a sharp increase in product quality; the production of defective semiconductor chips fell from 6,000 per million to 40 per million.[8] This quality improvement made Motorola's output more attractive to its customers. By redesigning the production system, Motorola managers increased the organization's ability to respond to customer demands for quality products; Motorola became more responsive to customers. As another example of the link between responsiveness to customers and an organization's production system, this time in a service organization, consider the case of Southwest Airlines.

MANAGEMENT INSIGHT   HOW SOUTHWEST AIRLINES KEEPS ITS CUSTOMERS HAPPY

Southwest Airlines (www.iflyswa.com) is one of the most successful airlines in the United States. During the early 1990s, it was one of the few airlines in the world to remain profitable in the face of a serious slump in airline travel. Part of the reason for Southwest's success is that CEO Herb Kelleher created a production system uniquely tailored to satisfying the demands of its customers: people who want low-priced, reliable (on-time), and convenient air travel. Southwest is able to command high customer loyalty precisely because its production system delivers products, such as flights from Houston to Dallas, that have desired attributes: reliability, convenience, and low price.

Southwest's low-cost production system focuses not only on improving the maintenance of aircraft but also on the company's ticket reservation system, route structure, flight frequency, baggage-handling system, and in-flight services. Each of these elements of Southwest's production system is geared toward satisfying customer demands for low-priced, reliable, and convenient air travel. For example, Southwest offers a no-frills approach to in-flight customer service. No meals are served on board, and there are no first-class seats. Southwest does not subscribe to the big reservation computers used by travel agents because it believes the booking fees are too costly. Also, the airline flies only one type of aircraft, the fuel-efficient Boeing 737, which keeps training and maintenance costs down. All this translates into low prices to the customer.

Southwest's reliability derives from the fact that it has the quickest aircraft turnaround time in the industry. A Southwest ground crew needs only 15 minutes to turn around an incoming aircraft and prepare it for departure. This speedy operation helps to keep flights on time. Southwest has such quick turnaround because it has a flexible workforce that has been cross-trained to perform multiple tasks. Thus, the person who checks tickets might also help with baggage loading if time is short.

Southwest's convenience comes from its scheduling multiple flights every day between its popular locations, such as Dallas and Houston, and its use of airports that are close to downtown (Hobby at Houston and Love Field at Dallas) instead of more distant major airports.[9]   ■ ■ ■

Although managers must seek to improve the responsiveness to customers of their organization by improving its production system, they should *not* offer a level of responsiveness to customers that is more than that production system can profitably sustain. The company that customizes every product to the unique demands of individual customers is likely to see its cost structure become so high that unit costs exceed unit revenues.

Something like this appears to have occurred at Toyota (www.toyota.com) in the early 1990s. Toyota's flexible production system allows the company to produce a wide range of variations on a basic automobile model (for example, different colors and options). Extreme customization at first attracted many new customers and raised revenues. Toyota managers, however, seem to have pushed customization to the point where it increased costs faster than it generated additional revenues. At one point, literally thousands of different variations of Toyota's basic models, such as the Camry and Corolla, were being produced by Toyota factories. When a recession hit in Japan in the early 1990s, Toyota reexamined its approach to customization, and managers decided to reduce the number of model specifications by 20 percent, and the options offered with models by 30 percent. Managers at Toyota apparently concluded that the costs of extreme customization were exceeding the benefits.[10]

IMPROVING QUALITY

As noted earlier, high-quality products are reliable, dependable, and satisfying; they do the job they were designed for and meet customer requirements.[11] Quality is a concept that can be applied to the products of both manufacturing and service organizations——goods such as a Toyota car or a McDonald's hamburger or services such as Southwest Airlines's flight service or customer service in a bank. Why do managers seek to control and improve the quality of their organization's products?[12] There are two reasons (see Figure 4).

First, customers usually prefer a higher-quality product to a lower-quality product. So an organization able to provide, *for the same price,* a product of higher quality than a competitor's product is serving its customers better——it is being more responsive to its customers. Often, providing high-quality products creates a brand-name reputation for an organization's products. In turn, this enhanced reputation may allow the organization to charge more for its products than its competitors are

Figure 4 *The Impact of Increased Quality on Organizational Performance*

able to charge and thus make even greater profits. In 1993, 6 of the top 10 places in the J. D. Power list of the 10 most reliable cars sold in the U.S. market were captured by Toyota vehicles.[13] The high quality of Toyota vehicles has enabled Toyota to charge higher prices for its cars than the prices charged by rival automakers.

The second reason for trying to boost product quality is that higher product quality can increase efficiency and thereby lower operating costs and boost profits. Many managers in Western companies did not appreciate this relationship until the mid-to-late 1980s. They were operating with the belief, now known to be incorrect, that improving product quality *raised* operating costs. This belief was based on the (mistaken) assumption that building quality into a product is expensive. By contrast, managers in many Japanese companies had long operated on the assumption that achieving high product quality *lowered* operating costs because of the effect of quality on employee productivity: Higher product quality means that less employee time is wasted making defective products that must be discarded or providing substandard services, and less time has to be spent fixing mistakes. This translates into higher employee productivity, which means lower costs.

Total Quality Management

Total quality management a management technique that focuses on improving the quality of an organization's products and services.

At the forefront of the drive to improve product quality is a technique known as total quality management.[14] **Total quality management (TQM)** focuses on improving the quality of an organization's products and services and stresses that all of an organization's functional activities should be directed toward this goal. Conceived as an organizationwide management program, TQM requires the cooperation of managers in every function of an organization if it is to succeed. The TQM concept was first developed by a number of American consultants, including the late W. Edwards Deming, Joseph Juran, and A. V. Feigenbaum.[15] Originally, these consultants won few converts in the United States but were enthusiastically embraced by the Japanese, who named their premier annual prize for manufacturing excellence after Deming. Deming identified 14 steps that should be part of any TQM program (see Table 1).[16]

In essence, to increase quality, Deming urged managers to develop strategic plans that state goals exactly and spell out how they will be achieved. He argued that managers should embrace the philosophy that mistakes, defects, and poor-quality materials are not acceptable and should be eliminated. He suggested that first-level supervisors be allowed to spend more time working with employees and providing them with the tools they need to do the job. He recommended that management create an environment in which employees will not be afraid to report problems or recommend improvements. He believed that output goals and targets needed to include not only numbers or quotas but also some notion of quality to promote the production of defect-free output. Deming also argued that management has the responsibility to train employees in new skills to keep pace with changes in the workplace. Furthermore, he believed that achieving better quality requires that managers develop organizational values and norms centered on improving quality and that every manager and worker in an organization must commit to the goal of quality.

From the early 1980s, as word of the remarkable production successes resulting from TQM practices spread, many Western managers began implementing TQM within their organizations. In some organizations the results have been nothing short of spectacular. For example, when managers at Xerox first introduced a TQM program in conjunction with suppliers in 1983, the suppliers were producing about 25,000 defective parts per million. By 1992 the defect rate on parts from

Table 1 *Deming's 14 Steps to Quality*

1. Create constancy of purpose toward improvement of product and service, with the aim to become competitive, to stay in business, and to provide jobs.	**9.** Break down barriers between departments. People in research, design, sales, and production must work as a team, to foresee problems of production and in use that may be encountered with the product or service.
2. Adopt the new philosophy. We are in a new economic age. Western management must awaken to the challenge, must learn its responsibilities, and must take on leadership for change.	**10.** Eliminate slogans, exhortations, and targets for the workforce asking for zero defects and new levels of productivity. Such exhortations only create adversarial relationships. The bulk of the causes of low quality and low productivity belong to the system and thus lie beyond the power of the workforce.
3. Cease dependence on inspection to achieve quality. Eliminate the need for inspection on a mass basis by building quality into the product from the start.	**11.** (a) Eliminate work standards on the factory floor. Substitute leadership. (b) Eliminate management by objectives. Eliminate management by numbers, numerical goals. Substitute leadership.
4. End the practice of awarding business on the basis of price tag. Instead, minimize total cost.	**12.** (a) Remove barriers that rob the hourly worker of his or her right to pride of workmanship. The responsibility of supervisors must be changed from sheer numbers to quality. (b) Remove barriers that rob people in management and in engineering of their right to pride of workmanship.
5. Improve constantly and forever the system of production and service, to improve quality and productivity and thus constantly decrease costs.	**13.** Institute a vigorous program of education and self-improvement.
6. Institute training on the job.	**14.** Put everybody in the company to work to accomplish the transformation. The transformation is everybody's job.
7. Institute leadership. The aim of leadership should be to help people and machines and gadgets do a better job. Leadership of management is in need of an overhaul, as well as leadership of production workers.	
8. Drive out fear, so that everyone may work effectively for the company.	

suppliers was under 300 per million.[17] Ford Motor Company claims that its companywide implementation of a TQM program reduced the company's operating budget by over $40 billion over a ten-year period.[18] Partly as a consequence, in 1994 Ford emerged from a period of financial turmoil as the most profitable car company in the world. The positive effect that a TQM program can have on an organization can also be seen in the example of McDevitt Street Bovis, a construction services company, whose adoption of TQM led to a major improvement in the company's competitive position.

MANAGEMENT INSIGHT   MCDEVITT STREET BOVIS APPLIES TQM

In November 1987, managers at McDevitt Street Bovis, a construction services company based in Charlotte, North Carolina, received a shock. One of their largest clients, Hospital Corporation of America, informed McDevitt that its managers were going to award all future construction contracts on the basis of construction companies' commitment to total quality management. Managers at McDevitt were floored. They had no idea what TQM was or how it could be applied to a construction services company. Despite their ignorance, at 3:30 in the afternoon of November 13, 1987, top management of McDevitt decided to embrace TQM.

Top managers soon discovered that a principal objective of TQM was to eliminate costly mistakes, which are very common in the construction industry. Cost and time overruns, poor-quality work, and legal disputes among construction companies, subcontractors, and architects and their clients are commonplace in the industry. As they embarked on a TQM program, managers at McDevitt came to realize that many wasteful and costly mistakes resulted from misunderstandings caused by a lack of communication among the parties involved in a construction project. To improve communication, McDevitt's managers decided to develop a total quality plan for each contract that they worked on; they called their plan "Jobsite Quality Planning" (JQP).

JQP brings together clients, architects, the construction company, and subcontractors to agree on a written mission statement for a job and on tangible performance measures that will allow them to evaluate the success of a project. Performance measures typically include the frequency with which architects and engineers have to visit the job to correct mistakes; the manner of resolving disputes among subcontractors; coordination among mechanical, electrical, and plumbing contractors; and the cost method for measuring progress. As of 1995, managers at McDevitt had used Jobsite Quality Planning on over 400 projects. Seven years down the total quality management road, they found that TQM had produced some interesting results:

- Virtually every company with which JQP has been used has awarded McDevitt additional business.

- There has not been a single construction-related lawsuit arising from a JQP project. By 1993, McDevitt's legal expenses were down 50 percent, and the number of legal disputes has declined more than 60 percent since their peak in 1989.[19]

- McDevitt has made money each year since 1987, despite turmoil in the industry and widespread financial troubles among competing companies.

- Clients, subcontractors, architects, and engineers have all informed McDevitt that the JQP process truly improves the quality of a job.

It would be wrong to think that these achievements have been easy or cost less to attain. McDevitt continues to invest $500,000 per year in JQP training efforts. Moreover, it took years to get people at all levels of the company to buy into total quality management. Initial resistance ranged from middle managers who saw huge expenditures associated with JQP with no immediate payback, to job-site workers who did not understand the concept. Indeed, getting JQP widely accepted within McDevitt has involved major changes in the culture of the company. To this end, Luther Cochran, the CEO of McDevitt, really supported early adopters of JQP in the company, making heroes out of them for their successes. The result? Over time, most of the doubters were converted to JQP, and an obsession with quality has become a central value of McDevitt's culture. ■ ■ ■

Despite the many TQM success stories such as those of Xerox, Motorola, and McDevitt Street Bovis, there is mounting evidence that there is still a long way to go before TQM practices are widely accepted by Western managers. A 1992 study by the American Quality Foundation found that only 20 percent of U.S. companies regularly review the consequences of quality performance, compared with 70 percent of Japanese companies.[20] A study by Arthur D. Little of 500 American companies that use TQM found that only 36 percent believed that TQM was increasing their competitiveness.[21] The main reason for this finding, according to the study, was that many managers failed to fully understand or embrace the TQM concept. A survey of European companies by the European Foundation for Quality Management revealed that only 30 percent of European companies claimed to have adopted TQM practices, and a mere 5 or 10 percent said they were still actively pursuing TQM programs.[22] The European Foundation study also found that many TQM programs fail because of a lack of commitment by managers, who frequently talk up the importance of TQM but do not act on it.

Putting TQM into Action: The Management Challenge

Given the mixed track record of TQM, what actions can managers take to increase the probability of successful implementation of a TQM program? Studies of companies that have successfully implemented TQM programs, such as Xerox, Motorola, and McDevitt Street Bovis, suggest that the following 10 steps are necessary to make a TQM control system work.

1. *Build organizational commitment to quality.* TQM will do little to improve the performance of an organization unless all employees embrace it, and this often requires a change in an organization's culture.[23] Getting TQM thinking to become part of everyday thinking took a change in McDevitt's culture. The need to engineer a cultural change was also at the forefront of management thinking at Xerox when its managers first introduced TQM. When Xerox launched its total quality program, managers' first actions were to educate the entire workforce, from top management down, about the importance and operation of TQM. Managers formed groups. The first was a group of top managers, including the CEO. Outside consultants were hired to give this group basic TQM training. Each member of the top-management group was then given the responsibility to train a group at the next level in the hierarchy, and so on down throughout the organization until all 100,000 employees had received basic TQM training.

It is important to emphasize the ongoing nature of the effort to build commitment to TQM. The TQM philosophy needs to be continually emphasized, applied, and reinforced, for changing the culture of a company can take years. If TQM is treated as the hot management technique of the moment, pursued for a year, and then forgotten, it will fail to deliver on its promise to improve organizational performance.

2. *Focus on the customer.* TQM practitioners see a focus on the customer as the starting point.[24] According to TQM philosophy, the *customer* "defines" what quality is——not managers in quality control or engineering. The challenge is fourfold: (1) to identify what customers want from the good or service that the company provides; (2) to identify what the company actually provides to customers; (3) to identify the gap that exists between what customers want and what they actually get (the *quality gap*); and (4) to formulate a plan for closing the quality gap.

3. *Find ways to measure quality.* Another crucial element of any TQM program is the creation of a measuring system that managers can consistently use to evaluate quality. Devising appropriate measures is relatively easy in manufacturing companies where quality can be measured by criteria such as defects per million parts. It is more difficult in service companies where outputs are less tangible. But with a little creativity, suitable measures can be devised. For example, one of the measures that managers at Florida Power & Light use to evaluate quality is the number of meter-reading errors per month; another is the frequency and duration of power outages. At L. L. Bean, the Freeport, Maine, mail-order retailer of outdoor gear, managers use the percentage of orders that are correctly filled as one of their quality measures. Some banks use measures such as the number of customer defections per year or the number of statement errors per thousand customers to evaluate quality. The common theme running through all of these examples is that managers must identify what quality means from a customer's perspective and devise some measure that captures this.

4. *Set goals and create incentives.* Once a measure has been devised, managers' next step is to set a challenging quality goal and to create incentives for reaching that goal. At Xerox, the CEO set an initial goal of reducing defective parts from 25,000 per million to 1,000 per million. One way of creating incentives to attain a goal is to link rewards, such as bonus pay and promotional opportunities, to the goal.

5. *Solicit input from employees.* Employees can be a major source of information about the sources of poor quality. Therefore, it is important for managers to establish a framework for soliciting employee suggestions about improvements that can be made. **Quality circles**——groups of employees who meet regularly to discuss ways to increase quality——are often created to achieve this goal. Other companies create self-managed teams to further quality improvement efforts. Whatever the means chosen to solicit input from lower-level employees, managers must be open to receiving, and acting on, bad news and criticism from employees. According to Deming, however, Western managers have grown used to "killing the bearer of bad tidings."[25] Deming argued that managers who are committed to the quality concept must be open to bad news, for as he put it, bad news is a gold mine of information.

6. *Identify defects and trace them to their source.* A major source of product defects is the production system. TQM preaches the need for managers to identify defects in the work process, trace those defects back to their source, find out why they occurred, and make corrections so that they do not occur again. To identify defects, Deming advocated the use of statistical procedures to spot variations in the quality of goods or services. Deming considered variation to be the enemy of quality.[26] Once variations have been identified, he said, they need to be traced back to their source and eliminated.

One technique that helps greatly in the process of finding the source of defects is reducing the lot sizes of manufactured products (*lot size* is the number of units of a product produced in a particular run). When lot sizes are small, defects show up immediately, they can be quickly traced back to their source, and the problem can be fixed. Also, reducing lot sizes means that when defective products are produced, their number will be small, thereby reducing waste. Flexible manufacturing techniques (discussed later in this chapter) can be used to reduce lot sizes without raising costs. Thus the adoption of flexible manufacturing techniques may be an important aspect of a TQM program.

7. *Introduce just-in-time inventory systems.* **Inventory** is the stock of raw materials, inputs, and component parts that an organization has on hand at a particular point in time. Just-in-time (JIT) inventory systems play a major role in the process of identifying and finding the source of defects in inputs. When an organization has a **just-in-time inventory system,** parts or supplies arrive at the organization when they are needed, not before. This system can be contrasted with a *just-in-case* view of inventory, which leads an organization to stockpile excess inputs in a warehouse just in case it needs them to meet sudden upturns in demand. Under a JIT inventory system, defective parts enter an organization's production system immediately; they are not warehoused for months before use. This means that defective inputs can be quickly spotted. Managers can then trace the problem back to the supply source and fix it before more defective parts are produced.

Just-in-time systems were originally developed in Japan during the 1950s and 1960s. As this "Managing Globally" explains, they were developed in an attempt to improve product quality.

Quality circles groups of employees who meet regularly to discuss ways to increase quality.

Inventory the stock of raw materials, inputs, and component parts that an organization has on hand at a particular point in time.

Just-in-time inventory system a system in which parts or supplies arrive at an organization when they are needed, not before.

MANAGING GLOBALLY   THE *KANBAN* SYSTEM IN JAPAN

The Japanese *kanban* system of just-in-time inventory was originally developed at the Toyota Motor Company (www.toyota.com) during the 1950s by a mechanical engineer, Ohno Taiichi. At the time Taiichi was a middle manager in charge of one of Toyota's machine shops, which produced component parts for Toyota's automobile assembly lines. In developing the *kanban* system, Taiichi was trying to achieve two goals. First, he wanted to reduce the costs associated with stockpiling inventory before it was used in an automobile assembly line. Second, and more important from his perspective, he wanted to improve the quality of Toyota's cars. Taiichi reasoned that this required an improvement in the quality of component parts.

At the time, vast amounts of component parts were produced at once and then stored in a warehouse until they were needed. Taiichi saw a major problem with this approach. He reasoned that if there was a defect in a part, it would not be discovered for weeks or months, when the part was needed in the assembly process. But by that time, it might be too late to determine why the defect had occurred, and it would be difficult to correct the problem that had produced the defect. Moreover, if the defect was due to initial machine settings, the production of large volumes of defective individual parts implied enormous waste, which the frugal Taiichi saw as costly.

Taiichi decided to experiment with a new production system. Starting in his small machine shop, he developed a simple system of levers and pulleys that allowed him to reduce the time required to set up production machinery from hours to minutes and made the production of small lots of component parts economical. He then produced and sent component parts to the assembly line just as they were needed. The parts traveled from his machine shop to the assembly line in a small wheeled container known as a *kanban*. The assembly-line workers emptied the *kanban* and then sent the container back to Taiichi's machine shop. The return of the *kanban* container was treated as the signal to produce another small batch of component parts, and so the process repeated itself.

The system worked beautifully, and Taiichi was able to get rid of most of the warehouse space needed to store inventory. Moreover, the short production runs meant that defects in parts showed up at the assembly line almost immediately, which helped enormously in the process of identifying and eliminating the source of a defect. As a result, Taiichi's machine shop quickly gained a reputation for quality within Toyota.

Over the years, Taiichi was repeatedly promoted for his efforts (when he ended his career in the mid-1980s, he was Toyota's chief engineer) and given the authority to spread his *kanban* innovation, first within Toyota and then to Toyota's suppliers. During the 1970s other companies in Japan copied Toyota's revolutionary *kanban* system. Much of the subsequent success of Japanese companies globally during the 1980s can be attributed to the improvements in product quality that were brought about by the wide-scale adoption of the *kanban* system in Japan, a full decade before managers in Western companies imitated the idea.[27]   ■ ■ ■

8. *Work closely with suppliers.* As the "Managing Globally" feature makes clear, a major source of poor-quality finished goods is poor-quality component parts. To decrease product defects, managers must work closely with suppliers to improve the quality of the parts they supply. Managers at Xerox worked closely with suppliers to get them to adopt TQM programs, and the result was a huge reduction in the defect rate of component parts. Managers also need to work closely with suppliers to get them to adopt a JIT inventory system, also required for high quality.

To implement JIT systems with suppliers, and to get suppliers to set up their own TQM programs, two steps are necessary. First, managers must reduce the number of suppliers with which their organization does business. Managers at Xerox, for example, reduced the number of suppliers from 5,000 to 325, greatly streamlining their interactions with suppliers. Second, managers need to develop cooperative long-term relationships with remaining suppliers. Asking suppliers to invest in JIT and TQM systems means asking them to make major investments that tie them to the company. For example, to fully implement a JIT system, a company may ask a supplier to relocate its manufacturing plant so that it is next door to the company's assembly plant. Suppliers will be hesitant about making such investments unless they feel that the company is committed to an enduring long-term relationship with them.

9. *Design for ease of manufacture.* The more steps that are required to assemble a product, the more opportunities there are for making a mistake. It follows that designing products that have fewer parts and thus making their assembly easier should be linked to fewer defects. For example, after Texas Instruments redesigned an infrared sighting mechanism that it supplies to the Pentagon, the company found that it had reduced the number of parts from 47 to 12 and the number of assembly steps from 56 to 13. The consequence of this redesign was a fall in assembly costs and marked improvement in product quality.

10. *Break down barriers between functions.* Successful implementation of TQM requires organizationwide commitment from managers to quality and substantial cooperation between the different functions of an organization. R&D managers have to cooperate with manufacturing managers to design products that are easy to manufacture; marketing managers have to cooperate with manufacturing and R&D managers so that customer problems identified by marketing can be acted on; human resource managers have to cooperate with all of the other functions of the company in order to devise suitable quality training programs, and so on.

The Role of Top and Functional-Level Managers in TQM

All managers have critical roles to play in the TQM process. Normally, top managers initiate a TQM program, and a continuing emphasis on TQM requires their long-term commitment and willingness to make TQM an organizationwide priority. What cannot be stressed strongly enough, however, is that it is functional-level managers who carry prime responsibility for implementing most of the steps outlined above. Although top managers may be the ones who establish the initial TQM program, much of the actual work required to make a TQM program succeed is done by functional-level managers. It is functional-level managers who

- Identify defects, trace them back to their source, and fix quality problems
- Design products that are easy to assemble
- Identify customer needs, translate those needs into quality requirements, and see that these quality requirements shape the production system of the organization
- Work to break down the barriers between functional departments
- Solicit suggestions from lower-level employees about how to improve the quality of the organization's output

If the TQM philosophy is to become part of an organization's culture, functional-level managers must learn how to live and breathe the TQM philosophy. In those organizations where TQM has failed to deliver on its promise to improve product quality, lack of commitment by functional-level managers may be the reason. To develop a successful TQM program, managers must first involve employees at all levels in the organization. They then must clearly assign responsibility for improving quality to each employee and create a goal-setting system that allows them to evaluate how well each employee has achieved these goals. Finally, they must try to develop cultural values and norms that make quality an important goal and create organizational ceremonies to reward employees when quality targets are met.

IMPROVING EFFICIENCY

The third goal of operations management is to increase the efficiency of an organization's production system. The fewer the inputs required to produce a given output, the higher will be the level of production system efficiency. Managers can measure efficiency at the organization level in two ways. The measure known as *total factor productivity* looks at how well an organization utilizes all of its resources——such as labor, capital, materials, energy——to produce its outputs. It is expressed in the following equation:

$$\text{Total factor productivity} = \frac{\text{outputs}}{\text{all inputs}}$$

The problem with total factor productivity is that each input is typically measured in different units: Labor's contribution to producing an output is measured by hours worked; the contribution of materials is measured by the amount consumed (for example, tons of iron ore required to make a ton of steel); the contribution of energy is measured by the units of energy consumed (for example, kilowatt-hours), and so on. To compute total factor productivity, managers must convert all the inputs to a common unit, such as dollars, before they can work the equation.

Though sometimes a useful measure of efficiency overall, total factor productivity obscures the exact contribution of an individual input——such as labor——to the production of a given output. Consequently, most organizations focus on specific measures of efficiency, known as *partial productivity*, that measure the efficiency of an individual unit. For example, the efficiency of labor inputs is expressed as

$$\text{Labor productivity} = \frac{\text{outputs}}{\text{direct labor}}$$

Labor productivity is most commonly used to draw efficiency comparisons between different organizations. For example, a 1994 study found that it took the average Japanese company in the automobile components industry half as many labor hours to produce a component part such as a car seat or exhaust system as the average British company.[28] Thus, the study concluded, Japanese companies use their labor more efficiently than British companies.

The management of efficiency is an extremely important issue in most organizations, because increased efficiency lowers production costs, thereby allowing the organization to make a greater profit or to attract more customers by lowering its price. In the U.S. personal computer industry, for example, in 1990 the average personal computer sold for $3,000, by 1995 it sold for around $1,800. This decrease in price occurred despite the fact that the features of the average personal computer increased over this time period (that is, microprocessors became more powerful, memory increased, communication facilities such as built-in modems were added). The decrease in price was possible because personal computer manufacturers took several steps to boost their efficiency, which allowed them to lower their costs and prices and still make a profit. At Compaq Computer, for example, managers redesigned personal computers so that they were easier to assemble; this reduced the time it took to assemble a ProLine desktop computer from 20.85 minutes in 1991 to 10.49 minutes by 1994, a significant increase in efficiency.[29] Managers can boost efficiency in their organizations by focusing on a number of areas.

Total Quality Management and Efficiency

Increased product quality, obtained through the adoption of a TQM program, can have a major positive impact on labor productivity: When quality rises, less employee time is wasted making defective products that have to be discarded or fixing defective products. Moreover, a major source of quality improvement can come from designing products that have fewer parts and are therefore easier to assemble. Designing products with fewer parts also cuts down on total assembly time and increases efficiency.[30] When managers at Texas Instruments redesigned the infrared sighting mechanism for the Pentagon, for example, they achieved a significant increase in efficiency.

Facilities Layout, Flexible Manufacturing, and Efficiency

Another factor that influences efficiency is the way managers decide to lay out or design an organization's physical work facilities. This is important for two reasons. First, the way in which machines and workers are organized or grouped together into workstations affects the efficiency of the production system. Second, a major determinant of efficiency is the cost associated with setting up the equipment needed to make a particular product. **Facilities layout** is the operations management technique whose goal is to design the machine-worker interface to increase production system efficiency. **Flexible manufacturing** is the set of operations management techniques that attempt to reduce the setup costs associated with a production system.

FACILITIES LAYOUT   The way in which machines, robots, and people are grouped together affects how productive they can be. Figure 5 shows three basic ways of arranging workstations: product layout, process layout, and fixed-position layout.

In a *product layout,* machines are organized so that each operation needed to manufacture a product is performed by workstations arranged in a fixed sequence. Typically, workers are stationary in this arrangement, and a moving conveyor belt takes the product being worked on to the next workstation so that it is progressively assembled. *Mass production* is the familiar name of this form of facilities layout; car assembly lines are probably the best-known example. It used to be that product layout was efficient only when products were produced in large quantities; however, as the "Case in Contrast" indicates, the introduction of modular assembly lines controlled by computers is making it efficient to make products in small batches.

In a *process layout,* workstations are not organized in a fixed sequence. Rather, each workstation is relatively self-contained, and a product goes to whichever workstation is needed to perform the next operation to complete the product. Process layout is often suited to manufacturing settings that produce a variety of custom-made products, each tailored to the needs of a different kind of customer.

Facilities layout the operations management technique whose goal is to design the machine-worker interface to increase production system efficiency.
Flexible manufacturing operations management techniques that attempt to reduce the setup costs associated with a production system.

Figure 5 *Three Facilities Layouts*

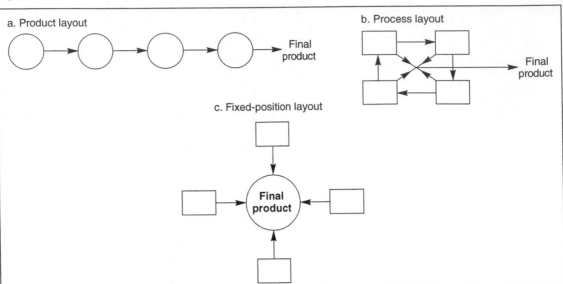

For example, a custom furniture manufacturer might use a process layout so that different teams of workers can produce a variety of different styles of chairs or tables made from different kinds of woods and finishes. Process layout provides the flexibility needed to change the product being produced. Such flexibility, however, often reduces efficiency because it is expensive.

In a *fixed-position layout*, the product being produced stays in a fixed position. Its component parts are produced in remote workstations and brought to the production area for final assembly. Increasingly, self-managed teams are being used in fixed-position layouts. Different teams assemble each component part and then send these parts to the final assembly team, which makes the final product. A fixed-position layout is commonly used for products such as jet airlines, mainframe computers, and gas turbines——products that are complex and difficult to assemble or so large that moving them from one workstation to another would be difficult.

FLEXIBLE MANUFACTURING   In a manufacturing company, a major source of costs is the costs associated with the setting up of the equipment needed to make a particular product. These costs include the cost of production that is forgone because nothing is actually produced while equipment is being set up. In the case of Federal-Mogul, for example, discussed in the "Case in Contrast," employees needed as much as half a day to set up the automated production equipment when switching from production of one product (such as a washer ring for the steering column of a car) to another (such as a washer ring for the steering column of a truck). During this half-day, the plant was not producing anything, but employees still had to be paid for this "nonproductive" time.

It follows that if setup times for complex production equipment can be reduced, so can setup costs, and efficiency will rise. In other words, if setup times can be reduced, the time that plant and employees spend in actually producing something will increase. This simple insight has been the driving force behind the development of flexible manufacturing techniques.

Flexible manufacturing aims to reduce the time required to set up production equipment.[31] The positive effects of flexible manufacturing techniques are evident in the case of Federal-Mogul. By redesigning its production system so that equipment geared for manufacturing one product could be quickly wheeled away and replaced with equipment geared to produce another product, Federal-Mogul was able to reduce setup times from as much as half a day in 1987 to 10 minutes in 1993. One result was a dramatic improvement in efficiency because there was now far less "nonproductive" time. Another favorable result was that flexible manufacturing enabled Federal-Mogul to produce three times as many different product varieties as before, in the same amount of time. In other words, flexible manufacturing increased Federal-Mogul's ability to be responsive to its customers.

Increasingly, organizations are experimenting with new designs for production systems that not only allow workers to be more productive but also make the work process more flexible, thus reducing setup costs. Some Japanese companies are experimenting with facilities layouts arranged as a spiral, as the letter Y, and as the number 6, to see how these various configurations affect setup costs and worker productivity. At a camcorder plant in Kohda, Japan, for example, Sony changed from a fixed-position layout in which 50 workers sequentially built a camcorder to a spiral process design in which 4 workers perform all the operations necessary to produce the camcorder. This new layout allows the most efficient workers to work at the highest pace, and it reduces setup costs because workers can easily switch from one model to another, increasing efficiency by 10 percent.[32]

Just-in-Time Inventory and Efficiency

Although JIT systems, such as Toyota's *kanban* system, were originally developed as part of the effort to improve product quality, they have major implications for efficiency. Major cost savings can result from increasing inventory turnover and reducing inventory holding costs, such as warehousing and storage costs and the cost of capital tied up in inventory. Ford's switch to JIT systems in the 1980s, for example, reportedly bought the company a huge one-time saving of $3 billion, and inventory holding costs have been reduced by one-third.

More recently, several service companies have adopted the JIT concept, often with great success. Wal-Mart, the fastest-growing general retailer in the United States, uses JIT systems to replenish the stock in its stores at least twice a week. Many Wal-Mart stores receive daily deliveries. Wal-Mart's main competitors, Kmart and Sears, typically replenish their stock every two weeks. Wal-Mart can maintain the same service levels as these competitors, but at one-fourth the inventory holding cost, a major source of cost saving. Thus, faster inventory turnover has helped Wal-Mart achieve an efficiency-based competitive advantage in the retailing industry.[33]

One drawback of JIT systems is that they leave an organization without a buffer stock of inventory.[34] Although buffer stocks of inventory can be expensive to store, they can help an organization when it is affected by shortages of inputs brought about by a disruption among suppliers (such as a labor dispute in a key supplier). Moreover, buffer stocks can help an organization respond quickly to increases in customer demand——that is, they can increase an organization's responsiveness to customers.

Because holding a buffer stock of inventory does have advantages, some early adopters of JIT systems have recently pulled back from a complete commitment to JIT. One such example is GE Appliances, profiled in the next "Management Insight."

MANAGEMENT INSIGHT   PROBLEMS WITH JIT AT GE APPLIANCES

GE (www.ge.com) Appliances' managers first became interested in Japan's *kanban* system of just-in-time inventory in the early 1980s when General Electric CEO Jack Welsh was urging GE's various divisions to boost their efficiency by adopting Japanese-style manufacturing techniques. At first the system seemed to be working well; the appliances division realized a one-time saving of over $50 million from inventory reductions as inventory holding costs fell by close to one-half. Moreover, managers found that JIT systems helped them identify defective inputs from suppliers, trace problems back to their source, and fix problems that caused defects so that they would not occur again.

By the early 1990s, however, managers at GE were becoming disillusioned with some aspects of their JIT system. One problem was that low inventories of some critical parts prevented GE from responding quickly to customer demands. GE gets 475 parts from 75 suppliers——some of which are located several thousand miles from GE's assembly plant. Getting critical parts from some of these suppliers often took so long that GE was unable to promptly fill orders from important customers, who then turned to GE's competitors.

In 1993 managers decided to increase by 24 percent their inventory of critical parts that had long delivery times. This change helped the company to respond more rapidly to customer orders. By 1994 GE was filling orders in 3.6 weeks, down from 18 weeks in 1990.[35] According to managers, the benefits of a faster order-to-delivery cycle more than offset the cost of stocking additional parts.   ■ ■ ■

Self-Managed Work Teams and Efficiency

Another efficiency-boosting innovation that is gaining wide acceptance in the workplace is the use of self-managed work teams.[36] The typical team consists of from 5 to 15 employees who produce an entire product instead of just parts of it.[37] Team members learn all team tasks and move from job to job. The result is a flexible workforce, because team members can fill in for absent coworkers. The members of each team also assume responsibility for work and vacation scheduling, ordering materials, and hiring new members——previous responsibilities of first-line managers. Because people often respond well to being given greater autonomy and responsibility, the use of empowered self-managed teams can increase productivity and efficiency. Moreover, cost savings arise from eliminating supervisors and creating a flatter organizational hierarchy, which further increases efficiency.

The effect of introducing self-managed teams is often an increase in efficiency of 30 percent or more, sometimes much more. After the introduction of flexible manufacturing technology and self-managed teams, a GE plant in Salisbury, North Carolina, increased efficiency by 250 percent compared with other GE plants producing the same products.[38]

Kaizen *(Continuous Improvement)* and Efficiency

Kaizen an all-embracing operations management philosophy that emphasizes the need for continuous improvement in the efficiency of an organization's production system.

Kaizen is the Japanese term for an all-embracing operations management philosophy that emphasizes the need for continuous improvement in the efficiency of an organization's production system.[39] Unlike TQM or JIT, *kaizen* is not a specific operations management technique; rather, *kaizen* stresses the contribution to improving efficiency and quality that can come from numerous small, incremental improvements in production processes.

The central principle of kaizen is the elimination of waste: wasted materials, piles of excess inventory, time wasted when a production employee makes more moves than are necessary to complete a task because, for example, his or her machine is poorly positioned, and time wasted in activities that do not add value, such as moving parts from one machine to another. According to representatives from the Kaizen Institute, a European management consultancy, in the average factory for every second spent adding value by, for example, assembling a product, another 1,000 seconds are spent not adding value.[40]

The *kaizen* philosophy emphasizes that managers and other employees should be taught to critically analyze all aspects of their organization's production system, to identify any sources of waste and to suggest ways to eliminate the waste. Often, self-managed work teams perform this analysis. They take time out once a week or once a month to analyze the design of their jobs and to suggest potential improvements to functional managers.[41]

Increasingly, as part of the *kaizen* process, managers are experimenting with changing facilities layouts to try to increase efficiency. In Paddy Hopkirk's car accessory factory, located in Bedfordshire, England, and profiled in the next "Managing Globally," the application of *kaizen* resulted in a change in facilities layout that reduced the time wasted in moving parts from workstation to workstation.

MANAGING GLOBALLY APPLYING *KAIZEN* TO IMPROVE FACILITIES LAYOUT

Paddy Hopkirk established his car accessories business in the 1960s, shortly after he had shot to motor car racing fame by winning the Monte Carlo Rally. Sales of Hopkirk's accessories, such as bicycle racks and axle stands, were always brisk, and by 1993 his company was doing over $6 million worth of business. Hopkirk, however, was the first to admit that his production system left a lot to be desired. So in 1993, after hearing about *kaizen* from a customer, he invited consultants from the Kaizen Institute to help him reorganize his production system.

After analyzing his factory's production system, the consultants realized that the source of the problem was the facilities layout Hopkirk had established. Over time, as sales had grown, Hopkirk had simply added new workstations to the production system as and when they were needed. The result was a process layout in which the product being assembled moved in the irregular sequences shown in the "before *Kaizen*" half of Figure 6. The consultants suggested that to save time and effort, the workstations should be reorganized into the sequential product layout shown in the "after *Kaizen*" illustration.

Once this change was made, the results were dramatic. One morning the factory was an untidy sprawl of workstations surrounded by piles of crates holding semifinished components. Two days later, when the 170-strong workforce came back to work, the machines had been brought together into tightly grouped workstations arranged in the fixed sequence shown in the illustration. The piles of components had disappeared, and the newly cleared floor space was neatly marked with color-coded lines mapping out the new flow of materials between workstations.

In the first full day of production, efficiency increased by as much as 30 percent. The space needed for some operations had been cut in half, and work-in-progress had been cut considerably. Moreover, the improved layout allowed for some jobs to be combined, freeing up operators for deployment elsewhere in the factory. An amazed Hopkirk exclaimed, "I was expecting a change but nothing as dramatic as this . . . it is fantastic."[42] ■ ■ ■

Figure 6 *The Application of Kaizen to Facilities Layout*

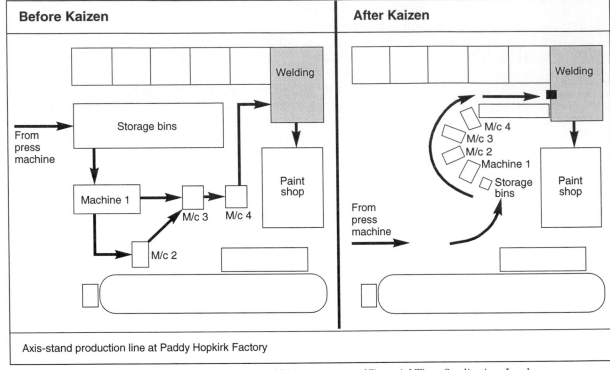

Axis-stand production line at Paddy Hopkirk Factory

Source: Reprinted from Financial Times *of January 4, 1994 by permission of Financial Times Syndication, London.*

The implementation of self-managed teams, flexible manufacturing systems and facilities layouts, TQM, and JIT are all consistent with the *kaizen* approach: All seek to reduce wasted materials and time. Indeed, these techniques were originally developed by Toyota and other Japanese companies that had adopted the *kaizen* philosophy and were looking for specific ways to improve their production processes.

Process Reengineering and Efficiency

Process reengineering the fundamental rethinking and radical redesign of business processes to achieve dramatic improvement in critical measures of performance such as cost, quality, service, and speed.

Think of the major activities of businesses as processes that take one or more kinds of inputs and create an output that is of value to the customer.[43] **Process reengineering** is the fundamental rethinking and radical redesign of business processes to achieve dramatic improvements in critical measures of performance such as cost, quality, service, and speed.[44] Order fulfillment, for example, can be thought of as a business process: Once a customer's order is received (the input), all the activities necessary to process the order are performed, and the ordered goods are delivered to the customer (the output).

Like *kaizen*, process reengineering can boost efficiency because it eliminates the time devoted to activities that do not add value. Unlike *kaizen*, with its emphasis on continuous incremental improvements, process reengineering is about redesigning business processes from scratch. It is concerned with the radical redesign of business processes, not incremental changes in those processes. Because process reengineering burst on the management scene in 1993, it is too early to evaluate its effectiveness as a management tool. Some interesting examples of reengineering, however, suggest that if properly implemented it can have a major impact on efficiency. Consider the case of Ford Motor Company, profiled in the following "Management Insight."

MANAGEMENT INSIGHT REENGINEERING OF PROCUREMENT AT FORD

Ford (www.ford.com) has a strategic alliance with Mazda (www.mazda.com). One day a Ford manager discovered, quite by accident, that the Japanese car company had only five people in its accounts payable department. The Ford manager was shocked, for Ford's U.S. operation alone had 500 employees in accounts payable. He reported his discovery to Ford's U.S. managers, who decided to form a task force to analyze Ford's procurement process and to see whether it could be reengineered.

Ford managers discovered that procurement began when the purchasing department sent a purchase order to a supplier and sent a copy of the purchase order to Ford's accounts payable department. When the supplier shipped the goods and they arrived at Ford, a clerk at the receiving dock completed a form describing the goods and sent the form to accounts payable. The supplier, meanwhile, sent accounts payable an invoice. Thus, accounts payable received three documents relating to these goods: a copy of the original purchase order, the receiving document, and the invoice. If the information in all three was in agreement (most of the time it was), a clerk in accounts payable issued payment. Occasionally, however, all three documents did not agree. And Ford discovered that accounts payable clerks spent most of their time straightening out the 1 percent of instances in which the purchase order, receiving document, and invoice contained conflicting information.[45]

Ford managers decided to reengineer the procurement process to simplify it. Now when a buyer in the purchasing department issues a purchase order to a supplier, that buyer also enters the order into an on-line data base. As before, suppliers send goods to the receiving dock. When the goods arrive, the clerk at the receiving dock checks a computer terminal to see whether the received shipment matches the description on the purchase order. If it does, the clerk accepts the goods and pushes a button on the terminal keyboard that tells the data base that the goods have arrived. Receipt of the goods is recorded in the data base, and a computer automatically issues and sends a check to the supplier. If the goods do not correspond to the description on the purchase order in the data base, the clerk at the dock refuses the shipment and sends it back to the supplier.

Payment authorization, which used to be performed by accounts payable, is now accomplished at the receiving dock. The new process has come close to eliminating the need for an accounts payable department. In some parts of Ford, the size of the accounts payable department has been cut by 95 percent. By reducing the head count in accounts payable, the reengineering effort reduced the amount of time wasted on unproductive activities, thereby increasing the efficiency of the total organization. ■ ■ ■

The Role of Top and Functional-Level Managers in Efficiency

As with TQM, managers at all levels have important roles to play in the effort to boost efficiency. Top management's role is to encourage efficiency improvements by, for example, emphasizing the need for continuous improvement (*kaizen*) or reengineering. Top management also must ensure that managers from different functional departments work together to find ways to increase efficiency. Achieving functional cooperation is important because many of the steps that must be taken to raise efficiency involve actions that cut across functional boundaries. Reengineering, for example, may require personnel from different departments to cooperate on the design of a new process.

As with TQM, however, it is middle managers who bear the prime responsibility for identifying and implementing many of the efficiency-enhancing improvements to a production system. It is typically functional-level managers who identify opportunities for continuous improvement or reengineering. Top managers might recognize the need for such actions, but functional-level managers are in the best position to identify opportunities for making efficiency-enhancing improvements (especially *kaizen* ones) to an organization's production systems. They are the managers who are involved in an organization's production system on a day-to-day basis.

OPERATIONS MANAGEMENT: SOME REMAINING ISSUES

Achieving superior responsiveness to customers through quality and efficiency often requires a profound shift in management operations and in the culture of an organization. The message of both TQM and *kaizen* for improving operations management in the future is that all employees need to constantly evaluate an organization's production system in an ongoing and never-ending search for improvements. Many reports are appearing in the popular press about widespread disillusionment with TQM, JIT, flexible manufacturing, *kaizen,* and reengineering. It is possible that many of the disillusioned organizations are those that failed to understand that implementing these systems requires a marked shift in organizational culture.[46] None of these systems is a panacea that can be taken once like a pill to cure industrial ills. Making these techniques work within an organization can pose a significant challenge that calls for hard work and years of persistence by the sponsoring managers.

Managers also need to understand the ethical implications of the adoption of many of the production techniques discussed here. TQM, JIT, flexible manufacturing, *kaizen,* and reengineering can all increase quality, efficiency, and responsiveness to customers, but they may do so at great cost to employees. Employees may see the demands of their job increase as the result of TQM or *kaizen,* or, worse, they may see themselves reengineered out of a job. Consider, for example, the incidents described in the following "Ethics in Action."

ETHICS IN ACTION   THE HUMAN COST OF IMPROVING PRODUCTIVITY

Toyota (www.toyota.com) may be the most productive automobile company in the world, but some of its gains have been achieved at a significant cost to its employees. Take Hisashi Tomiki, the leader of a four-man self-managed team in Toyota's huge Toyota City production plant, 200 miles south of Tokyo, Japan. Tomiki and his team work at a grueling pace to build cowls (steel chambers onto which windshields and steering columns are attached). Consider this description of Tomiki at work:

> *In two minutes Tomiki fits 24 metal pieces into designated slots on three welding machines; runs two large metal sheets through each of the machines, which weld on the parts; and fuses the two sheets together with two spot welds. There is little room for error.*

Once or twice an hour a mistake is made or a machine sticks, causing the next machine in line to stop. A yellow light flashes. Tomiki runs over. The squad must fix the part and work faster to catch up. A red button halts the production line if the problems are severe, but there is an unspoken rule against pushing it. Only once this day does Tomiki call in a special maintenance worker.[47]

The experience of workers like Tomiki makes many Western workers nervous about the spread of Japanese management techniques. Workers are heard to complain that constant improvement really means continuous speedup and added job stress. Consider this comment on *kaizen* from one employee at Mazda's auto plant in Flat Rock, Michigan. "Under *kaizen* management constantly reduces the parts, the resources, the manpower, to do the job. We are building 1,000 good cars a day, an incredible effort. But if we learn to do it with 90 percent [of the time and resources], they go to 80 percent. They take away another person, they take away another part."[48] The implication, of course, is that there is no end to the search for continuous improvement (which, in essence, is what the *kaizen* philosophy recommends) and therefore no end to the steady increase in the pressure put on employees to perform. Although some pressure is good, past a certain point it can seriously harm employees.

Nor is it just Japanese techniques that have such an impact. Process reengineering, first developed in America, is also taking its toll. Consider the following quote from Jerry Miller, a former employee of US West, whose team of billing clerks reengineered themselves out of a job in 1994: "When we first formed our teams, the company came in talking teams and empowerment and promised that we wouldn't lose any jobs. It turns out all this was a big cover. The company had us all set up for reengineering. We showed them how to streamline the work, and now 9,000 people are gone. It was cut-your-own-throat. It makes you feel used."[49] ■ ■ ■

The problems highlighted in the previous "Ethics in Action" raise serious questions about the introduction of *kaizen* and reengineering: They may constitute a violation of basic ethics, principally because they may require some deception. With regard to *kaizen*, one must ask whether it is ethical to continually increase the demands placed on employees, regardless of the human cost in terms of job stress. It is obvious that the answer is no. Employees are important stakeholders in an organization, and their support is vital if the organization is to function effectively. What are the limits to *kaizen;* what kind of work pressures are legitimate, and what pressures are excessive? There is no clear answer to this question. Ultimately the issue comes down to the judgment of responsible managers acting ethically toward all their stakeholders.

SUMMARY

CHAPTER SUMMARY

Operations Management and Competitive Advantage

Improving Responsiveness to Customers

What Do Customers Want?

Designing Production Systems that Are Responsive to Customers

Improving Quality

Total Quality Management

Putting TQM into Action: The Management Challenge

The Role of Top and Functional-Level Managers in TQM

Improving Efficiency

Total Quality Management and Efficiency

Facilities Layout, Flexible Manufacturing, and Efficiency

Just-in-Time Inventory and Efficiency

Self-Managed Work Teams and Efficiency

Kaizen (Continuous Improvement) and Efficiency

Process Reengineering and Efficiency

The Role of Top and Functional-Level Managers in Efficiency

Operations Management: Some Remaining Issues

CHAPTER REVIEW

OPERATIONS MANAGEMENT AND COMPETITIVE ADVANTAGE To achieve high performance, managers try to improve their responsiveness to customers, the quality of their products, and the efficiency of their organization. To achieve these goals, managers can use a number of operations management techniques to improve the way an organization's production system operates.

IMPROVING RESPONSIVENESS TO CUSTOMERS To achieve high performance in a competitive environment, it is imperative that the production system of an organization respond to customer demands. Managers try to design production systems that produce outputs that have the attributes that customers desire. One of the central tasks of operations management is to develop new and improved production systems that enhance the ability of the organization to economically deliver more of the product attributes that customers desire for the same price. Techniques such as TQM, JIT, flexible manufacturing, *kaizen,* and process reengineering are popular because they promise to do this. Managers should carefully analyze the links between responsiveness to customers and the production system of an organization. The ability of an organization to satisfy the demands of its customers for lower prices, acceptable quality, better features, and so on, critically depends on the nature of the organization's production system. As important as responsiveness to customers is, however, managers need to recognize that there are limits to how responsive an organization can be and still cover its costs.

IMPROVING QUALITY Managers seek to improve the quality of their organization's output because this enables them to better serve customers, to raise prices, and to lower production costs. Total quality management focuses on improving the quality of an organization's products and services and stresses that all of an organization's operations should be directed toward this goal. Putting TQM into practice requires an organizationwide commitment to TQM, a strong customer focus, finding ways to measure quality, setting quality improvement goals, soliciting input from employees about how to improve product quality, identifying defects and tracing them to their source, introducing just-in-time inventory systems, getting suppliers to adopt TQM practices, designing products for ease of manufacture, and breaking down barriers between functional departments.

IMPROVING EFFICIENCY Improving efficiency requires one or more of the following: the introduction of a TQM program, the adoption of flexible manufacturing technologies, the introduction of just-in-time inventory systems, the establishment of self-managed work teams, the institutionalization of a *kaizen* philosophy of continuous improvement within the organization, and process reengineering. Top management is responsible for setting the context within which efficiency improvements can take place by, for example, emphasizing the need for a *kaizen* philosophy. Functional-level managers bear prime responsibility for identifying and implementing efficiency-enhancing improvements in production systems.

TOPICS FOR DISCUSSION

- What are the main challenges to be overcome in implementing a successful total quality management program?
- Ask a manager how quality, efficiency, and responsiveness to customers are defined and measured in his or her organization.
- Go into a local store, restaurant, or supermarket and list the ways in which you think the organization is being responsive or unresponsive to the needs of its customers. How could this business's responsiveness to customers be improved?
- Widespread dissatisfaction with the results of TQM programs has been reported in the popular press.

Why do you think TQM programs frequently fail to deliver their promised benefits?
- What is efficiency, and what are some of the techniques that managers can use to increase it?
- Why is it important for managers to pay close attention to their organization's production system if they wish to be responsive to their customers?
- What, if any, are the ethical limitations to the aggressive implementation of the *kaizen* philosophy of continuous improvement?
- Total customer service is the goal toward which most organizations should strive." To what degree is this statement correct?

BUILDING MANAGEMENT SKILLS

MANAGING A PRODUCTION SYSTEM

Choose an organization with which you are familiar—one that you have worked in or patronized or one that has received extensive coverage in the popular press. The organization should be involved in only one industry or business. Answer these questions about the organization.

1 What is the output of the organization?
2 Describe the production system that the organization uses to produce this output.

3 What product attributes do customers of the organization desire?
4 Does its production system allow the organization to deliver the desired product attributes?
5 Try to identify improvements that might be made to the organization's production system to boost the organization's responsiveness to customers, quality, and efficiency.

SMALL GROUP BREAKOUT EXERCISE

HOW TO COMPETE IN THE SANDWICH BUSINESS

Form groups of three or four people, and appoint one member as the spokesperson who will communicate your findings to the whole class when called on by the instructor. Then discuss the following scenario.

You and your partners are thinking about opening a new kind of sandwich shop that will compete head-to-head with Subway and Thundercloud Subs. Because these chains have good brand-name recognition, it is vital that you find some source of competitive advantage

for your new sandwich shop, and you are meeting to brainstorm ways of obtaining one.

1 Identify the product attributes that a typical sandwich shop customer wants the most.
2 In what ways do you think you will be able to improve on the operations and processes of existing sandwich shops and achieve a competitive advantage through better (a) product quality, (b) efficiency, or (c) responsiveness to customers?

EXPLORING THE WORLD WIDE WEB

Enter the Web site of Kaizen Inc. (www.zaks/com/ kaizen) and click on the *kaizen* button.

1 What elements of the *kaizen* techniques does this company use?

2 How does the *kaizen* technique help give the company a competitive advantage?

Search for the Web site of a company that outlines the way it tries to improve customer responsiveness, quality, or efficiency. What specific techniques does the company use to improve the way it operates? How have those techniques helped the company improve its performance?

REFERENCES

1. Amal Kumar Naj, "Shifting Gears," *The Wall Street Journal,* May 7, 1993, A1.

2. The view of quality as including reliability goes back to the work of W. Edwards Deming and Joseph Juran. See A. Gabor, *The Man Who Discovered Quality* (New York: Times Books, 1990).

3. D. F. Abell, *Defining the Business: The Starting Point of Strategic Planning* (Englewood Cliffs, NJ: Prentice-Hall, 1980).

4. For details, see "Johnson & Johnson (A)," *Harvard Business School Case* #384-053.

5. M. E. Porter, *Competitive Advantage* (New York: Free Press, 1985).

6. According to Richard D'Aveni, the process of pushing price/attribute curves to the right is a characteristic of the competitive process. See R. D'Aveni, *Hypercompetition* (New York: Free Press, 1994).

7. This is a central insight of the modern manufacturing literature. See R. H. Hayes and S. C. Wheelwright, "Link Manufacturing Process and Product Life Cycles," *Harvard Business Review,* (January–February 1979): pp. 127–136; R. H. Hayes and S. C. Wheelwright, "Competing Through Manufacturing," *Harvard Business Review* (January–February 1985): pp. 99–109.

8. L. Therrien, "Spreading the Message," *Business Week,* October 25, 1991, p. 60.

9. B. O'Brian, "Flying on the Cheap," *The Wall Street Journal,* October 26, 1992, A1; B. O'Reilly, "Where Service Flies Right," *Fortune,* August 24, 1992, pp. 116–117; A. Salpukas, "Hurt in Expansion, Airlines Cut Back and May Sell Hubs," *The Wall Street Journal,* April 1, 1993, A1, C8.

10. K. Done, "Toyota Warns of Continuing Decline," *Financial Times,* November 23, 1993, p. 23.

11. The view of quality as reliability goes back to the work of Deming and Juran; see Gabor, *The Man Who Discovered Quality.*

12. See D. Garvin, "What Does Product Quality Really Mean?" *Sloan Management Review* 26 (Fall 1984): pp. 25–44; P. B. Crosby, *Quality Is Free* (New York: Mentor, 1980); Gabor, *The Man Who Discovered Quality.*

13. N. Templin, "Toyota Is Standout Once Again," *The Wall Street Journal,* May 28, 1993, B1.

14. See J. W. Dean and D. E. Bowen, "Management Theory and Total Quality: Improving Research and Practice Through Theory Development," *Academy of Management Review,* no. 19 (1994): pp. 392–418.

15. For general background information, see J. C. Anderson, M. Rungtusanatham, and R. G. Schroeder, "A Theory of Quality Management Underlying the Deming Management Method," *Academy of Management Review,* no. 19 (1994): pp. 472–509; "How to Build Quality," *The Economist,* September 23, 1989,

pp. 91–92; Gabor, *The Man Who Discovered Quality;* Crosby, *Quality Is Free.*

16. W. E. Deming, "Improvement of Quality and Productivity Through Action by Management," *National Productivity Review,* no. 1 (Winter 1981–1982): pp. 12–22.

17. D. Kearns, "Leadership Through Quality," *Academy of Management Executive,* no. 4 (1990): pp. 86–89; J. Sheridan, "America's Best Plants," *Industry Week,* October 15, 1990, pp. 27–40.

18. R. Winslow, "Exercising Waste," *The Wall Street Journal,* November 3, 1993, A1.

19. L. Cochrane, "Not Just Another Quality Snowjob," *The Wall Street Journal,* May 24, 1993, A10.

20. J. Bowles, "Is American Management Really Committed to Quality?" *Management Review* (April 1992): pp. 42–46.

21. O. Port and G. Smith, "Quality," *Business Week,* November 30, 1992, pp. 66–75.

22. V. Houlder, "Two Steps Forward, One Step Back," *Financial Times,* October 31, 1994, p. 8.

23. Bowles, "Is American Management Really Committed to Quality?"

24. Gabor, *The Man Who Discovered Quality.*

25. Deming, "Improvement of Quality and Productivity."

26. W. E. Deming, *Out of the Crisis* (Cambridge, MA: MIT Center for Advanced Engineering Study, 1986).

27. M. A. Cusumano, *The Japanese Automobile Industry* (Cambridge, MA: Harvard University Press, 1989); Ohno Taiichi, *Toyota Production System.* (Cambridge, MA: Productivity Press, 1990) (Japanese edition, 1978); J. P. Womack, D. T. Jones, and D. Roos, *The Machine that Changed the World* (New York: Macmillan, 1990).

28. J. Griffiths, "Europe's Manufacturing Quality and Productivity Still Lag Far Behind Japan's," *Financial Times,* November 4, 1994, p. 11.

29. S. McCartney, "Compaq Borrows Wal-Mart's Idea to Boost Production," *The Wall Street Journal,* June 17, 1994, B4.

30. S. C. Wheelwright and K. B. Clark, *Managing New Product and Process Development* (New York: Free Press, 1993).

31. P. Nemetz and L. Fry, "Flexible Manufacturing Organizations: Implications for Strategy Formulation," *Academy of Management Review,* no. 13 (1988): pp. 627–638; N. Greenwood, *Implementing Flexible Manufacturing Systems* (New York: Halstead Press, 1986).

32. M. Williams, "Back to the Past," *The Wall Street Journal,* 1994, October 24, 1994, A1.

33. G. Stalk and T. M. Hout, *Competing Against Time* (New York: Free Press, 1990).

34. For an interesting discussion of some other drawbacks of JIT and other "Japanese" manufacturing techniques, see S. M. Young, "A Framework for Successful Adoption and Performance of Japanese Manufacturing Practices in the United States," *Academy of Management Review,* no. 17 (1992): pp. 677–701.

35. A. Kumar Naj, "Shifting Gears," *The Wall Street Journal,* May 7, 1993, A1; B. Dumaine, "The Trouble with Teams," *Fortune,* September 5, 1994, pp. 86–92.

36. Dumaine, "The Trouble with Teams."

37. See C. W. L. Hill, "Transaction Cost Economizing as a Source of National Competitive Advantage: The Case of Japan," *Organization Science* (1994): M. Aoki, *Information, Incentives, and Bargaining in the Japanese Economy* (Cambridge: Cambridge University Press, 1989).

38. J. Hoerr, "The Payoff from Teamwork," *Business Week,* July 10, 1989, pp. 56–62.

39. M. Imai, *Kaizen: The Key to Japan's Competitive Success* (New York: Random House, 1987).

40. R. Gourlay, "Back to Basics on the Factory Floor," *Financial Times,* January 4, 1994, p. 12.

41. S. M. Young, "A Framework for Successful Adoption and Performance of Japanese Manufacturing Practices in the United States," *Academy of Management Review,* no. 17 (1992): pp. 677–700.

42. R. Gourlay, "Back to Basics on the Factory Floor," *Financial Times,* January 4, 1994, p. 12.

43. M. Hammer and J. Champy, *Reengineering the Corporation* (New York: Harper Business, 1993), p. 35.

44. Ibid., p. 46.

45. Ibid.

46. For example, see Houlder, "Two Steps Forward, One Step Back"; A. K. Naj, "Shifting Gears," *The Wall Street Journal,* May 7, 1993, A1; D. Greising, "Quality: How to Make It Pay," *Business Week,* August 8, 1994, pp. 54–59.

47. L. Helm and M. Edid, "Life on the Line: Two Auto Workers Who Are Worlds Apart," *Business Week,* September 30, 1994, pp. 76–78.

48. J. Flint, "'Constant Improvement' or Speedup?" *Forbes,* April 17, 1989, p. 94.

49. Dumaine, "The Trouble with Teams."

50. K. K. Reiste and A. Hubrich, "Work-Team Implementation," *Hospital Management Quarterly* (February 1996): pp. 47–53.

MANAGEMENT CASE

KAIZEN AT FRIGIDAIRE

Until 1990, the Frigidaire Company (www.frigidaire.com) plant in Jefferson, Iowa, used a traditional mass-production assembly system to produce transmissions. One hundred sixty employees, working in shifts, stood along a straight conveyor belt assembling transmissions, and supervisors were responsible for monitoring their performance and making all production-related decisions. According to managers, the management approach was like Theory X (management's negative assumption that all workers are lazy and need management's supervision), and although productivity was acceptable, quality was poor.

This situation changed rapidly in 1991 when a new plant manager took control of the Jefferson plant. The newcomer had experience with *kaizen* and the use of teams, or "cells," as the basis of the production system, rather than a conveyor belt. The production manager moved quickly to implement a new team-based approach in the factory based on *kaizen* principles.

He instructed his managers to examine the current production system and machinery layout and figure out how to divide the workforce into teams to produce the transmissions. Managers went to work and found that the most efficient way to group machines and workers into teams would be to divide the workforce into 28 teams.[50] The 28 teams were positioned so that they could efficiently exchange the component parts necessary to produce the final transmission.

The supervisors' role was totally changed. Responsibility for all assembly-related decision making was passed down the line to team members. Supervisors were renamed "primary facilitators," and their new role was to support a team and to provide it with the resources it needed. Each team and its facilitator was instructed to meet once a week to set production goals and to discuss ways to increase productivity and quality. Facilitators also were responsible for meeting together as a team once a week to share their knowledge and information and so spread the new learning among teams across the organization. By 1996, the new work system had succeeded dramatically. The performance of some teams had increased by 50 percent, and quality was up sharply too.

QUESTIONS

1 What changes did managers at Frigidaire make to the work system?
2 Why do you think the new work system was successful?

MANAGEMENT CASE IN THE NEWS

SELLING A BRIGHT IDEA— ALONG WITH THE KILOWATTS

D. Greising, Business Week

By the time Florida Power & Light (FPL) Co. (www.fpl.com) became the first U.S. company to capture Japan's prestigious W. E. Deming Prize in 1989, the Miami-based utility had become a kind of mecca for corporate America's quality mavens. Visitors marveled at FPL's quality department, numbering 80 staffers. And they were awestruck by the utility's 1,800 quality-improvement teams. "We had checkers checking checkers in everything we did," says J. Thomas Petillo, then an executive in the quality office.

In the end, however, FPL kept better tabs on quality than it did on its basic business. The utility's managers, preoccupied with such quality issues as timely billing and preventing downed power lines, woke up too late to the population explosion in southern Florida and the sudden surge in demand for power. FPL had to buy electricity from nearby utilities. It even had to initiate rolling brownouts to conserve power. The year it won the Deming, FPL's profits fell 8%, to $412 million, even though its revenues climbed 13% to $5.3 billion.

Talking Cure. With results like that, many companies would have turned out the lights on quality programs. Not FPL. Instead, the utility revamped its entire quality approach—this time with an emphasis on cost reduction. Nowadays, FPL's bottom line is much brighter. Its profits rose 23% last year, to $572.4 million. And building on its reputation as a Deming winner, FPL has launched a thriving return-on-quality

consulting business. FPL's Qualtec Quality Services Inc. unit has 52 consultants, annual billings of more than $13 million, and a list of 100 clients worldwide, from US West Inc. to Britain's Nuclear Electric PLC.

Qualtec's approach is straightforward. First, it tries to persuade managers to throw out their old views of quality. The consultants break up management—from top executives through middle managers—into groups to talk about quality and how it should be used only as a means to produce healthier results. The message is spread through teams made up of managers and blue-collar workers. Then, with everyone in agreement on how to define quality, Qualtec does a top-to-bottom review of the way a company operates, identifying potential quality improvements that could yield financial benefits.

At American President Co., a shipping company based in Oakland, Calif., Qualtec consultant Joe L. Webb made three transpacific voyages before singling out 45 processes that were key to keeping American President's ships running smoothly. Of those, Webb figured that 25, including loading cargo and meeting schedules, were critical to customers—and therefore likely candidates for quality improvements. Since then, Webb has recommended a number of measures, such as streamlining paperwork to reduce the time it takes customs officials to clear cargo.

"Turbo Teams." Not all of Qualtec's consultants have time for cruises. As more companies look for tangible payoffs from quality, they are also demanding speedier results. "Twelve to 18 months? Surely you

can do better than that" is the common refrain from clients, says Petillo, now Qualtec's president. In response, Qualtec has formed "turbo teams" of consultants and managers to develop quality programs in a matter of weeks, not months. Gauging the financial impact of quality improvements is still a challenge. To help its clients, Qualtec is developing new computer software to measure the cost of quality against projected financial results, such as sales and return on capital.

As for the old Deming process that FPL once championed, Petillo thinks it still has merits. But even the Japanese quality devotees he sees these days are no longer blind to cost. Japan's weakened economy has seen to that. "Before, the Japanese wouldn't talk about cost," says Petillo. "Now they understand." It's a revelation that Qualtec is helping to spread.

Source: D. Greising, "Selling a Bright Idea—Along with the Kilowatts," **Business Week,** *August 8, 1994, p. 59.*

QUESTIONS

1 What were the positive aspects of Florida Power & Light's obsession with total quality management? What were the negative aspects?

2 The Florida Power & Light case highlights a potential flaw in the TQM philosophy. What is this flaw?

3 Given the information in this case, how do you think the TQM philosophy needs to be modified in order to improve its effectiveness as a management tool?

CHAPTER 19

The Global Environment

A CASE IN CONTRAST

WHY EXPAND GLOBALLY?

During the 1980s, The Limited emerged as one of the top women's clothing chains in the United States, and Toys 'R' Us (www.tru.com) became the largest toy retailer. Founded by entrepreneurial managers in the 1970s, The Limited by Leslie Wexner and Toys 'R' Us by Charles Lazarus, both companies grew at the expense of traditional retailers such as Sears, J. C. Penney, and Kmart. By charging low prices, and by pioneering new ways to retail goods to customers, such as The Limited's boutique-like stores and Toys 'R' Us's toy supermarkets, Wexner and Lazarus charged past their competitors. For most of the 1980s, sales at both companies grew at an annual rate of over 20 percent, and both companies opened hundreds of new stores around the country.

In the early 1990s, both Wexner and Lazarus realized that their companies were likely to grow more slowly because they already had captured as large a share of customers for their respective products as they could reasonably expect. However, CEOs Wexner and Lazarus wanted to grow their companies even more and searched for ways to expand sales and attract new customers. They chose very different routes: Lazarus decided that Toys 'R' Us should expand internationally and open toy stores around the globe; Wexner decided that The Limited should stay within the United States and open different kinds of retail stores.

Lazarus's idea was that Toys 'R' Us should transfer its retailing skills, which had served the company so well in the United States, to other countries and become a major competitor in foreign markets. By mid-1994, Toys 'R' Us had opened 234 stores internationally, in addition to its 581 stores in the United States. The international expansion included 50 stores in Canada, 45 in Britain, 44 in Germany, 25 in France, 17 in Spain, and 16 in Japan.

Expansion into foreign markets has not been easy for Toys 'R' Us managers. They have had to work hard to respond to unfamiliar political, economic, and sociocultural forces present in foreign countries. The Japanese venture is an example of the difficulties the company has faced. Toys 'R' Us decided to enter the Japanese market in the mid-1980s but was unable to open a single store until late 1991. What caused the delay? Quite simply, the delay was due to Japan's Large Scale Retail Store Law, which allowed small Japanese retailers to block the opening of new stores in their neighborhoods for 10 years or more. As a result of pressure from the U.S. government, the Japanese government changed the law in 1990 so that local store owners could delay a store opening for only 18 months. Shortly after that, Toys 'R' Us opened its first Japanese stores.

Another challenge facing Toys 'R' Us managers was Japan's system of distributing Japanese products. Traditionally, Japanese manufacturers sold their products only by means of wholesalers with which they had developed long-term business relationships. Because the wholesalers added their own price markup, the price Toys 'R' Us had to pay for Japanese toys increased and thus thwarted the U.S. company's attempt to establish a competitive advantage in Japan based on price discounting. As a result, to keep its costs low, Toys 'R' Us insisted on buying directly from Japanese manufacturers, but the manufacturers refused. This stand-off was finally broken by Japan's deep recession in the early 1990s. Faced with slumping orders, computer-game maker Nintendo reversed its earlier decision and agreed to sell merchandise directly to Toys 'R' Us. Soon a host of other Japanese toy companies followed Nintendo's lead. With these major problems solved, Toys 'R' Us's average sales in its Japanese stores were between $15 million and $20 million a year, roughly double the sales per store in the United States. The company plans to open 100 stores in Japan by 2002. However, because of the problems managers experienced in responding to the forces in the Japanese environment, the company did not break even on its Japan operations until 1995.

At The Limited, Leslie Wexner watched as many companies, including Toys 'R' Us, ventured into international expansion in the 1980s. Wexner decided against a global approach to increasing sales. Instead, he decided to broaden The Limited's presence in the United States. Believing that customer and shareholder interests would be served best by focusing on opportunities in the United States, Wexner initiated the opening of new kinds of stores, including Victoria's Secret (lingerie), The Bath & Body Works (toiletries), and Structure (men's clothing). Many of these new stores performed well enough to become market leaders and greatly contributed to sales and profits. However, by the mid-1990s, overall sales growth for The Limited's flagship clothing stores had stalled and earnings were declining.[1]

Facing the prospect of limited future expansion in the United States, Wexner and The Limited have been criticized by analysts for not seizing the opportunity for international expansion in the early 1990s.[2] Analysts pointed to the success of Toys 'R' Us and other companies that overcame many of the problems associated with managing the global environment and, as a result, benefited greatly from their foreign operations. In response to this criticism, Wexner decided to take The Limited global. In 1995, the company launched its first international retailing venture by opening four Bath & Body Works stores in Britain, with plans for perhaps as many as 100 international stores by 2001.[3] Then Wexner announced plans to open foreign stores for each of The Limited's different store chains. The Limited appears poised to become a major player in the global marketplace, a strategy that it hopes will allow it to grow and prosper well into the next century.[4]

OVERVIEW

Just a decade ago, many U.S. managers and organizations, not just Wexner and The Limited, decided against investing in the global environment because of the problems associated with expanding abroad. Instead, they chose to operate as if the United States were a closed system, detached from the rest of the world. Events of the last ten years, however, have shown managers of organizations large and small, for-profit and not-for-profit, that they cannot afford to ignore the forces in the global environment. Many organizations and managers have concluded that in order to survive into the next century, they need to adopt a global perspective. Most organizations must become **global organizations,** organizations that operate and compete in more than one country.

Global organization an organization that operates and competes in more than one country.

If organizations are to adapt to the global environment, their managers must learn to understand the global forces that operate in it and how these forces give rise to opportunities and threats. In this chapter, we examine why the global environment is becoming more open, vibrant, and competitive. We examine how forces in the global task and general environments affect global organizations and their managers. We examine the different ways in which organizations can expand internationally. And we examine impediments to the creation of an even more open global environment. By the end of this chapter, you will appreciate the changes that have been taking place in the global environment and understand why it is important for managers to develop a global perspective as they strive to increase organizational efficiency and effectiveness.

THE CHANGING GLOBAL ENVIRONMENT

Until relatively recently, many managers did not regard the global environment as a significant source of opportunities and threats. Traditionally, managers regarded the global environment as *closed*—that is, as a set of distinct national markets and countries that were isolated physically, economically, and culturally from one another. As a result, they did not think much about global competition, exporting, obtaining inputs from foreign suppliers, or the challenges of managing in a foreign culture. These issues were simply outside the experience of the majority of managers, whose organizations remained firmly focused on competing at home, in the domestic marketplace.

Today, more and more managers regard the global environment as a source of important opportunities and threats that they must respond to (see Figure 1). Managers now view the global environment as *open*——that is, as an environment in which they and their organizations are free to buy goods and services from, and sell goods and services to, whichever countries they choose. An open environment is also one in which global organizations are free not only to compete against each other to attract customers but also to establish foreign subsidiaries to become the strongest competitors throughout the world. Coca-Cola and PepsiCo, for example, are currently competing to develop the strongest global soft-drinks empire.

In this section, we explain why the global environment is becoming more open and competitive and why this development is so significant for managers today. We

Figure 1 *The Global Environment*

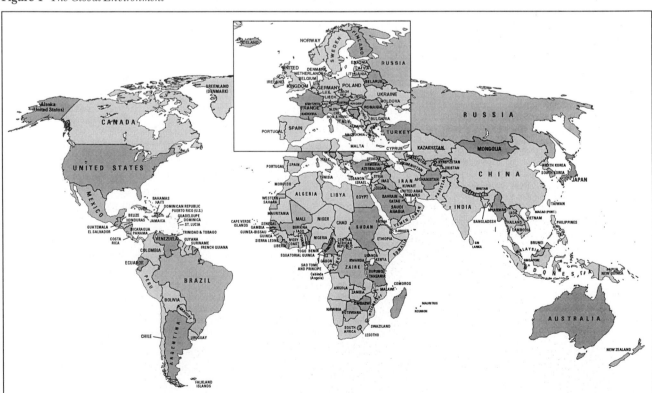

examine how economic changes such as the lowering of barriers to trade and investment have led to greater interaction and exchanges between organizations and countries. We discuss how declines in barriers of distance and culture have increased the interdependencies between organizations and countries. And we consider the specific implications of these changes for managers and organizations.

Declining Barriers to Trade and Investment

During the 1920s and 1930s, many countries erected formidable barriers to international trade and investment in the belief that this was the best way to promote their economic well-being. Many of these barriers were high tariffs on imports of manufactured goods. A **tariff** is a tax that a government imposes on imported or, occasionally, exported goods. The U.S. government, for example, currently levies a 25 percent tariff on four-wheel-drive vehicles imported to the United States. The aim of import tariffs is to protect domestic industries and jobs, such as those in the auto industry, from foreign competition by raising the price of goods from abroad.

Tariff a tax that a government imposes on imported or, occasionally, exported goods.

Very often, however, when one company imposes an import tariff, others follow suit and the result is a series of retaliatory moves as countries progressively raise tariff barriers against each other. In the 1920s this behavior depressed world demand and helped usher in the Great Depression of the 1930s and massive unemployment. In short, rather than protecting jobs and promoting economic well-being, governments of countries that resorted to raising high tariff barriers ultimately reduce employment and undermine economic growth.[5]

GATT AND THE RISE OF FREE TRADE Having learned from the Great Depression, advanced Western industrial countries after the Second World War committed themselves to the goal of removing barriers to the free flow of resources between countries. This commitment was reinforced by acceptance of a principle that predicted that free trade, rather than tariff barriers, was the best way to foster a healthy domestic economy and low unemployment.[6]

Free-trade doctrine the idea that if each country specializes in the production of the goods and services that it can produce most efficiently this will make the best use of global resources.

The **free-trade doctrine** predicts that if each country agrees to specialize in the production of the goods and services that it can produce most efficiently, this will make the best use of global resources, which will result in lower prices. For example, if Indian companies are more efficient in the production of textiles and U.S. companies are more efficient in the production of computer software, then under a free-trade agreement production of textiles would shift to India and computer software to the United States. Under these conditions, prices of textiles and software should fall because both goods are being produced in the location where they can be made at the lowest cost, benefiting consumers and making better use of scarce resources.

Countries that accepted this free-trade doctrine set as their goal the removal of barriers to the free flow of goods between countries. They attempted to achieve this through an international treaty known as the General Agreement on Tariffs and Trade (GATT). In the half-century since World War II, there have been eight rounds of GATT negotiations aimed at lowering tariff barriers. The latest round, the Uruguay Round, involved 117 countries and was completed in December 1993. This round succeeded in lowering tariffs by over 30 percent from the previous level. The average decline in tariff barriers achieved among the governments of developed countries since 1947 is more than 94 percent (similar in theory to a 94 percent reduction in taxes on imports).

Declining Barriers of Distance and Culture

Barriers of distance and culture also "closed" the global environment and kept managers inward looking. The management problems Unilever, a large British soap and detergent maker, experienced at the turn of the century illustrate the effect of these barriers.

Founded in London during the 1880s by William Lever, Unilever had a worldwide reach by the early 1900s and operated subsidiaries in most major countries of the British empire, including India, Canada, and Australia. Lever had a very hands-on, autocratic management style and found his far-flung business empire difficult to control. The reason for Lever's control problems was that communication over great distances was difficult. It took six weeks to reach India by ship from England, and international telephone and telegraph services were very unreliable.

Another problem that Unilever encountered was the difficulty of doing business in societies that were separated from Britain by barriers of language and culture. Different countries have different sets of national beliefs, values, and norms, and Lever found that a management approach that worked in Britain did not necessarily work in India or Persia (now Iran). As a result, management practices had to be tailored to suit each unique national culture. After Lever's death in 1925, top management at Unilever decentralized decision-making authority to the managers of the various national subsidiaries so that they could develop a management approach that suited the country in which they were operating. One result of this strategy was that the subsidiaries grew distant and remote from one another.[7]

Since the end of World War II, major advances in communications and transportation technology have been reducing the barriers of distance and culture that affected Unilever and other global organizations. Over the last thirty years, global communications have been revolutionized by developments in satellites, digital switching, and optical fiber telephone lines. Satellites and optical fibers can carry hundreds of thousands of messages simultaneously.[8] As a result of such developments, reliable and instantaneous communication is now possible with nearly any location in the world. Fax machines in Sri Lanka, cellular phones in the Brazilian rain forest, satellite dishes in Russia, video phones in Manhattan, and videoconferencing facilities in Japan are all part of the communications revolution that is changing the way the world works. This revolution has made it possible for a global organization——a tiny garment factory or a huge company such as Unilever——to do business anywhere, anytime, and to search out customers and suppliers from around the world.

Several major innovations in transportation technology since World War II also have made the global environment more open. Most significant, the growth of commercial jet travel has reduced the time it takes to get from one location to another. Because of jet travel, New York is now closer to Tokyo than it was to Philadelphia in the days of the thirteen colonies——a fact that makes control of far-flung international businesses much easier today than in William Lever's era.

In addition to making travel faster, modern communications and transportation technologies have also helped reduce the cultural distance between countries. Global communications networks and global media are helping to create a *worldwide culture* above and beyond unique national cultures. U.S. television networks such as CNN, MTV, and HBO can now be received in many countries around the world, and Hollywood films are shown around the globe.

Effects of Free Trade on Managers

The lowering of barriers to trade and investment and the decline of distance and culture barriers have created enormous opportunities for organizations to expand the market for their goods and services through exports and investments in foreign countries. Although managers at some organizations, such as Leslie Wexner at The Limited, have shied away from trying to sell their goods and services overseas, the case of Toys 'R' Us is more typical. Not only has the shift toward a more open global economy created more opportunities to sell goods and services in foreign markets; it also has created the opportunity to buy more from foreign countries. Indeed, the success in the United States of both The Limited and Toys 'R' Us has been based in part on their managers' willingness to import low-cost clothes and toys from foreign manufacturers. The Limited, for example, purchases most of its clothing from Hong Kong, Taiwan, and China because, according to CEO Wexner, U.S. textile makers do not offer the same quality, styling, flexibility or price.[9] So, despite Wexner's reluctance to expand his retail-store empire into foreign markets, his company is still a player in the global environment by virtue of its purchasing activities.

The manager's job is also more challenging in a dynamic global environment because of the increased intensity of competition that goes hand in hand with the lowering of barriers to trade and investment. Thus, the job of the average manager in a U.S. car company became a lot harder from the mid-1970s on as a result of the penetration of the U.S. market by efficient Japanese and German competitors and the increase in competition that resulted from it.

NAFTA The growth of regional trade agreements such as the North American Free Trade Agreement (NAFTA) also presents opportunities and threats for managers and their organizations. NAFTA, which became effective on January 1, 1994, will abolish within 10 years the tariffs on 99 percent of the goods traded between Mexico, Canada, and the United States. NAFTA will also remove most barriers on the cross-border flow of resources, giving, for example, financial institutions and retail businesses in Canada and the United States unrestricted access to the Mexican marketplace by the year 2000. After NAFTA was signed, there was a flood of investment from the United States into Mexico. Wal-Mart, Kmart, Price Club, Radio Shack, and other major U.S. retail chains plan to expand their operations in Mexico.

The establishment of free-trade areas creates an opportunity for manufacturing organizations because it allows them to reduce their costs. They can do this either by shifting production to the lowest cost-location within the free-trade area (for example, U.S. textile companies shifting production to Mexico) or by serving the whole region from one location, rather than establishing separate operations in each country.

Some managers, however, might see regional free-trade agreements as a threat because they expose a company based in one member country to increased competition from companies based in the other member countries. Managers in Mexico, the United States, and Canada are experiencing this now that NAFTA is here. For the first time, Mexican managers find themselves facing a threat: head-to-head competition in some industries against efficient U.S. and Canadian organizations. But the opposite is true as well: U.S. and Canadian managers are experiencing threats in labor-intensive industries, such as the textile industry, where Mexican businesses have a cost advantage.

In essence, the shift toward a more open, competitive global environment has increased both the opportunities that managers can take advantage of and the threats they must respond to in performing their jobs effectively. Next, we look in detail at the forces in the global task and general environments to see where these opportunities and threats are arising.

THE GLOBAL TASK ENVIRONMENT

As managers operate in the global environment, they confront forces that differ from country to country and from world region to world region.[10] In this section, we examine some of the forces in the global task environment that increase opportunities or threats for managers (see Figure 2).

Suppliers

At a global level, managers have the opportunity to buy products from foreign suppliers or to become their own suppliers and manufacture their own products abroad. For example, as noted in the "Case in Contrast," to lower costs and increase product quality, The Limited and Toys 'R' Us, respectively, imported low-cost clothes and toys from foreign manufacturers. Organizations such as Levi Strauss and AT&T also have prospered by manufacturing their own low-cost products abroad, which has enabled them to charge their U.S. customers lower prices.

A common problem facing managers of large global organizations such as Ford, Procter & Gamble, and IBM is the development of a global network of suppliers that will allow their companies to keep costs down and quality high. For example, the building of Boeing's new commercial jet aircraft, the 777, requires 132,500 engineered parts that are produced around the world by 545 different suppliers.[11] Boeing makes the majority of these parts. But eight Japanese suppliers make parts for the 777's fuselage, doors, and wings; a Singapore supplier makes the doors for the plane's forward landing gear; and three Italian suppliers manufacture wing flaps. Boeing's rationale for buying so many inputs from foreign suppliers is that these suppliers are the best in the world at performing their particular activity, and doing business with them helps Boeing to produce a high-quality final product, a vital requirement given the need for aircraft safety and

Figure 2 *Forces in the Global Task Environment*

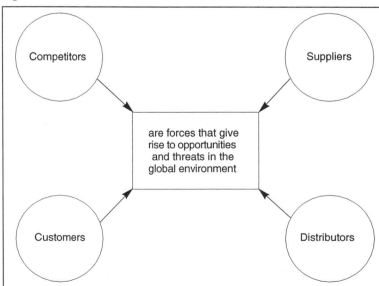

reliability.[12] Small organizations must also be alert to global opportunities to buy or manufacture low-cost products abroad in order to prosper, as the following example of Swan Optical suggests.

MANAGING GLOBALLY   SWAN OPTICAL SPREADS ITS WINGS

With annual sales of $30 million, Swan Optical is a small company that manufactures and distributes eyewear. Swan began its drive to become a global organization in the 1970s. At that time, the strong dollar made U.S.-based manufacturing expensive, and sales of low-priced imported eyewear were increasing rapidly in the U.S. eyewear market. Swan realized that it could not survive unless it also began to import inexpensive eyewear made abroad. At first, Swan bought from independent overseas manufacturers, primarily in Hong Kong. Swan's managers, however, were not satisfied with the quality of the eyewear or its slow delivery. Management decided that the best way to guarantee quality and on-time delivery was to set up its own foreign manufacturing operations and thus control quality and delivery schedules. Accordingly, in conjunction with a Chinese partner, Swan opened a manufacturing facility in Hong Kong to supply its own eyewear.

The choice of Hong Kong was influenced by the combination of low labor costs, a skilled workforce, and tax breaks given by the Hong Kong government.[13] The arrangement was successful for several years. By 1986, however, the increasing industrialization of Hong Kong and a growing labor shortage caused wage rates to increase and Hong Kong could no longer be considered a low-cost location. In response, Swan's managers opened a manufacturing plant in China to take advantage of China's lower wage rates. The Chinese plant manufactures parts for eyewear frames, which are shipped to the Hong Kong factory for final assembly and then distributed to markets in both North and South America.

Obtaining and selling low-cost eyewear was not the managers' only goal; they were also interested in launching a line of high-quality "designer" eyewear but lacked the necessary in-house skills. Therefore, they looked for opportunities to invest in foreign eyewear companies that enjoyed reputations for fashionable design and high-quality products. They found such eyewear companies in Japan, France, and Italy and invested in a minority shareholding in each company.[14] These eyewear factories supply Swan's Status Eye division, which has successfully marketed high-priced designer eyewear to its U.S. customers.   ■ ■ ■

Global outsourcing the purchase of inputs from foreign suppliers, or the production of inputs abroad, to lower production costs and improve product quality or design.

Global outsourcing is the process by which organizations purchase inputs from other companies or produce inputs themselves throughout the world, to lower their production costs and improve the quality or design of their products. To take advantage of national differences in the cost and quality of resources such as labor or raw materials, General Motors might build its own engines in one country, transmissions in another, brakes in a third, and buy other components from hundreds of global suppliers. Robert Reich, U.S. secretary of labor in the first Clinton administration, once calculated that of the $20,000 that customers pay GM for a Pontiac Le Mans, about $6,000 goes to South Korea, where the Le Mans is assembled; $3,500 to Japan for advanced components such as engines, transaxles, and electronics; $1,500 to Germany, where the Le Mans was designed; $800 to Taiwan, Singapore, and Japan for small components; $500 to Britain for advertising and marketing services; and about $100 to Ireland for data-processing services. The remaining $7,000 goes to GM——and to the lawyers, bankers, and insurance agents that GM retains in the United States.[15] Is the Le Mans a U.S.

product? Yes, but it is also a Korean product, a Japanese product, and a German product.

Distributors

Another force that creates opportunities and threats for global managers is the nature of a country's distribution system. As Toys 'R' Us discovered in Japan, the traditional means by which goods and services are distributed and sold to customers can present challenges to managers of organizations pursuing international expansion. Managers must identify the hidden problems surrounding the distribution and sale of goods and services——such as anticompetitive government regulations——in order to discover hidden threats early and find ways to overcome them before significant resources are invested.

Customers

The most obvious opportunity associated with expanding into the global environment is the prospect of selling goods and services to new customers, as Toys 'R' Us CEO Lazarus realized. Similarly, Arthur Andersen and Price Waterhouse, two large accounting companies, have established foreign operations throughout the world and recruit and train thousands of foreign accountants to serve the needs of customers in a wide variety of countries.

Today, once-distinct national markets are merging into one huge global marketplace where the same basic product can be sold to customers worldwide. This consolidation is occurring both for consumer goods and for business products and has created enormous opportunities for managers. The global acceptance of Coca-Cola, Levi's blue jeans, Sony Walkmans, McDonald's hamburgers, and Motorola pagers and flip phones is a sign that the tastes and preferences of consumers in different countries are beginning to become more similar.[16] Similarly, large global markets currently exist for business products such as telecommunications equipment, electronic components, computer services, and financial services. Thus, Motorola sells its telecommunications equipment, Intel its microprocessors, and Computer Associates its business systems management software, to customers throughout the world.

Nevertheless, despite evidence that the same goods and services are receiving acceptance from customers worldwide, it is important not to place too much emphasis on this development. Because national cultures differ in many ways, significant differences between countries in consumer tastes and preferences still remain. These differences often require managers to customize goods and services to suit the preferences of local consumers. For example, despite McDonald's position as a leading global organization, its management has recognized a need for local customization. In Brazil, McDonald's sells a soft drink made from the guarana, an exotic berry that grows along the Amazon River (in 1996, Pepsi announced that it was test-marketing a drink made from this berry in the United States). In Malaysia, McDonald's sells milk shakes flavored with durian, a strong-smelling fruit that local people consider an aphrodisiac.[17] Similarly, when Mattel decided to begin selling Barbie Dolls in Japan, it had to redesign the doll's appearance (color of hair, facial features, and so on) to suit the tastes of its prospective customers.

Competitors

Although finding less-expensive or higher-quality supplies and attracting new customers are global opportunities for managers, entry into the global environment also leads to major threats in the form of increases in competition both at home and abroad. U.S. managers in foreign markets, for example, face the problem of competing against local companies that are familiar with the local market and have generated considerable brand loyalty. As a result, U.S. managers might find it difficult to break into a foreign market and obtain new customers. Of course, foreign competitors trying to enter a U.S. company's domestic market face the same challenges. U.S. car companies faced strong global competition at home in the 1970s, when foreign competitors aggressively entered the U.S. market. In the global environment, the level of competition can increase rapidly, and managers must be alert to the changes taking place in order to respond appropriately.

THE GLOBAL GENERAL ENVIRONMENT

Despite evidence that countries are becoming more similar to one another and that the world is on the verge of becoming a "global village," countries still differ across a range of political, legal, economic, and cultural dimensions. When an organization operates in the global environment, it confronts in the global general environment a series of forces that differ from country to country and world region to world region. In this section we consider how forces in the global general environment, such as political and legal, economic, and sociocultural forces, create opportunities and threats for managers of global organizations (see Figure 3).

Political and Legal Forces

Representative democracy
a political system in which representatives elected by citizens form a government whose function is to make decisions on behalf of the electorate, and are legally accountable to the electorate.

Global political and legal forces result from the diverse and changing nature of various countries' political and legal systems. The global range of political systems includes everything from representative democracies to totalitarian regimes, and in order to manage global organizations effectively, managers must understand how these different political systems work. In **representative democracies,** such as Britain, Canada, Germany, and the United States, citizens periodically elect individuals to represent their interests. These elected representatives form a govern-

Figure 3 *Forces in the Global General Environment*

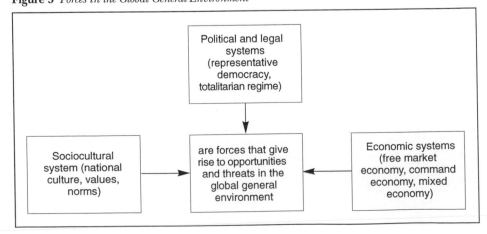

ment whose function is to make decisions on behalf of the electorate. To guarantee that voters can hold elected representatives legally accountable for their actions, an ideal representative democracy incorporates a number of safeguards into the law. These include (1) an individual's right to freedom of expression, opinion, and organization; (2) free media; (3) regular elections in which all eligible citizens are allowed to vote; (4) limited terms for elected representatives; (5) a fair court system that is independent from the political system; (6) a nonpolitical police force and armed service; and (7) relatively free access to state information.

Totalitarian regime a political system in which a single party, individual, or group holds all political power and neither recognizes nor permits opposition.

In contrast, in **totalitarian regimes** a single political party, individual, or group of individuals holds all political power. Typically, totalitarian regimes neither recognize nor permit opposition from individuals or groups. Most of the constitutional guarantees on which representative democracies are based are denied to the citizens of totalitarian states. In most totalitarian countries, political repression is widespread. Those who question the policies of the rulers and their right to rule find themselves imprisoned or worse. Totalitarian regimes are found in countries such as China, Iraq, and Iran.

Why must managers be concerned about the political makeup of a foreign country in which they are doing business? First, stable democratic countries with a high degree of political freedom tend to be characterized by economic freedom and a well-defined legal system. In turn, economic freedom and a well-defined legal system protect the rights of individuals and corporations and are conducive to business.[19] Second, totalitarian regimes' lack of respect for human rights raises the question of whether it is ethical to trade with, or invest in, those countries.

Economic Forces

Economic forces are caused by the changing nature of countries' economic systems. Around the globe, economic systems range from free-market economies to command economies, and managers must learn how different economic systems work in order to understand the opportunities and threats associated with them. In a **free-market economy,** the production of goods and services is left in the hands of *private* (as opposed to *government*) enterprise. The goods and services that are produced, and the quantities that are produced, are not specified by a central authority. Rather, production is determined by the interaction of the forces of supply and demand. If demand for a product exceeds supply, the price of the product will rise, prompting managers and organizations to produce more. If supply exceeds demand, prices will fall, causing managers and organizations to produce less. In a free-market economy the purchasing patterns of consumers, as signaled to managers by changes in demand, determine what and how much is produced.

Free-market economy an economic system in which private enterprise controls production and the interaction of supply and demand determines which and how many goods and services are produced and how much consumers pay for them.

Command economy an economic system in which the government owns all businesses and specifies which and how many goods and services are produced and the prices at which they are sold.

In a **command economy,** the goods and services that a country produces, the quantity in which they are produced, and the prices at which they are sold are all planned by the government. In a pure command economy, all businesses are government owned and private enterprise is forbidden. A decade ago, the communist countries of eastern Europe and the Soviet Union all had command economies, as did other communist countries such as China and Vietnam. The overall failure of these economies to perform as well as the free-market-oriented systems of western Europe, North America, and areas of the Pacific Rim helped precipitate the collapse of communism in many of these countries and the subsequent dismantlement of command economies. Even in China and Vietnam, which remain communist controlled, there has been a marked shift away from a command economy.

Mixed economy an economic system in which some sectors of the economy are left to private ownership and free-market mechanisms and others are owned by the government and subject to government planning.

Between the free market and command economies are mixed economies. In a **mixed economy,** certain sectors of the economy are left to private ownership and free-market mechanisms, and other sectors are characterized by significant government ownership and government planning. Mixed economies are most commonly found in the democratic countries of western Europe, but they are disappearing as these countries shift toward the free-market model. For example, in Britain in the early 1980s the government owned a majority stake in many important industries, including airlines, health care, steel, and telecommunications. Since then, following a trend toward privatization, the British government has sold its airline, steel, and telecommunications interests to private investors, and a significant private health care sector has emerged to compete with government-provided health care. Similar privatization efforts have been undertaken in other western European countries.

The manager of a global organization generally prefers a free-market system, for two reasons. First, because much of the economy is in private hands, there tend to be few restrictions on organizations that decide to invest in countries with free-market economies. For example, U.S. companies face fewer impediments to investing in Britain, with its largely free-market system, than they do in China, where a free market is allowed in only certain sectors of the economy. Second, free-market economies tend to be more economically developed and have higher rates of economic growth than command or mixed economies, so their citizens tend to have higher per capita incomes and more spending power.[20] As a result, for companies attempting to export or to establish foreign subsidiaries, they are more attractive markets than are mixed economies or command economies, which are closely regulated by government.

Changes in Political and Legal and Economic Forces

In recent years, two large and related shifts in political and economic forces have occurred globally (see Figure 4).[21] One——the shift away from totalitarian dictatorships and toward more democratic regimes——has been most dramatic in east-

Figure 4 *Changes in Political and Economic Forces*

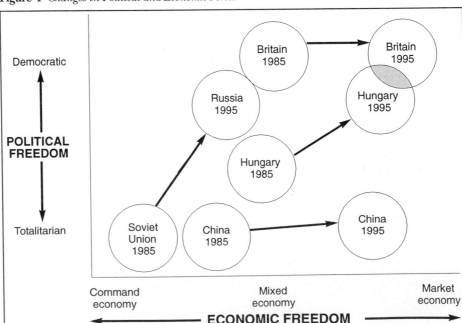

ern Europe and the former Soviet Union, where totalitarian communist regimes collapsed during the late 1980s and early 1990s. The other——the shift toward representative democracy——has occurred from Latin America to Africa. For the most part, the movement toward democracy has been precipitated by the failure of totalitarian regimes with command or mixed economies to improve the well-being of their citizens. This failure has been particularly noticeable in comparisons of these countries with democratic, free-market countries such as Germany, Japan, and the United States.

Accompanying this change in political forces has been a worldwide shift away from command and mixed economies and toward the free-market model, as noted previously.[22] This economic shift was triggered by the realization that government involvement in economic activity often impedes economic growth. Thus, a wave of privatization and deregulation has swept throughout the world, from the former communist countries to Latin America, Asia, and western Europe. Governments have sold off government-owned organizations to private investors and have dismantled regulations that inhibit the operation of the free market.

These trends are good news for managers of global organizations because they result in the expansion of opportunities for exporting and investment abroad. A decade ago, few Western companies exported to or invested in eastern Europe because the combination of totalitarian political regimes and command economies created a hostile environment for Western businesses. Since 1990, however, the environment in eastern Europe has become far more favorable for Western businesses; and from 1990 to 1993, Western businesses invested $15 billion in eastern Europe.[23] A similar story is unfolding in China, where despite the continued presence of a totalitarian communist regime, a move toward greater economic freedom has occurred and has produced a surge of Western and Japanese business activity in this region of the world. From 1990 to 1993, foreign companies invested nearly $40 billion in China.[24]

The managers of many Western companies have experienced considerable difficulty in their attempts to establish business operations in eastern Europe and China, however. For example, when the Chiquita banana company entered the Czech Republic in 1990, the company was hoping to take advantage of that nation's rapid move toward a free-market economy. However, Chiquita found that the premium bananas it sold in the West could not be marketed in the Czech Republic. After decades of communism, Czech citizens apparently had difficulty understanding why something of better quality should cost more. Chiquita was forced to switch to lower-quality bananas after discovering that consumers were unwilling to pay higher prices for superior bananas.[25] The experience of General Electric's managers in Hungary provides another example of the problems that managers may encounter when doing business in eastern Europe.

MANAGING GLOBALLY   GE'S U.S. MANAGERS STUMBLE IN HUNGARY

In 1989, General Electric (GE) (www.ge.com) agreed to acquire 51 percent of Tungsram, a maker of lighting products and widely regarded as one of Hungary's best companies, at a cost of $150 million. GE was attracted to Tungsram because of Hungary's low wage rates and the possibility of using the company as a base from which to export lighting products to western Europe. At the time, many analysts believed that GE would show other Western companies how to turn organizations once run by communist party officials into capitalist moneymakers. GE transferred some of its best managers to Tungsram and waited for the miracle to happen. Unfortunately, the company is still waiting!

One of the problems resulted from major misunderstandings between the American managers and the Hungarian workers. The Americans complained that the Hungarians were lazy; the Hungarians thought the Americans were pushy. GE's management system depends on extensive communication between workers and managers, a practice uncommon in the previous communist system. Changing behavior at Tungsram has proved to be difficult. The Americans wanted strong sales and marketing functions that would pamper customers. In the prior command economy, these activities were unnecessary. In addition, Hungarians expected GE to deliver Western-style wages, but GE came to Hungary to take advantage of the country's low-wage structure.[26]

As Tungsram's losses mounted, GE learned what happens when grand expectations collide with the grim reality of inefficiency and indifference toward customers and quality. Looking back, GE managers admit that, because of differences in basic attitudes between countries, they underestimated the difficulties they would face in turning Tungsram around. GE now believes that it has turned the corner, but this progress has not come easily. General Electric laid off half of Tungsram's 20,000 employees, including two out of every three managers, and invested $400 million in a new plant and equipment and in retraining the remaining employees and managers to help them learn the work attitudes and behaviors that a company needs in order to survive in a competitive global environment.   ■ ■ ■

As the example of GE and Tungsram illustrates, managers who want to take advantage of the opportunities created by changing global political and legal and economic forces face a major challenge.

Sociocultural Forces

What is interesting about the experiences of companies such as General Electric in Hungary and Chiquita in the Czech Republic is that many of their problems are the result of critical differences in the values, norms, and attitudes of Western cultures and eastern European cultures conditioned by communism and a command economy. National culture is an important sociocultural force that global managers must take into account when they do business in foreign countries. **National culture** includes the values, norms, knowledge, beliefs, moral principles, laws, customs, and other practices that unite the citizens of a country.[27] National culture shapes individual behavior by specifying appropriate and inappropriate behavior and interaction with others. People learn national culture in their everyday lives by interacting with those around them. This learning starts at an early age and continues throughout a person's life.

National culture the set of values that a society considers important and the norms of behavior that are approved or sanctioned in that society.

VALUES AND NORMS The basic building blocks of national culture are values and norms. **Values** are ideas about what a society believes to be good, right, desirable, or beautiful. They provide the basic underpinnings for notions of individual freedom, democracy, truth, justice, honesty, loyalty, social obligation, collective responsibility, the appropriate roles for men and women, love, sex, marriage, and so on. Values are more than merely abstract concepts; they are invested with considerable emotional significance. People argue, fight, and even die over values such as "freedom."

Values ideas about what a society believes to be good, right, desirable, or beautiful.

Though deeply embedded in society, values are not static——although change in a country's values is likely to be slow and painful. For example, the value systems of many formerly communist states, such as Russia, are undergoing significant changes as those countries move away from a value system that emphasizes the state and toward one that emphasizes individual freedom. Social turmoil often results when countries undergo major changes in their values.

Norms unwritten, informal codes of conduct that prescribe how people should act in particular situations.

Folkways the routine social conventions of everyday life.

Norms are unwritten social rules and codes of conduct that prescribe appropriate behavior in particular situations and shape the behavior of people toward one another. Two types of norms play a major role in national culture: folkways and mores. **Folkways** are the routine social conventions of everyday life. They concern customs and practices such as dressing appropriately for particular situations, good social manners, eating with the correct utensils, and neighborly behavior. Although folkways define the way people are expected to behave, violation of folkways is not a serious or moral matter. People who violate folkways are often thought to be eccentric or ill mannered, but they are not usually considered to be evil or bad. In many countries, foreigners may be excused initially for violating folkways because they are unaccustomed to local behavior, but repeated violations will not be excused because foreigners are expected to learn appropriate behavior.

Mores norms that are considered to be central to the functioning of society and to social life.

Mores are norms that are considered to be central to the functioning of society and to social life. They have much greater significance than folkways. Accordingly, the violation of mores can be expected to bring serious retribution. Mores include proscriptions against theft, adultery, and incest. In many societies mores have been enacted into law. Thus, all advanced societies have laws against theft and incest. However, there are many differences in mores from one society to another.[28] In the United States, for example, drinking alcohol is widely accepted; but in Saudi Arabia, the consumption of alcohol is viewed as a violation of an important traditional custom and is punishable by imprisonment (as many U.S. citizens working in Saudi Arabia have discovered).

HOFSTEDE'S MODEL OF NATIONAL CULTURE Researchers have spent considerable time and effort identifying similarities and differences in the values and norms of different countries. One model of national culture was developed by Gert Hofstede.[29] As a psychologist for IBM, Hofstede collected data on employee values and norms from more than 100,000 IBM employees in 64 countries. Based on his research, Hofstede developed five dimensions along which national cultures can be placed (see Figure 5).

INDIVIDUALISM VERSUS COLLECTIVISM The first dimension, which Hofstede labeled *individualism versus collectivism*, has a long history in human thought. **In-**

Figure 5 *Hofstede's Model of National Culture*

Individualism ←——————→ Collectivism	
Low power distance ←——————→ High power distance	
Achievement oriented ←——————→ Nurturing oriented	
Low uncertainty avoidance ←——————→ High uncertainty avoidance	
Short-term orientation ←——————→ Long-term orientation	

Individualism a worldview that values individual freedom and self-expression and adherence to the principle that people should be judged by their individual achievements rather than by their social background.
Collectivism a worldview that values subordination of the individual to the goals of the group and adherence to the principle that people should be judged by their contribution to the group.

dividualism is a worldview that values individual freedom and self-expression and adherence to the principle that people should be judged by their individual achievements rather than by their social background. In Western countries, individualism usually includes admiration for personal success, a strong belief in individual rights, and high regard for individual entrepreneurs.[30]

In contrast, **collectivism** is a worldview that values subordination of the individual to the goals of the group and adherence to the principle that people should be judged by their contribution to the group. Collectivism was widespread in communist countries but has become less prevalent since the collapse of communism in those countries. Japan is a noncommunist country where collectivism is highly valued.

Collectivism in Japan traces its roots to the fusion of Confucian, Buddhist, and Shinto thought that occurred during the Tokugawa period in Japanese history (1600–1870s).[31] One of the central values that emerged during this period was strong attachment to the group—whether a village, a work group, or a company. Strong identification with the group is said to create pressures for collective action in Japan, as well as strong pressure for conformity to group norms and a relative lack of individualism.[32]

Managers must realize that organizations and organizational members reflect their national culture's emphasis on individualism or collectivism. Indeed, one of the major reasons why Japanese and American management practices differ is that Japanese culture values collectivism and U.S. culture values individualism.[33]

Power distance the degree to which societies accept the idea that inequalities in the power and well-being of their citizens are due to differences in individuals' physical and intellectual capabilities and heritage.

POWER DISTANCE By **power distance** Hofstede meant the degree to which societies accept the idea that inequalities in the power and well-being of their citizens are due to differences in individuals' physical and intellectual capabilities and heritage. This concept also encompasses the degree to which societies accept the economic and social differences in wealth, status, and well-being that result from differences in individual capabilities.

Societies in which inequalities are allowed to persist or grow over time have *high power distance.* In high-power-distance societies, workers who are professionally successful amass wealth and pass it on to their children, and as a result, inequalities may grow over time. In such societies, the gap between rich and poor, with all the attendant political and social consequences, grows very large. In contrast, societies with *low power distance,* large inequalities between citizens are not allowed to develop. In low-power-distance countries, the government uses taxation and social welfare programs to reduce inequality and improve the welfare of the least fortunate. These societies are more attuned to preventing a large gap between rich and poor and discord between different classes of citizens.

Advanced Western countries such as the United States, Germany, the Netherlands, and the United Kingdom have relatively low power distance and high individualism. Economically poor Latin American counties such as Guatemala and Panama, and Asian countries such as Malaysia and the Philippines, have high power distance and low individualism.[34] These findings suggest that the cultural values of richer countries emphasize protecting the rights of individuals and, at the same time, provide a fair chance of success to every member of society.

Achievement orientation a worldview that values assertiveness, performance, success, and competition.
Nurturing orientation a worldview that values the quality of life, warm personal friendships, and services and care for the weak.

ACHIEVEMENT VERSUS NURTURING ORIENTATION Societies that have an **achievement orientation** value assertiveness, performance, success, competition, and results. Societies that have a **nurturing orientation** value the quality of life, warm personal relationships, and services and care for the weak. Japan and the United States tend to be achievement oriented; the Netherlands, Sweden, and Denmark are more nurturing oriented.

Uncertainty avoidance the degree to which societies are willing to tolerate uncertainty and risk.

UNCERTAINTY AVOIDANCE Societies as well as individuals differ in their tolerance for uncertainty and risk. Societies low on **uncertainty avoidance** (such as the United States and Hong Kong) are easygoing, value diversity, and tolerate differences in personal beliefs and actions. Societies high on uncertainty avoidance (such as Japan and France) are more rigid and skeptical about people whose behaviors or beliefs differ from the norm. In these societies, conformity to the values of the social and work groups to which a person belongs is the norm, and structured situations are preferred because they provide a sense of security.

Long-term orientation a worldview that values thrift and persistence in achieving goals.
Short-term orientation worldview that values personal stability or happiness and living for the present.

LONG-TERM VERSUS SHORT-TERM ORIENTATION The last dimension that Hofstede described is orientation toward life and work.[35] A national culture with a **long-term orientation** rests on values such as thrift (saving) and persistence in achieving goals. A national culture with a **short-term orientation** is concerned with maintaining personal stability or happiness and living for the present. Societies with long-term orientations include Taiwan and Hong Kong, well known for their high rate of per capita savings. The United States and France have a short-term orientation, and their citizens tend to spend more and save less.

NATIONAL CULTURE AND GLOBAL MANAGEMENT Differences among national cultures have important implications for managers. First, because of cultural differences, management practices that are effective in one country might be troublesome in another. GE managers learned this while trying to manage Tungsram, their Hungarian subsidiary. Often, management practices must be tailored to suit the cultural contexts within which an organization operates. An approach effective in the United States might not work in Japan, Hungary, or Mexico, because of differences in national culture. For example, American-style pay-for-performance systems that emphasize the performance of individuals alone might not work well in Japan, where individual performance in pursuit of group goals is the value that receives emphasis.

Managers doing business with individuals from another country must be sensitive to the value systems and norms of that country and behave accordingly. For example, Friday is the Islamic Sabbath. Thus, it would be impolite and inappropriate for a U.S. manager to schedule a busy day of activities for Saudi Arabian managers visiting on a Friday.

A culturally diverse management team can be a source of strength for an organization participating in the global marketplace. Organizations that employ managers from a variety of cultures appreciate better than do organizations with culturally homogeneous management teams how national cultures differ, and they tailor their management systems and behaviors to these differences. Indeed, one of the advantages that many Western companies have over their Japanese competitors is greater willingness to build an international team of senior managers.[36] For example, Compaq, one of America's most successful computer companies, is headed by a German-born CEO, and Ford Motor Company is headed by a British-born CEO. Japanese companies, in contrast, tend to be dominated by Japanese managers and consequently have a more culturally narrow view of doing business across borders.

Culture shock the feelings of surprise and disorientation that people experience when they do not understand the values, folkways, and mores that guide behavior in a culture.

Culture shock is a phrase that sums up the feelings of surprise and disorientation that people experience when they enter a foreign culture and do not understand the values, folkways, and mores that guide behavior in that culture. Many managers and their families experience culture shock when they move abroad. If they have received no training, they may not understand how to do business in a foreign country or how local stores and school systems operate. Learning a differ-

Expatriate managers managers who go abroad to work for a global organization.

ent culture takes time and effort, and global organizations must devote considerable resources to helping **expatriate managers** (managers who go abroad to work for a global organization) adapt to local conditions and learn the local culture.

CHOOSING A WAY TO EXPAND INTERNATIONALLY

As we have discussed, the trend toward a more open, competitive global environment has proved to be both an opportunity and a threat for organizations and managers. The opportunity is that organizations that expand globally are able to open new markets and reach more customers and gain access to new sources of raw materials and to low-cost suppliers of inputs. The threat is that organizations that expand globally are likely to encounter new competitors in the foreign countries they enter and must respond to new political, economic, and cultural conditions.

Before setting up foreign operations, managers of companies such as Toys 'R' Us, Boeing, and Swan Optical needed to analyze the forces in a particular country's environment (such as Korea or Brazil) in order to choose the right method to expand and respond to those forces in the most appropriate way. In general, there are four basic ways to operate in the global environment: importing and exporting, licensing and franchising, strategic alliances, and wholly owned foreign subsidiaries. We briefly discuss each one, moving from the lowest level of foreign involvement and investment required of a global organization and its managers, and the least amount of risk, to the high end of the spectrum (see Figure 6).[37]

Importing and Exporting

Exporting making products at home and selling them abroad.

The least complex global operations are exporting and importing. A company engaged in **exporting** makes products at home and sells them abroad. An organization might sell its own products abroad or allow a local organization in the foreign country to distribute its products. Compaq and Microsoft, for example, control the distribution of their products to foreign computer retailers, and makers of many luxury products, such as producers of French wine and spirits, allow local organizations to take responsibility for distribution activities. Few risks are associated with exporting because a company does not have to invest in developing manufacturing facilities abroad. It can further reduce its investment abroad if it allows a local company to distribute its products.

Importing selling at home products that are made abroad.

A company engaged in **importing** sells at home products that are made abroad (products it makes itself or buys from other companies). For example, most of the products that companies such as Pier 1 Imports, The Bombay Company, and The Limited sell to their customers are made abroad. In many cases the appeal of a product——for example, Irish glass, French wine, Italian furniture, or Indian silk——is that it is made abroad.

Figure 6 *Four Ways of Expanding Internationally*

Licensing and Franchising

In **licensing,** a company (the licenser) allows a foreign organization (the licensee) to take charge of both manufacturing and distributing one or more of its products in the licensee's country or world region in return for a negotiated fee. Chemical maker Du Pont might license a local factory in India to produce nylon or Teflon. The advantage of licensing is that the licenser does not have to bear the development costs associated with opening up in a foreign country; the licensee bears the costs. The risks associated with this strategy are that the company granting the license has to give its foreign partner access to its technological know-how and so risks losing control over its secrets.

Whereas licensing is pursued primarily by manufacturing companies, franchising is pursued primarily by service organizations. In **franchising,** a company (the franchiser) sells to a foreign organization (the franchisee) the rights to use its brand name and operating know-how in return for a lump-sum payment and share of the franchiser's profits. Hilton Hotels might sell a franchise to a local company in Chile to operate hotels under the Hilton name in return for a franchise payment. The advantage of franchising is that the franchiser does not have to bear the development costs of overseas expansion and avoids the many problems associated with setting up foreign operations. The downside is that the organization that grants the franchise may lose control over the way in which the franchisee operates and product quality may fall. In this way, franchisers, such as Hilton, Avis, and McDonald's, risk losing their good names. Customers who buy McDonald's hamburgers in Korea may reasonably expect those burgers to be as good as the ones they get at home. If they are not, McDonald's reputation will suffer over time.

Strategic Alliances

One way to overcome the loss-of-control problems associated with exporting, licensing, and franchising is to expand globally by means of a strategic alliance. In a **strategic alliance,** managers pool or share their organization's resources and know-how with those of a foreign company, and the two organizations share the rewards or risks of starting a new venture in a foreign country. Sharing resources allows a U.S. company, for example, to take advantage of the high-quality skills of foreign manufacturers and the specialized knowledge of foreign managers about the needs of local customers, and to reduce the risks involved in a venture. At the same time, the terms of the alliance give the U.S. company more control over how the good or service is produced or sold in the foreign country than it would have as a franchiser or licenser.

A strategic alliance can take the form of a written contract between two or more companies to exchange resources, or it can result in the creation of a new organization. A **joint venture** is a strategic alliance among two or more companies that agree to jointly establish and share the ownership of a new business.[38] An organization's level of involvement abroad increases in a joint venture because it normally involves a capital investment in production facilities abroad in order to produce goods or services outside its home country. Risk, however, is reduced.

Wholly Owned Foreign Subsidiaries

When managers decide to establish a **wholly owned foreign subsidiary,** they invest in establishing production operations in a foreign country independent of any local direct involvement. Many Japanese car component companies, for example, have established their own operations in the United States to supply U.S.-based Japanese car makers such as Toyota with high-quality inputs.

Operating alone, without any direct involvement from foreign companies, an organization receives all of the rewards and bears all of the risks associated with operating abroad.[39] This method of international expansion is much more expensive than the others because it requires a higher level of foreign investment and presents managers with many more threats. However, investment in a foreign subsidiary or division also gives an organization high potential returns because it does not have to share its profits with a foreign organization and its managers have full control over all aspects of their foreign subsidiary's operations, thus reducing the level of risk. Moreover, it allows managers to protect their technology and know-how from foreign organizations. Large, well-known companies like Du Pont, General Motors, and Arthur Andersen, which have plenty of resources, make extensive use of wholly owned subsidiaries. However, they are not the only kind of organization that embarks on a global adventure, as the story of Harry Ramsden's fish and chips makes clear.

MANAGING GLOBALLY   HOW TO GET THE WORLD HOOKED ON FISH AND CHIPS

Deep-fried fish and chips is one of the most popular foods in England. Harry Ramsden's first fish and chips shop was located in Guiseley, Yorkshire, and the company has long been considered one of the premium fish and chips shops in England. In addition, it is one of the few shops to open in multiple locations. In 1995, the company had 12 branches in Britain, including one in Dublin. Its busiest U.K. location, the beach resort town of Blackpool, generates annual sales of £1.5 million ($2.3 million).[40] Harry Ramsden's managers, however, are not satisfied with their organization's success. They want to turn Harry Ramsden's into a global organization.

Thus, in 1992 in Hong Kong, the company opened its first wholly owned international operation, marketing its product as Britain's "fast food." Fish and chips, salted and doused with vinegar according to Ramsden's standard recipe, proved to be popular in Hong Kong, and in 1994 the Hong Kong location generated annual sales equivalent to those at the Blackpool operation. Moreover, although half of the initial customers at the Hong Kong location were British expatriates (British citizens who live and work in Hong Kong), by 1994 more than 80 percent of its customers were of Chinese origin.[41] Harry Ramsden's seemed to be well on the way to changing the tastes and preferences of Hong Kong's Chinese community.

Encouraged by their success, Harry Ramsden's managers planned to open additional subsidiaries in Singapore and Melbourne, Australia. However, their biggest target market was Japan, whose citizens consume more fish per person than are eaten in any other country in the world. To establish a presence in Japan, Harry Ramsden's set up a temporary fish and chips shop in Tokyo's Yoyagi Park to serve fish and chips covered with the standard salt and vinegar. Despite Japanese consumers' traditional dislike of greasy food, Ramsden's fish and chips were accepted, and word spread that it was indeed a tasty treat.

Harry Ramsden's managers decided that the best way to expand into Japan was to seek a Japanese partner and establish a joint venture. Their rationale was that they could take advantage of their joint-venture partner's in-depth knowledge of the market and local consumer tastes. The company found a venture partner and opened its first fish and chips shop in Japan in 1995.

No matter whether it expands globally by establishing wholly owned subsidiaries or by establishing joint ventures, Harry Ramsden's managers have recognized the need for some local product customization to suit local tastes. In each fish and chips shop, at least one dish caters to local tastes. In Glasgow, Scotland, the local item is haggis, a blended meat and grain product cooked in a sheep's stomach; in Hong Kong it is an exotic salad; and in Japan it is sushi.   ■■■

IMPEDIMENTS TO AN OPEN GLOBAL ENVIRONMENT

To this point, we have emphasized the trend toward the creation of a more open, competitive global environment and the advantages that result from this, such as access to more customers or to higher-quality or cheaper inputs. However, as every manager of a global organization knows, we live in an imperfect world, and significant barriers to cross-border exchanges between countries continue to make global expansion risky and expensive.

Government-Imposed Impediments

One reason why barriers exist is that there are ways of getting around free-trade agreements such as the GATT. GATT aims primarily to lower tariff barriers, but there are various nontariff barriers to trade that governments can erect. In other words, there are many loopholes in the GATT that countries can exploit. One class of nontariff impediments to international trade and investment is known as *administrative barriers.* Administrative barriers are government policies that in theory have nothing to do with international trade and investment but in practice have the intended effect of limiting imports of goods and inward investment by foreign corporations.

One example of an administrative trade barrier is mentioned in the "Case in Contrast." Japan's Large Scale Retail Store Law prior to 1991 allowed small retailers to block the establishment of a large retail establishment for up to 10 years and was used to slow the entry of Toys 'R' Us into the Japanese market. Another kind of administrative trade barrier prevents Dutch companies from exporting tulip bulbs to Japan. Why do Dutch companies export tulip bulbs to almost every country in the world except Japan? Japanese customs inspectors insist on checking every tulip bulb by cutting the stems vertically down the middle, and even Japanese ingenuity cannot put them back together.[42]

Of course, Japan is not the only country with administrative barriers to trade. Another example closer to home is apparent in Mexico's effort to slow the expansion of Wal-Mart in Mexico.

MANAGING GLOBALLY   WAL-MART RUNS INTO RED TAPE

Wal-Mart (www.wal-mart.com), the largest U.S. discount retail chain, viewed the January 1, 1994, passage of the North American Free Trade Agreement (NAFTA) as an opportunity to expand operations into Mexico. Only five years before, Mexican regulations had severely limited any direct investment by foreign companies into Mexico. Wal-Mart's managers took the passage of NAFTA as a green light for investment. They launched an ambitious expansion program in Mexico and opened four Wal-Mart stores in 1994 and 10 warehouse-style Sam's Clubs in 1994 and had many more planned.

Reality struck in the early summer of 1994, however, when Mexican government inspectors made a surprise visit to Wal-Mart's new superstore in Mexico City. The inspectors found thousands of products that they claimed were improperly labeled. The inspectors charged that at least 11,700 pieces of merchandise lacked proper labels and that each product had to be labeled in Spanish to indicate the product's country of origin, content, and instructions for use——and also, in some cases, an import permit number.[43] Wal-Mart's managers pointed out that much of the merchandise——40 percent or more——was purchased from a local Mexican distributor. Nevertheless, the regulators insisted that Wal-Mart had the ultimate responsibility for labeling the products, and they closed the store for 72 hours until the problems were corrected.

This brush with administrative barriers and overzealous inspectors has sobered Wal-Mart's managers. They view this kind of bureaucratic red tape as a deliberate attempt by government officials to raise Wal-Mart's costs of doing business in Mexico and thereby slowing the company's expansion plans.   ■ ■ ■

Self-Imposed Ethical Impediments

Other impediments to cross-border trade and investment are self-imposed by organizations. Why would managers choose to limit their own options for engaging in international trade and investment? In many countries, human rights, workers' rights, and environmental protection are of such low priority that managers decline to have their organizations trade with, or invest in, these countries on ethical grounds.

The human rights issue has recently been raised in the United States in connection with the importing of goods from China. China is not a democracy, and its human rights record is poor. Some of the goods imported into the United States from China are made by prison labor. Many prisoners in China are political prisoners, locked up because of their opposition to the communist-controlled state. Learning of this use of prisoners, many organizations broke off their ties with Chinese companies.

Similarly, U.S. investment in Mexico has fallen as a result of revelations about Mexico's poor environmental record and labor laws. Many critics argue that U.S. businesses investing in Mexico are doing so to take advantage of that nation's lax (by U.S. standards) environmental and labor laws.

There are arguments in favor of investing in countries that have poor records on human rights, environmental protection, and workers' rights. One is that economic growth increases a country's concern for human rights, environmental protection, and workers' rights, and that rich countries tend to have better records in these areas than poor countries. Thus, trade or investment in a poor country eventually might improve its stance on human rights, environmental protection, and workers' rights.[44] One manager using trade and investment to improve conditions in poor countries is Anita Roddick, founder of The Body Shop International. As illustrated in the following "Ethics in Action" feature, Roddick has long espoused a fair-trade philosophy that is designed to improve the welfare of people in less-developed countries while at the same time giving The Body Shop products for its stores.

ETHICS IN ACTION   ANITA RODDICK'S FAIR-TRADE PHILOSOPHY

Anita Roddick started The Body Shop (www.the-body-shop.com) in 1976 with a single store in the south of England. Today, the company is one of the world's largest retail chains in the skin and hair care market. From the beginning, Roddick has espoused a set of New Age business values that emphasize human, animal, and environmental rights. Thus, for example, The Body Shop goes to great lengths to ensure that neither its product nor its ingredients have been tested on animals for the cosmetics industry, the company includes natural, botanical ingredients in many of its preparations, and actively encourages its customers to refill or recycle its containers. One of Roddick's most interesting positions, however, is her "Trade, not Aid" policy.

Underlying the "Community Trade" concept is the belief that by establishing sustainable trading relationships with communities in need, companies such as The Body Shop can help improve the welfare of poor people. Roddick's idea of Community Trade or "Trade, Not Aid" does not denigrate the concept of humanitarian aid. She is simply making a statement that fair trade, not aid, is the better option for long-term economic development in less developed communities.

As an example of the policy in operation, a few years ago the Kayapo Indians in the Brazilian rain forest were faced with offers of logging and mining in their traditional area from both Brazilian and foreign companies. The Kayapo invited The Body Shop to identify an economic and sustainable alternative that would provide jobs and help preserve their indigenous homeland. Roddick believed that Brazil nuts could be sustainably harvested and the oil used as a conditioner in a Body Shop hair care product. She asked the Indians to gather Brazil nuts for The Body Shop. However, the Indians felt that at $8 per kilo, the price of Brazil nuts was too low to make this option economically viable. In response, The Body Shop purchased some simple machinery for the Kayapo that can be used to grind the nuts, cook them, and squash them until the oil is extracted. The pure, cold-pressed Brazil nut oil can be sold for $38 per kilo.[45] As a result, the Kayapo Indians have been able to earn a living while also preserving their native culture and environment. Their relationship with The Body Shop has also helped them establish and maintain dental, cultural, and health care programs. Thus, The Body Shop's trade with producers in less developed countries seeks to ensure the people's right to control their own resources, land, and lives. ■ ■ ■

SUMMARY

CHAPTER SUMMARY

The Changing Global Environment
Declining Barriers to Trade and Investment
Declining Barriers of Distance and Culture
Effects of Free Trade on Managers

The Global Task Environment
Suppliers
Distributors
Customers
Competitors

CHAPTER REVIEW

THE GLOBAL ENVIRONMENT In recent years there has been a marked shift away from a closed global environment, in which countries are cut off from each other by barriers to international trade and investment and by barriers of distance and culture, and toward a more open global environment. The emergence of an open global environment and the reduction of barriers to the free flow of goods, services, and investment owes much to the rise of global trade agreements such as GATT; to the growing global acceptance of a free-market philosophy; and to the poor performance of countries that protected their markets from international trade and investment.

THE GLOBAL TASK ENVIRONMENT Forces in the global task environment are more complex than those inside just one country and pre-

The Global General Environment

Political and Legal Forces

Economic Forces

Changes in Political and Legal and
   Economic Forces

Sociocultural Forces

Choosing a Way to Expand Internationally

Importing and Exporting

Licensing and Franchising

Strategic Alliances

Wholly Owned Foreign Subsidiaries

**Impediments to an Open Global
Environment**

Government Imposed Impediments

Self-Imposed Ethical Impediments

sent managers with greater opportunities and threats. Managers must analyze forces in their global task environment to determine how best to operate abroad.

THE GLOBAL GENERAL ENVIRONMENT In the general environment, managers must recognize the substantial differences that exist among countries' political, legal, economic, and sociocultural systems. Political, legal, and economic differences range from democratic states with free-market systems to totalitarian states with mixed or command economies. These differences impact on the attractiveness of a nation as a trading partner or as a target for foreign investment. Substantial differences in national culture can also be observed, such as those described in Hofstede's model of national culture. Management practices must be tailored to the particular culture in which they are to be applied. What works in the United States, for example, might not be appropriate in France, Peru, or Vietnam.

IMPEDIMENTS TO AN OPEN GLOBAL ENVIRONMENT Despite the shift toward a more open, competitive global environment, many impediments to international trade and investment still remain.

TOPICS FOR DISCUSSION AND ACTION

- In what ways does a more open global environment increase opportunities and threats in the global task environment?
- How do political, legal, and economic forces shape national culture? What characteristics of national culture do you think have the most important effect on how successful a country is in doing business abroad?
- Ask an expatriate manager about the most important problems and challenges that he or she confronted during an assignment abroad.
- The textile industry has a labor-intensive manufacturing process that utilizes unskilled and semiskilled workers. What are the implications of the shift to a more open global environment for textile companies whose manufacturing operations are based in high-wage countries such as Australia, Britain, and the United States?
- "Over the next decade we will see the emergence of enormous global markets for standardized products such as cars, blue jeans, food products, and recorded

music." In your view is this an accurate statement or an exaggeration?
- After the passage of the North American Free Trade Agreement, many U.S. companies shifted production operations to Mexico to take advantage of lower labor costs and lower standards for environmental and worker protection. As a result, they cut their costs and were better able to survive in an increasingly competitive global environment. Was their behavior ethical—that is, do the ends justify the means?
- Go to the library and gather information that allows you to compare and contrast the political, economic, and cultural systems of the United States, Mexico, and Canada. In what ways are the countries similar? How do they differ? How might the similarities and differences influence the activities of managers at an enterprise such as Wal-Mart, which does business in all three countries?

SMALL GROUP BREAKOUT EXERCISES

HOW TO BECOME GLOBALLY AWARE

Form groups of three to five people, and appoint one group member as the spokesperson who will communicate your findings to the whole class when called on by the instructor. Then, discuss the following scenario.

You are store managers who work for a large U.S. retailer that is planning to open a chain of new stores in France. Each of you has been given the responsibility to manage one of these stores, and you are meeting to develop a plan of action to help you and your families adjust to the conditions that you will encounter in France. As a group:

1 Decide which forces in the environment you think will most affect your ability and your family's ability to adjust to the French culture.
2 What are the best ways to gather information about the French business and social environment to enable you to understand these forces?
3 Before you and your family leave for France, what steps can you take to smooth your transition into the French culture and help you avoid culture shock?

BUILDING MANAGEMENT SKILLS

STUDYING A GLOBAL ORGANIZATION

Pick one of the following companies—Ford Motor Company, Compaq Computer, Procter & Gamble, or Kellogg. Collect information about the company from its annual reports or from articles in business magazines such as *Fortune* or *Business Week;* then do the following.

1 Identify the three largest foreign markets in which the company operates.
2 List the forces in the global task environment that you think have most affected the company's organization, and try to determine how its managers have responded to those forces.

3 Identify the political, economic, and sociocultural forces that have the most effect on the company, paying particular attention to differences in national culture. What implications, if any, do such differences have for the way in which this company sells its product in different national markets?
4 Determine how the shift toward a more open global environment has affected the opportunities and threats facing managers in the company.

EXPLORING THE WORLD WIDE WEB

This exercise deals with the global activities of Goodyear Tire and Rubber Company. Research Goodyear's Web site (goodyear.com), and click on all paths to access information about Goodyear's global presence. In particular look at the 1995 annual report, and the section on strategic developments.

1 What is Goodyear's method of expanding into the global environment, and why do you think this approach was chosen?

2 How will declining barriers of distance and culture affect the way Goodyear operates?

Search for the Web site of a company with a strong global presence. What are the main forces in the task and general global environments that most affect the way this company operates?

REFERENCES

1. R. Tomkins, "A Long Walk for the Shops," *Financial Times,* April 11, 1994, p. 13; W. Dawkins, "Revolution in Toyland," *Financial Times,* April 8, 1993, p. 9; L. Zinn, "The Limited: All Grown Up and Nowhere to Go?" *Business Week,* December 20, 1993, p. 44.

2. Zinn, "The Limited"; *Value Line* (August 1994): p. 1716.

3. "Limited Inc. to Open Bath & Body Stores in UK Joint Venture," *The Wall Street Journal,* June 23, 1994, B3.

4. M. Pacelle, "Limited Unveils Buyback Plan of $1.62 Billion," *The Wall Street Journal,* January 29. 1996, B5.

5. J. Bhagwati, *Protectionism* (Cambridge, MA: MIT Press, 1988).

6. For a summary of these theories, see P. Krugman and M. Obstfeld, *International Economics: Theory and Policy* (New York: HarperCollins, 1991). Also see C. W. L. Hill, *International Business* (Homewood, IL: Irwin, 1994), ch. 4.

7. C. A. Bartlett and S. Ghoshal, *Managing Across Borders* (Boston: Harvard Business School Press, 1989).

8. C. Arnst and G. Edmondson, "The Global Free for All," *Business Week,* September 26, 1994, pp. 118–126.

9. W. Konrads, "Why Leslie Wexner Shops Overseas," *Business Week,* February 3, 1992, p. 30.

10. R. Dore, *Taking Japan Seriously: A Confusion Perspective on Leading Economic Issues* (Stanford, CA: Stanford University Press, 1987).

11. "Boeing's Worldwide Supplier Network," *Seattle Post-Intelligence,* April 9, 1994, p. 13.

12. I. Metthee, "Playing a Large Part," *Seattle-Post Intelligence,* April 9, 1994, p. 13.

13. "The Gains from Trade," *The Economist,* September 23, 1989, pp. 25–26.

14. C. S. Tranger, "Enter the Mini-Multinational," *Northeast International Business* (March 1989): pp. 13–14.

15. R. B. Reich, *The Work of Nations* (New York: Knopf, 1991).

16. T. Levitt, "The Globalization of Markets," *Harvard Business Review* (May–June 1983): pp. 92–102.

17. T. Deveny et al., "McWorld?" *Business Week,* October 13, 1986, pp. 78–86.

18. R. Wesson, *Modern Government— Democracy and Authoritarianism,* 2d ed. (Englewood Cliffs, NJ: Prentice-Hall, 1992).

19. Nobel prize–winning economist Douglas North makes this argument. See D. C. North, *Institutions, Institutional Change, and Economic Performance* (Cambridge: Cambridge University Press, 1990).

20. For an accessible discussion of the reasons for this, see M. Friedman and R. Friedman, *Free to Choose* (London: Penguin Books, 1990).

21. P. M. Sweezy and H. Magdoff, *The Dynamics of U.S. Capitalism* (New York: Monthly Review Press, 1972).

22. The ideology is that of individualism, which dates back to Adam Smith, John Stuart Mill, and the like. See H. W. Spiegel, *The Growth of Economic Thought* (Durham, NC: Duke University Press, 1991).

23. P. Hofheinz, "Yes, You Can Win in Eastern Europe," *Fortune,* May 16, 1994, pp. 110–112.

24. T. Walker, "Crucial Stage of the Reform Program," *Financial Times,* November 18, 1993, sec. 3, p. 1.

25. M. Magnier, "Chiquita Bets Czechoslovakia Can Produce Banana Bonanza," *Journal of Commerce,* August 29, 1991, pp. 1, 3.

26. J. Perlez, "GE Finds Tough Going in Hungary," *The New York Times,* July 25, 1994, C1, C3.

27. E. B. Tylor, *Primitive Culture* (London: Murray, 1871).

28. For details on the forces that shape culture, see Hill, *International Business* (ch. 2).

29. G. Hofstede, B. Neuijen, D. D. Ohayv, and G. Sanders, "Measuring Organizational Cultures: A Qualitative and Quantitative Study Across Twenty Cases," *Administrative Science Quarterly,* no. 35 (1990): pp. 286–316.

30. R. Bellah, *Habits of the Heart: Individualism and Commitment in American Life* (Berkeley: University of California Press, 1985).

31. R. Bellah, *The Tokugawa Religion* (New York: Free Press, 1957).

32. C. Nakane, *Japanese Society* (Berkeley: University of California Press, 1970).

33. For example, see Dore, *Taking Japan Seriously.*

34. G. Hofstede, "The Cultural Relativity of Organizational Practices and Theories," *Journal of International Business Studies* (Fall 1983): pp. 75–89.

35. Hofstede, Neuijen, Ohayv, and Sanders, "Measuring Organizational Cultures."

36. J. P. Fernandez, and M. Barr, *The Diversity Advantage* (New York: Lexington Books, 1994).

37. R. E. Caves, *Multinational Enterprise and Economic Analysis* (Cambridge: Cambridge University Press, 1982).

38. B. Kogut, "Joint Ventures: Theoretical and Empirical Perspectives," *Strategic Management Journal* no. 9 (1988): pp. 319–33.

39. N. Hood and S. Young, *The Economics of the Multinational Enterprise* (London: Longman, 1979).

40. P. Abrahams, "Getting Hooked on Fish and Chips in Japan," *Financial Times,* May 17, 1994, p. 6.

41. "Another World," *The Economist,* September 19, 1992, pp. 15–18.

42. Bhagwati, *Protectionism.*

43. G. Smith, "NAFTA: A Green Light for Red Tape," *Business Week,* July 25, 1994, p. 48.

44. "Free Trade or Foul," *The Economist,* June 4, 1994, 70. Also see Krugman and Obstfeld, *International Economics.*

45. A. Roddick, "Not Free Trade but Fair Trade," *Across the Board* (June 1994): p. 58; A. Jack and N. Buckley, "Halo Slips on the Raspberry Bubbles," *Financial Times,* August 27–28, 1994, p. 12.

46. A. Choi, "GM Seeds Grow Nicely in Eastern Europe," *The Wall Street Journal,* April 3, 1995, A11.

MANAGEMENT CASE

GM'S MANAGERS TACKLE EASTERN EUROPE

After the collapse of totalitarian regimes in eastern Europe, many formerly communist-controlled companies were sold to foreign investors. In the car industry, for example, companies such as Skoda, the largest Czech car company, and FSM, Poland's largest car maker, were put up for sale. Managers of western European and U.S. car companies took very different approaches to taking advantage of the opportunities that such sales offered.

At the end of the cold war, the managers of companies such as Volkswagen of Germany and Fiat of Italy rushed into eastern Europe and bought Skoda and FSM along with other car companies. The main reason why European managers took over the formerly communist car companies was the extremely low labor costs in eastern Europe. Managers at Volkswagen and Fiat hoped to quickly turn around the eastern European car plants to produce inexpensive cars for sale to customers in western European countries. What they found when they took control of their new companies, however, shocked them: outdated machinery and equipment operated by a demoralized workforce that lacked the skills necessary to produce cars that met the high quality standards expected by Western consumers. Both Volkswagen and Fiat were forced to pour billions of dollars into modernizing plants

and equipment and retraining workers. They quickly learned how costly the strategy of large-scale foreign investment can be.

When managers at General Motors (GM) looked at eastern Europe, they saw not only the opportunities, but also the threats. In the early 1900s, GM had established a major western European car division under the Vauxhall name in Britain and the Opel name in Germany. In the 1980s, GM's European car division was experiencing many of the same problems as its U.S. parent: Both were plagued by inefficient, high-cost car-making operations. Despite many attempts to restructure operations, GM's huge size and bureaucratic approach made change difficult and slow, especially in the United States. In Europe, GM had more success under the control of Jack Smith, head of European operations and a master of the art of Japanese-style lean production. In fact, Smith turned around GM's European operations, and his success as a global manager led to his appointment as the CEO of GM in 1993. These experiences influenced GM managers' approach to expansion into eastern Europe—an approach very different from that of their European counterparts.

Unlike managers at Volkswagen and Fiat, GM's managers anticipated the difficulty of restructuring eastern European car companies that had operated in totalitarian regimes and had been shaped by communistic political, economic, and sociocul-

tural values. So, rather than simply taking over existing car-making operations and letting both managers and workers continue to operate under the old communist values and norms, GM's managers decided to start fresh ventures but do so in a small-scale way to test the waters. They established small factories in Warsaw, Poland; Szentgottard, Hungary; and Eisenach, Germany. Workers at these plants were trained to assemble cars from prefabricated car parts made in the West.[46] GM hoped to get the benefit of low-cost eastern European labor with high quality Western-made car parts.

GM's ventures were successful and, unlike Volkswagen and Fiat, General Motors avoided the problems associated with changing outdated attitudes and behaviors. Having succeeded in this small way, GM's managers then decided to make low-cost car parts in Poland and Hungary and ship them abroad for use in GM's worldwide assembly operations. This venture also succeeded, and GM is currently expanding both its assembly and its car parts manufacturing operations in Europe.

QUESTIONS

1 What problems did GM's managers avoid by choosing a small-scale method of expansion into eastern Europe?
2 What kinds of problems do you think GM's managers are likely to encounter as their eastern European operations grow?

MANAGEMENT CASE IN THE NEWS

HOW A GLOBAL MANAGER OPERATES

Fortune magazine

Chad Holliday grew up in Nashville playing football, mowing lawns, dating—the usual. It was a comfortable life. He fully expected to take over his father's industrial equipment distribution business. Never did he imagine he would one day work for a multinational corporation and live in Japan. But during his senior year at the University of Tennessee in Knoxville, his dad called one day and said, "How're your grades, son? They'd better be good, because I just sold the business."

Holliday didn't miss a beat. With the flexibility that has come to be his trademark, he simply parlayed a summer job at Du Pont into a full-time career at the Delaware chemical giant, which has seen him rise through various plant-level supervisory jobs and executive positions to his current duties. At Du Pont he now has responsibility for eight global businesses generating $10 billion in revenues and producing everything from fabric to paper coatings. A second hat, chairman of Du Pont Asia Pacific, puts him in Tokyo and in charge of 7,000 employees and businesses totaling $3.5 billion in sales.

Holliday is truly an internationalist with substantial foreign experience—Brenneman had a Mexico assignment with Bain, for example, and Hapka did an overseas stint for McKinsey. A foreign assignment, it seems, is no longer considered a backwater but rather a fast track to the top. Holliday has to oversee Du Pont's doings in 15 Far Eastern countries. Not surprisingly, he devotes roughly half his time to personnel decisions. "For me to be knowledgeable about any single business decision is almost impossible," he says, his Southern drawl in evidence even halfway around the world. "I have to try to put the right people in place."

Exhibit A is Holliday's decision in 1991 to recruit local talent to head up Du Pont in Japan. It was a controversial move and provoked grumblings by several of Du Pont's top managers back at headquarters in Wilmington, Delaware. They worried about loyalty. And what about the possibility that valuable trade secrets might be stolen?

Holliday stuck to his decision. He homed in on Akira Imamichi, president of a joint venture between Du Pont and Mitsui Petrochemical. Because Imamichi spoke virtually no English and Holliday's Japanese wasn't much better, the interview was conducted with the help of translators. Prior to hiring Imamichi, Holliday, as a trust-building exercise, took him on a tour of Japan (translators in tow). The two visited plants and got to know each other. They even stopped at the Hiroshima Peace Memorial Museum, dedicated to the World War II atom bomb explosion. "We got that out of the way," Holliday says with a sigh. "That's probably the most sensitive subject between an American and a Japanese person."

Imamichi has worked out well. Earnings have been growing more than twice as fast since he took the reins, even as the Japanese economy has been in a rut. And as Holliday had hoped, Imamichi has been able to eliminate some biases of Du Pont's American managers in Japan toward the local work force, which is 98% Japanese. Holliday feared that favoritism was being shown toward employees who spoke English well or demonstrated "Western" traits, such as taking personal credit for business success. "Sure enough, Imamichi came in and made many personnel changes," says Holliday. "People we thought weren't very good he thought outstanding, and vice versa."

Perhaps the most telling tribute to Holliday's natural adaptability is his current living arrangement. He and his wife, Ann, live in downtown Tokyo, a far cry from John Overton High School in Nashville, where they met. Their apartment is just 800 square feet, with low tables and screens and no dishwasher. Ann has become an excellent Japanese cook and is fond of ikebana, the Japanese art of flower arrangement. As for the couple's two sons, well, they are fluent in Japanese, unlike Dad, who's still working hard on it.

Source: "How a Global Manager Operates," *Fortune* magazine, June 24, 1996, pp. 84–86.

QUESTIONS

1 What is Chad Holliday's approach to global management?
2 What kind of skills does a global manager like Holliday need?

INDEX